The Seven Storey Mountain

THOMAS MERTON

The Seven Storey Mountain

First published in the United States in 1948
by Harcourt, Brace and Company, New York

First published in Great Britain in 1975 by Sheldon Press

Reprinted five times

This edition published in 1990

Society for Promoting Christian Knowledge
36 Causton Street
London SW1P 4ST

British Library Cataloguing-in-Publication Data
A catalogue record for this book is available from the British Library

ISBN 978-0-281-04474-0

7 9 10 8

First printed in Great Britain by
Bookcraft, Midsomer Norton
Reprinted in Great Britain by
Antony Rowe Limited

Produced on paper from sustainable forests

Contents

Illustrations

Part One

1

Prisoner's Base

ON THE LAST day of January 1915, under the sign of the Water Bearer, in a year of a great war, and down in the shadow of some French mountains on the borders of Spain, I came into the world. Free by nature, in the image of God, I was nevertheless the prisoner of my own violence and my own selfishness, in the image of the world into which I was born. That world was the picture of Hell, full of men like myself, loving God and yet hating Him; born to love Him, living instead in fear and hopeless self-contradictory hungers.

Not many hundreds of miles away from the house where I was born, they were picking up the men who rotted in the rainy ditches among the dead horses and the ruined seventy-fives, in a forest of trees without branches along the river Marne.

My father and mother were captives in that world, knowing they did not belong with it or in it, and yet unable to get away from it. They were in the world and not of it—not because they were saints, but in a different way: because they were artists. The integrity of an artist lifts a man above the level of the world without delivering him from it.

My father painted like Cézanne and understood the southern French landscape the way Cézanne did. His vision of the world was sane, full of balance, full of veneration for structure, for the relations of masses and for all the circumstances that impress an individual identity on each created thing. His vision was religious and clean, and therefore his paintings were without decoration or superfluous comment, since a religious man respects the power of God's creation to bear witness for itself. My father was a very good artist.

Neither of my parents suffered from the little spooky prejudices that devour the people who know nothing but automobiles and movies and what's in the ice-box and what's in the papers and which neighbors are getting a divorce.

I inherited from my father his way of looking at things and some of his integrity and from my mother some of her dissatisfaction with the mess the world is in, and some of her versatility. From both I got capacities for work and vision and enjoyment and expression that ought to have made me some kind of a King, if the standards the world lives by were the real ones. Not that we ever had any money: but any fool knows that you don't need money to get enjoyment out of life.

If what most people take for granted were really true—if all you needed to be happy was to grab everything and see everything and investigate every experience and then talk about it, I should have been a very happy person, a spiritual millionaire, from the cradle even until now.

If happiness were merely a matter of natural gifts, I would never have entered a Trappist monastery when I came to the age of a man.

ii

My father and mother came from the ends of the earth, to Prades, and though they came to stay, they stayed there barely long enough for me to be born and get on my small feet, and then they left again. And they continued and I began a somewhat long journey: for all three of us, one way and another, it is now ended.

And though my father came from the other side of the earth, beyond many oceans, all the pictures of Christchurch, New Zealand, where he was born, look like the suburbs of London, but perhaps a little cleaner. There is more sunlight in New Zealand, and I think the people are healthier.

My father's name was Owen Merton. Owen because his mother's family had lived for a generation or two in Wales, though I believe they were originally Lowland Scotch. And my father's father was a music master, and a pious man, who taught at Christ's College, Christchurch, on the South Island.

My father had a lot of energy and independence. He told me how it was in the hill country and in the mountains of the South Island, out on the sheep farms and in the forests where he had been, and once, when one of the Antarctic expeditions came that way, my father nearly joined it, to go to the South Pole. He would have been frozen to death along with all the others, for that was the one from which no one returned.

When he wanted to study art, there were many difficulties in his way, and it was not easy for him to convince his people that that was really his vocation. But eventually he went to London, and then to Paris, and in Paris he met my mother, and married her, and never went back to New Zealand.

My mother was an American. I have seen a picture of her as a rather slight, thin, sober little person with a serious and somewhat anxious and very sensitive face. And this corresponds with my memory of her—worried, precise, quick, critical of me, her son. Yet in the family she has always been spoken of as gay and very light-hearted. My grandmother kept great locks of Mother's red hair, after she died, and Mother's happy laughter as a boarding-school girl was what never ceased to echo in my grandmother's memory.

It seems to me, now, that Mother must have been a person full of insatiable dreams and of great ambition after perfection: perfection in art, in interior decoration, in dancing, in housekeeping, in raising children. Maybe that is why I remember her mostly as worried: since the imperfection of myself, her first son, had been a great deception. If this book does not prove anything else, it will certainly show that I was nobody's dream-child. I have seen a diary Mother was keeping, in the time of my infancy and first childhood, and it reflects some astonishment at the stubborn and seemingly spontaneous development of completely unpredictable features in my character, things she had never bargained for: for example, a deep and serious urge to adore the gas-light in the kitchen, with no little ritualistic veneration, when I was about four. Churches and formal religion were things to which Mother attached not too much importance in the training of a modern child, and my guess is that she thought, if I were left to myself, I would grow up into a nice, quiet Deist of some sort, and never be perverted by superstition.

My baptism, at Prades, was almost certainly Father's idea, because he had grown up with a deep and well-developed faith, according to the doctrines of the Church of England. But I don't think there was much power, in the waters of the baptism I got in Prades, to untwist the warping of my essential freedom, or loose me from the devils that hung like vampires on my soul.

My father came to the Pyrenees because of a dream of his own: more single, more concrete and more practical than Mother's numerous and haunting ideals of perfection. Father wanted to get some place where he could settle in France, and raise a family, and paint, and live on practically nothing, because we had practically nothing to live on.

Father and Mother had many friends at Prades, and when they had moved there, and had their furniture in their flat, and the canvasses piled up in the corner, and the whole place smelling of fresh oil-paints and water-color and cheap pipe tobacco and cooking, more friends came down from Paris. And Mother would paint in the hills, under a large canvas parasol, and Father would paint in the sun, and the friends would drink red wine and gaze out over the valley at Canigou, and at the monastery on the slopes of the mountain.

There were many ruined monasteries in those mountains. My mind goes back with great reverence to the thought of those clean, ancient stone cloisters, those low and mighty rounded arches hewn and set in place by monks who have perhaps prayed me where I now am. St. Martin and St. Michael the Archangel, the great patron of monks, had churches in those mountains. Saint Martin-du-Canigou; Saint Michel-de-Cuxa. Is it any wonder I should have a friendly feeling about those places?

One of them, stone by stone, followed me across the Atlantic a score of years later, and got itself set up within convenient reach of me when I most needed to see what a cloister looked like, and what kind of place a man might live in, to live according to his rational nature, and not like a stray dog. St. Michel-de-Cuxa is all fixed up in a special and considerably tidy little museum in an uptown park, in New York, overlooking the Hudson River, in such a way that you don't recall what kind of a city you are in. It is called The Cloisters. Synthetic as it is, it still preserves enough of its own reality to be a reproach to everything else around it, except the trees and the Palisades.

But when the friends of my father and mother came to Prades, they brought the newspapers, rolled up in their coat pockets, and they had many postcards carrying patriotic cartoons, representing the Allies overcoming the Germans. My grandparents—that is, my mother's father and mother in America—were worried about her being in a land at war, and it was evident that we could not stay much longer at Prades.

I was barely a year old. I remember nothing about the journey, as we went to Bordeaux, to take the boat that had a gun mounted on the foredeck. I remember nothing about the crossing of the sea, nothing of the anxiety about U-boats, or the arrival in New York, and in the land where there was no war. But I can easily reconstruct the first encounter between my American grandparents and their new son-in-law and their grandson.

For Pop, as my American grandfather was called in the family, was a buoyant and excitable man who, on docks, boats, trains, in stations, in elevators, on busses, in hotels, in restaurants, used to get keyed up and start ordering everybody around, and making new arrangements, and changing them on the spur of the moment. My grandmother, whom we called Bonnemaman, was just the opposite, and her natural deliberateness and hesitancy and hatred of activity always seemed to increase in proportion to Pop's excesses in the opposite direction. The more active Pop became and the more he shouted and gave directions, the more hesitant and doubtful and finally inert was my grandmother. But perhaps this obscure and innocent and wholly subconscious conflict had not yet developed, in 1916, to the full pitch of complications which it was to attain some fifteen years later.

I have no doubt that there was a certain amount of conflict between the two generations when Father and Mother determined that they were going to find their own kind of a house and live in it. It was a small house, very old and rickety, standing under two or three high pine trees, in Flushing, Long Island, which was then a country town. We were out in the fields in the direction of Kiljordan and Jamaica and the old Truant School. The house had four rooms, two downstairs and two upstairs, and two of the rooms were barely larger than closets. It must have been very cheap.

Our landlord, Mr. Duggan, ran a nearby saloon. He got in trouble with Father for helping himself to the rhubarb which we were growing in the garden. I remember the grey summer dusk in which this happened. We were at the supper table, when the bended Mr. Duggan was observed, like some whale in the sea of green rhubarb, plucking up the red stalks. Father rose to his feet and hastened out into the garden. I could hear indignant words. We sat at the supper table, silent, not eating, and when Father returned I began to question him, and to endeavour to work out the morality of the situation. And I still remember it as having struck me as a difficult case, with much to be said on both sides. In fact, I had assumed that if the landlord felt like it, he could simply come and harvest all our vegetables, and there was nothing we could do about it. I mention this with the full consciousness that someone will use it against me, and say that the real reason I became a monk in later years was that I had the mentality of a medieval serf when I was barely out of the cradle.

Father did as much painting as he could. He filled several sketch books and finished some water-colors along the waterfront in New York, and eventually even had an exhibition in a place in Flushing which was maintained by some artists there. Two doors away from us, up the road, in a white house with pointed gables, surrounded by a wide sweep of sloping lawn, and with a stable that had been turned into a studio, lived Bryson Burroughs, who painted pale, classical pictures something like Puvis de Chavannes and who, with some of the gentleness you could see in his work, was very kind to us.

Father could not support us by painting. During the war years we lived on his work as a landscape gardener: which was mostly plain manual labor, for he not only laid out the gardens of some rich people in the neighborhood, but did most of the work planting and caring for them: and that was how we lived. Father did not get this money under false pretenses. He was a very good gardener, understood flowers, and knew how to make things grow. What is more, he liked this kind of work almost as much as painting.

Then in November 1918, about a week before the Armistice of that particular World War, my younger brother was born. He was a child with a much serener nature than mine, with not so many obscure drives and impulses. I remember that everyone was impressed by his constant and unruffled happiness. In the long evenings, when he was put to bed before the sun went down, instead of protesting and fighting, as I did when I had to go to bed, he would lie upstairs in his crib, and we would hear him singing a little tune. Every evening it was the same tune, very simple, very primitive; a nice little tune, very suitable for the time of day and for the season. Downstairs, we would all fall more or less silent, lulled by the singing of the child in the crib, and we would see the sunrays slanting across the fields and through the windows as the day ended.

I had an imaginary friend, called Jack, who had an imaginary dog, called Doolittle. The chief reason why I had an imaginary friend was that there were no other children to play with, and my brother John Paul was still a baby. When I tried to seek diversion watching the gentlemen who played pool at Mr. Duggan's saloon, I got into much trouble. On the other hand, I could go and play at Burroughs' place, in their garden and in the room full of old lumber over the studio. Betty Burroughs knew how to join in games in a way that did not imply patronage, though she was practically grown up. But for friends of my own age, I had to fall back on my imagination, and it was perhaps not a good thing.

Mother did not mind the company I kept in my imagination, at least to begin with, but once I went shopping with her, and refused to cross Main Street, Flushing, for fear that the imaginary dog, Doolittle, might get run over by real cars. This I later learned from her record of the affair in her diary.

By 1920 I could read and write and draw. I drew a picture of the house, and everybody sitting under the pine trees, on a blanket, on the grass, and sent it to Pop in the mail. He lived at Douglaston, which was about five miles away. But most of the time I drew pictures of boats. Ocean liners with many funnels and hundreds of portholes, and waves all around as jagged as a saw, and the air full of "v's" for the sea-gulls.

Things were stimulated by the momentous arrival of my New Zealand grandmother, who had come from the Antipodes to visit her scattered children in England and America, as soon as the war had ended. I think she brought one of my aunts along with her, but I was most of all impressed by Granny. She must have talked to me a great deal, and asked me many questions and told me a great number of things, and though there are few precise details I remember about that visit, the general impression she left was one of veneration and awe—and love. She was very good and kind, and there was nothing effusive and overwhelming about her affection. I have no precise memory of what she looked like, except that she wore dark clothes, grey and dark brown, and had glasses and grey hair and spoke quietly and earnestly. She had been a teacher, like her husband, my New Zealand grandfather.

The clearest thing I remember about her was the way she put salt on her oatmeal at breakfast. Of this I am certain: it made a very profound impression on me. Of one other thing I am less certain, but it is in itself much more important: she taught me the Lord's Prayer. Perhaps I had been taught to say the "Our Father" before, by my earthly father. I never used to say it. But evidently Granny asked me one night if I had said my prayers, and it turned out that I did not know the "Our Father," so she taught it to me. After that I did not forget it, even though I went for years without saying it at all.

It seems strange that Father and Mother, who were concerned almost to the point of scrupulosity about keeping the minds of their sons uncontaminated by error and mediocrity and ugliness and sham, had not bothered to give us any formal religious training. The only explanation I have is the guess that Mother must have had strong views on the subject. Possibly she considered any organized religion below the standard of intellectual perfection she demanded of any child of hers. We never went to church in Flushing.

In fact, I remember having an intense desire to go to church one day, but we did not go. It was Sunday. Perhaps it was an Easter Sunday, probably in 1920. From across the fields, and beyond the red farmhouse of our neighbor, I could see the spire of St. George's church, above the trees. The sound of the churchbells came to us across the bright fields. I was playing in front of the house, and stopped to listen. Suddenly, all the birds began to sing in the trees above my head, and the sound of birds singing and churchbells ringing lifted up my heart with joy. I cried out to my father:

"Father, all the birds are in their church."

And then I said: "Why don't we go to church?"

My father looked up and said: "We will."

"Now?" said I.

"No, it is too late. But we will go some other Sunday."

And yet Mother did go somewhere, sometimes, on Sunday mornings, to worship God. I doubt that Father went with her; he probably stayed at home to take care of me and John Paul, for we never went. But anyway, Mother went to the Quakers, and sat with them in their ancient meeting house. This was the only kind of religion for which she had any use, and I suppose it was taken for granted that, when we grew older, we might be allowed to tend in that direction too. Probably no influence would have been brought to bear on us to do so. We would have been left to work it out more or less for ourselves.

Meanwhile, at home, my education was progressing along the lines laid down by some progressive method that Mother had read about in one of those magazines. She answered an advertisement that carried an oval portrait of some bearded scholar with a pince-nez, and received from Baltimore a set of books and some charts and even a small desk and blackboard. The idea was that the smart modern child was to be turned loose amid this apparatus, and allowed to develop spontaneously into a midget university before reaching the age of ten.

The ghost of John Stuart Mill must have glided up and down the room with a sigh of gratification as I opened the desk and began. I forget what came of it all, except that one night I was sent to bed early for stubbornly spelling "which" without the first "h": "w-i-c-h." I remember brooding about this as an injustice. "What do they think I am, anyway?" After all, I was still only five years old.

Still, I retain no grudge against the fancy method or the desk that went with it. Maybe that was where my geography book came from—the favorite book of my childhood. I was so fond of playing prisoner's base all over those maps that I wanted to become a sailor. I was only too eager for the kind of foot-loose and unstable life I was soon to get into.

My second best book confirmed me in this desire. This was a collection of stories called the *Greek Heroes*. It was more than I could do to read the Victorian version of these Greek myths for myself, but Father read them aloud, and I learned of Theseus and the Minotaur, of the Medusa, of Perseus and Andromeda. Jason sailed to a far land, after the Golden Fleece. Theseus returned victorious, but forgot to change the black sails, and the King of Athens threw himself down from the rock, believing that his son was dead. In those days I learned the name Hesperides, and it was from these things that I unconsciously built up the vague fragments of a religion and of a philosophy, which remained hidden and implicit in my acts, and which, in due time, were to assert themselves in a deep and all-embracing attachment to my own judgement and my own will and a constant turning away from subjection, towards the freedom of my own ever-changing horizons.

In a sense, this was intended as the fruit of my early training. Mother wanted me to be independent, and not to run with the herd. I was to be original, individual, I was to have a definite character and ideals of my own. I was not to be an article thrown together, on the common bourgeois pattern, on everybody else's assembly line.

If we had continued as we had begun, and if John Paul and I had grown up in that house, probably this Victorian-Greek complex would have built itself up gradually, and we would have turned into good-mannered and earnest sceptics, polite, intelligent, and perhaps even in some sense useful. We might have become successful authors, or editors of magazines, professors at small and progressive colleges. The way would have been all smooth and perhaps I would never have ended up as a monk.

But it is not yet the time to talk about that happy consummation, the thing for which I most thank and praise God, and which is of all things the ultimate paradoxical fulfilment of my mother's ideas for me—the last thing she would ever have dreamed of: the boomerang of all her solicitude for an individual development.

But oh, how many possibilities there were ahead of me and my brother in that day! A brand-new conscience was just coming into existence as an actual, operating function of a soul. My choices were just about to become responsible. My mind was clean and unformed enough to receive any set of standards, and work with the most perfect of them, and work with grace itself, and God's own values, if I had ever had the chance.

Here was a will, neutral, undirected, a force waiting to be applied, ready to generate tremendous immanent powers of light or darkness, peace or conflict, order or confusion, love or sin. The bias which my will was to acquire from the circumstances of all its acts would eventually be the direction of my whole being towards happiness or misery, life or death, heaven or hell.

More than that: since no man ever can, or could, live by himself and for himself alone, the destinies of thousands of other people were bound to be affected, some remotely, but some very directly and near-at-hand, by my own choices and decisions and desires, as my own life would also be formed and modified according to theirs. I was entering into a moral universe in which I would be related to every other rational being, and in which whole masses of us, as thick as swarming bees, would drag one another along towards some common end of good or evil, peace or war.

I think it must have been after Mother went to the hospital that, one Sunday, I went to the Quaker meeting house with Father. He had explained to me that the people came and sat there, silent, doing nothing, saying nothing, until the Holy Spirit moved someone to speak. He also told me that a famous old gentleman, who was one of the founders of the Boy Scouts of America, would be there. That was Dan Beard. Consequently I sat among the Quakers with three more or less equal preoccupations running through my mind. Where was Dan Beard? Would he not only be called beard, but have one on his chin? And what was the Holy Spirit going to move all these people to do or say?

I forget how the third question was answered. But after the man sitting in the high wooden rostrum, presiding over the Quakers, gave the signal that the meeting was ended, I saw Dan Beard among the people under the low sunny porch, outside the meeting-house door. He had a beard.

It was almost certainly in the last year or so of Mother's life, 1921, that Father got a job as organist at the Episcopalian church in Douglaston. It was not a job that made him very happy or enthusiastic. He did not get along very well with the minister. But I began to go to the church on Sundays, which makes me think that Mother was in the hospital, because I must have been living with Pop and Bonnemaman in Douglaston.

The old Zion church was a white wooden building, with a squat, square little belfry, standing on a hill, surrounded by high trees and a large graveyard, and in a crypt underneath it were buried the original Douglas family, who had settled there on the shore of the Sound some hundred years before. It was pleasant enough on Sundays. I remember the procession that came out of the sacristy, a choir of men and women, dressed in black, with white surplices, and led by a Cross. There were stained glass windows up behind the altar, one had an anchor on it, for its design, which interested me because I wanted to go to sea, and travel all over the world. Strange interpretation of a religious symbol ordinarily taken to signify stability in Hope: the theological virtue of Hope, dependence on God. To me it suggested just the opposite. Travel, adventure, the wide sea, and unlimited possibilities of human heroism, with myself as the hero.

Then there was a lectern, shaped like an eagle with outspread wings, on which rested a huge Bible. Nearby was an American flag, and above that was one of those little boards they have in Protestant churches, on which the numbers of the hymns to be sung are indicated by black and white cards. I was impressed by the lighting of candles on the altar, by the taking up of the collection, and by the singing of hymns, while Father, hidden behind the choir somewhere, played the organ.

One came out of the church with a kind of comfortable and satisfied feeling that something had been done that needed to be done, and that was all I knew about it. And now, as I consider it after many years, I see that it was very good that I should have got at least that much of religion in my childhood. It is a law of man's nature, written into his very essence, and just as much a part of him as the desire to build houses and cultivate the land and marry and have children and read books and sing songs, that he should want to stand together with other men in order to acknowledge their common dependence on God, their Father and Creator. In fact, this desire is much more fundamental than any purely physical necessity.

At this same time my father played the piano every evening in a small movie theater which had been opened in the next town, Bayside. We certainly needed money.

iii

And probably the chief reason why we needed money was that Mother had cancer of the stomach.

That was another thing that was never explained to me. Everything about sickness and death was more or less kept hidden from me, because consideration of these things might make a child morbid. And since I was destined to grow up with a nice, clear, optimistic and well-balanced outlook on life, I was never even taken to the hospital to see Mother, after she went there. And this was entirely her own idea.

How long she had been ill and suffering, still keeping house for us, not without poverty and hardship, without our knowing anything of what it was, I cannot say. But her sickness probably accounts for my memory of her as thin and pale and rather severe.

With a selfishness unusual even in a child, I was glad to move from Flushing to my grandparents' house at Douglaston. There I was allowed to do more or less as I pleased, there was plenty of food, and we had two dogs and several cats to play with. I did not miss Mother very much, and did not weep when I was not allowed to go and see her. I was content to run in the woods with the dogs, or climb trees, or pester the chickens, or play around in the clean little studio where Bonnemaman sometimes painted china, and fired it in a small kiln.

Then one day Father gave me a note to read. I was very surprised. It was for me personally, and it was in my mother's handwriting. I don't think she had ever written to me before—there had never been any occasion for it. Then I understood what was happening, although, as I remember, the language of the letter was confusing to me. Nevertheless, one thing was quite evident. My mother was informing me, by mail, that she was about to die, and would never see me again.

I took the note out under the maple tree in the back yard, and worked over it, until I had made it all out, and had gathered what it really meant. And a tremendous weight of sadness and depression settled on me. It was not the grief of a child, with pangs of sorrow and many tears. It had something of the heavy perplexity and gloom of adult grief, and was therefore all the more of a burden because it was, to that extent, unnatural. I suppose one reason for this was that I had more or less had to arrive at the truth by induction.

Prayer? No, prayer did not even occur to me. How fantastic that will seem to a Catholic—that a six-year-old child should find out that his mother is dying, and not know enough to pray for her! It was not until I became a Catholic, twenty years later, that it finally occurred to me to pray for my mother.

My grandparents did not have a car, but they hired one to go in to the hospital, when the end finally came. I went with them in the car, but was not allowed to enter the hospital. Perhaps it was just as well. What would have been the good of my being plunged into a lot of naked suffering and emotional crisis without any prayer, any Sacrament to stabilize and order it, and make some kind of meaning out of it? In that sense, Mother was right. Death, under those circumstances, was nothing but ugliness, and if it could not possibly have any ultimate meaning, why burden a child's mind with the sight of it?

I sat outside, in the car, with the hired driver. Again, I knew nothing definite about what was going on. But I think there was also by this time no little subconscious rejection of everything that might have given me any certainty that Mother was really dying: for if I had wanted to find out, I would not have had much trouble.

It seemed like a very long time.

The car was parked in a yard entirely enclosed by black brick buildings, thick with soot. On one side was a long, low shed, and rain dripped from the eaves, as we sat in silence, and listened to the drops falling on the roof of the car. The sky was heavy with mist and smoke, and the sweet sick smell of hospital and gas-house mingled with the stuffy smell of the automobile.

But when Father and Pop and Bonnemaman and my Uncle Harold came out of the hospital door, I did not need to ask any questions. They were all shattered by sorrow.

When we got home to Douglaston, Father went into a room alone, and I followed him and found him weeping, over by the window.

He must have thought of the days before the war, when he had first met Mother in Paris, when she had been so happy, and gay, and had danced, and had been full of ideas and plans and ambitions for herself and for him and for their children. It had not turned out as they had planned. And now it was all over. And Bonnemaman was folding away the big heavy locks of red hair that had fallen from the shears when my mother was a girl, folding them away now in tissue paper, in the spare room, and weeping bitterly.

They hired the same car again a day or so later, for another journey, and this time I am definitely glad I stayed in the car.

Mother, for some reason, had always wanted to be cremated. I suppose that fits in with the whole structure of her philosophy of life: a dead body was simply something to be put out of the way as quickly as possible. I remember how she was, in the house at Flushing, with a rag tied tightly around her head to keep the dust out of her hair, cleaning and sweeping and dusting the rooms with the greatest energy and intensity of purpose: and it helps one to understand her impatience with useless and decaying flesh. That was something to be done away with, without delay. When life was finished, let the whole thing be finished, definitely, for ever.

Once again, the rain fell, the sky was dark. I cannot remember if Cousin Ethel (my mother's cousin, called Mrs. McGovern, who was a nurse) remained in the car to keep me from getting too gloomy. Nevertheless I was very sad. But I was not nearly so unhappy as I would have been if I had gone up to that mournful and appalling place and stood behind a big pane of glass to watch my mother's coffin glide slowly between the steel doors that led to the furnace.

iv

Mother's death had made one thing evident: Father now did not have to do anything but paint. He was not tied down to any one place. He could go wherever he needed to go, to find subjects and get ideas, and I was old enough to go with him.

And so, after I had been a few months in the local school at Douglaston, and had already been moved up to the second grade, in the evil-smelling grey annex on top of the hill, Father came back to New York and announced that he and I were going somewhere new.

It was with a kind of feeling of triumph that I watched the East River widen into Long Island Sound, and waited for the moment when the Fall River boat, in all her pride, would go sweeping past the mouth of Bayside Bay and I would view Douglaston, as I thought, from the superiority of the open water and pass it by, heading for a new horizon called Fall River and Cape Cod and Provincetown.

We could not afford a cabin, but slept down below decks in the crowded steerage, if you could call it that, among the loud Italian families and the colored boys who spent the night shooting craps under the dim light, while the waters spoke loudly to us, above our heads, proclaiming that we were well below the waterline.

And in the morning we got off the boat at Fall River, and walked up the street beside the textile mills, and found a lunch wagon crowded with men getting something to eat on the way to work; and we sat at the counter and ate ham and eggs.

All day long after that we were in a train. Just before we crossed the great black drawbridge over the Cape Cod Canal, Father got off at a station and went to a store across the street and bought me a bar of Baker's chocolate, with a blue wrapper and a picture of a lady in an old-fashioned cap and apron, serving cups of chocolate. I was almost completely overwhelmed with surprise and awe at the fact of such tremendous largesse. Candy had always been strictly rationed.

Then came the long, long journey through the sand dunes, stopping at every station, while I sat, weary and entranced, with the taste of chocolate thick and stale in my mouth, turning over and over in my mind the names of places where we were going: Sandwich, Falmouth, Truro, Provincetown. The name Truro especially fascinated me. I could not get it out of my mind: Truro. Truro. It was a name as lonely as the edge of the sea.

That summer was full of low sand dunes, and coarse grasses as sharp as wires, growing from the white sand. And the wind blew across the sand. And I saw the breakers of the grey sea come marching in towards the land, and I looked out at the ocean. Geography had begun to become a reality.

The whole town of Provincetown smelled of dead fish, and there were countless fishing boats, of all sizes, tied up along the wharves; and you could run all day on the decks of the schooners, and no one would prevent you, or chase you away. I began to know the smell of ropes and of pitch and of the salt, white wood of decks, and the curious smell of seaweed, under the docks.

When I got the mumps, Father read to me out of a book by John Masefield, which was full of pictures of sailing ships, and the only punishment I remember getting that summer was a mild reproof for refusing to eat an orange.

By the time we returned to Douglaston, and Father left me with my grandparents, where John Paul had been all the time, I had learned how to draw pictures of schooners and barks and clippers and brigs, and knew far more about all these distinctions than I do now.

Perhaps I went back to the rickety grey annex of the Public School for a couple of weeks—not for longer. Because Father had found a new place where he wanted to go and paint pictures, and having found it, came back to get his drawing boards and me, and there we went together. It was Bermuda.

Bermuda in those days had no big hotels and no golf-courses to speak of. It was not famous for anything. It was simply a curious island, two or three days out of New York, in the Gulf Stream, where the British had a small naval base and where there were no automobiles and not much of anything else either.

We took a small boat called the *Fort Victoria,* with a red and black funnel, and surprisingly soon after we had left New York harbor, the flying fishes began to leap out of the foam before her bows and skid along over the surface of the warm waves. And although I was very eager for my first sight of the island, it came upon us suddenly before I was aware, and stood up before us in the purple waters, green and white. You could already see the small white houses, made of coral, cleaner than sugar, shining in the sun, and all around us the waters paled over the shallows and became the color of emeralds, where there was sand, or lavender where there were rocks below the surface. We threaded our way in a zig-zag between the buoys that marked the path through the labyrinthine reefs.

The *H.M.S. Calcutta* lay at anchor off Ireland Island dockyard, and Father pointed to Somerset where, among the dark green cedars, was the place where we would live. Yet it was evening before we finally got there. How quiet and empty it was, in Somerset, in the gathering dusk! Our feet padded softly in the creamy dust of the deserted road. No wind stirred the paper leaves of the banana trees, or in the oleanders. Our voices seemed loud, as we spoke. Nevertheless it was a very friendly island. Those who occasionally came by saluted us as if we were old acquaintances.

The boarding house had a green verandah and many rocking chairs. The dark green paint needed renewing. The British officers, or whatever they were who lived in the place, sat and smoked their pipes, and talked, if they talked at all, about matters extremely profane. And here Father put down our bags. They were expecting us. In the shadows, we sat down to dinner. I quickly adjusted myself to the thought that this was home.

It is almost impossible to make much sense out of the continual rearrangement of our lives and our plans from month to month in my childhood. Yet every new development came to me as a reasonable and worthy change. Sometimes I had to go to school, sometimes I did not. Sometimes Father and I were living together, sometimes I was with strangers and only saw him from time to time. People came into our lives and went out of our lives. We had now one set of friends, now another. Things were always changing. I accepted it all. Why should it ever have occurred to me that nobody else lived like that? To me, it seemed as natural as the variations of the weather and the seasons. And one thing I knew: for days on end I could run where I pleased, and do whatever I liked, and life was very pleasant.

When Father left the boarding house, I remained there, and continued to live in it, because it was near the school. He was living in some other part of Somerset, with some people he had met, and he spent his days at work, painting landscapes. In fact, after that winter in Bermuda he had finished enough work to have an exhibition, and this made him enough money to go back to Europe. But meanwhile, I was going to the local school for white children, which was next to a large public cricket field, and I was constantly being punished for my complete inability to grasp the principles of multiplication and division.

It must have been very difficult for Father to try to make all these decisions. He wanted me to go to school, and he wanted me to be with him. When both these things ceased to be possible at the same time, he first decided in favor of the school: but then, after considering at length the nature of the place where I had to live, and the kind of talk I heard there, all day long, with my wide-open and impassive understanding, he took me out of the school, and brought me to live where he was. And I was very glad, because I was relieved of the burden of learning multiplication and long division.

The only worry was that my former teacher passed along that road on her bicycle on her way home, and if I was playing by the road, I had to get out of sight for fear that she would send the truant officer around and make me come back to school. One evening I did not see her coming, and I was a little late in diving into the bushes that filled a deserted quarry and, as I peeked out between the branches, I could see her looking back over her shoulder as she slowly pedalled up the white hill.

Day after day the sun shone on the blue waters of the sea, and on the islands in the bay, and on the white sand at the head of the bay, and on the little white houses strung along the hillside. I remember one day looking up into the sky, and taking it into my head to worship one of the clouds, which was shaped at one end like the head of Minerva with a helmet—like the head of the armed lady on the big British pennies.

Father left me in Bermuda with his friends, who were literary people and artists, and went to New York and had an exhibition.

It got a good press and he sold many pictures. His style had developed, since Mother's death had delivered him from landscape gardening. It was becoming at the same time more abstract, more original, and simpler, and more definite in what it had to say. I think that the people in New York did not yet see the full force of his painting, or the direction in which he was going, because the Brooklyn Museum, for instance, bought the kind of pictures of Bermuda that might be thought remotely to resemble Winslow Homer, rather than the things that indicated Father's true originality. And anyway, there was not much in common between him and Winslow Homer, except the bare fact of having painted watercolors of sub-tropical scenes. As a water-colorist, he was more like John Marin, without any of Marin's superficiality.

After the exhibition was over, and the pictures were sold, and Father had the money in his pocket, I returned from Bermuda, and found out that Father was going to sail for France, with his friends, and leave me in America.

V

Pop's office always seemed to me a fine place. The smell of typewriters and glue and office stationery had something clean and stimulating about it. The whole atmosphere was bright and active, and everybody was especially friendly, because Pop was very well liked. The term "live-wire" was singularly appropriate for him. He was always bristling with nervous energy, and most people were happy when he came shouting through their departments, snapping his fingers and whacking all the desks with a rolled-up copy of the *Evening Telegram.*

Pop worked for Grosset and Dunlap, publishers who specialized in cheap reprints of popular novels, and in children's books of an adventurous cast. They were the ones who gave the world Tom Swift and all his electrical contrivances, together with the Rover Boys and Jerry Todd and all the rest. And there were several big showrooms full of these books, where I could go and curl up in a leather armchair and read all day without being disturbed until Pop came along to take me down to Childs and eat chicken à la king.

This was nineteen-twenty-three and Grosset and Dunlap were at a peak of prosperity. As a matter of fact, it was just about this time that Pop had carried off the one great stroke of his career.

He had sold his employers the notion of printing the books of popular movies illustrated with stills from the film, to be sold in connection with the publicity given to the picture itself. This idea took on very quickly and remained popular all through the twenties, and made a lot of money for the company, and it was to be the cornerstone of Pop's own economic stability and, in fact, of the whole family's for fifteen years to come.

And so, *Black Oxen* and the *Ten Commandments* and the *Eternal City* and I forget what else went forth into all the drugstores and bookstores in all the small towns from Boston to San Francisco, full of pictures of Pola Negri and other stars of the time.

In those days movies were still occasionally made on Long Island, and more than once, my brother and I and all our friends in the neighborhood would hear they were taking some scene or other down at Alley Pond. Once, under the trees, we witnessed what was supposed to be a gypsy wedding between Gloria Swanson and some forgotten hero. The idea was that the two of them allowed their wrists to be slashed, and bound together, so that their blood would mingle: that was the gypsy wedding, according to the ideas of whoever was producing this immortal masterpiece. Frankly, however, we were not very much interested in all this. As children, we had enough sense to find the whole concept extremely heavy. We were much more excited when W. C. Fields came to Alley Pond to make part of a short comedy. First they set up the cameras in front of an old tumbledown house. I don't remember whether our hero was supposed to be drunk or scared, but the door of the house would fly open, and W. C. Fields would come hurtling out and go careering down the steps in a way that made you wonder how he got to the bottom of them without breaking both legs and all of his ribs. After he had done this over and over again innumerable times, with a singular patience and philosophical tenacity, the men moved their cameras up on top of a big pile of old lumber that was standing by, and filmed what was evidently part of the same sequence. There was a steep wooded slope, full of trees and bushes, ending in a sheer drop of about six feet. At the bottom of this, they planted a couple of extremely tame cows. Then W. C. Fields came blundering through the bushes, in his same hysterical, stumbling flight from some unseen menace. Looking behind him, he failed to see the drop, and went plunging over, landing on top of the two tame cows, which were supposed to run madly away with him on their backs. However, they just let Fields land on top of them with a heavy thud, and then stood there, chewing on the grass, and looking bored, until he fell off, and climbed stoically back up the hill to start all over again.

I mention all this because, as a matter of fact, the movies were really the family religion at Douglaston.

That summer, 1923, Pop and Bonnemaman had taken John Paul with them, and had gone to California, and had visited Hollywood, with the status of something more than simple tourists, since Pop knew a lot of movie people in a business way. The trip had something of the nature of a pilgrimage, however, and we never heard the end of what Jackie Coogan had personally said to them and how he had acted personally in their presence, in a real actual personal face-to-face-meeting-with-Jackie-Coogan.

Pop and Bonnemaman's other heroes were Doug and Mary. I admit, that what with *Robin Hood* and the *Thief of Baghdad* we all paid Douglas Fairbanks a somewhat corrupt form of hyperdulia, although neither I nor John Paul could get excited over Mary Pickford. But to Pop and Bonnemaman, Doug and Mary seemed to sum up every possible human ideal: in them was all perfection of beauty and wit, majesty, grace and decorum, bravery and love, gaiety and tenderness, all virtues and every admirable moral sentiment, truth, justice, honor, piety, loyalty, zeal, trust, citizenship, valor and, above all, marital fidelity. Day after day these two gods were extolled for the perfection of their mutual love, their glorious, simple, sincere, pious, faithful conjugal devotion to one another. Everything that good, plain, trusting middle-class optimism could devise, was gathered up into one big sentimental holocaust of praise, by my innocent and tender-hearted grandparents, and laid at the feet of Doug and Mary. It was a sad day in our family when Doug and Mary were divorced.

My grandfather's favorite place of worship was the Capitol theatre, in New York. When the Roxy theatre was built, he transferred his allegiance to that huge pile of solidified caramel, and later on there was no shrine that so stirred his devotion as the Music Hall.

There is no need to go into details of the trouble and confusion my brother and I often managed to create in the Douglaston household. When guests came whom we did not like, we would hide under the tables, or run upstairs and throw hard and soft objects down into the hall and into the living room.

One thing I would say about my brother John Paul. My most vivid memories of him, in our childhood, all fill me with poignant compunction at the thought of my own pride and hard-heartedness, and his natural humility and love.

I suppose it is usual for elder brothers, when they are still children, to feel themselves demeaned by the company of a brother four or five years younger, whom they regard as a baby and whom they tend to patronise and look down upon. So when Russ and I and Bill made huts in the woods out of boards and tar-paper which we collected around the foundations of the many cheap houses which the speculators were now putting up, as fast as they could, all over Douglaston, we severely prohibited John Paul and Russ's little brother Tommy and their friends from coming anywhere near us. And if they did try to come and get into our hut, or even to look at it, we would chase them away with stones.

When I think now of that part of my childhood, the picture I get of my brother John Paul is this: standing in a field, about a hundred yards away from the clump of sumachs where we have built our hut, is this little perplexed five-year-old kid in short pants and a kind of a leather jacket, standing quite still, with his arms hanging down at his sides, and gazing in our direction, afraid to come any nearer on account of the stones, as insulted as he is saddened, and his eyes full of indignation and sorrow. And yet he does not go away. We shout at him to get out of there, to beat it, and go home, and wing a couple of more rocks in that direction, and he does not go away. We tell him to play in some other place. He does not move.

And there he stands, not sobbing, not crying, but angry and unhappy and offended and tremendously sad. And yet he is fascinated by what we are doing, nailing shingles all over our new hut. And his tremendous desire to be with us and to do what we are doing will not permit him to go away. The law written in his nature says that he must be with his elder brother, and do what he is doing: and he cannot understand why this law of love is being so wildly and unjustly violated in his case.

Many times it was like that. And in a sense, this terrible situation is the pattern and prototype of all sin: the deliberate and formal will to reject disinterested love for us for the purely arbitrary reason that we simply do not want it. We will to separate ourselves from that love. We reject it entirely and absolutely, and will not acknowledge it, simply because it does not please us to be loved. Perhaps the inner motive is that the fact of being loved disinterestedly reminds us that we all need love from others, and depend upon the charity of others to carry on our own lives. And we refuse love, and reject society, in so far as it seems, in our own perverse imagination, to imply some obscure kind of humiliation.

There was a time when I and my magnificent friends, in our great hut, having formed a "gang," thought we were sufficiently powerful to antagonize the extremely tough Polish kids who had formed a real gang in Little Neck, a mile away. We used to go over in their neighborhood, and stand, facing in the general direction of the billboards, behind which they had their headquarters, and, from a very safe distance, we would shout defiance and challenge them to come out and fight.

Nobody came out. Perhaps there was nobody at home.

But then, one cold and rainy afternoon, we observed that numbers of large and small figures, varying in age from ten to sixteen, most of them very brawny, with caps pulled down over their eyes in a business-like way, were filtering in, by the various streets, and gathering in the vacant lot outside our house. And there they stood, with their hands in their pockets. They did not make any noise, or yell, or shout any challenges, they just stood around, looking at the house.

There were twenty or twenty-five of them. There were four of us. The climax of the situation came when Frieda, our German maid, told us that she was very busy with house-cleaning, and that we must all get out of the house immediately. Without listening to our extremely nervous protests, she chased us out the back way. We made a dash through several back yards and went down the other block, and ended up safely in the house where Bill lived, which was at the other end of the vacant lot, and from which we viewed the silent and pugnacious group from Little Neck, still standing around, and with the evident determination of staying there for quite a while.

And then an extraordinary thing happened.

The front door of our house, at the other end of the lot, opened. My little brother John Paul came walking down the steps, with a certain amount of dignity and calm. He crossed the street, and started across the lot. He walked towards the Little Neck gang. They all turned towards him. He kept on walking, and walked right into the middle of them. One or two of them took their hands out of their pockets. John Paul just looked at them, turning his head on one side, then on the other. And he walked right through the middle of them, and nobody even touched him.

And so he came to the house where we were. We did not chase him away.

vi

My grandparents were like most other Americans. They were Protestants, but you could never find out precisely what kind of Protestants they were. I, their own grandson, was never able to ascertain. They put money in the little envelopes that came to them from Zion church, but they never went near the place itself. And they also contributed to the Salvation Army and a lot of other things: so you could not tell what they were by the places which they helped to support. Of course, they had sent my uncle in his boyhood to the choir school of the Cathedral of St. John the Divine, on the rock above Harlem, which was then a peaceful bourgeois neighborhood. And they sent John Paul there too, in due course. Indeed, there was even some talk of sending me there. Yet that did not make them Episcopalians. It was not the religion that they patronised, but the school and the atmosphere. In practice, Bonnemaman used to read the little black books of Mary Baker Eddy, and I suppose that was the closest she got to religion.

On the whole, the general attitude around that house was the more or less inarticulate assumption that all religions were more or less praiseworthy on purely natural or social grounds. In any decent suburb of a big city you would expect to run across some kind of a church, once in a while. It was part of the scenery, like the High School and the Y.M.C.A. and the big whale-back roof and water-tank of the movie theater.

The only exceptions to this general acceptability of religions were the Jews and Catholics. Who would want to be a Jew? But then, that was a matter of race more than of religion. The Jews were Jews, but they could not very well help it. But as for the Catholics—it seemed, in Pop's mind, that there was a certain sinister note of malice connected with the profession of anything like the Catholic faith. The Catholic Church was the only one against which I ever heard him speak with any definite bitterness or animosity.

The chief reason was that he himself belonged to some kind of a Masonic organization, called, oddly enough, the Knights Templars. Where they picked up that name, I do not know: but the original Knights Templars were a military religious Order in the Catholic Church, who had an intimate connection with the Cistercians, of which the Trappists are a reform.

Being Knights, the Knights Templars had a sword. Pop kept his sword first in the closet in his den, and then, for a while, it was in the coat closet by the front door, mixed up with the canes and umbrellas, and with the huge policeman's club which Pop evidently believed would be useful if a burglar came around.

I suppose that at the meetings of the Knights Templars to which Pop went less and less frequently, he heard how wicked the Catholic Church was. He had probably heard that from his childhood up. It is what all Protestant children hear. It is part of their religious training.

If there was another reason why he feared the Church of Rome, it was because of the accident that some of the most corrupt politicians that ever passed a bribe in a New York election were known to be Catholics. To Pop, the word "Catholic" and "Tammany" meant just about the same thing. And since this fitted in very well with what every Protestant child is told about the duplicity and hypocrisy of Catholics, Catholicism had become associated, in his mind, with everything dishonest and crooked and immoral.

This was an impression that probably remained with him to the end of his days, but it ceased to be explicit when a Catholic lady came to live with us as a sort of companion to Bonnemaman, and a general nurse and housekeeper to the whole family. This was no temporary addition to the household. I think we were all very fond of Elsie from the beginning, and Bonnemaman got to depending on her so much that she stayed around and became more and more a part of the family, until she finally entered it altogether by marrying my uncle. With her arrival, Pop no longer let loose any of his tirades against Rome unless some bitter word happened to slip out without deliberation.

This was one of the few things I got from Pop that really took root in my mind, and became part of my mental attitude: this hatred and suspicion of Catholics. There was nothing overt about it. It was simply the deep, almost subconscious aversion from the vague and evil thing, which I called Catholicism, which lived back in the dark corners of my mentality with the other spooks, like death and so on. I did not know precisely what the word meant. It only conveyed a kind of a cold and unpleasant feeling.

The devil is no fool. He can get people feeling about heaven the way they ought to feel about hell. He can make them fear the means of grace the way they do not fear sin. And he does so, not by light but by obscurity, not by realities but by shadows; not by clarity and substance, but by dreams and the creatures of psychosis. And men are so poor in intellect that a few cold chills down their spine will be enough to keep them from ever finding out the truth about anything.

As a matter of fact, by this time I was becoming more and more positively averse to the thought of any religion, although I was only nine. The reason was that once or twice I had to go to Sunday School, and found it such a bore that from then on I went to play in the woods instead. I don't think the family was very grieved.

All this time, Father was abroad. He had gone first to the South of France, to the Roussillon, where I was born. He was living first at Banyuls, then at Collioure, painting landscapes along the Mediterranean shore, and in the red mountains, all the way down to Port Vendres and the borders of Catalonia. Then, after a while, he and the people he was with crossed over into Africa and went inland in Algeria, to a place on the edge of the desert, and there he painted some more.

Letters came from Africa. He sent me a package containing a small burnous, which I could wear, and a stuffed lizard of some sort. At that time I had gathered a small natural history museum of pieces of junk that are to be found around Long Island, like arrowheads and funny-looking stones.

During those years, he was painting some of the best pictures he had ever painted in his life. But then something happened, and we got a letter from one of his friends, telling us that he was seriously ill. He was, in fact, dying.

When Bonnemaman told me this news, I was old enough to understand what it meant, and I was profoundly affected, filled with sorrow and with fear. Was I never to see my father again? This could not happen. I don't know whether or not it occurred to me to pray, but I think by this time it must have, at least once or twice, although I certainly had very little of anything that could be called faith. If I did pray for my father it was probably only one of those blind, semi-instinctive movements of nature that will come to anyone, even an atheist in a time of crisis, and which do not prove the existence of God, exactly, but which certainly show that the need to worship and acknowledge Him is something deeply ingrained in our dependent natures, and simply inseparable from our essence.

It seems that for days Father lay in delirium. Nobody appeared to know what was the matter with him. He was expected to die from moment to moment. But he did not die.

Finally he got past the crisis of this strange sickness, and recovered his consciousness, and began to improve and get well. And when he was on his feet again, he was able to finish some more pictures, and get his things together, and go to London, where he held his most successful exhibition, at the Leicester Galleries, early in 1925.

When he returned to New York, in the early summer of that year, he came in a kind of triumph. He was beginning to be a successful artist. Long ago he had been elected to one of those more or less meaningless British societies, so that he could write F.R.B.A. after his name—which he never did—and I think he was already in *Who's Who*, although that was the kind of thing for which he had supreme contempt.

But now, what was far more useful to an artist, he had gained the attention and respect of such an important and venerable critic as Roger Fry, and the admiration of people who not only knew what a good painting was, but had some money with which to buy one.

As he landed in New York, he was a very different person—more different than I realized—from the man who had taken me to Bermuda two years before. All I noticed, at the moment, was the fact that he had a beard, to which I strenuously objected, being filled with the provincial snobbery so strong in children and adolescents.

"Are you going to shave it off now, or later?" I inquired, when we got to the house in Douglaston.

"I am not going to shave it off at all," said my father.

"That's crazy," I said. But he was not disturbed. He did shave it off, a couple of years later, by which time I had got used to it.

However, he had something to tell me that upset my complacency far more than the beard. For by now, having become more or less acclimatised in Douglaston, after the unusual experience of remaining some two years in the same place, I was glad to be there, and liked my friends, and liked to go swimming in the bay. I had been given a small camera with which I took pictures, which my uncle caused to be developed for me at the Pennsylvania Drug Store, in the city. I possessed a baseball bat with the word "Spalding" burnt on it in large letters. I thought maybe I would like to become a Boy Scout and, indeed, I had seen a great competition of Boy Scouts in the Flushing Armory, just next door to the Quaker meeting-house where I had once got a glimpse of Dan Beard, with his beard.

My father said: "We are going to France."

"France!" I said, in astonishment. Why should anybody want to go to France? I thought: which shows that I was a very stupid and ignorant child. But he persuaded me that he meant what he said. And when all my objections were useless, I burst into tears. Father was not at all unsympathetic about it. He kindly told me that I would be glad to be in France, when I got there, and gave me many reasons why it was a good idea. And finally he admitted that we would not start right away.

With this compromise I was temporarily comforted, thinking perhaps the plan would be dropped after a while. But fortunately it was not. And on August the twenty-fifth of that year the game of Prisoner's Base began again, and we sailed for France. Although I did not know it, and it would not have interested me then, it was the Feast of St. Louis of France.

2

Our Lady of the Museums

How DID IT ever happen that, when the dregs of the world had collected in western Europe, when Goth and Frank and Norman and Lombard had mingled with the rot of old Rome to form a patchwork of hybrid races, all of them notable for ferocity, hatred, stupidity, craftiness, lust and brutality—how did it happen that, from all this, there should come Gregorian chant, monasteries and cathedrals, the poems of Prudentius, the commentaries and histories of Bede, the *Moralia* of Gregory the Great, St. Augustine's *City of God*, and his *Trinity*, the writings of St. Anselm, St. Bernard's sermons on the Canticles, the poetry of Caedmon and Cynewulf and Langland and Dante, St. Thomas' *Summa*, and the *Oxoniense* of Duns Scotus?

How does it happen that even today a couple of ordinary French stonemasons, or a carpenter and his apprentice, can put up a dovecote or a barn that has more architectural perfection than the piles of eclectic stupidity that grow up at the cost of hundreds of thousands of dollars on the campuses of American universities?

When I went to France, in 1925, returning to the land of my birth, I was also returning to the fountains of the intellectual and spiritual life of the world to which I belonged. I was returning to the spring of natural waters, if you will, but waters purified and cleaned by grace with such powerful effect that even the corruption and decadence of the French society of our day has never been able to poison them entirely, or reduce them once again to their original and barbarian corruption.

And yet it was France that grew the finest flowers of delicacy and grace and intelligence and wit and understanding and proportion and taste. Even the countryside, even the landscape of France, whether in the low hills and lush meadows and apple orchards of Normandy or in the sharp and arid and vivid outline of the mountains of Provence, or in the vast, rolling red vineyards of Languedoc, seems to have been made full of a special perfection, as a setting for the best of the cathedrals, the most interesting towns, the most fervent monasteries, and the greatest universities.

But the wonderful thing about France is how all her perfections harmonize so fully together. She has possessed all the skills, from cooking to logic and theology, from bridge-building to contemplation, from vine-growing to sculpture, from cattle-breeding to prayer: and possessed them more perfectly, separately and together, than any other nation.

Why is it that the songs of the little French children are more graceful, their speech more intelligent and sober, their eyes calmer and more profound than those of the children of other nations? Who can explain these things?

France, I am glad I was born in your land, and I am glad God brought me back to you, for a time, before it was too late.

I did not know all these things about France the rainy September evening when we landed at Calais, coming from England through which we had passed on our way.

Nor did I share or understand the enthusiastic satisfaction with which Father got off the boat and walked into the noise of the French station, filled with the cries of porters and with the steam of the French trains.

I was tired, and fell asleep long before we got to Paris. I woke up long enough to be impressed by the welter of lights in the wet streets, and the dark sweep of the Seine, as we crossed one of the countless bridges, while far away the fires on the Eiffel tower spelled "C-I-T-R-O-Ë-N."

The words Montparnasse, Rue des Saints Pères, Gare d'Orléans filled my mind with their unmeaning, and spelled me no certitude concerning the tall grey houses, and the wide shady awnings of the cafés, and the trees, and the people, and the churches, and the flying taxis, and the green and white busses full of noise.

I did not have time, at the age of ten, to make anything out of this city, but already I knew I was going to like France: and then, once more, we were on a train.

That day, on that express, going into the south, into the Midi, I discovered France. I discovered that land which is really, as far as I can tell, the one to which I do belong, if I belong to any at all, by no documentary title but by geographical birth.

We flew over the brown Loire, by a long, long bridge at Orléans, and from then on I was home, although I had never seen it before, and shall never see it again. It was there, too, that Father told me about Joan of Arc, and I suppose the thought of her was with me, at least in the back of my mind, all the day long. Maybe the thought of her, acting as a kind of implicit prayer by the veneration and love it kindled in me, won me her intercession in heaven, so that through her I was able to get some sort of actual grace out of the sacrament of her land, and to contemplate God without realizing it in all the poplars along those streams, in all the low-roofed houses gathered about the village churches, in the woods and the farms and the bridged rivers. We passed a place called Châteaudun. When the land became rockier, we came to Limoges, with a labyrinth of tunnels, ending in a burst of light and a high bridge and a panorama of the city crowding up the side of a steep hill to the feet of the plain-towered cathedral. And all the time we were getting deeper and deeper into Aquitaine: towards the old provinces of Quercy and Rouergue, where, although we were not sure yet of our destination, I was to live and drink from the fountains of the Middle Ages.

In the evening we came to a station called Brive. Brive-la-Gaillarde. The dusk was gathering. The country was hilly, and full of trees, yet rocky, and you knew that the uplands were bare and wild. In the valleys were castles. It was too dark for us to see Cahors.

And then: Montauban.

What a dead town! What darkness and silence, after the train. We came out of the station into an empty, dusty square, full of shadows, and a dim light, here and there. The hoofs of a cab-horse clopped away along the empty street, taking some of the other people who had descended from the express off into the mysterious town. We picked up our bags and crossed the square to a hotel that was there, one of those low, undefined, grey little hotels, with a dim bulb burning in a downstairs window, illuminating a small café, with a lot of iron tables and a few calendars covered with fly-specks and the big volumes of the Bottin crowding the rickety desk of the sourfaced lady in black who presided over the four customers.

And yet, instead of being dreary, it was pleasant. And although I had no conscious memory of anything like this, it was familiar, and I felt at home. Father threw open the wooden shutters of the room, and looked out into the quiet night, without stars, and said:

"Do you smell the woodsmoke in the air? That is the smell of the Midi."

ii

When we woke up in the morning, and looked out into the bright sunlit air, and saw the low tiled roofs, we realized that we had come upon a scene different from the last kind of landscape we had seen by the light of the previous evening in the train.

We were at the borders of Languedoc. Everything was red. The town was built of brick. It stood on a kind of low bluff, over the clay-colored eddies of the river Tarn. We might almost have been in a part of Spain. But oh! It was dead, that town!

Why were we there? It was not only that Father wanted to continue painting in the south of France. He had come back to us that year with more than a beard. Whether it was his sickness or what, I do not know, but something had made him certain that he could not leave the training and care of his sons to other people, and that he had a responsibility to make some kind of a home, somewhere, where he could at the same time carry on his work and have us living with him, growing up under his supervision. And, what is more, he had become definitely aware of certain religious obligations for us as well as for himself.

I am sure he had never ceased to be a religious man: but now—a thing which I did not remember from my earlier years—he told me to pray, to ask God to help us, to help him paint, to help him have a successful exhibition, to find us a place to live.

When we were settled then, perhaps after a year or two, he would bring John Paul over to France too. Then we would have a home. So far, of course, everything was indefinite. But the reason why he had come to Montauban was that he had been advised that there was a very good school there.

The school in question was called the Institut Jean Calvin, and the recommendation had come from some prominent French Protestants whom Father knew.

I remember we went and visited the place. It was a big, clean, white building overlooking the river. There were some sunny cloisters, full of greenery, and all the rooms were empty, because it was still the time of summer vacation. However, there was something about it that Father did not like, and I was, thank God, never sent there. As a matter of fact it was not so much a school as a kind of Protestant residence where a lot of youths (who belonged, mostly, to fairly well-to-do families) boarded and received religious instruction and supervision and, for the rest, attended the classes of the local Lycée.

And so I obscurely began to realize that, although Father was anxious for me to get some kind of religious training, he was by no means in love with French Protestantism. As a matter of fact, I learned later from some of his friends, that at that time there had been not a little likelihood that he might become a Catholic. He seems to have been much attracted to the Church, but in the end he resisted the attraction because of the rest of us. I think he felt that his first duty was to take the ordinary means at his disposal to get me and John Paul to practise whatever religion was nearest at hand to us, for if he became a Catholic there might have been immense complications with the rest of the family, and we would perhaps have remained without any religion at all.

He would have felt far less hesitant if he had only had some Catholic friends of his own intellectual level—someone who would be able to talk to him intelligently about the faith. But as far as I know, he had none. He had a tremendous respect for the good Catholic people we met, but they were too inarticulate about the Church to be able to tell him anything about it that he could understand—and also, they were generally far too shy.

Then, too, after the first day, it became clear that Montauban was no place for us. There was really nothing there worth painting. It was a good enough town, but it was dull. The only thing that interested Father was the Musée Ingres, filled with meticulous drawings by that painter, who had been born in Montauban: and that collection of cold and careful sketches was not enough to keep anyone at a high pitch of inspiration for much more than fifteen minutes. More characteristic of the town was a nightmarish bronze monument by Bourdelle, outside the museum, which seemed to represent a group of cliff-dwellers battling in a mass of molten chocolate.

However, when we happened to inquire at the Syndicat d'Initiative about places to live, we saw photographs of some little towns which, as we were told, were in a valley of a river called the Aveyron not very far away to the northeast of the city.

The afternoon we took the peculiar, antiquated train out of Montauban into the country, we felt something like the three Magi after leaving Herod and Jerusalem when they caught sight once again of their star.

The locomotive had big wheels and a low, squat boiler, and an inordinately high smoke-stack, so that it seemed to have escaped from the museum, except that it was very sturdy and did its work well. And the three or four little coaches sped us quickly into a territory that was certainly sacramental.

The last town that had a brick campanile to its church, after the manner of all Languedoc, was Montricoux. Then the train entered the Aveyron valley. After that, we were more or less in Rouergue. And then we began to see something.

I did not realize what we were getting into until the train swept around a big curve of the shallow river, and came to stop under the sunny plane trees along the platform of a tiny station, and we looked out the window, and saw that we had just passed along the bottom of a sheer cliff one or two hundred feet high, with a thirteenth-century castle on the top of it. That was Bruniquel. All around us, the steep hills were thick with woods, small gnarled oaks, clinging to the rock. Along the river, the slender poplars rippled with the light of late afternoon, and green waters danced on the stones. The people who got on and off the train were peasants with black smocks, and on the roads we saw men walking beside teams of oxen, drawing their two-wheeled carts: and they guided the placid beasts with their long sticks. Father told me that the people were all talking, not French, but the old patois, langue d'oc.

The next place was Penne. At the meeting of two valleys, a thin escarpment of rock soared up boldly over the river, bent and sharply rising, like an open wing. On the top were the ruins of another castle. Further down, straggling along the ridge, went the houses of the village and somewhere among them the small square tower of a church, an open iron belfry on top, with a visible bell.

The valley seemed to get narrower and deeper as the train followed its narrow single track between the river and the rocks. Sometimes there was enough space between us and the river to contain a small hayfield. Occasionally a deserted dirt road or cattle track would cross our way, and there would be a house and a crossing-gate and one of furious French bells, throwing the sudden scare of its clangor through the windows of the carriage as we passed by.

The valley widened a little to contain the village of Cazals, hanging on to the foot of the hill across the river, and then we were back in the gorge. If you went to the window and looked up, you could see the grey and yellow cliffs towering up so high they almost blocked out the sky. And now we could begin to distinguish caves high up on the rock. Later I would climb up there and visit some of them. Passing through tunnel after tunnel, and over many bridges, through bursts of light and greenery followed by deep shadow, we came at last to the town of our destination.

It was an old, old town. Its history went back to the Roman days—which were the times of the martyred saint, its patron. Antoninus had brought Christianity to the Roman colony in this valley, and later he had been martyred in another place, Pamiers, down in the foothills of the Pyrenees, near Prades, where I was born.

Even in 1925, St. Antonin preserved the shape of a round, walled *bourg:* only the walls themselves were gone, and were replaced on three sides by a wide circular street lined with trees and spacious enough to be called a Boulevard, although you hardly ever saw anything on it but ox-carts and chickens. The town itself was a labyrinth of narrow streets, lined by old thirteenth-century houses, mostly falling into ruins. Nevertheless, the medieval town was there, but for the fact that the streets were no longer crowded and busy, and the houses and shops were no longer occupied by prosperous merchants and artisans, and there was nothing left of the color and gaiety and noise of the Middle Ages. Nevertheless, to walk through those streets was to be in the Middle Ages: for nothing had been touched by man, only by ruin and by the passage of time.

It seems that one of the busiest guilds of the town had been that of the tanners and the old tanneries were still there, along a narrow foul-smelling sewer of a stream that ran through a certain section of the town. But in those old days the whole place had been filled with the activity of all the work belonging to a free and prosperous commune.

And as I say, the center of it all was the church.

Unfortunately, the very importance of the ancient shrine of St. Antonin had drawn down violence upon it in the days of the religious wars. The church that now stood on the ruins was entirely modern, and we could not judge what the old one had been like, or see, reflected in its work and construction, the attitude of the citizens who had built it. Even now, however, the church dominated the town, and each noon and evening sent forth the Angelus bells over the brown, ancient tiled roofs reminding people of the Mother of God who watched over them.

And even now, although I never thought of it and was, indeed, incapable of doing so, since I had no understanding of the concept of Mass, even now, several times each morning, under those high arches, on the altar over the relics of the martyr, took place that tremendous, secret and obvious immolation, so secret that it will never be thoroughly understood by a created intellect, and yet so obvious that its very obviousness blinds us by excess of clarity: the unbloody Sacrifice of God under the species of bread and wine.

Here, in this amazing, ancient town, the very pattern of the place, of the houses and streets and of nature itself, the circling hills, the cliffs and trees, all focussed my attention upon the one, important central fact of the church and what it contained. Here, everywhere I went, I was forced, by the disposition of everything around me, to be always at least virtually conscious of the church. Every street pointed more or less inward to the center of the town, to the church. Every view of the town, from the exterior hills, centered upon the long grey building with its high spire.

The church had been fitted into the landscape in such a way as to become the keystone of its intelligibility. Its presence imparted a special form, a particular significance to everything else that the eye beheld, to the hills, the forests, the fields, the white cliff of the Rocher d'Anglars and to the red bastion of the Roc Rouge, to the winding river, and the green valley of the Bonnette, the town and the bridge, and even to the white stucco villas of the modern bourgeois that dotted the fields and orchards outside the precinct of the vanished ramparts: and the significance that was thus imparted was a supernatural one.

The whole landscape, unified by the church and its heavenward spire, seemed to say: this is the meaning of all created things: we have been made for no other purpose than that men may use us in raising themselves to God, and in proclaiming the glory of God. We have been fashioned, in all our perfection, each according to his own nature, and all our natures ordered and harmonized together, that man's reason and his love might fit in this one last element, this God-given key to the meaning of the whole.

Oh, what a thing it is, to live in a place that is so constructed that you are forced, in spite of yourself, to be at least a virtual contemplative! Where all day long your eyes must turn, again and again, to the House that hides the Sacramental Christ!

I did not even know who Christ was, that He was God. I had not the faintest idea that there existed such a thing as the Blessed Sacrament. I thought churches were simply places where people got together and sang a few hymns. And yet now I tell you, you who are now what I once was, unbelievers, it is that Sacrament, and that alone, the Christ living in our midst, and sacrificed by us, and for us and with us, in the clean and perpetual Sacrifice, it is He alone Who holds our world together, and keeps us all from being poured headlong and immediately into the pit of our eternal destruction. And I tell you there is a power that goes forth from that Sacrament, a power of light and truth, even into the hearts of those who have heard nothing of Him and seem to be incapable of belief.

iii

We soon rented an apartment in a three-story house at the edge of the town, on the Place de la Condamine, where they held the cattle market. But Father planned to build a house of his own, and soon he bought some land nearby on the lower slopes of the big hill that closed off the western arm of the valley of the Bonnette. On top of the hill was a little chapel, now abandoned, called Le Calvaire, and indeed up the rocky path through the vineyards behind our land there had once been a series of shrines, making the fourteen Stations of the Cross between the town and the top of the hill. But that kind of piety had died away in the nineteenth-century: there were not enough good Catholics left to keep it alive.

And then when Father began to make plans for building his house, we travelled all over the countryside looking at places, and also visiting villages where there might be good subjects for pictures.

Thus I was constantly in and out of old churches, and stumbled upon the ruins of ancient chapels and monasteries. We saw wonderful hill towns like Najac and Cordes. Cordes was even more perfectly preserved than St. Antonin, but it did not have the form of our town built around its shrine, although Cordes was, of course, centered upon its church too. But Cordes had been built as a sort of fortified summer resort for the Counts of Languedoc, and its chief attraction were the more or less fancy houses of the court officials who came out there for the hunting with their Lord.

Then, too, we went down into the plains to the south, and came to Albi, with the red cathedral of St. Cecilia frowning over the Tarn like a fortress, and from the top of that tower we looked out over the plains of Languedoc, where all the churches were forts. This land was long wild with heresy, and with the fake mysticism that tore men away from the Church and from the Sacraments, and sent them into hiding to fight their way to some strange, suicidal nirvana.

There was a factory in St. Antonin—the only factory in the place—employing the only proletarians, three or four men, one of whom was also the only Communist. The factory made some kind of a machine for raising hay effortlessly from the surface of a field on to the top of a wagon. The man who owned it was called Rodolausse, the town capitalist. He had two sons who ran his plant for him. One of them was a tall, lanky, solemn, dark-haired man with horn-rimmed spectacles.

One evening we were sitting in one of the cafés of the town, a deserted place run by a very old man. Rodolausse got to talking with Father, and I remember his polite enquiry as to whether we were Russians. He got that idea from the beard.

When he found out we had come there to live, he immediately offered to sell us his house, and invited us out there to dinner, that we might see it. The House of Simon de Montfort, as it was called, was a big farm a mile or two out of town on the road to Caylus. It stood up the slope of a hill overlooking the valley of the Bonnette and was itself in the mouth of a deep circular valley full of woods where, as we found, a small stream full of watercress rose from a clear spring. The house itself was an ancient place, and looked as if De Montfort might indeed have lived in it. But it also looked as if he might still be haunting it. It was very dark and gloomy: and, being dark, was no place for a painter. Besides, it was too expensive for us. And Father preferred to build a house of his own.

It was not long after I had started to go to the local elementary school, where I sat with great embarrassment among the very smallest children, and tried to pick up French as we went along, that Father had already drawn up plans for the house we would build on the land he had now bought at the foot of Calvary. It would have one big room, which would be a studio and dining room and living room, and then upstairs there would be a couple of bedrooms. That was all.

We traced out the foundations and Father and a workman began to dig. Then a water diviner came in and found us water and we had a well dug. Near the well Father planted two poplar trees—one for me, one for John Paul—and to the east of the house he laid out a large garden when the following spring came around.

Meanwhile, we had made a lot of friends. I do not know whether it was through the capitalist, Rodolausse, or through the radical-socialist teamster Pierrot, that we got in contact with the local rugby football club, or they with us: but one of the first things that happened after our arrival was that a delegation from the club, the "Avant-Garde de Saint-Antonin," presented themselves to Father and asked him to become president of the club. He was English, and therefore he was an expert, they assumed, in every type of sport. As a matter of fact, he had played rugby for his school in New Zealand. So he became president of the club, and occasionally refereed their wild games, at the risk of his life. It was not only that the rules had changed, since his time, but there was a special interpretation of the rules in St. Antonin which no one could discover without a private revelation or the gift of the discernment of souls. However, he lived through the season.

I used to accompany him and the team to all the games they played away from home, going as far as Figeac to the northeast, deep in the hill country of Rouergue; or Gaillac, on the plains of Languedoc, to the south, a town with one of those fortress-churches and a real stadium for its rugby team. St. Antonin was not, of course, called in to play the Gaillac first-fifteen, but only to play an opener, while the crowds were coming in for the principal game.

In those days the whole south of France was infected with a furious and violent passion for rugby football, and played it with a blood-thirsty energy that sometimes ended in mortal injuries. In the really important games, the referee usually had to be escorted from the grounds afterwards by a special bodyguard, and not infrequently had to make his escape over the fence and through the fields. The only sport that raised a more universal and more intense excitement than rugby, was long-distance bicycle racing. St. Antonin was off the circuit of the big road races, but occasionally there would be a race that came through our hills, and we would stand at the end of the long climb to the top of Rocher d'Anglars, and watch them coming slowly up the hill, with their noses almost scraping the front wheels of their bikes as they bent far down and toiled, with all their muscles clenched into tremendous knots. And the veins stood out on their foreheads.

One of the members of the rugby team was a small, rabbit-like man, the son of the local hay and feed dealer, who owned a car and drove most of the team back and forth from the games. One night he nearly killed himself and about six of us when a rabbit got into the lights on the road ahead of us and kept running in front of the car. Immediately, this wild Frenchman jammed his foot down on the gas and started after the rabbit. The white tail bobbed up and down in the light, always just a few feet ahead of the wheels, and whipping from one side of the road to the other, to throw the auto off his scent: only the auto didn't hunt that way. It just kept roaring after the rabbit, zig-zagging from one side of the road to the other and nearly spilling us all into the ditch.

Those of us who were piled up in the back seat began to get a little nervous, especially when we observed that we were coming to the top of the long steep hill that went winding down into the valley where St. Antonin was. If we kept after that rabbit, we would surely go over the bank, and then we wouldn't stop turning over until we landed in the river, a couple of hundred feet below.

Somebody growled a modest complaint:

"C'est assez, hein? Tu ne l'attraperas pas!"

The son of the hay and feed dealer said nothing. He bent over the wheel with his eyes popping at the road, and the white tail in front of us kept darting away from the wheels of the car, zig-zagging from the high bank on one side to the ditch on the other.

And then we came over the hill. The darkness and emptiness of the valley was before us. The road began to descend.

The complaints in the back seat increased, became a chorus. But the driver stepped on the gas even harder. The car careened wildly across the road; we had nearly caught the rabbit. But not quite. He was out there ahead of us again.

"We'll get him on the hill," exclaimed the driver. "Rabbits can't run down-hill, their hind legs are too long."

The rabbit ahead of us was doing a fine job of running down-hill, just about five feet ahead of our front wheels.

Then somebody began to yell: "Look out, look out!"

We were coming to a fork in the road. The main road went on to the left, and an older road sloped off at a steeper incline to the right. In between them was a wall. And the rabbit headed straight for the wall.

"Stop! Stop!" we implored. Nobody could tell which way the rabbit was going to go: and the wall was flying straight at us.

"Hold on!" somebody shouted.

The car gave a wild lurch, and if there had been any room in the back we would all have fallen on the floor. But we were not dead. The car was still on the main road, roaring down into the valley and, to our immense relief, there was no rabbit, out there in the lights.

"Did you catch him?" I asked hopefully. "Maybe you caught him back there?"

"Oh, no," replied the driver sadly, "he took the other road."

Our friend the teamster Pierrot was a huge, powerful man, but he did not play on the football team. He was too lazy and too dignified, although he would have been a decorative addition to the outfit. There were three or four others like him, big men with huge black moustaches and bristling eyebrows, as wild as the traditional representations of Gog and Magog. One of them used to play whole games wearing a grey, peaked street-cap. I suppose if we had ever played on a really hot day he would have come out on the field with a straw hat on. Anyway, this element of the team would have made a fine subject for Douanier-Rousseau, and Pierrot would have fitted in admirably. Only his sport was sitting at the table of a café imbibing cognac. Sometimes, too, he made excursions to Toulouse, and once, while we were standing on the bridge, he gave me a bloodcurdling description of a fight he had had with an Arab, with a knife, in the big city.

It was Pierrot who took us to a wedding feast at a farm up by Caylus. I went to several of these feasts, during the time when I was at St. Antonin, and I never saw anything so Gargantuan: and yet it was never wild or disordered. The peasants and the foresters and the others who were there certainly ate and drank tremendously: but they never lost their dignity as human beings. They sang and danced and played tricks on one another, and the language was often fairly coarse, but in a manner which was more or less according to custom, and on the whole the atmosphere was good and healthy, and all this pleasure was sanctified by a Sacramental occasion.

On this occasion Pierrot put on his good black suit and his clean cap and hitched up a gig, and we drove to Caylus. It was the farm of his uncle or cousin. The place was crowded with carts and carriages, and the feast was a more or less communal affair. Everybody had provided something towards it, and Father brought a bottle of strong, black Greek wine which nearly pulverized the host.

There were too many guests to be contained in the big dining room and kitchen of the farm, with its blood-sausages and strings of onions hanging from the beams. One of the barns had been cleaned out and tables had been set up in there, and about one o'clock in the afternoon everybody sat down and began to eat. After the soups, the women began to bring in the main courses from the kitchen: and there were plates and plates of every kind of meat. Rabbit, veal, mutton, lamb, beef, stews and steaks, and fowl, fried, boiled, braised, roasted, sautéed, fricasseed, dished this way and that way, with wine sauces and all other kinds of sauces, with practically nothing else to go with it except an occasional piece of potato or carrot or onion in the garnishing.

"All the year round they live on bread and vegetables and bits of sausage," Father explained, "so now they don't want anything but meat." And I suppose he had the right explanation. But before the meal was half over, I got up from the table and staggered out into the air, and leaned against the wall of the barn, and watched the huge, belligerent geese parading up and down the barn-yard, dragging their tremendous overstuffed livers in the dirt, those livers which would soon be turned into the kind of pâté de foie gras which even now made me sick.

The feast lasted until late in the afternoon, and even when night fell some were still at it there in the barn. But meanwhile the owner of the farm and Pierrot and Father and I had gone out to see an old abandoned chapel that stood on the property. I wonder what it had been: a shrine, a hermitage perhaps? But now, in any case, it was in ruins. And it had a beautiful thirteenth- or fourteenth-century window, empty of course of its glass. Father bought the whole thing, with some of the money he had saved up from his last exhibition, and we eventually used the stones and the window and the door-arches and so on in building our house at St. Antonin.

By the time the summer of 1926 came around, we were well established in St. Antonin, although work on the house had not yet really begun. By this time I had learned French, or all the French that a boy of eleven was expected to use in the ordinary course of his existence, and I remember how I had spent hours that winter reading books about all the other wonderful places there were in France.

Pop had sent us money, at Christmas, and we used some of it to buy a big expensive three volume set of books, full of pictures, called *Le Pays de France*. And I shall never forget the fascination with which I studied it, and filled my mind with those cathedrals and ancient abbeys and those castles and towns and monuments of the culture that had so captivated my heart.

I remember how I looked at the ruins of Jumièges and Cluny, and wondered how those immense basilicas had looked in the days of their glory. Then there was Chartres, with its two unequal spires; the long vast nave of Bourges; the soaring choir of Beauvais; the strange fat romanesque cathedral of Angouleme, and the white byzantine domes of Perigueux. And I gazed upon the huddled buildings of the ancient Grande Chartreuse, crowded together in their solitary valley, with the high mountains loaded with firs, soaring up to their rocky summits on either side. What kind of men had lived in those cells? I cannot say that I wondered much about that, as I looked at the pictures. I had no curiosity about monastic vocations or religious rules, but I know my heart was filled with a kind of longing to breathe the air of that lonely valley and to listen to its silence. I wanted to be in all these places, which the pictures of

Le Pays de France showed me: indeed, it was a kind of a problem to me and an unconscious source of obscure and half-realized woe, that I could not be in all of them at once.

iv

That summer, 1926, much to Father's distress—because he wanted to stay at St. Antonin and work on the house and at his painting—Pop gathered up a great mountain of baggage in New York, stirred Bonnemaman into action, dressed up my brother John Paul in a new suit and, armed with passports and a whole sheaf of tickets from Thomas Cook and Son, boarded the liner *Leviathan* and started for Europe.

News of this invasion had been disturbing Father for some time. Pop was not content to come and spend a month or two in St. Antonin with us. In fact, he was not particularly anxious to come to this small, forgotten town at all. He wanted to keep on the move and, since he had two months at his disposal, he saw no reason why he could not cover the whole of Europe from Russia to Spain and from Scotland to Constantinople. However, being dissuaded from this Napoleonic ambition, he consented to restrict his appetite for sight-seeing to England, Switzerland and France.

In May or June the information reached us that Pop had descended in force upon London, had scoured the Shakespeare country and other parts of England—and was now preparing to cross the channel and occupy the north of France.

We were instructed to get ourselves together and to move northward, join forces with him in Paris, after which we would proceed together to the conquest of Switzerland.

Meanwhile at St. Antonin we had peaceful visitors, two gentle old ladies, friends of the family in New Zealand, and with them we started out, with no haste, on our northward journey. We all wanted to see Rocamadour.

Rocamadour is a shrine to the Mother of God, where an image of Our Lady is venerated in a cave-chapel half way up a cliff, against the side of which a monastery was built in the Middle Ages. The legend says that the place was first settled by the publican Zacchaeus, the man who climbed the sycamore tree to see Christ as He came by, and whom Christ told to climb down again, and entertain Him in his own house.

At the moment when we were leaving Rocamadour, after a short visit that filled my mind with memory of a long summer evening, with swallows flying around the wall of the old monastery up against the cliff, and around the tower of the new shrine on top of it, Pop was riding around all the châteaux of the Loire in a bus full of Americans. And as they went whizzing through Chenonceaux and Blois and Tours, Pop, who had his pockets crammed full of two- and five-sou pieces, and even francs and two-franc pieces, would dig in and scatter handfuls of coins into the streets whenever they passed a group of playing children. And the dusty wake of the bus would ring with his burst of laughter as all the kids plunged after the coins in a wild scramble.

It was that way all through the valley of the Loire.

When we got to Paris, having left the two old ladies from New Zealand in an obscure town called Saint Céré down in the south, we found Pop and Bonnemaman entrenched in the most expensive hotel they could find. The *Continental* was far beyond their means, but it was 1926 and the franc was so low that Pop's head was completely turned by it, and he had lost all sense of values.

The first five minutes in that hotel room in Paris told us all we needed to know about the way it was going to be for the next two weeks, in the whirlwind tour of Switzerland that was just about to begin.

The room was crammed to the doors with so much useless luggage that you could hardly move around in it. And Bonnemaman and John Paul let it be known that they had sunk into a state of more or less silent opposition and passive resistance to all of Pop's enthusiastic displays of optimism and pep.

When Pop told us about the Loire campaign and the largesse with which he had showered every village from Orleans to Nantes, we realized from the mute pain in Bonnemaman's expression, as she turned an eloquent and pleading look to my father, just how the rest of the family felt about all this. And, seeing what we were in for, we more or less instinctively took sides with the oppressed. It was clear that every move, from now on, was going to be rich in public and private humiliation for the more or less delicate sensibilities of the rest of us, from Bonnemaman who was extremely touchy by nature, to John Paul and myself who were quick to see or imagine that others were laughing at Pop and felt ourselves included in the derision by implication.

And thus we started out for the Swiss frontier, travelling in easy stages seven or eight hours a day in the train and stopping overnight. There was the constant embarkation and debarkation from trains and taxis and hotel busses and each time every one of the sixteen pieces of luggage had to be accounted for, and the voice of my grandfather would be heard echoing along the walls of the greatest railway stations in Europe. "Martha, where the dickens did you leave that pigskin bag?"

On every piece of luggage, by way of identification, Pop had pasted a pink American two-cent stamp, a device which had aroused sharp and instantaneous criticism from myself and John Paul. "What are you trying to do, Pop," we asked with sarcasm. "Are you going to send that stuff through the mail?"

The first day was not so bad for me and Father, because we were still in France. We saw a little of Dijon, and the train passed through Besançon on the way to Basle. But as soon as we got into Switzerland, things were different.

For some reason, we found Switzerland extremely tedious. It was not Father's kind of landscape, and anyway he had no time to sketch or paint anything, even if he had wanted to. In every city we hunted, first thing of all, for the museum. But the museums were never satisfactory. They were filled mostly with huge canvasses by some modern Swiss national artist, paintings representing monstrous great executioners trying to chop the heads off Swiss patriots. Besides, it was always hard for us to find the museum in the first place, because we did not know German, and we couldn't make any sense out of the answers people gave us. Then when we finally did get there, instead of the comfort of a few decent pictures, we would immediately be confronted by another immense red and yellow cartoon by this Swiss jingo whose name I have forgotten.

Finally we took to making fun of everything in the museums, and playing around, and putting our hats on the statues, which was all right because the place was always totally deserted anyway. But once or twice we nearly got in trouble with the stuffy Swiss custodians, who came around the corner by surprise and found us mocking the hatted masterworks, kidding the busts of Beethoven and the rest.

As a matter of fact, the only pleasure Father got out of the whole expedition was a jazz concert he heard in Paris, given by a big American Negro orchestra—I cannot imagine who it was. I think it was too far back for Louis Armstrong: but Father was very happy with that. I did not go. Pop did not approve of jazz. But when we got to Lucerne, there was an orchestra in the hotel, and our table in the dining room was so close to it that I could reach out and touch the drum. And the drummer was a Negro with whom I immediately made friends, although he was rather shy. Meals were very interesting with all this business-like drumming going on right in my ear, and I was more fascinated by the activities of the drummer than I was by the melons and meats that were set before us. This was the only pleasure I got out of Switzerland and then, almost immediately, Pop got our table changed.

The rest of the time was one long fight. We fought on pleasure steamers, we fought on funicular railways, we fought on the tops of mountains and at the foot of mountains and by the shores of lakes and under the heavy branches of the evergreens.

In the hotel at Lucerne, John Paul and I nearly came to blows (Bonnemaman being on John Paul's side) over the question as to whether the English had stolen the tune of *God Save the King* from *My Country 'Tis of Thee* or whether the Americans had cribbed *My Country 'Tis of Thee* from *God Save the King*. By this time, since I was on Father's British passport, I considered myself English.

Perhaps the worst day of all was the day we climbed the Jungfrau—in a train. All the way up I was arguing with Pop, who thought we were being cheated, for he contended that the Jungfrau was not nearly so high as all the other mountains around us, and he had embarked on this excursion on the more or less tacit assumption that the Jungfrau was the highest mountain around these parts: and now look, the Eiger and the Monch were much higher! I was vehement in explaining that the Jungfrau looked lower because it was further away, but Pop did not believe in my theory of perspective.

By the time we got to the Jungfrau *joch*, everybody was ready to fall down from nervous exhaustion, and the height made Bonnemaman faint, and Pop began to feel sick, and I had a big crisis of tears in the dining room, and then when Father and I and John Paul walked out into the blinding white-snow field without dark glasses we all got headaches; and so the day, as a whole, was completely horrible.

Then, in Interlaken, although Pop and Bonnemaman had the intense consolation of being able to occupy the same rooms that had been used only a few months before by Douglas Fairbanks and Mary Pickford, John Paul humiliated the whole family by falling fully dressed into a pond full of gold-fish and running through the hotel dripping with water and green-weeds. Finally, we were all scared out of our wits when one of the maids, exhausted by the strain of waiting on so many hundreds of English and American tourists, fainted, while carrying a loaded tray, and crashed to the floor in a tornado of dishes right behind my chair.

We were glad to get out of Switzerland, and back into France, but by the time we reached Avignon, I had developed such a disgust for sightseeing that I would not leave the hotel to go and see the Palace of the Popes. I remained in the room and read *Tarzan of the Apes*, finishing the whole book before Father and John Paul returned from what was probably the only really interesting thing we had struck in the whole miserable journey.

V

Pop had come very unwillingly to St. Antonin, and as soon as he got there he tried to leave again. The streets were too dirty. They disgusted him. But Bonnemaman refused to move until the full month, or whatever time they had planned to stay, had passed.

However, one of the official family acts that took place during this time was an excursion to Montauban, and the inspection of the Lycée to which I was to be sent in the fall.

I suppose those brick cloisters looked innocent enough in the afternoon sun of late August, when they were empty of the fiends in black smocks who were to fill them in late September. I was to get my fill of bitterness in those buildings, in due time.

Pop and Bonnemaman and John Paul and all the luggage left on the express for Paris as August came to an end. Then, in the first week of September, came the patronal feast of Saint Antonin, with torchlight processions, and everybody dancing the polka and the schottische under the Japanese lanterns on the esplanade. There were many other attractions and excitements, including a certain fanciful novelty in shooting galleries. At one end of town, there was a pigeon tied by the leg to the top of a tree, and everybody blasted at it with a shotgun until it was dead. At the other end of town, by the river bank, men were shooting at a chicken which was tied to a floating box, moored out in the center of the stream.

For my own part, I entered a great competition with most of the boys and youths of the town, in which we all jumped into the river and swam after a duck that was thrown off the bridge. It was finally caught by a respectable fellow called Georges who was studying to be a school-teacher at the normal school in Montauban.

At this time, too, being eleven and a half years old, I fell in love with a mousy little girl with blonde locks called Henriette. It was a rather desultory affair. She went home and told her parents that the son of the Englishman was in love with her, and her mother clapped her hands and their household rang with alleluias on that day. The next time I saw her she was very friendly, and during one of the dances, with a kind of official artfulness, she allowed me to chase her 'round and 'round a tree.

Then the artificiality of the business dawned on me and I went home. Father said to me: "What's this I hear about you chasing after girls at your age?" After that life became very serious, and a few weeks later I put on my new blue uniform and went off to the Lycée.

Although by this time I knew French quite well, the first day in the big, gravelled yard, when I was surrounded by those fierce, cat-like little faces, dark and morose, and looked into those score of pairs of glittering and hostile eyes, I forgot every word, and could hardly answer the furious questions that were put to me. And my stupidity only irritated them all the more. They began to kick me, and to pull and twist my ears, and push me around, and shout various kinds of insults. I learned a great deal of obscenity and blasphemy in the first few days, simply by being the direct or indirect object of so much of it.

After this everybody accepted me and became quite friendly and pleasant, once they were used to my pale, blue-eyed and seemingly stupid English face. Nevertheless, when I lay awake at night in the huge dark dormitory and listened to the snoring of the little animals all around me, and heard through the darkness and the emptiness of the night the far screaming of the trains, or the mad iron cry of a bugle in a distant *caserne* of Senegalese troops, I knew for the first time in my life the pangs of desolation and emptiness and abandonment.

At first I used to go home nearly every Sunday taking the early train from Montauban-Villenouvelle, at about five-thirty in the morning. And I would plead with Father to let me out of that miserable school, but it was in vain. After about two months I got used to it and ceased to be so unhappy. The wound was no longer so raw: but I was never happy or at peace in the violent and unpleasant atmosphere of those brick cloisters.

The children I had associated with at St. Antonin had not been by any means angels, but there had at least been a certain simplicity and affability about them. Of course, the boys who went to the Lycée were of the same breed and the same stamp: there was no specific difference, except that they came from families that were better off. All my friends at St. Antonin had been the children of workmen and peasants, with whom I sat in the elementary school. But when a couple of hundred of these southern French boys were thrown together in the prison of that Lycée, a subtle change was operated in their spirit and mentality. In fact, I noticed that when you were with them separately, outside the school, they were mild and peaceable and humane enough. But when they were all together there seemed to be some diabolical spirit of cruelty and viciousness and obscenity and blasphemy and envy and hatred that banded them together against all goodness and against one another in mockery and fierce cruelty and in vociferous, uninhibited filthiness. Contact with that wolf-pack felt very patently like contact with the mystical body of the devil: and, especially in the first few days, the members of that body did not spare themselves in kicking me around without mercy.

The students were divided into two strictly segregated groups, and I was among "les petits," those in "quatrième," the fourth class, and below it. The oldest among us were fifteen and sixteen, and among these were five or six big morose bullies with thick black hair growing out of their foreheads almost down to the eyebrows. They were physically stronger than anybody else and, though less intelligent, they were craftier in the works of evil, louder in obscenity and completely unrestrained in their brutality, when the mood was on them. Of course, they were not always unpleasant and hostile: but in a sense their friendship was more dangerous than their enmity and, in fact, it was this that did the most harm: because the good children who came to the school quickly got into the habit of tolerating all the unpleasantness of these individuals, in order not to get their heads knocked off for failing to applaud. And so the whole school, or at least our part of it, was dominated by their influence.

When I think of the Catholic parents who sent their children to a school like that, I begin to wonder what was wrong with their heads. Down by the river, in a big clean white building, was a college run by the Marist Fathers. I had never been inside it: indeed, it was so clean that it frightened me. But I knew a couple of boys who went to it. They were sons of the little lady who ran the pastry shop opposite the church at St. Antonin and I remember them as exceptionally nice fellows, very pleasant and good. It never occurred to anyone to despise them for being pious. And how unlike the products of the Lycée they were!

When I reflect on all this, I am overwhelmed at the thought of the tremendous weight of moral responsibility that Catholic parents accumulate upon their shoulders by not sending their children to Catholic schools. Those who are not of the Church have no understanding of this. They cannot be expected to. As far as they can see, all this insistence on Catholic schools is only a moneymaking device by which the Church is trying to increase its domination over the minds of men, and its own temporal prosperity. And of course most non-Catholics imagine that the Church is immensely rich, and that all Catholic institutions make money hand over fist, and that all the money is stored away somewhere to buy gold and silver dishes for the Pope and cigars for the College of Cardinals.

Is it any wonder that there can be no peace in a world where everything possible is done to guarantee that the youth of every nation will grow up absolutely without moral and religious discipline, and without the shadow of an interior life, or of that spirituality and charity and faith which alone can safeguard the treaties and agreements made by governments?

And Catholics, thousands of Catholics everywhere, have the consummate audacity to weep and complain because God does not hear their prayers for peace, when they have neglected not only His will, but the ordinary dictates of natural reason and prudence, and let their children grow up according to the standards of a civilization of hyenas.

The experience of living with the kind of people I found in the Lycée was something new to me, but in degree, rather than in kind. There was the same animality and toughness and insensitivity and lack of conscience that existed to some extent in my own character, and which I had found more or less everywhere.

But these French children seemed to be so much tougher and more cynical and more precocious than anyone else I had ever seen. How, then, could I fit them in with the ideal of France which my father had, and which even I had then in an obscure and inchoate form? I suppose the only answer is *corruptio optimi pessima.* Since evil is the defect of good, the lack of a good that ought to be there, and nothing positive in itself, it follows that the greatest evil is found where the highest good has been corrupted. And I suppose the most shocking thing about France is the corruption of French spirituality into flippancy and cynicism; of French intelligence into sophistry; of French dignity and refinement into petty vanity and theatrical self-display; of French charity into a disgusting fleshly concupiscence, and of French faith into sentimentality or puerile atheism. There was all of this in the Lycée Ingres, at Montauban.

However, as I say, I adjusted myself to the situation, and got into a group of more or less peaceful friends who had more wit than obscenity about them and were, in fact, the more intelligent children in the three lower classes. I say intelligent; I mean, also, precocious.

But they had ideals and ambitions and, as a matter of fact, by the middle of my first year, I remember we were all furiously writing novels. On the days when we went out for walks, two by two into the country in a long line which broke up into groups at the edge of town, my friends and I would get together, walking in a superior way, with our caps on the backs of our heads and our hands in our pockets, like the great intellectuals that we were, discussing our novels. The discussion was not merely confined to telling the plot of what we were writing: a certain amount of criticism was passed back and forth.

For instance—I was engaged in a great adventure story, the scene of which was laid in India, and the style of which was somewhat influenced by Pierre Loti. It was written in French. At one point in the story I had the hero, who was in financial difficulties, accept a loan of some money from the heroine. This concept evoked loud cries of protest from my confrères, who found that it offended all the most delicate standards required in a romantic hero. What do you mean, accept money from the heroine! *Allons donc, mon vieux, c'est impossible, ça! C'est tout à fait inoui!* I had not thought of that at all, but I made the change.

That particular novel was never finished, as I remember. But I know I finished at least one other, and probably two, besides one which I wrote at St. Antonin before coming to the Lycée. They were all scribbled in exercise books, profusely illustrated in pen and ink—and the ink was generally bright blue.

One of the chief of these works, I remember, was inspired by Kingsley's *Westward Ho!* and by *Lorna Doone*, and it was about a man living in Devonshire in the sixteenth century. The villains were all Catholics, in league with Spain, and the book ended in a tremendous naval battle off the coast of Wales, which I illustrated with great care. At one point in the book a priest, one of the villains, set fire to the house of the heroine. I did not tell my friends this. I think they would have been offended. They were at least nominal Catholics, and were among the students who lined up two by two to go to Mass at the Cathedral on Sunday mornings.

On the other hand, I do not think they can have been very well instructed Catholics, for one day, as we were emerging from the Lycée, on the way out to one of those walks, we passed two religious in black soutanes, with black bushy beards, standing in the square before the school, and one of my friends hissed in my ear: "Jesuits!" For some reason or other he was scared of Jesuits. And, as a matter of fact, now that I know more about religious Orders, I realize that they were not Jesuits but Passionist missionaries, with the white insignia of the Passionists on their breasts.

At first, on the Sundays when I remained at the Lycée, I stayed in *Permanence* with the others who did not go to Mass at the Cathedral. That is, I sat in the study hall reading the novels of Jules Verne or Rudyard Kipling (I was very much affected by a French translation of *The Light That Failed*). But later on, Father arranged for me to receive instructions, with a handful of others, from a little fat Protestant minister who came to the Lycée to evangelize us.

On Sunday mornings we gathered around the stove in the bleak, octagonal edifice which had been erected in one of the courts as a Protestant "temple" for the students. The minister was a serious little man, and he explained the parables of the Good Samaritan and the Pharisee and the Publican and so on. I don't remember that there was any particularly deep spirituality about it, but there was nothing to prevent him from showing us the obvious moral lessons.

I am grateful that I got at least that much of religion, at an age when I badly needed it: it was years since I had even been inside a church for any other purpose than to look at the stained glass windows or the Gothic vaulting. However, it was practically useless. What is the good of religion without personal spiritual direction? Without Sacraments, without any means of grace except a desultory prayer now and then, at intervals, and an occasional vague sermon?

There was also a Catholic chapel in the Lycée, but it was falling into ruins and the glass was out of most of the windows. Nobody ever saw the inside of it, because it was locked up tight. I suppose back in the days when the Lycée was built the Catholics had managed, at the cost of several years of patient effort, to get this concession out of the government people who were erecting the school: but in the long run it did not do them much good.

The only really valuable religious and moral training I ever got as a child came to me from my father, not systematically, but here and there and more or less spontaneously, in the course of ordinary conversations. Father never applied himself, of set purpose, to teach me religion. But if something spiritual was on his mind, it came out more or less naturally. And this is the kind of religious teaching, or any other kind of teaching, that has the most effect. "A good man out of the good treasure of his heart, bringeth forth good fruit; and an evil man out of the evil treasure bringeth forth that which is evil. For out of the abundance of the heart the mouth speaketh."

And it is precisely this speech "out of the abundance of the heart" that makes an impression and produces an effect in other people. We give ear and pay at least a partially respectful attention to anyone who is really sincerely convinced of what he is saying, no matter what it is, even if it is opposed to our own ideas.

I have not the slightest idea what the little *pasteur* told us about the Pharisee and the Publican, but I shall never forget a casual remark Father happened to make, in which he told me of St. Peter's betrayal of Christ, and how, hearing the cock crow, Peter went out and wept bitterly. I forget how it came up, and what the context was that suggested it: we were just talking casually, standing in the hall of the flat we had taken on the Place de la Condamine.

I have never lost the vivid picture I got, at that moment, of Peter going out and weeping bitterly. I wonder how I ever managed to forget, for so many years, the understanding I acquired at that moment of how St. Peter felt, and of what his betrayal meant to him.

Father was not afraid to express his ideas about truth and morality to anybody that seemed to need them,—that is, if a real occasion arose. He did not, of course, go around interfering with everybody else's business. But once his indignation got the better of him, and he gave a piece of his mind to a shrew of a French-woman, one of those spiteful sharp-tongued *bourgeoises,* who was giving free expression to her hatred of one of her neighbors who very much resembled herself.

He asked her why she thought Christ had told people to love their enemies. Did she suppose God commanded this for His benefit? Did He get anything out of it that He really needed from us? Or was it not rather for our own good that he had given us this commandment? He told her that if she had any sense, she would love other people if only for the sake of the good and health and peace of her own soul, instead of tearing herself to pieces with her own envy and spitefulness. It was St. Augustine's argument, that envy and hatred try to pierce our neighbor with a sword, when the blade cannot reach him unless it first passes through our own body. I suppose Father had never read any of St. Augustine, but he would have liked him.

This incident with the shrew reminds one a little of Léon Bloy. Father had not read him either, but he would have liked him too. They had much in common, but Father shared none of Bloy's fury. If he had been a Catholic, his vocation as a lay-contemplative would certainly have developed along the same lines. For I am sure he had that kind of a vocation. But unfortunately it never really developed, because he never got to the Sacraments. However, there were in him the latent germs of the same spiritual poverty and all of Bloy's hatred of materialism and of false spiritualities and of worldly values in people who called themselves Christians.

In the winter of 1926 Father went to Murat. Murat is in the Cantal, the old Province of Auvergne, a Catholic province. It is in the mountains of central France, green mountains, old volcanoes. The valleys are full of rich pastures and the mountains are heavy with fir trees or raise their green domes into the sky, bare of woods, covered with grass. The people of this land are Celts, mostly. The Auvergnats have been more or less laughed at, in French tradition, for their simplicity and rusticity. They are very stolid people, but very good people.

At Murat, Father boarded with a family who had a little house, a sort of a small farm, on the slope of one of the steep hills outside the town, and I went up there to spend the Christmas holidays, that year.

Murat was a wonderful place. It was deep in snow, and the houses with their snow-covered roofs relieved the grey and blue and slate-dark pattern of the buildings crowded together on the sides of three hills. The town huddled at the foot of a rock crowned by a colossal statue of the Immaculate Conception, which seemed to me, at the time, to be too big, and to bespeak too much religious enthusiasm. By now I realize that it did not indicate any religious excess at all. These people wanted to say in a very obvious way that they loved Our Lady, who should indeed be loved and revered, as a Queen of great power and a Lady of immense goodness and mercy, mighty in her intercession for us before the throne of God, tremendous in the glory of her sanctity and her fullness of grace as Mother of God. For she loves the children of God, who are born into the world with the image of God in their souls, and her powerful love is forgotten, and it is not understood, in the blindness and foolishness of the world.

However, I did not bring up the subject of Murat in order to talk about this statue, but about M. and Mme. Privat. They were the people with whom we boarded, and long before we got to Murat, when the train was climbing up the snowy valley, from Aurillac, on the other side of the Puy du Cantal, Father was telling me: "Wait until you see the Privats."

In a way, they were to be among the most remarkable people I ever knew.

The Auvergnats are, as a rule, not tall. The Privats were both of them not much taller than I was, being then twelve, but tall for my age. I suppose M. Privat was about five foot three or four, but not more. But he was tremendously broad, a man of great strength. He seemed to have no neck, but his head rose from his shoulders in a solid column of muscle and bone, and for the rest, his shadow was almost completely square. He wore a black broad-brimmed hat, like most of the peasants of the region, and it gave his face an added solemnity when his sober and judicious eyes looked out at you peacefully from under the regular brows and that regular brim above them. These two decks, two levels of regularity, added much to the impression of solidity and immobility and impassiveness which he carried with him everywhere, whether at work or at rest.

His little wife was more like a bird, thin, serious, earnest, quick, but also full of that peacefulness and impassiveness which, as I now know, came from living close to God. She wore a funny little headdress which I find it almost impossible to describe, except to say that it looked like a little sugar-loaf perched on top of her head, and garnished with a bit of black lace. The women of Auvergne still wear that headdress.

It is a great pleasure for me to remember such good and kind people and to talk about them, although I no longer possess any details about them. I just remember their kindness and goodness to me, and their peacefulness and their utter simplicity. They inspired real reverence, and I think, in a way, they were certainly saints. And they were saints in that most effective and telling way: sanctified by leading ordinary lives in a completely supernatural manner, sanctified by obscurity, by usual skills, by common tasks, by routine, but skills, tasks, routine which received a supernatural form from grace within, and from the habitual union of their souls with God in deep faith and charity.

Their farm, their family, and their Church were all that occupied these good souls; and their lives were full.

Father, who thought more and more of my physical and moral health, realized what a treasure he had found in these two, and consequently Murat was more and more in his mind as a place where I should go and get healthy.

That winter, at the Lycée, I had spent several weeks in the infirmary with various fevers, and the following summer, when Father had to go to Paris, he took the opportunity to send me once again to Murat, to spend a few weeks living with the Privats, who would feed me plenty of butter and milk and would take care of me in every possible way.

Those were weeks that I shall never forget, and the more I think of them, the more I realize that I must certainly owe the Privats for more than butter and milk and good nourishing food for my body. I am indebted to them for much more than the kindness and care they showed me, the goodness and the delicate solicitude with which they treated me as their own child, yet without any assertive or natural familiarity. As a child, and since then too, I have always tended to resist any kind of a possessive affection on the part of any other human being—there has always been this profound instinct to keep clear, to keep free. And only with truly supernatural people have I ever felt really at my ease, really at peace.

That was why I was glad of the love the Privats showed me, and was ready to love them in return. It did not burn you, it did not hold you, it did not try to imprison you in demonstrations, or trap your feet in the snares of its interest.

I used to run in the woods, and climb the mountains. I went up the Plomb du Cantal, which is nothing more than a huge hill, with a boy who was, I think, the Privats' nephew. He went to a Catholic school taught, I suppose, by priests. It had not occurred to me that every boy did not talk like the brats I knew at the Lycée. Without thinking, I let out some sort of a remark of the kind you heard all day long at Montauban, and he was offended and asked where I had picked up that kind of talk. And yet, while being ashamed of myself, I was impressed by the charitableness of his reaction. He dismissed it at once, and seemed to have forgotten all about it, and left me with the impression that he excused me on the grounds that I was English and had used the expression without quite knowing what it meant.

After all, this going to Murat was a great grace. Did I realize it? I did not know what a grace was. And though I was impressed with the goodness of the Privats, I could not fail to realize what was its root and its foundation. And yet it never occurred to me at the time to think of being like them, of profiting in any way by their example.

I think I only talked to them once about religion. We were all sitting on the narrow balcony looking out over the valley, at the hills turning dark blue and purple in the September dusk. Somehow, something came up about Catholics and Protestants and immediately I had the sense of all the solidity and rectitude of the Privats turned against me, accusing me like the face of an impregnable fortification.

So I began to justify Protestantism, as best I could. I think they had probably said that they could not see how I managed to go on living without the faith: for there was only one Faith, one Church. So I gave them the argument that every religion was good: they all led to God, only in different ways, and every man should go according to his own conscience, and settle things according to his own private way of looking at things.

They did not answer me with any argument. They simply looked at one another and shrugged and Monsieur Privat said quietly and sadly: "*Mais c'est impossible.*"

It was a terrible, a frightening, a very humiliating thing to feel all their silence and peacefulness and strength turned against me, accusing me of being estranged from them, isolated from their security, cut off from their protection and from the strength of their inner life by my own fault, by my own wilfulness, by my own ignorance, and my uninstructed Protestant pride.

One of the humiliating things about it was that I wanted them to argue, and they despised argument. It was as if they realized, as I did not, that my attitude and my desire of argument and religious discussion implied a fundamental and utter lack of faith, and a dependence on my own lights, and attachment to my own opinion.

What is more, they seemed to realize that I did not believe in anything, and that anything I might say I believed would be only empty talk. Yet they did not give me the feeling that this was some slight matter, something to be indulged in a child, something that could be left to work itself out in time, of its own accord. I had never met people to whom belief was a matter of such moment. And yet there was nothing they could do for me directly. But what they could do, I am sure they did, and I am glad they did it. And I thank God from the bottom of my heart that they were concerned, and so deeply and vitally concerned, at my lack of faith.

Who knows how much I owe to those two wonderful people? Anything I say about it is only a matter of guessing but, knowing their charity, it is to me a matter of moral certitude that I owe many graces to their prayers, and perhaps ultimately the grace of my conversion and even of my religious vocation. Who shall say? But one day I shall know, and it is good to be able to be confident that I will see them again and be able to thank them.

vi

Father had gone to Paris to be best man at the wedding of one of his friends from the old days in New Zealand. Capt. John Chrystal had made himself a career in the British army and was an officer in the hussars. Later on he became Governor of a prison: but he was not as dreary as that might imply. After the wedding, the Captain and his wife went off on their honeymoon, and the mother of the new Mrs. Chrystal came down to St. Antonin with Father.

Mrs. Stratton was an impressive kind of a person. She was a musician, and a singer, but I forget whether she had been on the stage: in any case, she was not a very theatrical character, rather the opposite, although she had a certain amount of dash about her. She was not what you would call elderly, by any means, and besides she was a woman of great vitality and strength of character, with rich intelligence and talent, and strong and precise ideas about things. Her convictions commanded respect, as did her many talents, and above all her overwhelming personal dignity. You felt that she ought to have been called Lady Stratton, or the Countess of something.

At first I was secretly resentful of the great influence she at once began to exercise over our lives, and thought she was bossing our affairs too much, but even I was able to realize that her views and advice and guidance were very valuable things. But so strong was her influence that I think it was due to her more than to anyone else that we gave up the idea of living permanently in St. Antonin.

The house was almost finished and ready for occupation, and it was a beautiful little house too, simple and solid. It looked good to live in, with that one big room with the medieval window and a huge medieval fireplace. Father had even managed to procure a winding stone stair and it was by that that you went up to the bedroom. The garden around the house, where Father had done much work, would have been fine.

On the other hand, Father was travelling too much for the house to be really useful. In the winter of 1927 he was some months at Marseilles and the rest of the time at Cette, another Mediterranean port. Soon he would have to go to England, for by this time he was ready for another exhibition. All this time I was at the Lycée, becoming more and more hard-boiled in my precocity, and getting accustomed to the idea of growing up as a Frenchman.

Then Father went to London for the exhibition.

It was the spring of 1928. The school year would soon be over. I was not thinking much about the future. All I knew was that Father would be back from England in a few days.

It was a bright, sunny morning in May when he arrived at the Lycée, and the first thing he told me was to get my things packed: we were going to England.

I looked around me like a man that has had chains struck from his hands. How the light sang on the brick walls of the prison whose gates had just burst open before me, sprung by some invisible and beneficent power: my escape from the Lycée was, I believe, providential.

In the last moments in which I had an opportunity to do so, I tasted the ferocious delights of exultant gloating over the companions I was about to leave. They stood around me in the sun, with their hands hanging at their sides, wearing their black smocks and their berets, and laughing and sharing my excitement, not without envy.

And then I was riding down the quiet street in a carriage, with my luggage beside me, and Father talking about what we were going to do. How lightly the cab-horse's hoofs rang out in the hard, white dirt of the street! How gaily they echoed along the pale smug walls of the dusty houses! "Liberty!" they said, "liberty, liberty, liberty, liberty," all down the street.

We passed the big polygonal barn of a post-office, covered with the tatters of ancient posters, and entered under the dappled shadow of the plane trees. I looked ahead, up the long street to Villenouvelle station, where I had taken the train so many times in the small hours of the morning, on my way home to spend the Sunday in St. Antonin.

When we got on the little train, and travelled the way we had first come to the Aveyron valley, I did indeed feel my heart tighten at the loss of my thirteenth century: but oh, it had long ceased to belong to us. We had not been able to hold on, for very long, to the St. Antonin of the first year: and the bitter lye of the Lycée had burned all its goodness out of me again, and I was cauterized against it, and had become somewhat insensitive to it: not so much so, however, that I did not feel a little sad at leaving it for ever.

It is sad, too, that we never lived in the house that Father built.

But never mind! The grace of those days has not been altogether lost, by any means.

Before I was really able to believe that I was out of the Lycée for good, we were racing through Picardy on the Nord railway. Pretty soon the atmosphere would take on that dim pearlish grey that would tell us we were nearing the Channel, and all along the line we would read the big billboards saying, in English: "Visit Egypt!"

Then, after that, the channel steamer, Folkestone cliffs, white as cream in the sunny haze, the jetty, the grey-green downs and the line of prim hotels along the top of the rock: these things all made me happy. And the cockney cries of the porters and the smell of strong tea in the station refreshment room spelled out all the associations of what had, up to now, always been a holiday country for me, a land heavy with awe-inspiring proprieties, but laden with all kinds of comforts, and in which every impact of experience seemed to reach the soul through seven or eight layers of insulation.

England meant all this for me, in those days, and continued to do so for a year or two more, because going to England meant going to Aunt Maud's house in Ealing.

The red brick house at 18 Carlton Road, with the little lawn that was also a bowling green and the windows looking out on the enclosed patch of grass which was the Durston House cricket field, was a fortress of nineteenth-century security. Here in Ealing, where all the Victorian standards stood entrenched in row upon row of identical houses, Aunt Maud and Uncle Ben lived in the very heart and the center of the citadel, and indeed Uncle Ben was one of the commanders.

The retired headmaster of Durston House Preparatory School for Boys, on Castlebar Road, looked like almost all the great, tearful, solemn war-lords of Victorian society. He was a stoop-shouldered man with a huge, white waterfall moustache, a pince-nez, ill-fitting tweeds. He walked slowly and with a limp, because of his infirmities, and required much attention from everybody, especially Aunt Maud. When he spoke, although he spoke quietly and distinctly, you knew he had a booming voice if he wanted to use it, and sometimes when he had a particularly dramatic statement to make, his eyes would widen, and he would stare you in the face, and shake his finger at you, and intone the words like the ghost in Hamlet: then, if that had been the point of some story, he would sit back in his chair, and laugh quietly, displaying his great teeth, and gazing from face to face of those who sat at his feet.

As for Aunt Maud, I think I have met very few people in my life so like an angel. Of course, she was well on in years, and her clothes, especially her hats, were of a conservatism most extreme. I believe she had not forsaken a detail of the patterns that were popular at the time of the Diamond Jubilee. She was a sprightly and charming person, a tall, thin, quiet, meek old lady who still, after all the years, had something about her of the sensible and sensitive Victorian girl. Nice, in the strict sense, and in the broad colloquial sense, was a word made for her: she was a very nice person. In a way, her pointed nose and her thin smiling lips even suggested the expression of one who had just finished pronouncing that word. "How nice!"

Now that I was going to go to school in England, I would be more and more under her wing. In fact, I had barely landed when she took me on one of those shopping expeditions in Oxford Street that was the immediate prelude to Ripley Court—a school in Surrey which was now in the hands of her sister-in-law, Mrs. Pearce, the wife of Uncle Ben's late brother, Robert. He had been killed in a cycling accident when, coming to the bottom of a hill, he had failed to turn the corner and had run straight into a brick wall. His brakes had gone back on him halfway down.

It was on one of those mornings in Oxford Street, perhaps not the very first one, that Aunt Maud and I had a great conversation about my future. We had just bought me several pairs of grey flannel trousers and a sweater and some shoes and some grey flannel shirts and one of those floppy flannel hats that English children have to wear, and now, having emerged from D. H. Evans, were riding down Oxford Street on the top of an open bus, right up in the front, where one could see simply everything.

"I wonder if Tom has thought at all about his future," Aunt Maud said and looked at me, winking and blinking with both eyes as a sign of encouragement. I was Tom. She sometimes addressed you in the third person, like that, perhaps as a sign of some delicate, inward diffidence about bringing the matter up at all.

I admitted that I had thought a little about the future, and what I wanted to be. But I rather hesitated to tell her that I wanted to be a novelist.

"Do you think writing would be a good profession for anyone?" I said tentatively.

"Yes indeed, writing is a very fine profession! But what kind of writing would you like to do?"

"I have been thinking that I might write stories," I said.

"I imagine you would probably do quite well at that, some day," said Aunt Maud, kindly, but added: "Of course, you know that writers sometimes find it very difficult to make their way in the world."

"Yes, I realize that," I said reflectively.

"Perhaps if you had some other occupation, as a means of making a living, you might find time to write in your spare moments. Novelists sometimes get their start that way, you know."

"I might be a journalist," I suggested, "and write for the newspapers."

"Perhaps that is a good idea," she said. "A knowledge of languages would be very valuable in that field, too. You could work your way up to the position of a foreign correspondent."

"And I could write books in my spare time."

"Yes, I suppose you probably could manage it that way."

I think we rode all the way out to Ealing, talking in this somewhat abstract and utopian strain, and finally we got off, and crossed Haven Green to Castlebar Road where we had to stop in at Durston House for something or other.

It was not the first time I had met Mrs. Pearce, the headmistress of Ripley Court. She was a bulky and rather belligerent-looking woman with great pouches under her eyes. She was standing in a room in which were hung several of my father's paintings. She had probably been looking at them, and considering the error and instability of an artist's way of life when Aunt Maud mentioned the fact that we had been talking about my own future.

"Does he want to be a dilettante like his father?" said Mrs. Pearce roughly, surveying me with a rather outraged expression through the lenses of her spectacles.

"We were thinking that perhaps he might become a journalist," said Aunt Maud gently.

"Nonsense," said Mrs. Pearce, "let him go into business and make a decent living for himself. There's no use in his wasting his time and deceiving himself. He might as well get some sensible ideas into his head from the very start, and prepare himself for something solid and reliable and not go out into the world with his head full of dreams." And then, turning to me, she cried out: "Boy! Don't become a dilettante, do you hear?"

I was received at Ripley Court, although the summer term was almost over, more or less as if I were an orphan or some kind of a stray that required at once pity and a special, not unsuspicious kind of attention. I was the son of an artist, and had just come from two years in a French school, and the combination of artist and France added up to practically everything that Mrs. Pearce and her friends suspected and disliked. Besides, to crown it all, I did not know any Latin. What was to be made of a boy who was already in the middle of his fourteenth year and could not decline *mensa*—had never even opened a Latin grammar?

So I had the humiliation of once again descending to the lowest place and sitting with the smallest boys in the school and beginning at the beginning.

But Ripley was a pleasant and happy place after the prison of the Lycée. The huge, dark green sweep of the cricket field, and the deep shadows of the elm trees where one sat waiting for his innings, and the dining room where we crammed ourselves with bread and butter and jam at tea-time and listened to Mr. Onslow reading aloud from the works of Sir Arthur Conan Doyle, all this was immense luxury and peace after Montauban.

And the mentality of the red-faced, innocent English boys was a change. They seemed to be much pleasanter and much happier—and indeed they had every reason to be so, since they all came from the shelter of comfortable and secure homes and were so far protected from the world by a thick wall of ignorance—a wall which was to prove no real protection against anything as soon as they passed on to their various Public Schools, but which, for the time being, kept them children.

On Sundays, we all dressed up in the ludicrous clothes that the English conceive to be appropriate to the young, and went marching off to the village church, where a whole transept was reserved for us. There we all sat in rows, in our black Eton jackets and our snow-white Eton collars choking us up to the chin, and bent our well-brushed and combed heads over the pages of our hymnals. And at last I was really going to Church.

On Sunday evenings, after the long walk in the country, through the lush Surrey fields, we gathered again in the wooden drill-room of the school, and sat on benches, and sang hymns, and listened to Mr. Onslow reading aloud from *Pilgrim's Progress*.

Thus, just about the time when I most needed it, I did acquire a little natural faith, and found many occasions of praying and lifting up my mind to God. It was the first time I had ever seen people kneel publicly by their beds before getting into them, and the first time I had ever sat down to meals after a grace.

And for about the next two years I think I was almost sincerely religious. Therefore, I was also, to some extent, happy and at peace. I do not think there was anything very supernatural about it, although I am sure grace was working in all our souls in some obscure and uncertain way. But at least we were fulfilling our natural duties to God—and therefore satisfying a natural need: for our duties and our needs, in all the fundamental things for which we were created, come down in practise to the same thing.

Later on, like practically everyone else in our stupid and godless society, I was to consider these two years as "my religious phase." I am glad that that now seems very funny. But it is sad that it is funny in so few cases. Because I think that practically everybody does go through such a phase, and for the majority of them, that is all that it is, a phase and nothing more. If that is so, it is their own fault: for life on this earth is not simply a series of "phases" which we more or less passively undergo. If the impulse to worship God and to adore Him in truth by the goodness and order of our own lives is nothing more than a transitory and emotional thing, that is our own fault. It is so only because we make it so, and because we take what is substantially a deep and powerful and lasting moral impetus, supernatural in its origin and in its direction, and reduce it to the level of our own weak and unstable and futile fancies and desires.

Prayer is attractive enough when it is considered in a context of good food, and sunny joyous country churches, and the green English countryside. And, as a matter of fact, the Church of England means all this. It is a class religion, the cult of a special society and group, not even of a whole nation, but of the ruling minority in a nation. That is the principal basis for its rather strong coherence up to now. There is certainly not much doctrinal unity, much less a mystical bond between people many of whom have even ceased to believe in grace or Sacraments. The thing that holds them together is the powerful attraction of their own social tradition, and the stubborn tenacity with which they cling to certain social standards and customs, more or less for their own sake. The Church of England depends, for its existence, almost entirely on the solidarity and conservatism of the English ruling class. Its strength is not in anything supernatural, but in the strong social and racial instincts which bind the members of this caste together; and the English cling to their Church the way they cling to their

King and to their old schools: because of a big, vague, sweet complex of subjective dispositions regarding the English countryside, old castles and cottages, games of cricket in the long summer afternoons, tea-parties on the Thames, croquet, roast-beef, pipe-smoking, the Christmas panto, *Punch* and the London *Times* and all those other things the mere thought of which produces a kind of a warm and inexpressible ache in the English heart.

I got mixed up in all this as soon as I entered Ripley Court, and it was strong enough in me to blur and naturalize all that might have been supernatural in my attraction to pray and to love God. And consequently the grace that was given me was stifled, not at once, but gradually. As long as I lived in this peaceful hothouse atmosphere of cricket and Eton collars and synthetic childhood, I was pious, perhaps sincerely. But as soon as the frail walls of this illusion broke down again—that is, as soon as I went to a Public School and saw that, underneath their sentimentality, the English were just as brutal as the French—I made no further effort to keep up what seemed to me to be a more or less manifest pretense.

At the time, of course, I was not capable of reasoning about all this. Even if my mind had been sufficiently developed to do so, I would never have found the perspective for it. Besides, all this was going on in my emotions and feelings, rather than in my mind and will—thanks to the vagueness and total unsubstantiality of Anglican doctrine as it gets preached, in practice, from most pulpits.

It is a terrible thing to think of the grace that is wasted in this world, and of the people that are lost. Perhaps one explanation of the sterility and inefficacy of Anglicanism in the moral order is, besides its lack of vital contact with the Mystical Body of the True Church, the social injustice and the class oppression on which it is based: for, since it is mostly a class religion, it contracts the guilt of the class from which it is inseparable. But this is a guess which I am not prepared to argue out.

I was already nearly too old for Ripley Court, being by now fourteen, but I had to pick up enough Latin to be able to make at least a presentable showing in a scholarship examination for some Public School. As to the school where I should go, Uncle Ben made a more or less expert choice, in his capacity as retired headmaster of a prep school. Since Father was poor, and an artist, there would be no thinking of one of the big schools like Harrow or Winchester—though Winchester was the one for which Uncle Ben had the greatest respect, having achieved his ambition of sending many of his pupils there with scholarships. The reason was twofold: not merely that Father could not be considered able to pay the bills (although, in fact, Pop was to pay them, from America) but the scholarship examinations would be altogether too hard for me.

The final choice was regarded by everyone as very suitable. It was an obscure but decent little school in the Midlands, an old foundation, with a kind of a little tradition of its own. It had recently gone up slightly in its rating because of the work of its greatest headmaster, who was just about to retire—all of this was the kind of thing Uncle Ben knew and told me, and Aunt Maud confirmed it, saying:

"I am sure you will find Oakham a very nice school."

3

The Harrowing of Hell

In the autumn of 1929 I went to Oakham. There was something very pleasant and peaceful about the atmosphere of this little market town, with its school and its old fourteenth-century church with the grey spire, rising in the middle of a wide Midland vale.

Obscure it certainly was. Oakham's only claim to fame was the fact that it was the county town, and in fact the only real town in the smallest county in England. And there were not even any main roads or main railway lines running through Rutland, except for the Great North Road which skirted the Lincolnshire border.

In this quiet back-water, under the trees full of rooks, I was to spend three and a half years getting ready for a career. Three and a half years were a short time: but when they were over, I was a very different person from the embarrassed and clumsy and more or less well-meaning, but interiorly unhappy fourteen-year-old who came there with a suitcase and a brown felt hat and a trunk and a plain wooden tuck-box.

Meanwhile, before I entered Oakham, and took up my abode in the ratty, gaslit corner of Hodge Wing that was called the "Nursery," things had happened to complicate and sadden my life still further.

In the Easter vacation of 1929 I had been with Father at Canterbury, where he was working, painting pictures mostly in the big, quiet Cathedral close. I had spent most of my days walking in the country around Canterbury, and the time went quietly except for the momentous occasion of a big Charlie Chaplin movie which came, late indeed, to Canterbury. It was *The Gold Rush*.

When the holidays were over and I went back to Ripley Court, Father crossed over to France. The last I heard about him was that he was at Rouen. Then, one day, towards the end of the summer term, when the school cricket eleven went in to Ealing to play Durston House, I was surprised to find myself appointed to go along as scorer. There was, of course, no likelihood of my ever going as a member of the team, since I was a hopeless cricketer from the start. On the way into town, on the bus or somewhere, I learned that my father was in Ealing, at Aunt Maud's, and that he was ill. This was why they had sent me along, I suppose: during the tea-interval I would have a chance to run in to the house which overlooked the cricket field and see Father.

The bus unloaded us in the lane that led to the field. In the tiny pavilion, the other scorer and I opened our large, green-ruled books, and wrote down the names of one another's team in the boxes down the side of the big rectangular page. Then, with our pencils all sharpened we waited, as the first pair went in to bat, striding heavily in their big white pads.

The dim June sun shone down on the field. Over yonder, where the poplars swayed slightly in the haze, was Aunt Maud's house, and I could see the window in the brick gable where Father probably was.

So the match began.

I could not believe that Father was very ill. If he were, I supposed that they would have made more fuss about it. During the tea interval, I went over, and passed through the green wooden door in the wall to Aunt Maud's garden and entered the house and went upstairs. Father was in bed. You could not tell from his appearance how ill he was: but I managed to gather it from the way he talked and from his actions. He seemed to move with difficulty and pain, and he did not have much to say. When I asked him what was the matter, he said nobody seemed to know.

I went back to the cricket pavilion a little saddened and unquiet. I told myself that he would probably get better in a week or two. And I thought this guess had proved to be right when, at the end of term, he wrote to me that we would be spending the summer in Scotland, where an old friend of his, who had a place in Aberdeenshire, had invited him to come and rest and get well.

We took one of those night trains from King's Cross. Father seemed well enough, although by the time we got to Aberdeen the following noon, after stopping at a lot of grey and dreary Scotch stations, he was weary and silent.

We had a long wait at Aberdeen, and we thought of going out and taking a look at the city. We stepped out of the station into a wide, deserted cobbled street. In the distance there was a harbor. We saw gulls, and the masts and funnel of what appeared to be a couple of trawlers. But the place seemed to have been struck by a plague. There was no one in sight. Now that I think of it, it must have been Sunday, for dead as Aberdeen is, it surely could not have been so completely deserted on a week day. The whole place was as grey as a tomb, and the forbidding aspect of all that hostile and untenanted granite depressed us both so much that we immediately returned to the station, and sat down in the refreshment room, and ordered some hotch-potch, which did little or nothing to lighten our spirits.

It was late afternoon by the time we got to Insch. The sun came out, and slanted a long ray at the far hills of heather which constituted our host's grouse-moor. The air was clear and silent as we drove out of the forsaken town that seemed to us more of a settlement than a town, and headed into the wilderness.

For the first few days Father kept to his room, coming down for meals. Once or twice he went out into the garden. Soon he could not even come down for meals. The doctor paid frequent visits, and soon I understood that Father was not getting better at all.

Finally, one day he called me up to the room.

"I have to go back to London," he said.

"London?"

"I must go to a hospital, son."

"Are you worse?"

"I don't get any better."

"Have they still not found out what it is that is the matter with you, Father?"

He shook his head. But he said: "Pray God to make me well. I think I ought to be all right in due course. Don't be unhappy."

But I was unhappy.

"You like it here, don't you?" he asked me.

"Oh, it's all right, I suppose."

"You'll stay here. They are very nice. They will take care of you, and it will do you good. Do you like the horses?"

I admitted without any undue excitement or enthusiasm that the ponies were all right. There were two of them. The two nieces of the family and I spent part of the day grooming them and cleaning out their stalls, and part of the day riding them. But, as far as I was concerned, it was too much work. The nieces, divining this unsportsmanlike attitude of mine, tended to be a little hostile and to boss me around in a patronising sort of a way. They were sixteen or seventeen, and seemed to have nothing whatever on their minds except horses, and they did not even look like their normal selves when they were not in riding breeches.

And so Father said good-bye, and we put him on the train, and he went to London to the Middlesex Hospital.

The summer days dragged on, cold days full of mist, some days bright with sun. I became less and less interested in the stable and the ponies, and before August was half done, the nieces had given me up in disgust and I was allowed to drop away into my own unhappy isolation, my world without horses, without hunting and shooting, without tartans and without the Braemar gathering and all those other noble institutions.

Instead, I sat in the branches of a tree reading the novels of Alexandre Dumas, volume after volume, in French, and later, in rebellion against the world of horses, I would borrow a bicycle that happened to be around the place, and go off into the country and look at the huge ancient stone circles where the druids had once congregated to offer human sacrifice to the rising sun—when there *was* a rising sun.

One day I was in the deserted house all by myself with Athos, Porthos, Aramis and D'Artagnan (Athos being my favorite and, in a sense, the one into whom I tended to project myself). The telephone rang. I thought for a while of letting it ring and not answering it, but eventually I did. It turned out to be a telegram for me.

At first I could not make out the words, as the Scotch lady in the telegraph office was pronouncing them. Then, when I did make them out, I did not believe them.

The message ran: "Entering New York harbor. All well." And it came from Father, in the hospital, in London. I tried to argue the woman at the other end of the wire into telling me that it came from my Uncle Harold, who had been travelling in Europe that year. But she would not be argued into anything but what she saw right in front of her nose. The telegram was signed Father, and it came from London.

I hung up the receiver and the bottom dropped out of my stomach. I walked up and down in the silent and empty house. I sat down in one of the big leather chairs in the smoking room. There was nobody there. There was nobody in the whole huge house.

I sat there in the dark, unhappy room, unable to think, unable to move, with all the innumerable elements of my isolation crowding in upon me from every side: without a home, without a family, without a country, without a father, apparently without any friends, without any interior peace or confidence or light or understanding of my own—without God, too, without God, without heaven, without grace, without anything. And what was happening to Father, there in London? I was unable to think of it.

The first thing that Uncle Ben did when I entered the house at Ealing was to tell me the news with all the dramatic overtones he gave to his most important announcements.

His eyes widened and he stared at me and bared his great teeth, pronouncing every syllable with tremendous distinctness and emphasis, saying: "Your father has a malignant tumor on the brain."

Father lay in a dark ward in the hospital. He did not have much to say. But it was not as bad as I had feared, from the telegram he had sent me. Everything he said was lucid and intelligible and I was comforted, in the sense that a clearly apparent physiological cause seemed to me to exclude the thought of insanity in the strict sense. Father was not out of his mind. But you could already see the evil, swelling lump on his forehead.

He told me, weakly, that they were going to try and operate on him, but they were afraid they could not do very much. Again he told me to pray.

I did not say anything about the telegram.

Leaving the hospital, I knew what was going to happen. He would lie there like that for another year, perhaps two or three years. And then he would die—unless they first killed him on an operating table.

Since those days, doctors have found out that you can cut away whole sections of the brain, in these operations, and save lives and minds and all. In 1929 they evidently did not yet know this. It was Father's lot to die slowly and painfully in the years when the doctors were just reaching the point of the discovery.

ii

Oakham, Oakham! The grey murk of the winter evenings in that garret where seven or eight of us moiled around in the gaslight, among the tuck-boxes, noisy, greedy, foul-mouthed, fighting and shouting! There was one who had a ukulele which he did not know how to play. And Pop used to send me the brown rotogravure sections of the New York Sunday papers, and we would cut out the pictures of the actresses and paste them up on the walls.

And I toiled with Greek verbs. And we drank raisin wine and ate potato chips until we fell silent and sat apart, stupefied and nauseated. And under the gaslight I would write letters to Father in the hospital, letters on cream-colored notepaper, stamped with the school crest in blue.

After three months it was better. I was moved up into the Upper Fifth, and changed to a new study downstairs, with more light, though just as crowded and just as much of a mess. And we had Cicero and European history—all about the nineteenth century, with a certain amount of cold scorn poured on Pio Nono. In the English class we read *The Tempest* and the *Nun's Priest's Tale* and the *Pardoner's Tale* and Buggy Jerwood, the school chaplain, tried to teach us trigonometry. With me, he failed. Sometimes he would try to teach us something about religion. But in this he also failed.

In any case, his religious teaching consisted mostly in more or less vague ethical remarks, an obscure mixture of ideals of English gentlemanliness and his favorite notions of personal hygiene. Everybody knew that his class was liable to degenerate into a demonstration of some practical points about rowing, with Buggy sitting on the table and showing us how to pull an oar.

There was no rowing at Oakham, since there was no water. But the chaplain had been a rowing "blue" at Cambridge, in his time. He was a tall, powerful, handsome man, with hair greying at the temples, and a big English chin, and a broad, uncreased brow, with sentences like "I stand for fair-play and good sportsmanship" written all over it.

His greatest sermon was on the thirteenth chapter of First Corinthians—and a wonderful chapter indeed. But his exegesis was a bit strange. However, it was typical of him and, in a way, of his whole church. "Buggy's" interpretation of the word "charity" in this passage (and in the whole Bible) was that it simply stood for "all that we mean when we call a chap a 'gentleman.'" In other words, charity meant good-sportsmanship, cricket, the decent thing, wearing the right kind of clothes, using the proper spoon, not being a cad or a bounder.

There he stood, in the plain pulpit, and raised his chin above the heads of all the rows of boys in black coats, and said: "One might go through this chapter of St. Paul and simply substitute the word 'gentleman' for 'charity' wherever it occurs. 'If I talk with the tongues of men and of angels, and be not a gentleman, I am become as sounding brass, or a tinkling cymbal . . . A gentleman is patient, is kind; a gentleman envieth not, dealeth not perversely; is not puffed up. . . . A gentleman never falleth away.' . . ."

And so it went. I will not accuse him of finishing the chapter with "Now there remain faith, hope and gentlemanliness, and the greatest of these is gentlemanliness . . ." although it was the logical term of his reasoning.

The boys listened tolerantly to these thoughts. But I think St. Peter and the twelve Apostles would have been rather surprised at the concept that Christ had been scourged and beaten by soldiers, cursed and crowned with thorns and subjected to unutterable contempt and finally nailed to the Cross and left to bleed to death in order that we might all become gentlemen.

As time went on, I was to get into fierce arguments with the football captain on this subject, but that day was yet to come. As long as I was among the fourteen- and fifteen-year-olds in Hodge Wing, I had to mind my behaviour with the lords of the school, or at least in their presence. We were disciplined by the constant fear of one of those pompous and ceremonious sessions of bullying, arranged with ritualistic formality, when a dozen or so culprits were summoned into one of the hollows around Brooke hill, or up the Braunston road, and beaten with sticks, and made to sing foolish songs and to hear themselves upbraided for their moral and social defects.

When I got into the sixth form, which I did after a year, I came more directly under the influence and guidance of the new Headmaster, F. C. Doherty. He was a young man for a Headmaster, about forty, tall, with a great head of black hair, a tremendous smoker of cigarettes and a lover of Plato. Because of the cigarettes, he used to like to give his class in his own study, when he decently could, for there he could smoke one after another, while in the classrooms he could not smoke at all.

He was a broad-minded man, and I never realized how much I owed to him until I left Oakham. If it had not been for him, I would probably have spent years in the fifth form trying to pass the School Certificate in mathematics. He saw that I could far easier pass the Higher Certificate, specializing in French and Latin where, although the examination in these subjects would be very hard, there would be no maths. And the Higher Certificate meant far more than the other. It was he who began, from the start, to prepare me for the university, getting me to aim at a Cambridge scholarship. And it was he who let me follow the bent of my own mind, for Modern Languages and Literature, although that meant that I spent much of my time studying alone in the library, since there was no real "Modern" course at Oakham at the time.

This was all the more generous of him for the fact that he really was very much attached to the Classics, and especially Plato, and he would have liked all of us to catch some of that infection. And yet this infection—which, in my eyes, was nothing short of deadly—was something I resisted with all my will. I do not exactly know why I hated Plato: but after the first ten pages of *The Republic* I decided that I could not stand Socrates and his friends, and I don't think I ever recovered from that repugnance. There can hardly have been any serious intellectual reason for my dislike of these philosophers, although I do have a kind of congenital distaste for philosophic idealism. But we were reading *The Republic* in Greek, which meant that we never got far enough into it to be able to grasp the ideas very well. Most of the time I was too helpless with the grammar and syntax to have time for any deeper difficulties.

Nevertheless, after a couple of months of it, I got to a state where phrases like "the Good, the True, and the Beautiful" filled me with a kind of suppressed indignation, because they stood for the big sin of Platonism: the reduction of all reality to the level of pure abstraction, as if concrete, individual substances had no essential reality of their own, but were only shadows of some remote, universal, ideal essence filed away in a big card-index somewhere in heaven, while the demiurges milled around the Logos piping their excitement in high, fluted, English intellectual tones. Platonism entered very much into the Headmaster's ideas of religion, which were deeply spiritual and intellectual. Also he was slightly more High-Church than most of the people at Oakham. However, it was no easier to find out, concretely, what he believed than it was to find out what anybody else believed in that place.

I had several different Masters in the one hour a week devoted to religious instruction (outside of the daily chapel). The first one just plodded through the third Book of Kings. The second, a tough little Yorkshireman, who had the virtue of being very definite and outspoken in everything he said, once exposed to us Descartes' proof of his own and God's existence. He told us that as far as he was concerned, that was the foundation of what religion meant to him. I accepted the *Cogito ergo sum* with less reserve than I should have, although I might have had enough sense to realize that any proof of what is self-evident must necessarily be illusory. If there are no self-evident first principles, as a foundation for reasoning to conclusions that are not immediately apparent, how can you construct any kind of a philosophy? If you have to prove even the basic axioms of your metaphysics, you will never have a metaphysics, because you will never have any strict proof of anything, for your first proof will involve you in an infinite regress, proving that you are proving what you are proving and so on, into the exterior darkness where there is wailing and gnashing of teeth. If Descartes thought it was necessary to prove his own existence, by the fact that he was thinking, and that his thought therefore existed in some subject, how did he prove that he was thinking in the first place? But as to the second step, that God must exist because Descartes had a clear idea of him—that never convinced me, then or at any other time, or now either. There are much better proofs for the existence of God than that one.

As for the Headmaster, when he gave us religious instruction, as he did in my last year or so at Oakham, he talked Plato, and told me to read A. E. Taylor, which I did, but under compulsion, and taking no trouble to try and understand what I was reading.

In 1930, after I had turned fifteen, and before most of these things happened, the way began to be prepared for my various intellectual rebellions by a sudden and very definite sense of independence, a realization of my own individuality which, while being natural at that age, took an unhealthy egotistic turn. And everything seemed to conspire to encourage me to cut myself off from everybody else and go my own way. For a moment, in the storms and confusion of adolescence, I had been humbled by my own interior sufferings, and having a certain amount of faith and religion, I had subjected myself more or less willingly and even gladly to the authority of others, and to the ways and customs of those around me.

But in Scotland I had begun to bare my teeth and fight back against the humiliation of giving in to other people, and now I was rapidly building up a hard core of resistance against everything that displeased me: whether it was the opinions or desires of others, or their commands, or their very persons. I would think what I wanted and do what I wanted, and go my own way. If those who tried to prevent me had authority to prevent me, I would have to be at least externally polite in my resistance: but my resistance would be no less determined, and I would do my own will, have my own way.

When Pop and Bonnemaman came to Europe again in 1930, they practically threw the doors of the world wide open to me and gave me my independence. The economic crisis of 1929 had not altogether ruined Pop: he did not have all his substance invested in companies that crashed, but the indirect effect on him was just as serious as it was on every other ordinary business man.

In June 1930, they all came down to Oakham—Pop, Bonne-maman and John Paul. It was a quiet visit. They no longer took towns by storm. The depression had changed all that. Besides, they were used to travelling in Europe by now. The fear and trepidation that had been so strong an element in their excitement in the old days were somewhat allayed. Their voyages were comparatively—but only comparatively—serene.

They had a couple of big rooms in the labyrinthine "Crown Inn" at Oakham, and one of the first things Pop did was to take me apart into one of them and talk to me in a way that amounted to an emancipation.

I think it was the first time in my life I had ever been treated as if I were completely grown up and able to take care of myself in everything, and to hold my own in a business conversation. In reality, I have never been able to talk intelligently about business. But I listened to Pop exposing our financial affairs as if I understood every word about it, and when it was over I had, indeed, grasped all the essentials.

No one knew what was going to happen in the world in the next ten or twenty years. Grosset and Dunlap was still in business, and so was Pop: but one could never tell when the business itself might fold up, or if he himself would be turned out. But in order to make sure that John Paul and I would be able to finish school, and even go on to the university, and have something to keep us from starving while we were looking for a job afterwards, Pop had taken the money he had planned to leave us in his will, and had put it away for us where it would be as safe as possible, in some kind of insurance policy which would pay us so much a year. He worked it out on a piece of paper and showed me all the figures and I nodded wisely. I didn't grasp the details but I understood that I ought to be able to get along all right until about 1940. And in any case, before a couple of years had gone by, Pop discovered that the big magic insurance policy did not work as neatly as he had expected, so he had to change his plans again, with a loss of a little money somewhere.

When it was all done, Pop gave me the piece of paper with all the figures on it, and sat up straight in his chair, and looked out the window, running his hand over the top of his bald head and said: "So now it's all settled. No matter what happens to me, you will both be taken care of. You've got nothing to worry about for a few years, anyway."

I was a bit dazed by the momentousness of it, and by Pop's own great generosity. Because, after all, he really meant it that way. What he was trying to do was to arrange everything so that even if he were ruined, we would be able to take care of ourselves. Fortunately, he was never ruined.

That day at Oakham, Pop crowned his generosity and his recognition of my maturity by an altogether astounding concession. He not only told me he was in favor of my smoking, but even bought me a pipe. I was fifteen, mind you, and Pop had always hated smoking anyway. Besides, it was forbidden by the rules of the school —rules which I had been systematically breaking all that year, more for the sake of asserting my independence than for the pleasure of lighting and relighting those cold, biting pipefuls of Rhodesian cut-plug.

When the holidays came there was another big change. It was decided that I would no longer spend my holidays with Aunt Maud or other relatives in the suburbs or outside of London. My godfather, an old friend of Father's from New Zealand, who was by now a Harley Street specialist, offered to let me stay at his place in town when I was in London: and that meant that most of the day and night I was more or less free to do what I liked.

Tom—my godfather—was to be the person I most respected and admired and consequently the one who had the greatest influence on me at this time in my life. He too gave me credit for being more intelligent and mature than I was, and this of course pleased me very much. He was later to find out that his trust in me was misplaced.

Life in the flat where Tom and his wife lived was very well-ordered and amusing. You got breakfast in bed, served by a French maid, on a small tray: coffee or chocolate in a tiny pot, toast or rolls, and, for me, fried eggs. After breakfast, which came in at about nine, I knew I would have to wait a little to get a bath, so I would stay in bed for an hour or so more reading a novel by Evelyn Waugh or somebody like that. Then I would get up and take my bath and get dressed and go out and look for some amusement—walk in the park, or go to a museum, or go to some gramophone shop and listen to a lot of hot records—and then buy one, to pay for the privilege of listening to all the rest. I used to go to Levy's, on the top floor of one of those big buildings in the crescent of Regent Street, because they imported all the latest Victors and Brunswicks and Okeh's from America, and I would lock myself up in one of those little glass-doored booths, and play all the Duke Ellingtons and Louis Armstrongs and the old King Olivers and all the other things I have forgotten. Basin Street Blues, Beale Street Blues, Saint James Infirmary, and all the other places that had blues written about them: all these I suddenly began to know much of by indirection and woeful hearsay, and I guess I lived vicariously in all the slums in all the cities of the South: Memphis and New Orleans and Birmingham, places which I have never yet seen. I don't know where those streets were, but I certainly knew something true about them, which I found out on that top floor in Regent Street and in my study at Oakham.

Then I would go back to my godfather's place, and we would have lunch in the dining room, sitting at the little table that always seemed to me so small and delicate that I was afraid to move for fear the whole thing would collapse and the pretty French dishes would smash on the floor and scatter the French food on the waxed floorboards. Everything in that flat was small and delicate. It harmonised with my godfather and his wife. Not that he was delicate, but he was a little man who walked quietly and quickly on small feet, or stood at the fireplace with a cigarette between his fingers, neat and precise as a decent doctor ought to be. And he had something of the pursed lips of medical men—the contraction of the lips that they somehow acquire leaning over wide-open bodies.

Tom's wife was delicate. In fact, she looked almost brittle. She was French, and the daughter of a great Protestant patriarch with a long white beard who dominated French Calvinism from the Rue des Saints-Pères.

Everything in their flat was in proportion to their own stature and delicacy and precision and neatness and wit. Yet I do not say it looked like a doctor's place—still less like an English doctor's place. English doctors always seem to go in for very heavy and depressing kinds of furniture. But Tom was not the kind of specialist that always wears a frock coat and a wing-collar. His flat was bright and full of objects I was afraid to break and, on the whole, I was scared to walk too heavily for fear I might suddenly go through the floor.

What I most admired about Tom and Iris, from the start, was that they knew everything and had everything in its proper place. From the first moment when I discovered that one was not only allowed to make fun of English middle-class notions and ideals but encouraged to do so in that little bright drawing-room, where we balanced coffee-cups on our knees, I was very happy. I soon developed a habit of wholesale and glib detraction of all the people with whom I did not agree or whose taste and ideas offended me.

They, in turn, lent me all the novels and told me about the

various plays, and listened with amusement to Duke Ellington, and played me their records of La Argentina. It was from them that I was to discover all the names that people most talked about in modern writing: Hemingway, Joyce, D. H. Lawrence, Evelyn Waugh, Céline with his *Voyage au Bout de la Nuit*, Gide and all the rest, except that they did not bother much with poets. I heard about T. S. Eliot from the English Master at Oakham who had just come down from Cambridge and read me aloud "The Hollow Men."

It was Tom who, once when we were in Paris, took me to see a lot of pictures by Chagall and several others like him, although he did not like Braque and the Cubists and never developed any of my enthusiasm for Picasso. It was he who showed me that there was some merit in Russian movies and in René Clair: but he never understood the Marx Brothers. It was from him that I discovered the difference between the Café Royal and the Café Anglais, and many other things of the same nature. And he also could tell you what members of the English nobility were thought to take dope.

Really, all these things implied a rather strict standard of values: but values that were entirely worldly and cosmopolitan. Values they were, however, and one kept to them with a most remarkably nice fidelity. I only discovered much later on that all this implied not only esthetic but a certain worldly moral standard, the moral and artistic values being fused inseparably in the single order of taste. It was an unwritten law, and you had to be very smart and keenly attuned to their psychology to get it: but there it was, a strict moral law, which never expressed any open hatred of evil, or even any direct and explicit condemnation of any other sins than bourgeois pharisaism and middle-class hypocrisy, which they attacked without truce. Nevertheless their code disposed of other deordinations with quiet and pointed mockery. The big difficulty with me and my failure was that I did not see, for instance, that their interest in D. H. Lawrence as art was, in some subtle way, disconnected from any endorsement of his ideas about how a man ought to live. Or rather, the distinction was more subtle still: and it was between their interest in and amusement at those ideas, and the fact, which they took for granted, that it was rather vulgar to practice them the way Lawrence did. This was a distinction which I did not grasp until it was too late.

Until the time I went to Cambridge, I developed rapidly under their influence, and in many ways the development was valuable and good: and of course, there must be no question of the kindness and sincerity of the interest which they took in me, or their generosity in devoting themselves so whole-heartedly to my care and to my training, in their informal and unofficial way.

It was Tom who definitely assured me that I should prepare for the English diplomatic or at least consular service, and did not spare any effort to see that I advanced steadily, in every possible way, towards that end. He was able to foresee an infinity of little details that would have to be taken care of long before they arose—the value, for instance, of "reading for the bar" which simply meant eating a certain number of dinners at one of the Inns of Court, so as to fulfil the minimum residence requirements of a London Law student, and the payment of a fee for a minor distinction which would be useful in the diplomatic service. As it happened, I never got around to eating those dinners, and I dare to hope I shall be no lower in heaven for my failure to do so.

iii

It was the summer of 1930, before most of these things had happened. I mean, the summer when Pop had made over to me the portion of my inheritance and threw open the door for me to run away and be a prodigal, or be a prodigal without running away from any earthly home, for that matter. I could very well eat the husks of swine without the inconvenience of going into a far country to look for them.

Most of that summer we were all together in London. The reason was, that we could be near the hospital and visit Father. I remember the first of those visits.

It was several months since I had been in London, and then only in passing, so I had really hardly seen Father at all since he had entered the hospital the autumn before.

So all of us went to the hospital. Father was in a ward. We had arrived much too early, and had to wait. We were in a new wing of the big hospital. The floor was shiny and clean. Vaguely depressed by the smell of sickness and disinfectant and the general medical smell that all hospitals have, we sat in a corridor downstairs for upwards of half an hour. I had just bought Hugo's *Italian Self-Taught*, and began to teach myself some verbs, sitting there in the hall, with John Paul restive on the bench beside me. And the time dragged.

Finally the clock we had been watching got around to the appropriate hour; we went up in an elevator. They all knew where the ward was—it was a different ward. I think they had changed his ward two or three times. And he had had more than one operation. But none of them had been successful.

We went into the ward. Father was in bed, to the left, just as you went in the door.

And when I saw him, I knew at once there was no hope of his living much longer. His face was swollen. His eyes were not clear but, above all, the tumor had raised a tremendous swelling on his forehead.

I said: "How are you, Father?"

He looked at me and put forth his hand, in a confused and unhappy way, and I realized that he could no longer even speak. But at the same time, you could see that he knew us, and knew what was going on, and that his mind was clear, and that he understood everything.

But the sorrow of his great helplessness suddenly fell upon me like a mountain. I was crushed by it. The tears sprang to my eyes. Nobody said anything more.

I hid my face in the blanket and cried. And poor Father wept, too. The others stood by. It was excruciatingly sad. We were completely helpless. There was nothing anyone could do.

When I finally looked up and dried my tears, I noticed that the attendants had put screens all around the bed. I was too miserable to feel ashamed of my un-English demonstration of sorrow and affection. And so we went away.

What could I make of so much suffering? There was no way for me, or for anyone else in the family, to get anything out of it. It was a raw wound for which there was no adequate relief. You had to take it, like an animal. We were in the condition of most of the world, the condition of men without faith in the presence of war, disease, pain, starvation, suffering, plague, bombardment, death. You just had to take it, like a dumb animal. Try to avoid it, if you could. But you must eventually reach the point where you can't avoid it any more. Take it. Try to stupefy yourself, if you like, so that it won't hurt so much. But you will always have to take some of it. And it will all devour you in the end.

Indeed, the truth that many people never understand, until it is too late, is that the more you try to avoid suffering, the more you suffer, because smaller and more insignificant things begin to torture you, in proportion to your fear of being hurt. The one who does most to avoid suffering is, in the end, the one who suffers most: and his suffering comes to him from things so little and so trivial that one can say that it is no longer objective at all. It is his own existence, his own being, that is at once the subject and the source of his pain, and his very existence and consciousness is his greatest torture. This is another of the great perversions by which the devil uses our philosophies to turn our whole nature inside out, and eviscerate all our capacities for good, turning them against ourselves.

All summer we went regularly and faithfully to the hospital once or twice a week. There was nothing we could do but sit there, and look at Father and tell him things which he could not answer. But he understood what we said.

In fact, if he could not talk, there were other things he could still do. One day I found his bed covered with little sheets of blue notepaper on which he had been drawing. And the drawings were real drawings. But they were unlike anything he had ever done before—pictures of little, irate Byzantine-looking saints with beards and great halos.

Of us all, Father was the only one who really had any kind of a faith. And I do not doubt that he had very much of it, and that behind the walls of his isolation, his intelligence and his will, unimpaired, and not hampered in any essential way by the partial obstruction of some of his senses, were turned to God, and communed with God Who was with him and in him, and Who gave him, as I believe, light to understand and to make use of his suffering for his own good, and to perfect his soul. It was a great soul, large, full of natural charity. He was a man of exceptional intellectual honesty and sincerity and purity of understanding. And this affliction, this terrible and frightening illness which was relentlessly pressing him down even into the jaws of the tomb, was not destroying him after all.

Souls are like athletes, that need opponents worthy of them, if they are to be tried and extended and pushed to the full use of their powers, and rewarded according to their capacity. And my father was in a fight with this tumor, and none of us understood the battle. We thought he was done for, but it was making him great. And I think God was already weighing out to him the weight of reality that was to be his reward, for he certainly believed far more than any theologian would require of a man to hold explicitly as "necessity of means," and so he was eligible for this reward, and his struggle was authentic, and not wasted or lost or thrown away.

In the Christmas holidays I only saw him once or twice. Things were about the same. I spent most of the holidays in Strasbourg, where Tom had arranged for me to go for the sake of the languages: German and French. I stayed in a big Protestant *pension* in the

Rue Finkmatt, and was under the unofficial tutelage of a professor at the University, a friend of Tom's family and of the Protestant patriarch.

Professor Hering was a kind and pleasant man with a red beard, and one of the few Protestants I have ever met who struck one as being at all holy: that is, he possessed a certain profound interior peace, which he probably got from his contact with the Fathers of the Church, for he was a teacher of theology. We did not talk much about religion, however. Once when some students were visiting him, one of them explained to me the essentials of Unitarianism, and when I asked the professor about it afterwards, he said it was all right, in a way which indicated that he approved, in a sort of academic and eclectic way, of all these different forms of belief: or rather that he was interested in them as objectively intriguing manifestations of a fundamental human instinct, regarding them more or less through the eyes of a sociologist. As a matter of fact, sometimes Protestant theology does, in certain circumstances, amount to little more than a combination of sociology and religious history, but I will not accuse him of teaching it altogether in that sense, for I really have no idea how he taught it.

Under the inspiration of the environment, I went to a Lutheran church and sat through a long sermon in German which I did not understand. But I think that was all the worship of God I did in Strasbourg. I was more interested in Josephine Baker, a big skinny colored girl from some American city like St. Louis, who came to one of the theaters and sang *J'ai deux amours, mon pays et Paris.*

So I went back to school, after seeing Father for a moment on the way through London. I had been back for barely a week when I was summoned, one morning, to the Headmaster's study, and he gave me a telegram which said that Father was dead.

The sorry business was all over. And my mind made nothing of it. There was nothing I seemed to be able to grasp. Here was a man with a wonderful mind and a great talent and a great heart: and, what was more, he was the man who had brought me into the world, and had nourished me and cared for me and had shaped my soul and to whom I was bound by every possible kind of bond of affection and attachment and admiration and reverence: killed by a growth on his brain.

Tom got an obituary printed in the *Times*, and he saw to it that the funeral went off more or less decently: but it was still another one of those cremations. This time it was at Golders Green. The only difference was that the minister said more prayers, and the chapel looked a little more like a chapel, and Tom had got them to hide the coffin under a very beautiful shroud of silk from the Orient somewhere, China or Bali or India.

But in the end they took the shroud off and rolled the coffin through one of those sliding doors and then, in the sinister secrecy of the big, intricate crematory, out of our sight, the body was burned, and we went away.

Nevertheless, all that is of no importance, and it can be forgotten. For I hope that, in the living Christ, I shall one day see my father again: that is, I believe that Christ, Who is the Son of God, and Who is God, has power to raise up all those who have died in His grace, to the glory of His own Resurrection, and to share, body and soul, in the glory of His Divine inheritance, at the last day.

The death of my father left me sad and depressed for a couple of months. But that eventually wore away. And when it did, I found myself completely stripped of everything that impeded the movement of my own will to do as it pleased. I imagined that I was free. And it would take me five or six years to discover what a frightful captivity I had got myself into. It was in this year, too, that the hard crust of my dry soul finally squeezed out all the last traces of religion that had ever been in it. There was no room for any God in that empty temple full of dust and rubbish which I was now so jealously to guard against all intruders, in order to devote it to the worship of my own stupid will.

And so I became the complete twentieth-century man. I now belonged to the world in which I lived. I became a true citizen of my own disgusting century: the century of poison gas and atomic bombs. A man living on the doorsill of the Apocalypse, a man with veins full of poison, living in death. Baudelaire could truly address me, then, reader: *Hypocrite lecteur, mon semblable, mon frère . . .*

iv

Meanwhile there was one discovery of mine, one poet who was a poet indeed, and a Romantic poet, but vastly different from those contemporaries, with whom he had so little to do. I think my love for William Blake had something in it of God's grace. It is a love that has never died, and which has entered very deeply into the development of my life.

Father had always liked Blake, and had tried to explain to me what was good about him when I was a child of ten. The funny thing about Blake is that although the *Songs of Innocence* look like children's poems, and almost seem to have been written for children, they are, to most children, incomprehensible. Or at least, they were so to me. Perhaps if I had read them when I was four or five, it would have been different. But when I was ten, I knew too much. I knew that tigers did not burn in the forests of the night. That was very silly, I thought. Children are very literal-minded.

I was less literal when I was sixteen. I could accept Blake's metaphors and they already began, a little, to astound and to move me, although I had no real grasp of their depth and power. And I liked Blake immensely. I read him with more patience and attention than any other poet. I thought about him more. And I could not figure him out. I do not mean, I could not figure out the Prophetic Books —nobody can do that! But I could not place him in any kind of a context, and I did not know how to make his ideas fit together.

One grey Sunday in the spring, I walked alone out the Brooke Road and up Brooke Hill, where the rifle range was. It was a long, bare hog-back of a hill, with a few lone trees along the top, and it commanded a big sweeping view of the Vale of Catmos, with the town of Oakham lying in the midst of it, gathered around the grey, sharp church spire. I sat on a stile on the hill top, and contemplated the wide vale, from the north, where the kennels of the Cottesmore hounds were, to Lax Hill and Manton in the south. Straight across was Burley House, on top of its hill, massed with woods. At my feet, a few red brick houses straggled out from the town to the bottom of the slope.

And all the time I reflected, that afternoon, upon Blake. I remember how I concentrated and applied myself to it. It was rare that I ever really thought about such a thing of my own accord. But I was trying to establish what manner of man he was. Where did he stand? What did he believe? What did he preach?

On one hand he spoke of the "priests in black gowns who were going their rounds binding with briars my joys and desires." And yet on the other hand he detested Voltaire and Rousseau and everybody like them and everything that they stood for, and he abominated all materialistic deism, and all the polite, abstract natural religions of the eighteenth century, the agnosticism of the nineteenth, and, in fact, most of the common attitudes of our day.

> The atoms of Democritus
> And Newton's particles of light
> Are sands upon the Red-Sea shore
> Where Israel's tents do shine so bright. . .

I was absolutely incapable of reconciling, in my mind, two things that seemed so contrary. Blake was a revolutionary, and yet he detested the greatest and most typical revolutionaries of his time, and declared himself opposed without compromise to people who, as I thought, seemed to exemplify some of his own most characteristic ideals.

How incapable I was of understanding anything like the ideals of a William Blake! How could I possibly realize that his rebellion, for all its strange heterodoxies, was fundamentally the rebellion of the saints. It was the rebellion of the lover of the living God, the rebellion of one whose desire of God was so intense and irresistible that it condemned, with all its might, all the hypocrisy and petty sensuality and skepticism and materialism which cold and trivial minds set up as unpassable barriers between God and the souls of men.

The priests that he saw going their rounds in black gowns—he knew no Catholics at the time, and had probably never even seen a Catholic priest—were symbols, in his mind, of the weak, compromising, pharisaic piety of those whose god was nothing but an objectification of their own narrow and conventional desires and hypocritical fears.

He did not distinguish any particular religion or sect as the objects of his disdain: he simply could not stand false piety and religiosity, in which the love of God was stamped out of the souls of men by formalism and conventions, without any charity, without the light and life of a faith that brings man face to face with God. If on one page of Blake these priests in black gowns were frightening and hostile figures, on another, the "Grey Monk of Charlemaine" was a saint and a hero of charity and of faith, fighting for the peace of the true God with all the ardent love that was the only reality Blake lived for. Towards the end of his life, Blake told his friend Samuel Palmer that the Catholic Church was the only one that taught the love of God.

I am not, of course, recommending the study of William Blake to all minds as a perfect way to faith and to God. Blake is really extraordinarily difficult and obscure and there is, in him, some of the confusion of almost all the heterodox and heretical mystical systems that ever flourished in the west—and that is saying a lot. And yet, by the grace of God, at least in my opinion, he was kept very much uncontaminated by all his crazy symbols precisely because he was such a good and holy man, and because his faith was so real and his love for God so mighty and so sincere.

The Providence of God was eventually to use Blake to awaken something of faith and love in my own soul—in spite of all the misleading notions, and all the almost infinite possibilities of error that underlie his weird and violent figures. I do not, therefore, want to seem to canonize him. But I have to acknowledge my own debt to him, and the truth which may appear curious to some, although it is really not so: that through Blake I would one day come, in a round-about way, to the only true Church, and to the One Living God, through His Son, Jesus Christ.

V

In three months, the summer of 1931, I suddenly matured like a weed.

I cannot tell which is the more humiliating: the memory of the half-baked adolescent I was in June or the glib and hard-boiled specimen I was in October when I came back to Oakham full of a thorough and deep-rooted sophistication of which I was both conscious and proud.

The beginning was like this: Pop wrote to me to come to America. I got a brand-new suit made. I said to myself, "On the boat I am going to meet a beautiful girl, and I am going to fall in love."

So I got on the boat. The first day I sat in a deck chair and read the correspondence of Goethe and Schiller which had been imposed on me as a duty, in preparation for the scholarship examinations at the university. What is worse, I not only tolerated this imposition but actually convinced myself that it was interesting.

The second day I had more or less found out who was on the boat. The third day I was no longer interested in Goethe and Schiller. The fourth day I was up to my neck in the trouble that I was looking for.

It was a ten-day boat.

I would rather spend two years in a hospital than go through that anguish again! That devouring, emotional, passionate love of adolescence that sinks its claws into you and consumes you day and night and eats into the vitals of your soul! All the self-tortures of doubt and anxiety and imagination and hope and despair that you go through when you are a child, trying to break out of your shell, only to find yourself in the middle of a legion of full-armed emotions against which you have no defense! It is like being flayed alive. No one can go through it twice. This kind of a love affair can really happen only once in a man's life. After that he is calloused. He is no longer capable of so many torments. He can suffer, but not from so many matters of no account. After one such crisis he has experience and the possibility of a second time no longer exists, because the secret of the anguish was his own utter guilelessness. He is no longer capable of such complete and absurd surprises. No matter how simple a man may be, the obvious cannot go on astonishing him for ever.

I was introduced to this particular girl by a Catholic priest who came from Cleveland and played shuffleboard in his shirt sleeves without a Roman collar on. He knew everybody on the boat in the first day, and as for me, two days had gone by before I even realized that she was on board. She was travelling with a couple of aunts and the three of them did not mix in with the other passengers very much. They kept to themselves in their three deck chairs and had nothing to do with the gentlemen in tweed caps and glasses who went breezing around and around the promenade deck.

When I first met her I got the impression she was no older than I was. As a matter of fact she was about twice my age: but you could be twice sixteen without being old, as I now realize, sixteen years after the event. She was small and delicate and looked as if she were made out of porcelain. But she had big wide-open California eyes and was not afraid to talk in a voice that was at once ingenuous and independent and had some suggestion of weariness about it as if she habitually stayed up too late at night.

To my dazzled eyes she immediately became the heroine of every novel and I all but flung myself face down on the deck at her feet. She could have put a collar on my neck and led me around from that time forth on the end of a chain. Instead of that I spent my days telling her and her aunts all about my ideals and my ambitions and she in her turn attempted to teach me how to play bridge. And that is the surest proof of her conquest, for I never allowed anyone else to try such a thing as that on me, never! But even she could not succeed in such an enterprise.

We talked. The insatiable wound inside me bled and grew, and I was doing everything I could to make it bleed more. Her perfume and the peculiar smell of the denicotinized cigarettes she smoked followed me everywhere and tortured me in my cabin.

She told me how once she was in a famous night club in a famous city when a famous person, a prince of the royal blood, had stared very intently at her for a long time and had finally got up and started to lurch in the direction of her table when his friends had made him sit down and behave himself.

I could see that all the counts and dukes who liked to marry people like Constance Bennett would want also to marry her. But the counts and dukes were not here on board this glorified cargo boat that was carrying us all peacefully across the mild dark waves of the North Atlantic. The thing that crushed me was that I had never learned to dance.

We made Nantucket Light on Sunday afternoon and had to anchor in quarantine that night. So the ship rode in the Narrows on the silent waters, and the lights of Brooklyn glittered in the harbor like jewels. The boat was astir with music and with a warm glowing life that pulsated within the dark hull and poured out into the July night through every porthole. There were parties in all the cabins. Everywhere you went, especially on deck where it was quiet, you were placed in the middle of movie scenery—the setting for the last reel of the picture.

I made a declaration of my undying love. I would not, could not, ever love anyone else but her. It was impossible, unthinkable. If she went to the ends of the earth, destiny would bring us together again. The stars in their courses from the beginning of the world had plotted this meeting which was the central fact in the whole history of the universe. Love like this was immortal. It conquered time and outlasted the futility of human history. And so forth.

She talked to me, in her turn, gently and sweetly. What it sounded like was: "You do not know what you are saying. This can never be. We shall never meet again." What it meant was: "You are a nice kid. But for heaven's sake grow up before someone makes a fool of you." I went to my cabin and sobbed over my diary for a while and then, against all the laws of romance, went peacefully to sleep.

However, I could not sleep for long. At five o'clock I was up again, and walking restlessly around the deck. It was hot. A grey mist lay on the Narrows. But when it became light, other anchored ships began to appear as shapes in the mist. One of them was a Red Star liner on which, as I learned from the papers when I got on shore, a passenger was at that precise moment engaged in hanging himself.

At the last minute before landing I took a snapshot of her which, to my intense sorrow, came out blurred. I was so avid for a picture of her that I got too close with the camera and it was out of focus. It was a piece of poetic justice that filled me with woe for months.

Of course the whole family was there on the dock. But the change was devastating. With my heart ready to explode with immature emotions I suddenly found myself surrounded by all the cheerful and peaceful and comfortable solicitudes of home. Everybody wanted to talk. Their voices were full of questions and information. They took me for a drive on Long Island and showed me where Mrs. Hearst lived and everything. But I only hung my head out of the window of the car and watched the green trees go swirling by, and wished that I were dead.

I would not tell anybody what was the matter with me, and this reticence was the beginning of a kind of estrangement between us. From that time on no one could be sure what I was doing or thinking. I would go to New York and I would not come home for meals and I would not tell anyone where I had been.

Most of the time I had not been anywhere special; I would go to the movies, and then wander around the streets and look at the crowds of people and eat hot dogs and drink orange juice at Nedicks. Once with great excitement I got inside a speak-easy. And when I found out that the place was raided a few days later I grew so much in my own estimation that I began to act as if I had shot my way out of the wildest joints in town.

Bonnemaman was the one who suffered most from my reticence. For years she had been sitting at home wondering what Pop was doing in the city all day, and now that I was developing the same wandering habits it was quite natural for her to imagine strange things about me, too.

But the only wickedness I was up to was that I roamed around the city smoking cigarettes and hugging my own sweet sense of independence.

I found out that Grosset and Dunlap published more than the Rover Boys. They brought out reprints of writers like Hemingway and Aldous Huxley and D. H. Lawrence and I devoured them all, on the cool sleeping porch of the house at Douglaston, while the moths of the summer darkness came batting and throbbing against the screens, attracted by my light that burned until all hours.

Most of the time I was running into my uncle's room to borrow his dictionary, and when he found out what words I was looking up he arched his eyebrows and said: "What are you reading, anyway?"

At the end of the summer I started back for England on the same boat on which I had come. This time the passenger list included some girls from Bryn Mawr and some from Vassar and some from somewhere else, all of whom were going to a finishing school in France. It seems as if all the rest of the people on board were detectives. Some of them were professional detectives. Others were amateurs; all of them made me and the Bryn Mawr girls the object of their untiring investigations. But in any case the ship was divided into these two groups: on the one hand the young people, on the other the elders. We sat in the smoking room all the rainy days playing Duke Ellington records on the portable vic that belonged to one of the girls. When we got tired of that we wandered all over the ship looking for funny things to do. The hold was full of cattle, and there was also a pack of fox-hounds down there. We used to go down and play with the dogs. At Le Havre, when the cattle were unloaded, one of the cows broke loose and ran all over the dock in a frenzy. One night three of us got up in the crow's nest on the foremast, where we certainly did not belong. Another time we had a party with the radio operators and I got into a big argument about Communism.

That was another thing that had happened that summer: I had begun to get the idea that I was a Communist, although I wasn't quite sure what Communism was. There are a lot of people like that. They do no little harm by virtue of their sheer, stupid inertia, lost in between all camps, in the no-man's-land of their own confusion. They are fair game for anybody. They can be turned into fascists just as quickly as they can be pulled into line with those who are really Reds.

The other group was made up of the middle-aged people. At their core were the red-faced, hard-boiled cops who spent their time drinking and gambling and fighting among themselves and spreading scandal all over the boat about the young ones who were so disreputable and wild.

The truth is that we did have quite a big bar bill, the Bryn Mawr girls and myself, but we were never drunk, because we drank slowly and spent the whole time stuffing ourselves with sardines on toast and all the other dainties which are the stock in trade of English liners.

In any case, I set foot once more on the soil of England dressed up in a gangster suit which Pop had bought me at Wallach's, complete with padded shoulders. And I had a new, pale grey hat over my eye and walked into England pleased with the consciousness that I had easily acquired a very lurid reputation for myself with scarcely any trouble at all.

The separation of the two generations on board the ship had pleased me. It had flattered me right down to the soles of my feet. It was just what I wanted. It completed my self-confidence, guaranteed my self-assertion. Anyone older than myself symbolized authority. And the vulgarity of the detectives and the stupidity of the other middle-aged people who had believed all their stories about us fed me with a pleasantly justifiable sense of contempt for their whole generation. Therefore I concluded that I was now free of all authority, and that nobody could give me any advice that I had to listen to. Because advice was only the cloak of hypocrisy or weakness or vulgarity or fear. Authority was constituted by the old and weak, and had its roots in their envy for the joys and pleasures of the young and strong. . . .

Finally, when I arrived at Oakham several days after the beginning of the term I was convinced that I was the only one in the whole place who knew anything about life, from the Headmaster on down.

I was now a house prefect in Hodge Wing with a great big study and a lot of slightly lop-sided wicker armchairs full of cushions. On the walls I hung Medici prints of Manet and some other impressionists and photographs of various Greco-Roman Venuses from museums in Rome. And my bookshelf was full of a wide variety of strange bright-colored novels and pamphlets, all of which were so inflammatory that there would never be any special need for the Church to put them on the *Index*, for they would all be damned *ipso jure*—most of them by the natural law itself. I will not name the ones I remember, because some fool might immediately go and read them all: but I might mention that one of the pamphlets was Marx's Communist Manifesto—not because I was seriously exercised about the injustices done to the working class, which were and are very real, but were too serious for my empty-headed vanity—but simply because I thought it fitted in nicely with the décor in which I now moved in all my imaginings.

For it had become evident to me that I was a great rebel. I fancied that I had suddenly risen above all the errors and stupidities and mistakes of modern society—there are enough of them to rise above, I admit—and that I had taken my place in the ranks of those who held up their heads and squared their shoulders and marched into the future. In the modern world, people are always holding up their heads and marching into the future, although they haven't the slightest idea what they think the "future" is or could possibly mean. The only future we seem to walk into, in actual fact, is full of bigger and more terrible wars, wars well calculated to knock our upraised heads off those squared shoulders.

Here in this study I edited the school magazine which had fallen into my hands that autumn, and read T. S. Eliot, and even tried to write a poem myself about Elpenor, in Homer, getting drunk and falling off the roof of a palace. And his soul fled into the shades of hell. And the rest of the time I played Duke Ellington's records or got into arguments about politics and religion.

All those vain and absurd arguments! My advice to an ordinary religious man, supposing anyone were to desire my advice on this point, would be to avoid all arguments about religion, and especially about the existence of God. However, to those who know some philosophy I would recommend the study of Duns Scotus' proofs for the actual existence of an Infinite Being, which are given in the Second Distinction of the First Book of the *Opus Oxoniense*—in Latin that is hard enough to give you many headaches. It is getting to be rather generally admitted that, for accuracy and depth and scope, this is the most perfect and complete and thorough proof for the existence of God that has ever been worked out by any man.

I doubt if it would have done much good to bring these considerations before me in those days, when I was just turning seventeen, and thought I knew all about philosophy without ever having learned any. However, I did have a desire to learn. I was attracted to philosophy. It was an attraction the Headmaster had worked hard to implant in our souls: but there was, and could be, no course in philosophy at Oakham. I was left to my own devices.

I remember once mentioning all this to Tom, my guardian. We were walking out of his front door, into Harley Street, and I told him of my desire to study philosophy, and to know the philosophers.

He, being a doctor, told me to leave philosophy alone: there were few things, he told me, that were a greater waste of time.

Fortunately, this was one of the matters in which I decided to ignore his advice. Anyway, I went ahead and tried to read some philosophy. I never got very far with it. It was too difficult for me to master all by myself. People who are immersed in sensual appetites and desires are not very well prepared to handle abstract ideas. Even in the purely natural order, a certain amount of purity of heart is required before an intellect can get sufficiently detached and clear to work out the problems of metaphysics. I say a certain amount, however, because I am sure that no one needs to be a saint to be a clever metaphysician. I dare say there are plenty of metaphysicians in hell.

However, the philosophers to whom I was attracted were not the best. For the most part, I used to take their books out of libraries, and return them without ever having opened them. It was just as well. Nevertheless during the Easter vacation, when I was seventeen, I earnestly and zealously set about trying to figure out Spinoza.

I had gone to Germany, by myself as usual, for the vacation. In Cologne I had bought a big rucksack and slung it over my shoulders and started up the Rhine valley on foot, in a blue jersey and an old pair of flannel bags, so that people in the inns along the road asked me if I was a Dutch sailor off one of the river barges. In the rucksack, which was already heavy enough, I had a couple of immoral novels and the Everyman Library edition of Spinoza. Spinoza and the Rhine valley! I certainly had a fine sense of appropriateness. The two go very well together. However I was about eighty years too late. And the only thing that was lacking was that I was not an English or American student at Heidelberg: then the mixture would have been perfect in all its mid-nineteenth-century ingredients.

I picked up more, on this journey, than a few intellectual errors, half understood. Before I got to Koblenz, I had trouble in one foot. Some kind of an infection seemed to be developing under one of the toenails. But it was not especially painful, and I ignored it. However, it made walking unpleasant, and so, after going on as far as St. Goar, I gave up in disgust. Besides, the weather had turned bad, and I had got lost in the forest, trying to follow the imaginary hiker's trail called the Rheinhöhenweg.

I went back to Koblenz, and sat in a room over a big beer hall called the Neuer Franziskaner and continued my desultory study of Spinoza and my modern novelists. Since I understood the latter much better than the philosopher, I soon gave him up and concentrated on the novels.

After a few days, I returned to England, passing through Paris, where Pop and Bonnemaman were. There I picked up some more and even worse books, and went back to school.

I had not been back for more than a few days when I began to feel ill. At first, I thought I was only out of sorts because of the sore foot and a bad toothache, which had suddenly begun to afflict me.

They sent me down to the school dentist, Dr. McTaggart, who lived in a big brick building like a barracks, on the way to the station. Dr. McTaggart was a lively little fellow. He knew me well, for I was always having trouble with my teeth. He had a theory that you should kill the nerves of teeth, and he had already done so to half a dozen of mine. For the rest, he would trot gaily around and around the big chair in which I sat, mute and half frozen with terror. And he would sing, as he quickly switched his drills: "It won't be a stylish marriage— We can't afford a carriage— But you'll look sweet— Upon the seat— Of a bicycle built for two."

Then he would start wrecking my teeth once again, with renewed gusto.

This time he tapped at the tooth, and looked serious.

"It will have to come out," he said.

I was not sorry. The thing was hurting me, and I wanted to get rid of it as soon as possible.

But Dr. McTaggart said: "I can't give you anything to deaden the pain, you know."

"Why not?"

"There is a great deal of infection, and the matter has spread far beyond the roots of the tooth."

I accepted his reasoning on trust and said: "Well, go ahead."

And I sat back in the chair, mute with misgivings, while he happily trotted over to his tool-box singing "It won't be a stylish marriage" and pulled out an ugly-looking forceps.

"All ready?" he said, jacking back the chair, and brandishing the instrument of torture. I nodded, feeling as if I had gone pale to the roots of my hair.

But the tooth came out fast, in one big, vivid flash of pain and left me spitting a lot of green and red business into the little blue whispering whirlpool by the side of the dentist's chair.

"Oh, goodness," said Dr. McTaggart, "I don't like that very much, I must say."

I walked wearily back to school, reflecting that it was not really so terrible after all to have a tooth pulled out without novocain. However, instead of getting better, I got worse. By evening, I was really ill, and that night—that sleepless night—was spent in a fog of sick confusedness and general pain. The next morning they took my temperature and put me to bed in the sick-room, where I eventually got to sleep.

That did not make me any better. And I soon gathered in a vague way that our matron, Miss Harrison, was worried about me, and communicated her worries to the Headmaster, in whose own house this particular sick-room was.

Then the school doctor came around. And he went away again, returning with Dr. McTaggart who, this time, did not sing.

And I heard them agreeing that I was getting to be too full of gangrene for my own good. They decided to lance a big hole in my gum, and see if they could not drain the pocket of infection there and so, having given me a little ether, they went ahead. I awoke with my mouth full of filth, both doctors urging me to hurry up and get rid of it.

When they had gone, I lay back in bed and closed my eyes and thought: "I have blood-poisoning."

And then my mind went back to the sore foot I had developed in Germany. Well, I would tell them about it when they came back the next time.

Sick, weary, half asleep, I felt the throbbing of the wound in my mouth. Blood-poisoning.

The room was very quiet. It was rather dark, too. And as I lay in bed, in my weariness and pain and disgust, I felt for a moment the shadow of another visitor pass into the room.

It was death, that came to stand by my bed.

I kept my eyes closed, more out of apathy than anything else. But anyway, there was no need to open one's eyes to see the visitor, to see death. Death is someone you see very clearly with eyes in the center of your heart: eyes that see not by reacting to light, but by reacting to a kind of a chill from within the marrow of your own life.

And, with those eyes, those interior eyes, open upon that coldness, I lay half asleep and looked at the visitor, death.

What did I think? All I remember was that I was filled with a deep and tremendous apathy. I felt so sick and disgusted that I did not very much care whether I died or lived. Perhaps death did not come very close to me, or give me a good look at the nearness of his coldness and darkness, or I would have been more afraid.

But at any rate, I lay there in a kind of torpor and said: "Come on, I don't care." And then I fell asleep.

What a tremendous mercy it was that death did not take me at my word, that day, when I was still only seventeen years old. What a thing it would have been if the trapdoors that were prepared for me had yawned and opened their blackness and swallowed me down in the middle of that sleep! Oh, I tell you, it is a blessing beyond calculation that I woke up again, that day, or the following night, or in the week or two that came after.

And I lay there with nothing in my heart but apathy—there was a kind of pride and spite in it: as if it was life's fault that I had to suffer a little discomfort, and for that I would show my scorn and hatred of life, and die, as if that were a revenge of some sort. Revenge upon what? What was life? Something existing apart from me, and separate from myself? Don't worry, I did not enter into any speculations. I only thought: "If I have to die—what of it. What do I care? Let me die, then, and I'm finished."

Religious people, those who have faith and love God and realize what life is and what death means, and know what it is to have an immortal soul, do not understand how it is with the ones who have no faith, and who have already thrown away their souls. They find it hard to conceive that anyone could enter into the presence of death without some kind of compunction. But they should realize that millions of men die the way I was then prepared to die, the way I then might have died.

They might say to me: "Surely you thought of God, and you wanted to pray to Him for mercy."

No. As far as I remember, the thought of God, the thought of prayer did not even enter my mind, either that day, or all the rest of the time that I was ill, or that whole year, for that matter. Or if the thought did come to me, it was only as an occasion for its denial and rejection. I remember that in that year, when we stood in the chapel and recited the Apostles' Creed, I used to keep my lips tight shut, with full deliberation and of set purpose, by way of declaring my own creed which was: "I believe in nothing." Or at least I thought I believed in nothing. Actually, I had only exchanged a certain faith, faith in God, Who is Truth, for a vague uncertain faith in the opinions and authority of men and pamphlets and newspapers—wavering and varying and contradictory opinions which I did not even clearly understand.

I wish I could give those who believe in God some kind of an idea of the state of a soul like mine was in then. But it is impossible to do it in sober, straight, measured, prose terms. And, in a sense, image and analogy would be even more misleading, by the very fact that they would have life in them, and convey the notion of some real entity, some kind of energy, some sort of activity. But my soul was simply dead. It was a blank, a nothingness. It was empty, it was a kind of a spiritual vacuum, as far as the supernatural order was concerned. Even its natural faculties were shrivelled husks of what they ought to have been.

A soul is an immaterial thing. It is a principle of activity, it is an "act," a "form," an energizing principle. It is the life of the body, and it must also have a life of its own. But the life of the soul does not inhere in any physical, material subject. So to compare a soul without grace to a corpse without life is only a metaphor. But it is very true.

St. Theresa had a vision of hell. She saw herself confined in a narrow hole in a burning wall. The vision terrified her above all with the sense of the appalling stress of this confinement and heat. All this is symbolic, of course. But a poetic grasp of the meaning of the symbol should convey something of the experience of a soul which is reduced to an almost infinite limit of helplessness and frustration by the fact of dying in sin, and thus being eternally separated from the principle of all vital activity which, for the soul in its own proper order, means intellection and love.

But I now lay on this bed, full of gangrene, and my soul was rotten with the corruption of my sins. And I did not even care whether I died or lived.

The worst thing that can happen to anyone in this life is to lose all sense of these realities. The worst thing that had ever happened to me was this consummation of my sins in abominable coldness and indifference, even in the presence of death.

What is more, there was nothing I could do for myself. There was absolutely no means, no natural means within reach, for getting out of that state. Only God could help me. Who prayed for me? One day I shall know. But in the economy of God's love, it is through the prayers of other men that these graces are given. It was through the prayers of someone who loved God that I was, one day, to be delivered out of that hell where I was already confined without knowing it.

The big gift God gave me was that I got well. They bundled me up and put me on a stretcher with blankets all up around my face and nothing sticking out but my nose, and carried me across the stone quadrangle where my friends were playing "quad-cricket" with a sawed-off bat and a grey tennis ball. They stood aside in awe as I passed on the way to the school sanatorium.

I had explained to the doctor about my foot, and they came and cut off the toenail and found the toe full of gangrene. But they gave me some anti-toxin and did not have to cut off the toe. Dr. McTaggart came around every day or two to treat the infected place in my mouth, and gradually I began to get better, and to eat, and sit up, and read my filthy novels again. Nobody thought of prohibiting them, because nobody else had heard of the authors.

It was while I was in the sanatorium that I wrote a long essay on the modern novel—Gide, Hemingway, Dos Passos, Jules Romains, Dreiser, and so on, for the Bailey English Prize, and won a lot of books bound in tree-calf for my efforts.

Two attempts were made to convert me to less shocking tastes. The music master lent me a set of records of Bach's B Minor Mass, which I liked, and sometimes played on my portable gramophone, which I had with me in the big airy room looking out on the Headmaster's garden. But most of the time I played the hottest and loudest records, turning the vic towards the classroom building, eighty yards away across the flowerbeds, hoping that my companions, grinding out the syntax of Virgil's *Georgics*, would be very envious of me.

The other loan was that of a book. The Headmaster came along, one day, and gave me a little blue book of poems. I looked at the name on the back. "Gerard Manley Hopkins." I had never heard of him. But I opened the book, and read the "Starlight Night" and the Harvest poem and the most lavish and elaborate early poems. I noticed that the man was a Catholic and a priest and, what is more, a Jesuit.

I could not make up my mind whether I liked his verse or not. It was elaborate and tricky and in places it was a little lush and overdone, I thought. Yet it was original and had a lot of vitality and music and depth. In fact the later poems were all far too deep for me, and I could not make anything out of them at all.

Nevertheless, I accepted the poet, with reservations. I gave the book back to the Head, and thanked him, and never altogether forgot Hopkins, though I was not to read him again for several years.

I got out of the sanatorium in a month or six weeks. With the end of June, came our big examination—the higher certificate, which I took in French and German and Latin. Then we went away for the vacation, and I settled down to wait until September for the results of the exam. Pop and Bonnemaman and John Paul were once again in Europe for the summer, and we all spent a couple of months in a big, dreary hotel in Bournemouth, standing on top of a cliff and facing the sea with a battery of white iron balconies, painted silver, so that they gleamed in the pale, English summer sun and in the morning mists. I will not go into the emotions of that summer, in which I and a girl I met there kept going through storms of sentiment alternating with adolescent quarrels, during which I used to escape from Bournemouth into the Dorset downs and wander around for the whole day in the country trying to recover my equilibrium.

But at the end of the summer, when she went back to London, and my family also took the boat at Southampton and went home, I packed up my rucksack and went into the New Forest, with a pup tent, and sat down under some pine trees at the edge of a common a couple of miles from Brockenhurst. Oh, the tremendous loneliness of that first night in the forest! The frogs sang in the brackish stream, and the fireflies played in the gorse, and occasionally a lone car would pass along the distant road, exaggerating the silence by the sound that died in the wake of its passing. And I sat in the door of my tent, uneasily trying to digest the eggs and bacon I had fried and the bottle of cider I had brought out from the village.

She had said she would write me a letter, addressed to the Post-office at Brockenhurst, as soon as she got home, but I thought this camp site at the edge of the common was too dreary. Besides, the water of the stream tasted funny and I thought maybe I might get poisoned, so I moved on down toward Beaulieu, where I did not have to eat my own cooking, but ate in an inn. And I spent the afternoon lying in the grass in front of the old Cistercian abbey, copiously pitying myself for my boredom and for the loneliness of immature love. At the same time, however, I was debating in my mind whether to go to a "Gymkhana," that is a sort of a polite amateur horse-show, and mingle with all the gentry of the county, perhaps meeting someone even more beautiful than the girl for whom I thought I was, at the moment, pining away even unto death. However, I wisely decided to avoid the tents of such a dull affair.

As for the Cistercian abbey, which was the scene of these meditations, I did not think much about it at all. I had wandered through the ruins of the old buildings, and had stood in the parish church that had taken over the old refectory of the monks, and I had tasted a little of the silence and peacefulness of the greensward under the trees, where the cloister used to be. But it was all in the usual picnic spirit with which the average modern Englishman visits one of his old abbeys. If he does happen to wonder what kind of men once lived in such places, or why they ever did so, he does not ask himself if people still try to do the same thing today. That would seem to him a kind of impertinence. But by this time I had practically lost all interest in such speculations. What did I care about monks and monasteries? The world was going to open out before me, with all its entertainments, and everything would be mine and with my intelligence and my five sharp senses I would rob all its treasures and rifle its coffers and empty them all. And I would take what pleased me, and the rest I would throw away. And if I merely felt like spoiling the luxuries I did not want to use, I would spoil them and misuse them, to suit myself, because I was master of everything. It did not matter that I would not have much money: I would have enough, and my wits would do.

the rest. And I was aware that the best pleasures can be had without very much money—or with none at all.

I was at the house of one of my friends from school when the results of the higher certificate came out in September, and I could not decently indulge all my vanity at my success, because he had failed. However, he and I were to go up to Cambridge together for the scholarship examinations that December.

Andrew was the son of a country parson in the Isle of Wight and he had been cricket captain at Oakham. He wore horn-rimmed spectacles and had a great chin that he held up in the air, and a lock of black hair fell down over his forehead, and he was one of the school intellectuals. He and I used to work, or rather sit, in the library at Oakham, with many books open before us, but talking about impertinent matters and drinking a foul purple concoction called Vimto out of bottles which we concealed under the table or behind the volumes of the Dictionary of National Biography.

He had discovered a black book called, as I think, *The Outline of Modern Knowledge*, which was something that had just come to the library and was full of information about psychoanalysis. Indeed, it went into some details of psychoanalytical fortune-telling by the inspection of faeces which I never ran into anywhere else, and which I still preserved enough sense to laugh at, at that time. But later, at Cambridge, psychoanalysis was to provide me with a kind of philosophy of life and even a sort of pseudo-religion which was nearly the end of me altogether. By that time, Andrew himself had lost interest in it.

When we went up to the university, to sit for the scholarship exam, in the dank heavy-hanging mists of December, I spent most of the time between papers devouring D. H. Lawrence's *Fantasia of the Unconscious* which, even as psychoanalysis, is completely irresponsible and, just as it says, a fantasia. Lawrence picked up a lot of terms like "lumbar ganglion" and threw them all together and stewed them up with his own worship of the sex-instinct to produce the weird mixture which I read as reverently as if it were some kind of sacred revelation, sitting in the rooms of an undergraduate who liked Picasso, but who had gone down for the Christmas vacation. Andrew, for his part, was at St. Catherine's, terrified of a tutor who had a reputation for being a very ferocious person. All that week I sat under the high, silent rafters of the Hall, at Trinity College, and covered long sheets of foolscap with my opinions concerning Molière and Racine and Balzac and Victor Hugo and Goethe and Schiller and all the rest, and a few days after it was all over, we looked in the *Times* and this time both Andrew and I had succeeded. We were exhibitioners, he at St. Catherine's and I at Clare, while his study-mate, Dickens, who was the only other person at Oakham besides myself who liked hot records, had another exhibition at St. John's.

My satisfaction was very great. I was finished with Oakham—not that I disliked the school, but I was glad of my liberty. Now, at last, I imagined that I really was grown up and independent, and I could stretch out my hands and take all the things I wanted.

So during the Christmas holidays I ate and drank so much and went to so many parties that I made myself sick.

But I picked myself up, and dusted myself off, and on January 31st of the New Year, my eighteenth birthday, Tom took me to the Café Anglais and treated me to champagne and the next day I was off on the way to Italy.

vi

Already at Avignon I foresaw that I was going to run out of money before I got to Genoa. I had a letter of credit on a bank there. So from Avignon I wrote back to Tom asking for money. From Marseilles I started out on foot along the coast, walking on the white mountain road, overlooking the bright blue water, having on my hip a flask of rum and in the rucksack some more of the same novels. At Cassis all the restaurants were crammed with people who had come out from Marseilles for the day, since it was Sunday, and I had to wait long for my *bouillabaisse*. It was dark by the time I arrived at the grim little port of La Ciotat, under its sugar-loaf rock. Tired, I sat on the jetty and contemplated the moon.

At Hyères I had to wait a couple of days before the money arrived, and when it did, the letter that went with it was filled with sharp reproofs. Tom, my guardian, took occasion of my impracticality to call attention to most of my other faults as well, and I was very humiliated. So after a month of my precious liberty, I received my first indication that my desires could never be absolute: they must necessarily be conditioned and modified by contacts and conflicts with the desires and interests of others. This was something that it would take me a long time to find out, and indeed in the natural order alone I would never really get to understand it. I believed in the beautiful myth about having a good time so long as it does not hurt anybody else. You cannot live for your own pleasure and your own convenience without inevitably hurting and injuring the feelings and the interests of practically everybody you meet. But, as a matter of fact, in the natural order no matter what ideals may be theoretically possible, most people more or less live for themselves and for their own interests and pleasures or for those of their own family or group, and therefore they are constantly interfering with one another's aims, and hurting one another and injuring one another, whether they mean it or not.

I started out from Hyères again, this time more weary and depressed, walking among the pines, under the hot sun, looking at the rocks and the yellow mimosas and the little pink villas and the light blazing on the sea. That night I came down a long hill in the dusk to a hamlet called Cavalaire, and slept in a boarding house full of sombre retired accountants who drank vin-rosé with their wives under the dim light of weak electric bulbs, and I went to bed and dreamt that I was in jail.

At Saint Tropez I had a letter of introduction to a friend of Tom's, a man with t.b., living in a sunny house on top of a hill, and there I met a couple of Americans who had rented a villa in the hills behind Cannes and they invited me there, when I came that way.

On the way to Cannes, I got caught by a storm, towards evening, in the mountains of the Esterel, and was picked up by a chauffeur driving a big fancy Delage. I slung my rucksack off my shoulder and threw it in the back seat and settled down, with the warmth of the motor seeping up through the boards and into my wet, tired feet. The chauffeur was an Englishman who had an auto-hiring business in Nice and said he had just picked up the Lindbergh family off the liner at Villefranche and had taken them somewhere down the road here. At Cannes he took me to a very dull place, a club for English chauffeurs and sailors off the yachts of the rich people who were wintering on the Riviera. There I ate ham and eggs and watched the chauffeurs politely playing billiards, and grew depressed at the smell of London that lingered in the room—the smell of English cigarettes and English beer. It reminded me of the fogs I thought I had escaped.

Then I found the villa of the people I had met at Saint Tropez, and stayed there a couple of days, and finally, fed up with walking, and seeing that I would probably be bored with the rest of the road along the coast, I got on the train and went to Genoa.

Perhaps the boredom that I felt had its roots in some physical cause, because the first morning I woke up in Genoa, with a bunch of Italian housepainters working on the roof outside my window,

I was out of sorts and had a great boil on my elbow, which I clumsily tried to heal by my own private treatments, which did not work.

So I cashed my letter of credit and got on another train and went to Florence, where I had another letter of introduction to a man who was a sculptor. Florence was freezing. I took a trolley out across the Arno, and found the steep road up the hill where my man lived, and climbed it in the icy silence of a Tuscan winter evening. At first I thought nobody was going to answer my knock on the big hollow-sounding door, but presently an old Italian cook came out, and led me in to the studio where I made myself known and explained that I had a boil on my elbow. So the cook got some hot water and I sat in the dry dust of plaster and among the stone chips around the base of some half-finished work, and talked to the sculptor while his cook fixed up a poultice for my boil.

The artist was the brother of the former Headmaster of Oakham, the one who had preceded Doherty. I had seen some of his bas-reliefs which decorated the front of the school chapel. He was not as old as his brother, the ex-head. But he was a kind, stoop-shouldered person with greying hair, and had most of the old head's geniality. He said to me: "I was thinking of going down and seeing the Greta Garbo film in town this evening. Do you like Greta Garbo?"

I admitted that I did. "Very well, then," he said, "we will go."

But Florence was too cold, and I thought the boil was getting better. So the next day I left, on the way to Rome. I was tired of passing through places. I wanted to get to the term of my journey, where there was some psychological possibility that I would stop in one place and remain.

The train ambled slowly through the mountains of Umbria. The blue sky glared down upon the rocks. The compartment was empty save for myself, and nobody got in until one of the last stations before Rome. All day I stared out at the bare hills, at the wild, ascetic landscape. Somewhere out there, on one of those mountains, St. Francis had been praying and the seraph with the fiery, blood-red wings had appeared before him with the Christ in the midst of those wings: and from the wounds, other wounds had been nailed in Francis's hands and feet and side. If I had thought of that, that day, it would have been all I needed to complete the discouragement of my pagan soul, for it turned out that the boil was no better after all, and that I had another toothache. For that matter, my head felt as if I had a fever as well, and I wondered if the old business of blood-poisoning was starting once again.

So there I was, with all the liberty that I had been promising myself for so long. The world was mine. How did I like it? I was doing just what I pleased, and instead of being filled with happiness and well-being, I was miserable. The love of pleasure is destined by its very nature to defeat itself and end in frustration. But I was one of the last men in the world who would have been convinced by the wisdom of a St. John of the Cross in those strange days.

But now I was entering a city which bears living testimony to these truths, to those who can see it, to those who know where to look for it—to those who know how to compare the Rome of the Caesars with the Rome of the martyrs.

I was entering the city that had been thus transformed by the Cross. Square white apartment houses were beginning to appear in thick clusters at the foot of the bare, grey-green hills, with clumps of cypress here and there, and presently over the roofs of the buildings, I saw, rising up in the dusk, the mighty substance of St. Peter's dome. The realization that it was not a photograph filled me with great awe.

My first preoccupation in Rome was to find a dentist. The people in the hotel sent me to one nearby. There were a couple of nuns in the waiting room. After they left, I entered. The dentist had a brown beard. I did not trust my Italian for so important a matter as a toothache. I spoke to him in French. He knew a little French. And he looked at the tooth.

He knew what he thought was wrong with it, but he did not know the technical word in French.

"Ah," he said, "vous avez un *colpo d'aria*."

I figured it out easily enough to mean that I had caught a chill in my tooth—according to this man with the brown beard. But still, cowardice closed my mouth, and I was content not to argue that I thought it was by no means a chill, but an abscess.

"I shall treat it with ultra-violet rays," said the dentist. With a mixture of relief and scepticism, I underwent this painless and futile process. It did nothing whatever to relieve the toothache. But I left with warm assurances from the dentist that it would all disappear during the night.

Far from disappearing during the night, the toothache did what all toothaches do during the night: kept me awake, in great misery, cursing my fate.

The next morning I got up and staggered back to my friend *colpo d'aria* next door. I met him coming down the stairs with his beard all brushed and a black hat on his head, with gloves and spats and everything. Only then did I realize that it was Sunday. However, he consented to give a look at the chilled tooth.

In a mixture of French and Italian he asked me if I could stand ether. I said yes, I could. He draped a clean handkerchief over my nose and mouth and dropped a couple of drops of ether on it. I breathed deeply, and the sweet sick knives of the smell reached in to my consciousness and the drumming of the heavy dynamos began. I hoped that he wasn't breathing too deeply himself, or that his hand wouldn't slip, and spill the whole bottle of it in my face.

However, a minute or two later I woke up again and he was waving the red, abscessed roots of the tooth in my face and exclaiming: "*C'est fini!*"

I moved out of my hotel and found a *pensione* with windows that looked down on the sunny Triton fountain in the middle of the Piazza Barberini and the Bristol Hotel and the Barberini Cinema and the Barberini Palace, and the maid brought me some hot water to treat the boil on my arm. I went to bed and tried to read a novel by Maxim Gorki which very quickly put me to sleep.

I had been in Rome before, on an Easter vacation from school, for about a week. I had seen the Forum and the Colosseum and the Vatican museum and St. Peter's. But I had not really seen Rome.

This time, I started out again, with the misconception common to Anglo-Saxons, that the real Rome is the Rome of the ugly ruins, the Rome of all those grey cariated temples wedged in between the hills and the slums of the city. I tried to reconstruct the ancient city, in my mind—a dream which did not work very well, because of the insistent shouting of the sellers of postcards who beset me on every side. After a few days of trying the same thing, it suddenly struck me that it was not worth the trouble. It was so evident, merely from the masses of stone and brick that still represented the palaces and temples and baths, that imperial Rome must have been one of the most revolting and ugly and depressing cities the world has ever seen. In fact, the ruins with cedars and cypresses and umbrella pines scattered about among them were far more pleasant than the reality must have been.

However, I still roamed about the museums, especially the one in the Baths of Diocletian, which had also been, at one time, a Carthusian monastery—probably not a very successful one—and I studied Rome in a big learned book that I had bought, together with an old second-hand Baedeker in French.

And after spending the day in museums and libraries and bookstores and among the ruins, I would come home again and read my novels. In fact, I was also beginning to write one of my own, although I did not get very far with it as long as I was at Rome.

I had a lot of books with me—a strange mixture: Dryden, the poems of D. H. Lawrence, some Tauchnitz novels, and James Joyce's *Ulysses* in a fancy India-paper edition, slick and expensive, which I lent to someone, later on, and never got back.

Things were going on as they usually did with me. But after about a week—I don't know how it began—I found myself looking into churches rather than into ruined temples. Perhaps it was the frescoes on the wall of an old chapel—ruined too—at the foot of the Palatine, at the edge of the Forum, that first aroused my interest in another and a far different Rome. From there it was an easy step to Sts. Cosmas and Damian, across the Forum, with a great mosaic, in the apse, of Christ coming in judgement in a dark blue sky, with a suggestion of fire in the small clouds beneath His feet. The effect of this discovery was tremendous. After all the vapid, boring, semi-pornographic statuary of the Empire, what a thing it was to come upon the genius of an art full of spiritual vitality and earnestness and power—an art that was tremendously serious and alive and eloquent and urgent in all that it had to say. And it was without pretentiousness, without fakery, and had nothing theatrical about it. Its solemnity was made all the more astounding by its simplicity—and by the obscurity of the places where it lay hid, and by its subservience to higher ends, architectural, liturgical and spiritual ends which I could not even begin to understand, but which I could not avoid guessing, since the nature of the mosaics themselves and their position and everything about them proclaimed it aloud.

I was fascinated by these Byzantine mosaics. I began to haunt the churches where they were to be found, and, as an indirect consequence, all the other churches that were more or less of the same period. And thus without knowing anything about it I became a pilgrim. I was unconsciously and unintentionally visiting all the great shrines of Rome, and seeking out their sanctuaries with some of the eagerness and avidity and desire of a true pilgrim, though not quite for the right reason. And yet it was not for a wrong reason either. For these mosaics and frescoes and all the ancient altars and thrones and sanctuaries were designed and built for the instruction of people who were not capable of immediately understanding anything higher.

I never knew what relics and what wonderful and holy things were hidden in the churches whose doors and aisles and arches had become the refuge of my mind. Christ's cradle and the pillar of the Flagellation and the True Cross and St. Peter's chains, and the tombs of the great martyrs, the tomb of the child St. Agnes and the martyr St. Cecilia and of Pope St. Clement and of the great deacon St. Lawrence who was burned on a gridiron. . . . These things did not speak to me, or at least I did not know they spoke to me. But the churches that enshrined them did, and so did the art on their walls.

And now for the first time in my life I began to find out something of Who this Person was that men called Christ. It was obscure, but it was a true knowledge of Him, in some sense, truer than I knew and truer than I would admit. But it was in Rome that my conception of Christ was formed. It was there I first saw Him, Whom I now serve as my God and my King, and Who owns and rules my life.

It is the Christ of the Apocalypse, the Christ of the Martyrs, the Christ of the Fathers. It is the Christ of St. John, and of St. Paul, and of St. Augustine and St. Jerome and all the Fathers—and of the Desert Fathers. It is Christ God, Christ King, "*for in Him dwelleth the fulness of the Godhead corporeally, and you are filled in Him, Who is the Head of all principality and power . . . For in Him were all things created in heaven and on earth, visible and invisible, whether thrones or dominations or principalities or powers, all things were created by Him and in Him. And He is before all, and by Him all things consist . . . because in Him it hath well pleased the Father that all fulness should dwell . . . Who is the image of the invisible God, the first-born of every creature . . .*[1]" "*The first-begotten of the dead, and the prince of the kings of the earth, Who hath loved us, and washed us from our sins in His own Blood, and hath made us a kingdom and priests to God His Father.*" [2]

The saints of those forgotten days had left upon the walls of their churches words which by the peculiar grace of God I was able in some measure to apprehend, although I could not decode them all. But above all, the realest and most immediate source of this grace was Christ Himself, present in those churches, in all His power, and in His Humanity, in His Human Flesh and His material, physical, corporeal Presence. How often I was left en-

[1] Col. I and II. [2] Apoc. I.

tirely alone in these churches with the tremendous God, and knew nothing of it—except I had to know something of it, as I say, obscurely. And it was He Who was teaching me Who He was, more directly than I was capable of realising.

These mosaics told me more than I had ever known of the doctrine of a God of infinite power, wisdom and love Who had yet become Man, and revealed in His Manhood the infinity of power, wisdom and love that was His Godhead. Of course I could not grasp and believe these things explicitly. But since they were implicit in every line of the pictures I contemplated with such admiration and love, surely I grasped them implicitly—I had to, in so far as the mind of the artist reached my own mind, and spoke to it his conception and his thought. And so I could not help but catch something of the ancient craftsman's love of Christ, the Redeemer and Judge of the World.

It was more or less natural that I should want to discover something of the meaning of the mosaics I saw—of the Lamb standing as though slain, and of the four-and-twenty elders casting down their crowns. And I had bought a Vulgate text, and was reading the New Testament. I had forgotten all about the poems of D. H. Lawrence except for the fact that he had four poems about the Four Evangelists, based on the traditional symbols from Ezechiel and the Apocalypse of the four mystical creatures. One evening, when I was reading these poems, I became so disgusted with their falseness and futility that I threw down the book and began to ask myself why I was wasting my time with a man of such unimportance as this. For it was evident that he had more or less completely failed to grasp the true meaning of the New Testament, which he had perverted in the interests of a personal and home-made religion of his own which was not only fanciful, but full of unearthly seeds, all ready to break forth into hideous plants like those that were germinating in Germany's unweeded garden, in the dank weather of Nazism.

So for once I put my favorite aside. And I read more and more of the Gospels, and my love for the old churches and their mosaics grew from day to day. Soon I was no longer visiting them merely for the art. There was something else that attracted me: a kind of interior peace. I loved to be in these holy places. I had a kind of deep and strong conviction that I belonged there: that my rational nature was filled with profound desires and needs that could only find satisfaction in churches of God. I remember that one of my favorite shrines was that of St. Peter in Chains, and I did not love it for any work of art that was there, since the big attraction, the big "number," the big "feature" in that place is Michelangelo's Moses. But I had always been extremely bored by that horned and pop-eyed frown and by the crack in the knee. I'm glad the thing couldn't speak, for it would probably have given out some very heavy statements.

Perhaps what was attracting me to that Church was the Apostle himself to whom it is dedicated. And I do not doubt that he was praying earnestly to get me out of my own chains: chains far heavier and more terrible than ever were his.

Where else did I like to go? St. Pudenziana, St. Praxed's, above all St. Mary Major and the Lateran, although as soon as the atmosphere got heavy with baroque melodrama I would get frightened, and the peace and the obscure, tenuous sense of devotion I had acquired would leave me.

So far, however, there had been no deep movement of my will, nothing that amounted to a conversion, nothing to shake the iron tyranny of moral corruption that held my whole nature in fetters. But that also was to come. It came in a strange way, suddenly, a way that I will not attempt to explain.

I was in my room. It was night. The light was on. Suddenly it seemed to me that Father, who had now been dead more than a year, was there with me. The sense of his presence was as vivid and as real and as startling as if he had touched my arm or spoken to me. The whole thing passed in a flash, but in that flash, instantly, I was overwhelmed with a sudden and profound insight into the misery and corruption of my own soul, and I was pierced deeply with a light that made me realize something of the condition I was in, and I was filled with horror at what I saw, and my whole being rose up in revolt against what was within me, and my soul desired escape and liberation and freedom from all this with an intensity and an urgency unlike anything I had ever known before. And now I think for the first time in my whole life I really began to pray—praying not with my lips and with my intellect and my imagination, but praying out of the very roots of my life and of my being, and praying to the God I had never known, to reach down towards me out of His darkness and to help me to get free of the thousand terrible things that held my will in their slavery.

There were a lot of tears connected with this, and they did me good, and all the while, although I had lost that first vivid, agonizing sense of the presence of my father in the room, I had him in my mind, and I was talking to him as well as to God, as though he were a sort of intermediary. I do not mean this in any way that might be interpreted that I thought he was among the saints. I did not really know what that might mean then, and now that I do know I would hesitate to say that I thought he was in Heaven. Judging by my memory of the experience I should say it was "as if" he had been sent to me out of Purgatory. For after all, there is no reason why the souls in Purgatory should not help those on earth by their prayers and influence, just like those in Heaven: although usually they need our help more than we need theirs. But in this case, assuming my guess has some truth in it, things were the other way 'round.

However, this is not a thing on which I would place any great stress. And I do not offer any definite explanation of it. How do I know it was not merely my own imagination, or something that could be traced to a purely natural, psychological cause—I mean the part about my father? It is impossible to say. I do not offer any explanation. And I have always had a great antipathy for everything that smells of necromancy—table-turning and communications with the dead, and I would never deliberately try to enter in to any such thing. But whether it was imagination or nerves or whatever else it may have been, I can say truly that I did feel, most vividly, as if my father were present there, and the consequences that I have described followed from this, as though he had communicated to me without words an interior light from God, about the condition of my own soul—although I wasn't even sure I had a soul.

The one thing that seems to me morally certain is that this was really a grace, and a great grace. If I had only followed it through, my life might have been very different and much less miserable for the years that were to come.

Before now I had never prayed in the churches I had visited. But I remember the morning that followed this experience. I remember how I climbed the deserted Aventine, in the spring sun, with my soul broken up with contrition, but broken and clean, painful but sanitary like a lanced abscess, like a bone broken and re-set. And it was true contrition, too, for I don't think I was capable of mere attrition, since I did not believe in hell. I went to the Dominicans' Church, Santa Sabina. And it was a very definite experience, something that amounted to a capitulation, a surrender, a conversion, not without struggle, even now, to walk deliberately into the church with no other purpose than to kneel down and pray to God. Ordinarily, I never knelt in these churches, and never paid any formal or official attention to Whose house it was. But now I took holy water at the door and went straight up to the altar rail and knelt down and said, slowly, with all the belief I had in me, the Our Father.

It seems almost unbelievable to me that I did no more than this, for the memory remains in me as that of such an experience that it would seem to have implied at least a half hour of impassioned prayer and tears. The thing to remember is that I had not prayed at all for some years.

Another thing which Catholics do not realize about converts is the tremendous, agonizing embarrassment and self-consciousness which they feel about praying publicly in a Catholic Church. The effort it takes to overcome all the strange imaginary fears that everyone is looking at you, and that they all think you are crazy or ridiculous, is something that costs a tremendous effort. And that day in Santa Sabina, although the church was almost entirely empty, I walked across the stone floor mortally afraid that a poor devout old Italian woman was following me with suspicious eyes. As I knelt to pray, I wondered if she would run out and accuse me at once to the priests, with scandalous horror, for coming and praying in their church—as if Catholics were perfectly content to have a lot of heretic tourists walking about their churches with complete indifference and irreverence, and would get angry if one of them so far acknowledged God's presence there as to go on his knees for a few seconds and say a prayer!

However, I prayed, then I looked about the church, and went into a room where there was a picture by Sassoferrato, and stuck my face out a door into a tiny, simple cloister, where the sun shone down on an orange tree. After that I walked out into the open feeling as if I had been reborn, and crossed the street, and strolled through the suburban fields to another deserted church where I did not pray, being scared by some carpenters and scaffolding. I sat outside, in the sun, on a wall and tasted the joy of my own inner peace, and turned over in my mind how my life was now going to change, and how I would become better.

vii

It was a wan hope, however. But the last week or ten days that I was in Rome were very happy and full of joy, and on one of those afternoons I took the trolley out to San Paolo, and after that got on a small rickety bus which went up a country road into a shallow saucer of a valley in the low hills south of the Tiber, to the Trappist monastery of Tre Fontane. I went in to the dark, austere old church, and liked it. But I was scared to visit the monastery. I thought the monks were too busy sitting in their graves beating themselves with disciplines. So I walked up and down in the silent afternoon, under the eucalyptus trees, and the thought grew on me: "I should like to become a Trappist monk."

There was very little danger of my doing so, then. The thought was only a daydream—and I suppose it is a dream that comes to many men, even men who don't believe in anything. Is there any man who has ever gone through a whole lifetime without dressing himself up, in his fancy, in the habit of a monk and enclosing himself in a cell where he sits magnificent in heroic austerity and solitude, while all the young ladies who hitherto were cool to his affections in the world come and beat on the gates of the monastery crying, "Come out, come out!"

Ultimately, I suppose, that is what my dream that day amounted to. I had no idea what Trappist monks were, or what they did, except that they kept silence. In fact, I also thought they lived in cells like the Carthusians, all alone.

In the bus, going back to San Paolo, I ran into a student from the American Academy whom I knew. He was riding with his mother, and introduced me to her, and we talked about the monastery, and I said I wished I were a monk. The student's mother looked at me with a horror and astonishment so extreme that I was really a little shocked by it.

The days went by. Letters came from America, telling me to take the boat and come there. Finally I bade farewell to the Italian typewriter salesman and the other inhabitants of the *pensione*, including the lady who ran the place and whose mother had been overwhelmed with thoughts of death when I played *St. Louis Blues* on the piano, sending in the maid to ask me to desist.

With sorrow in my heart I saw the last of the Piazza Barberini and the big curved boulevard that ran into it; and the last of the Pincio gardens, and St. Peter's dome in the distance and the Piazza di Spagna; but above all, I had sorrow and emptiness in my heart at leaving my beloved churches—San Pietro in Vincoli, Santa Maria Maggiore, San Giovanni in Laterano, Santa Pudenziana, Santa Prassede, Santa Sabina, Santa Maria sopra Minerva, Santa Maria in Cosmedin, Santa Maria in Trastevere, Santa Agnese, San Clemente, Santa Cecilia . . .

The train crossed the Tiber. The little pyramid and the cypresses of the English cemetery where Keats was buried disappeared. I remembered some allusion in Plautus to a big hill of rubbish and potsherds that had once stood in this part of the city. Then we came out into the bare plain between Rome and the sea. In this distance were San Paolo, and the low hills that concealed the Trappist monastery of Tre Fontane. "O Rome," I said in my heart, "will I ever see you again?"

The first two months after I landed in New York, and went to the house in Douglaston, I continued to read the Bible surreptitiously—I was afraid someone might make fun of me. And since I slept on the sleeping porch, which opened on the upstairs hall through glass doors and which, in any case, I shared with my uncle, I no longer dared to pray on my knees before going to sleep, though I am sure everybody would have been pleased and edified. The real reason for this was that I did not have the humility to care nothing about what people thought or said. I was afraid of their remarks, even kind ones, even approving ones. Indeed, it is a kind of quintessence of pride to hate and fear even the kind and legitimate approval of those who love us! I mean, to resent it as a humiliating patronage.

There is no point in telling all the details of how this real but temporary religious fervor of mine cooled down and disappeared. At Easter we went to the church where my father had once been organist, Zion Church, with the white spire standing among the locust trees on the hill between us and the station. And there I was very irritated by the services, and my own pride increased the irritation and complicated it. And I used to walk about the house or sit at the dinner table telling everybody what a terrible place Zion Church was, and condemning everything that it stood for.

One Sunday I went to the Quaker meeting house in Flushing, where Mother had once sat and meditated with the Friends. I sat down there too, in a deep pew in the back, near a window. The place was about half full. The people were mostly middle-aged or old, and there was nothing that distinguished them in any evident way from the congregation in a Methodist or a Baptist or an Episcopalian or any other Protestant church, except that they sat silent, waiting for the inspiration of the Holy Ghost. I liked that. I liked the silence. It was peaceful. In it, my shyness began to die down, and I ceased to look about and criticize the people, and entered, somewhat superficially, into my own soul, and some nebulous good resolutions began to take shape there.

But it did not get very far, for presently one of the middle-aged ladies thought the Holy Ghost was after her to get up and talk.

I secretly suspected that she had come to the meeting all prepared to make a speech anyway, for she reached into her handbag, as she stood up, and cried out in a loud earnest voice:

"When I was in Switzerland I took this snapshot of the famous Lion of Lucerne. . . ." With that she pulled out a picture. Sure enough, it was the famous Lion of Lucerne. She held it up and tried to show it around to the Friends, at the same time explaining that she thought it was a splendid exemplification of Swiss courage and manliness and patience and all the other virtues of the watch-making Swiss which she mentioned and which I have now forgotten.

The Friends accepted it in patience, without enthusiasm or resentment. But I went out of the meeting house saying to myself: "They are like all the rest. In other churches it is the minister who hands out the commonplaces, and here it is liable to be just anybody."

Still, I think I had enough sense to know that it would be madness to look for a group of people, a society, a religion, a church from which all mediocrity would absolutely be excluded. But when I read the works of William Penn and found them to be about as supernatural as a Montgomery Ward catalogue I lost interest in the Quakers. If I had run across something by Evelyn Underhill it might have been different.

I think that one could find much earnest and pure and humble worship of God and much sincere charity among the Quakers. Indeed, you are bound to find a little of this in every religion. But I have never seen any evidence of its rising above the natural order. They are full of natural virtues and some of them are contemplatives in a natural sense of the word. Nor are they excluded from God's graces if He wills. For He loves them, and He will not withhold His light from good people anywhere. Yet I cannot see that they will ever be anything more than what they claim to be—a "Society of Friends."

That summer, when I went on a slow and dirty train in a roundabout way to Chicago to see the World's Fair, I picked up two pamphlets on the Mormons in the Hall of Religion, but the story of the holy books discovered through revelation on a hill in upper New York State did not convince me and I was not converted. The thin red and yellow walls of the palaces of the Fair, scattered between the lake and the slums and freight-yards, amused me with their noise, and for the first time I walked in the wide-open air of the flat and endless Middle West.

Out of sheer bravado I got myself a job for a few days as a barker in front of a side-show in a part of the Fair called the Streets of Paris, the nature of which is sufficiently evident from that name. The ease with which I got the job astounded and flattered me, and it gave me a sense of power and importance to be so suddenly transported from the order of those who were fleeced of their money to the level of those who did the fleecing. However, in a couple of days I also discovered that perhaps I had not risen above the ranks of the "suckers" after all, since the boss of the side-show was more ready to pay me in promises and fancy words than in dollars, for my services. Besides, it was very tiring to stand in the heat and dust from noon to midnight shouting at the sea of straw-hatted heads and shoulders dressed in duck and seersucker or in open-necked shirts and dresses soaked with healthy Middle-Western sweat. The absolutely open and undisguised and non-committal frankness of the paganism of Chicago and of this Fair and of this particular part of the Fair and, apparently, of the whole country which it represented, amazed me after the complicated reticences of England and the ornate pornography of France.

When I got back to New York I had lost most of my temporary interest in religion. My friends in that city had a religion of their own: a cult of New York itself, and of the peculiar manner in which Manhattan expressed the bigness and gaudiness and noisiness and frank animality and vulgarity of this American paganism.

I used to go to the Burlesque and hang around Fourteenth Street with Reg Marsh, who was an old friend of my father's, and who is famous for painting all these things in his pictures. Reginald Marsh was (and I suppose still is) a thick-set man of short stature who gave the impression that he was a retired light-weight prize-fighter. He had a way of talking out of the corner of his mouth, and yet at the same time his face had something babyish and cherubic about it, as he looked out at the world through the simple and disinterested and uncritical eyes of the artist, taking everything as he found it, and considering everything as possible subject matter for one of his Hogarthian compositions, provided only it was alive.

We got along very well together, because of the harmony of our views, I worshipping life as such, and he worshipping it especially in the loud, wild bedlam of the crowded, crazy city that he loved. His favorite places of devotion were Union Square and the Irving Place Burlesque, stinking of sweat and cheap cigars and ready to burn down or collapse at any minute. But I guess his cathedral was Coney Island. Everybody who has ever seen his pictures, knows that much about Reg Marsh.

All that summer I hung around his Fourteenth Street studio, and went with him to many of the parties to which he was invited, and got to know my way around New York.

But when September came I sailed for England once more. This time I made the crossing on the *Manhattan,* a garish and turbulent cabin class steamer full of Nazi spies working as stewards and detesting the Jewish passengers. The voyage was a violent one. One night I looked down one of the deep stair-wells and saw six or seven half-drunk passengers having a general fight on the swaying linoleum floor of E deck. And one afternoon in the middle of one of those paralyzing synthetic amusements that are fixed up for the passengers on Atlantic liners—I think it must have been the "horse race"—an American dentist stood up with a loud roar and challenged a French tailor to come out and fight him on the promenade deck. The challenge was not taken up, but all the business men and tourists savored the delicious scandal, for there was no one on board who was not aware that behind it all stood the six-foot daughter of someone prominent in Washington, D. C.

At Plymouth they put those of us who were bound for London on to a fat launch in the middle of the harbor, and once again I looked upon the pale green downs of England. I landed with one of the worst colds I ever had in my life.

And so on the tide of all these circumstances of confusion I swept into the dark, sinister atmosphere of Cambridge and began my university career.

viii

Perhaps to you the atmosphere of Cambridge is neither dark nor sinister. Perhaps you were never there except in May. You never saw anything but the thin Spring sun half veiled in the mists and blossoms of the gardens along the Backs, smiling on the lavender bricks and stones of Trinity and St. John's, or my own college, Clare.

I am even willing to admit that some people might live there for three years, or even a lifetime, so protected that they never sense the sweet stench of corruption that is all around them—the keen, thin scent of decay that pervades everything and accuses with a terrible accusation the superficial youthfulness, the abounding undergraduate noise that fills those ancient buildings. But for me, with my blind appetites, it was impossible that I should not rush in and take a huge bite of this rotten fruit. The bitter taste is still with me after not a few years.

My freshman year went by very fast. It was a dizzy business that began in the dark, brief afternoons of the English autumn and ended after a short series of long summer evenings on the river. All those days and nights were without romance, horrible. They could not help being everything that I did not want them to be.

I was breaking my neck trying to get everything out of life that you think you can get out of it when you are eighteen. And I ran with a pack of hearties who wore multicolored scarves around their necks and who would have barked all night long in the echoing shadows of the Petty Cury if they had not been forced to go home to bed at a certain time.

At first it was confusing. It took me a month or two to find my level in this cloudy semi-liquid medium in whose dregs I was ultimately destined to settle. There were my friends from Oakham. At first we clung together for protection, and used to spend much time in one another's rooms, although Andrew's digs were far away in the wilds beyond Addenbrooke's hospital. To get there I cycled through a mysterious world of new buildings dedicated to chemistry, and at the end of the journey drank tea and played *St. Louis Blues* on the piano. Dickens was much nearer. He was around the corner from my lodgings. You travelled through two or three courts of St. John's College and crossed the river. He was in the so-called New Building. His room directly overlooked the river and he and I and Andrew would eat breakfast there and throw bits of toast to the ducks while he told us all about Pavlov and conditioned reflexes.

As the year went on I drifted apart from them, especially from Andrew who ended up as the leading man in the Footlights show that year. He was something of a singer. My crowd had no interest in singing and a certain amount of contempt, indeed, for the Footlights and all that it represented. I remember that I almost made friends with one or two serious and somewhat complicated young men who were reading modern languages with me and belonged to my own college, but their reticences bored me. And they, in their turn, were rather shocked by the two-handed heartiness with which I was grabbing at life.

In the room underneath mine, in my lodgings, was a round red-faced Yorkshireman who was a pacifist. He too was full of reticences. But on Armistice Day he got into some kind of a demonstration and all the rugger players and oarsmen threw eggs at him. I knew nothing about it until I saw the pictures in the evening paper.

I would not have been interested in making friends with him

either—he was too tame and shy. But in any case the landlord took to coming into my room and calumniating the poor man while I listened patiently, knowing of no way to shut him up. Before the end of the year the landlord was much more disgusted with me than with any lodger he had ever had before or, probably, since.

I think it was after Armistice Day, when I had finally become acquainted with some two hundred different people, that I drifted into the crowd that had been gravitating around the nether pole of Cambridge life.

We were the ones who made all the noise when there was a "bump supper." We lived in the Lion Inn. We fought our way in and out of the "Red Cow."

In that year most of my friends were gated at one time or another, and by the end of it not a few of us were sent down. I cannot even clearly remember who most of them were—except for Julian. He stands out vividly enough. He wore horn-rimmed spectacles and looked, I will not say like an American, but like a Frenchman trying to look like an American. He could tell long complicated stories in an American accent too nasal to be true. He was the grandson or the great-grandson of a Victorian poet and lived in the old man's house on the Isle of Wight. He roomed in a big rabbit warren of a place on Market Hill which was going to be torn down at the end of the year to make room for a new building, belonging to Caius College. Before the wreckers came in, Julian's friends had already begun the ruin of the house by attempting to destroy the precarious section of it where he himself lived. I seem to remember some trouble when somebody threw a teapot out of the window of these rooms and nearly brained the Dean of Kings who was passing by in the street below.

Then there was a laconic, sallow-faced fellow who came from Oundle and drove a racing car. He sat still and quiet most of the time with the strange, fevered mysticism of the racing driver in his veins while the rest of us talked and yelled. But when he got under the wheel of his car—which he was not allowed to drive as a freshman—he was transformed into a strange sort of half-spiritual being, possessed by a weird life belonging to another frightening world. The prohibition on driving could not, of course, hold him. Once in a while he would disappear. Then he would come back relatively happy, and sit down and play poker with anybody who would take him on. I think he was finally sent down altogether for the wildest of his expeditions which ended with him trying to drive his car down one of the zig-zag cliff paths at Bournemouth.

But why dig up all this old scenery and reconstruct the stews of my own mental Pompeii after enough years have covered them up? Is it even worth the obvious comment that in all this I was stamping the last remains of spiritual vitality out of my own soul, and trying with all my might to crush and obliterate the image of the divine liberty that had been implanted in me by God? With every nerve and fibre of my being I was laboring to enslave myself in the bonds of my own intolerable disgust. There is nothing new or strange about the process. But what people do not realize is that this is the crucifixion of Christ: in which He dies again and again in the individuals who were made to share the joy and the freedom of His grace, and who deny Him.

Aunt Maud died that November. I found my way to London and to Ealing, and was at the funeral.

It was a grey afternoon, and rainy, almost as dark as night. Everywhere the lights were on. It was one of those short, dark, foggy days of the early English winter.

Uncle Ben sat in a wheel-chair, broken and thin, with a black skull-cap on his head, and this time he really did look like a ghost. He seemed to have lost the power of speech, and looked about him with blank uncomprehension, as if all this story of a funeral were a gratuitous insult to his intelligence. Why were they trying to tell him that Maud was dead?

They committed the thin body of my poor Victorian angel to the clay of Ealing, and buried my childhood with her. In an obscure, half-conscious way I realized this and was appalled. She it was who had presided in a certain sense over my most innocent days. And now I saw those days buried with her in the ground.

Indeed the England I had seen through the clear eyes of her own simplicity, that too had died for me here. I could no longer believe in the pretty country churches, the quiet villages, the elm-trees along the common where the cricketers wait in white while the bowler pensively paces out a run for himself behind the wicket. The huge white clouds that sail over Sussex, the bell-charmed spires of the ancient county towns, the cathedral closes full of trees, the deaneries that ring with rooks—none of this any longer belonged to me, for I had lost it all. Its fragile web of charmed associations had been broken and blown away and I had fallen through the surface of old England into the hell, the vacuum and the horror that London was nursing in her avaricious heart.

It was the last time that I saw any of my family in England.

I took the last train back to Cambridge and was so exhausted that I fell asleep and woke up at Ely, and had to turn back, so that I got in long after midnight. And I felt offended at being gated for what was not, as I thought, my fault. It was the first of the two times I was gated that year.

Shall I follow the circle of the season down into the nadir of winter darkness, and wake up the dirty ghosts under the trees of the Backs, and out beyond the Clare New Building and in some rooms down on the Chesterton Road? When it began to be spring, I was trying to row in the Clare fourth boat, although it nearly killed me. But at least, since we were supposed to be in training, I got up early for a few weeks and went to the College for breakfast, and went to bed without being too dizzy in the nighttime.

In these days I seem to remember there was a little sunlight. It fell through the ancient windows of Professor Bullough's room in Caius. It was a large, pleasant room, lined with books, and with windows opening on the grass of two courts. It was below the level of those lawns and you had to go down a couple of steps to get into his sitting room. In fact I think his sitting room itself was on two levels, and in the corner he had a high medieval lectern. There he stood, a tall, thin, grey, somewhat ascetic scholar, placidly translating Dante to us, while ten or a dozen students, men and women, sat about in the chairs and followed in our Italian texts.

In the winter term we had begun with the *Inferno*, and had progressed slowly, taking each day part of a Canto. And now Dante and Virgil had come through the icy heart of hell, where the three-headed devil chewed the greatest traitors, and had climbed out to the peaceful sea at the foot of the seven-circled mountain of Purgatory. And now, in the Christian Lent, which I was observing without merit and without reason, for the sake of a sport which I had grown to detest because I was so unsuccessful in it, we were climbing from circle to circle of Purgatory.

I think the one great benefit I got out of Cambridge was this acquaintance with the lucid and powerful genius of the greatest Catholic poet—greatest in stature, though not in perfection or sanctity. Because of his genius, I was ready to accept all that he said about such things as Purgatory and Hell at least provisionally, as long as I had the book under my eyes, in his own terms. That was already much. I suppose it would have been too much to expect some kind of an application of his ideas to myself, in the moral order, just because I happened to have a sort of esthetic sensitiveness to them. No, it seems to me that I was armored and locked in within my own defectible and blinded self by seven layers of imperviousness, the capital sins which only the fires of Purgatory or of Divine Love (they are about the same) can burn away. But now I was free to keep away from the attack of those flames merely by averting my will from them: and it was by now permanently and habitually turned away and immunized. I had done all that I could to make my heart untouchable by charity and had fortified it, as I hoped, impregnably in my own impenetrable selfishness.

At the same time, I could listen, and listen with gladness and a certain intentness, to the slow and majestic progress of the myths and symbols in which Dante was building up a whole poetic synthesis of scholastic philosophy and theology. And although not one of his ideas took firm root in my mind, which was both too coarse and too lazy to absorb anything so clean, nevertheless, there remained in me a kind of armed neutrality in the presence of all these dogmas, which I tended to tolerate in a vague and general way, in bulk, in so far as that was necessary to an understanding of the poem.

This, as I see it, was also a kind of a grace: the greatest grace in the positive order that I got out of Cambridge.

All the rest were negative. They were only graces in the sense that God in His mercy was permitting me to fly as far as I could from His love but at the same time preparing to confront me, at the end of it all, and in the bottom of the abyss, when I thought I had gone farthest away from Him. *Si ascendero in coelum, tu illic es. Si descendero in infernum, ades.* For in my greatest misery He would shed, into my soul, enough light to see how miserable I was, and to admit that it was my own fault and my own work. And always I was to be punished for my sins by my sins themselves, and to realize, at least obscurely, that I was being so punished and burn in the flames of my own hell, and rot in the hell of my own corrupt will until I was forced at last, by my own intense misery, to give up my own will.

I had tasted something of this before: but that was nothing compared to the bitterness that soon began to fill me in that year at Cambridge.

The mere realization of one's own unhappiness is not salvation: it may be the occasion of salvation, or it may be the door to a deeper pit in Hell, and I had much deeper to go than I realized. But now, at least, I realized where I was, and I was beginning to try to get out.

Some people may think that Providence was very funny and very cruel to allow me to choose the means I now chose to save my soul.

But Providence, that is the love of God, is very wise in turning away from the self-will of men, and in having nothing to do with them, and leaving them to their own devices, as long as they are intent on governing themselves, to show them to what depths of futility and sorrow their own helplessness is capable of dragging them.

And all the irony and cruelty of this situation came, not from Providence, but from the devil, who thought he was cheating God of my stupid and uninteresting little soul.

So it was, then, that I began to get all the books of Freud and Jung and Adler out of the big redecorated library of the Union and to study, with all the patience and application which my hangovers allowed me, the mysteries of sex-repression and complexes and introversion and extroversion and all the rest. I, whose chief trouble was that my soul and all its faculties were going to seed because there was nothing to control my appetites—and they were pouring themselves out in an incoherent riot of undirected passion—came to the conclusion that the cause of all my unhappiness was sex-repression! And, to make the thing more subtly intolerable, I came to the conclusion that one of the biggest crimes in this world was introversion, and, in my efforts to be an extrovert, I entered upon a course of reflections and constant self-examinations, studying all my responses and analyzing the quality of all my emotions and reactions in such a way that I could not help becoming just what I did not want to be: an introvert.

Day after day I read Freud, thinking myself to be very enlightened and scientific when, as a matter of fact, I was about as scientific as an old woman secretly poring over books about occultism, trying to tell her own fortune, and learning how to dope out the future from the lines in the palm of her hand. I don't know if I ever got very close to needing a padded cell: but if I ever had gone crazy, I think psychoanalysis would have been the one thing chiefly responsible for it.

Meanwhile, I had received several letters from my guardian. They were sharp, and got sharper as they went on, and finally, in March or April, I got a curt summons to come to London.

I had to wait a long time, a long, long time in the waiting-room, where I turned over the pages of all the copies of *Punch* for two years back. I suppose this was part of a deliberate plan to sap my morale, this leaving me alone in a dismal, foggy room, with all those copies of that dreary magazine.

Finally, after about an hour and a half, I was summoned to

climb the narrow stairs to the consulting room immediately above. The floor was waxed, and once again I got this sense of precariousness in my footing, and was glad to get across the room to the chair by the desk without falling down and breaking a hip.

With polished and devastating coolness, which carried with it a faint suggestion of contempt, Tom offered me a cigarette. The implication was that I was going to need it. Therefore, obviously, I refused it.

Nevertheless, the fifteen or twenty minutes that followed were among the most painful and distressing I have ever lived through: not because of anything that he said to me, for he was not angry or even unkind. In fact I do not even remember exactly what he did say. The thing that made me suffer was that he asked me very bluntly and coldly for an explanation of my conduct and left me to writhe. For as soon as I was placed in the position of having to give some kind of positive explanation or defence of so much stupidity and unpleasantness, as if to justify myself by making it seem possible for a rational creature to live that way, the whole bitterness and emptiness of it became very evident to me, and my tongue would hardly function. And the words I murmured about my "making mistakes" and "not wanting to hurt others" sounded extremely silly and cheap.

So I was very glad to get out of there, and as soon as I was in the street I smoked plenty of cigarettes.

Months went by, and things did not change at all. After the Easter vacation, I was called in to my tutor to explain why I was not attending most of my lectures, and a few other things besides. This time I was not so uncomfortable. As to the exams that were soon to come—I was to take the first part of the Modern Language Tripos in French and Italian—I thought I would be able to pass them, which as a matter of fact I did, getting a second in both. The results were wired to me by one of my friends when I was already on the boat for America—one of those ten-day boats out of London. We were going through the Straits of Dover, and the sun was on the white cliffs, and my lungs were filling with the fresh air.

I was planning to come back the next year, and had already arranged for a room in the Old Court of Clare, right over the gate that led out to Clare bridge. I would have looked out over the President's garden. But certainly, considering the kind of undergraduate I was, that was the worst possible place for me to have wanted to room: for I was right in between the President and the

Senior Tutor. However, I never went up to Cambridge again as a member of the University.

That summer Tom sent me a letter in New York suggesting that I had better give up the idea of ever entering the British Diplomatic service, and that Cambridge was, henceforth, useless. To return would be to waste my time and money. He thought it would be very sensible if I stayed in America.

It did not take me five minutes to come around to agreeing with him. I do not know whether it was entirely subjective, but it seemed to me that there was some kind of a subtle poison in Europe, something that corrupted me, something the very thought and scent of which sickened me, repelled me.

What was it? Some kind of a moral fungus, the spores of which floated in that damp air, in that foggy and half-lighted darkness?

The thought that I was no longer obliged to go back into those damp and fetid mists filled me with an immense relief—a relief that far overbalanced the pain of my injured pride, the shame of comparative failure. I say I was no longer obliged to return: I would have to go back long enough to get on the quota and enter America permanently, for now I was only in the country on a temporary visa. But that did not matter so much. The feeling that I did not have to stay was another liberation.

Once again, I ask myself if it was not mostly subjective—perhaps it was. For I do not accuse the whole of England of the corruption that I had discovered in only a part of it. Nor do I blame England for this as a nation, as if it alone were infected with the sweet and nasty disease of the soul that seemed to be rotting the whole of Europe, in high places above all.

It was something I had not known or seen, in the England of those first days when I had been a child, and walked in the innocent countryside, and looked at the old village churches and read the novels of Dickens and wandered by the streams on picnics with my aunt and cousins.

What was wrong with this place, with all these people? Why was everything so empty?

Above all, why did the very boisterousness of the soccer blues, the rugger players, the cricketers, the oarsmen, the huntsmen and drinkers in the Lion and the clumsy dancers in the Rendezvous—why was all their noise so oafish and hollow and ridiculous? It seemed to me that Cambridge and, to some extent, the whole of England was pretending, with an elaborate and intent and conscious, and perhaps in some cases a courageous effort, to act as if it were alive.

And it took a lot of acting. It was a vast and complicated charade, with expensive and detailed costuming and scenery and a lot of inappropriate songs: and yet the whole thing was so intolerably dull, because most of the people were already morally dead, asphyxiated by the steam of their own strong yellow tea, or by the smell of their own pubs and breweries, or by the fungus on the walls of Oxford and Cambridge.

I speak of what I remember: perhaps the war that grew out of all this did something to cure it or to change it.

For those who had nothing but this emptiness in the middle of them, no doubt the things they had to do and to suffer during the war filled that emptiness with something stronger and more resilient than their pride—either that or it destroyed them utterly. But when I had been away from Cambridge about a year, I heard what had happened to one of them, a friend of mine.

Mike was a beefy and red-faced and noisy youth who came from somewhere in Wales, and was part of the crowd in which I milled around in the daytime and the nighttime during that year at Cambridge. He was full of loud laughter and a lot of well-meaning exclamations, and in his quieter moments he got into long and complicated sentences about life. But what was more characteristic of him was that he liked to put his fist through windows. He was the noisy and hearty type; he was altogether jolly. A great eater and drinker, he chased after girls with an astounding heaviness of passion and emotion. He managed to get into a lot of trouble. That was the way it was when I left Cambridge. The next year I heard how he ended up. The porter, or somebody, went down into the showers, under the buildings of the Old Court at Clare, and found Mike hanging by his neck from a rope slung over one of the pipes, with his big hearty face black with the agony of strangulation. He had hanged himself.

The Europe I finally left for good, in the late November of 1934, was a sad and unquiet continent, full of forebodings.

Of course, there were plenty of people who said: "There will not be a war . . ." But Hitler had now held power in Germany for some time, and that summer all the New York evening papers had been suddenly filled with the news of Dollfuss' murder in Austria, and the massing of Italian troops on the Austrian borders. It was one of the nights when I was down at Coney Island, with Reginald Marsh, and I walked in the whirl of lights and noise and drank glasses of thin, icy beer, and ate hot dogs full of mustard, and wondered if I would soon be in some army or other, or perhaps dead.

It was the first time I had felt the cold steel of the war-scare in my vitals. There was a lot more to come. It was only 1934.

And now, in November, when I was leaving England forever—the ship sailed quietly out of Southampton water by night—the land I left behind me seemed silent with the silence before a storm. It was a land all shut up and muffled in layers of fog and darkness, and all the people were in the rooms behind the thick walls of their houses, waiting for the first growl of thunder as the Nazis began to warm up the motors of a hundred thousand planes.

Perhaps they did not know they were waiting for all this. Perhaps they thought they had nothing better to occupy their minds than the wedding of Prince George and Princess Marina which had taken place the day before. Even I myself was more concerned with the thought of some people I was leaving than with the political atmosphere at that precise moment. And yet that atmosphere was something that would not allow itself to be altogether ignored.

I had seen enough of the things, the acts and appetites, that were to justify and to bring down upon the world the tons of bombs that would someday begin to fall in millions. Did I know that my own sins were enough to have destroyed the whole of England and Germany? There has never yet been a bomb invented that is half so powerful as one mortal sin—and yet there is no positive power in sin, only negation, only annihilation: and perhaps that is why it is so destructive, it is a nothingness, and where it is, there is nothing left—a blank, a moral vacuum.

It is only the infinite mercy and love of God that has prevented us from tearing ourselves to pieces and destroying His entire creation long ago. People seem to think that it is in some way a proof that no merciful God exists, if we have so many wars. On the contrary, consider how in spite of centuries of sin and greed and lust and cruelty and hatred and avarice and oppression and injustice, spawned and bred by the free wills of men, the human race can still recover, each time, and can still produce men and women who overcome evil with good, hatred with love, greed with charity, lust and cruelty with sanctity. How could all this be possible without the merciful love of God, pouring out His grace upon us? Can there be any doubt where wars come from and where peace comes from, when the children of this world, excluding God from their peace conferences, only manage to bring about greater and greater wars the more they talk about peace?

We have only to open our eyes and look about us to see what our sins are doing to the world, and have done. But we cannot see. We are the ones to whom it is said by the prophets of God: "Hearing hear, and understand not; and see the vision, and know it not."

There is not a flower that opens, not a seed that falls into the ground, and not an ear of wheat that nods on the end of its stalk in the wind that does not preach and proclaim the greatness and the mercy of God to the whole world.

There is not an act of kindness or generosity, not an act of sacrifice done, or a word of peace and gentleness spoken, not a child's prayer uttered, that does not sing hymns to God before His throne, and in the eyes of men, and before their faces.

How does it happen that in the thousands of generations of murderers since Cain, our dark bloodthirsty ancestor, that some of us can still be saints? The quietness and hiddenness and placidity of the truly good people in the world all proclaim the glory of God.

All these things, all creatures, every graceful movement, every ordered act of the human will, all are sent to us as prophets from God. But because of our stubbornness they come to us only to blind us further.

"Blind the heart of this people and make their ears heavy, and shut their eyes: lest they see with their eyes, and hear with their ears and understand with their heart and be converted, and I heal them."

We refuse to hear the million different voices through which God speaks to us, and every refusal hardens us more and more against His grace—and yet He continues to speak to us: and we say He is without mercy!

"But the Lord dealeth patiently for your sake, not willing that any should perish, but that all should return to penance."

Mother of God, how often in the last centuries have you not come down to us, speaking to us in our mountains and groves and hills, and telling us what was to come upon us, and we have not heard you. How long shall we continue to be deaf to your voice, and run our heads into the jaws of the hell that abhors us?

Lady, when on that night I left the Island that was once your England, your love went with me, although I could not know it, and could not make myself aware of it. And it was your love, your intercession for me, before God, that was preparing the seas before my ship, laying open the way for me to another country.

I was not sure where I was going, and I could not see what I would do when I got to New York. But you saw further and clearer than I, and you opened the seas before my ship, whose track lead me across the waters to a place I had never dreamed of, and which you were even then preparing for me to be my rescue and my shelter and my home. And when I thought there was no God and no love and no mercy, you were leading me all the while into the midst of His love and His mercy, and taking me, without my knowing anything about it, to the house that would hide me in the secret of His Face.

Glorious Mother of God, shall I ever again distrust you, or your God, before Whose throne you are irresistible in your intercession? Shall I ever turn my eyes from your hands and from your face and from your eyes? Shall I ever look anywhere else but in the face of your love, to find out true counsel, and to know my way, in all the days and all the moments of my life?

As you have dealt with me, Lady, deal also with all my millions of brothers who live in the same misery that I knew then: lead them in spite of themselves and guide them by your tremendous influence, O Holy Queen of souls and refuge of sinners, and bring them to your Christ the way you brought me. *Illos tuos misericordes oculos ad nos converte, et Jesum, benedictum fructum ventris tui, nobis ostende.* Show us your Christ, Lady, after this our exile, yes: but show Him to us also now, show Him to us here, while we are still wanderers.

4

The Children in the Market Place

I HAD A long way to go. I had more to cross than the Atlantic. Perhaps the Styx, being only a river, does not seem so terribly wide. It is not its width that makes it difficult to cross, especially when you are trying to get out of hell, and not in. And so, this time, even though I got out of Europe, I still remained in hell. But it was not for want of trying.

It was a stormy crossing. When it was possible, I walked on the wide, empty decks that streamed with spray. Or I would get up forward where I could see the bows blast their way headfirst into the mountains of water that bore down upon us. And I would hang on to the rail while the ship reeled and soared into the wet sky, riding the sea that swept under us while every stanchion and bulkhead groaned and complained.

When we got on to the Grand Banks, the seas calmed and there was a fall of snow, and the snow lay on the quiet decks, and made them white in the darkness of the evening. And because of the peacefulness of the snow, I imagined that my new ideas were breeding within me an interior peace.

The truth is, I was in the thick of a conversion. It was not the right conversion, but it was a conversion. Perhaps it was a lesser evil. I do not doubt much that it was. But it was not, for all that, much of a good. I was becoming a Communist.

Stated like that, it sounds pretty much the same as if I said: "I was growing a moustache." As a matter of fact, I was still unable to grow a moustache. Or I did not dare to try. And, I suppose, my Communism was about as mature as my face—as the sour, perplexed, English face in the photo on my quota card. However, as far as I know, this was about as sincere and complete a step to moral conversion as I was then able to make with my own lights and desires, such as they then were.

A lot of things had happened to me since I had left the relative seclusion of Oakham, and had been free to indulge all my appetites in the world, and the time had come for a big readjustment in my values. I could not evade that truth. I was too miserable, and it was evident that there was too much wrong with my strange, vague, selfish hedonism.

It did not take very much reflection on the year I had spent at Cambridge to show me that all my dreams of fantastic pleasures and delights were crazy and absurd, and that everything I had reached out for had turned to ashes in my hands, and that I myself, into the bargain, had turned out to be an extremely unpleasant sort of a person—vain, self-centered, dissolute, weak, irresolute, undisciplined, sensual, obscene and proud. I was a mess. Even the sight of my own face in a mirror was enough to disgust me.

When I came to ask myself the reasons for all this, the ground was well prepared. My mind was already facing what seemed to be an open door out of my spiritual jail. It was some four years since I had first read the Communist Manifesto, and I had never entirely forgotten about it. One of those Christmas vacations at Strasbourg I had read some books about Soviet Russia, how all the factories were working overtime, and all the ex-moujiks wore great big smiles on their faces, welcoming Russian aviators on their return from Polar flights, bearing the boughs of trees in their hands. Then I often went to Russian movies, which were pretty good from the technical point of view, although probably not so good as I thought they were, in my great anxiety to approve of them.

Finally, I had in my mind the myth that Soviet Russia was the friend of all the arts, and the only place where true art could find a refuge in a world of bourgeois ugliness. Where I ever got that idea is hard to find out, and how I managed to cling to it for so long is harder still, when you consider all the photographs there were, for everyone to see, showing the Red Square with gigantic pictures of Stalin hanging on the walls of the world's ugliest buildings—not to mention the views of the projected monster monument to Lenin, like a huge mountain of soap-sculpture, and the Little Father of Communism standing on top of it, and sticking out one of his hands. Then, when I went to New York in the summer, I found the *New Masses* lying around the studios of my friends and, as a matter of fact, a lot of the people I met were either party members or close to being so.

So now, when the time came for me to take spiritual stock of myself, it was natural that I should do so by projecting my whole spiritual condition into the sphere of economic history and the class-struggle. In other words, the conclusion I came to was that it was not so much I myself that was to blame for my unhappiness, but the society in which I lived.

I considered the person that I now was, the person that I had been at Cambridge, and that I had made of myself, and I saw clearly enough that I was the product of my times, my society and my class. I was something that had been spawned by the selfishness and irresponsibility of the materialistic century in which I lived. However, what I did not see was that my own age and class only had an accidental part to play in this. They gave my egoism and pride and my other sins a peculiar character of weak and supercilious flippancy proper to this particular century: but that was only on the surface. Underneath, it was the same old story of greed and lust and self-love, of the three concupiscences bred in the rich, rotted undergrowth of what is technically called "the world," in every age, in every class.

"If any man love the world, the charity of the Father is not in him. For all that is in the world is the concupiscence of the flesh and the concupiscence of the eyes and the pride of life." That is to say, all men who live only according to their five senses, and seek nothing beyond the gratification of their natural appetites for pleasure and reputation and power, cut themselves off from that charity which is the principle of all spiritual vitality and happiness because it alone saves us from the barren wilderness of our own abominable selfishness.

It is true that the materialistic society, the so-called culture that has evolved under the tender mercies of capitalism, has produced what seems to be the ultimate limit of this worldliness. And nowhere, except perhaps in the analogous society of pagan Rome, has there ever been such a flowering of cheap and petty and disgusting lusts and vanities as in the world of capitalism, where there is no evil that is not fostered and encouraged for the sake of making money. We live in a society whose whole policy is to excite every nerve in the human body and keep it at the highest pitch of artificial tension, to strain every human desire to the limit and to create as many new desires and synthetic passions as possible, in order to cater to them with the products of our factories and printing presses and movie studios and all the rest.

Being the son of an artist, I was born the sworn enemy of everything that could obviously be called "bourgeois," and now I only had to dress up that aversion in economic terms and extend it to cover more ground than it had covered before—namely, to include anything that could be classified as semi-fascist, like D. H. Lawrence and many of the artists who thought they were rebels without really being so—and I had my new religion all ready for immediate use.

It was an easy and handy religion—too easy in fact. It told me that all the evils in the world were the product of capitalism. Therefore, all that had to be done to get rid of the evils of the world was to get rid of capitalism. This would not be very hard, for capitalism contained the seeds of its own decay (and that indeed is a very obvious truth which nobody would trouble to deny, even some of the most stupid defenders of the system now in force: for our wars are altogether too eloquent in what they have to say on the subject). An active and enlightened minority—and this minority was understood to be made up of the most intelligent and vital elements of society, was to have the two-fold task of making the oppressed class, the proletariat, conscious of their own power and destiny as future owners of all the means of production, and to "bore from within" in order to gain control of power by every possible means. Some violence, no doubt, would probably be necessary, but only because of the inevitable reaction of capitalism by the use of fascist methods to keep the proletariat in subjection.

It was capitalism that was to blame for everything unpleasant, even the violence of the revolution itself. Now, of course, the revolution had already taken the first successful step in Russia. The Dictatorship of the Proletariat was already set up there. It would have to spread through the rest of the world before it could be said that the revolution had really been a success. But once it had, once capitalism had been completely overthrown, the semi-state, or Dictatorship of the Proletariat, would itself only be a temporary matter. It would be a kind of guardian of the revolution, a tutor of the new classless society, during its minority. But as soon as the citizens of the new, classless world had had all the greed educated out of them by enlightened methods, the last vestiges of the "state" would wither away, and there would be a new world, a new golden age, in which all property would be held in common, at least all capital goods, all the land, means of production and so on, and nobody would desire to seize them for himself: and so there would be no more poverty, no more wars, no more misery, no more starvation, no more violence. Everybody would be happy. Nobody would be overworked. They would all amicably exchange wives whenever they felt like it, and their offspring would be brought up in big shiny incubators, not by the state because there wouldn't be any state, but by that great, beautiful surd, the lovely, delicious unknown quantity of the new "Classless Society."

I don't think that even I was gullible enough to swallow all the business about the ultimate bliss that would follow the withering away of the state—a legend far more naive and far more oversimplified than the happy hunting ground of the most primitive Indian. But I simply assumed that things would be worked out by the right men at the right time. For the moment, what was needed was to get rid of capitalism.

The thing that made Communism seem so plausible to me was my own lack of logic which failed to distinguish between the reality of the *evils* which Communism was trying to overcome and the validity of its diagnosis and the chosen cure.

For there can be no doubt that modern society is in a terrible condition, and that its wars and depressions and its slums and all its other evils are principally the fruits of an unjust social system, a system that must be reformed and purified or else replaced. However, if you are wrong, does that make me right? If you are bad, does that prove that I am good? The chief weakness of Communism is that it is, itself, only another breed of the same materialism which is the source and root of all the evils which it so clearly sees, and it is evidently nothing but another product of the breakdown of the capitalist system. Indeed, it seems to be pieced together out of the ruins of the same ideology that once went into the vast, amorphous, intellectual structure underlying capitalism in the nineteenth century.

I don't know how anybody who pretends to know anything about history can be so naive as to suppose that after all these centuries of corrupt and imperfect social systems, there is eventually to evolve something perfect and pure out of them—the good out of the evil, the unchanging and stable and eternal out of the variable and mutable, the just out of the unjust. But perhaps revolution is a contradiction of evolution, and therefore means the replacement of the unjust by the just, of the evil by the good. And yet it is still just as naive to suppose that members of the same human species, without having changed anything but their minds, should suddenly turn around and produce a perfect society, when they have never been able, in the past, to produce anything but imperfection and, at best, the barest shadow of justice.

However, as I say, perhaps the hopefulness that suddenly began to swell in my breast as I stood on the deck of this ten-day liner going to New York, via Halifax, was largely subjective and imaginary. The chance association, in my mind, with fresh air and the sea and a healthy feeling and a lot of good resolutions, coinciding with a few superficial notions of Marxism, had made me—like so many others—a Communist in my own fancy, and I would become one of the hundreds of thousands of people living in America who are willing to buy an occasional Communist pamphlet and listen without rancor to a Communist orator, and to express open dislike of those who attack Communism, just because they are aware that there is a lot of injustice and suffering in the world, and somewhere got the idea that the Communists were the ones who were most sincerely trying to do something about it.

Added to this was my own personal conviction, the result of the uncertain and misdirected striving for moral reform, that I must now devote myself to the good of society, and apply my mind, at least to some extent, to the tremendous problems of my time.

I don't know how much good there was in this: but I think there was some. It was, I suppose, my acknowledgment of my selfishness, and my desire to make reparation for it by developing some kind of social and political consciousness. And at the time, in my first fervor, I felt myself willing to make sacrifices for this end. I wanted to devote myself to the causes of peace and justice in the world. I wanted to do something positive to interrupt and divert the gathering momentum that was dragging the whole world into another war—and I felt there was something I could do, not alone, but as the member of an active and vocal group.

It was a bright, icy-cold afternoon when, having passed Nantucket Light, we first saw the long, low, yellow shoreline of Long Island shining palely in the December sun. But when we entered New York harbor the lights were already coming on, glittering like jewels in the hard, clear buildings. The great, debonair city that was both young and old, and wise and innocent, shouted in the winter night as we passed the Battery and started up the North River. And I was glad, very glad to be an immigrant once again.

I came down on to the dock with a great feeling of confidence and possessiveness. "New York, you are mine! I love you!" It is the glad embrace she gives her lovers, the big, wild city: but I guess ultimately it is for their ruin. It certainly did not prove to be any good for me.

With my mind in the ferment in which it was, I thought for a moment of registering for courses at the New School for Social Research, in the shiny, black building on Twelfth Street, but I was easily persuaded that I had better finish out a regular university course and get a degree. And therefore I entered upon all the complicated preambles to admission to Columbia.

I came out of the subway at 116th Street. All around the campus were piles of dirty snow, and I smelled the wet, faintly exhilarating air of Morningside Heights in the winter time. The big, ugly buildings faced the world with a kind of unpretentious purposefulness, and people hurried in and out the glass doors with none of the fancy garments of the Cambridge undergraduate—no multicolored ties and blazers and scarfs, no tweeds and riding breeches, no affectations of any kind, but only the plain, drab overcoats of city masses. You got the impression that all these people were at once more earnest and more humble, poorer, smarter perhaps, certainly more diligent than those I had known at Cambridge.

Columbia was, for the most part, stripped of fancy academic ritual. The caps and gowns were reserved for occasions which, as a matter of fact, nobody really had to attend. I only got mixed up in one of them purely by accident, several months after I had acquired my degree, rolled up in a cardboard container, through one of the windows of the post-office-like registration bureau in University Hall.

Compared with Cambridge, this big sooty factory was full of light and fresh air. There was a kind of genuine intellectual vitality in the air—at least relatively speaking. Perhaps the reason was that most of the students had to work hard to pay for every classroom hour. Therefore they appreciated what they got, even when there was not much in it to appreciate. Then there was the big, bright, shiny, new library, with a complicated system of tickets and lights, at the main loan desk: and there I soon came out with a great armful of things, books which excited me more than I now can understand. I think it was not the books themselves but my own sense of energy and resolve that made me think everything was more interesting than it was.

What, for instance, did I find to enthrall me in a book about esthetics by a man called Yrjö Hirn? I cannot remember. And even in spite of my almost congenital dislike for Platonism, I was happy with the *Enneads* of Plotinus, in Marsilio Ficino's Latin translation. The truth is that there is a considerable difference between Plato and Plotinus, but I am not enough of a philosopher to know what it is. Thank God I shall never again have to try and find out, either. But anyway, I dragged this huge volume into the subway and out on the Long Island railroad to the house in Douglaston, where I had a room with a big glass-enclosed bookcase full of Communist pamphlets and books on psychoanalysis, in which the little Vulgate I had once bought in Rome lay neglected and out of place . . .

For some reason I became intensely interested in Daniel Defoe, and read his whole life and dipped into most of the strange journalistic jobs of writing which he did besides *Robinson Crusoe*. I made a hero for myself out of Jonathan Swift, because of his writing. Towards May of that year I remember going in to the Columbia Bookstore and selling them a copy of T. S. Eliot's essays and a lot of other things which I was getting rid of in a conscious reaction against artiness—as if all that were too bourgeois for my serious and practical new-self.

Then, because of the wide general curriculum of an American university, which, instead of trying to teach you any one thing completely, strives to give its students a superficial knowledge of everything, I found myself mildly interested in things like geology and economics, and interiorly cursing a big, vague course in current events called "Contemporary Civilization," which was imposed on all the sophomores whether they liked it or not.

Soon I was full of all the economic and pseudo-scientific jargon appropriate to a good Columbia man, and was acclimated to the new atmosphere which I found so congenial. That was true. Columbia, compared with Cambridge, was a friendly place. When you had to go and see a professor or an advisor or a dean about something, he would tell you, more or less simply, what you needed to know. The only trouble was that you usually had to wait around for about half an hour before you got a chance to see anybody. But once you did, there were no weird evasions and none of the pompous beating about the bush, mixed up with subtle academic allusions and a few dull witticisms which was what you were liable to get out of almost anybody at Cambridge, where everybody cultivated some special manner of his own, and had his own individual and peculiar style. I suppose it is something that you have to expect around a university, this artificiality. For a man to be absolutely sincere with generation after generation of students requires either supernatural simplicity or, in the natural order, a kind of heroic humility.

There was—and still is—one man at Columbia, or rather one among several, who was most remarkable for this kind of heroism. I mean Mark Van Doren.

The first semester I was at Columbia, just after my twentieth birthday, in the winter of 1935, Mark was giving part of the "English sequence" in one of those rooms in Hamilton Hall with windows looking out between the big columns on to the wired-in track on South Field. There were twelve or fifteen people with more or less unbrushed hair, most of them with glasses, lounging around. One of them was my friend Robert Gibney.

It was a class in English literature, and it had no special bias of any kind. It was simply about what it was supposed to be about: the English literature of the eighteenth century. And in it literature was treated, not as history, not as sociology, not as economics, not as a series of case-histories in psychoanalysis but, *mirabile dictu,* simply as literature.

I thought to myself, who is this excellent man Van Doren who being employed to teach literature, teaches just that: talks about writing and about books and poems and plays: does not get off on a tangent about the biographies of the poets or novelists: does not read into their poems a lot of subjective messages which were never there? Who is this man who does not have to fake and cover up a big gulf of ignorance by teaching a lot of opinions and conjectures and useless facts that belong to some other subject? Who is this who really loves what he has to teach, and does not secretly detest all literature, and abhor poetry, while pretending to be a professor of it?

That Columbia should have in it men like this who, instead of subtly destroying all literature by burying and concealing it under a mass of irrelevancies, really purified and educated the perceptions of their students by teaching them how to read a book and how to tell a good book from a bad, genuine writing from falsity and pastiche: all this gave me a deep respect for my new university.

Mark would come into the room and, without any fuss, would start talking about whatever was to be talked about. Most of the time he asked questions. His questions were very good, and if you tried to answer them intelligently, you found yourself saying excellent things that you did not know you knew, and that you had not, in fact, known before. He had "educed" them from you by his question. His classes were literally "education"—they brought things out of you, they made your mind produce its own explicit ideas. Do not think that Mark was simply priming his students with thoughts of his own, and then making the thought stick to their minds by getting them to give it back to him as their own. Far from it. What he did have was the gift of communicating to them something of his own vital interest in things, something of his manner of approach: but the results were sometimes quite unexpected—and by that I mean good in a way that he had not anticipated, casting lights that he had not himself foreseen.

Now a man who can go for year after year—although Mark was young then and is young now—without having any time to waste in flattering and cajoling his students with any kind of a fancy act, or with jokes, or with storms of temperament, or periodic tirades—whole classes spent in threats and imprecations, to disguise the fact that the professor himself has come in unprepared—one who can do without all these non-essentials both honors his vocation and makes it fruitful. Not only that, but his vocation, in return, perfects and ennobles him. And that is the way it should be, even in the natural order: how much more so in the order of grace!

Mark, I know, is no stranger to the order of grace: but considering his work as teacher merely as a mission on the natural level—I can see that Providence was using him as an instrument more directly than he realized. As far as I can see, the influence of Mark's sober and sincere intellect, and his manner of dealing with his subject with perfect honesty and objectivity and without evasions, was remotely preparing my mind to receive the good seed of scholastic philosophy. And there is nothing strange in this, for Mark himself was familiar at least with some of the modern scholastics, like Maritain and Gilson, and he was a friend of the American neo-Thomists, Mortimer Adler and Richard McKeon, who had started out at Columbia but had had to move to Chicago, because Columbia was not ripe enough to know what to make of them.

The truth is that Mark's temper was profoundly scholastic in the sense that his clear mind looked directly for the quiddities of things, and sought being and substance under the covering of accident and appearances. And for him poetry was, indeed, a virtue of the practical intellect, and not simply a vague spilling of the emotions, wasting the soul and perfecting none of our essential powers.

It was because of this virtual scholasticism of Mark's that he would never permit himself to fall into the naive errors of those who try to read some favorite private doctrine into every poet they like of every nation or every age. And Mark abhorred the smug assurance with which second-rate left-wing critics find adumbrations of dialectical materialism in everyone who ever wrote from Homer and Shakespeare to whomever they happen to like in recent times. If the poet is to their fancy, then he is clearly seen to be preaching the class struggle. If they do not like him, then they are able to show that he was really a forefather of fascism. And all their literary heroes are revolutionary leaders, and all their favorite villains are capitalists and Nazis.

It was a very good thing for me that I ran into someone like Mark Van Doren at that particular time, because in my new reverence for Communism, I was in danger of docilely accepting any kind of stupidity, provided I thought it was something that paved the way to the Elysian fields of classless society.

ii

There was a sort of a legend in New York, fostered by the Hearst papers, that Columbia was a hotbed of Communists. All the professors and students were supposed to be Reds, except perhaps the president of the university, Nicholas Murray Butler, living in solitary misery in his big brick house on Morningside Drive. I have no doubt that the poor old man's misery was real, and that his isolation from most of the university was very real. But the statement that everybody in the university was a Communist was far from true.

I know that, as far as the faculty was concerned, Columbia University was built up in concentric rings, about a solid core of well-meaning, unenlightened stuffiness, the veterans, the beloved of the trustees and the alumni, and Butler's intellectual guard of honor. Then there was an inner circle of sociologists and economists and lawyers, whose world was a mystery to me, and who exercised a powerful influence in Washington under the New Deal. About all of them and their satellites I never knew anything, except that they were certainly not Communists. Then there was the little galaxy of pragmatists in the school of philosophy, and all the thousands of their pale spiritual offspring in the jungles of Teachers College and New College. They were not Communists either. They cast a mighty influence over the whole American Middle West, and were to a great extent conditioned by the very people whom they were trying to condition, so that Teachers College always stood for colorlessness and mediocrity and plain, hapless behaviorism. These three groups were then the real Columbia. I suppose they all prided themselves on their liberalism, but that is precisely what they were: "liberals," not Communists, and they brought down upon their heads all the scorn the Communists could pour upon them for their position of habitual compromise.

I do not understand much about politics. Besides, it would be outside the scope of my present vocation if I tried to make any political analysis of anything. But I can say that there were, at that time, quite a few Communists or Communist sympathizers among the undergraduates, and especially in Columbia College where most of the smartest students were Reds.

The Communists had control of the college paper and were strong on some of the other publications and on the Student Board. But this campus Communism was more a matter of noise than anything else, at least as far as the rank and file were concerned.

The Spectator was always starting some kind of a fight and calling for mass-meetings and strikes and demonstrations. Then the fraternity boys, who elected to play "Fascist" in this children's game, would get up in the classroom buildings and turn the firehoses on the people who were standing around the Communist speaker. Then the whole thing would come out in the New York *Journal* that evening and all the alumni would choke on their mock turtle soup down at the Columbia Club.

By the time I arrived at Columbia, the Communists had taken to holding their meetings at the sundial on 116th Street, in the middle of the wide-open space between the old domed library and South Field. This was well out of the range of the firehoses in the Journalism building and Hamilton Hall. The first meeting I went to, there, was very tame. It was against Italian Fascism. There were one or two speeches—by students practising the art. Those who stood around were mostly members of the National Students' League, who were there out of a sense of duty or partisanship. A few curious passers-by stopped a while on their way to the subway. There was not much excitement. A girl with a mop of black hair stood by, wearing a placard pronouncing some kind of a judgement on Fascism. Someone sold me a pamphlet.

Presently I picked out the quiet, earnest, stocky little man in the grey overcoat, a hatless, black-haired Communist from downtown, who was running the affair. He was not a student. He was the real article. This was his assignment: forming and training the material that offered itself to him at Columbia. He had an assistant, a younger man, and the two of them were kept pretty busy. I went up to him and started to talk. When he actually listened to me, and paid attention to my ideas, and seemed to approve of my interest, I was very flattered. He got my name and address and told me to come to the meetings of the N.S.L.

Soon I was walking up and down in front of the Casa Italiana wearing two placards, front and back, accusing Italy of injustice in the invasion of Ethiopia that had either just begun or was just about to begin. Since the accusation was manifestly true, I felt a certain satisfaction in thus silently proclaiming it as a picket. There were two or three of us. For an hour and a half or two hours we walked up and down the pavement of Amsterdam Avenue, in the grey afternoon, bearing our dire accusations, while the warm sense of justification in our hearts burned high, even in spite of the external boredom.

For during that whole time no one even came near the Casa Italiana, and I even began to wonder if there were anyone at all inside of it. The only person who approached us was a young Italian who looked as if he might be a Freshman football player, and tried to get into an argument. But he was too dumb. He went away mumbling that the Hearst papers were very excellent because of the great prizes which they offered, in open competition, to their many readers.

I forget how the picketing ended: whether we waited for someone else to come and take over, or whether we just decided we had done enough and took off our signs and went away. But any way I had the feeling that I had done something that was good, if only as a gesture: for it certainly did not seem to have accomplished anything. But at least I had made a kind of public confession of faith. I had said that I was against war—against all war. That I believed wars to be unjust. That I thought they could only ruin and destroy the world. . . . Someone will ask where I managed to get all that out of the placard I was carrying. But as far as I remember, that was the party line that year—at least it was the line that was handed out to the public.

I can still hear the tired, determined chanting of students at campus demonstrations: "Books, not Battleships!" "No More WAR!" There was no distinction made. It was war as such that we hated and said we wanted no more of. We wanted books, not battleships, we said. We were all burned up with the thirst for knowledge, for intellectual and spiritual improvement. And here the wicked capitalists were forcing the government to enrich them by buying armaments and building battleships and planes and tanks, when the money ought to be spent on volumes of lovely cultural books for us students. Here we were on the threshold of life, we cried: our hands were reaching out for education and culture. Was the government going to put a gun in them, and send us off on another imperialistic war? And the line of reasoning behind all this definitely held, in 1935, that all war was imperialistic war. War, according to the party line in 1935, was an exclusively capitalist amusement.

It was purely and simply a device to enrich the armament manufacturers and the international bankers, coining fortunes for them with the blood of the workers and students.

One of the big political events of that spring was a "Peace Strike." I was never quite able to understand by virtue of what principle a student could manage to consider himself on strike by cutting a class. Theoretically, I suppose, it amounted to a kind of defiance of authority: but it was a defiance that did not cost anybody anything except perhaps the student himself. And besides, I was quite used to cutting classes whenever I felt like it, and it seemed to me rather bombastic to dress it up with the name of "strike." However, on another of those grey days, we went on "strike," and this time there were several hundred people in the gymnasium, and even one or two members of the faculty got up on the platform and said something.

They were not all Communists, but all the speeches had more or less the same burden: that it was absurd to even think of such a thing as a just war in our time. Nobody wanted war: there was no justification for any war of any kind on the part of anybody, and consequently, if a war did start, it would certainly be the result of a capitalist plot, and should be firmly resisted by everybody with any kind of a conscience.

That was just the kind of a position that attracted me, that appealed to my mind at that time. It seemed to cut across all complexities by its sweeping and uncompromising simplicity. All war was simply unjust, and that was that. The thing to do was to fold your arms and refuse to fight. If everybody did that, there would be no more wars.

That cannot seriously have been the Communist position, but at least I thought it was. And anyway, the theme of this particular meeting was the "Oxford Pledge." The words of that pledge were written out in huge letters on a great big placard that hung limply in the air over the speakers' platform, and all the speakers waved their arms at it and praised it, and repeated it, and urged it upon us, and in the end we all took it, and acclaimed it, and solemnly pledged ourselves to it.

Perhaps everybody has, by now, forgotten what the Oxford Pledge was. It was a resolution that had been passed by the Oxford Union, which said that they, these particular Oxford undergraduates, simply would refuse to fight for King and Country in any war whatever. The fact that a majority of those who happened to be at a meeting of a university debating society, one evening, voted that way certainly did not commit the whole university, or even any one of the voters, to what the resolution said, and it was only other student groups, all over the world, that had transformed it into a "pledge." And this "pledge" was then taken by hundreds of thousands of students in all kinds of schools and colleges and universities with some of the solemnity that might make it look as if they intended to bind themselves by it—the way we were doing at Columbia that day. All this was usually inspired by the Reds, who were very fond of the Oxford Pledge that year. . . .

However, the next year the Spanish Civil war broke out. The first thing I heard about that war was that one of the chief speakers at the 1935 Peace Strike, and one who had been so enthusiastic about this glorious pledge that we would never fight in any war, was now fighting for the Red Army against Franco, and all the N.S.L. and the Young Communists were going around picketing everybody who seemed to think that the war in Spain was not holy and sacrosanct and a crusade for the workers against Fascism.

The thing that perplexes me is: what did all the people in the gymnasium at Columbia, including myself, think we were doing when we took that pledge? What did a pledge mean to us? What was, in our minds, the basis of such an obligation? How could we be obliged? Communists don't believe in any such thing as a natural law, or the law of conscience, although they seem to. They are always crying out against the injustice of capitalism and yet, as a matter of fact, they very often say in the same breath that the very concept of justice is simply a myth devised by the ruling classes to beguile and deceive the proletariat.

As far as I can remember, it seems that what most of us thought we were doing, when we took that pledge, was simply making a public statement, and doing so in sufficient numbers, as we hoped, to influence politicians. There was no intention of binding ourselves under any obligation. The notion never even occurred to us. Most of us probably secretly thought we were gods anyway, and therefore the only law we had to obey was our own ineffable little wills. It was sufficient to say that we did not intend to go to war for anybody: and that was enough. And if, afterwards, we changed our minds—well, were we not our own gods?

It's a nice, complex universe, the Communist universe: it gravitates towards stability and harmony and peace and order on the poles of an opportunism that is completely irresponsible and erratic. Its only law is, it will do whatever seems to be profitable to itself at the moment. However, that seems to have become the rule of all modern political parties. I have nothing to say about it. I do not profess to be either amazed or broken-hearted that such a thing should be possible. Let the dead bury their dead: they have certainly got enough to bury. It is the fruit of their philosophy that they should: and that is all that they need to be reminded of. But you cannot make them believe it.

I had formed a kind of an ideal picture of Communism in my mind, and now I found that the reality was a disappointment. I suppose my daydreams were theirs also. But neither dream is true.

I had thought that Communists were calm, strong, definite people, with very clear ideas as to what was wrong with everything. Men who knew the solution, and were ready to pay any price to apply the remedy. And their remedy was simple and just and clean, and it would definitely solve all the problems of society, and make men happy, and bring the world peace.

It turned out that some of them indeed were calm, and strong, and had a kind of peace of mind that came from definite convictions and from a real devotion to their cause, out of motives of a kind of vague natural charity and sense of justice. But the trouble with their convictions was that they were mostly strange, stubborn prejudices, hammered into their minds by the incantation of statistics, and without any solid intellectual foundation. And having decided that God is an invention of the ruling classes, and having excluded Him, and all moral order with Him, they were trying to establish some kind of a moral system by abolishing all morality in its very source. Indeed, the very word morality was something repugnant to them. They wanted to make everything right, and they denied all the criteria given us for distinguishing between right and wrong.

And so it is an indication of the intellectual instability of Communism, and the weakness of its philosophical foundations, that most Communists are, in actual fact, noisy and shallow and violent people, torn to pieces by petty jealousies and factional hatreds and envies and strife. They shout and show off and generally give the impression that they cordially detest one another even when they are supposed to belong to the same sect. And as for the inter-sectional hatred prevailing between all the different branches of radicalism, it is far bitterer and more virulent than the more or less sweeping and abstract hatred of the big general enemy, capitalism. All this is something of a clue to such things as the wholesale executions of Communists who have moved their chairs to too prominent a position in the ante-chamber of Utopia which the Soviet Union is supposed to be.

iii

My active part in the world revolution was not very momentous. It lasted, in all, about three months. I picketed the Casa Italiana, I went to the Peace Strike, and I think I made some kind of a speech in the big classroom on the second floor of the Business School, where the N.S.L. had their meetings. Maybe it was a speech on Communism in England—a topic about which I knew absolutely nothing; in that case, I was loyally living up to the tradition of Red oratory. I sold some pamphlets and magazines. I don't know what was in them, but I could gather their contents from the big black cartoons of capitalists drinking the blood of workers.

Finally, the Reds had a party. And, of all places, in a Park Avenue apartment. This irony was the only amusing thing about it. And after all it was not so ironical. It was the home of some Barnard girl who belonged to the Young Communist League and her parents had gone away for the week-end. I could get a fair picture of them from the way the furniture looked, and from the volumes of Nietszche and Schopenhauer and Oscar Wilde and Ibsen that filled the bookcases. And there was a big grand piano on which someone played Beethoven while the Reds sat around on the floor. Later we had a sort of Boy Scout campfire group in the living room, singing heavy Communist songs, including that delicate anti-religious classic, "There'll be pie in the sky when you die."

One little fellow with buck teeth and horn-rimmed glasses pointed to two windows in a corner of one of the rooms. They commanded a whole sweep of Park Avenue in one direction and the cross-town street in another. "What a place for a machine-gun nest," he observed. The statement came from a middle-class adolescent. It was made in a Park Avenue apartment. He had evidently never even seen a machine-gun, except in the movies. If there had been a revolution going on at the time, he would have probably been among the first to get his head knocked off by the revolutionists. And in any case he, like all the rest of us, had just finished making the famous Oxford Pledge that he would not fight in any war whatever . . .

One reason why I found the party so dull was that nobody was very enthusiastic about getting something to drink except me.

Finally one of the girls encouraged me, in a businesslike sort of a way, to go out and buy bottles of rye at a liquor store around the corner on Third Avenue, and when I had drunk some of the contents she invited me into a room and signed me up as a member of the Young Communist League. I took the party name of Frank Swift. When I looked up from the paper the girl had vanished like a not too inspiring dream, and I went home on the Long Island Railroad with the secret of a name which I have been too ashamed to reveal to anyone until this moment when I am beyond humiliation.

I only went to one meeting of the Young Communist League, in the apartment of one of the students. It was a long discussion as to why Comrade So-and-so did not come to any of the meetings. The answer was that his father was too bourgeois to allow it. So after that, I walked out into the empty street, and let the meeting end however it would.

It was good to be in the fresh air. My footsteps rang out on the dark stones. At the end of the street, the pale amber light of a bar-room beckoned lovingly to me from under the steel girders of the elevated. The place was empty. I got a glass of beer and lit a cigarette and tasted the first sweet moment of silence and relief.

And that was the end of my days as a great revolutionary. I decided that it would be wiser if I just remained a "fellow-traveller." The truth is that my inspiration to do something for the good of mankind had been pretty feeble and abstract from the start. I was still interested in doing good for only one person in the world—myself.

May came, and all the trees on Long Island were green, and when the train from the city got past Bayside and started across the meadows to Douglaston, you could see the pale, soft haze of summer beginning to hang over the bay, and count the boats that had been set afloat again after the winter, and were riding jauntily at their moorings off the end of the little dock. And now in the lengthening evenings the dining room was still light with the rays of the sun when Pop came home for dinner, slamming the front door and whooping at the dog and smacking the surface of the hall table with the evening paper to let everybody know that he had arrived.

Soon John Paul was home from his school in Pennsylvania, and my exams were over, and we had nothing to do but go swimming and hang around the house playing hot records. And in the evening we would wander off to some appalling movie where we nearly died of boredom. We did not have a car, and my uncle would not let us touch the family Buick. It would not have done me any good anyway, because I never learned to drive. So most of the time, we would get a ride to Great Neck and then walk back the two or three miles along the wide road when the show was over.

Why did we ever go to all those movies? That is another mystery. But I think John Paul and I and our various friends must have seen all the movies that were produced, without exception, from 1934 to 1937. And most of them were simply awful. What is more, they got worse from week to week and from month to month, and day after day we hated them more. My ears are ringing with the false, gay music that used to announce the Fox movietone and the Paramount newsreels with the turning camera that slowly veered its aim right at your face. My mind still echoes with the tones of Pete Smith and Fitzpatrick of the Travel-talks saying, "And now farewell to beautiful New South Wales."

And yet I confess a secret loyalty to the memory of my great heroes: Chaplin, W. C. Fields, Harpo Marx, and many others whose names I have forgotten. But their pictures were rare, and for the rest, we found ourselves perversely admiring the villains and detesting the heroes. The truth is that the villains were almost always the better actors. We were delighted with everything they did. We were almost always in danger of being thrown out of the theater for our uproarious laughter at scenes that were supposed to be most affecting, tender and appealing to the finer elements in the human soul—the tears of Jackie Cooper, the brave smile of Alice Faye behind the bars of a jail.

The movies soon turned into a kind of hell for me and my brother and indeed for all my closest friends. We could not keep away from them. We were hypnotised by those yellow flickering lights and the big posters of Don Ameche. Yet as soon as we got inside, the suffering of having to sit and look at such colossal stupidities became so acute that we sometimes actually felt physically sick. In the end, it got so that I could hardly sit through a show. It was like lighting cigarettes and taking a few puffs and throwing them away, appalled by the vile taste in one's mouth.

In 1935 and 1936, without my realizing it, life was slowly, once more, becoming almost intolerable.

In the fall of 1935, John Paul went to Cornell, and I went back to Columbia, full of all kinds of collegiate enthusiasms, so that in a moment of madness I even gave my name for the Varsity lightweight crew. After a couple of days on the Harlem River and then on the Hudson, when we tried to row to Yonkers and back in what seemed to me to be a small hurricane, I decided that I did not wish to die so young, and after that carefully avoided the Boat-House all the rest of the time I was in college.

However, October is a fine and dangerous season in America. It is dry and cool and the land is wild with red and gold and crimson, and all the lassitudes of August have seeped out of your blood, and you are full of ambition. It is a wonderful time to begin anything at all. You go to college, and every course in the catalogue looks wonderful. The names of the subjects all seem to lay open the way to a new world. Your arms are full of new, clean notebooks, waiting to be filled. You pass through the doors of the library, and the smell of thousands of well-kept books makes your head swim with a clean and subtle pleasure. You have a new hat, a new sweater perhaps, or a whole new suit. Even the nickels and the quarters in your pocket feel new, and the buildings shine in the glorious sun.

In this season of resolutions and ambitions, in 1935, I signed up for courses in Spanish and German and Geology and Constitutional Law and French Renaissance Literature and I forget what else besides. And I started to work for *The Spectator* and the yearbook and *The Review* and I continued to work for *Jester* as I had already done the spring before. And I found myself pledging one of the fraternities.

It was a big, gloomy house behind the new library. On the ground floor there was a pool-room as dark as a morgue, a dining room, and some stairs led up to a big dark wainscotted living room where they held dances and beer-parties. Above that were two floors of bedrooms where telephones were constantly ringing and all day long somebody or other was singing in the showerbath. And there was somewhere in the building a secret room which I must not reveal to you, reader, at any price, even at the cost of life itself. And there I was eventually initiated. The initiation with its various tortures lasted about a week, and I cheerfully accepted penances which, if they were imposed in a monastery, for a supernatural motive, and for some real reason, instead of for no reason at all, would cause such an uproar that all religious houses would be closed and the Catholic Church would probably have a hard time staying in the country.

When that was over I had a gold and enamel pin on my shirt. My name was engraved on the back of it, and I was quite proud of it for about a year, and then it went to the laundry on a shirt and never came back.

I suppose there were two reasons why I thought I ought to join a fraternity. One was the false one, that I thought it would help me to "make connections" as the saying goes, and get a marvelous job on leaving college. The other, truer one was that I imagined that I would thus find a multitude of occasions for parties and diversions, and that I would meet many very interesting young ladies at the dances that would be held in that mausoleum. Both these hopes turned out to be illusory. As a matter of fact, I think the only real explanation was that I was feeling the effects of October.

Anyway, when John Paul went to Cornell the whole family, except me, drove up to Ithaca in the Buick and came back with words and concepts that filled the house with a kind of collegiate tension for a couple of weeks to come. Everybody was talking about football and courses and fraternities.

As a matter of fact, John Paul's first year at Cornell turned out to be sad in the same way as my first year at Cambridge—a thing that was not long in becoming apparent, when the bills he could not pay began to show up at home. But it was even more obvious to me when I saw him again.

He was naturally a happy and optimistic sort of a person and he did not easily get depressed. And he had a clear, quick intelligence and a character as sensitive as it was well-balanced. Now his intelligence seemed a little fogged with some kind of an obscure, interior confusion, and his happiness was perverted by a sad, lost restlessness. Although he maintained all his interests and increased them, the increase was in extent, not in depth, and the result was a kind of scattering of powers, a dissipation of the mind and will in a variety of futile aims.

He stood for some time, with great uncertainty, on the threshold of a fraternity house at Cornell, and even let them put a pledge pin on him, and then after a couple of weeks he took it off again and ran away. And with three friends he rented a house on one of those steep, shady Ithaca streets, and after that the year was a long and sordid riot, from which he derived no satisfaction. They called the place Grand Hotel, and had stationery printed with that title, on which desultory and fragmentary letters would come to Douglaston, and fill everyone with unquiet. When he came back from Cornell, John Paul looked tired and disgusted.

I suppose it is true, at least theoretically, the brothers watch over one another and help one another along in the fraternity house. In my fraternity house at Columbia, I know that the wiser members used to get together and shake their heads a little when somebody was carrying his debauchery too far. And when there was any real trouble, the concern of the brothers was sincere and dramatic, but it was useless. And there is always trouble in a fraternity house. The trouble, which came in the year after I was initiated, was the disappearance of one of the brothers, whom we shall call Fred.

Fred was a tall, stoop-shouldered, melancholy individual, with dark hair growing low on his brows. He never had much to say, and he liked to go apart and drink in mournful solitude. The only vivid thing I remember about him was that he stood over me, during one of the peculiar ceremonies of the initiation, when all the pledges had to stuff themselves with bread and milk for a special reason. And while I tried with despairing efforts to get the huge mouthfuls swallowed down, this Fred was standing over me with woeful cries of: "EAT, EAT, EAT!" It must have been sometime after Christmas that he disappeared.

I came into the house one night, and they were sitting around in the leather chairs talking earnestly. "Where's Fred?" was the burden of the discussion. He had not been seen anywhere for a couple of days. Would his family be upset if someone called up his home to see if he was there? Evidently, but it had to be done: he had not gone home either. One of the brothers had long since visited all his usual haunts. People tried to reconstruct the situation in which he had last been seen. With what dispositions had he last walked out of the front door. The usual ones, of course: silence, melancholy, the probable intention of getting drunk. A week passed and Fred was not found. The earnest concern of the brothers was fruitless. The subject of Fred was more or less dropped and, after a month, most of us had forgotten it. After two months, the whole thing was finally settled.

"They found Fred," somebody told me.

"Yes? Where?"

"In Brooklyn."

"Is he all right?"

"No, he's dead. They found him in the Gowanus Canal."

"What did he do, jump in?"

"Nobody knows what he did. He'd been there a long time."

"How long?"

"I don't know, a couple of months. They figured out who it was from the fillings in his teeth."

It was a picture that was not altogether vague to me. Our famous course in Contemporary Civilization had involved me, one winter afternoon, in a visit to the Bellevue Morgue, where I had seen rows and rows of iceboxes containing the blue, swollen corpses of drowned men along with all the other human refuse of the big, evil city: The dead that had been picked up in the streets, ruined by raw alcohol. The dead that had been found starved and frozen lying where they had tried to sleep in a pile of old newspapers. The pauper dead from Randalls Island. The dope-fiend dead. The murdered dead. The run-over. The suicides. The dead Negroes and Chinese. The dead of venereal disease. The dead from unknown causes. The killed by gangsters. They would all be shipped for burial up the East River in a barge to one of those islands where they also burned garbage.

Contemporary Civilization! One of the last things we saw on the way out of the morgue was the hand of a man pickled in a jar, brown and vile. They were not sure whether he was a criminal or not, and they wanted to have some part of him, after they had sent the rest of him up to the ghats. In the autopsy room a man on the table with his trunk wide open pointed his sharp, dead nose at the ceiling. The doctors held his liver and kidneys in their hands and sprayed them over with a trickle of water from a little rubber hose. I have never forgotten the awful, clammy silence of the city morgue at Bellevue, where they collect the bodies of those who died of contemporary civilization, like Fred.

Nevertheless, during that year I was so busy and so immersed in activities and occupations that I had no time to think for very long on these things. The energy of that golden October and the stimulation of the cold, bright winter days when the wind swept down as sharp as knives from the shining Palisades kept driving me through the year in what seemed to be fine condition. I had never done so many different things at the same time or with such apparent success. I had discovered in myself something of a capacity for work and for activity and for enjoyment that I had never dreamed of. And everything began to come easy, as the saying goes.

It was not that I was really studying hard or working hard: but all of a sudden I had fallen into a kind of a mysterious knack of keeping a hundred different interests going in the air at the same time. It was a kind of a stupendous juggling act, a tour-de-force, and what surprised me most was that I managed to keep it up without collapsing. In the first place, I was carrying about eighteen points in my courses—the average amount. I had found out the simplest way of fulfilling the minimum requirements for each one.

Then there was the "Fourth Floor." The fourth floor of John Jay

Hall was the place where all the offices of the student publications and the Glee Club and the Student Board and all the rest were to be found. It was the noisiest and most agitated part of the campus. It was not gay, exactly. And I hardly ever saw, anywhere, antipathies and contentions and jealousies at once so petty, so open and so sharp. The whole floor was constantly seething with the exchange of insults from office to office. Constantly, all day long, from morning to night, people were writing articles and drawing cartoons calling each other Fascists. Or else they were calling one another up on the phone and assuring one another in the coarsest terms of their undying hatred. It was all intellectual and verbal, as vicious as it could be, but it never became concrete, never descended into physical rage. For this reason, I think that it was all more or less of a game which everybody played for purposes that were remotely esthetic.

The campus was supposed to be, in that year, in a state of "intellectual ferment." Everybody felt and even said that there were an unusual number of brilliant and original minds in the college. I think that it was to some extent true. Ad Reinhardt was certainly the best artist that had ever drawn for *Jester*, perhaps for any other college magazine. His issues of *Jester* were real magazines. I think that in cover designs and layouts he could have given lessons to some of the art-editors downtown. Everything he put out was original, and it was also funny, because for the first time in years *Jester* had some real writers contributing to it, and was not just an anthology of the same stale and obscene jokes that have been circulating through the sluggish system of American college magazines for two generations. By now Reinhardt had graduated, and so had the editor of the 1935 *Spectator*, Jim Wechsler.

My first approach to the Fourth Floor had been rather circumspect, after the manner of Cambridge. I went to my adviser, Prof. McKee, and asked him how to go about it, and he gave me a letter of introduction to Leonard Robinson who was editor of *The Columbia Review*, the literary magazine. I don't know what Robinson would have made of a letter of introduction. Anyway, I never got to meeting him after all. When I went to the *Review* office I gave the note to Bob Giroux, an associate editor, and he looked at it and scratched his head some bit and told me to write something if I got an idea.

By 1936 Leonard Robinson had vanished. I always heard a lot about Robinson, and it all adds up to nothing very clear, so that

I have always had the impression that he somehow lives in the trees. I pray that he may go to heaven.

As for *Review,* Robert Paul Smith and Robert Giroux were both editing it together, and it was good. I don't know whether you would use the term "ferment" in their case, but Smith and Giroux were both good writers. Also, Giroux was a Catholic and a person strangely placid for the Fourth Floor. He had no part in its feuds and, as a matter of fact, you did not see him around there very much. John Berryman was more or less the star on *Review* that year. He was the most earnest-looking man on the campus.

There was not an office on that floor where I did not have something to do, except the Glee Club and Student Board and the big place where all the football coaches had their desks. I was writing stories for *Spectator,* and columns that were supposed to be funny; I was writing things for the yearbook and trying to sell copies of it—a thankless task. The yearbook was the one thing nobody wanted: it was expensive and dull. Of this I eventually became editor, without any evident benefit to myself or to the book or to Columbia or to the world.

I was never particularly drawn to the Varsity show: but they had a piano in their room, and the room was almost always empty, so I used to go in there and play furious jazz, after the manner I had taught myself—a manner which offended every ear but my own. It was a way of letting off steam—a form of athletics if you like. I have ruined more than one piano by this method.

The place where I was busiest was the *Jester* office. Nobody really worked there, they just congregated about noontime and beat violently with the palms of their hands on the big empty filing cabinets, making a thunderous sound that echoed up and down the corridor, and was sometimes answered from the *Review* office across the hall. There I usually came and drew forth from the bulging leather bag of books that I carried, copy and drawings which I put into the editor's hand. The editor that year was Herb Jacobson, and he printed all my worst cartoons very large in the most prominent parts of the magazine.

I thought I had something to be proud of when I became art-editor of *Jester* at the end of that year. Robert Lax was to be editor and Ralph Toledano managing editor, and we got along well together. The next year *Jester* was well put together because of Toledano and well written because of Lax and sometimes popular with the masses because of me. When it was really funny, it was not popular at all. The only really funny issues were mostly the work of Lax and Bob Gibney, the fruit of ideas that came to them at four o'clock in the morning in their room on the top floor of Furnald Hall.

The chief advantage of *Jester* was that it paid most of our bills for tuition. We were happy about it all, and wandered around the campus with little golden crowns dangling on our watch chains. Indeed, that was the only reason why I had a watch chain. I did not have a watch.

I have barely begun the list of all the things that occupied me in those days. For example, I gave my name to Miss Wegener at the appointments office. Miss Wegener was—and I hope she still is—a kind of a genius. She sat all day long behind her desk in that small, neat office in the Alumni house. No matter how many people she had talked to, she always looked unruffled and at peace. Every time you went to see her, one or two phone calls would come in, and she would make a note on a little pad of paper. In summer she never seemed to be worried by the hot weather. And she always smiled at you with a smile that was at the same time efficient and kind, pleasant and yet a little impersonal. She was another one who had a vocation and was living up to it!

One of the best jobs she ever got for me was that of guide and interpreter on the observation roof of the R.C.A. building, Rockefeller Center. It was an easy job. So easy in fact that it was boring. You simply had to stand there and talk to the people who came pouring out of the elevator with all their questions. And for this you got twenty-seven and a half dollars a week, which was very good pay in 1936. I also worked in another office in Radio City, for some people who handled publicity for all the manufacturers of Paper Cups and Containers. For them I did cartoons that said you would surely get trench mouth if you ever drank out of an ordinary glass. For each cartoon I was paid six dollars. It made me feel like an executive, to go walking in and out of the doors of the R.C.A. building with my pockets full of money. Miss Wegener would also send me off on the subway with little slips of paper with the addresses of apartments where I would interview rich Jewish ladies about tutoring their children in Latin, which meant that I got two or two and a half dollars an hour for sitting with them and doing their homework.

I also handed in my name for the Cross Country team. The fact that the coach was not sorry to get me is sufficient indication of one reason why we were the worst college Cross Country team in the East that year. And so, in my afternoons, I would run around and around South Field on the cinder path. And when winter came, I would go round and round the board track until I had blisters all over the soles of my feet and was so lame I could hardly walk. Occasionally I would go up to Van Cortlandt Park and run along the sandy and rocky paths through the woods. When we raced any other college, I was never absolutely the last one home—there were always two or three other Columbia men behind me. I was one of those who never came in until the crowd had lost interest and had begun to disperse. Perhaps I would have been more of a success as a long-distance runner if I had gone into training, and given up smoking and drinking, and kept regular hours.

But no. Three or four nights a week my fraternity brothers and I would go flying down in the black and roaring subway to 52nd Street, where we would crawl around the tiny, noisy and expensive nightclubs that had flowered on the sites of the old speakeasies in the cellars of those dirty brownstone houses. There we would sit, for hours, packed in those dark rooms, shoulder to shoulder with a lot of surly strangers and their girls, while the whole place rocked and surged with storms of jazz. There was no room to dance. We just huddled there between the blue walls, shoulder to shoulder and elbow to elbow, crouching and deafened and taciturn. If you moved your arm to get your drink you nearly knocked the next man off his stool. And the waiters fought their way back and forth through the sea of unfriendly heads, taking away the money of all the people.

It was not that we got drunk. No, it was this strange business of sitting in a room full of people and drinking without much speech, and letting yourself be deafened by the jazz that throbbed through the whole sea of bodies binding them all together in a kind of fluid medium. It was a strange, animal travesty of mysticism, sitting in those booming rooms, with the noise pouring through you, and the rhythm jumping and throbbing in the marrow of your bones. You couldn't call any of that, *per se*, a mortal sin. We just sat there, that was all. If we got hangovers the next day, it was more because of the smoking and nervous exhaustion than anything else.

How often, after a night of this, I missed all the trains home to Long Island and went and slept on a couch somewhere, at the Fraternity House, or in the apartment of somebody I knew around town. What was worst of all was going home on the subway, on the chance that one might catch a bus at Flushing! There is nothing so dismal as the Flushing bus station, in the grey, silent hour just before the coming of dawn. There were always at least one or two of those same characters whose prototypes I had seen dead in the morgue. And perhaps there would be a pair of drunken soldiers trying to get back to Fort Totten. Among all these I stood, weary and ready to fall, lighting the fortieth or fiftieth cigarette of the day—the one that took the last shreds of lining off my throat.

The thing that depressed me most of all was the shame and despair that invaded my whole nature when the sun came up, and all the laborers were going to work: men healthy and awake and quiet, with their eyes clear, and some rational purpose before them. This humiliation and sense of my own misery and of the fruitlessness of what I had done was the nearest I could get to contrition. It was the reaction of nature. It proved nothing except that I was still, at least, morally alive: or rather that I had still some faint capacity for moral life in me. The term "morally alive" might obscure the fact that I was spiritually dead. I had been that long since!

iv

In the fall of 1936 Pop died. The manner of his death was this. I had been on a geology field trip in Pennsylvania, and had come back, late one Sunday night after a long cold ride through New Jersey, back from the coal mines and the slate quarries, in an open Ford. The icy wind of the Delaware Water Gap was still in my flesh. I went to bed without seeing anybody. They were all in their rooms by the time I got home.

The next morning I looked in Pop's room, and he was sitting up in bed looking strangely unhappy and confused.

"How do you feel?" I said.

"Rotten," he answered. There was nothing surprising about that. He was always getting ill. I supposed he had caught another cold. I said:

"Take some more sleep, then."

"Yes," he said, "I guess I will."

I went back into the bathroom, and hastened to dress and drink my coffee and run for the train.

That afternoon I was on the track, in the pale November sun, taking an easy work-out. I came down the shady side of the field, in front of the library. There was one of the juniors who worked for the Yearbook standing behind the high wire fence, at the corner nearest John Jay, where the bushes and poplar trees were. As I came down to the bend he called out to me and I went over to the fence.

"Your aunt was on the phone just now," he told me. "She said your grandfather is dead."

There was nothing I could say.

I trotted back along the field and went down and took a quick shower and got into my clothes and went home. There was no train but one of those slow ones, that ambled out on to the Island half empty, with long stops at every station. But I knew there was no particular hurry. I could not bring him back to life.

Poor old Pop. I was not surprised that he was dead, or that he had died that way. I supposed his heart had failed. It was typical of him, that kind of death: he was always in a hurry, always ahead of time. And now, after a whole long lifetime of impatience, waiting for Bonnemaman to get ready to go to the theater, or to come to dinner, or to come down and open the Christmas presents, after all that, he had brooked no delay about dying. He had slipped out on us, in his sleep, without premeditation, on the spur of the moment.

I would miss Pop. In the last year or two we had drawn rather close together. He often got me to come to lunch with him downtown and there he would tell me all his troubles, and talk over the prospects for my future—I had returned to the old idea of becoming a newspaper man. There was a great deal of simplicity about Pop. It was a simplicity, an ingenuousness that belonged to his nature: and it was something peculiarly American. Or at least, it belonged to the Americans of his generation, this kind and warm-hearted and vast and universal optimism.

When I got to the house, I knew where I would find his body. I went up to his bed-room and opened the door. The only shock was to find that the windows were all open and the room was full of the cold November air. Pop, who in his life had feared all draughts and had lived in overheated houses, now lay under a sheet in this icy cold death-chamber. It was the first death that had been in the house that he had built for his family twenty-five years before.

Now a strange thing happened. Without my having thought about it, or debating about it in my mind, I closed the door and got on my knees by the bed and prayed. I suppose it was just the spontaneous response of my love for poor Pop—the obvious way to do something for him, to acknowledge all his goodness to me. And yet, I had seen other deaths without praying or being even drawn to pray. Two or three summers before an old relative of mine had died, and the only thing that had occurred to me was the observation that her lifeless corpse was no more than a piece of furniture.

I did not feel that there was anybody there, only a *thing*. This did not teach me what it taught Aristotle, about the existence of the soul . . .

But now I only wanted to pray.

Unfortunately, I knew that Bonnemaman was going to come in and tell me to look at the body, and soon I heard her steps in the hall. I got off my knees before she opened the door.

"Aren't you going to look at him?" she said to me.

I said nothing. She raised the corner of the sheet, and I looked at Pop's dead face. It was pale, and it was dead. She let the sheet fall back, and together we walked out of the room, and I sat and talked to her for an hour or so, while the sun was going down.

Everybody knew that now this would be the end of Bonnemaman too. Although our family had been one of those curious modern households in which everybody was continually arguing and fighting, and in which there had been for years an obscure and complicated network of contentions and suppressed jealousies, Bonnemaman had been tremendously attached to her husband. She soon began to languish, but it was months before she finally died.

First, she fell down and broke her arm. It mended slowly and painfully. But as it did, she turned into a bent and silent old woman, with a rather haggard face. When the summer came, she could no longer get out of bed. Then came the alarms at night when we thought she was dying, and stood for hours by her bed, listening to the harsh gasp in her throat. And then too I was praying, looking into the mute, helpless face she turned towards my face. This time I was more conscious of what I was doing, and I prayed for her to live, although in some sense it was obviously better that she should die.

I was saying, within myself: "You Who made her, let her go on living." The reason I said this was that life was the only good I was certain of. And if life was the one big value, the one chief reality, its continuance depended on the will (otherwise why pray?) of the supreme Principle of all life, the ultimate Reality, He Who is Pure Being. He Who is Life Itself. He Who, simply, is. By praying, I was implicitly acknowledging all this. And now twice I had prayed, although I continued to think I believed in nothing.

Bonnemaman lived. I hope it had something to do with grace, with something that was given to Bonnemaman from God, in those last weeks that she continued to live, speechless and helpless on her bed, to save her soul. Finally, in August, she died, and they took her away and made an end of her body like all the rest. That was the summer of 1937.

Pop had died in November 1936. Already, in that fall, I had begun to feel ill. Still I kept on trying to do all the things I was doing—following my courses, editing the Yearbook, working, and running on the Cross Country Team without going into training. . . .

One day we raced Army and Princeton. I was not last, but as usual I was about twenty-third or -fourth out of thirty or so. When I got to the end of the course, I simply fell down and lay on the ground, waiting for my stomach to turn inside out within me. I felt so bad that I did not even mind what the people thought. I did not try to look brave, or to make any jokes about myself, or to hide the way I felt. I lay there until I felt better, then I got up and went away, and never came back to the locker rooms again. The coach did not bother to come looking for me. Nobody tried to persuade me to go back on the team. We were all equally satisfied: I was through. However, it did not help much to get rid of this burden.

One day I was coming into town on the Long Island train. I had a bagful of work that was already late, and had to be handed in that day. After that, I had a date with someone with whom I liked very much to have a date. While the train was going through the freight yards in Long Island City my head suddenly began to swim. It was not that I was afraid of vomiting, but it was as if some center of balance within me had been unexpectedly removed, and as if I were about to plunge into a blind abyss of emptiness without end. I got up and stood in the gap between the cars to get some air, but my knees were shaking so much that I was afraid I would slip through the chains between the cars and end up under the wheels, so I got back and propped myself against the wall and held on. This strange vertigo came and went, while the train dived into the tunnel under the river, and everything around me went dark and began to roar. I think the business had passed over by the time we got to the station.

I was scared. And the first thing that occurred to me was to go and find the house physician in the Pennsylvania Hotel. He examined me and listened to my heart and took my blood pressure, and gave me something to drink and told me I was over-stimulated. What did I do for a living, he asked me. I told him I went to college and did quite a few other things besides. He told me to give some of them up. And then he suggested that I ought to go to bed and get some sleep, and then go home when I felt better.

So next I found myself in a room in the Pennsylvania Hotel, lying on a bed, trying to go to sleep. But I could not.

It was a small, narrow room, rather dark, even though the window seemed to occupy most of the wall that was in front of me. You could hear the noise of the traffic coming up from far below, on 32nd Street. But the room itself was quiet, with a quietness that was strange, ominous.

I lay on the bed and listened to the blood pounding rapidly inside my head. I could hardly keep my eyes closed. Yet I did not want to open them, either. I was afraid that if I even looked at the window, the strange spinning inside my head would begin again.

That window! It was huge. It seemed to go right down to the floor. Maybe the force of gravity would draw the whole bed, with me on it, to the edge of that abyss, and spill me headlong into the emptiness.

And far, far away in my mind was a little, dry, mocking voice that said: "What if you threw yourself out of that window. . . ."

I turned over on the bed, and tried to go to sleep. But the blood drummed and drummed in my head. I could not sleep.

I thought to myself: "I wonder if I am having a nervous breakdown."

Then, again, I saw that window. The mere sight of it made my head spin. The mere thought that I was high above the ground almost knocked me out again.

The doctor came in and saw me lying there wide awake and said: "I thought I told you to go to sleep."

"I couldn't sleep," I said. He gave me a bottle of medicine, and went away again. All I wanted was to get out of that room.

When he was gone, I got up and went downstairs and paid for the room and took a train home. I did not feel bad in the train going home. The house was empty. I lay down on a thing in the living room that they called the chaise-longue, and went to sleep.

When Else came home, she said: "I thought you were going to stay up town for dinner."

But I said: "I felt bad, so I came home."

What was the matter with me? I never found out. I suppose it was a sort of a nervous breakdown. In connection with it, I developed gastritis, and thought I was beginning to get a stomach ulcer.

The doctors gave me a diet and some medicine. The effect of both was more psychological than anything else. Every time I went to eat anything, I studied what was there, and only chose certain things and ate them with a sort of conscious scrupulosity. I remember one of the things that I was told to eat: it was ice-cream. I had no objection to eating ice-cream, especially in summer. How delightful not only to enjoy this dish, but also to feed my imagination with thoughts of its healthfulness and wholesomeness. I could almost see it kindly and blandly and mercifully covering the incipient ulcer with its cool, health-giving substance.

The whole result of this diet was to teach me this trivial amusement, this cult of foods that I imagined to be bland and healthful. It made me think about myself. It was a game, a hobby, something like psychoanalysis had been. I even sometimes fell into the discussion of foods and their values and qualities in relation to health, as if I were an authority on the subject. And for the rest, I went around with my mind in my stomach and ate quarts and quarts of ice-cream.

Now my life was dominated by something I had never really known before: fear. Was it really something altogether new? No, for fear is inseparable from pride and lust. They may hide it for a time: but it is the reverse of the coin. The coin had turned over and I was looking at the other side: the eagle that was to eat out my insides for a year or so, cheap Prometheus that I had become! It was humiliating, this strange wariness that accompanied all my actions, this self-conscious watchfulness. It was a humiliation I had deserved more than I knew. There was more justice in it than I could understand.

I had refused to pay any attention to the moral laws upon which all our vitality and sanity depend: and so now I was reduced to the condition of a silly old woman, worrying about a lot of imaginary rules of health, standards of food-value, and a thousand minute details of conduct that were in themselves completely ridiculous and stupid, and yet which haunted me with vague and terrific sanctions. If I eat this, I may go out of my mind. If I do not eat that, I may die in the night.

I had at last become a true child of the modern world, completely tangled up in petty and useless concerns with myself, and almost incapable of even considering or understanding anything that was really important to my own true interests.

Here I was, scarcely four years after I had left Oakham and walked out into the world that I thought I was going to ransack and rob of all its pleasures and satisfactions. I had done what I intended, and now I found that it was I who was emptied and robbed and gutted. What a strange thing! In filling myself, I had emptied myself. In grasping things, I had lost everything. In devouring pleasures and joys, I had found distress and anguish and fear. And now, finally, as a piece of poetic justice, when I was reduced to this extremity of misery and humiliation, I fell into a love affair in which I was at last treated in the way I had treated not a few people in these last years.

This girl lived on my own street, and I had the privilege of seeing her drive off with my rivals ten minutes after she had flatly refused to go out with me, asserting that she was tired and wanted to stay home. She did not even bother to conceal the fact that she found me amusing when there was nothing better to occupy her mind. She used to regale me with descriptions of what she considered to be a good time, and of the kind of people she admired and liked—they were precisely the shallow and superficial ones that gave me goose-flesh when I saw them sitting around in the Stork Club. And it was the will of God that for my just punishment I should take all this in the most abject meekness, and sit and beg like some kind of a pet dog until I finally got a pat on the head or some small sign of affection.

This could not last long, and it did not. But I came out of it chastened and abject, though not nearly as abject as I ought to have been, and returned to the almost equal humiliation of my quarts of ice-cream.

Such was the death of the hero, the great man I had wanted to be. Externally (I thought) I was a big success. Everybody knew who I was at Columbia. Those who had not yet found out, soon did when the Yearbook came out, full of pictures of myself. It was enough to tell them more about me than I intended, I suppose. They did not have to be very acute to see through the dumb self-satisfied expression in all those portraits. The only thing that surprises me is that no one openly reproached or mocked me for such ignominious vanity. No one threw any eggs at me, nobody said a word. And yet I know how capable they were of saying many words, not tastefully chosen, perhaps, but deadly enough.

The wounds within me were, I suppose, enough. I was bleeding to death.

If my nature had been more stubborn in clinging to the pleasures that disgusted me: if I had refused to admit that I was beaten by this futile search for satisfaction where it could not be found, and if my moral and nervous constitution had not caved in under the weight of my own emptiness, who can tell what would eventually have happened to me? Who could tell where I would have ended?

I had come very far, to find myself in this blind-alley: but the very anguish and helplessness of my position was something to which I rapidly succumbed. And it was my defeat that was to be the occasion of my rescue.

Part Two

1

With a Great Price

THERE IS A paradox that lies in the very heart of human existence. It must be apprehended before any lasting happiness is possible in the soul of a man. The paradox is this: man's nature, by itself, can do little or nothing to settle his most important problems. If we follow nothing but our natures, our own philosophies, our own level of ethics, we will end up in hell.

This would be a depressing thought, if it were not purely abstract. Because in the concrete order of things God gave man a nature that was ordered to a supernatural life. He created man with a soul that was made not to bring itself to perfection in its own order, but to be perfected by Him in an order infinitely beyond the reach of human powers. We were never destined to lead purely natural lives, and therefore we were never destined in God's plan for a purely natural beatitude. Our nature, which is a free gift of God, was given to us to be perfected and enhanced by another free gift that is not due it.

This free gift is "sanctifying grace." It perfects our nature with the gift of a life, an intellection, a love, a mode of existence infinitely above its own level. If a man were to arrive even at the abstract pinnacle of natural perfection, God's work would not even be half done: it would be only about to begin, for the real work is the work of grace and the infused virtues and the gifts of the Holy Ghost.

What is "grace"? It is God's own life, shared by us. God's life is Love. *Deus caritas est.* By grace we are able to share in the infinitely self-less love of Him Who is such pure actuality that He needs nothing and therefore cannot conceivably exploit anything for selfish ends. Indeed, outside of Him there is nothing, and whatever exists exists by His free gift of its being, so that one of the notions that is absolutely contradictory to the perfection of God is selfishness. It is metaphysically impossible for God to be selfish, because the existence of everything that is depends upon His gift, depends upon His unselfishness.

When a ray of light strikes a crystal, it gives a new quality to the crystal. And when God's infinitely disinterested love plays upon a human soul, the same kind of thing takes place. And that is the life called sanctifying grace.

The soul of man, left to its own natural level, is a potentially lucid crystal left in darkness. It is perfect in its own nature, but it lacks something that it can only receive from outside and above itself. But when the light shines in it, it becomes in a manner transformed into light and seems to lose its nature in the splendor of a higher nature, the nature of the light that is in it.

So the natural goodness of man, his capacity for love which must always be in some sense selfish if it remains in the natural order, becomes transfigured and transformed when the Love of God shines in it. What happens when a man loses himself completely in the Divine Life within him? This perfection is only for those who are called the saints—for those rather who *are* the saints and who live in the light of God alone. For the ones who are called saints by human opinion on earth may very well be devils, and their light may very well be darkness. For as far as the light of God is concerned, we are owls. It blinds us and as soon as it strikes us we are in darkness. People who look like saints to us are very often not so, and those who do not look like saints very often are. And the greatest saints are sometimes the most obscure—Our Lady, St. Joseph.

Christ established His Church, among other reasons, in order that men might lead one another to Him and in the process sanctify themselves and one another. For in this work it is Christ Who draws us to Himself through the action of our fellow men.

We must check the inspirations that come to us in the depths of our own conscience against the revelation that is given to us with divinely certain guarantees by those who have inherited in our midst the place of Christ's Apostles—by those who speak to us in the Name of Christ and as it were in His own Person. *Qui vos audit me audit; qui vos spernit, me spernit.*

When it comes to accepting God's own authority about things that cannot possibly be known in any other way except as revealed by His authority, people consider it insanity to incline their ears and listen. Things that cannot be known in any other way, they will not accept from this source. And yet they will meekly and passively accept the most appalling lies from newspapers when they scarcely need to crane their necks to see the truth in front of them, over the top of the sheet they are holding in their hands.

For example, the very thought of an *imprimatur* on the front of a book—the approbation of a bishop, allowing the book to be printed on the grounds that it contains safe doctrine—is something that drives some people almost out of their minds with indignation.

One day, in the month of February 1937, I happened to have five or ten loose dollars burning a hole in my pocket. I was on Fifth Avenue, for some reason or other, and was attracted by the window of Scribner's bookstore, all full of bright new books.

That year I had signed up for a course in French Medieval Literature. My mind was turning back, in a way, to the things I remembered from the old days in Saint Antonin. The deep, naive, rich simplicity of the twelfth and thirteenth centuries was beginning to speak to me again. I had written a paper on a legend of a "Jongleur de Notre Dame," compared with a story from the Fathers of the Desert, in Migne's *Latin Patrology*. I was being drawn back into the Catholic atmosphere, and I could feel the health of it, even in the merely natural order, working already within me.

Now, in Scribner's window, I saw a book called *The Spirit of Medieval Philosophy*. I went inside, and took it off the shelf, and looked at the table of contents and at the title page which was deceptive, because it said the book was made up of a series of lectures that had been given at the University of Aberdeen. That was no recommendation, to me especially. But it threw me off the track as to the possible identity and character of Etienne Gilson, who wrote the book.

I bought it, then, together with one other book that I have completely forgotten, and on my way home in the Long Island train, I unwrapped the package to gloat over my acquisitions. It was only then that I saw, on the first page of *The Spirit of Medieval Philosophy*, the small print which said: "Nihil Obstat . . . Imprimatur."

The feeling of disgust and deception struck me like a knife in the pit of the stomach. I felt as if I had been cheated! They should have warned me that it was a Catholic book! Then I would never have bought it. As it was, I was tempted to throw the thing out the window at the houses of Woodside—to get rid of it as something dangerous and unclean. Such is the terror that is aroused in the enlightened modern mind by a little innocent Latin and the signature of a priest. It is impossible to communicate, to a Catholic, the number and complexity of fearful associations that a little thing like this can carry with it. It is in Latin—a difficult, ancient and obscure tongue. That implies, to the mind that has roots in Protestantism, all kinds of sinister secrets, which the priests are supposed to cherish and to conceal from common men in this unknown language. Then, the mere fact that they should pass judgement on the character of a book, and permit people to read it: that in itself is fraught with terror. It immediately conjures up all the real and imaginary excesses of the Inquisition.

That is something of what I felt when I opened Gilson's book: for you must understand that while I admired Catholic *culture*, I had always been afraid of the Catholic Church. That is a rather common position in the world today. After all, I had not bought a book on medieval philosophy without realizing that it would be Catholic philosophy: but the imprimatur told me that what I read would be in full conformity with that fearsome and mysterious thing, Catholic Dogma, and the fact struck me with an impact against which everything in me reacted with repugnance and fear.

Now in the light of all this, I consider that it was surely a real grace that, instead of getting rid of the book, I actually read it. Not all of it, it is true: but more than I used to read of books that deep. When I think of the numbers of books I had on my shelf in the little room at Douglaston that had once been Pop's "den"—books which I had bought and never even read, I am more astounded than ever at the fact that I actually read this one: and what is more, remembered it.

And the one big concept which I got out of its pages was something that was to revolutionize my whole life. It is all contained in one of those dry, outlandish technical compounds that the scholastic philosophers were so prone to use: the word *aseitas*. In this one word, which can be applied to God alone, and which expresses His most characteristic attribute, I discovered an entirely new concept of God—a concept which showed me at once that the belief of Catholics was by no means the vague and rather superstitious hangover from an unscientific age that I had believed it to be. On the contrary, here was a notion of God that was at the same time deep, precise, simple and accurate and, what is more, charged with implications which I could not even begin to appreciate, but which I could at least dimly estimate, even with my own lack of philosophical training.

Aseitas—the English equivalent is a transliteration: aseity—simply means the power of a being to exist absolutely in virtue of itself, not as caused by itself, but as requiring no cause, no other justification for its existence except that its very nature is to exist. There can be only one such Being: that is God. And to say that God exists *a se*, of and by and by reason of Himself, is merely to say that God is Being Itself. *Ego sum qui sum.* And this means that God must enjoy "complete independence not only as regards everything outside but also as regards everything within Himself."

This notion made such a profound impression on me that I made a pencil note at the top of the page: "Aseity of God—God is being *per se*." I observe it now on the page, for I brought the book to the monastery with me, and although I was not sure where it had gone, I found it on the shelves in Father Abbot's room the other day, and I have it here before me.

I marked three other passages, so perhaps the best thing would be to copy them down. Better than anything I could say, they will convey the impact of the book on my mind.

> When God says that He is being [reads the first sentence so marked] and if what He says is to have any intelligible meaning to our minds, it can only mean this: that He is the pure act of existing.

Pure act: therefore excluding all imperfection in the order of existing. Therefore excluding all change, all "becoming," all beginning or end, all limitation. But from this fulness of existence, if I had been capable of considering it deeply enough, I would soon have found that the fulness of all perfection could easily be argued.

But another thing that struck me was an important qualification the author made. He distinguished between the concepts of *ens in genere*—the abstract notion of being in general—and *ens infinitum*, the concrete and real Infinite Being, Who, Himself, transcends all our conceptions. And so I marked the following words, which were to be my first step towards St. John of the Cross:

> Beyond all sensible images, and all conceptual determinations, God affirms Himself as the absolute act of being in its pure actuality. Our concept of God, a mere feeble analogue of a reality which overflows it in every direction, can be made explicit only in the judgement: Being is Being, an absolute positing of that which, lying beyond every object, contains in itself the sufficient reason of objects. And that is why we can rightly say that the very excess of positivity which hides the divine being from our eyes is nevertheless the light which lights up all the rest: *ipsa caligo summa est mentis illuminatio.*

His Latin quotation was from St. Bonaventure's *Itinerarium.*

The third sentence of Gilson's that I marked in those few pages read as follows:

When St. Jerome says that God is His own origin and the cause of His own substance, he does not mean, as Descartes does, that God in a certain way posits Himself in being by His almighty power as by a cause, but simply that we must not look outside of God for a cause of the existence of God.

I think the reason why these statements, and others like them, made such a profound impression on me, lay deep in my own soul. And it was this: I had never had an adequate notion of what Christians meant by God. I had simply taken it for granted that the God in Whom religious people believed, and to Whom they attributed the creation and government of all things, was a noisy and dramatic and passionate character, a vague, jealous, hidden being, the objectification of all their own desires and strivings and subjective ideals.

The truth is, that the concept of God which I had always entertained, and which I had accused Christians of teaching to the world, was a concept of a being who was simply impossible. He was infinite and yet finite; perfect and imperfect; eternal and yet changing—subject to all the variations of emotion, love, sorrow, hate, revenge, that men are prey to. How could this fatuous, emotional thing be without beginning and without end, the creator of all? I had taken the dead letter of Scripture at its very deadest, and it had killed me, according to the saying of St. Paul: "The letter killeth, but the spirit giveth life."

I think one cause of my profound satisfaction with what I now read was that God had been vindicated in my own mind. There is in every intellect a natural exigency for a true concept of God: we are born with the thirst to know and to see Him, and therefore it cannot be otherwise.

I know that many people are, or call themselves, "atheists" simply because they are repelled and offended by statements about God made in imaginary and metaphorical terms which they are not able to interpret and comprehend. They refuse these concepts of God, not because they despise God, but perhaps because they demand a notion of Him more perfect than they generally find: and because ordinary, figurative concepts of God could not satisfy them, they turn away and think that there are no other: or, worse still, they refuse to listen to philosophy, on the ground that it is nothing but a web of meaningless words spun together for the justification of the same old hopeless falsehoods.

What a relief it was for me, now, to discover not only that no idea of ours, let alone any image, could adequately represent God, but also that we *should not* allow ourselves to be satisfied with any such knowledge of Him.

The result was that I at once acquired an immense respect for Catholic philosophy and for the Catholic faith. And that last thing was the most important of all. I now at least recognized that faith was something that had a very definite meaning and a most cogent necessity.

If this much was a great thing, it was about all that I could do at the moment. I could recognize that those who thought about God had a good way of considering Him, and that those who believed in Him really believed in someone, and their faith was more than a dream. Further than that it seemed I could not go, for the time being.

How many there are in the same situation! They stand in the stacks of libraries and turn over the pages of St. Thomas's *Summa* with a kind of curious reverence. They talk in their seminars about "Thomas" and "Scotus" and "Augustine" and "Bonaventure" and they are familiar with Maritain and Gilson, and they have read all the poems of Hopkins—and indeed they know more about what is best in the Catholic literary and philosophical tradition than most Catholics ever do on this earth. They sometimes go to Mass, and wonder at the dignity and restraint of the old liturgy. They are impressed by the organization of a Church in which everywhere the priests, even the most un-gifted, are able to preach at least something of a tremendous, profound, unified doctrine, and to dispense mysteriously efficacious help to all who come to them with troubles and needs.

In a certain sense, these people have a better appreciation of the Church and of Catholicism than many Catholics have: an appreciation which is detached and intellectual and objective. But they never come into the Church. They stand and starve in the doors of the banquet—the banquet to which they surely realize that they are invited—while those more poor, more stupid, less gifted, less educated, sometimes even less virtuous than they, enter in and are filled at those tremendous tables.

When I had put this book down, and had ceased to think explicitly about its arguments, its effect began to show itself in my life. I began to have a desire to go to church—and a desire more sincere and mature and more deep-seated than I had ever had before. After all, I had never before had so great a need.

The only place I could think of was the Episcopal Church down the road, old Zion Church, among the locust trees, where Father had once played the organ. I think the reason for this was that God wanted me to climb back the way I had fallen down. I had come to despise the Church of England, the "Protestant Episcopal Church," and He wanted me to do away with what there was of pride and self-complacency even in that. He would not let me become a Catholic, having behind me a rejection of another church that was not the right kind of a rejection, but one that was sinful in itself, rooted in pride, and expressed in contumely.

This time I came back to Zion Church, not to judge it, not to condemn the poor minister, but to see if it could not do something to satisfy the obscure need for faith that was beginning to make itself felt in my soul.

It was a nice enough church. It was pleasant to sit there, in the pretty little white building, with the sun pouring through the windows, on Sunday mornings. The choir of surpliced men and women and the hymns we all sang did not exactly send me up into ecstasy: but at least I no longer made fun of them in my heart. And when it came time to say the Apostles' Creed, I stood up and said it, with the rest, hoping within myself that God would give me the grace someday to really believe it.

The minister was called Mr. Riley. Pop had always called him "Dr. Riley" to his great embarrassment. Despite the Irish name, he detested Catholics, like most Protestant ministers. He was always very friendly to me and used to get into conversations about intellectual matters and modern literature, even men like D. H. Lawrence with whom he was thoroughly familiar.

It seems that he counted very much on this sort of thing—considered it an essential part of his ministry to keep up with the latest books, and to be able to talk about them, to maintain contact with people by that means. But that was precisely one of the things that made the experience of going to his church such a sterile one for me. He did not like or understand what was considered most "advanced" in modern literature and, as a matter of fact, one did not expect him to; one did not demand that of him. Yet it was modern literature and politics that he talked about, not religion and God. You felt that the man did not know his vocation, did not know what he was supposed to be. He had taken upon himself some function in society which was not his and which was, indeed, not a necessary function at all.

When he did get around to preaching about some truth of the Christian religion, he practically admitted in the pulpit, as he did in private to anyone who cared to talk about it, that he did not believe most of these doctrines, even in the extremely diluted form in which they are handed out to Protestants. The Trinity? What did he want with the Trinity? And as for the strange medieval notions about the Incarnation, well, that was simply too much to ask of a reasonable man.

Once he preached a sermon on "Music at Zion Church" and sent me word that I must be sure to be there, for I would hear him make mention of my father. That is just about typical of Protestant pulpit oratory in the more "liberal" quarters. I went, dutifully, that morning, but before he got around to the part in which I was supposed to be personally interested, I got an attack of my head-spinning and went out into the air. When the sermon was being preached, I was sitting on the church steps in the sun, talking to the black-gowned verger, or whatever he was called. By the time I felt better, the sermon was over.

I cannot say I went to this church very often: but the measure of my zeal may be judged by the fact that I once went even in the middle of the week. I forget what was the occasion: Ash Wednesday or Holy Thursday. There were one or two women in the place, and myself lurking in one of the back benches. We said some prayers. It was soon over. By the time it was, I had worked up courage to take the train into New York and go to Columbia for the day.

ii

Now I come to speak of the real part Columbia seems to have been destined to play in my life in the providential designs of God. Poor Columbia! It was founded by sincere Protestants as a college predominantly religious. The only thing that remains of that is the university motto: *In lumine tuo videbimus lumen*—one of the deepest and most beautiful lines of the psalms. "In Thy light, we shall see light." It is, precisely, about grace. It is a line that might serve as the foundation stone of all Christian and Scholastic learning, and which simply has nothing whatever to do with the standards of education at modern Columbia. It might profitably be changed to *In lumine Randall videbimus Dewey*.

Yet, strangely enough, it was on this big factory of a campus that the Holy Ghost was waiting to show me the light, in His own light. And one of the chief means He used, and through which he operated, was human friendship.

God has willed that we should all depend on one another for our salvation, and all strive together for our own mutual good and our own common salvation. Scripture teaches us that this is especially true in the supernatural order, in the doctrine of the Mystical Body of Christ, which flows necessarily from Christian teaching on grace.

"You are the body of Christ and members one of another. . . . And the eye cannot say to the hand: I need not thy help: nor again the head to the feet, I have no need of you. . . . And if one member suffer anything, all the members suffer with it; and if one member glory all the others rejoice with it."

So now is the time to tell a thing that I could not realize then, but which has become very clear to me: that God brought me and a half a dozen others together at Columbia, and made us friends, in such a way that our friendship would work powerfully to rescue us from the confusion and the misery in which we had come to find ourselves, partly through our own fault, and partly through a complex set of circumstances which might be grouped together under the heading of the "modern world," "modern society." But the qualification "modern" is unnecessary and perhaps unfair. The traditional Gospel term, "the world," will do well enough.

All our salvation begins on the level of common and natural and ordinary things. (That is why the whole economy of the Sacraments, for instance, rests, in its material element, upon plain and ordinary things like bread and wine and water and salt and oil.) And so it was with me. Books and ideas and poems and stories, pictures and music, buildings, cities, places, philosophies were to be the materials on which grace would work. But these things are themselves not enough. The more fundamental instinct of fear for my own preservation came in, in a minor sort of a way, in this strange, half-imaginary sickness which nobody could diagnose completely.

The coming war, and all the uncertainties and confusions and fears that followed necessarily from that, and all the rest of the violence and injustice that were in the world, had a very important part to play. All these things were bound together and fused and vitalized and prepared for the action of grace, both in my own soul and in the souls of at least one or two of my friends, merely by our friendship and association together. And it fermented in our sharing of our own ideas and miseries and headaches and perplexities and fears and difficulties and desires and hangovers and all the rest.

I have already mentioned Mark Van Doren. It would not be exactly true to say that he was a kind of nucleus around whom this concretion of friends formed itself: that would not be accurate. Not all of us took his courses, and those who did, did not do so all at the same time. And yet nevertheless our common respect for Mark's sanity and wisdom did much to make us aware of how much we ourselves had in common.

Perhaps it was for me, personally, more than for the others, that Mark's course worked in this way. I am thinking of one particular incident.

It was the fall of 1936, just at the beginning of the new school year—on one of those first, bright, crazy days when everybody is full of ambition. It was the beginning of the year in which Pop was going to die and my own resistance would cave in under the load of pleasures and ambitions I was too weak to carry: the year in which I would be all the time getting dizzy, and in which I learned to fear the Long Island railroad as if it were some kind of a monster, and to shrink from New York as if it were the wide-open mouth of some burning Aztec god.

That day, I did not foresee any of this. My veins were still bursting with the materialistic and political enthusiasms with which I had first come to Columbia and, indeed, in line with their general direction, I had signed up for courses that were more or less sociological and economic and historical. In the obscurity of the strange, half-conscious semi-conversion that had attended my retreat from Cambridge, I had tended more and more to be suspicious of literature, poetry—the things towards which my nature drew me—on the grounds that they might lead to a sort of futile estheticism, a philosophy of "escape."

This had not involved me in any depreciation of people like Mark. However, it had just seemed more important to me that I should take some history course, rather than anything that was still left of his for me to take.

So now I was climbing one of the crowded stairways in Hamilton Hall to the room where I thought this history course was to be given. I looked in to the room. The second row was filled with the unbrushed heads of those who every day at noon sat in the *Jester* editorial offices and threw paper airplanes around the room or drew pictures on the walls.

Taller than them all, and more serious, with a long face, like a horse, and a great mane of black hair on top of it, Bob Lax meditated on some incomprehensible woe, and waited for someone to come in and begin to talk to them. It was when I had taken off my coat and put down my load of books that I found out that this was not the class I was supposed to be taking, but Van Doren's course on Shakespeare.

So I got up to go out. But when I got to the door I turned around again and went back and sat down where I had been, and stayed there. Later I went and changed everything with the registrar, so I remained in that class for the rest of the year.

It was the best course I ever had at college. And it did me the most good, in many different ways. It was the only place where I ever heard anything really sensible said about any of the things that were really fundamental—life, death, time, love, sorrow, fear, wisdom, suffering, eternity. A course in literature should never be a course in economics or philosophy or sociology or psychology: and I have explained how it was one of Mark's great virtues that he did not make it so. Nevertheless, the material of literature and especially of drama is chiefly human acts—that is, free acts, moral acts. And, as a matter of fact, literature, drama, poetry, make certain statements about these acts that can be made in no other way. That is precisely why you will miss all the deepest meaning of Shakespeare, Dante, and the rest if you reduce their vital and creative statements about life and men to the dry, matter-of-fact terms of history, or ethics, or some other science. They belong to a different order.

Nevertheless, the great power of something like *Hamlet, Coriolanus,* or the *Purgatorio* or Donne's *Holy Sonnets* lies precisely in the fact that they are a kind of commentary on ethics and psychology and even metaphysics, even theology. Or, sometimes, it is the other way 'round, and those sciences can serve as a commentary on these other realities, which we call plays, poems.

All that year we were, in fact, talking about the deepest springs of human desire and hope and fear; we were considering all the most important realities, not indeed in terms of something alien to Shakespeare and to poetry, but precisely in his own terms, with occasional intuitions of another order. And, as I have said, Mark's balanced and sensitive and clear way of seeing things, at once simple and yet capable of subtlety, being fundamentally scholastic, though not necessarily and explicitly Christian, presented these things in ways that made them live within us, and with a life that was healthy and permanent and productive. This class was one of the few things that could persuade me to get on the train and go to Columbia at all. It was, that year, my only health, until I came across and read the Gilson book.

It was this year, too, that I began to discover who Bob Lax was, and that in him was a combination of Mark's clarity and my confusion and misery—and a lot more besides that was his own.

To name Robert Lax in another way, he was a kind of combination of Hamlet and Elias. A potential prophet, but without rage. A king, but a Jew too. A mind full of tremendous and subtle intuitions, and every day he found less and less to say about them, and resigned himself to being inarticulate. In his hesitations, though without embarrassment or nervousness at all, he would often curl his long legs all around a chair, in seven different ways, while he was trying to find a word with which to begin. He talked best sitting on the floor.

And the secret of his constant solidity I think has always been a kind of natural, instinctive spirituality, a kind of inborn direction to the living God. Lax has always been afraid he was in a blind alley, and half aware that, after all, it might not be a blind alley, but God, infinity.

He had a mind naturally disposed, from the very cradle, to a kind of affinity for Job and St. John of the Cross. And I now know that he was born so much of a contemplative that he will probably never be able to find out how much.

To sum it up, even the people who have always thought he was "too impractical" have always tended to venerate him—in the way people who value material security unconsciously venerate people who do not fear insecurity.

In those days one of the things we had most in common, although perhaps we did not talk about it so much, was the abyss that walked around in front of our feet everywhere we went, and kept making us dizzy and afraid of trains and high buildings. For some reason, Lax developed an implicit trust in all my notions about what was good and bad for mental and physical health, perhaps because I was always very definite in my likes and dislikes. I am afraid it did not do him too much good, though. For even though I had my imaginary abyss, which broadened immeasurably and became ten times dizzier when I had a hangover, my ideas often tended to some particular place where we would hear this particular band and drink this special drink until the place folded up at four o'clock in the morning.

The months passed by, and most of the time I sat in Douglaston, drawing cartoons for the paper-cup business, and trying to do all the other things I was supposed to do. In the summer, Lax went to Europe, and I continued to sit in Douglaston, writing a long, stupid novel about a college football player who got mixed up in a lot of strikes in a textile mill.

I did not graduate that June, although I nominally belonged to that year's class: I had still one or two courses to take, on account of having entered Columbia in February. In the fall of 1937 I went back to school, then, with my mind a lot freer, since I was not burdened with any more of those ugly and useless jobs on the fourth floor. I could write and do the drawings I felt like doing for *Jester*.

I began to talk more to Lax and to Ed Rice who was now drawing better and funnier pictures than anybody else for the magazine. For the first time I saw Sy Freedgood, who was full of a fierce and complex intellectuality which he sometimes liked to present in the guise of a rather suspicious suavity. He was in love with a far more technical vocabulary than any of the rest of us possessed, and was working at something in the philosophy graduate school. Seymour used consciously to affect a whole set of different kinds of duplicity, of which he was proud, and he had carried the *mendacium jocosum* or "humorous lie" to its utmost extension and frequency. You could sometimes gauge the falsity of his answers by their promptitude: the quicker the falser. The reason for this was, probably, that he was thinking of something else, something very abstruse and far from the sphere of your question, and he could not be bothered to bring his mind all that way back, to think up the real answer.

For Lax and myself and Gibney there was no inconvenience about this, for two reasons. Since Seymour generally gave his false answers only to practical questions of fact, their falsity did not matter: we were all too impractical. Besides his false answers were generally more interesting than the truth. Finally, since we knew they were false anyway, we had the habit of seeing all his statements, in the common factual order by a kind of double standard, instituting a comparison between what he had said and the probable truth, and this cast many interesting and ironical lights upon life as a whole.

In his house at Long Beach, where his whole family lived in a state of turmoil and confusion, there was a large, stupid police dog that got in everybody's way with his bowed head and slapped-down ears and amiable, guilty look. The first time I saw the dog, I asked: "What's his name?"

"Prince," said Seymour, out of the corner of his mouth.

It was a name to which the beast responded gladly. I guess he responded to any name, didn't care what you called him, so flattered was he to be called at all, being as he knew an extremely stupid dog.

So I was out on the boardwalk with the dog, shouting: "Hey, Prince; hey, Prince!"

Seymour's wife, Helen, came along and heard me shouting all this and said nothing, imagining, no doubt, that it was some way I had of making fun of the brute. Later, Seymour or someone told me that "Prince" wasn't the dog's name, but they told me in such a way that I got the idea that his name was really "Rex." So for some time after that I called him: "Hey, Rex; hey, Rex!" Several months later, after many visits to the house, I finally learned that the dog was called nothing like Prince nor Rex, but "Bunky."

Moral theologians say that the *mendacium jocosum* in itself does not exceed a venial sin.

Seymour and Lax were rooming together in one of the dormitories, for Bob Gibney, with whom Lax had roomed the year before, had now graduated, and was sitting in Port Washington with much the same dispositions with which I had been sitting in Douglaston, facing a not too dissimilar blank wall, the end of his own blind-alley. He occasionally came in to town to see Dona Eaton who had a place on 112th Street, but no job, and was more cheerful about her own quandary than the rest of us, because the worst that could happen to her was that she would at last run completely out of money and have to go home to Panama.

Gibney was not what you would call pious. In fact, he had an attitude that would be commonly called impious, only I believe God understood well enough that his violence and sarcasms covered a sense of deep metaphysical dismay—an anguish that was real, though not humble enough to be of much use to his soul. What was materially impiety in him was directed more against common ideas and notions which he saw or considered to be totally inadequate, and maybe it subjectively represented a kind of oblique zeal for the purity of God, this rebellion against the commonplace and trite, against mediocrity, religiosity.

During the year that had passed, I suppose it must have been in the spring of 1937, both Gibney and Lax and Bob Gerdy had all been talking about becoming Catholics. Bob Gerdy was a very smart sophomore with the face of a child and a lot of curly hair on top of it, who took life seriously, and had discovered courses on Scholastic Philosophy in the graduate school, and had taken one of them.

Gibney was interested in Scholastic Philosophy in much the same way as James Joyce was—he respected its intellectuality, particularly that of the Thomists, but there was not enough that was affective about his interest to bring about any kind of a conversion.

For the three or four years that I knew Gibney, he was always holding out for some kind of a "sign," some kind of a sensible and tangible interior jolt from God, to get him started, some mystical experience or other. And while he waited and waited for this to come along, he did all the things that normally exclude and nullify the action of grace. So in those days, none of them became Catholics.

The most serious of them all, in this matter, was Lax: he was the one that had been born with the deepest sense of Who God was. But he would not make a move without the others.

And then there was myself. Having read *The Spirit of Medieval Philosophy* and having discovered that the Catholic conception of God was something tremendously solid, I had not progressed one step beyond this recognition, except that one day I had gone and looked up St. Bernard's *De Diligendo Deo* in the catalogue of the University Library. It was one of the books Gilson had frequently mentioned: but when I found that there was no good copy of it, except in Latin, I did not take it out.

Now it was November 1937. One day, Lax and I were riding downtown on one of those busses you caught at the corner of 110th Street and Broadway. We had skirted the southern edge of Harlem, passing along the top of Central Park, and the dirty lake full of rowboats. Now we were going down Fifth Avenue, under the trees. Lax was telling me about a book he had been reading, which was Aldous Huxley's *Ends and Means*. He told me about it in a way that made me want to read it too.

So I went to Scribner's bookstore and bought it, and read it, and wrote an article about it, and gave the article to Barry Ulanov who was editor of *Review* by that time. He accepted the article with a big Greek smile and printed it. The smile was on account of the conversion it represented, I mean the conversion in me, as well as in Huxley, although one of the points I tried to make was that perhaps Huxley's conversion should not have been taken as so much of a surprise.

Huxley had been one of my favorite novelists in the days when I had been sixteen and seventeen and had built up a strange, ignorant philosophy of pleasure based on all the stories I was reading. And now everybody was talking about the way Huxley had changed. The chatter was all the more pleasant because of Huxley's agnostic old grandfather—and his biologist brother. Now the man was preaching mysticism.

Huxley was too sharp and intelligent and had too much sense of humor to take any of the missteps that usually make such conversions look ridiculous and oafish. You could not laugh at him, very well—at least not for any one concrete blunder. This was not one of those Oxford Group conversions, complete with a public confession.

On the contrary, he had read widely and deeply and intelligently in all kinds of Christian and Oriental mystical literature, and had come out with the astonishing truth that all this, far from being a mixture of dreams and magic and charlatanism, was very real and very serious.

Not only was there such a thing as a supernatural order, but as a matter of concrete experience, it was accessible, very close at hand, an extremely near, an immediate and most necessary source of moral vitality, and one which could be reached most simply, most readily by prayer, faith, detachment, love.

The point of his title was this: we cannot use evil means to attain a good end. Huxley's chief argument was that we were using the means that precisely made good ends impossible to attain: war, violence, reprisals, rapacity. And he traced our impossibility to use the proper means to the fact that men were immersed in the material and animal urges of an element in their nature which was blind and crude and unspiritual.

The main problem is to fight our way free from subjection to this more or less inferior element, and to reassert the dominance of our mind and will: to vindicate for these faculties, for the spirit as a whole, the freedom of action which it must necessarily have if we are to live like anything but wild beasts, tearing each other to pieces. And the big conclusion from all this was: we must practice prayer and asceticism.

Asceticism! The very thought of such a thing was a complete revolution in my mind. The word had so far stood for a kind of weird and ugly perversion of nature, the masochism of men who had gone crazy in a warped and unjust society. What an idea! To deny the desires of one's flesh, and even to practice certain disciplines that punished and mortified those desires: until this day, these things had never succeeded in giving me anything but gooseflesh. But of course Huxley did not stress the physical angle of mortification and asceticism—and that was right, in so far as he was more interested in striking to the very heart of the matter, and showing the ultimate positive principle underlying the need for detachment.

He showed that this negation was not something absolute, sought for its own sake: but that it was a freeing a vindication of our real selves, a liberation of the spirit from limits and bonds that were intolerable, suicidal—from a servitude to flesh that must ultimately destroy our whole nature and society and the world as well.

Not only that, once the spirit was freed, and returned to its own element, it was not alone there: it could find the absolute and perfect Spirit, God. It could enter into union with Him: and what is more, this union was not something vague and metaphorical, but it was a matter of real experience. What that experience amounted to, according to Huxley, might or might not have been the nirvana of the Buddhists, which is the ultimate negation of all experience and all reality whatever: but anyway, somewhere along the line, he quoted proofs that it was and could be a real and positive experience.

The speculative side of the book—its strongest—was full, no doubt, of strange doctrines by reason of its very eclecticism. And the practical element, which was weak, inspired no confidence, especially when he tried to talk about a concrete social program. Huxley seemed not to be at home with the Christian term "Love" which sounded extraordinarily vague in his contexts—and which must nevertheless be the heart and life of all true mysticism. But out of it all I took these two big concepts of a supernatural, spiritual order, and the possibility of real, experimental contact with God.

Huxley was thought, by some people, to be on the point of entering the Church, but *Ends and Means* was written by a man who was not at ease with Catholicism. He quoted St. John of the Cross and St. Teresa of Avila indiscriminately with less orthodox Christian writers like Meister Eckhart: and on the whole he preferred the Orient. It seems to me that in discarding his family's tradition of materialism he had followed the old Protestant groove back into the heresies that make the material creation evil of itself, although I do not remember enough about him to accuse him of formally holding such a thing. Nevertheless, that would account for his sympathy for Buddhism, and for the nihilistic character which he preferred to give to his mysticism and even to his ethics. This also made him suspicious, as the Albigensians had been, and for the same reason, of the Sacraments and Liturgical life of the Church, and also of doctrines like the Incarnation.

With all that I was not concerned. My hatred of war and my

own personal misery in my particular situation and the general crisis of the world made me accept with my whole heart this revelation of the need for a spiritual life, an interior life, including some kind of mortification. I was content to accept the latter truth purely as a matter of theory: or at least, to apply it most vociferously to one passion which was not strong in myself, and did not need to be mortified: that of anger, hatred, while neglecting the ones that really needed to be checked, like gluttony and lust.

But the most important effect of the book on me was to make me start ransacking the university library for books on Oriental mysticism.

I remember those winter days, at the end of 1937 and the beginning of 1938, peaceful days when I sat in the big living room at Douglaston, with the pale sun coming in the window by the piano, where one of my father's water-colors of Bermuda hung on the wall.

The house was very quiet, with Pop and Bonnemaman gone from it, and John Paul away trying to pass his courses at Cornell. I sat for hours, with the big quarto volumes of the Jesuit Father Wieger's French translations of hundreds of strange Oriental texts.

I have forgotten the titles, even the authors, and I never understood a word of what they said in the first place. I had the habit of reading fast, without stopping, or stopping only rarely to take a note, and all these mysteries would require a great deal of thought, even were a man who knew something about them to puzzle them out. And I was completely unfamiliar with anything of the kind. Consequently, the strange great jumble of myths and theories and moral aphorisms and elaborate parables made little or no real impression on my mind, except that I put the books down with the impression that mysticism was something very esoteric and complicated, and that we were all inside some huge Being in whom we were involved and out of whom we evolved, and the thing to do was to involve ourselves back in to him again by a system of elaborate disciplines subject more or less to the control of our own will. The Ábsolute Being was an infinite, timeless, peaceful, impersonal Nothing.

The only practical thing I got out of it was a system for going to sleep, at night, when you couldn't sleep. You lay flat in bed, without a pillow, your arms at your sides and your legs straight out, and relaxed all your muscles, and you said to yourself:

"Now I have no feet, now I have no feet . . . no feet . . . no legs . . . no knees."

Sometimes it really worked: you did manage to make it feel as if your feet and legs and the rest of your body had changed into air and vanished away. The only section with which it almost never worked was my head: and if I had not fallen asleep before I got that far, when I tried to wipe out my head, instantly chest and stomach and legs and feet all came back to life with a most exasperating reality and I did not get to sleep for hours. Usually, however, I managed to get to sleep quite quickly by this trick. I suppose it was a variety of auto-suggestion, a kind of hypnotism, or else simply muscular relaxation, with the help of a little work on the part of an active fancy.

Ultimately, I suppose all Oriental mysticism can be reduced to techniques that do the same thing, but in a far more subtle and advanced fashion: and if that is true, it is not mysticism at all. It remains purely in the natural order. That does not make it evil, *per se*, according to Christian standards: but it does not make it good, in relation to the supernatural. It is simply more or less useless, except when it is mixed up with elements that are strictly diabolical: and then of course these dreams and annihilations are designed to wipe out all vital moral activity, while leaving the personality in control of some nefarious principle, either of his own, or from outside himself.

It was with all this in my mind that I went and received my diploma of Bachelor of Arts from one of the windows in the Registrar's office, and immediately afterwards put my name down for some courses in the Graduate School of English.

The experience of the last year, with the sudden collapse of all my physical energy and the diminution of the brash vigor of my worldly ambitions, had meant that I had turned in terror from the idea of anything so active and uncertain as the newspaper business. This registration in the graduate school represented the first remote step of a retreat from the fight for money and fame, from the active and worldly life of conflict and competition. If anything, I would now be a teacher, and live the rest of my life in the relative peace of a college campus, reading and writing books.

That the influence of the Huxley book had not, by any means, lifted me bodily out of the natural order overnight is evident from the fact that I decided to specialize in eighteenth century English Literature, and to choose my subject for a Master of Arts Thesis from somewhere in that century. As a matter of fact, I had already half decided upon a subject, by the time the last pile of dirty snow had melted from the borders of South Field. It was an unknown novelist of the second half of the eighteenth century called Richard Graves. The most important thing he wrote was a novel called the *Spiritual Quixote,* which was in the Fielding tradition, a satire on the more excited kind of Methodists and other sects of religious enthusiasts in England at that time.

I was to work under Professor Tyndall, and this would have been just his kind of a subject. He was an agnostic and rationalist who took a deep and amused interest in all the strange perversions of the religious instinct that our world has seen in the last five hundred years. He was just finishing a book on D. H. Lawrence which discussed, not too kindly, Lawrence's attempt to build up a synthetic, home-made religion of his own out of all the semi-pagan spiritual jetsam that came his way. All Lawrence's friends were very much annoyed by it when it was published. I remember that in that year one of Tyndall's favorite topics of conversation was the miracles of Mother Cabrini, who had just been beatified. He was amused by these, too, because, as for all rationalists, it was for him an article of faith that miracles cannot happen.

I remember with what indecision I went on into the spring, trying to settle the problem of a subject with finality. Yet the thing worked itself out quite suddenly: so suddenly that I do not remember what brought it about. One day I came running down out of the Carpenter Library, and passed along the wire fences by the tennis courts, in the sun, with my mind made up that there was only one possible man in the eighteenth century for me to work on: the one poet who had least to do with his age, and was most in opposition to everything it stood for.

I had just had in my hands the small, neatly printed Nonesuch Press edition of the *Poems of William Blake,* and I now knew what my thesis would probably be. It would take in his poems and some aspect of his religious ideas.

In the Columbia bookstore I bought the same edition of Blake, on credit. (I paid for it two years later.) It had a blue cover, and I suppose it is now hidden somewhere in our monastery library, the part to which nobody has access. And that is all right. I think the ordinary Trappist would be only dangerously bewildered by the "Prophetic Books," and those who still might be able to profit by Blake, have a lot of other things to read that are still better. For my own part, I no longer need him. He has done his work for me: and he did it very thoroughly. I hope that I will see him in heaven.

But oh, what a thing it was to live in contact with the genius and the holiness of William Blake that year, that summer, writing the thesis! I had some beginning of an appreciation of his greatness above the other men of his time in England: but from this distance, from the hill where I now stand, looking back I can really appreciate his stature.

To assimilate him to the men of the ending eighteenth century would be absurd. I will not do it: all those conceited and wordy and stuffy little characters! As for the other romantics: how feeble and hysterical their inspirations seem next to the tremendously genuine and spiritual fire of William Blake. Even Coleridge, in the rare moments when his imagination struck the pitch of true creativeness, was still only an artist, an imaginer, not a seer; a maker, but not a prophet.

Perhaps all the great romantics were capable of putting words together more sensibly than Blake, and yet he, with all his mistakes of spelling, turned out the greater poet, because his was the deeper and more solid inspiration. He wrote better poetry when he was twelve than Shelley wrote in his whole life. And it was because at twelve he had already seen, I think, Elias, standing under a tree in the fields south of London.

It was Blake's problem to try and adjust himself to a society that understood neither him nor his kind of faith and love. More than once, smug and inferior minds conceived it to be their duty to take this man Blake in hand and direct and form him, to try and canalize what they recognized as "talent" in some kind of a conventional channel. And always this meant the cold and heartless disparagement of all that was vital and real to him in art and in faith. There were years of all kinds of petty persecution, from many different quarters, until finally Blake parted from his would-be patrons, and gave up all hope of an alliance with a world that thought he was crazy, and went his own way.

It was when he did this, and settled down as an engraver for good, that the Prophetic Books were no longer necessary. In the latter part of his life, having discovered Dante, he came in contact, through him, with Catholicism, which he described as the only religion that really taught the love of God, and his last years were relatively full of peace. He never seems to have felt any desire to hunt out a priest in the England where Catholicism was still practically outlawed: but he died with a blazing face and great songs of joy bursting from his heart.

As Blake worked himself into my system, I became more and more conscious of the necessity of a vital faith, and the total unreality and unsubstantiality of the dead, selfish rationalism which had been freezing my mind and will for the last seven years. By the time the summer was over, I was to become conscious of the fact that the only way to live was to live in a world that was charged with the presence and reality of God.

To say that, is to say a great deal: and I don't want to say it in a way that conveys more than the truth. I will have to limit the statement by saying that it was still, for me, more an intellectual realization than anything else: and it had not yet struck down into the roots of my will. The life of the soul is not knowledge, it is love, since love is the act of the supreme faculty, the will, by which man is formally united to the final end of all his strivings—by which man becomes one with God.

iii

On the door of the room in one of the dormitories, where Lax and Sy Freedgood were living in a state of chaos, was a large grey picture, a lithograph print. Its subject was a man, a Hindu, with wide-open eyes and a rather frightened expression, sitting cross-legged in white garments. I asked about it, and I could not figure out whether the answer was derisive or respectful. Lax said someone had thrown a knife at the picture and the knife had bounced back and nearly cut all their heads off. In other words, he gave me to understand that the picture had something intrinsically holy about it: that accounted for the respect and derision manifested towards it by all my friends. This mixture was their standard acknowledgment of the supernatural, or what was considered to be supernatural. How that picture happened to get on that door in that room is a strange story.

It represented a Hindu messiah, a savior sent to India in our own times, called Jagad-Bondhu. His mission had to do with universal peace and brotherhood. He had died not very long before, and had left a strong following in India. He was, as it were, in the role of a saint who had founded a new religious Order, although he was considered more than a saint: he was the latest incarnation of the godhead, according to the Hindu belief in a multiplicity of incarnations.

In 1932 a big official sort of letter was delivered to one of the monasteries of this new "Order," outside of Calcutta. The letter came from the Chicago World's Fair, which was to be held in the following year. How they ever heard of this monastery, I cannot imagine. The letter was a formal announcement of a "World Congress of Religions." I am writing this all from memory but that is the substance of the story: they invited the abbot of this monastery to send a representative to Congress.

I get this picture of the monastery: it is called Sri Angan, meaning "the Playground." It consists of an enclosure and many huts or "cells," to use an Occidental term. The monks are quiet, simple men. They live what we would call a liturgical life, very closely integrated with the cycle of the seasons and of nature: in fact, the chief characteristic of their worship seems to be this deep, harmonious identification with all living things, in praising God. Their praise itself is expressed in songs, accompanied by drums and primitive instruments, flutes, pipes. There is much ceremonial dancing. In addition to that, there is a profound stress laid on a form of "mental prayer" which is largely contemplative. The monk works himself into it, by softly chanting lyrical aspirations to God and then remains in peaceful absorption in the Absolute.

For the rest, their life is extremely primitive and frugal. It is not so much what we would call austere. I do not think there are any fierce penances or mortifications. But nevertheless, the general level of poverty in Hindu society as a whole imposes on these monks a standard of living which most Occidental religious would probably find unlivable. Their clothes consist of a turban and something thrown around the body and a robe. No shoes. Perhaps the robe is only for travelling. Their food—some rice, a few vegetables, a piece of fruit.

Of all that they do, they attach most importance to prayer, to praising God. They have a well-developed sense of the power and efficacy of prayer, based on a keen realization of the goodness of God. Their whole spirituality is childlike, simple, primitive if you like, close to nature, ingenuous, optimistic, happy. But the point is, although it may be no more than the full flowering of the natural virtue of religion, with the other natural virtues, including a powerful natural charity, still the life of these pagan monks is one of such purity and holiness and peace, in the natural order, that it may put to shame the actual conduct of many Christian religious, in spite of their advantages of constant access to all the means of grace.

So this was the atmosphere into which the letter from Chicago dropped like a heavy stone. The abbot was pleased by the letter. He did not know what the Chicago World's Fair was. He did not understand that all these things were simply schemes for accumulating money. The "World Congress of Religions" appeared to him as something more than the fatuous scheme of a few restless, though probably sincere, minds. He seemed to see in it the first step towards the realization of the hopes of their beloved messiah, Jagad-Bondhu: world peace, universal brotherhood. Perhaps, now, all religions would unite into one great universal religion, and all men would begin to praise God as brothers, instead of tearing each other to pieces.

At any rate, the abbot selected one of his monks and told him that he was to go to Chicago, to the World Congress of Religions.

This was a tremendous assignment. It was something far more terrible than an order given, for instance, to a newly ordained Capuchin to proceed to a mission in India. That would merely be a matter of a trained missionary going off to occupy a place that had been prepared for him. But here was a little man who had been born at the edge of a jungle told to start out from a contemplative monastery and go not only into the world, but into the heart of a civilization the violence and materialism of which he could scarcely evaluate, and which raised gooseflesh on every square inch of his body. What is more, he was told to undertake this journey *without money*. Not that money was prohibited to him, but they simply did not have any. His abbot managed to raise enough to get him a ticket for a little more than half the distance. After that heaven would have to take care of him.

By the time I met this poor little monk who had come to America without money, he had been living in the country for about five years, and had acquired, of all things, the degree of Doctor of Philosophy from the University of Chicago. So that people referred to him as Doctor Bramachari, although I believe that Bramachari is simply a generic Hindu term for monk—and one that might almost be translated: "Little-Brother-Without-the-Degree-of-Doctor."

How he got through all the red tape that stands beween America and the penniless traveller is something that I never quite understood. But it seems that officials, after questioning him, being completely overwhelmed by his simplicity, would either do something dishonest in his favor, or else would give him a tip as to how to beat the various technicalities. Some of them even lent him fairly large sums of money. In any case he landed in America.

The only trouble was that he got to Chicago after the World Congress of Religions was all over.

By that time, one look at the Fair buildings, which were already being torn down, told him all he needed to know about the World Congress of Religions. But once he was there, he did not have much trouble. People would see him standing around in the middle of railway stations waiting for Providence to do something about his plight. They would be intrigued by his turban and white garments (which were partly concealed by a brown overcoat in winter). They observed that he was wearing a pair of sneakers, and perhaps that alone was enough to rouse their curiosity. He was frequently invited to give lectures to religious and social clubs, and to schools and colleges, and he more than once spoke from the pulpits of Protestant churches. In this way he managed to make a living for himself. Besides, he was always being hospitably entertained by people that he met, and he financed the stages of his journey by artlessly leaving his purse lying open on the living room table, at night, before his departure.

The open mouth of the purse spoke eloquently to the hearts of his hosts, saying: "As you see, I am empty," or, perhaps, "As you see, I am down to my last fifteen cents." It was often enough filled up in the morning. He got around.

How did he run into Sy Freedgood? Well, Seymour's wife was studying at Chicago, and she met Bramachari there, and then Seymour met Bramachari, and Bramachari came to Long Beach once or twice, and went out in Seymour's sailboat, and wrote a poem which he gave to Seymour and Helen. He was very happy with Seymour, because he did not have to answer so many stupid questions and, after all, a lot of the people who befriended him were cranks and semi-maniacs and theosophists who thought they had some kind of a claim on him. They wearied him with their eccentricities, although he was a gentle and patient little man. But at Long Beach he was left in peace, although Seymour's ancient grandmother was not easily convinced that he was not the hereditary enemy of the Jewish people. She moved around in the other room, lighting small religious lamps against the intruder.

It was the end of the school year, June 1938, when Lax and Seymour already had a huge box in the middle of the room, which they were beginning to pack with books, when we heard Bramachari was again coming to New York.

I went down to meet him at Grand Central with Seymour, and it was not without a certain suppressed excitement that I did so, for Seymour had me all primed with a superb selection of lies about Bramachari's ability to float in the air and walk on water. It was a long time before we found him in the crowd, although you would think that a Hindu in a turban and a white robe and a pair of Keds would have been a rather memorable sight. But all the people we asked, concerning such a one, had no idea of having seen him.

We had been looking around for ten or fifteen minutes, when a cat came walking cautiously through the crowd, and passed us by with a kind of a look, and disappeared.

"That's him," said Seymour. "He changed himself into a cat. Doesn't like to attract attention. Looking the place over. Now he knows we're here."

Almost at once, while Seymour was asking a porter if he had seen anything like Bramachari, and the porter was saying no, Bramachari came up behind us.

I saw Seymour swing around and say, in his rare, suave manner: "Ah, Bramachari, how are you!"

There stood a shy little man, very happy, with a huge smile, all teeth, in the midst of his brown face. And on the top of his head was a yellow turban with Hindu prayers written all over it in red. And, on his feet, sure enough: sneakers.

I shook hands with him, still worrying lest he give me some kind of an electric shock. But he didn't. We rode up to Columbia in the subway, with all the people goggling at us, and I was asking Bramachari about all the colleges he had been visiting. Did he like Smith, did he like Harvard? When we were coming out into the air at 116th Street, I asked him which one he liked best, and he told me that they were all the same to him: it had never occurred to him that one might have any special preference in such things.

I lapsed into a reverent silence and pondered on this thought.

I was now twenty-three years old and, indeed, I was more mature than that in some respects. Surely by now it ought to have dawned on me that places did not especially matter. But no, I was very much attached to places, and had very definite likes and dislikes for localities as such, especially colleges, since I was always thinking of finding one that was altogether pleasant to live and teach in.

After that, I became very fond of Bramachari, and he of me. We got along very well together, especially since he sensed that I was trying to feel my way into a settled religious conviction, and into some kind of a life that was centered, as his was, on God.

The thing that strikes me now is that he never attempted to explain his own religious beliefs to me—except some of the externals of the cult, and that was later on. He would no doubt have told me all I wanted to know, if I had asked him, but I was not curious enough. What was most valuable to me was to hear his evaluation of the society and religious beliefs he had come across in America: and to put all that down on paper would require another book.

He was never sarcastic, never ironical or unkind in his criticisms: in fact he did not make many judgements at all, especially adverse ones. He would simply make statements of fact, and then burst out laughing—his laughter was quiet and ingenuous, and it expressed his complete amazement at the very possibility that people should live the way he saw them living all around him.

He was beyond laughing at the noise and violence of American city life and all the obvious lunacies like radio-programs and bill-board advertising. It was some of the well-meaning idealisms that he came across that struck him as funny. And one of the things that struck him as funniest of all was the eagerness with which Protestant ministers used to come up and ask him if India was by now nearly converted to Protestantism. He used to tell us how far India was from conversion to Protestantism—or Catholicism for that matter. One of the chief reasons he gave for the failure of any Christian missionaries to really strike deep into the tremendous populations of Asia was the fact that they maintained themselves on a social level that was too far above the natives. The Church of England, indeed, thought they would convert the Indians by maintaining a strict separation—white men in one church, natives in a different church: both of them listening to sermons on brotherly love and unity.

But all Christian missionaries, according to him, suffered from this big drawback: they lived too well, too comfortably. They took care of themselves in a way that simply made it impossible for the Hindus to regard them as holy—let alone the fact that they ate meat, which made them repugnant to the natives.

I don't know anything about missionaries: but I am sure that, by our own standards of living, their life is an arduous and difficult one, and certainly not one that could be regarded as comfortable. And by comparison with life in Europe and America it represents a tremendous sacrifice. Yet I suppose it would literally endanger their lives if they tried to subsist on the standard of living with which the vast majority of Asiatics have to be content. It seems hard to expect them to go around barefoot and sleep on mats and live in huts. But one thing is certain: the pagans have their own notions of holiness, and it is one that includes a prominent element of asceticism. According to Bramachari, the prevailing impression among the Hindus seems to be that Christians don't know what asceticism means. Of course, he was talking principally of Protestant missionaries, but I suppose it would apply to anyone coming to a tropical climate from one of the so-called "civilized" countries.

For my own part, I see no reason for discouragement. Bramachari was simply saying something that has long since been familiar to readers of the Gospels. Unless the grain of wheat, falling in the ground, die, itself remaineth alone: but if it die, it bringeth forth much fruit. The Hindus are not looking for us to send them men who will build schools and hospitals, although those things are good and useful in themselves—and perhaps very badly needed in India: they want to know if we have any saints to send them.

There is no doubt in my mind that plenty of our missionaries are saints: and that they are capable of becoming greater saints too. And that is all that is needed. And, after all, St. Francis Xavier converted hundreds of thousands of Hindus in the sixteenth century and established Christian societies in Asia strong enough to survive for several centuries without any material support from outside the Catholic world.

Bramachari was not telling me anything I did not know about the Church of England, or about the other Protestant sects he had come in contact with. But I was interested to hear his opinion of the Catholics. They, of course, had not invited him to preach in their pulpits: but he had gone into a few Catholic churches out of curiosity. He told me that these were the only ones in which he really felt that people were praying.

It was only there that religion seemed to have achieved any degree of vitality, among us, as far as he could see. It was only to Catholics that the love of God seemed to be a matter of real concern, something that struck deep in their natures, not merely pious speculation and sentiment.

However, when he described his visit to a big Benedictine monastery in the Mid-West he began to grin again. He said they had showed him a lot of workshops and machinery and printing presses and taken him over the whole "plant" as if they were very wrapped up in all their buildings and enterprises. He got the impression that they were more absorbed in printing and writing and teaching than they were in praying.

Bramachari was not the kind of man to be impressed with such statements as: "There's a quarter of a million dollars' worth of stained glass in this church . . . the organ has got six banks of keys and it contains drums, bells and a mechanical nightingale . . . and the retable is a genuine bas-relief by a real live Italian artist."

The people he had the least respect for were all the borderline cases, the strange, eccentric sects, the Christian Scientists, the Oxford Group and all the rest of them. That was, in a sense, very comforting. Not that I was worried about them: but it confirmed me in my respect for him.

He did not generally put his words in the form of advice: but the one counsel he did give me is something that I will not easily forget: "There are many beautiful mystical books written by the Christians. You should read St. Augustine's *Confessions*, and *The Imitation of Christ*."

Of course I had heard of both of them: but he was speaking as if he took it for granted that most people in America had no idea that such books ever existed. He seemed to feel as if he were in possession of a truth that would come to most Americans as news—as if there was something in their own cultural heritage that they had long since forgotten: and he could remind them of it. He repeated what he had said, not without a certain earnestness:

"Yes, you must read those books."

It was not often that he spoke with this kind of emphasis.

Now that I look back on those days, it seems to me very probable that one of the reasons why God had brought him all the way from India, was that he might say just that.

After all, it is rather ironical that I had turned, spontaneously to the east, in reading about mysticism, as if there were little or nothing in the Christian tradition. I remember that I ploughed through those heavy tomes of Father Wieger's with the feeling that all this represented the highest development of religion on earth. The reason may have been that I came away from Huxley's *Ends and Means* with the prejudice that Christianity was a less pure religion, because it was more "immersed in matter"—that is, because it did not scorn to use a Sacramental liturgy that relied on the appeal of created things to the senses in order to raise the souls of men to higher things.

So now I was told that I ought to turn to the Christian tradition, to St. Augustine—and told by a Hindu monk!

Still, perhaps if he had never given me that piece of advice, I would have ended up in the Fathers of the Church and Scholasticism after all: because a fortunate discovery in the course of my work on my M.A. thesis put me fairly and definitely on that track at last.

That discovery was one book that untied all the knots in the problem which I had set myself to solve by my thesis. It was Jacques Maritain's *Art and Scholasticism.*

iv

The last week of that school year at Columbia had been rather chaotic. Lax and Freedgood had been making futile efforts to get their belongings together and go home. Bramachari was living in their room, perched on top of a pile of books. Lax was trying to finish a novel for Professor Nobbe's course in novel-writing, and all his friends had volunteered to take a section of the book and write it, simultaneously: but in the end the book turned out to be more or less a three-cornered affair—by Lax and me and Dona Eaton. When Nobbe got the thing in his hands he could not figure it out at all, but he gave us a B-minus, with which we were more than satisfied.

Then Lax's mother had come to town to live near him in the last furious weeks before graduation and catch him if he collapsed. He had to take most of his meals in the apartment she had rented in Butler Hall. I sometimes went along and helped him nibble the various health-foods.

At the same time, we were planning to get a ride on an oil barge up the Hudson and the Erie Canal to Buffalo—because Lax's brother-in-law was in the oil business. After that we would go to the town where Lax lived, which was Olean, up in that corner of New York state.

On "Class Day" we leaned out the window of Lax's room and drank a bottle of champagne, looking at the sun on South Field, and watching the people beginning to gather under the trees in front of Hamilton, where we would all presently hear some speeches and shake hands with Nicholas Murray Butler.

It was not my business to graduate that June at all. My graduation was all over when I picked up my degree in the registrar's office last February. However, I borrowed the cap and gown with which Dona Eaton had graduated from Barnard a year before, and went and sat with all the rest, mocking the speeches, with the edge of my sobriety slightly dulled by the celebration that had just taken place with the champagne in Furnald.

Finally we all got up and filed slowly up the rickety wooden steps to the temporary platform to shake hands with all the officials. President Butler was a much smaller man than I had expected. He looked intensely miserable, and murmured something or other to each student, as he shook hands. It was inaudible. I was given to understand that for the past six or seven years people had been in the habit of insulting him, on these occasions, as a kind of a farewell.

I didn't say anything. I just shook his hand, and passed on. The next one I came to was Dean Hawkes who looked up with surprise, from under his bushy white eyebrows, and growled:

"What are *you* doing here, anyway?"

I smiled and passed on.

We did not get the ride on the oil barge, after all, but went to Olean on a train, and for the first time I saw a part of the world in which I was one day going to learn how to be very happy—and that day was not now very far away.

It is the association of that happiness which makes upper New York state seem, in my memory, to be so beautiful. But it is objectively so, there is no doubt of that. Those deep valleys and miles and miles of high, rolling wooded hills: the broad fields, the big red barns, the white farm houses and the peaceful towns: all this looked more and more impressive and fine in the long slanting rays of the sinking sun after we had passed Elmira.

And you began to get some of the feeling of the bigness of America, and to develop a continental sense of the scope of the country and of the vast, clear sky, as the train went on for mile after mile, and hour after hour. And the color, and freshness, and bigness, and richness of the land! The cleanness of it. The wholesomeness. This was new and yet it was old country. It was mellow country. It had been cleared and settled for much more than a hundred years.

When we got out at Olean, we breathed its health and listened to its silence.

I did not stay there for more than a week, being impatient to get back to New York on account of being, as usual, in love.

But one of the things we happened to do was to turn off the main road, one afternoon on the way to the Indian reservation, to look at the plain brick buildings of a college that was run by the Franciscans.

It was called St. Bonaventure's. Lax had a good feeling about the place. And his mother was always taking courses there, in the evenings—courses in literature from the Friars. He was a good friend of the Father Librarian and liked the library. We drove in to the grounds and stopped by one of the buildings.

But when Lax tried to make me get out of the car, I would not.

"Let's get out of here," I said.

"Why? It's a nice place."

"It's O.K., but let's get out of here. Let's go to the Indian reservation."

"Don't you want to see the library?"

"I can see enough of it from here. Let's get going."

I don't know what was the matter. Perhaps I was scared of the thought of nuns and priests being all around me—the elemental fear of the citizen of hell, in the presence of anything that savors of the religious life, religious vows, official dedication to God through Christ. Too many crosses. Too many holy statues. Too much quiet and cheerfulness. Too much pious optimism. It made me very uncomfortable. I had to flee.

When I got back to New York, one of the first things I did was to break away, at last, from the household in Douglaston. The family had really practically dissolved with the death of my grandparents, and I could get a lot more work done if I did not have to spend so much time on subways and the Long Island train.

One rainy day in June, then, I made a bargain with Herb, the colored taximan at Douglaston, and he drove me and all my bags and books and my portable vic and all my hot records and pictures to put on the wall and even a tennis racquet which I never used, uptown to a rooming-house on 114th Street, just behind the Columbia library.

All the way up we discussed the possible reasons for the mysterious death of Rudolph Valentino, once a famous movie star: but it was certainly not what you would call a live issue. Valentino had died at least ten years before.

"This is a nice spot you got here," said Herb, approving of the room I was renting for seven-fifty a week. It was shiny and clean and filled with new furniture and had a big view of a pile of coal, in a yard by the campus tennis courts, with South Field and the steps of the old domed library beyond. The panorama even took in a couple of trees.

"I guess you're going to have a pretty hot time, now you got away from your folks," Herb remarked, as he took his leave.

Whatever else may have happened in that room, it was also there that I started to pray again more or less regularly, and it was there that I added, as Bramachari had suggested, *The Imitation of Christ* to my books, and it was from there that I was eventually to be driven out by an almost physical push, to go and look for a priest.

July came, with its great, misty heats, and Columbia filled with all the thousands of plump, spectacled ladies in pink dresses, from the Middle-West, and all the grey gents in seersucker suits, all the dried-up high-school principals from Indiana and Kansas and Iowa and Tennessee, with their veins shrivelled up with positivism and all the reactions of the behaviorist flickering behind their spectacles as they meditated on the truths they learned in those sweltering halls.

The books piled higher and higher on my desk in the Graduate reading room and in my own lodgings. I was in the thick of my thesis, making hundreds of mistakes that I would not be able to detect for several years to come, because I was far out of my depth. Fortunately, nobody else detected them either. But for my own part, I was fairly happy, and learning many things. The discipline of the work itself was good for me, and helped to cure me, more than anything else did, of the illusion that my health was poor.

And it was in the middle of all this that I discovered Scholastic philosophy.

The subject I had finally chosen was "Nature and Art in William Blake." I did not realize how providential a subject it actually was! What it amounted to, was a study of Blake's reaction against every kind of literalism and naturalism and narrow, classical realism in art, because of his own ideal which was essentially mystical and supernatural. In other words, the topic, if I treated it at all sensibly, could not help but cure me of all the naturalism and materialism in my own philosophy, besides resolving all the inconsistencies and self-contradictions that had persisted in my mind for years, without my being able to explain them.

After all, from my very childhood, I had understood that the artistic experience, at its highest, was actually a natural analogue of mystical experience. It produced a kind of intuitive perception of reality through a sort of affective identification with the object contemplated—the kind of perception that the Thomists call "connatural." This means simply a knowledge that comes about as it were by the identification of natures: in the way that a chaste man understands the nature of chastity because of the very fact that his soul is full of it—it is a part of his own nature, since habit is second nature. Non-connatural knowledge of chastity would be that of a philosopher who, to borrow the language of the *Imitation*, would be able to define it, but would not possess it.

I had learned from my own father that it was almost blasphemy to regard the function of art as merely to reproduce some kind of a sensible pleasure or, at best, to stir up the emotions to a transitory thrill. I had always understood that art was contemplation, and that it involved the action of the highest faculties of man.

When I was once able to discover the key to Blake, in his rebellion against literalism and naturalism in art, I saw that his Prophetic Books and the rest of his verse at large represented a rebellion against naturalism in the moral order as well.

What a revelation that was! For at sixteen I had imagined that Blake, like the other romantics, was glorifying passion, natural energy, for their own sake. Far from it! What he was glorifying was the transfiguration of man's natural love, his natural powers, in the refining fires of mystical experience: and that, in itself, implied an arduous and total purification, by faith and love and desire, from all the petty materialistic and commonplace and earthly ideals of his rationalistic friends.

Blake, in his sweeping consistency, had developed a moral insight that cut through all the false distinctions of a worldly and interested morality. That was why he saw that, in the legislation of men, some evils had been set up as standards of right by which other evils were to be condemned: and the norms of pride or greed had been established in the judgement seat, to pronounce a crushing and inhuman indictment against all the normal healthy strivings of human nature. Love was outlawed, and became lust, pity was swallowed up in cruelty, and so Blake knew how:

> The harlot's cry from street to street
> Shall weave old England's winding-sheet.

I had heard that cry and that echo. I had seen that winding sheet. But I had understood nothing of all that. I had tried to resolve it into a matter of sociological laws, of economic forces. If I had been able to listen to Blake in those old days, he would have told me that sociology and economics, divorced from faith and charity, become nothing but the chains of his aged, icy demon Urizen! But now, reading Maritain, in connection with Blake, I saw all these difficulties and contradictions disappear.

I, who had always been anti-naturalistic in art, had been a pure naturalist in the moral order. No wonder my soul was sick and torn apart: but now the bleeding wound was drawn together by the notion of Christian virtue, ordered to the union of the soul with God.

The word virtue: what a fate it has had in the last three hundred years! The fact that it is nowhere near so despised and ridiculed in Latin countries is a testimony to the fact that it suffered mostly from the mangling it underwent at the hands of Calvinists and Puritans. In our own days the word leaves on the lips of cynical high-school children a kind of flippant smear, and it is exploited in theaters for the possibilities it offers for lewd and cheesy sarcasm. Everybody makes fun of virtue, which now has, as its primary meaning, an affectation of prudery practiced by hypocrites and the impotent.

When Maritain—who is by no means bothered by such trivialities—in all simplicity went ahead to use the term in its Scholastic sense, and was able to apply it to art, a "virtue of the practical intellect," the very newness of the context was enough to disinfect my mind of all the miasmas left in it by the ordinary prejudice against "virtue" which, if it was ever strong in anybody, was strong in me. I was never a lover of Puritanism. Now at last I came around to the sane conception of virtue—without which there can be no happiness, because virtues are precisely the powers by which we can come to acquire happiness: without them, there can be no joy, because they are the habits which coordinate and canalize our natural energies and direct them to the harmony and perfection and balance, the unity of our nature with itself and with God, which must, in the end, constitute our everlasting peace.

By the time I was ready to begin the actual writing of my thesis, that is, around the beginning of September 1938, the groundwork of conversion was more or less complete. And how easily and sweetly it had all been done, with all the external graces that had been arranged, along my path, by the kind Providence of God! It had taken little more than a year and a half, counting from the time I read Gilson's *The Spirit of Medieval Philosophy* to bring me up from an "atheist"—as I considered myself—to one who accepted all the full range and possibilities of religious experience right up to the highest degree of glory.

I not only accepted all this, intellectually, but now I began to desire it. And not only did I begin to desire it, but I began to do so efficaciously: I began to want to take the necessary means to achieve this union, this peace. I began to desire to dedicate my life to God, to His service. The notion was still vague and obscure, and it was ludicrously impractical in the sense that I was already dreaming of mystical union when I did not even keep the simplest rudiments of the moral law. But nevertheless I was convinced of the reality of the goal, and confident that it could be achieved: and whatever element of presumption was in this confidence I am sure God excused, in His mercy, because of my stupidity and helplessness, and because I was really beginning to be ready to do whatever I thought He wanted me to do to bring me to Him.

But, oh, how blind and weak and sick I was, although I thought I saw where I was going, and half understood the way! How deluded we sometimes are by the clear notions we get out of books. They make us think that we really understand things of which we have no practical knowledge at all. I remember how learnedly and enthusiastically I could talk for hours about mysticism and the experimental knowledge of God, and all the while I was stoking the fires of the argument with Scotch and soda.

That was the way it turned out that Labor Day, for instance. I went to Philadelphia with Joe Roberts, who had a room in the same house as I, and who had been through all the battles on the Fourth Floor of John Jay for the past four years. He had graduated and was working on some trade magazine about women's hats. All one night we sat, with a friend of his, in a big dark roadhouse outside of Philadelphia, arguing and arguing about mysticism, and smoking more and more cigarettes and gradually getting drunk. Eventually, filled with enthusiasm for the purity of heart which begets the vision of God, I went on with them into the city, after the closing of the bars, to a big speak-easy where we completed the work of getting plastered.

My internal contradictions were resolving themselves out, indeed, but still only on the plane of theory, not of practice: not for lack of good-will, but because I was still so completely chained and fettered by my sins and my attachments.

I think that if there is one truth that people need to learn, in the world, especially today, it is this: the intellect is only theoretically independent of desire and appetite in ordinary, actual practice. It is constantly being blinded and perverted by the ends and aims of passion, and the evidence it presents to us with such a show of impartiality and objectivity is fraught with interest and propaganda. We have become marvelous at self-delusion; all the more so, because we have gone to such trouble to convince ourselves of our own absolute infallibility. The desires of the flesh—and by that I mean not only sinful desires, but even the ordinary, normal appetites for comfort and ease and human respect, are fruitful sources of every kind of error and misjudgement, and because we have these yearnings in us, our intellects (which, if they operated all alone in a vacuum, would indeed, register with pure impartiality what they saw) present to us everything distorted and accommodated to the norms of our desire.

And therefore, even when we are acting with the best of intentions, and imagine that we are doing great good, we may be actually doing tremendous material harm and contradicting all our good intentions. There are ways that seem to men to be good, the end whereof is in the depths of hell.

The only answer to the problem is grace, grace, docility to grace. I was still in the precarious position of being my own guide and my own interpreter of grace. It is a wonder I ever got to the harbor at all!

Sometime in August, I finally answered an impulsion that had been working on me for a long time. Every Sunday, I had been going out on Long Island to spend the day with the same girl who had brought me back in such a hurry from Lax's town Olean. But every week, as Sunday came around, I was filled with a growing desire to stay in the city and go to some kind of a church.

At first, I had vaguely thought I might try to find some Quakers, and go and sit with them. There still remained in me something of the favorable notion about Quakers that I had picked up as a child, and which the reading of William Penn had not been able to overcome.

But, naturally enough, with the work I was doing in the library, a stronger drive began to assert itself, and I was drawn much more imperatively to the Catholic Church. Finally the urge became so strong that I could not resist it. I called up my girl and told her that I was not coming out that week-end, and made up my mind to go to Mass for the first time in my life.

The first time in my life! That was true. I had lived for several years on the continent, I had been to Rome, I had been in and out of a thousand Catholic cathedrals and churches, and yet I had never heard Mass. If anything had ever been going on in the churches I visited, I had always fled, in wild Protestant panic.

I will not easily forget how I felt that day. First, there was this sweet, strong, gentle, clean urge in me which said: "Go to Mass! Go to Mass!" It was something quite new and strange, this voice that seemed to prompt me, this firm, growing interior conviction of what I needed to do. It had a suavity, a simplicity about it that I could not easily account for. And when I gave in to it, it did not exult over me, and trample me down in its raging haste to land on its prey, but it carried me forward serenely and with purposeful direction.

That does not mean that my emotions yielded to it altogether quietly. I was really still a little afraid to go to a Catholic church, of set purpose, with all the other people, and dispose myself in a pew, and lay myself open to the mysterious perils of that strange and powerful thing they called their "Mass."

God made it a very beautiful Sunday. And since it was the first time I had ever really spent a sober Sunday in New York, I was surprised at the clean, quiet atmosphere of the empty streets uptown. The sun was blazing bright. At the end of the street, as I came out the front door, I could see a burst of green, and the blue river and the hills of Jersey on the other side.

Broadway was empty. A solitary trolley came speeding down in front of Barnard College and past the School of Journalism. Then, from the high, grey, expensive tower of the Rockefeller Church, huge bells began to boom. It served very well for the eleven o'clock Mass at the little brick Church of Corpus Christi, hidden behind Teachers College on 121st Street.

How bright the little building seemed. Indeed, it was quite new. The sun shone on the clean bricks. People were going in the wide open door, into the cool darkness and, all at once, all the churches of Italy and France came back to me. The richness and fulness of the atmosphere of Catholicism that I had not been able to avoid apprehending and loving as a child, came back to me with a rush: but now I was to enter into it fully for the first time. So far, I had known nothing but the outward surface.

It was a gay, clean church, with big plain windows and white columns and pilasters and a well-lighted, simple sanctuary. Its style was a trifle eclectic, but much less perverted with incongruities than the average Catholic church in America. It had a kind of a seventeenth-century, oratorian character about it, though with a sort of American colonial tinge of simplicity. The blend was effective and original: but although all this affected me, without my thinking about it, the thing that impressed me most was that the place was full, absolutely full. It was full not only of old ladies and broken-down gentlemen with one foot in the grave, but of men and women and children young and old—especially young: people of all classes, and all ranks on a solid foundation of workingmen and -women and their families.

I found a place that I hoped would be obscure, over on one side, in the back, and went to it without genuflecting, and knelt down. As I knelt, the first thing I noticed was a young girl, very pretty too, perhaps fifteen or sixteen, kneeling straight up and praying quite seriously. I was very much impressed to see that someone who was young and beautiful could with such simplicity make prayer the real and serious and principal reason for going to church. She was clearly kneeling that way because she meant it, not in order to show off, and she was praying with an absorption which, though not the deep recollection of a saint, was serious enough to show that she was not thinking at all about the other people who were there.

What a revelation it was, to discover so many ordinary people in a place together, more conscious of God than of one another: not there to show off their hats or their clothes, but to pray, or at least to fulfil a religious obligation, not a human one. For even those who might have been there for no better motive than that they were obliged to be, were at least free from any of the self-conscious and human constraint which is never absent from a Protestant church where people are definitely gathered together as people, as neighbors, and always have at least half an eye for one another, if not all of both eyes.

Since it was summer time, the eleven o'clock Mass was a Low Mass: but I had not come expecting to hear music. Before I knew it, the priest was in the sanctuary with the two altar boys, and was busy at the altar with something or other which I could not see very well, but the people were praying by themselves, and I was engrossed and absorbed in the thing as a whole: the business at the altar and the presence of the people. And still I had not got rid of my fear. Seeing the late-comers hastily genuflecting before entering the pew, I realised my omission, and got the idea that people had spotted me for a pagan and were just waiting for me to miss a few more genuflections before throwing me out or, at least, giving me looks of reproof.

Soon we all stood up. I did not know what it was for. The priest was at the other end of the altar, and, as I afterwards learned, he was reading the Gospel. And then the next thing I knew there was someone in the pulpit.

It was a young priest, perhaps not much over thirty-three or -four years old. His face was rather ascetic and thin, and its asceticism was heightened with a note of intellectuality by his horn-rimmed glasses, although he was only one of the assistants, and he did not consider himself an intellectual, nor did anyone else apparently consider him so. But anyway, that was the impression he made on me: and his sermon, which was simple enough, did not belie it.

It was not long: but to me it was very interesting to hear this young man quietly telling the people in language that was plain, yet tinged with scholastic terminology, about a point in Catholic Doctrine. How clear and solid the doctrine was: for behind those words you felt the full force not only of Scripture but of centuries of a unified and continuous and consistent tradition. And above all, it was a vital tradition: there was nothing studied or antique about it. These words, this terminology, this doctrine, and these convictions fell from the lips of the young priest as something that were most intimately part of his own life. What was more, I sensed that the people were familiar with it all, and that it was also, in due proportion, part of their life also: it was just as much integrated into their spiritual organism as the air they breathed or the food they ate worked in to their blood and flesh.

What was he saying? That Christ was the Son of God. That, in Him, the Second Person of the Holy Trinity, God, had assumed a Human Nature, a Human Body and Soul, and had taken Flesh and dwelt amongst us, full of grace and truth: and that this Man, Whom men called the Christ, was God. He was both Man and God: two Natures hypostatically united in one Person or suppositum, one individual Who was a Divine Person, having assumed to Himself a Human Nature. And His works were the works of God: His acts were the acts of God. He loved us: God, and walked among us: God, and died for us on the Cross, God of God, Light of Light, True God of True God.

Jesus Christ was not simply a man, a good man, a great man, the greatest prophet, a wonderful healer, a saint: He was something that made all such trivial words pale into irrelevance. He was God. But nevertheless He was not merely a spirit without a true body, God hiding under a visionary body: He was also truly a Man, born of the Flesh of the Most Pure Virgin, formed of her Flesh by the Holy Spirit. And what He did, in that Flesh, on earth, He did not only as Man but as God. He loved us as God, He suffered and died for us, God.

And how did we know? Because it was revealed to us in the Scriptures and confirmed by the teaching of the Church and of the powerful unanimity of Catholic Tradition from the First Apostles, from the first Popes and the early Fathers, on down through the Doctors of the Church and the great scholastics, to our own day. *De Fide Divina.* If you believed it, you would receive light to grasp it, to understand it in some measure. If you did not believe it, you would never understand: it would never be anything but scandal or folly.

And no one can believe these things merely by wanting to, of his own volition. Unless he receive grace, an actual light and impulsion of the mind and will from God, he cannot even make an act of living faith. It is God Who gives us faith, and no one cometh to Christ unless the Father draweth him.

I wonder what would have happened in my life if I had been given this grace in the days when I had almost discovered the Divinity of Christ in the ancient mosaics of the churches of Rome. What scores of self-murdering and Christ-murdering sins would have been avoided—all the filth I had plastered upon His image in my soul during those last five years that I had been scourging and crucifying God within me?

It is easy to say, after it all, that God had probably foreseen my infidelities and had never given me the grace in those days because He saw how I would waste and despise it: and perhaps that rejection would have been my ruin. For there is no doubt that one of the reasons why grace is not given to souls is because they have so hardened their wills in greed and cruelty and selfishness that their refusal of it would only harden them more. . . . But now I had been beaten into the semblance of some kind of humility by misery and confusion and perplexity and secret, interior fear, and my ploughed soul was better ground for the reception of good seed.

The sermon was what I most needed to hear that day. When the Mass of the Catechumens was over, I, who was not even a catechumen, but only a blind and deaf and dumb pagan as weak and dirty as anything that ever came out of the darkness of Imperial Rome or Corinth or Ephesus, was not able to understand anything else.

It all became completely mysterious when the attention was refocussed on the altar. When the silence grew more and more profound, and little bells began to ring, I got scared again and, finally, genuflecting hastily on my left knee, I hurried out of the church in the middle of the most important part of the Mass. But it was just as well. In a way, I suppose I was responding to a kind of liturgical instinct that told me I did not belong there for the celebration of the Mysteries as such. I had no idea what took place in them: but the fact was that Christ, God, would be visibly present on the altar in the Sacred Species. And although He was there, yes, for love of me: yet He was there in His power and His might, and what was I? What was on my soul? What was I in His sight?

It was liturgically fitting that I should kick myself out at the end of the Mass of the Catechumens, when the ordained *ostiarii* should have been there to do it. Anyway, it was done.

Now I walked leisurely down Broadway in the sun, and my eyes looked about me at a new world. I could not understand what it was that had happened to make me so happy, why I was so much at peace, so content with life for I was not yet used to the clean savor that comes with an actual grace—indeed, there was no impossibility in a person's hearing and believing such a sermon and being justified, that is, receiving sanctifying grace in his soul as a habit, and beginning, from that moment, to live the divine and supernatural life for good and all. But that is something I will not speculate about.

All I know is that I walked in a new world. Even the ugly buildings of Columbia were transfigured in it, and everywhere was peace in these streets designed for violence and noise. Sitting outside the gloomy little Childs restaurant at 111th Street, behind the dirty, boxed bushes, and eating breakfast, was like sitting in the Elysian Fields.

V

My reading became more and more Catholic. I became absorbed in the poetry of Hopkins and in his notebooks—that poetry which had only impressed me a little six years before. Now, too, I was deeply interested in Hopkins' life as a Jesuit. What was that life? What did the Jesuits do? What did a priest do? How did he live? I scarcely knew where to begin to find out about all such things: but they had started to exercise a mysterious attraction over me.

And here is a strange thing. I had by now read James Joyce's *Ulysses* twice or three times. Six years before—on one of those winter vacations in Strasbourg—I had tried to read *Portrait of the Artist* and had bogged down in the part about his spiritual crisis. Something about it had discouraged, bored and depressed me. I did not want to read about such a thing: and I finally dropped it in the middle of the "Mission." Strange to say, sometime during this summer—I think it was before the first time I went to Corpus Christi—I reread *Portrait of the Artist* and was fascinated precisely by that part of the book, by the "Mission," by the priest's sermon on hell. What impressed me was not the fear of hell, but the expertness of the sermon. Now, instead of being repelled by the thought of such preaching—which was perhaps the author's intention—I was stimulated and edified by it. The style in which the priest in the book talked, pleased me by its efficiency and solidity and drive: and once again there was something eminently satisfying in the thought that these Catholics knew what they believed, and knew what to teach, and all taught the same thing, and taught it with coordination and purpose and great effect. It was this that struck me first of all, rather than the actual subject matter of their doctrine—until, that is, I heard the sermon at Corpus Christi.

So then I continued to read Joyce, more and more fascinated by the pictures of priests and Catholic life that came up here and there in his books. That, I am sure, will strike many people as a strange thing indeed. I think Joyce himself was only interested in rebuilding the Dublin he had known as objectively and vitally as he could. He was certainly very alive to all the faults in Irish Catholic society, and he had practically no sympathy left for the Church he had abandoned: but in his intense loyalty to the vocation of artist for which he had abandoned it (and the two vocations are not *per se* irreconcilable: they only became so because of peculiar subjective circumstances in Joyce's own case) he meant to be as accurate as he could in rebuilding his world as it truly was.

Therefore, reading Joyce, I was moving in his Dublin, and breathing the air of its physical and spiritual slums: and it was not the most Catholic side of Dublin that he always painted. But in the background was the Church, and its priests, and its devotions, and the Catholic life in all its gradations, from the Jesuits down to those who barely clung to the hem of the Church's garments. And it was this background that fascinated me now, along with the temper of Thomism that had once been in Joyce himself. If he had abandoned St. Thomas, he had not stepped much further down than Aristotle.

Then, of course, I was reading the metaphysical poets once again—especially Crashaw—and studying his life, too, and his conversion. That meant another avenue which led more or less directly to the Jesuits. So in the late August of 1938, and September of that year, my life began to be surrounded, interiorly, by Jesuits. They were the symbols of my new respect for the vitality and coordination of the Catholic Apostolate. Perhaps, in the back of my mind, was my greatest Jesuit hero: the glorious Father Rothschild of Evelyn Waugh's *Vile Bodies*, who plotted with all the diplomats, and rode away into the night on a motorcycle when everybody else was exhausted.

Yet with all this, I was not yet ready to stand beside the font. There was not even any interior debate as to whether I ought to become a Catholic. I was content to stand by and admire. For the rest, I remember one afternoon, when my girl had come in to town to see me, and we were walking around the streets uptown, I subjected her to the rather disappointing entertainment of going to Union Theological Seminary, and asking for a catalogue of their courses which I proceeded to read while we were walking around on

Riverside Drive. She was not openly irritated by it: she was a very good and patient girl anyway. But still you could see she was a little bored, walking around with a man who was not sure whether he ought to enter a theological seminary.

There was nothing very attractive in that catalogue. I was to get much more excited by the article on the Jesuits in the *Catholic Encyclopaedia*—breathless with the thought of so many novitiates and tertianships and what not—so much scrutiny, so much training. What monsters of efficiency they must be, these Jesuits, I kept thinking to myself, as I read and reread the article. And perhaps, from time to time, I tried to picture myself with my face sharpened by asceticism, its pallor intensified by contrast with a black cassock, and every line of it proclaiming a Jesuit saint, a Jesuit master-mind. And I think the master-mind element was one of the strongest features of this obscure attraction.

Apart from this foolishness, I came no nearer to the Church, in practice, than adding a "Hail Mary" to my night prayers. I did not even go to Mass again, at once. The following week-end I went to see my girl once again; it was probably after that that I went on the expedition to Philadelphia. It took something that belongs to history to form and vitalize these resolutions that were still only vague and floating entities in my mind and will.

One of those hot evenings at the end of summer the atmosphere of the city suddenly became terribly tense with some news that came out of the radios. Before I knew what the news was, I began to feel the tension. For I was suddenly aware that the quiet, disparate murmurs of different radios in different houses had imperceptibly merged into one big, ominous unified voice, that moved at you from different directions and followed you down the street, and came to you from another angle as soon as you began to recede from any one of its particular sources.

I heard "Germany—Hitler—at six o'clock this morning the German Army . . . the Nazis . . ." What had they done?

Then Joe Roberts came in and said there was about to be a war. The Germans had occupied Czechoslovakia, and there was bound to be a war.

The city felt as if one of the doors of hell had been half opened, and a blast of its breath had flared out to wither up the spirits of men. And people were loitering around the newsstands in misery.

Joe Roberts and I sat in my room, where there was no radio, until long after midnight, drinking canned beer and smoking cigarettes, and making silly and excited jokes but, within a couple of days, the

English Prime Minister had flown in a big hurry to see Hitler and had made a nice new alliance at Munich that cancelled everything that might have caused a war, and returned to England. He alighted at Croydon and came stumbling out of the plane saying "Peace in our time!"

I was very depressed. I was beyond thinking about the intricate and filthy political tangle that underlay the mess. I had given up politics as more or less hopeless, by this time. I was no longer interested in having any opinion about the movement and interplay of forces which were all more or less iniquitous and corrupt, and it was far too laborious and uncertain a business to try and find out some degree of truth and justice in all the loud, artificial claims that were put forward by the various sides.

All I could see was a world in which everybody said they hated war, and in which we were all being rushed into a war with a momentum that was at last getting dizzy enough to affect my stomach. All the internal contradictions of the society in which I lived were at last beginning to converge upon its heart. There could not be much more of a delay in its dismembering. Where would it end? In those days, the future was obscured, blanked out by war as by a dead-end wall. Nobody knew if anyone at all would come out of it alive. Who would be worse off, the civilians or the soldiers? The distinction between their fates was to be abolished, in most countries, by aerial warfare, by all the new planes, by all the marvelous new bombs. What would the end of it be?

I knew that I myself hated war, and all the motives that led to war and were behind wars. But I could see that now my likes or dislikes, beliefs or disbeliefs meant absolutely nothing in the external, political order. I was just an individual, and the individual had ceased to count. I meant nothing, in this world, except that I would probably soon become a number on the list of those to be drafted. I would get a piece of metal with my number on it, to hang around my neck, so as to help out the circulation of red-tape that would necessarily follow the disposal of my remains, and that would be the last eddy of mental activity that would close over my lost identity.

The whole business was so completely unthinkable that my mind, like almost all the other minds that were in the same situation, simply stopped trying to cope with it, and refixed its focus on the ordinary routine of life.

I had my thesis to type out, and a lot of books to read, and I was thinking of preparing an article on Crashaw which perhaps I would send to T. S. Eliot for his *Criterion.* I did not know that *Criterion* had printed its last issue, and that Eliot's reaction to the situation that so depressed me was to fold up his magazine.

The days went on and the radios returned to their separate and individual murmuring, not to be regimented back into their appalling shout for yet another year. September, as I think, must have been more than half gone.

I borrowed Father Leahy's life of Hopkins from the library. It was a rainy day. I had been working in the library in the morning. I had gone to buy a thirty-five-cent lunch at one of those little pious kitchens on Broadway—the one where Professor Gerig, of the graduate school of French, sat daily in silence with his ancient, ailing mother, over a very small table, eating his Brussels sprouts. Later in the afternoon, perhaps about four, I would have to go down to Central Park West and give a Latin lesson to a youth who was sick in bed, and who ordinarily came to the tutoring school run by my landlord, on the ground floor of the house where I lived.

I walked back to my room. The rain was falling gently on the empty tennis courts across the street, and the huge old domed library stood entrenched in its own dreary greyness, arching a cyclops eyebrow at South Field.

I took up the book about Gerard Manley Hopkins. The chapter told of Hopkins at Balliol, at Oxford. He was thinking of becoming a Catholic. He was writing letters to Cardinal Newman (not yet a cardinal) about becoming a Catholic.

All of a sudden, something began to stir within me, something began to push me, to prompt me. It was a movement that spoke like a voice.

"What are you waiting for?" it said. "Why are you sitting here? Why do you still hesitate? You know what you ought to do? Why don't you do it?"

I stirred in the chair, I lit a cigarette, looked out the window at the rain, tried to shut the voice up. "Don't act on impulses," I thought. "This is crazy. This is not rational. Read your book."

Hopkins was writing to Newman, at Birmingham, about his indecision.

"What are you waiting for?" said the voice within me again. "Why are you sitting there? It is useless to hesitate any longer. Why don't you get up and go?"

I got up and walked restlessly around the room. "It's absurd," I thought. "Anyway, Father Ford would not be there at this time of day. I would only be wasting time."

Hopkins had written to Newman, and Newman had replied to him, telling him to come and see him at Birmingham.

Suddenly, I could bear it no longer. I put down the book, and got into my raincoat, and started down the stairs. I went out into the street. I crossed over, and walked along by the grey wooden fence, towards Broadway, in the light rain.

And then everything inside me began to sing—to sing with peace, to sing with strength and to sing with conviction.

I had nine blocks to walk. Then I turned the corner of 121st Street, and the brick church and presbytery were before me. I stood in the doorway and rang the bell and waited.

When the maid opened the door, I said:

"May I see Father Ford, please?"

"But Father Ford is out."

I thought: well, it is not a waste of time, anyway. And I asked when she expected him back. I would come back later, I thought.

The maid closed the door. I stepped back into the street. And then I saw Father Ford coming around the corner from Broadway. He approached, with his head down, in a rapid, thoughtful walk. I went to meet him and said:

"Father, may I speak to you about something?"

"Yes," he said, looking up, surprised. "Yes, sure, come into the house."

We sat in the little parlor by the door. And I said: "Father, I want to become a Catholic."

vi

I came out of the presbytery with three books under my arm. I had hoped that I could begin taking instructions at once, but the pastor had told me to read these books, and pray and think and see how I felt about it in a week or ten days' time. I did not argue with him: but the hesitation that had been in my mind only an hour or so before seemed to have vanished so completely that I was astonished and a little abashed at this delay. So it was arranged that I should come in the evenings, twice a week.

"Father Moore will be your instructor," said the Pastor.

There were four assistants at Corpus Christi, but I guessed that Father Moore was going to be the one whom I had heard preaching the sermon on the divinity of Christ and, as a matter of fact, he was the one who, in the designs of Providence, had been appointed for this work of my salvation.

1
Thomas Merton at
about the time he wrote
The Seven Storey Mountain

2
Fr Irenaeus Herscher, OFM
Librarian 1934–1970
now Librarian Emeritus
at St Bonaventure
University

3
Thomas Merton
and Bob Lax
in 1939

4 St Bonaventure University Commencement, 8 June 1941
Left to right: Fr Peter R. Biasiotto, OFM, Lawrence Kenney, Thomas Merton, Dennis Lane, Fr Gabriel Naughton, OFM

5 Devereux Hall—a Residence on St Bonaventure University Campus where Thomas Merton lived during his teaching career there

If people had more appreciation of what it means to be converted from rank, savage paganism, from the spiritual level of a cannibal or of an ancient Roman, to the living faith and to the Church, they would not think of catechism as something trivial or unimportant. Usually the word suggests the matter-of-course instructions that children have to go through before First Communion and Confirmation. Even where it is a matter-of-course, it is one of the most tremendous things in the world, this planting of the word of God in a soul. It takes a conversion to really bring this home.

I was never bored. I never missed an instruction, even when it cost me the sacrifice of some of my old amusements and attractions, which had such a strong hold over me and, while I had been impatient of delay from the moment I had come to that first sudden decision, I now began to burn with desire for Baptism, and to throw out hints and try to determine when I would be received into the Church.

My desire became much greater still, by the end of October, for I made the Mission with the men of the parish, listening twice a day to sermons by two Paulist Fathers and hearing Mass and kneeling at Benediction before the Christ Who was gradually revealing Himself to me.

When the sermon on hell began, I was naturally making mental comparisons with the one in Joyce's *Portrait of the Artist* and reflecting on it in a kind of detached manner, as if I were a third and separate person watching myself hearing this sermon and seeing how it affected me. As a matter of fact this was the sermon which should have done me the most good and did, in fact, do so.

My opinion is that it is a very extraordinary thing for anyone to be upset by such a topic. Why should anyone be shattered by the thought of hell? It is not compulsory for anyone to go there. Those who do, do so by their own choice, and against the will of God, and they can only get into hell by defying and resisting all the work of Providence and grace. It is their own will that takes them there, not God's. In damning them He is only ratifying their own decision—a decision which He has left entirely to their own choice. Nor will He ever hold our weakness alone responsible for our damnation. Our weakness should not terrify us: it is the source of our strength. *Libenter gloriabor in infirmitatibus meis ut inhabitet in me virtus Christi.* Power is made perfect in infirmity, and our very helplessness is all the more potent a claim on that Divine Mercy Who calls to Himself the poor, the little ones, the heavily burdened.

My reaction to the sermon on hell was, indeed, what spiritual writers call "confusion"—but it was not the hectic, emotional confusion that comes from passion and from self-love. It was a sense of quiet sorrow and patient grief at the thought of these tremendous and terrible sufferings which I deserved and into which I stood a very good chance of entering, in my present condition: but at the same time, the magnitude of the punishment gave me a special and particular understanding of the greatness of the evil of sin. But the final result was a great deepening and awakening of my soul, a real increase in spiritual profundity and an advance in faith and love and confidence in God, to Whom alone I could look for salvation from these things. And therefore I all the more earnestly desired Baptism.

I went to Father Moore after the sermon on hell and said that I hoped he was going to baptize me really soon. He laughed, and said that it would not be much longer. By now, it was the beginning of November.

Meanwhile, there had been another thought, half forming itself in the back of my mind—an obscure desire to become a priest. This was something which I tended to hold separate from the thought of my conversion, and I was doing my best to keep it in the background. I did not mention it either to Father Ford or Father Moore, for the chief reason that in my mind it constituted a kind of admission that I was taking the thought more seriously than I wanted to—it almost amounted to a first step towards application for admission to a seminary.

However, it is a strange thing: there was also in my mind a kind of half-formed conviction that there was one other person I should consult about becoming a priest before I took the matter to the rectory. This man was a layman, and someone I had never yet seen, and it was altogether strange that I should be inclined so spontaneously to put the matter up to him, as if he were the only logical one to give me advice. In the end, he was the one I first consulted—I mean, the one from whom I first seriously asked advice, for I had long been talking about it to my friends, before I came around to him.

This man was Daniel Walsh, about whom I had heard a great deal from Lax and Gerdy. Gerdy had taken his course on St. Thomas Aquinas in the graduate school of Philosophy: and now as the new school year began, my attention centered upon this one course. It had nothing directly to do with my preparation for the exams for the M.A. degree in January. By now degrees and everything else to do with a university career had become very unimportant in comparison with the one big thing that occupied my mind and all my desires.

I registered for the course, and Dan Walsh turned out to be another one of those destined in a providential way to shape and direct my vocation. For it was he who pointed out my way to the place where I now am.

When I was writing about Columbia and its professors, I was not thinking of Dan Walsh: and he really did not belong to Columbia at all. He was on the faculty of the Sacred Heart College at Manhattanville, and came to Columbia twice a week to lecture on St. Thomas and Duns Scotus. His class was a small one and was, as far as Columbia was concerned, pretty much of an academic bypath. And that was in a sense an additional recommendation—it was off that broad and noisy highway of pragmatism which leads between its banks of artificial flowers to the gates of despair.

Walsh himself had nothing of the supercilious self-assurance of the ordinary professor: he did not need this frail and artificial armor for his own insufficiency. He did not need to hide behind tricks and vanities any more than Mark Van Doren did; he never even needed to be brilliant. In his smiling simplicity he used to efface himself entirely in the solid and powerful mind of St. Thomas. Whatever brilliance he allowed himself to show forth in his lectures was all thrown back upon its source, the Angel of the Schools.

Dan Walsh had been a student and collaborator of Gilson's and knew Gilson and Maritain well. In fact, later on he introduced me to Maritain at the Catholic Book Club, where this most saintly philosopher had been giving a talk on Catholic Action. I only spoke a few conventional words to Maritain, but the impression you got from this gentle, stooping Frenchman with much grey hair, was one of tremendous kindness and simplicity and godliness. And that was enough: you did not need to talk to him. I came away feeling very comforted that there was such a person in the world, and confident that he would include me in some way in his prayers.

But Dan himself had caught a tremendous amount of this simplicity and gentleness and godliness too: and perhaps the impression that he made was all the more forceful because his square jaw had a kind of potential toughness about it. Yet no: there he sat, this little, stocky man, who had something of the appearance of a good-natured prize fighter, smiling and talking with the most childlike delight and cherubic simplicity about the *Summa Theologica*.

His voice was low and, as he spoke, he half apologetically searched the faces of his hearers for signs of understanding and, when he found it, he seemed surprised and delighted.

I very quickly made friends with him, and told him all about my thesis and the ideas I was trying to work with, and he was very pleased. And one of the things he sensed at once was something that I was far from being able to realize: but it was that the bent of my mind was essentially "Augustinian." I had not yet followed Bramachari's advice to read St. Augustine and I did not take Dan's evaluation of my ideas as having all the directive force that was potentially in it—for it did not even come clothed in suggestion or advice.

Of course, to be called "Augustinian" by a Thomist might not in every case be a compliment. But coming from Dan Walsh, who was a true Catholic philosopher, it was a compliment indeed.

For he, like Gilson, had the most rare and admirable virtue of being able to rise above the petty differences of schools and systems, and seeing Catholic philosophy in its wholeness, in its variegated unity, and in its true Catholicity. In other words, he was able to study St. Thomas and St. Bonaventure and Duns Scotus side by side, and to see them as complementing and reinforcing one another, as throwing diverse and individual light on the same truths from different points of view, and thus he avoided the evil of narrowing and restricting Catholic philosophy and theology to a single school, to a single attitude, a single system.

I pray to God that there may be raised up more like him in the Church and in our universities, because there is something stifling and intellectually deadening about textbooks that confine themselves to giving a superficial survey of the field of philosophy according to Thomist principles and then discard all the rest in a few controversial objections. Indeed, I think it a great shame and a danger of no small proportions, that Catholic philosophers should be trained in division against one another, and brought up to the bitterness and smallness of controversy: because this is bound to narrow their views and dry up the unction that should vivify all philosophy in their souls.

Therefore, to be called an "Augustinian" by Dan Walsh was a compliment, in spite of the traditional opposition between the Thomist and Augustinian schools, Augustinian being taken not as confined to the philosophers of that religious order, but as embracing all the intellectual descendants of St. Augustine. It is a great compliment to find oneself numbered as part of the same spiritual heritage as St. Anselm, St. Bernard, St. Bonaventure, Hugh and Richard of St. Victor, and Duns Scotus also. And from the tenor of his course, I realized that he meant that my bent was not so much towards the intellectual, dialectical, speculative character of Thomism, as towards the spiritual, mystical, voluntaristic and practical way of St. Augustine and his followers.

His course and his friendship were most valuable in preparing me for the step I was about to take. But as time went on, I decided to leave the notion of becoming a priest out of the way for the time being. So I never even mentioned it to Dan in those days.

As November began, my mind was taken up with this one thought: of getting baptized and entering at last into the supernatural life of the Church. In spite of all my studying and all my reading and all my talking, I was still infinitely poor and wretched in my appreciation of what was about to take place within me. I was about to set foot on the shore at the foot of the high, seven-circled mountain of a Purgatory steeper and more arduous than I was able to imagine, and I was not at all aware of the climbing I was about to have to do.

The essential thing was to begin the climb. Baptism was that beginning, and a most generous one, on the part of God. For, although I was baptized conditionally, I hope that His mercy swallowed up all the guilt and temporal punishment of my twenty-three black years of sin in the waters of the font, and allowed me a new start. But my human nature, my weakness, and the cast of my evil habits still remained to be fought and overcome.

Towards the end of the first week in November, Father Moore told me I would be baptized on the sixteenth. I walked out of the rectory that evening happier and more contented than I had ever been in my life. I looked at a calendar to see what saint had that day for a feast, and it was marked for St. Gertrude.

It was only in the last days before being liberated from my slavery to death, that I had the grace to feel something of my own weakness and helplessness. It was not a very vivid light that was given to me on the subject: but I was really aware, at last, of what a poor and miserable thing I was. On the night of the fifteenth of November, the eve of my Baptism and First Communion, I lay in my bed awake and timorous for fear that something might go wrong the next day. And to humiliate me still further, as I lay there, fear came over me that I might not be able to keep the eucharistic fast. It only meant going from midnight to ten o'clock without drinking any water or taking any food, yet all of a sudden this little act of self-denial which amounts to no more, in reality, than a sort of an abstract token, a gesture of good-will, grew in my imagination until it seemed to be utterly beyond my strength—as if I were about to go without food and drink for ten days, instead of ten hours. I had enough sense left to realize that this was one of those curious psychological reactions with which our nature, not without help from the devil, tries to confuse us and avoid what reason and our will demand of it, and so I forgot about it all and went to sleep.

In the morning, when I got up, having forgotten to ask Father Moore if washing your teeth was against the eucharistic fast or not, I did not wash them, and, facing a similar problem about cigarettes, I resisted the temptation to smoke.

I went downstairs and out into the street to go to my happy execution and rebirth.

The sky was bright and cold. The river glittered like steel. There was a clean wind in the street. It was one of those fall days full of life and triumph, made for great beginnings, and yet I was not altogether exalted: for there were still in my mind these vague, half animal apprehensions about the externals of what was to happen in the church—would my mouth be so dry that I could not swallow the Host? If that happened, what would I do? I did not know.

Gerdy joined me as I was turning in to Broadway. I do not remember whether Ed Rice caught up with us on Broadway or not. Lax and Seymour came after we were in church.

Ed Rice was my godfather. He was the only Catholic among us—the only Catholic among all my close friends. Lax, Seymour, and Gerdy were Jews. They were very quiet, and so was I. Rice was the only one who was not cowed or embarrassed or shy.

The whole thing was very simple. First of all, I knelt at the altar of Our Lady where Father Moore received my abjuration of heresy and schism. Then we went to the baptistery, in a little dark corner by the main door.

I stood at the threshold.

"*Quid Petis ab ecclesia Dei?*" asked Father Moore.

"*Fidem!*"

"*Fides quid tibi praestat?*"

"*Vitam aeternam.*"

Then the young priest began to pray in Latin, looking earnestly and calmly at the page of the *Rituale* through the lenses of his glasses. And I, who was asking for eternal life, stood and watched him, catching a word of the Latin here and there.

He turned to me:

"*Abrenuntias Satanae?*"

In a triple vow I renounced Satan and his pomps and his works.

"Dost thou believe in God the Father almighty, Creator of heaven and earth?"

"*Credo!*"

"Dost thou believe in Jesus Christ His only Son, Who was born, and suffered?"

"*Credo!*"

"Dost thou believe in the Holy Spirit, in the Holy Catholic Church, the Communion of saints, the remission of sins, the resurrection of the body and eternal life?"

"*Credo!*"

What mountains were falling from my shoulders! What scales of dark night were peeling off my intellect, to let in the inward vision of God and His truth! But I was absorbed in the liturgy, and waiting for the next ceremony. It had been one of the things that had rather frightened me—or rather, which frightened the legion that had been living in me for twenty-three years.

Now the priest blew into my face. He said: "*Exi ab eo, spiritus immunde:* Depart from him, thou impure spirit, and give place to the Holy Spirit, the Paraclete."

It was the exorcism. I did not see them leaving, but there must have been more than seven of them. I had never been able to count them. Would they ever come back? Would that terrible threat of Christ be fulfilled, that threat about the man whose house was clean and garnished, only to be reoccupied by the first devil and many others worse than himself?

The priest, and Christ in him—for it was Christ that was doing these things through his visible ministry, in the Sacrament of my purification—breathed again into my face.

"Thomas, receive the good Spirit through this breathing, and receive the Blessing of God. Peace be with thee."

Then he began again to pray, and sign me with Crosses, and presently came the salt which he put on my tongue—the salt of wisdom, that I might have the savor of divine things, and finally he poured the water on my head, and named me Thomas, "if thou be not already baptized."

After that, I went into the confessional, where one of the other assistants was waiting for me. I knelt in the shadows. Through the dark, close-meshed wire of the grille between us, I saw Father McGough, his head bowed, and resting on his hand, inclining his ear towards me. "Poor man," I thought. He seemed very young and he had always looked so innocent to me that I wondered how he was going to identify and understand the things I was about to tell him.

But one by one, that is, species by species, as best I could, I tore out all those sins by their roots, like teeth. Some of them were hard, but I did it quickly, doing the best I could to approximate the number of times all these things had happened—there was no counting them, only guessing.

I did not have any time to feel how relieved I was when I came stumbling out, as I had to go down to the front of the church where Father Moore would see me and come out to begin his—and my—Mass. But ever since that day, I have loved confessionals.

Now he was at the altar, in his white vestments, opening the book. I was kneeling right at the altar rail. The bright sanctuary was all mine. I could hear the murmur of the priest's voice, and the responses of the server, and it did not matter that I had no one to look at, so that I could tell when to stand up and kneel down again, for I was still not very sure of these ordinary ceremonies. But when the little bells were rung I knew what was happening. And I saw the raised Host—the silence and simplicity with which Christ once again triumphed, raised up, drawing all things to Himself—drawing me to Himself.

Presently the priest's voice was louder, saying the *Pater Noster*. Then, soon, the server was running through the *Confiteor* in a rapid murmur. That was for me. Father Moore turned around and made a big cross in absolution, and held up the little Host.

"Behold the Lamb of God: behold Him Who taketh away the sins of the world."

And my First Communion began to come towards me, down the steps. I was the only one at the altar rail. Heaven was entirely mine—that Heaven in which sharing makes no division or diminution. But this solitariness was a kind of reminder of the singleness with which this Christ, hidden in the small Host, was giving Himself for me, and to me, and, with Himself, the entire Godhead and Trinity—a great new increase of the power and grasp of their indwelling that had begun only a few minutes before at the font.

I left the altar rail and went back to the pew where the others were kneeling like four shadows, four unrealities, and I hid my face in my hands.

In the Temple of God that I had just become, the One Eternal and Pure Sacrifice was offered up to the God dwelling in me: the sacrifice of God to God, and me sacrificed together with God, incorporated in His Incarnation. Christ born in me, a new Bethlehem, and sacrificed in me, His new Calvary, and risen in me: offering me to the Father, in Himself, asking the Father, my Father and His, to receive me into His infinite and special love—not the love He has for all things that exist—for mere existence is a token of God's love, but the love of those creatures who are drawn to Him in and with the power of His own love for Himself.

For now I had entered into the everlasting movement of that gravitation which is the very life and spirit of God: God's own gravitation towards the depths of His own infinite nature, His goodness without end. And God, that center Who is everywhere, and whose circumference is nowhere, finding me, through incorporation with Christ, incorporated into this immense and tremendous gravitational movement which is love, which is the Holy Spirit, loved me.

And He called out to me from His own immense depths.

2

The Waters of Contradiction

How BEAUTIFUL AND how terrible are the words with which God speaks to the soul of those He has called to Himself, and to the Promised Land which is participation in His own life—that lovely and fertile country which is the life of grace and glory, the interior life, the mystical life. They are words lovely to those who hear and obey them: but what are they to those who hear them without understanding or response?

For the Land which thou goest to possess is not like the land of Egypt from whence thou camest out where, when the seed is sown, waters are brought in to water it after the manner of gardens. But it is a land of hills and plains, expecting rain from heaven.

And the Lord thy God doth always visit it, and His eyes are on it from the beginning of the year unto the end thereof.

If then you obey my commandments, which I command you this day, that you love the Lord your God and serve Him with all your heart, and with all your soul:

He will give to your land the early rain and the latter rain, that you may gather in your corn, and your wine, and your oil, and your hay out of the fields to feed your cattle, and that you may eat and be filled.

Beware lest perhaps your heart be deceived and you depart from the Lord and serve strange Gods and adore them: and the Lord being angry shut up heaven and the rain come not down, nor the earth yield her fruit, and you perish quickly from the excellent land which the Lord will give you . . .

I had come, like the Jews, through the Red Sea of Baptism. I was entering into a desert—a terribly easy and convenient desert, with all the trials tempered to my weakness—where I would have a chance to give God great glory by simply trusting and obeying Him, and walking in the way that was not according to my own nature and my own judgement. And it would lead me to a land I could not imagine or understand. It would be a land that was not like the land of Egypt from which I had come out: the land of human nature blinded and fettered by perversity and sin. It would be a land in which the work of man's hands and man's ingenuity counted for little or nothing: but where God would direct all things, and where I would be expected to act so much and so closely under His guidance that it would be as if He thought with my mind, as if He willed with my will.

It was to this that I was called. It was for this that I had been created. It was for this Christ had died on the Cross, and for this that I was now baptized, and had within me the living Christ, melting me into Himself in the fires of His love.

This was the call that came to me with my Baptism, bringing with it a most appalling responsibility if I failed to answer it. Yet, in a certain sense, it was almost impossible for me to hear and answer it. Perhaps it demanded a kind of miracle of grace for me to answer it at once, spontaneously and with complete fidelity—and, oh, what a thing it would have been if I had done so!

For it was certainly true that the door into immense realms was opened to me on that day. And that was something I could not help realizing however obscurely and vaguely. The realization, indeed, was so remote and negative that it only came to me by way of contrast with the triviality and bathos of normal human experience—the talk of my friends, the aspect of the city, and the fact that every step down Broadway took me further and further into the abyss of anti-climax.

Father Moore had caught us just as we were going out the door and rushed us into the rectory for breakfast, and that was a good thing. It had something of the character of my good Mother, the Church, rejoicing at having found her lost groat. We all sat around the table and there was nothing incongruous about the happiness I then felt at all this gaiety, because charity cannot be incongruous with itself: and certainly everybody was glad at what had been done, first of all myself and Father Moore, and then, in different degrees, Lax, Gerdy, Seymour and Rice.

But after that we went out, and discovered that we had nowhere to go: this irruption of the supernatural had upset the whole tenor of a normal, natural day.

It was after eleven o'clock, and nearly time for lunch, and we had just had breakfast. How could we have lunch? And if, at twelve o'clock, we did not have lunch, what was there for us to do?

And then once and for all, the voice that was within me spoke again, and I looked once again into the door which I could not understand, into the country that was meaningless because it was too full of meanings that I could never grasp. "The land which thou goest to possess is not like the land of Egypt from whence thou camest out . . . For my thoughts are not your thoughts, nor your ways my ways, saith the Lord . . . Seek the Lord while He may be found, call upon Him while He is near . . . Why do you spend money for that which is not bread and your labor for that which doth not satisfy you?"

I heard all this, and yet somehow I seemed not to be able to grasp or understand it. Perhaps, in a way, there was a kind of moral impossibility of my doing what I should have done, because I simply did not yet know what it was to pray, to make sacrifices, to give up the world, to lead what is called the supernatural life. What were the things I should have done and that it could not even occur to me to do?

I should have begun at once, in the first place, to go to Communion every day. That did occur to me, but at first I thought that was not generally done. Besides I believed you had to go to confession every time you wanted to go to Communion. Of course, the simple way out of that would have been to keep going to Father Moore and asking him questions.

That was the second thing I should have done: I should have sought constant and complete spiritual direction. Six weeks of instructions, after all, were not much, and I certainly had nothing but the barest rudiments of knowledge about the actual practice of Catholic life, and if I had not made the absolutely tragic assumption that now my period of training was finished and done with, I would not have made such a mess of that first year after my Baptism. Probably the very worst thing I could have done was to hesitate about asking questions that occurred to me, and to have been too ashamed of my weakness to approach Father Moore about the real, fundamental needs of my soul.

Direction was the thing I most needed, and which I was least solicitous to avail myself of. And as far as I remember I only got around to asking Father Moore some trivial questions—what was a scapular, what was the difference between a breviary and a missal, and where could I get a missal?

The idea of the priesthood had been put aside, for the time being. I had good enough motives for doing so: it was too soon, perhaps, to think of that. Nevertheless, when I ceased to think of myself explicitly as a possible candidate for a high and arduous and special vocation in the Church, I tended automatically to slacken my will and to relax my vigilance, and to order my acts to nothing but an ordinary life. I needed a high ideal, a difficult aim, and the priesthood provided me with one. And there were many concrete factors in this. If I were going to enter a seminary or a monastery some day, I would have to begin to acquire some of the habits of religious or seminarians—to live more quietly, to give up so many amusements and such worldliness, and to be very careful to avoid things that threatened to provoke my passions to their old riot.

But without this ideal, I was in real and constant danger of carelessness and indifference, and the truth is, that after receiving the immense grace of Baptism, after all the struggles of persuasion and conversion, and after all the long way I had come, through so much of the no-man's land that lies around the confines of hell, instead of becoming a strong and ardent and generous Catholic, I simply slipped into the ranks of the millions of tepid and dull and sluggish and indifferent Christians who live a life that is still half animal, and who barely put up a struggle to keep the breath of grace alive in their souls.

I should have begun to pray, really pray. I had read books all about mysticism, and what is more, at the moment of Baptism, had I but known it, the real mystical life—the life of sanctifying grace and the infused theological virtues and the gifts of the Holy Ghost—was laid open to me in all its fulness: I had only to enter in to it and help myself, and I would soon have advanced rapidly in prayer. But I did not. I did not even know what was ordinary mental prayer, and I was quite capable of practising that from the start: but what is even worse, it was four or five months before I even learned how to say the Rosary properly, although I had one and used occasionally to say the *Paters* and *Aves* without knowing what else was required.

One of the big defects of my spiritual life in that first year was a lack of devotion to the Mother of God. I believed in the truths which the Church teaches about Our Lady, and I said the "Hail Mary" when I prayed, but that is not enough. People do not realize the tremendous power of the Blessed Virgin. They do not know who she is: that it is through her hands all graces come because God has willed that she thus participate in His work for the salvation of men.

To me, in those days, although I believed in her, Our Lady occupied in my life little more than the place of a beautiful myth—for in practice I gave her no more than the kind of attention one gives to a symbol or a thing of poetry. She was the Virgin who stood in the doors of the medieval cathedrals. She was the one I had seen in all the statues in the Musée de Cluny, and whose pictures, for that matter, had decorated the walls of my study at Oakham.

But that is not the place that belongs to Mary in the lives of men. She is the Mother of Christ still, His Mother in our souls. She is the Mother of the supernatural life in us. Sanctity comes to us through her intercession. God has willed that there be no other way.

But I did not have that sense of dependence or of her power. I did not know what need I had of trust in her. I had to find out by experience.

What could I do without love of the Mother of God, without a clear and lofty spiritual objective, without spiritual direction, without daily Communion, without a life of prayer? But the one thing I needed most of all was a sense of the supernatural life, and systematic mortification of my passions and of my crazy nature.

I made the terrible mistake of entering upon the Christian life as if it were merely the natural life invested with a kind of supernatural mode by grace. I thought that all I had to do was to continue living as I had lived before, thinking and acting as I did before, with the one exception of avoiding mortal sin.

It never occurred to me that if I continued to live as I had lived before, I would be simply incapable of avoiding mortal sin. For before my Baptism I had lived for myself alone. I had lived for the satisfaction of my own desires and ambitions, for pleasure and comfort and reputation and success. Baptism had brought with it the obligation to reduce all my natural appetites to subordination to God's will: "For the wisdom of the flesh is an enemy to God: for it is not subject to the law of God, neither can it be. And they who are in the flesh, cannot please God . . . and if you live according to the flesh, you shall die: but if by the Spirit you mortify the deeds of the flesh, you shall live. For whosoever are led by the Spirit of God, they are the sons of God." *Spiritu ambulate, et desideria carnis non perficietis.*

St. Thomas explains the words of the Epistle to the Romans very clearly and simply. The wisdom of the flesh is a judgement that the ordinary ends of our natural appetites are the goods to which the *whole of man's life* are to be ordered. Therefore it inevitably inclines the will to violate God's law.

In so far as men are prepared to prefer their own will to God's will, they can be said to hate God: for of course they cannot hate Him in Himself. But they hate Him in the Commandments which they violate. But God is our life: God's will is our food, our meat, our life's bread. To hate our life is to enter into death, and therefore the prudence of the flesh is death.

The only thing that saved me was my ignorance. Because in actual fact, since my life after my Baptism was pretty much what it had been before Baptism, I was in the condition of those who despise God by loving the world and their own flesh rather than Him. And because that was where my heart lay, I was bound to fall into mortal sin, because almost everything that I did tended, by virtue of my habitual intention to please myself before all else, to obstruct and deaden the work of grace in my soul.

But I did not clearly realize all this. Because of the profound and complete conversion of my intellect, I thought I was entirely converted. Because I believed in God, and in the teachings of the Church, and was prepared to sit up all night arguing about them with all comers, I imagined that I was even a zealous Christian.

But the conversion of the intellect is not enough. And as long as the will, the *domina voluntas*, did not belong completely to God, even the intellectual conversion was bound to remain precarious and indefinite. For although the will cannot force the intellect to see an object other than it is, it can turn it away from the object altogether, and prevent it from considering that thing at all.

Where was my will? "Where your treasure is, there will your heart be also," and I had not laid up any treasures for myself in heaven. They were all on earth. I wanted to be a writer, a poet, a critic, a professor. I wanted to enjoy all kinds of pleasures of the intellect and of the senses and in order to have these pleasures I did not hesitate to place myself in situations which I knew would end in spiritual disaster—although generally I was so blinded by my own appetites that I never even clearly considered this fact until it was too late, and the damage was done.

Of course, as far as my ambitions went, their objects were all right in themselves. There is nothing wrong in being a writer or a poet—at least I hope there is not: but the harm lies in wanting to be one for the gratification of one's own ambitions, and merely in order to bring oneself up to the level demanded by his own internal self-idolatry. Because I was writing for myself and for the world, the things I wrote were rank with the passions and selfishness and sin from which they sprang. An evil tree brings forth evil fruits, when it brings forth fruit at all.

I went to Mass, of course, not merely every Sunday, but sometimes during the week as well. I was never long from the Sacraments—usually I went to confession and Communion if not every week, every fortnight. I did a fair amount of reading that might be called "spiritual," although I did not read spiritually. I devoured books making notes here and there and remembering whatever I thought would be useful in an argument—that is, for my own aggrandizement, in order that I myself might take these things and shine by their light, as if their truth belonged to me. And I occasionally made a visit to a church in the afternoons, to pray or do the Stations of the Cross.

All this would have been enough for an ordinary Catholic, with a lifetime of faithful practice of his religion behind him: but for me it could not possibly be enough. A man who has just come out of the hospital, having nearly died there, and having been cut to pieces on an operating table, cannot immediately begin to lead the life of an ordinary working man. And after the spiritual mangle I have gone through, it will never be possible for me to do without the sacraments daily, and without much prayer and penance and meditation and mortification.

It took me time to find it out: but I write down what I have found out at last, so that anyone who is now in the position that I was in then may read it and know what to do to save himself from great peril and unhappiness. And to such a one I would say: Whoever you are, the land to which God has brought you is not like the land of Egypt from which you came out. You can no longer live here as you lived there. Your old life and your former ways are crucified now, and you must not seek to live any more for your own gratification, but give up your own judgement into the hands of a wise director, and sacrifice your pleasures and comforts for the love of God and give the money you no longer spend on those things, to the poor.

Above all, eat your daily Bread without which you cannot live, and come to know Christ Whose Life feeds you in the Host, and He will give you a taste of joys and delights that transcend anything you have ever experienced before, and which will make the transition easy.

ii

The first morning of 1939 was a grey morning. It was to turn out a grey year—very grey. But now a cold wind was blowing in off the sea, where I walked, among the white empty houses to the naked place where stands the church of St. Ignatius Martyr. The wind did something to help me to wake up, but it did not improve my temper much. The new year was beginning badly.

The night before being New Year's Eve, we had had a party in the house of Seymour's mother-in-law, who was a doctor, in Long Beach. It had been a mixed-up, desultory affair, in which we remained in a place that served as the doctor's waiting-room, sitting on the floor, playing different kinds of drums and drinking I forget what. But whatever it was we drank it put me in a bad temper.

The only person in the place not more or less fed up with everything was Bramachari, who had taken his turban off and sat in a chair and did not mind the noise. Later on, however, John Slate, who was also in a bad mood, having had a tooth torn out of his head, tried to tie me up in Bramachari's turban so the monk quietly went home—that is, to Seymour's house—and slept.

Later on, I threw a can of pineapple juice at a street light and also went to bed. I was sleeping in the same room with Bramachari, and consequently when it began to get light, he sat up and started chanting his morning prayers and I woke up. Since I could not get back to sleep even when his prayers trailed off into contemplation, I was going to an earlier Mass than I had expected. But it was a good thing. As usual, I found out that the only good thing about such days, or any other days, was Mass.

What a strange thing that I did not see how much that meant, and come at last to the realization that it was God alone I was supposed to live for, God that was supposed to be the center of my life and of all that I did.

It was to take me nearly a year to untangle that truth from all my disorganized and futile desires: and sometimes it seems to me that the hangovers I had while I was finding it out had something to do with what was going on in the history of the world.

For that was to be 1939, the year when the war that everybody had been fearing finally began to teach us with its inexorable logic that the dread of war is not enough. If you don't want the effect, do something to remove the causes. There is no use loving the cause and fearing the effect and being surprised when the effect inevitably follows the cause.

By this time, I should have acquired enough sense to realize that the cause of wars is sin. If I had accepted the gift of sanctity that had been put in my hands when I stood by the font in November 1938, what might have happened in the world? People have no idea what one saint can do: for sanctity is stronger than the whole of hell. The saints are full of Christ in the plenitude of His Kingly and Divine power: and they are conscious of it, and they give themselves to Him, that He may exercise His power through their smallest and seemingly most insignificant acts, for the salvation of the world.

But the world did not get very much of that out of me.

The end of January came. I remember, when I took my exams for the M.A., I went to Communion two days in a row, and both days I was very happy, and also I did quite well in the examinations. So after that I thought it was necessary for me to go to Bermuda for a week, and sit in the sun, and go swimming, and ride bicycles along those empty white roads, rediscovering the sights and smells that had belonged to a year of my early childhood. I met a lot of people who liked to ride around all night in a carriage singing: "Someone's in the kitchen with Dinah—strumming on the old banjo." The weather was so good that I came back to New York brown and full of health, with my pocket full of snapshots of the strangers with whom I had been dancing and sailing in yachts. And I was just in time to see Bramachari leave for India, at last, on the *Rex*. He was sailing with the Cardinals who were off to elect the new Pope.

Then I went to Greenwich Village and signed a lease for a one-room apartment and started work on my Ph.D. I suppose the apartment on Perry Street was part of the atmosphere appropriate to an intellectual such as I imagined myself to be and, as a matter of fact, I felt much more important in this large room with a bath and fireplace and French windows leading out on to a rickety balcony than I had felt in the little place ten feet wide behind the Columbia Library. Besides, I now had a shiny new telephone all my own which rang with a deep, discreet, murmuring sort of a bell as if to invite me suavely to expensive and sophisticated pursuits.

I don't, as a matter of fact, remember anything very important happening over that telephone, except that I used to make dates with a nurse who was stationed in one of the clinics out at the World's Fair which opened that year on Flushing Meadows. Also, it was the occasion of a series of furiously sarcastic letters to the telephone company because of various kinds of troubles, mechanical and financial.

The one I most talked to, over this phone, was Lax. He had a phone which did not even cost him anything, for he was living in the Hotel Taft, tutoring the children of the manager, and having access to an icebox full of cold chicken at all hours of the day and night. The two principal items of news which he communicated to me, from his point of vantage, were, first, the appearance of Joyce's *Finnegans Wake* and, second, the election of Pope Pius XII.

It was one of those first spring mornings when the new, warm sun is full of all kinds of delights, that I heard about the Pope. I had been sitting on the balcony in a pair of blue dungarees, drinking Coca-Cola, and getting the sun. When I say sitting on the balcony, I mean sitting on the good boards and letting my feet dangle through the place where the boards had broken. This was what I did a great deal of the time, in the mornings, that spring: surveying Perry Street from the east, where it ran up short against a block of brick apartments, to the west, where it ended at the river, and you could see the black funnels of the Anchor liners.

When I wasn't sitting on this balcony doing nothing, I was in the room, in the deepest armchair, studying the letters of Gerard Manley Hopkins and his Notebooks and trying to figure out various manuals on prosody and covering little white index cards with notes. For it was my plan to write a Ph.D. dissertation on Hopkins.

The typewriter that was always open on the desk was sometimes busy when I got a book to review: for I had been doing occasional reviews for the Sunday book sections of the *Times* and *Herald Tribune*. But what was better, I sometimes managed to grind out, with labor and anguish, some kind of a poem.

I had never been able to write verse before I became a Catholic. I had tried, but I had never really succeeded, and it was impossible to keep alive enough ambition to go on trying. I had started once or twice at Oakham, and I had written two or three miserable things at Cambridge. At Columbia, when I thought I was a Red, I got one stupid idea for a poem, about workers working on a dock and bombing planes flying overhead—you know: ominous. When it got on paper it was so silly that not even the magazines on the Fourth Floor would print it. The only other verse I had ever been able to turn out before my Baptism was an occasional line for the *Jester*.

In November 1938, I acquired a sudden facility for rough, raw Skeltonic verses—and that lasted about a month, and died. They were not much, but one of them took a prize which it did not deserve. But now I had many kinds of sounds ringing in my ears and they sometimes asked to get on paper. When their rhythms and tones followed Andrew Marvell, the results were best. I always liked Marvell; he did not mean as much to me as Donne or Crashaw (when Crashaw wrote well) but nevertheless there was something about his temper for which I felt a special personal attraction. His moods were more clearly my own than Crashaw's or even Donne's.

When I lived on Perry Street, it was hard to write poems. The lines came slow, and when it was all done, there were very few of them. They were generally rhymed iambic tetrameter, and because I was uneasy with any rhyme that sounded hackneyed, rhyming was awkward and sometimes strange.

I would get an idea, and walk around the streets, among the warehouses, towards the poultry market at the foot of Twelfth Street, and I would go out on the chicken dock trying to work out four lines of verse in my head, and sit in the sun. And after I had looked at the fireboats and the old empty barges and the other loafers and the Stevens Institute on its bluff across the river in Hoboken, I would write the poem down on a piece of scrap paper and go home and type it out.

I usually sent it at once to some magazine. How many envelopes I fed to the green mailbox at the corner of Perry Street just before you got to Seventh Avenue! And everything I put in there came back—except for the book reviews.

The more I failed, the more I was convinced that it was important for me to have my work printed in magazines like the *Southern Review* or *Partisan Review* or the *New Yorker*. My chief concern was now to see myself in print. It was as if I could not be quite satisfied that I was real until I could feed my ambition with these trivial glories, and my ancient selfishness was now matured and concentrated in this desire to see myself externalized in a public and printed and official self which I could admire at my ease. This was what I really believed in: reputation, success. I wanted to live in the eyes and the mouths and the minds of men. I was not so crude that I wanted to be known and admired by the whole world: there was a certain naive satisfaction in the idea of being only appreciated by a particular minority, which gave a special fascination to this urge within me. But when my mind was absorbed in all that, how could I lead a supernatural life, the life to which I was called? How could I love God, when everything I did was done not for Him but for myself, and not trusting in His aid, but relying on my own wisdom and talents?

Lax rebuked me for all this. His whole attitude about writing was purified of such stupidity, and was steeped in holiness, in charity, in disinterestedness. Characteristically he conceived the function of those who knew how to write, and who had something to say, in terms of the salvation of society. Lax's picture of America—before which he has stood for twelve years with his hands hanging in helplessness at his sides—is the picture of a country full of people who want to be kind and pleasant and happy and love good things and serve God, but do not know how. And they do not know where to turn to find out. They are surrounded by all kinds of sources of information which only conspire to bewilder them more and more. And Lax's vision is a vision of the day when they will turn on the radio and somebody will start telling them what they have really been wanting to hear and needing to know. They will find somebody who is capable of telling them of the love of God in language that will no longer sound hackneyed or crazy, but with authority and conviction: the conviction born of sanctity.

I am not sure whether this conception of his necessarily implied a specific vocation, a definite and particular mission: but in any case, he assumed that it was the sort of thing that should be open to me, to Gibney, to Seymour, to Mark Van Doren, to some writers he admired, perhaps even to somebody who did not know how to talk, but could only play a trumpet or a piano. And it was open to himself also: but for himself, he was definitely waiting to be "sent."

In any case, although I had gone before him to the fountains of grace, Lax was much wiser than I, and had clearer vision, and was, in fact, corresponding much more truly to the grace of God than I, and he had seen what was the only important thing. I think he has told what he had to say to many people besides myself: but certainly his was one of the voices through which the insistent Spirit of God was determined to teach me the way I had to travel.

Therefore, another one of those times that turned out to be historical, as far as my own soul is concerned, was when Lax and I were walking down Sixth Avenue, one night in the spring. The street was all torn up and trenched and banked high with dirt and marked out with red lanterns where they were digging the subway, and we picked our way along the fronts of the dark little stores, going downtown to Greenwich Village. I forget what we were arguing about, but in the end Lax suddenly turned around and asked me the question:

"What do you want to be, anyway?"

I could not say, "I want to be Thomas Merton the well-known writer of all those book reviews in the back pages of the *Times Book Review*," or "Thomas Merton the assistant instructor of Freshman English at the New Life Social Institute for Progress and Culture," so I put the thing on the spiritual plane, where I knew it belonged and said:

"I don't know; I guess what I want is to be a good Catholic."

"What do you mean, you want to be a good Catholic?"

The explanation I gave was lame enough, and expressed my confusion, and betrayed how little I had really thought about it at all.

Lax did not accept it.

"What you should say"—he told me—"what you should say is that you want to be a saint."

A saint! The thought struck me as a little weird. I said:

"How do you expect me to become a saint?"

"By wanting to," said Lax, simply.

"I can't be a saint," I said, "I can't be a saint." And my mind darkened with a confusion of realities and unrealities: the knowledge of my own sins, and the false humility which makes men say that they cannot do the things that they *must* do, cannot reach the level that they *must* reach: the cowardice that says: "I am satisfied to save my soul, to keep out of mortal sin," but which means, by those words: "I do not want to give up my sins and my attachments."

But Lax said: "No. All that is necessary to be a saint is to want to be one. Don't you believe that God will make you what He created you to be, if you will consent to let Him do it? All you have to do is desire it."

A long time ago, St. Thomas Aquinas had said the same thing—and it is something that is obvious to everybody who ever understood the Gospels. After Lax was gone, I thought about it, and it became obvious to me.

The next day I told Mark Van Doren:

"Lax is going around saying that all a man needs to be a saint is to want to be one."

"Of course," said Mark.

All these people were much better Christians than I. They understood God better than I. What was I doing? Why was I so slow, so mixed up, still, so uncertain in my directions and so insecure?

So at great cost I bought the first volume of the Works of St. John of the Cross and sat in the room on Perry Street and turned over the first pages, underlining places here and there with a pencil. But it turned out that it would take more than that to make me a saint: because these words I underlined, although they amazed and dazzled me with their import, were all too simple for me to understand. They were too naked, too stripped of all duplicity and compromise for my complexity, perverted by many appetites. However, I am glad that I was at least able to recognize them, obscurely, as worthy of the greatest respect.

iii

When the summer came I sub-let the apartment on Perry Street to Seymour's wife and went up-state, into the hills behind Olean. Lax's brother-in-law had a cottage, on top of a hill, from which you could see miles over New York and Pennsylvania—miles of blue hill-tops and wooded ridges, miles of forest smudged here and there, in the dry weeks, with smoke, and gashed open, in the neighboring valley, by the lumbermen. All day and all night the silence of the wood was broken by the coughing of oil-pumps, and when you passed through the trees you could see long metal arms moving back and forth clumsily in the shadows of the glade, because the hills were full of oil.

So Benjie, Lax's brother-in-law, gave us this place, and let us live there, trusting more than he should have in our ability to live in a house for more than a week without partially destroying it.

Lax and I and Rice moved in to the cottage, and looked around for places to put our typewriters. There was one big room with a huge stone fireplace and the works of Rabelais and a table which we presently ruined, feeding ourselves on it with hamburgers and canned beans and untold quarts of milk. There was a porch which looked out over the hills and where we eventually erected a trapeze. It was very pleasant to sit on the step of this porch, and look at the valley in the quiet evening, and play the drums. We had a pair of *bongós*, a Cuban double-drum, which is played two-handed and gives several different tones, depending where and how you hit it.

In order to make sure we would have plenty of books, we went down to the library at St. Bonaventure's College where this time, being baptized, I was no longer scared of the Friars. The librarian was Father Irenaeus, who looked up at us through his glasses and recognized Lax with ingenuous surprise. He always seemed to be surprised and glad to see everybody. Lax introduced us to him: "This is Ed Rice, this is Tom Merton."

"Ah! Mr. Rice. . . . Mr. Myrtle." Father Irenaeus took us both in, with the eyes of a rather bookish child, and shook hands without embarrassment.

"Merton," said Lax, "Tom Merton."

"Yes, glad to know you, Mr. Myrtle," said Father Irenaeus.

"They were at Columbia too," said Lax.

"Ah, Columbia," said Father Irenaeus. "I studied at the Columbia Library School," and then he took us into his own library and with reckless trust abandoned all the shelves to us. It never occurred to him to place any limit upon the appetites of those who seemed to like books. If they wanted books, well, this was a library. He had plenty of books, that was what a library was for. You could take as many as you liked, and keep them until you were through: he was astonishingly free of red tape, this happy little Franciscan. When I got to know the Friars a little better, I found out that this trait was fairly universal. Those who love rigid and methodical systems have their life of penance all cut out for them if they enter the Franciscans, and especially if they become superiors. But as far as I know, Father Irenaeus has never been robbed of his books on a larger scale than any other librarian, and on the whole, the little library at St. Bonaventure's was always one of the most orderly and peaceful I have ever seen.

Presently we came out of the stacks with our arms full.

"May we take all these, Father?"

"Sure, sure, that's fine; help yourself."

We signed a vague sort of a ticket, and shook hands.

"Good-bye, Mr. Myrtle," said the Friar, and stood in the open door and folded his hands as we started down the steps with our spoils.

I still did not know that I had discovered a place where I was going to find out something about happiness.

The books we took back to the cottage were hardly opened all summer: but anyway, they were there, lying around, in case we needed something to read. But really they were not necessary: for we eventually found places that proved very suitable for our typewriters, and all started writing novels. Rice wrote a novel called *The Blue Horse*. It took him about ten days. It was about a hundred and fifty pages long, illustrated. Lax wrote several fragments of novels which presently coalesced into one called *The Spangled Palace*. But the thing I got started on grew longer and longer and longer and eventually it was about five hundred pages long, and was called first *Straits of Dover* and then *The Night Before the Battle*, and then *The Labyrinth*. In its final form, it was shorter, and had been half rewritten, and it went to several publishers but to my great sorrow never got printed—at least I was sorry about it in those days, but now I am full of self-congratulation at the fact that those pages escaped the press.

It was partly autobiographical, and therefore it took in some of the ground that this present book had covered: but it took in much more of the ground that I have avoided covering this time. Besides, I found the writing of it easier and more amusing if I mixed up a lot of imaginary characters in my own story. It is a pleasant way to write. When the truth got dull, I could create a diversion with a silly man called Terence Metrotone. I later changed him to Terence Park, after I showed the first draft of the book to my uncle, who abashed me by concluding that Terence Metrotone was a kind of an acrostic for myself. That was, as a matter of fact, very humiliating, because I had made such a fool of the character.

The mere pleasure of sitting on top of this wooded mountain, with miles of country and cloudless sky to look at, and birds to listen to all day, and the healthy activity of writing page after page of novel, out under a tree facing the garage, made those weeks happy ones, in a natural sort of a way.

We could have made even more of it than we did. I think we all had a sort of a feeling that we could be hermits up on that hill: but the trouble was that none of us really knew how and I, who was in a way the most articulate, as well as the least sensible, whenever it came to matters of conduct and decisions concerning good and evil, still had the strongest urges to go down into the valleys and see what was on at the movies, or play the slot machines, or drink beer.

The best we could do about expressing our obscure desire of living lives that were separate and in some sense dedicated was to allow our beards to grow, which they did more or less slowly. Lax ended up with the best. It was black and solemn. Rice's was rather ragged, but it looked fine when he grinned, because he had big teeth and slanting eyes like an Eskimo. I myself entertained the secret belief that I looked like Shakespeare. I was still wearing the thing when I went to New York, later, and I took it to the World's Fair. I was standing thus bearded in a side-show that had something to do with Africa, and a young man who was not an explorer, but wore a white explorer's outfit, took me to be indeed an explorer because of the beard. Or at least he plied me with some knowing questions about central Africa. I think we were both trading on our knowledge of that wonderful movie, *Dark Rapture.*

The cottage would have made a good hermitage, and I now wish we had more exploited its possibilities. Lax was the only one who had the sense to get up, sometimes, very early in the morning, about sunrise. For my own part I usually slept until about eight, then fried a couple of eggs and swallowed a bowl of cornflakes and started at once to write. The closest I got to using the solitude for meditation was when I spent a few afternoons under a little peach tree in the high grass of what might have been a lawn, and read, at last, St. Augustine's *Confessions* and parts of St. Thomas's *Summa.*

I had accepted Lax's principle about sanctity being possible to those who willed it, and filed it away in my head with all my other principles—and still I did nothing about using it. What was this curse that was on me, that I could not translate belief into action, and my knowledge of God into a concrete campaign for possessing Him, Whom I knew to be the only true good? No, I was content to speculate and argue: and I think the reason is that my knowledge was too much a mere matter of natural and intellectual consideration. After all, Aristotle placed the highest natural felicity in the knowledge of God which was accessible to him, a pagan: and I think he was probably right. The heights that can be reached by metaphysical speculation introduce a man into a realm of pure and subtle pleasure that offers the most nearly permanent delights you can find in the natural order. When you go one step higher, and base your speculations on premises that are revealed, the pleasure gets deeper and more perfect still. Yet even though the subject matter may be the mysteries of the Christian faith, the manner of contemplating them, speculative and impersonal, may still not transcend the natural plane, at least as far as practical consequences go.

In such an event, you get, not contemplation, but a kind of intellectual and esthetic gluttony—a high and refined and even virtuous form of selfishness. And when it leads to no movement of the will towards God, no efficacious love of Him, it is sterile and dead, this meditation, and could even accidentally become, under certain circumstances, a kind of a sin—at least an imperfection.

Experience has taught me one big moral principle, which is this: it is totally impractical to plan your actions on the basis of a vast two-columned list of possibilities, with mortal sins on one side and things that are "not a mortal sin" on the other—the one to be avoided, the other to be accepted without discussion.

Yet this hopelessly misleading division of possibilities is what serves large numbers of Catholics as a whole moral theology. It is not so bad when they are so busy working for a living that the range of possibilities is more or less cut down and determined: but Heaven help them when they go on their vacation, or when Saturday night comes around. It is one reason for the number of drunken Irishmen in the world on Saturday nights for, as we know—and it is quite true—incomplete drunkenness is *per se* a venial sin. Therefore apply the two-column principle. You run your finger down the column of mortal sins *per se*. Going to a movie in which a man and woman maul each other at close range for hundreds of feet of film is not a mortal sin *per se*. Neither is incomplete drunkenness, nor gambling and so on. Therefore all these belong to the order of pursuits which are not illicit. Therefore they are licit. Therefore if anyone says, no matter with what qualifications, that you ought *not* to do these things—he is a heretic. If people are not careful, they get themselves into the position of arguing that it is virtuous to go to the movies, to gamble, to get half-drunk . . .

I know what I am talking about, because that was the way I was still trying to live in those days. Do you want to see the two-column principle in operation? Here is an example of a lot of things which were not mortal sins in themselves. What they were *per accidens* I am afraid to say: I leave them up to the mercy of God; but they were done by one whom He was calling to a life of perfection, a life dedicated to the joy of serving and loving Him alone . . .

A carnival came to Bradford. To us that meant a couple of Ferris wheels and a bingo game and the "Whip" and a man wearing a white uniform and a crash helmet being fired out of a cannon into a net. We got into the car and started out along the Rock City road, through the dark woods alive with the drumming of the oil pumps.

It was a big carnival. It seemed to fill the bottom of a narrow valley, one of the zig-zag valleys in which Bradford is hidden, and the place blazed with lights. The stacks of the oil refinery stood up, beyond the lights, like the guardians of hell. We walked into the white glare and the noise of crazy electric music and the thick sweet smell of candy.

"Hey, fellows, come over this way if you please."

We turned our beards shyly towards the man in shirt sleeves, hatted with a felt hat, leaning out of his booth. We could see the colored board, the numbers. We approached. He began to explain to us that, out of the kindness of his big foolish heart, he was conducting this game of chance which was so easy and simple that it really amounted to a kind of public charity, a means for endowing intelligent and honest young men like ourselves with a handsome patrimony.

We listened to his explanation. It was not one of those games where you won a box of popcorn, that was evident. In fact, although it started at a quarter, the ante doubled at every throw: of course, so did the prize, and the prize was in dollars.

"All you have to do is roll the little ball into these holes and . . ."

And he explained just what holes you had to roll the little ball into. Each time you had to get a new and different combination of numbers.

"You put down a quarter," said our benefactor, "and you are about to win two dollars and fifty cents. If you should happen to miss it the first time, it will be all the better for you, because for fifty cents you'll win five dollars—for one dollar you'll take ten—for two you'll take twenty."

We put down our quarters, and rolled the little balls into the wrong holes.

"Good for you," said the man, "now you stand a chance of winning twice as much." And we all put down fifty cents.

"Fine, keep it up, you're getting ready to win more and more each time—you can't miss, it's in-ev-i-table!"

He pocketed a dollar bill from each of us.

"That's the way, men, that's the way," he exclaimed, as we all rolled the little ball into the wrong holes again.

I paused and asked him to go over the rules of the game a second time. He did, and I listened closely. It was as I thought. I hadn't the vaguest idea what he was talking about. You had to get certain combinations of numbers, and for my own part I was completely unable to figure out what the combinations were. He simply told us what to shoot for, and then rapidly added up all the numbers and announced:

"You just missed it. Try again, you're so close you can't fail." And the combination changed again.

In about two and a half minutes he had taken all our money except for a dollar which I was earnestly saving for the rest of the carnival and for beer. How, he asked us, could we have the heart to quit now? Here we were right on the point of cleaning up, getting back all our losses, and winning a sum that made us dizzy: three hundred and fifty dollars.

"Men," he said, "you can't quit now, you're just throwing away your money if you quit. It doesn't make sense, does it? You didn't come all the way out here just to throw away your dough? Use your heads, boys. Can't you see you've *got* to win?"

Rice got that big grin on his face that meant "Let's get out of here."

"We haven't any more money," someone said.

"Have you any traveller's checks?" the philanthropist inquired.

"No."

But I never saw anyone so absorbed and solemn as Lax was, at that moment, in his black beard, with his head bowed over all those incomprehensible numbers. So he looked at me and I looked at him, and the man said:

"If you want to run home and get a little more money, I'll hold the game open for you—how's that?"

We said: "Hold the game open, we'll be back."

We got into the car and drove, in the most intense silence, fifteen miles or whatever the distance was to the cottage, and fifteen miles back, with thirty-five dollars and all the rest of the money we had: but the thirty-five alone were for the game.

When the benefactor of the poor saw the three of us come through that gate again, he really looked surprised and a little scared. The expressions on our faces must have been rather frightening, and perhaps he imagined that we had gone home not only to get our money but our guns.

We walked up to the booth.

"You held this game open for us, huh?"

"Yes, indeed, men, the game is open."

"Explain it over again."

He explained it over again. He told us what we had to get to win—it seemed impossible to miss. We put the money down on the counter and Lax rolled the little ball—into the wrong holes.

"Is that all, boys?" said the prince of charity.

"That's all." We turned on our heels and went away.

With the money I had kept in my pocket we went into the other places we would have done well to keep out of, and saw all of the carnival, and then went into Bradford where, drinking beer in a bar, we began to feel better and started to assuage our wounds by telling a lot of fancy lies to some girls we met in the bar—they were maids who worked at the t.b. sanatorium at Rocky Crest, on the mountain about a mile and a half from the cottage.

I remember that as the evening went on, there was a fairly large mixed audience of strangers gathered around the table where we were holding forth about the amusement ring which we managed and controlled. It was called the Panama-American Entertainment corporation, and was so magnificent that it made the present carnival in Bradford look like a sideshow. However, the effect was somewhat spoiled when a couple of Bradford strong men came up with no signs of interest in our story, and said:

"If we see you guys around here again with those beards we are going to knock your heads off."

So Rice stood up and said: "Yeah? Do you want to fight?"

Everybody went out into the alley, and there was a great deal of talk back and forth, but no fight, which was a good thing. They were quite capable of making us eat those beards.

We eventually found our way home but Rice did not dare try to drive the car into the garage for fear he would miss the door. He stopped short in the driveway and we opened the doors of the car and rolled out and lay on the grass, looking blindly up into the stars while the earth rolled and pitched beneath us like a foundering ship. The last thing I remember about that night was that Rice and I eventually got up and walked into the house, and found Lax sitting in one of the chairs in the living room, talking aloud, and uttering a lot of careful and well-thought-out statements directed to a pile of dirty clothes, bundled up and ready for the laundry, which somebody had left in another armchair on the other side of the room.

iv

When we went back to New York, in the middle of August, the world that I had helped to make was finally preparing to break the shell and put forth its evil head and devour another generation of men.

At Olean we never read any newspapers, and we kept away from radios on principle, and for my own part the one thing that occupied my mind was the publication of the new novel. Having found an old copy of *Fortune* lying around Benjie's premises, I had read an article in it on the publishing business: and on the basis of that article I had made what was perhaps the worst possible choice of a publisher—the kind of people who would readily reprint everything in the *Saturday Evening Post* in diamond letters on sheets of gold. They were certainly not disposed to be sympathetic to the wild and rambling thing I had composed on the mountain.

And it was going to take them a good long time to get around to telling me about it.

For my own part, I was walking around New York in the incomparable agony of a new author waiting to hear the fate of his first book—an agony which is second to nothing except the torments of adolescent love. And because of my anguish I was driven, naturally enough, to fervent though interested prayer. But after all God does not care if our prayers are interested. He wants them to be. Ask and you shall receive. It is a kind of pride to insist that none of our prayers should ever be petitions for our own needs: for this is only another subtle way of trying to put ourselves on the same plane as God—acting as if we had no needs, as if we were not creatures, not dependent on Him and dependent, by His will, on material things too.

So I knelt at the altar rail in the little Mexican church of Our Lady of Guadalupe on Fourteenth Street, where I sometimes went to Communion, and asked with great intensity of desire for the publication of the book, if it should be for God's glory.

The fact that I could even calmly assume that there was some possibility of the book giving glory to God shows the profound depths of my ignorance and spiritual blindness: but anyway, that was what I asked. But now I realize that it was a very good thing that I made that prayer.

It is a matter of common belief among Catholics that when God promises to answer our prayers, He does not promise to give us exactly what we ask for. But we can always be certain that if he does not give us that, it is because He has something much better to give us instead. That is what is meant by Christ's promise that we will receive all that we ask in His Name. *Quodcumque petimus adversus utilitatem salutis, non petimus in nomine Salvatoris.*

I think I prayed as well as I could, considering what I was, and with considerable confidence in God and in Our Lady, and I knew I would be answered. I am only just beginning to realize how well I was answered. In the first place the book was never published, and that was a good thing. But in the second place God answered me by a favor which I had already refused and had practically ceased to desire. He gave me back the vocation that I had half-consciously given up, and He opened to me again the doors that had fallen shut when I had not known what to make of my Baptism and the grace of that First Communion.

But before He did this I had to go through some little darkness and suffering.

I think those days at the end of August 1939 were terrible for everyone. They were grey days of great heat and sultriness and the weight of physical oppression by the weather added immeasurably to the burden of the news from Europe that got more ominous day by day.

Now it seemed that at last there really would be war in earnest. Some sense of the craven and perverted esthetic excitement with which the Nazis were waiting for the thrill of this awful spectacle made itself felt negatively, and with hundredfold force, in the disgust and nausea with which the rest of the world expected the embrace of this colossal instrument of death. It was a danger that had, added to it, an almost incalculable element of dishonor and insult and degradation and shame. And the world faced not only destruction, but destruction with the greatest possible defilement: defilement of that which is most perfect in man, his reason and his will, his immortal soul.

All this was obscure to most people, and made itself felt only in a mixture of disgust and hopelessness and dread. They did not realize that the world had now become a picture of what the majority of its individuals had made of their own souls. We had given our minds and wills up to be raped and defiled by sin, by hell itself: and now, for our inexorable instruction and reward, the whole thing was to take place all over again before our eyes, physically and morally, in the social order, so that some of us at least might have some conception of what we had done.

In those days, I realized it myself. I remember one of the nights at the end of August when I was riding on the subway, and suddenly noticed that practically nobody in the car was reading the evening paper, although the wires were hot with news. The tension had become so great that even this toughest of cities had had to turn aside and defend itself against the needles of such an agonizing stimulation. For once everybody else was feeling what Lax and I and Gibney and Rice had been feeling for two years about newspapers and news.

There was something else in my own mind—the recognition: "I myself am responsible for this. My sins have done this. Hitler is not the only one who has started this war: I have my share in it too . . ." It was a very sobering thought, and yet its deep and probing light by its very truth eased my soul a little. I made up my mind to go to confession and Communion on the First Friday of September.

The nights dragged by. I remember one, when I was driving in from Long Island where I had been having dinner at Gibney's house at Port Washington. The man with whom I was riding had a radio in the car, and we were riding along the empty Parkway, listening to a quiet, tired voice from Berlin. These commentators' voices had lost all their pep. There was none of that lusty and

6
Thomas Merton's
bedroom in the
hermitage at the
Abbey of Gethsemani

7
The Shrine of
St Thérèse on
St Bonaventure
Campus where
Thomas Merton
prayed for the
spiritual aid
which directed him
to Gethsemani

doctrinaire elation with which the news broadcasters usually convey the idea that they know all about everything. This time you knew that nobody knew what was going to happen, and they all admitted it. True, they were all agreed that the war was now going to break out. But when? Where? They could not say.

All the trains to the German frontier had been stopped. All air service had been discontinued. The streets were empty. You got the feeling that things were being cleared for the first great air-raid, the one that everyone had been wondering about, that H. G. Wells and all the other people had written about, the one that would wipe out London in one night . . .

The Thursday night before the first Friday of September I went to confession at St. Patrick's Cathedral and then, with characteristic stupidity, stopped in at Dillon's, which was a bar where we went all the time, across the street from the stage-door of the Center Theater. Gibney and I used to sit there waiting for the show to end, and we would hang around until one or two in the morning with several girls we knew who had bits to play in it. This evening, before the show was out, I ran into Jinny Burton, who was not in the show, but could have been in many better shows than that, and she said she was going home to Richmond over Labor Day. She invited me to come with her. We arranged to meet in Pennsylvania Station the following morning.

When it was morning, I woke up early and heard the radios. I could not quite make out what they were saying, but the voices were not tired any more: there was much metallic shouting which meant something had really happened.

On my way to Mass, I found out what it was. They had bombed Warsaw, and the war had finally begun.

In the Church of St. Francis of Assisi, near the Pennsylvania Station, there was a High Mass. The priest stood at the altar under the domed mosaic of the apse and his voice rose in the solemn cadences of the Preface of the Mass—those ancient and splendid and holy words of the Immortal Church. *Vere dignum et justum est aequum et salutare nos tibi semper et ubique gratias agere, Domine sancte, Pater omnipotens, aeterne Deus . . .*

It was the voice of the Church, the Bride of Christ who is in the world yet not of it, whose life transcends and outlives wars and persecutions and revolutions and all the wickedness and cruelty and rapacity and injustice of men. It is truly meet and just always and in all things to give Thee thanks, Holy Lord, omnipotent Father, eternal God: a tremendous prayer that reduces all wars to their real smallness and insignificance in the face of eternity. It is a prayer that opens the door to eternity, that springs from eternity and goes again into eternity, taking our minds with it in its deep and peaceful wisdom. Always and in all things to give Thee thanks, omnipotent Father. Was it thus that she was singing, this Church, this one Body, who had already begun to suffer and to bleed again in another war?

She was thanking Him *in* the war, *in* her suffering: not for the war and for the suffering, but for His love which she knew was protecting her, and us, in this new crisis. And raising up her eyes to Him, she saw the eternal God alone through all these things, was interested in His action alone, not in the bungling cruelty of secondary causes, but only in His love, His wisdom. And to Him the Church, His Bride, gave praise through Christ, through Whom all the angelic hierarchies praise Him . . .

I knelt at the altar rail and on this the first day of the Second World War received from the hand of the priest, Christ in the Host, the same Christ Who was being nailed again to the cross by the effect of my sins, and the sins of the whole selfish, stupid, idiotic world of men.

There was no special joy in that week-end in Virginia. On the Saturday afternoon when we started out from Richmond to go to Urbanna, where Jinny's family had a boat they were going to sail in a regatta, we got the news about the sinking of the *Athenia*, and then, that evening, I suddenly developed a pain in an impacted wisdom tooth. It raged all night and the next day I staggered off to the regatta, worn out with sleeplessness and holding a jaw full of pain.

Down at the dock where there was a gas-pump for the motor boats and a red tank full of Coca-Cola on ice, we stood out of the sun in the doorway of a big shed smelling of ropes and pitch, and listened to a man talking on the radio from London.

His voice was reassuring. The city had not yet been bombed.

We started out of the cove, and passed through the mouth into the open estuary of the Rappahannock, blazing with sun, and everybody was joking about the *Bremen*. The big German liner had sailed out of New York without warning and had disappeared. Every once in a while some high drawling Southern female voice would cry:

"There's the *Bremen*."

I had a bottle of medicine in my pocket, and with a match and a bit of cotton I swabbed the furious impacted tooth.

Nevertheless, when I got back to New York, it turned out that the war was not going to be so ruthless after all—at least so it seemed. The fighting was fierce in Poland, but in the west there was nothing doing. And now that the awful tension was over, people were quieter and more confident than they had been before the fighting had started.

I went to a dentist who hammered and chipped at my jaw until he got the wisdom tooth out of my head, and then I went back to Perry Street and lay on my bed and played some ancient records of Bix Beiderbecke, Paul Whiteman's trumpet player, and swabbed my bleeding mouth with purple disinfectant until the whole place reeked of it.

I had five stitches in my jaw.

The days went by. The city was quiet and confident. It even began to get gay again. Whatever happened, it was evident that America was not going to get into the war right away, and a lot of people were saying that it would just go on like this for years, a sort of state of armed waiting and sniping, with the big armies lined up in their impregnable fortified areas. It was as if the world were entering upon a strange new era in which the pretence of peace had defined itself out into what it was, a state of permanent hostility that was nevertheless not quite ready to fight. And some people thought we were just going to stay that way for twenty years.

For my own part, I did not think anything about it, except that the grim humor of Russia's position in the war could not help but strike me: for now, after a loud outcry and a great storm of crocodile tears over Chamberlain's betrayal of Czechoslovakia the year before, the Reds were comfortably allied with Germany and blessing, with a benign smile, the annihilation of Poland, ready themselves to put into effect some small designs of their own regarding the Finns.

The party line had evolved indeed, and turned itself into many knots since the days of the 1935 Peace Strike and the Oxford Pledge. We had once been led to believe that all wars were wars of aggression and wars of aggression were the direct product of capitalism, masking behind Fascism and all the other movements with colored shirts, and therefore no one should fight at all. It now turned out that the thing to do was support the aggressive war of the Soviets against Finland and approve the Russian support of German aggression in Poland.

The September days went by, and the first signs of fall were beginning to be seen in the clearing of the bright air. The days of heat were done. It was getting on toward that season of new beginnings, when I would get back to work on my Ph.D., and when I hoped possibly to get some kind of job as an instructor at Columbia, in the College or in Extension.

These were the things I was thinking about when one night Rice and Bob Gerdy and I were in Nick's on Sheridan Square, sitting at the curved bar while the room rocked with jazz. Presently Gibney came in with Peggy Wells, who was one of the girls in that show at the Center Theater, the name of which I have forgotten. We all sat together at a table and talked and drank. It was just like all the other nights we spent in those places. It was more or less uninteresting but we couldn't think of anything else to do and there seemed to be no point in going to bed.

After Rice and Gerdy went home, Gibney and Peggy and I still sat there. Finally it got to be about four o'clock in the morning. Gibney did not want to go out on Long Island, and Peggy lived uptown in the Eighties.

They came to Perry Street, which was just around the corner.

It was nothing unusual for me to sleep on the floor, or in a chair, or on a couch too narrow and too short for comfort—that was the way we lived, and the way thousands of other people like us lived. One stayed up all night, and finally went to sleep wherever there happened to be room for one man to put his tired carcass.

It is a strange thing that we should have thought nothing of it, when if anyone had suggested sleeping on the floor as a penance, for the love of God, we would have felt that he was trying to insult our intelligence and dignity as men! What a barbarous notion! Making yourself uncomfortable as a penance! And yet we somehow seemed to think it quite logical to sleep that way as part of an evening dedicated to pleasure. It shows how far the wisdom of the world will go in contradicting itself. "From him that hath not, it shall be taken away even that which he hath."

I suppose I got some five or six hours of fitful sleep, and at about eleven we were all awake, sitting around dishevelled and half stupefied, talking and smoking and playing records. The thin, ancient, somewhat elegiac cadences of the long dead Beiderbecke sang in the room. From where I sat, on the floor, I could see beyond the roofs to a patch of clear fall sky.

At about one o'clock in the afternoon I went out to get some breakfast, returning with scrambled eggs and toast and coffee in an armful of cardboard containers, different shapes and sizes, and pockets full of new packs of cigarettes. But I did not feel like smoking. We ate and talked, and finally cleared up all the mess and someone had the idea of going for a walk to the Chicken Dock. So we got ready to go.

Somewhere in the midst of all this, an idea had come to me, an idea that was startling enough and momentous enough by itself, but much more astonishing in the context. Perhaps many people will not believe what I am saying.

While we were sitting there on the floor playing records and eating this breakfast the idea came to me: "I am going to be a priest."

I cannot say what caused it: it was not a reaction of especially strong disgust at being so tired and so uninterested in this life I was still leading, in spite of its futility. It was not the music, not the fall air, for this conviction that had suddenly been planted in me full grown was not the sick and haunting sort of a thing that an emotional urge always is. It was not a thing of passion or of fancy. It was a strong and sweet and deep and insistent attraction that suddenly made itself felt, but not as movement of appetite towards any sensible good. It was something in the order of conscience, a new and profound and clear sense that this was what I really ought to do.

How long the idea was in my mind before I mentioned it, I cannot say. But presently I said casually:

"You know, I think I ought to go and enter a monastery and become a priest."

Gibney had heard that before, and thought I was fooling. The statement aroused no argument or comment, and anyway, it was not one to which Gibney was essentially unsympathetic. As far as he was concerned, any life made sense except that of a business man.

As we went out the door of the house I was thinking:

"I am going to be a priest."

When we were on the Chicken Dock, my mind was full of the same idea. Around three or four in the afternoon Gibney left and went home to Port Washington. Peggy and I sat looking at the dirty river for a while longer. Then I walked with her to the subway. In the shadows under the elevated drive over Tenth Avenue I said:

"Peggy, I mean it, I am going to enter a monastery and be a priest."

She didn't know me very well and anyway, she had no special ideas about being a priest. There wasn't much she could say. Anyway, what did I expect her to say?

I was glad, at last, to be alone. On that big wide street that is a continuation of Eighth Avenue, where the trucks run down very fast and loud—I forget its name—there was a little Catholic library and a German bakery where I often ate my meals. Before going to the bakery to get dinner and supper in one, I went to the Catholic library, St. Veronica's. The only book about religious Orders they seemed to have was a little green book about the Jesuits but I took it and read it while I ate in the bakery.

Now that I was alone, the idea assumed a different and more cogent form. Very well: I had accepted the possibility of the priesthood as real and fitting for me. It remained for me to make it, in some sense, more decisive.

What did that mean? What was required? My mind groped for some sort of an answer. What was I supposed to do, here and now?

I must have been a long time over the little book and these thoughts. When I came out into the street again, it was dusk. The side streets, in fact, were already quite dark. I suppose it was around seven o'clock.

Some kind of an instinct prompted me to go to Sixteenth Street, to the Jesuit Church of St. Francis Xavier. I had never been there. I don't know what I was looking for: perhaps I was thinking primarily of talking to some one of the Fathers there—I don't know.

When I got to Sixteenth Street, the whole building seemed dark and empty, and as a matter of fact the doors of the church were locked. Even the street was empty. I was about to go away disappointed, when I noticed a door to some kind of a basement under the church.

Ordinarily I would never have noticed such a door. You went down a couple of steps, and there it was, half hidden under the stairs that led up to the main door of the church. There was no sign that the door was anything but locked and bolted fast.

But something prompted me: "Try that door."

I went down the two steps, put my hand on the heavy iron handle. The door yielded and I found myself in a lower church, and the church was full of lights and people and the Blessed Sacrament was exposed in a monstrance on the altar, and at last I realized what I was supposed to do, and why I had been brought here.

It was some kind of a novena service, maybe a Holy Hour, I don't know: but it was nearly ending. Just as I found a place and fell on my knees, they began singing the *Tantum Ergo*. . . . All these people, workmen, poor women, students, clerks, singing the Latin hymn to the Blessed Sacrament written by St. Thomas Aquinas.

I fixed my eyes on the monstrance, on the white Host.

And then it suddenly became clear to me that my whole life was at a crisis. Far more than I could imagine or understand or conceive was now hanging upon a word—a decision of mine.

I had not shaped my life to this situation: I had not been building up to this. Nothing had been further from my mind. There was, therefore, an added solemnity in the fact that I had been called in here abruptly to answer a question that had been preparing, not in my mind, but in the infinite depths of an eternal Providence.

I did not clearly see it then, but I think now that it might have been something in the nature of a last chance. If I had hesitated or refused at that moment—what would have become of me?

But the way into the new land, the promised land, the land that was not like the Egypt where I persisted in living, was now thrown open again: and I instinctively sensed that it was only for a moment.

It was a moment of crisis, yet of interrogation: a moment of searching, but it was a moment of joy. It took me about a minute to collect my thoughts about the grace that had been suddenly planted in my soul, and to adjust the weak eyes of my spirit to its unaccustomed light, and during that moment my whole life remained suspended on the edge of an abyss: but this time, the abyss was an abyss of love and peace, the abyss was God.

It would be in some sense a blind, irrevocable act to throw myself over. But if I failed to do that . . . I did not even have to turn and look behind me at what I would be leaving. Wasn't I tired enough of all that?

So now the question faced me:

"Do you really want to be a priest? If you do, say so . . ."

The hymn was ending. The priest collected the ends of the humeral veil over his hands that held the base of the monstrance, and slowly lifted it off the altar, and turned to bless the people.

I looked straight at the Host, and I knew, now, Who it was that I was looking at, and I said:

"Yes, I want to be a priest, with all my heart I want it. If it is Your will, make me a priest—make me a priest."

When I had said them, I realized in some measure what I had done with those last four words, what power I had put into motion on my behalf, and what a union had been sealed between me and that power by my decision.

Part Three

1
Magnetic North

ONCE AGAIN, classes were beginning at the University. The pleasant fall winds played in the yellowing leaves of the poplars in front of the college dormitories and many young men came out of the subways and walked earnestly and rapidly about the campus with little blue catalogues of courses under their arms, and their hearts warm with the desire to buy books. But now, in this season of new beginnings, I really had something new to begin.

A year ago the conviction had developed in my mind that the one who was going to give me the best advice about where and how to become a priest was Dan Walsh. I had come to this conclusion before I had ever met him, or sat and listened to his happy and ingenuous lectures on St. Thomas. So on this September day, in 1939, the conviction was to bear its fruit.

Dan was not on the Columbia campus that day. I went into one of the phone booths at Livingston Hall and called him up.

He was a man with rich friends, and that night he had been invited to dinner with some people on Park Avenue, although there was certainly nothing of Park Avenue about him and his simplicity. But we arranged to meet downtown, and at about ten o'clock that evening I was standing in the lobby of one of those big, shiny, stuffy apartments, waiting for him to come down out of the elevator.

As soon as we walked out into the cool night, Dan turned to me and said: "You know, the first time I met you I thought you had a vocation to the priesthood."

I was astonished and ashamed. Did I really give that impression? It made me feel like a whited sepulchre, considering what I knew was inside me. On the whole, perhaps it would have been more reassuring if he had been surprised.

He was not surprised, he was very pleased. And he was glad to talk about my vocation, and about the priesthood and about religious Orders. They were things to which he had given a certain amount of thought, and on the whole, I think that my selection of an adviser was a very happy one. It was a good inspiration and, in fact, it was to turn out much better than I realized at first.

The quietest place we could think of in that neighborhood was the men's bar at the Biltmore, a big room full of comfortable chairs, hushed and panelled and half empty. We sat down in one of the far corners, and it was there, two being gathered together in His Name and in His charity, that Christ impressed the first definite form and direction upon my vocation.

It was very simply done. We just talked about several different religious Orders, and Dan suggested various priests I might consult and finally promised to give me a note of introduction to one of them.

I had read a little here and there about the Jesuits, the Franciscans, the Dominicans, the Benedictines, leafing through the *Catholic Encyclopaedia* in the reference library in South Hall, and shopping around in the stacks. I had put my nose into the Rule of St. Benedict and not derived much benefit from so cursory an acquaintance—all I remembered was that the saint seemed a little vexed at the fact that the monks of his day could not be persuaded to go without wine. I had looked into a little French book about the Dominicans, and there I met with a piece of information that gave me pause: it said they all slept together in a common dormitory, and I thought: "Who wants to sleep in a common dormitory?" The picture in my mind was that of the long, cold, green upstairs room in the Lycée, with row after row of iron beds and a lot of skinny people in night-shirts.

I spoke to Dan Walsh about the Jesuits, but he said he did not know any Jesuits, and for my own part, the mere fact that he did not seem to have any particular reaction, positive or negative, to that Order, did away with the weak and vague preference which I had hitherto given it in my own mind. I had instinctively turned that way first of all, because I had read the life of Gerard Manley Hopkins and studied his poems, but there had never been any real attraction calling me to that kind of a life. It was geared to a pitch of active intensity and military routine which were alien to my own needs. I doubt if they would have kept me in their novitiate—but if they had, they would probably have found me a great misfit. What I needed was the solitude to expand in breadth and depth and to be simplified out under the gaze of God more or less the way a plant spreads out its leaves in the sun. That meant that I needed a Rule that was almost entirely aimed at detaching me from the world and uniting me with God, not a Rule made to fit me to fight for God in the world. But I did not find out all that in one day.

Dan spoke of the Benedictines. In itself, the vocation attracted me: a liturgical life in some big abbey in the depths of the country. But in actual fact it might just mean being nailed down to a desk in an expensive prep-school in New Hampshire for the rest of my life—or, worse still, being a parish priest remotely attached to such a prep-school, and living in more or less permanent separation from the claustral and liturgical center which had first attracted me.

"What do you think of the Franciscans?" said Dan.

As soon as I mentioned St. Bonaventure's, it turned out that he had many friends there and knew the place fairly well; in fact they had given him some sort of an honorary degree there that summer. Yes, I liked the Franciscans. Their life was very simple and informal and the atmosphere of St. Bonaventure's was pleasant and happy and peaceful. One thing that attracted me to them was a sort of freedom from spiritual restraint, from systems and routine. No matter how much the original Rule of St. Francis has changed, I think his spirit and his inspiration are still the fundamental thing in Franciscan life. And it is an inspiration rooted in joy, because it is guided by the prudence and wisdom which are revealed only to the little ones—the glad wisdom of those who have had the grace and the madness to throw away everything in one uncompromising rush, and to walk around barefooted in the simple confidence that if they get into trouble, God will come and get them out of it again.

This is not something that is confined to the Franciscans: it is at the heart of every religious vocation, and if it is not, the vocation does not mean much. But the Franciscans, or at least St. Francis, reduced it to its logical limits, and at the same time invested it with a kind of simple thirteenth century lyricism which made it doubly attractive to me.

However, the lyricism must be carefully distinguished from the real substance of the Franciscan vocation, which is that tremendous and heroic poverty, poverty of body and spirit which makes the Friar literally a tramp. For, after all, "mendicant" is only a fancy word for tramp, and if a Franciscan cannot be a tramp in this full and complete and total mystical sense, he is bound to be a little unhappy and dissatisfied. As soon as he acquires a lot of special articles for his use and comfort and becomes sedate and respectable and spiritually sedentary he will, no doubt, have an easy and pleasant time, but there will be always gnawing in his heart the nostalgia for that uncompromising destitution which alone can give him joy because it flings him headlong into the arms of God.

Without poverty, Franciscan lyricism sounds tinny and sentimental and raw and false. Its tone is sour, and all its harmonies are somewhat strained.

I am afraid that at that time, it was the lyricism that attracted me more than the poverty, but really I don't think I was in a position to know any better. It was too soon for me to be able to make the distinction. However, I remember admitting that one of the advantages of their Rule, as far as I was concerned, was that it was easy.

After all, I was really rather frightened of all religious rules as a whole, and this new step, into the monastery, was not something that presented itself to me, all at once, as something that I would just take in my stride. On the contrary, my mind was full of misgivings about fasting and enclosure and all the long prayers and community life and monastic obedience and poverty, and there were plenty of strange spectres dancing about in the doors of my imagination, all ready to come in, if I would let them in. And if I did, they would show me how I would go insane in a monastery, and how my health would crack up, and my heart would give out, and I would collapse and go to pieces and be cast back into the world a hopeless moral and physical wreck.

All this, of course, was based on the assumption that I was in weak health, for that was something I still believed. Perhaps it was to some extent true, I don't know. But the fear of collapse had done nothing, in the past years, to prevent me from staying up all night and wandering around the city in search of very unhealthy entertainments. Nevertheless, as soon as there was question of a little fasting or going without meat or living within the walls of a monastery, I instantly began to fear death.

What I eventually found out was that as soon as I started to fast and deny myself pleasures and devote time to prayer and meditation and to the various exercises that belong to the religious life, I quickly got over all my bad health, and became sound and strong and immensely happy.

That particular night I was convinced that I could not follow anything but the easiest of religious rules.

When Dan began to talk about the one religious Order that filled him with the most enthusiasm, I was able to share his admiration but I had no desire to join it. It was the Order of Cistercians, the

Cistercians of the Strict Observance. The very title made me shiver, and so did their commoner name: The Trappists.

Once, six years before—and it seemed much longer than that—when I had barely glanced at the walls of the Trappist monastery of Tre Fontane, outside Rome, the fancy of becoming a Trappist had entered my adolescent mind: but if it had been anything but a pure day-dream, it would not have got inside my head at all. Now, when I was actually and seriously thinking of entering a monastery, the very idea of Trappists almost reduced me to a jelly.

"Last summer," said Dan, "I made a retreat at a Trappist monastery in Kentucky. It is called Our Lady of Gethsemani. Did you ever hear of it?"

And he began to tell me about the place—how he had been staying with some friends, and they had driven him over to the monastery. It was the first time they had ever been there. Although they lived in Kentucky, they hardly knew the Trappists existed. His hostess had been very piqued at the signs about women keeping out of the enclosure under pain of excommunication, and she had watched with awe as the heavy door closed upon him, engulfing him in that terrible, silent building.

(From where I sit and write at this moment, I look out the window, across the quiet guest-house garden, with the four banana trees and the big red and yellow flowers around Our Lady's statue. I can see the door where Dan entered and where I entered. Beyond the Porter's Lodge is a low green hill where there was wheat this summer. And out there, yonder, I can hear the racket of the diesel tractor: I don't know what they are ploughing.)

Dan had stayed in the Trappist monastery a week. He told me of the life of the monks. He told me of their silence. He said they never conversed, and the impression I got was that they never spoke at all, to anybody.

"Don't they even go to confession?" I asked.

"Of course. And they can talk to the abbot. The retreat master talked to the guests. He was Father James. He said that it was a good thing the monks didn't have to talk—with all the mixture of men they have there, they get along better without it: lawyers and farmers and soldiers and schoolboys, they all live together, and go everywhere together and do everything together. They stand in choir together, and go out to work together and sit together in the same place when they read and study. It's a good thing they don't talk."

"Oh, so they sing in choir?"

"Sure," said Dan, "they sing the Canonical hours and High Mass. They are in choir several hours a day."

I was relieved to think that the monks got to choir and exercised their vocal cords. I was afraid that so much silence would wither them up altogether.

"And they work in the fields," said Dan. "They have to make their own living by farming and raising stock. They grow most of what they eat, and bake their own bread, and make their own shoes . . ."

"I suppose they fast a lot," I said.

"Oh, yes, they fast more than half the year, and they never eat meat or fish, unless they get sick. They don't even have eggs. They just live on vegetables and cheese and things like that. They gave me a cheese when I was there, and I took it back to my friends' house. When we got there, they handed it to the colored butler. They said to him, 'Do you know what that is? That's monks' cheese.' He couldn't figure it out, and he looked at it for a while, and then he got an idea. So he looked up with a big smile and said: 'Oh, I know what you all mean: *monks!* Them's like goats.' "

But I was thinking about all that fasting. The life took my breath away, but it did not attract me. It sounded cold and terrible. The monastery now existed in my mind as a big grey prison with barred windows, filled with dour and emaciated characters with their hoods pulled down over their faces.

"They are very healthy," said Dan, "and they are big strong men. Some of them are giants."

(Since I came to the monastery I have tried to pick out Dan's "giants." I can account for one or two easily enough. But I think he must have seen the rest of them in the dark—or perhaps they are to be explained by the fact that Dan himself is not very tall.)

I sat in silence. In my heart, there was a kind of mixture of exhilaration and dejection, exhilaration at the thought of such generosity, and depression because it seemed such a drastic and cruel and excessive rejection of the rights of nature.

Dan said: "Do you think you would like that kind of a life?"

"Oh, no," I said, "not a chance! That's not for me! I'd never be able to stand it. It would kill me in a week. Besides, I have to have meat. I can't get along without meat, I need it for my health."

"Well," said Dan, "it's a good thing you know yourself so well."

For a moment it occurred to me that he was being ironical, but there was not a shadow of irony in his voice, and there never was. He was far too good and too kind and too simple for irony. He thought I knew what I was talking about, and took my word for it.

And so the conclusion of that evening was that I decided to go and see the Franciscans, and after all, we both agreed that they seemed to be the best for me.

So he gave me a note to his friend Father Edmund, at the monastery of St. Francis of Assisi on 31st Street.

ii

The Franciscan monastery on 31st Street, New York, is a grey unprepossessing place, crowded in among big buildings, and inhabited by very busy priests. Not the least busy of them in those days was Father Edmund, Dan Walsh's friend: and yet he was not too busy to talk to me practically any time I came around to see him. He was a big amiable man full of Franciscan cheerfulness, kind, disciplined by hard work yet not hardened by it, for his priesthood, which kept him close to Christ and to souls more than softened and humanized him.

From the first moment I met him, I knew I had a good friend in Father Edmund. He questioned me about my vocation, asking me how long it was since my Baptism, and what it was that attracted me to the Franciscans, and what I was doing at Columbia, and when I had talked to him for a while, he began to encourage me in the idea of becoming a Friar.

"I don't see any reason why you shouldn't eventually make application to enter the novitiate next August," he said.

Next August! That was a long way off. Now that my mind was made up, I was impatient to get started. However, I had not expected to be admitted immediately by any Order. But I asked him:

"Father, isn't there some chance of my entering sooner?"

"We admit all our novices together, in a group," he said. "They start out at Paterson, in August, then they go on together all the way through until ordination. It's the only way we can handle them. If you entered at any other time, you would miss out all along the line. Have you had much philosophy?"

I told him of Dan Walsh's courses, and he thought for a moment.

"Perhaps there might be a chance of starting you out in the novitiate in February," he said, but he did not seem to be very hopeful. No doubt what he was thinking of was that I might skip a half-year of philosophy and so catch up with the others at the house of studies up-state, where they would be sent after the year's noviceship.

"Are you living with your parents?" he asked me.

I told him they had long been dead, and that none of my family was left, except an uncle and a brother.

"Is your brother a Catholic too?"

"No, Father."

"Where is he? What does he do?"

"He goes to Cornell. He is supposed to get out of there next June."

"Well," said Father Edmund, "what about yourself? Have you got enough to live on? You aren't starving or anything, are you?"

"Oh, no, Father, I can get along. I've got a chance of a job teaching English in Extension at Columbia this year, and besides that they gave me a grant-in-aid to pay for my courses for the doctorate."

"You take that job," said the Friar; "that will do you a lot of good. And get busy on that doctorate, too. Do all the work you can, and study a little philosophy. Study won't hurt you at all. After all, you know, if you come into the Order you'll probably end up teaching at St. Bona's or Siena. You'd like that, wouldn't you?"

"Oh, sure," I said, and that was the truth.

I walked down the steps of the monastery into the noisy street, with my heart full of happiness and peace.

What a transformation this made in my life! Now, at last, God had become the center of my existence. And it had taken no less than this decision to make Him so. Apparently, in my case, it had to be that way.

I was still without any formal spiritual direction, but I went frequently to confession, especially at St. Francis' Church, where the Friars were more inclined to give me advice than secular priests had been. And it was in one of the confessionals at St. Francis' that a good priest one day told me, very insistently:

"Go to Communion every day, every day."

By that time, I had already become a daily communicant, but his words comforted and strengthened me, and his emphasis made me glad. And indeed I had reason to be, for it was those daily Communions that were transforming my life almost visibly, from day to day.

I did not realize any of this on those beautiful mornings: I scarcely was aware that I was so happy. It took someone else to draw my attention to it.

I was coming down Seventh Avenue one morning. It must have

been in December or January. I had just come from the little church of Our Lady of Guadalupe, and from Communion, and was going to get some breakfast at a lunch wagon near Loew's Sheridan Theater. I don't know what I was thinking of, but as I walked along I nearly bumped into Mark who was on his way to the subway, going to Columbia for his morning classes.

"Where are you going?" he said. The question surprised me, as there did not seem to be any reason to ask where I was going, and all I could answer was: "To breakfast."

Later on, Mark referred again to the meeting and said:

"What made you look so happy, on the street, there?"

So that was what had impressed him, and that was why he had asked me where I was going. It was not where I was going that made me happy, but where I was coming from. Yet, as I say, this surprised me too, because I had not really paid any attention to the fact that I was happy—which indeed I was.

Now every day began with Mass and Communion, either at Our Lady of Guadalupe or St. Francis of Assisi Church.

After that I went back to Perry Street, and got to work rewriting the novel which had been handed back to me politely by one of those tall, thin, anxious young men with horn-rimmed glasses who are to be found in the offices of publishers. (He had asked me if I was trying to write in some new experimental style, and then ducked behind his desk as if I might pull a knife on him for his impertinence.)

About twelve I would go out to get a sandwich at some drug-store, and read in the paper about the Russians and the Finns or about the French sitting in the Maginot Line, and sending out a party of six men somewhere in Loraine to fire three rifle shots at an imaginary German.

In the afternoon I usually had to go to Columbia and sit in a room and hear some lecture on English Literature, after which I went to the library and read St. Thomas Aquinas' commentary on Aristotle's *Metaphysics* which I had reserved for me on my desk in the graduate reading room. This was a matter of great consternation to some Sisters of St. Joseph who occupied nearby desks and who, after a while, became timidly friendly when they learned that I was going to become a Franciscan in the summer.

At about three in the afternoon I was in the habit of going to Corpus Christi, or to Our Lady of Lourdes which was even closer, and doing the Stations of the Cross. This meditative and easy prayer provided me with another way, more valuable than I realized, of entering into participation in the merits of Christ's Passion, and of renewing within me the life that had been set alight by that morning's Communion.

In those days it took a little effort to walk to a church and go around the fourteen stations saying vocal prayers, for I was still not used to praying. Therefore, doing the Stations of the Cross was still more laborious than consoling, and required a sacrifice. It was much the same with all my devotions. They did not come easily or spontaneously, and they very seldom brought with them any strong sensible satisfaction. Nevertheless the work of performing them ended in a profound and fortifying peace: a peace that was scarcely perceptible, but which deepened and which, as my passions subsided, became more and more real, more and more sure, and finally stayed with me permanently.

It was also at this time that I first attempted any kind of mental prayer. I had bought a copy of the *Spiritual Exercises* of St. Ignatius many months before, and it had remained idle on the shelf—except that when I came back from Olean and took over the apartment from Seymour's wife, to whom I had sub-let it, I found a couple of little pencil marks in the margin opposite passages that might be interpreted as sinister and Jesuitical. One of them was about death, and the other had something to do with pulling all the blinds down when you wanted to meditate.

For my own part I had long been a little scared of the *Spiritual Exercises*, having somewhere acquired a false impression that if you did not look out they would plunge you head first into mysticism before you were aware of it. How could I be sure that I would not fly up into the air as soon as I applied my mind to the first meditation? I have since found out that there is very little danger of my ever flying around the premises at mental prayer. The *Spiritual Exercises* are very pedestrian and practical—their chief purpose being to enable all the busy Jesuits to get their minds off their work and back to God with a minimum of wasted time.

I wish I had been able to go through the *Exercises* under the roof of some Jesuit house, directed by one of their priests. However, I went about it under my own direction, studying the rules of procedure that were given in the book, and following them in so far as I managed to grasp what they were all about. I never even breathed a word about what I was doing to any priest.

As far as I remember I devoted a whole month to the *Exercises*, taking one hour each day. I took a quiet hour, in the afternoon, in my room on Perry Street: and since I now lived in the back of the house, there were no street noises to worry me. It was really quite silent. With the windows closed, since it was winter, I could not even hear any of the neighborhood's five thousand radios.

The book said the room should be darkened, and I pulled down the blinds so that there was just enough light left for me to see the pages, and to look at the Crucifix on the wall over my bed. And the book also invited me to consider what kind of a position I should take for my meditation. It left me plenty of freedom of choice, so long as I remained more or less the way I was, once I had settled down, and did not go promenading around the room scratching my head and talking to myself.

So I thought and prayed awhile over this momentous problem, and finally decided to make my meditations sitting cross-legged on the floor. I think the Jesuits would have had a nasty shock if they had walked in and seen me doing their *Spiritual Exercises* sitting there like Mahatma Gandhi. But it worked very well. Most of the time I kept my eyes on the Crucifix or on the floor, when I did not have to look at the book.

And so, having prayed, sitting on the floor, I began to consider the reason why God had brought me into the world:

> Man was created to this end: that he should praise God, Our Lord, and reverence and serve Him, and by doing these things, should save his soul. And all the other things on the face of the earth were created for man, to help him in attaining the end for which he was created. Whence it follows that man must use these things only in so far as they help him towards his end, and must withdraw himself from them in so far as they are obstacles to his attaining his end. . . . Wherefore it is necessary that we make ourselves indifferent to all created things, in so far as it is permitted to our free will . . . in such a way that, as far as we are concerned, we should not desire health rather than sickness, riches rather than poverty, honor rather than ignominy, a long life rather than a short life, and so on, desiring and choosing only those things which more efficaciously lead us to the end for which we were created.

The big and simple and radical truths of the "Foundation" were, I think, too big and too radical for me. By myself, I did not even scratch the surface of them. I vaguely remember fixing my mind on this notion of indifference to all created things in themselves, to sickness and health, and being mildly appalled. Who was I to understand such a thing? If I got a cold I nearly choked myself with aspirins and hot lemonade, and dived into bed with undisguised alarm. And here was a book that might perhaps be telling me that I ought to be able to remain as cool as an icebox in the presence of a violent death. How could I figure out just what and how much that word "indifferent" meant, if there was no one to tell me? I did not have any way of seeing the distinction between indifference of the will and indifference of the feelings—the latter being practically a thing unknown, even in the experience of the saints. So, worrying about this big difficulty of my own creation, I missed the real fruit of this fundamental meditation, which would have been an application of its notions to all the things to which I myself was attached, and which always tended to get me into trouble.

However, the real value of the *Exercises* for me came when I got to the various contemplations, especially the mysteries of the life of Christ. I docilely followed all St. Ignatius's rules about the "composition of place" and sat myself down in the Holy House at Nazareth with Jesus and Mary and Joseph, and considered what they did, and listened to what they said and so on. And I elicited affections, and made resolutions, and ended with a colloquy and finally made a brief retrospective examination of how the meditation had worked out. All this was so new and interesting, and the labor of learning it engrossed me so much, that I was far too busy for distractions. The most vital part of each meditation was always the application of the senses (hearing the yelling of the damned in hell, smelling their burning rottenness, seeing the devils coming at you to drag you down with the rest, and so on).

As far as I remember, there was one theological point that made a very deep impression on me, greater than anything else. Somewhere in the first week, after having considered the malice of mortal sin, I had turned to the evil of venial sin. And there, suddenly, while the horror of mortal sin had remained somewhat abstract to me, simply because there were so many aspects and angles to the question, I clearly saw the malice of venial sin precisely as an offense against the goodness and loving kindness of God, without any respect to punishment. I left that meditation with a deep conviction of the disordination and malice there is in preferring one's own will and satisfaction to the will of God for Whose love we were created.

In the big meditation on the "Two Standards," where you are supposed to line up the army of Christ in one field and the army of the devil in the other, and ask yourself which one you choose, I got into too much of a Cecil B. De Mille atmosphere to make much out of it, but in the considerations on a choice of a state in life which followed, a strange thing happened, which scared me a little. It was the only incident that savored of externally supernatural intervention in the retreat.

I had already made my choice of a state of life. I was going to be a Franciscan. Consequently, I embarked on these thoughts without too much personal concern. I was meandering around in considerations of what a man ought to do with his earthly possessions—a meditation that might have been useful to someone who really had some possessions to dispose of—when my doorbell rang. I pressed the button that opened the street-door below, and went to the head of the stairs, thinking that perhaps it was Gibney or somebody like that.

It was a little man in a mouse-colored overcoat, whom I had never before seen.

"Are you Thomas Merton?" he said to me, as he arrived on my landing.

I did not deny it, and he entered my room and sat down on the bed.

"Did you write that review of that book about D. H. Lawrence in the *Times* book section last Sunday?" he asked me.

I thought I was in for it. I had favorably reviewed a book on Lawrence by Tyndall, under whom I had done my thesis at Columbia. He had written just the kind of a book that was calculated to drive all the people who had made a Messiah out of Lawrence clean out of their wits with pain and rage. I had already got an angry letter in the mail for even reviewing such a book, and I thought that now somebody had come around to shoot me if I did not recant.

"Yes," I said, "I wrote the review. Didn't you like it?"

"Oh, I didn't read it," said the little man, "but Mr. Richardson read it, and he told me all about it."

"Who is Mr. Richardson?"

"You don't know him? He lives in Norwalk. I was talking to him about your review only yesterday."

"I don't know anybody in Norwalk," I said. I could not figure out whether this Mr. Richardson liked the review or not, and did not bother. It did not seem to have any bearing on the man's visit after all.

"I have been travelling around all day," he said, thoughtfully. "I was in Elizabeth, New Jersey; then in Bayonne, New Jersey; then in Newark. Then, when I was coming back on the Hudson Tube I thought of Mr. Richardson and how he had been talking about you, and I thought I would come and see you."

So there he was. He had been in Elizabeth and Bayonne and Newark and now he was sitting on my bed, with his mouse-colored overcoat and his hat in his hand.

"Do you live in New Jersey?" I said, out of politeness.

"Oh, no, of course not, I live in Connecticut," he said quickly. But I had opened out only an avenue to further confusion. He went into intricate geographical details about where he lived and how he happened to be associated with this Mr. Richardson of Norwalk, and then he said:

"When I saw the ad in the paper, I decided to go over to New Jersey."

"The ad?"

"Yes, the ad about the job I was looking for in Elizabeth, and didn't get. And now I haven't even enough money to get back to Connecticut."

I finally began to see what it was all about.

The visitor was stumbling around in a long, earnest and infinitely complicated account of all the jobs he had failed to get in New Jersey, and I, with a strange awe and excitement, began to think two things: "How much money have I got to give him?" and "How did he happen to walk in here just when I was in the middle of that meditation about giving all your goods to the poor? . . ."

The possibility that he might even be an angel, disguised in that mouse-colored coat, struck me with a force that was all the more affecting because it was so obviously absurd. And yet the more I think about it, the more I am convinced of the propriety of God sending me an angel with instructions to try and fool me by talking like a character in one of those confusing short stories that get printed in the *New Yorker*.

Anyway, I reached into my pockets and started emptying them, putting quarters and pennies and nickels on the desk. Of course, if the man was an angel, then the whole affair was nothing but a set-up, and I should give him everything I had on me, and go without supper. Two things restrained me. First, the desire of supper, and, second, the fact that the stranger seemed to be aware that I was somewhat moved with secret thoughts, and apparently interpreted them as annoyance. Anyway, figuring that I was in some way upset, he showed himself to be in a hurry to take the little I had already collected for him, as if that were plenty.

He hastened away, stuffing a dollar bill and the change into his pockets, leaving me in such a state of bewilderment that I positively could not sit down cross-legged and continue the meditation. I was still wondering if I should not run down the street after him and give him the other dollar which I still had.

But still, applying St. Ignatius' standard to the present circumstances, I had done fairly well. I had given him about three-fifths of my liquid capital.

Perhaps, in a way, it is better that I didn't give him everything and go without supper. I would have preened myself with such consummate and disgusting vanity—assuming I did not die of fear, and call up one of my friends to lend me something—that there would have been no merit in it at all. For all that, even if his story was disconnected and very silly, and even if he was not an angel, he was much more than that if you apply Christ's own standard about whatsoever you have done to the least of His little ones.

Anyway, it certainly put some point into that meditation.

iii

That was also the season in which, three nights a week, I taught a class in English composition, in one of the rooms in the School of Business at Columbia. Like all Extension classes, it was a mixture of all flesh. There was a tough and bad-tempered chemist who was a center of potential opposition, because he was taking the course under duress—it was required of all the students who were following a systematic series of courses in anything at all. There was an earnest and sensitive Negro youth who sat in the front row, dressed in a neat grey suit, and peered at me intently through his glasses all the time the class was going on. There was an exchange student from the University of Rome, and there was one of those middle-aged ladies who had been taking courses like this for years and who handed in neat and punctilious themes and occupied, with a serene and conscious modesty, her rightful place as the star of the class. This entitled her to talk more than anybody else and ask more unpredictable questions.

Once, after I had been insisting that they should stick to concrete and tangible evidence, in describing places and things, an Irishman called Finegan who had been sitting in bewilderment and without promise in one of the back rows, suddenly blossomed out with a fecundity in minute and irrelevant material detail that it was impossible to check. He began handing in descriptions of shoe factories that made you feel as if you were being buried under fifty tons of machinery. And I learned, with wonder and fear, that teachers have a mysterious and deadly power of letting loose psychological forces in the minds of the young. The rapidity, the happy enthusiasm with which they responded to hints and suggestions—but with the wrong response—was enough to make a man run away and live in the woods.

But I liked teaching very much—especially teaching this kind of a class, in which most of the students had to work for their living, and valued their course because they had to pay for it out of their own savings. Teaching people like that is very flattering: the class is always so eager to get anything you have to give them, and the mere fact that they want so much, is liable to give you the impression that you are capable of giving them all they want.

For my part I was left more or less free to go ahead and teach them according to my own ideas. Now if people are going to write, they must first of all have something to write about, and if a man starts out to teach English composition, he implicitly obliges himself to teach the students how to get up enough interest in things to write about them. But it is also impossible for people to learn to write unless they also read. And so a course in composition, if it is not accompanied somewhere along the line by a course in literature, should also take a little time to teach people how to read, or at least how to get interested in a book.

Therefore, I spent most of the time throwing out ideas about what might or might not be important in life and in literature, and letting them argue about it. The arguments got better when they also included discussion of the students' favorite ideas, as expressed on paper. It soon turned out that although they did not all have ideas, they all had a definite hunger for ideas and for convictions, from the young man who wrote a theme about how happy he had been one summer when he had had a job painting a church, to the quiet Catholic housewife who sat in one of the middle rows viewing me with a reassuring smile and an air of friendly complicity whenever the discussion got around near the borders of religion. So it was a very lively class, on the whole.

But it was only to last a term. And when January came around, they told me, down in the office, that they were going to give me a class in straight, unalleviated grammar in the spring session.

Grammar was something I knew absolutely nothing about, and only the most constant vigilance had kept it out of sight in the composition class. Besides, since I was entering the monastery in the summer, I assured myself that I ought to take a last vacation, and I was already leafing through books about Mexico and Cuba, trying to decide where I would spend the money that I was no longer going to need to support myself in the world.

I told the heads of my department that I could not teach grammar in the spring, because I wanted to prepare myself for life in the cloister. They asked me what made me want to do such a thing as that, and sadly shook their heads, but did not try to argue me out of it. They told me I could come back if I changed my mind—and it almost sounded as if they were saying: "We'll take you back when you've been disillusioned and given up this fantastic notion as a bad job."

Since I still had some money coming to me from the University on my "Grant-in-Aid" I signed up for two courses in the spring. One of them was a seminar on St. Thomas, with Dan Walsh, which ended up with two of us sitting and reading the *De Ente et Essentia* with Dan in his room, in a house run by an old lady who had made a kind of career for herself by harboring the New York Giants under her roof in the baseball season.

While I was still wondering whether I could afford to go to Mexico or only to Cuba, Lent came in sight, and so I put it off until after Lent. And then, one day, when I was working in the library, I suddenly began to get pains in my stomach, and to feel weak and sick. I put away my books, and went to see a doctor, who put me on a table, and poked at my stomach and said, without hesitation:

"Yes, you've got it."

"Appendicitis?"

"Yes. You'd better have that thing out."

"Right away?"

"Well, you might as well. What's the use of waiting? You would only get into trouble with it."

And immediately he called up the hospital.

I walked down the brownstone stairs of the doctor's house, thinking that it would be nice, in the hospital, with nuns to look after me: but at the same time I was already having visions of mishaps, fatal accidents, slips of the knife that would land me in the grave. . . . I made a lot of prayers to Our Lady of Lourdes and went home to Perry Street to get a toothbrush and a copy of Dante's *Paradiso*.

And so I started back uptown. In the Fourteenth Street subway station there was a drunk. And he was really drunk. He was lying prostrate in the middle of the turnstiles, in everybody's way. Several people pushed him and told him to get up and get out of there, but he could not even get himself up on his feet.

I thought to myself: "If I try to lift him out of there, my appendix will burst, and I too will be lying there in the turnstiles along with him." With my nervousness tempered by a nice warm feeling of smugness and self-complacency, I took the drunk by the shoulders and laboriously hauled him backwards out of the turnstiles and propped him up against the wall. He groaned feebly in protest.

Then, mentally congratulating myself for my great solicitude and charity towards drunks, I entered the turnstile and went down to take the train to the hospital on Washington Heights. As I looked back, over my shoulder, from the bottom of the stairs, I could see the drunk slowly and painfully crawling back towards the turnstile, where he once again flung himself down, prostrate, across the opening, and blocked the passage as he had done before.

It was night when I got out of the station uptown, and started to climb scores of monumental steps to the top of the bluff where St. Elizabeth's Hospital was. Ice was shining in the branches of the trees, and here and there bright icicles would break off and fall and shatter in the street. I climbed the steps of the hospital, and entered the clean shiny hall and saw a crucifix and a Franciscan nun, all in white, and a statue of the Sacred Heart.

I was very sick when I came out of the ether, and I filled myself full of swords by taking a clandestine drink of water before I should have done so. But one of the nuns who was on night duty brought me a glass of what tasted like, and turned out to be, anisette. It braced me up considerably. After that, when I could eat again, I began to sit up and read Dante in bed, and the rest of the ten days were indeed a paradise.

Every morning, early, after I had washed my teeth and the nurse had fixed my bed, I would lie quiet, in happy expectancy, for the sound of the little bell coming down the hall which meant: Communion. I could count the doors the priest entered, as he stopped at the different rooms and wards. Then, with the nuns kneeling in the door, he came to my bedside with the ciborium.

"*Corpus Domini Nostri Jesu Christi custodiat animam tuam in vitam aeternam.*"

And he was gone. You could hear the bell disappear down the corridor. Under the sheet my hands folded quietly with my rosary between my fingers. It was a rosary John Paul had given me for Christmas: since he did not know the difference between one rosary and another, he had let himself be cheated in some pious store, and bought some beads that looked good but which fell to pieces in six months. It was the kind of rosary that was meant to be looked at rather than used. But the affection which it represented was as strong as the rosary itself was weak, and so, while the beads held together, I used them in preference to the strong, cheap, black wooden beads made for workmen and old Irish washwomen which I had bought for twenty-five cents in the basement of Corpus Christi during the mission.

"You go to Communion every day?" said the Italian in the next bed. He had got himself full of pneumonia shovelling snow all night for the WPA.

"Yes," I said, "I am going to be a priest."

"You see this book," I said to him, later in the day. "That's Dante's *Paradiso*."

"Dante," he said, "an Italian." And he lay on the bed with his eyes staring at the ceiling and said nothing more.

This lying in bed and being fed, so to speak, with a spoon was more than luxury: it was also full of meaning. I could not realize it at the time—and I did not need to: but a couple of years later I saw that this all expressed my spiritual life as it was then.

For I was now, at last, born: but I was still only new-born. I was living: I had an interior life, real, but feeble and precarious. And I was still nursed and fed with spiritual milk.

The life of grace had at last, it seemed, become constant, permanent. Weak and without strength as I was, I was nevertheless walking in the way that was liberty and life. I had found my spiritual freedom. My eyes were beginning to open to the powerful and constant light of heaven and my will was at last learning to give in to the subtle and gentle and loving guidance of that love which is Life without end. For once, for the first time in my life, I had been, not days, not weeks, but months, a stranger to sin. And so much health was so new to me, that it might have been too much for me.

And therefore I was being fed not only with the rational milk of every possible spiritual consolation, but it seemed that there was no benefit, no comfort, no innocent happiness, even of the material order, that could be denied me.

So I was all at once surrounded with everything that could protect me against trouble, against savagery, against suffering. Of course, while I was in the hospital, there were some physical pains, some very small inconveniences: but on the whole, everybody who has had an ordinary appendix operation knows that it is really only a picnic. And it was certainly that for me. I finished the whole *Paradiso*, in Italian, and read part of Maritain's *Preface to Metaphysics*.

After ten days I got out and went to Douglaston, to the house where my uncle and aunt still lived and where they invited me to rest until I was on my feet again. So that meant two more weeks of quiet, and undisturbed reading. I could shut myself up in the room that had once been Pop's "den," and make meditations, and pray, as I did, for instance, on the afternoon of Good Friday. And for the rest my aunt was willing to talk all day about the Redemptorists whose monastery had been just down the street when she had been a little girl in Brooklyn.

Finally, in the middle of Easter week, I went to my doctor and he ripped off the bandages and said it was all right for me to go to Cuba.

I think it was in that bright Island that the kindness and solicitude that surrounded me wherever I turned my weak steps, reached their ultimate limit. It would be hard to believe that anyone was so well taken care of as I was: and no one has ever seen an earthly child guarded so closely and so efficiently and cherished and guided and watched and led with such attentive and prevenient care as surrounded me in those days. For I walked through fires and put my head into the mouths of such lions as would bring grey hairs even to the head of a moral theologian, and all the while I was walking in my new simplicity and hardly knew what it was all about, so solicitous were my surrounding angels to whisk the scandals out from the path of my feet, and to put pillows under my knees wherever I seemed about to stumble.

I don't believe that a saint who had been elevated to the state of mystical marriage could walk through the perilous streets and dives of Havana with notably less contamination than I seem to have contracted. And yet this absence of trouble, this apparent immunity from passion or from accident, was something that I calmly took for granted. God was giving me a taste of that sense of proprietorship to which grace gives a sort of a right in the hearts of all His children. For all things are theirs, and they are Christ's, and Christ is God's. They own the world, because they have renounced proprietorship of anything in the world, and of their own bodies, and have ceased to listen to the unjust claims of passion.

Of course, with me there was no question of any real detachment. If I did not listen to my passions it was because, in the merciful dispensation of God, they had ceased to make any noise—for the time being. They did wake up, momentarily, but only when I was well out of harm's way in a very dull and sleepy city called Camagüey where practically everybody was in bed by nine o'clock at night, and where I tried to read St. Teresa's *Autobiography* in

Spanish under the big royal palms in a huge garden which I had all to myself.

I told myself that the reason why I had come to Cuba was to make a pilgrimage to Our Lady of Cobre. And I did, in fact, make a kind of a pilgrimage. But it was one of those medieval pilgrimages that was nine-tenths vacation and one-tenth pilgrimage. God tolerated all this and accepted the pilgrimage on the best terms in which it could be interpreted, because He certainly beset me with graces all the way around Cuba: graces of the kind that even a person without deep spirituality can appreciate as graces: and that is the kind of person I was then and still am.

Every step I took opened up a new world of joys, spiritual joys, and joys of the mind and imagination and senses in the natural order, but on the plane of innocence, and under the direction of grace.

There was a partial natural explanation for this. I was learning a thing that could not be completely learned except in a culture that is at least outwardly Catholic. One needs the atmosphere of French or Spanish or Italian Catholicism before there is any possibility of a complete and total experience of all the natural and sensible joys that overflow from the Sacramental life.

But here, at every turn, I found my way into great, cool, dark churches, some of them with splendid altars shining with carven retables or rich with mahogany and silver: and wonderful red gardens of flame flowered before the saints or the Blessed Sacrament.

Here in niches were those lovely, dressed-up images, those little carved Virgins full of miracle and pathos and clad in silks and black velvet, throned above the high altars. Here, in side chapels, were those *pietàs* fraught with fierce, Spanish drama, with thorns and nails whose very sight pierced the mind and heart, and all around the church were many altars to white and black saints: and everywhere were Cubans in prayer, for it is not true that the Cubans neglect their religion—or not as true as Americans complacently think, basing their judgements on the lives of the rich, sallow young men who come north from the island and spend their days in arduous gambling in the dormitories of Jesuit colleges.

But I was living like a prince in that island, like a spiritual millionaire. Every morning, getting up about seven or half-past, and walking out into the warm sunny street, I could find my way quickly to any one of a dozen churches, new churches or as old as the seventeenth century. Almost as soon as I went in the door I could receive Communion, if I wished, for the priest came out with a ciborium loaded with Hosts before Mass and during it and after it—and every fifteen or twenty minutes a new Mass was starting at a different altar. These were the churches of the religious Orders—Carmelites, Franciscans, the American Augustinians at El Santo Cristo, or the Fathers of Mercy—everywhere I turned, there was someone ready to feed me with the infinite strength of the Christ Who loved me, and Who was beginning to show me with an immense and subtle and generous lavishness how much He loved me.

And there were a thousand things to do, a thousand ways of easily making a thanksgiving: everything lent itself to Communion: I could hear another Mass, I could say the Rosary, do the Stations of the Cross, or if I just knelt where I was, everywhere I turned my eyes I saw saints in wood or plaster or those who seemed to be saints in flesh and blood—and even those who were probably not saints, were new enough and picturesque enough to stimulate my mind with many meanings and my heart with prayers. And as I left the church there was no lack of beggars to give me the opportunity of almsgiving, which is an easy and simple way of wiping out sins.

Often I left one church and went to hear another Mass in another church, especially if the day happened to be Sunday, and I would listen to the harmonious sermons of the Spanish priests, the very grammar of which was full of dignity and mysticism and courtesy. After Latin, it seems to me there is no language so fitted for prayer and for talk about God as Spanish: for it is a language at once strong and supple, it has its sharpness, it has the quality of steel in it, which gives it the accuracy that true mysticism needs, and yet it is soft, too, and gentle and pliant, which devotion needs, and it is courteous and suppliant and courtly, and it lends itself surprisingly little to sentimentality. It has some of the intellectuality of French but not the coldness that intellectuality gets in French: and it never overflows into the feminine melodies of Italian. Spanish is never a weak language, never sloppy, even on the lips of a woman.

The fact that while all this was going on in the pulpit, there would be Cubans ringing bells and yelling lottery numbers outside in the street seemed to make no difference. For a people that is supposed to be excitable, the Cubans have a phenomenal amount of patience with all the things that get on American nerves and drive people crazy, like persistent and strident noise. But for my own part, I did not mind any of that any more than the natives did.

When I was sated with prayers, I could go back into the streets, walking among the lights and shadows, stopping to drink huge glasses of iced fruit juices in the little bars, until I came home again and read Maritain or St. Teresa until it was time for lunch.

And so I made my way to Matanzas and Camagüey and Santiago—riding in a wild bus through the olive-grey Cuban countryside, full of sugar-cane fields. All the way I said rosaries and looked out into the great solitary ceiba trees, half expecting that the Mother of God would appear to me in one of them. There seemed to be no reason why she should not, for all things in heaven were just a little out of reach. So I kept looking, looking, and half expecting. But I did not see Our Lady appear, beautiful, in any of the ceiba trees.

At Matanzas I got mixed up in the *paseo* where the whole town walks around and around the square in the evening coolness, the men in one direction and the girls in the other direction, and immediately I made friends with about fifty-one different people of all ages. The evening ended up with me making a big speech in broken Spanish, surrounded by men and boys in a motley crowd that included the town Reds and the town intellectuals and the graduates of the Marist Fathers' school and some law students from the University of Havana. It was all about faith and morals and made a big impression and, in return, their acceptance of it made a big impression on me, too: for many of them were glad that someone, a foreigner, should come and talk about these things, and I heard someone who had just arrived in the crowd say:

"¿Es católico, ese Americano?"

"Man," said the other, "he is a Catholic and a very good Catholic," and the tone in which he said this made me so happy that, when I went to bed, I could not sleep. I lay in the bed and looked up through the mosquito netting at the bright stars that shone in upon me through the wide-open window that had no glass and no frame, but only a heavy wooden shutter against the rain.

In Camagüey I found a Church to La Soledad, Our Lady of Solitude, a little dressed-up image up in a shadowy niche: you could hardly see her. La Soledad! One of my big devotions, and you never find her, never hear anything about her in this country, except that one of the old California missions was dedicated to her.

Finally my bus went roaring across the dry plain towards the blue wall of mountains: Oriente, the end of my pilgrimage.

When we had crossed over the divide and were going down through the green valleys towards the Caribbean Sea, I saw the yellow Basilica of Our Lady of Cobre, standing on a rising above the tin roofs of the mining village in the depths of a deep bowl of green, backed by cliffs and sheer slopes robed in jungle.

"There you are, Caridad del Cobre! It is you that I have come to see; you will ask Christ to make me His priest, and I will give you my heart, Lady: and if you will obtain for me this priesthood, I will remember you at my first Mass in such a way that the Mass will be for you and offered through your hands in gratitude to the Holy Trinity, Who has used your love to win me this great grace."

The bus tore down the mountainside to Santiago. The mining engineer who had got on at the top of the divide was talking all the way down in English he had learned in New York, telling me of the graft that had enriched the politicians of Cuba and of Oriente.

In Santiago I ate dinner on the terrace of a big hotel in front of the cathedral. Across the square was the shell of a five-storey building that looked as if it had been gutted by a bomb: but the ruin had happened in an earthquake not so very long before. It was long enough ago so that the posters on the fence that had been put up in front of it had time to get tattered, and I was thinking: perhaps it is now getting to be time for another earthquake. And I looked up at the two towers of the cathedral, ready to sway and come booming down on my head.

The bus that took me to Cobre the next morning was the most dangerous of all the furious busses that are the terror of Cuba. I think it made most of the journey at eighty miles an hour on two wheels, and several times I thought it was going to explode. I said rosaries all the way up to the shrine, while the trees went by in a big greenish-yellow blur. If Our Lady had tried to appear to me, I probably would never even got a glimpse of her.

I walked up the path that wound around the mound on which the Basilica stands. Entering the door, I was surprised that the floor was so shiny and the place was so clean. I was in the back of the church, up in the apse, in a kind of oratory behind the high altar, and there, facing me, in a little shrine, was La Caridad, the little, cheerful, black Virgin, crowned with a crown and dressed in royal robes, who is the Queen of Cuba.

There was nobody else in the place but a pious middle-aged lady attendant in a black dress who was eager to sell me a lot of medals and so I knelt before La Caridad and made my prayer and made my promise. I sneaked down into the Basilica after that, and knelt where I could see La Caridad and where I could really be alone and pray, but the pious lady, impatient to make her deal, or perhaps afraid that I might get up to some mischief in the Basilica, came down and peeked through the door.

So, disappointed and resigned, I got up and came out and bought a medal and got some change for the beggars and went away, without having a chance to say all that I wanted to say to La Caridad or to hear much from her.

Down in the village I bought a bottle of some kind of *gaseosa* and stood under the tin roof of the porch of the village store. Somewhere in one of the shacks, on a harmonium, was played: "*Kyrie Eleison, Kyrie Eleison, Kyrie Eleison.*"

And I went back to Santiago.

But while I was sitting on the terrace of the hotel, eating lunch, La Caridad del Cobre had a word to say to me. She handed me an idea for a poem that formed so easily and smoothly and spontaneously in my mind that all I had to do was finish eating and go up to my room and type it out, almost without a correction.

So the poem turned out to be both what she had to say to me and what I had to say to her. It was a song for La Caridad del Cobre, and it was, as far as I was concerned, something new, and the first real poem I had ever written, or anyway the one I liked best. It pointed the way to many other poems; it opened the gate, and set me travelling on a certain and direct track that was to last me several years.

The poem said:

> The white girls lift their heads like trees,
> The black girls go
> Reflected like flamingoes in the street.
>
> The white girls sing as shrill as water,
> The black girls talk as quiet as clay.
>
> The white girls open their arms like clouds,
> The black girls close their eyes like wings:
> Angels bow down like bells,
> Angels look up like toys,
>
> Because the heavenly stars
> Stand in a ring:
> And all the pieces of the mosaic, earth,
> Get up and fly away like birds.

When I went back to Havana, I found out something else, too, and something vastly more important. It was something that made me realize, all of a sudden, not merely intellectually, but experimentally, the real uselessness of what I had been half deliberately looking for: the visions in the ceiba trees. And this experience opened another door, not a way to a kind of writing but a way into a world infinitely new, a world that was out of this world of ours entirely and which transcended it infinitely, and which was not a world, but which was God Himself.

I was in the Church of St. Francis at Havana. It was a Sunday. I had been to Communion at some other church, I think at El Cristo, and now I had come here to hear another Mass. The building was crowded. Up in front, before the altar, there were rows and rows of children, crowded together. I forget whether they were First Communicants or not: but they were children around that age. I was far in the back of the church, but I could see the heads of all those children.

It came time for the Consecration. The priest raised the Host, then he raised the chalice. When he put the chalice down on the altar, suddenly a Friar in his brown robe and white cord stood up in front of the children, and all at once the voices of the children burst out:

"*Creo en Diós. . . .*"

"I believe in God the Father Almighty, the creator of heaven and earth . . ."

The Creed. But that cry, "*Creo en Diós!*" It was loud, and bright, and sudden and glad and triumphant; it was a good big shout, that came from all those Cuban children, a joyous affirmation of faith.

Then, as sudden as the shout and as definite, and a thousand times more bright, there formed in my mind an awareness, an understanding, a realization of what had just taken place on the altar, at the Consecration: a realization of God made present by the words of Consecration in a way that made Him belong to me.

But what a thing it was, this awareness: it was so intangible, and yet it struck me like a thunderclap. It was a light that was so bright that it had no relation to any visible light and so profound and so intimate that it seemed like a neutralization of every lesser experience.

And yet the thing that struck me most of all was that this light was in a certain sense "ordinary"—it was a light (and this most of all was what took my breath away) that was offered to all, to everybody, and there was nothing fancy or strange about it. It was the light of faith deepened and reduced to an extreme and sudden obviousness.

It was as if I had been suddenly illuminated by being blinded by the manifestation of God's presence.

The reason why this light was blinding and neutralizing was that there was and could be simply nothing in it of sense or imagination. When I call it a light that is a metaphor which I am using, long after the fact. But at the moment, another overwhelming thing about this awareness was that it disarmed all images, all metaphors, and cut through the whole skein of species and phantasms with which we naturally do our thinking. It ignored all sense experience in order to strike directly at the heart of truth, as if a sudden and immediate contact had been established between my intellect and the Truth Who was now physically really and substantially before me on the altar. But this contact was not something speculative and abstract: it was concrete and experimental and belonged to the order of knowledge, yes, but more still to the order of love.

Another thing about it was that this light was something far above and beyond the level of any desire or any appetite I had ever yet been aware of. It was purified of all emotion and cleansed of everything that savored of sensible yearnings. It was love as clean and direct as vision: and it flew straight to the possession of the Truth it loved.

And the first articulate thought that came to my mind was:

"Heaven is right here in front of me: Heaven, Heaven!"

It lasted only a moment: but it left a breathless joy and a clean peace and happiness that stayed for hours and it was something I have never forgotten.

The strange thing about this light was that although it seemed so "ordinary" in the sense I have mentioned, and so accessible, there was no way of recapturing it. In fact, I did not even know how to start trying to reconstruct the experience or bring it back if I wanted to, except to make acts of faith and love. But it was easy to see that there was nothing I could do to give any act of faith that peculiar quality of sudden obviousness: that was a gift and had to come from somewhere else, beyond and above myself.

However, let no one think that just because of this light that came to me one day, at Mass, in the Church of St. Francis at Havana, I was in the habit of understanding things that clearly, or that I was far advanced in prayer. No, my prayer continued to be largely vocal. And the mental prayer I made was not systematic, but the more or less spontaneous meditating and affective prayer that came and went, according to my reading, here and there. And most of the time my prayer was not so much prayer as a matter of anticipating, with hope and desire, my entrance into the Franciscan novitiate, and a certain amount of imagining what it was going to be like, so that often I was not praying at all, but only day dreaming.

iv

The months passed quickly, but not quickly enough for me. Already it was June 1940: but the two months that remained until the date in August when the doors of the novitiate would open to receive thirty or forty new postulants seemed infinitely far away.

I did not stay long in New York when I came back from Cuba. I was there only a few days, in which I went to the monastery on 31st Street, and learned from Father Edmund that my application for admission had been accepted, and that some of the necessary papers had arrived. It was a very good thing that this was so, because postulants entering a religious Order need documents from every diocese where they have lived for a morally continuous year since their fourteenth year, as well as a birth certificate and a lot of other things as well.

But this was precisely the time when the German armies were pouring into France. At the moment when I stepped off the boat in New York, they had made their first great break through the French lines, and it had at last become obvious that the impregnable defence of the Maginot Line was a myth. Indeed, it was only a matter of very few days before the fierce armored divisions of the Nazis, following in the path broken out before them by the *Luftwaffe*, pierced the demoralized French army and embraced the betrayed nation in arms of steel. They had Paris within a fortnight, and then they were at the Loire, and finally the papers were full of blurred wirephotos of the dumb, isolated dining-car in the park at Compiègne where Hitler made the French eat the document on which the 1918 armistice had been written.

So, too, if my father and mother's marriage certificate from St. Anne's in Soho, London, had not come in that year, it might never have come at all. I don't know if the parish records of St. Anne's survived the blitzkrieg that was about to be let loose over the head of the huge, dark city full of sins and miseries, in whose fogs I had once walked with such wise complacency.

Everything seemed clear. A month would go by, and then another, and soon I would be walking, with my suitcase, up some drab, unimaginable street in Paterson, New Jersey, to a small brick monastery which I could not very well envisage. But the drabness of the city would be left behind at the door and I knew, although I had no special illusions about St. Anthony's novitiate either, that inside I would find peace. And I would begin my retreat, and after a month or so I would put on the brown robe and white cord of a friar and

I would be walking in sandals with a shaved head, in silence, to a not too beautiful chapel. But anyway, there I would have God, and possess Him, and belong to Him.

Meanwhile, I would go upstate. The best thing I could think of was to join Lax and Rice and Gerdy and Gibney and the red-headed Southerner Jim Knight who were all living at the cottage on the hill over Olean. But on the way, I went through Ithaca to see my brother at Cornell.

Perhaps this was the last time I would see John Paul before I entered the novitiate. I could not tell.

This was the year he was supposed to graduate from Cornell, but it turned out that things had gone wrong, and he was not graduating after all. The bored, lost, perplexed expression that wrinkled his forehead, the restlessness of his walk, and the joyless noisiness of his laughter told me all I needed to know about my brother's college career. I recognized all the tokens of the spiritual emptiness that had dogged my own steps from Cambridge to Columbia.

He had a big second-hand Buick in which he drove up and down all day under the heavy-hanging branches of the campus trees. His life was a constant reckless peregrination back and forth between the college and the town in the valley below it, from his classes to Willard Straight Hall to sit on the terrace with the co-eds and drink sodas in the sun, and look at the vast, luminous landscape as bright and highly colored as a plate in the *National Geographic Magazine*. He wandered from the university library to his rooms in the town, and thence to the movies, and thence to all those holes in the wall whose names I have forgotten or never knew, where Cornell students sit around tables in a dull, amber semi-darkness and fill the air with their noise and the smoke of their cigarettes and the din of their appalling wit.

I only stayed with him at Ithaca a couple of days, and when I got up in the morning to go to Mass and Communion, he came down and knelt with me and heard Mass, and watched me go to Communion. He told me he had been talking to the chaplain of the Catholic students, but I could not make out whether his real attraction was the faith, or the fact that the chaplain was interested in flying. And John Paul himself, as it turned out, was going down most days to the Ithaca airport and learning to fly a plane.

After we had had breakfast, he went back to the campus to take an examination in some such subject as Oriental history or Russian Literature, and I got on a bus that would take me to Elmira where I would get the train to Olean.

The cottage was crowded, and that meant that there were far more dirty dishes piling up in the kitchen after those perilous meals of fried, suspicious meats. But everybody was busy with something and the woods were quiet and the sun was as bright as ever on the wide, airy landscape of rolling mountains before our faces.

Presently Seymour came from New York, with Helen his wife, and Peggy Wells came to the cottage, and later came Nancy Flagg who went to Smith and for whom Lax had written a poem in the *New Yorker*. Gibney and Seymour climbed into the tops of thirty-foot trees and built a platform there about ten feet long between the trees, reached by a ladder up the side of one of the trees. It was so high that Lax would not even climb it.

Meanwhile, in the early mornings, outside the room where the girls lived, you would see Peggy Wells sitting and reading one of those fancy editions of the Bible as literature out loud to herself. And when Nancy Flagg was there, she sat in the same sun, and combed her long hair, which was marvelous red-gold and I hope she never cut it short for it gave glory to God. And on those days I think Peggy Wells read the Bible out loud to Nancy Flagg. I don't know. Later Peggy Wells walked through the woods by herself puzzling over Aristotle's *Categories*.

Rice and Knight and Gerdy sat apart, mostly in or around the garage, typing or discussing novels or commercial short stories, and Lax grew his beard, and thought, and sometimes put down on paper thoughts for a story, or talked with Nancy Flagg.

For my own part, I found a good place where I could sit on a rail of the fence along the stony driveway, and look at the far hills, and say the rosary. It was a quiet, sunny place, and the others did not come by that way much, and you could not hear the sounds of the house. This was where I was happiest, in those weeks in June.

It was too far from town to go down to Communion every morning—I had to hitch-hike down. And that was one reason why I asked one of my friends, Father Joseph, a Friar who had come to St. Bonaventure's from New York to teach summer school, if I could not come down there for a couple of weeks.

Seeing that I was going to enter the Order in August, it was not hard to persuade the Guardian to let me come down and stay in the big, dilapidated room in the gymnasium that was occupied by three or four poor students and seminarians who had odd jobs around the place as telephone operators and garage hands, for the summer.

At that time all the clerics from the different houses of studies in the Province came to St. Bonaventure's for the summer, and I suppose they are doing it again, now that the war is over. So in those weeks I really began to enter into Franciscan life, and get some taste of it as it is led in this country and to know some of its pleasant and cheerful and easy-going informality.

Summer school had not yet started, and the clerics had plenty of time to sit around on the steps of the library and gymnasium and tell me stories about how it had been with them in the novitiate. I began to get a picture of a life that was, in their estimation, somewhat severe, but was full of its own lighter moments.

St. Anthony's monastery, they said, was the hottest place they had ever seen, in the summer time, and the chapel was stuffy, and was filled with a sickening smell of wax from all the burning candles. Then there was a certain amount of work to be done. You had to scrub floors and wash dishes and work in the garden. But then you got some time to yourself and there was recreation too. I got dark hints of humiliations that were to be expected, here and there, but they all agreed that the novice master was a good sort of a fellow, and they liked him. They told me I would too.

The general impression I got was that all the unpleasantness and hardship was crowded into the year of the canonical novitiate, and that after that things opened out and became easy and pleasant as they were now: and certainly these clerics as I saw them were leading a life that could not by any stretch of the imagination be called hard. Here they were living at this college, among these beautiful green hills, surrounded by woods and fields, in a corner of America where the summer is never hot, and which they would leave long before the cold weather came. They had whole mornings and afternoons to read or study, and there were hours in which they could play baseball or tennis or go for walks in the woods, or even go in to town, walking two by two, solemnly in black suits and Roman collars.

They told me elaborate stories of the ways there were of getting around even the easy regulations that prohibited too much familiarity with seculars, and of course the good Catholic families in the town were falling over themselves in their anxiety to invite the young Franciscans to come and sit in their parlors and be made much of, with cookies and soft drinks.

For my part, I was already deciding in my mind that I would make use of all these opportunities to get away and read and pray and do some writing, when I was in my brown robe and wearing those same sandals.

Meanwhile, I got up when the clerics did—I suppose it was not much earlier than six in the morning—and went to Mass with them, and received Communion after them all, and then went to breakfast with the farm hands, where a little nun in a white and blue habit brought us cornflakes and fried eggs: for the cooking was done by some Sisters of one of those innumerable little Franciscan congregations.

After breakfast, I would walk over to the library, breathing the cold morning air as the dew melted on the lawns. Father Irenaeus gave me the key to the philosophy seminar room, and there I could spend the morning all alone reading St. Thomas, at my leisure, with a big, plain wooden crucifix at the end of the room for me to look at when I raised my eyes from the book.

I don't think I had ever been so happy in my life as I now was in that silent library, turning over the pages of the first part of the *Summa Theologica,* and here and there making notes on the goodness, the all-presence, the wisdom, the power, the love of God.

In the afternoons, I would walk in the woods, or along the Alleghany River that flowed among the trees, skirting the bottom of the wide pastures.

Turning over the pages of Butler's *Lives of the Saints,* I had looked for some name to take in religion—indeed, that was a problem over which I had wasted an undue amount of time. The Province was a big one, and there were so many Friars in it that they had run out of all the names—and you could not take a name that was already taken by someone else. I knew in advance that I could not be a John Baptist or an Augustine or Jerome or Gregory. I would have to find some outlandish name like Paphnutius (which was Father Irenaeus' suggestion). Finally I came across a Franciscan called Bl. John Spaniard and I thought that would sound fine.

I considered the possibility of myself running around in a brown robe and sandals, and imagined I heard the novice master saying: "Frater John Spaniard, go over there and scrub that floor." Or else he would put his head out of his room and say to one of the other novices: "Go and get Frater John Spaniard and bring him here," and then I would come humbly along the corridor in my sandals—or rather *our* sandals—with my eyes down, with the rapid but decorous gait of a young Friar who knew his business: Frater John Spaniard. It made a pleasant picture.

When I went back to the cottage on the hill, and timidly admitted that I thought I might take the name of Frater John Spaniard, Seymour at least thought it was a good choice. Seymour had a weakness for anything that seemed to have some sort of dash about it, and maybe in the back of his mind he was thinking of Torquemada and the Inquisition, although I don't think the John Spaniard in question had much to do with that. But I have forgotten where that saint actually did belong in history.

All this fuss about choosing a fancy name may seem like nothing but harmless foolishness, and I suppose that is true. But nevertheless I now realize that it was a sign of a profound and radical defect in the vocation which so filled my heart and occupied my imagination in those summer days of 1940.

It is true I was called to the cloister. That has been made abundantly clear. But the dispositions with which I was now preparing to enter the Franciscan novitiate were much more imperfect than I was able to realize. In choosing the Franciscans, I had followed what was apparently a perfectly legitimate attraction—an attraction which might very well have been a sign of God's will, even though it was not quite as supernatural as I thought. I had chosen this Order because I thought I would be able to keep its Rule without difficulty, and because I was attracted by the life of teaching and writing which it would offer me, and much more by the surroundings in which I saw I would probably live. God very often accepts dispositions that are no better than these, and even some that are far worse, and turns them into a true vocation in His own time.

But with me, it was not to be so. I had to be led by a way that I could not understand, and I had to follow a path that was beyond my own choosing. God did not want anything of my natural tastes and fancies and selections until they had been more completely divorced from their old track, their old habits, and directed to Himself, by His own working. My natural choice, my own taste in selecting a mode of life, was altogether untrustworthy. And already my selfishness was asserting itself, and claiming this whole vocation for itself, by investing the future with all kinds of natural pleasures and satisfactions which would fortify and defend my ego against the troubles and worries of life in the world.

Besides, I was depending almost entirely on my own powers and on my own virtues—as if I had any!—to become a good religious, and to live up to my obligations in the monastery. God does not want that. He does not ask us to leave the world as a favor to Himself.

God calls men—not only religious, but all Christians—to be the "salt of the earth." But the savor of the salt, says St. Augustine, is a supernatural life, and we lose our savor if, ceasing to rely on God alone, we are guided, in our actions, by the mere desire of temporal goods or the fear of their loss: "Be ye not solicitous, therefore, saying what shall we eat, or what shall we drink or wherewith shall we be clothed? For after all these things do the heathens seek. For your Father knoweth that you have need of all these things." "And he said to all: If any man will come after me, let him deny himself and take up his cross daily, and follow me. For whosoever will save his life shall lose it; for he that shall lose his life, for my sake, shall save it."

No matter what religious Order a man enters, whether its Rule be easy or strict in itself does not much matter; if his vocation is to be really fruitful it must cost him something, and must be a real sacrifice. It must be a cross, a true renunciation of natural goods, even of the highest natural goods.

Since I was the person that I happened to be, and since I was so strongly attached to material goods, and so immersed in my own self, and so far from God, and so independent of Him, and so dependent on myself and my own imaginary powers, it was necessary that I should not enter a monastery feeling the way I did about the Franciscans.

The truth of the matter is simply this: becoming a Franciscan, especially at that precise moment of history, meant absolutely no sacrifice at all, as far as I was concerned. Even the renunciation of legitimate pleasures of the flesh did not cost me as much as it might seem. I had suffered so much tribulation and unrest on their account that I rejoiced in the prospect of peace, in a life protected from the heat and anguish of passion by the vow of chastity. So even this was a boon rather than a matter of pain—all the more so because I imagined, in my stupid inexperience, that the fight against concupiscence had already been won, and that my soul was free, and that I had little or nothing to worry about any more.

No, all I would have to do would be to enter the novitiate, and undergo one year of inconveniences so slight that they would hardly be noticeable, and after that everything would be full of fine and easy delights—plenty of freedom, plenty of time to read and study and meditate, and ample liberty to follow my own tastes and desires in all things of the mind and spirit. Indeed, I was entering upon a life of the highest possible natural pleasures: for even prayer, in a certain sense, can be a natural pleasure.

Above all, it must be remembered that the world was at war, and even now, at the cottage, we sat around the fireplace at night and talked about the Selective Service Law that would soon be passed in Washington, wondering how it would be, and what we should do about it.

For Lax and Gibney this law involved a complicated problem of conscience. They were even asking themselves whether the war was licit at all: and if so, whether they could be justified in entering it as combatants. For my own part, no problems even arose, since I would be in a monastery, and the question would be settled automatically. . . .

I think it is very evident that such a vocation demanded more of a trial. God was not going to let me walk out of the miseries of the world into a refuge of my own choosing. He had another way prepared for me. He had several questions He wanted to ask me about this vocation of mine: questions which I would not be able to answer.

Then, when I failed to answer them, He would give me the answers, and I would find the problem solved.

It was a strange thing: I did not take it as a warning: but one night I was reading the ninth chapter of the Book of Job, and was amazed and stunned by a series of lines which I could not forget:

> And Job answered and said: "Indeed I know that it is so, and that man cannot be justified compared with God. If He will contend with him, he cannot answer Him, one for a thousand. . . . He is wise in heart and mighty in strength: who hath resisted Him and hath had peace? . . . Who shaketh the earth out of her place, and the pillars thereof tremble. Who commandeth the sun and it riseth not: and shutteth up the stars as it were under a seal."

It was a cool summer evening. I was sitting in the driveway outside the wide-open garage which had become a general dormitory, since we now had no car to put there. Rice and Lax and Seymour and I had all brought our beds out there to sleep in the air. With the book in my lap I looked down at the lights of the cars crawling up the road from the valley. I looked at the dark outline of the wooded hills and at the stars that were coming out in the eastern sky.

The words of the vulgate text rang and echoed in my heart: "*Qui facit Arcturum et Oriona* . . ." "Who maketh Arcturus and Orion and Hyades and the inner parts of the south. . . ."

There was something deep and disturbing in the lines. I thought they only moved me as poetry: and yet I also felt, obscurely enough, that there was something personal about them. God often talks to us directly in Scripture. That is, He plants the words full of actual graces as we read them and sudden undiscovered meanings are sown in our hearts, if we attend to them, reading with minds that are at prayer.

I did not yet have the art of reading that way, but nevertheless these words had a dark fire in them with which I began to feel myself burned and seared.

> If He come to me, I shall not see Him: if He depart, I shall not understand. . . . If He examine me on a sudden who shall answer Him? Or who can say: why dost Thou so?

There was something in the words that seemed to threaten all the peace that I had been tasting for months past, a kind of forewarning of an accusation that would unveil forgotten realities. I had fallen asleep in my sweet security. I was living as if God only existed to do me temporal favors . . .

> God whose wrath no man can resist, and under Whom they stoop that bear up the world.
>
> What am I then, that I should answer Him and have words with Him?
>
> And if He should hear me when I call, I should not believe that He had heard my voice.
>
> For He shall crush me in a whirlwind and multiply my wounds even without cause. . . .

"Even without cause!" And my uneasy spirit was already beginning to defend itself against this unfair God Who could not be unjust, could not be unfair.

> If I would justify myself, my own mouth shall condemn me: if I would shew myself innocent He shall prove me wicked.
>
> . . . *and multiply my wounds even without cause.*

I closed the book. The words struck deep. They were more than I would ever be able to understand. But the impression they made should have been a kind of warning that I was about to find out something about their meaning.

The blow fell suddenly.

I was within a few weeks of entering the novitiate. Already I was receiving those last minute letters from the novice-master, with the printed lists of things I was expected to bring with me to the monastery. They were few enough. The only perplexing item on the list was "one umbrella."

The list made me happy. I read it over and over. I began to feel the same pleased excitement that used to glow in the pit of my stomach when I was about to start out for camp in the summer, or to go to a new school. . . .

Then God asked me a question. He asked me a question about my vocation.

Rather, God did not have to ask me any questions. He knew all that He needed to know about my vocation. He allowed the devil, as I think, to ask me some questions, not in order that the devil should get any information, but in order that I might learn a thing or two.

There is a certain kind of humility in hell which is one of the worst things in hell, and which is infinitely far from the humility of the saints, which is peace. The false humility of hell is an unending, burning shame at the inescapable stigma of our sins. The sins of the damned are felt by them as vesture of intolerable insults from which they cannot escape, Nessus shirts that burn them up for ever and which they can never throw off.

The anguish of this self-knowledge is inescapable even on earth, as long as there is any self-love left in us: because it is pride that feels the burning of that shame. Only when all pride, all self-love has been consumed in our souls by the love of God, are we delivered from the thing which is the subject of those torments. It is only when we have lost all love of our selves for our own sakes that our past sins cease to give us any cause for suffering or for the anguish of shame.

For the saints, when they remember their sins, do not remember the sins but the mercy of God, and therefore even past evil is turned by them into a present cause of joy and serves to glorify God.

It is the proud that have to be burned and devoured by the horrible humility of hell. . . . But as long as we are in this life, even that burning anguish can be turned into a grace, and should be a cause of joy.

But anyway, one day I woke up to find out that the peace I had known for six months or more had suddenly gone.

The Eden I had been living in had vanished. I was outside the wall. I did not know what flaming swords barred my way to the gate whose rediscovery had become impossible. I was once more out in the cold and naked and alone.

Then everything began to fall apart, especially my vocation to the monastery.

Not that it occurred to me to doubt my desire to be a Franciscan, to enter the cloister, to become a priest. That desire was stronger than ever now that I was cast out into the darkness of this cold solitude. It was practically the only thing I had left, the only thing to cover me and keep me warm: and yet it was small comfort, because the very presence of the desire tortured me by contrast with the sudden hopelessness that had come storming up out of the hidden depths of my heart.

My desire to enter the cloister was small comfort indeed: for I had suddenly been faced with the agonizing doubt, the unanswerable question: Do I really have that vocation?

I suddenly remembered who I was, who I had been. I was astonished: since last September I seemed to have forgotten that I had ever sinned.

And now I suddenly realized that none of the men to whom I had talked about my vocation, neither Dan Walsh nor Father Edmund, knew who I really was. They knew nothing about my past. They did not know how I had lived before I entered the Church. They had simply accepted me because I was superficially presentable, I had a fairly open sort of a face and seemed to be sincere and to have an ordinary amount of sense and good will. Surely that was not enough.

Now the terrible problem faced me: "I have got to go and let Father Edmund know about all this. Perhaps it will make a big difference." After all, it is not enough merely to *desire* to enter the monastery.

An attraction to the cloister is not even the most important element in a religious vocation. You have to have the right moral and physical and intellectual aptitudes. And you have to be *accepted*, and accepted on certain grounds.

When I looked at myself in the light of this doubt, it began to appear utterly impossible that anyone in his right mind could consider me fit material for the priesthood.

I immediately packed my bag and started out for New York.

It seemed a long, long journey as the train crawled along the green valleys. As we were coming down the Delaware towards Callicoon, where the Franciscans had their minor seminary, the sky had clouded over. We were slowing down, and the first houses of the village were beginning to file past on the road beside the track. A boy who had been swimming in the river came running up a path through the long grass, from the face of the thunderstorm that was just about to break. His mother was calling to him from the porch of one of the houses.

I became vaguely aware of my own homelessness.

When we had gone around the bend and I could see the stone

tower of the seminary on the hilltop among the trees, I thought: "I will never live in you; it is finished."

I got into New York that evening and called up Father Edmund, but he was too busy to see me.

So I went out to the house at Douglaston.

"When are you going to the novitiate?" my aunt asked me.

"Maybe I'm not going," I said.

They did not ask me any questions.

I went to Communion and prayed earnestly that God's will should be done—and it was. But I was far from being able to understand it then.

Father Edmund listened to what I had to say. I told him about my past and all the troubles I had had. He was very friendly and very kind.

But if I had had any hope that he would wave all my doubts aside with a smile, I was soon disappointed. He said:

"Well, Tom, listen: suppose you let me think it over and pray a bit. Come back in a couple of days. All right?"

"In a couple of days?"

"Come back tomorrow."

So I waited for another day. My mind was full of anguish and restlessness. I prayed: "My God, please take me into the monastery. But anyway, whatever You want, Your will be done."

Of course I understand the whole business now. My own mind was full of strange, exaggerated ideas. I was in a kind of a nightmare. I could not see anything straight. But Father Edmund saw clearly enough for all that.

He saw that I was only a recent convert, not yet two years in the Church. He saw that I had had an unsettled life, and that my vocation was by no means sure, and that I was upset with doubts and misgivings. The novitiate was full, anyway. And when a novitiate is crammed with postulants year after year it is time for somebody to reflect about the quality of the vocations that are coming in. When there is such a crowd, you have to be careful that a few who are less desirable do not float in on the tide with the rest. . . .

So the next day he told me kindly enough that I ought to write to the Provincial and tell him that I had reconsidered my application.

There was nothing I could say. I could only hang my head and look about me at the ruins of my vocation.

I asked a few faint-hearted questions, trying to feel my way and find out if my case were altogether hopeless. Naturally, Father did not want to commit himself or his Order to anything, and I could not even get what might seem to be a vague promise for the future.

There seemed to me to be no question that I was now excluded from the priesthood for ever.

I promised I would write at once, and that I would proclaim my undying loyalty to the Friars Minor in doing so.

"Do that," Father said. "The Provincial will be pleased."

When I walked down the steps of the monastery, I was so dazed I didn't know what to do. All I could think of was to go over across Seventh Avenue to the Church of the Capuchins, next to the station. I went inside the church, and knelt in the back and, seeing there was a priest hearing confessions, I presently got up and took my place in the short line that led to his confessional.

I knelt in the darkness until the slide snapped back with a bang and I saw a thin, bearded priest who looked something like James Joyce. All the Capuchins in this country have that kind of a beard. The priest was in no mood to stand for any nonsense, and I myself was confused and miserable, and couldn't explain myself properly, and so he got my story all mixed up. Evidently he decided that I was only complaining and trying to get around the decision that had been made by some religious Order that had fired me out of their novitiate, probably for some good reason.

The whole thing was so hopeless that finally, in spite of myself, I began to choke and sob and I couldn't talk any more. So the priest, probably judging that I was some emotional and unstable and stupid character, began to tell me in very strong terms that I certainly did not belong in the monastery, still less the priesthood and, in fact, gave me to understand that I was simply wasting his time and insulting the Sacrament of Penance by indulging my self-pity in his confessional.

When I came out of that ordeal, I was completely broken in pieces. I could not keep back the tears, which ran down between the fingers of the hands in which I concealed my face. So I prayed before the Tabernacle and the big stone crucified Christ above the altar.

The only thing I knew, besides my own tremendous misery, was that I must no longer consider that I had a vocation to the cloister.

2

True North

It was very hot on Church Street. The street was torn up, and the dust swirled in the sun like gold around the crawling busses and the trucks and taxis. There were crowds of people on the sidewalks.

I stood under the relatively cool, white walls of the new Post Office building. And then, suddenly, walking in the crowd I saw my brother who was supposed to be at Ithaca. He was coming out of the building, and walking with more of a purpose, more of a swing. He almost ran into me.

"Oh," he said, "hello. Are you going out to Douglaston? I'll give you a ride. I've got the car here, just around the corner."

"What are you doing here?" I said.

Under the arching door of the big building were placards about joining the Navy, the Army, the Marines. The only question in my mind was which one he had been trying to join.

"Did you read about this new Naval Reserve scheme they've got?" he said. I knew something about it. That was what he was trying to get into. It was practically settled.

"You go on a cruise," he said, "and then you get a commission."

"Is it as easy as that?"

"Well, I guess they're anxious to get men. Of course, you have to be a college man."

When I told him I was not going to enter the novitiate after all, he said: "Why don't you come in to the Naval Reserve."

"No," I said, "no, thanks."

Presently he said: "What's that package you've got under your arm? Buy some books?"

"Yes."

When he had unlocked the car, I ripped the paper off the package, and took out the cardboard box containing the set of four books, bound in black leather, marked in gold.

I handed him one of the volumes. It was sleek and smelled new. The pages were edged in gold. There were red and green markers.

"What are they?" said John Paul.

"Breviaries."

The four books represented a decision. They said that if I could not live in the monastery, I should try to live in the world as if I were a monk in a monastery. They said that I was going to get as close as possible to the life I was not allowed to lead. If I could not wear the religious habit, I would at least join a Third Order and would try my best to get a job teaching in some Catholic College where I could live under the same roof as the Blessed Sacrament.

There could be no more question of living just like everybody else in the world. There could be no more compromises with the life that tried, at every turn, to feed me poison. I had to turn my back on these things.

God had kept me out of the cloister: that was His affair. He had also given me a vocation to live the kind of a life that people led in cloisters. If I could not be a religious, a priest—that was God's affair. But nevertheless He still wanted me to lead something of the life of a priest or of a religious.

I had said something to Father Edmund about it, in a general way, and he had agreed. But I did not tell him about the Breviaries. It did not even occur to me to do so. I had said: "I am going to try to live like a religious."

He thought that was all right. If I was teaching, and living in a college, that would be all right, it would be fine. And he was glad I wanted to join the Third Order, although he did not seem to attach much importance to it.

For my own part, I was not quite sure what a Third Order secular amounted to in modern America. But thinking of the Franciscan Tertiaries of the Middle Ages, and of their great saints, I realized in some obscure way that there were, or at least should be, great possibilities of sanctification in a Third Order.

I did have a sort of a suspicion that it might turn out, after all, to be little more, in the minds of most of its members, than a society for gaining Indulgences. But in any case, I did not despise Indulgences either, or any of the other spiritual benefits that came with the cord and scapular. However, it was going to be a long time before I got them, and in the meantime I did not hesitate to shape out the new life I thought God wanted of me.

It was a difficult and uncertain business, and I was starting again to make a long and arduous climb, alone, and from what seemed to be a great depth.

If I had ever thought I had become immune from passion, and that I did not have to fight for freedom, there was no chance of that illusion any more. It seemed that every step I took carried me painfully forward under a burden of desires that almost crushed me with the monotony of their threat, the intimate, searching familiarity of their ever-present disgust.

I did not have any lofty theories about the vocation of a lay-contemplative. In fact, I no longer dignified what I was trying to do by the name of a vocation. All I knew was that I wanted grace, and that I needed prayer, and that I was helpless without God, and that I wanted to do everything that people did to keep close to Him.

It was no longer possible to consider myself, abstractly, as being in a certain "state of life" which had special technical relations to other "states of life." All that occupied me now was the immediate practical problem of getting up my hill with this terrific burden I had on my shoulders, step by step, begging God to drag me along and get me away from my enemies and from those who were trying to destroy me.

I did not even reflect how the Breviary, the Canonical Office, was the most powerful and effective prayer I could possibly have chosen, since it is the prayer of the whole Church, and concentrates in itself all the power of the Church's impetration, centered around the infinitely mighty Sacrifice of the Mass—the jewel of which the rest of the Liturgy is the setting: the soul which is the life of the whole Liturgy and of all the Sacramentals. All this was beyond me, although I grasped it at least obscurely. All I knew was that I needed to say the Breviary, and say it every day.

Buying those books at Benziger's that day was one of the best things I ever did in my life. The inspiration to do it was a very great grace. There are few things I can remember that give me more joy.

The first time I actually tried to say the Office was on the feast of the Curé of Ars, St. John Vianney. I was on the train, going back to Olean—to Olean because the cottage was, for the time being, the safest place I could think of, and because anyway my best prospect for a job was at St. Bonaventure's.

As soon as the train was well started on its journey, and was climbing into the hills towards Suffern, I opened up the book and began right away with Matins, in the Common of a Confessor-non-pontiff.

"*Venite exultemus Domino, jubilemus Deo salutari nostro . . .*" It was a happy experience, although its exultancy was subdued and lost under my hesitations and external confusion about how to find my way around in the jungle of the rubrics. To begin with, I did not know enough to look for the general rubrics at the beginning of the *Pars Hiemalis* and anyway, when I did eventually find them, there was too much information in small-print and obscure canonical Latin for me to make much out of them.

The train climbed slowly into the Catskills, and I went on from psalm to psalm, smoothly enough. By the time I got to the Lessons of the Second Nocturn, I had figured out whose feast it was that I was celebrating.

This business of saying the Office on the Erie train, going up through the Delaware valley, was to become a familiar experience in the year that was ahead. Of course, I soon found out the ordinary routine by which Matins and Lauds are anticipated the evening of the day before. Usually, then, on my way from New York to Olean, I would be saying the Little Hours around ten o'clock in the morning when the train had passed Port Jervis and was travelling at the base of the steep, wooded hills that hemmed in the river on either side. If I looked up from the pages of the book, I would see the sun blazing on the trees and moist rocks, and flashing on the surface of the shallow river and playing in the forest foliage along the line. And all this was very much like what the book was singing to me, so that everything lifted up my heart to God.

> Thou sendest forth springs in the vales: between the midst of the hills the waters shall pass. . . . Over them the birds of the air shall dwell, from the midst of the rocks they shall give forth their voices. Thou waterest the hills from Thy upper rooms: the earth shall be filled with the fruit of Thy works. . . . The trees of the field shall be filled and the cedars of Libanus which He hath planted: there the sparrows shall make their nests. The highest of them is the house of the heron. The high hills are a refuge for the harts, the rocks for the irchins. . . . All expect from Thee that Thou give them food in season. What Thou givest them they shall gather up: when Thou openest Thy hand they shall all be filled with good. . . . Thou shalt send forth Thy Spirit and they shall be created, and Thou shalt renew the face of the earth.

Yes, and from the secret places of His essence, God began to fill my soul with grace in those days, grace that sprung from deep within me, I could not know how or where. But yet I would be able, after not so many months, to realize what was there, in the peace and the strength that were growing in me through my constant immersion in this tremendous, unending cycle of prayer, ever renewing its vitality, its inexhaustible, sweet energies, from hour to hour, from season to season in its returning round. And I, drawn into that atmosphere, into that deep, vast universal movement of vitalizing prayer, which is Christ praying in men to His Father, could not help but begin at last to live, and to know that I was alive. And my heart could not help but cry out within me: "I will sing to the Lord as long as I live: I will sing praise to my God while I have my being. Let my speech be acceptable to Him: but I will take delight in the Lord."

Truly, He was sending forth His Spirit, uttering His divine Word and binding me to Himself through His Spirit preceding from the Word spoken within me. As the months went on, I could not help but realize it.

Then, when I finished the Little Hours and closed the Breviary at the end of None reciting the *Sacrosancte*, and looked up out of the window to see the seminary of Callicoon momentarily appear on its distant hilltop, at the end of a long avenue of river, I no longer felt so much anguish and sorrow at not being in the monastery.

But I am getting ahead of my story. For in these days, in the late summer of 1940, it was not yet that way. The Breviary was hard to learn, and every step was labor and confusion, not to mention the mistakes and perplexities I got myself into. However, Father Irenaeus helped to straighten me out, and told me how the various feasts worked together, and how to say first Vespers for the proper feast, and all the other things one needs to find out. Apart from him, however, I didn't even speak of the Breviary to any other priest. I kept quiet about it, half fearing that someone would make fun of me, or think I was eccentric, or try to snatch my books away from me on some pretext. I would have been better off if I had been acting under the guidance of a director, but I had no understanding of such a thing in those days.

Meanwhile, I put on my best blue suit and hitch-hiked out to St. Bonaventure and spoke with Father Thomas Plassman, who was the president of the college, and the picture of benevolence. He listened kindly and soberly to my answers to his questions, filling a chair with his huge frame and looking at me through his glasses, out of a great kind face built on pontifical lines and all set for smiles paternal enough to embrace an archdiocese. Father Thomas would make a wonderful prelate, and, as a matter of fact, all the students and seminarians at St. Bonaventure held him in great awe for his learning and piety.

Back in Olean his reputation was even greater. Once I had someone whisper to me that Father Thomas was the third best educated man in America. I was not able to find out who were the other two ahead of him, or how it was possible to determine who was the best educated, or what that might precisely mean.

But in any case, he gave me a job at St. Bonaventure's, teaching English, for it fell out that Father Valentine Long, who wrote books and taught literature to the sophomores, had been transferred to Holy Name College, in Washington.

In the second week of September, with a trunkful of books and a typewriter and the old portable phonograph that I had bought when I was still at Oakham, I moved in to the little room that was assigned to me on the second floor of the big, red-brick building that was both a dormitory and a monastery. Out of my window I could look beyond the chapel front to the garden and fields and the woods. There was a little astronomical observatory out there behind the greenhouses, and in the distance you could tell where the river was by the line of trees at the end of the pasture. And then, beyond that, were the high, wooded hills, and my gaze travelled up Five Mile Valley beyond the farms to Martinny's Rocks. My eyes often wandered out there, and rested in that peaceful scene, and the landscape became associated with my prayers, for I often prayed looking out of the window. And even at night, the tiny, glowing light of a far farmhouse window in Five Mile Valley attracted my eye, the only visible thing in the black darkness, as I knelt on the floor and said my last prayer to Our Lady.

And as the months went on, I began to drink poems out of those hills.

Yet the room was not quiet, either. It was right on a corner next to the stairs, and when anybody on our floor was wanted on the telephone, someone would rush up the stairs and stick his head into the corridor right by my door and yell down the echoing hall. All day long I heard those voices bellowing, "Hey, Cassidy! Hey, Cassidy!" but I did not mind. It did not stop me from doing twice as much work in that room, in one year, as I had done in all the rest of my life put together.

It amazed me how swiftly my life fell into a plan of fruitful and pleasant organization, here under the roof with these Friars, in this house dedicated to God. The answer to this was, of course, the God Who lived under that same roof with me, hidden in His

Sacrament, the heart of the house, diffusing His life through it from the chapel Tabernacle: and also the Office I recited every day was another answer. Finally, there was the fact of my seclusion.

By this time, I had managed to get myself free from all the habits and luxuries that people in the world think they need for their comfort and amusement. My mouth was at last clean of the yellow, parching salt of nicotine, and I had rinsed my eyes of the grey slops of movies, so that now my taste and my vision were clean. And I had thrown away the books that soiled my heart. And my ears, too, had been cleansed of all wild and fierce noises and had poured into them peace, peace—except for that yell, "Hey, Cassidy," which, after all, did not make much difference.

Best of all, my will was in order, my soul was in harmony with itself and with God, though not without battle, and not without cost. That was a price I had to pay, or lose my life altogether, so there was no alternative but wait in patience, and let myself be ground out between the upper and nether millstones of the two conflicting laws within me. Nor could I taste anything of the sense that this is really a martyrdom full of merit and pleasing to God: I was still too obsessed with the sheer, brute difficulty of it, and the crushing humiliation that faced me all the time. *Peccatum meum contra me est semper.*

Yet, in spite of all that, there was in me the profound, sure certitude of liberty, the moral certitude of grace, of union with God, which bred peace that could not be shattered or overshadowed by any necessity to stand armed and ready for conflict. And this peace was all-rewarding. It was worth everything. And every day it brought me back to Christ's altars, and to my daily Bread, that infinitely holy and mighty and secret wholesomeness that was cleansing and strengthening my sick being through and through, and feeding, with His infinite life, my poor shredded sinews of morality.

I was writing a book—it was not much of a book—and I had classes to prepare. It was the latter work that had the most in it of health and satisfaction and reward. I had three big classes of sophomores, ninety students in all, to bring through English Literature from Beowulf to the Romantic Revival in one year. And a lot of them didn't even know how to spell. But that did not worry me very much, and it could not alter my happiness with *Piers Plowman* and the *Nun's Priest's Tale* and *Sir Gawain and the Green Knight:* I was back again in that atmosphere that had enthralled me as a child, the serene and simple and humorous Middle Ages, not the lute and goblin and moth-ball Middle Ages of Tennyson, but the real Middle Ages, the twelfth and thirteenth and fourteenth centuries, full of fresh air and simplicity, as solid as wheat bread and grape wine and water-mills and ox-drawn wagons: the age of Cistercian monasteries and of the first Franciscans.

And so, in my innocence, I stood up and talked about all these things in front of those rooms full of football players with long, unpronounceable names: and because they saw that I myself liked my own subject matter, they tolerated it, and even did a certain amount of work for me without too much complaint.

The classes were a strange mixture. The best elements in them were the football players and the seminarians. The football players were mostly on scholarships, and they did not have much money, and they stayed in at night most of the time. As a group, they were the best-natured and the best-tempered and worked as hard as the seminarians. They were also the most vocal. They liked to talk about these books when I stirred them up to argue. They liked to open their mouths and deliver rough, earnest and sometimes sardonic observations about the behavior of these figures in literature.

Also, some of them were strong and pious Catholics with souls full of faith and simplicity and honesty and conviction, yet without the violence and intemperance that come from mere prejudice. At Columbia it had been pretty much the fashion to despise football players as stupid: and I don't maintain that they are, as a class, geniuses. But the ones at St. Bona's taught me much more about people than I taught them about books, and I learned to have a lot of respect and affection for these rough, earnest, good-natured and patient men who had to work so hard and take so many bruises and curses to entertain the Friars and the Alumni on the football field, and to advertise the school.

I wonder what has happened to them all: how many of them got shot up in Africa or the Philippines? What became of that black-haired, grinning Mastrigiacomo who confided to me all his ambitions about being a band-leader; or that lanky, cat-faced villain Chapman whom I saw one night, after a dance, walking around chewing on a whole ham? What have they done with that big, quiet Irishman Quinn, or Woody McCarthy with his long bulbous nose and eyebrows full of perplexity and his sallies of gruff wit? Then there was Red Hagerman who was not a Catholic, and who looked like all the big cheerful muscle-bound football players they believed in in the nineteen twenties. He went off and got himself married towards the end of that year. Another one called "Red" was Red McDonald, and he was one of the best students in the class, and one of the best people: a serious young Irishman with a wide-open face, all full of sincerity and hard work. Then there was the big round-faced Polish boy whose name I have forgotten, who grabbed hold of the tail of a cow which dragged him all around the pasture on the day of the sophomore beer-party at the end of the year.

The most intelligent students were the seminarians or the ones that were going to enter the seminary: and they were the quietest. They kept pretty much to themselves, and handed in neat papers which you could be relatively sure were their own original work. Probably by now they are all priests.

The rest of the class was a mixture of all kinds of people, some of them disgruntled, some of them penniless and hard-working, some of them rich and dumb and too fond of beer. Some of them liked to play the drums and knew how. Others liked to play them and did not know how. Some of them were good dancers and danced a lot. Others just went uptown and played the slot machines until the last minute before midnight, when they came back to the college in a panic-stricken rush to get in before the time limit was up. One of them, Joe Nastri, thought he was a Communist. I don't suppose he had a very clear idea of what a Communist was. One day he went to sleep in class and one of the football players gave him the hot-foot.

Of all the crowd, it could not be said that they were very different from the students I had known in other colleges. With a few exceptions, they were certainly no holier. They got drunk just as much, but they made more noise about it, and had less money to spend, and were handicapped by the necessity of getting back to the dormitory at a certain time. Twice a week they had to get up and hear Mass, which was a burden to most of them. Only very few of them heard Mass and went to Communion every day —outside of the seminarians.

However, most of them clung with conviction to the Catholic faith, a loyalty which was resolute and inarticulate. It was hard to tell just how much that loyalty was a matter of conscious faith, and how much it was based on attachment to their class and social environment: but they were all pretty definite about being Catholics. One could not say of them that, as a whole, they led lives that went beyond the ordinary level demanded of a Christian. Some of the most intelligent of them often startled me with statements that showed they had not penetrated below the surface of Catholicism and did not really appreciate its spirit . . . One, for instance, argued that the virtue of humility was nonsense, and that it sapped a man of all his vitality and initiative. Another one did not think there were any such things as devils. . . .

All of them were serene in their conviction that the modern world was the highest point reached by man in his development, and that our present civilization left very little to be desired. I wonder if the events of 1943 and the two following years did anything to change their opinions.

That winter, when I was talking about the England of Langland and Chaucer and Shakespeare and Webster, the war-machine of totalitarian Germany had turned to devour that island, and morning after morning when I glanced at the New York *Times* in the library, between classes, I read the headlines about the cities that had been cut to pieces with bombs. Night after night the huge dark mass of London was bursting into wide areas of flame that turned its buildings into empty craters and cariated those miles and miles of slums. Around St. Paul's the ancient City was devastated, and there was no acre of Westminster, Bloomsbury, Camden Town, Mayfair, Bayswater, Paddington that had not been deeply scarred. Coventry was razed to the ground. Bristol, Birmingham, Sheffield, Newcastle were all raided, and the land was full of blood and smoke.

The noise of that fearful chastisement, the fruit of modern civilization, penetrated to the ears and minds of very few at St. Bonaventure's. The Friars understood something of what was going on: but they lost themselves, for the most part, in futile political arguments if they talked about it at all. But the students were more concerned with the movies and beer and the mousy little girls that ran around Olean in ankle socks, even when the snow lay deep on the ground.

I think it was in November that we all lined up, students and secular professors, in De la Roche Hall and gave our names in to be drafted. The whole process was an extremely quiet and unmomentous one. The room was not even crowded. You didn't even have the boredom of waiting.

I gave my name and my age and all the rest, and got a small white card. It was quickly over. It did not bring the war very close.

Yet it was enough to remind me that I was not going to enjoy this pleasant and safe and stable life forever. Indeed, perhaps now that I had just begun to taste my security, it would be taken away again, and I would be cast back into the midst of violence and uncertainty and blasphemy and the play of anger and hatred and all passion, worse than ever before. It would be the wages of my own twenty-five years: this war was what I had earned for myself and the world. I could hardly complain that I was being drawn into it.

ii

If we were all being pulled into the vortex of that fight, it was being done slowly and gradually. I was surprised when my brother was cast back into the solid area of peace—relative peace. It was one rainy night in the fall that he appeared in Olean in a new shiny Buick convertible roadster with a long black hood and a chassis that crouched low on the road, built for expensive and silent speed. The thing was all fixed up with searchlights, and as for my brother, he was not in uniform.

"What about the Navy?" I asked him.

It turned out that they were not giving out commissions in the Naval Reserve as freely as he had supposed, and he had had some differences of opinion with his commanding officers and, at the end of a cruise to the West Indies and after an examination of some sort, both my brother and the Naval Reserve were mutually delighted to end their association with one another.

I was not sorry.

"What are you going to do now, wait until you are drafted?"

"I suppose so," he said.

"And in the meantime? . . ."

"Maybe I'll go to Mexico," he said. "I want to take some pictures of those Mayan temples."

And, as a matter of fact, that was where he went when the weather got cold: to Yucatan, to find out one of those lost cities in the jungle and take a pile of kodachromes of those evil stones, soaked in the blood that was once poured out in libation to the devils by forgotten generations of Indians. He did not get rid of any of his restlessness in Mexico or Yucatan. He only found more of it among those blue volcanoes.

Snow comes early to St. Bonaventure's, and when the snow came, I used to say the little hours of the Breviary walking in the deep untrodden drifts along the wood's edge, towards the river. No one would ever come and disturb me out there in all that silence, under the trees, which made a noiseless, rudimentary church over my head, between me and the sky. It was wonderful out there when the days were bright, even though the cold bit down into the roots of my fingernails as I held the open Breviary in my hands. I could look up from the book, and recite the parts I already knew by heart, gazing at the glittering, snow-covered hills, white and gold and planted with bare woods, standing out bright against the blinding blue sky. Oh, America, how I began to love your country! What miles of silences God has made in you for contemplation! If only people realized what all your mountains and forests are really for!

The new year came, 1941. In its January, I was to have my twenty-sixth birthday, and enter upon my twenty-seventh, most momentous year.

Already, in February, or before that, the idea came to me that I might make a retreat in some monastery for Holy Week and Easter. Where would it be? The first place that came into my mind was the Trappist abbey Dan Walsh had told me about, in Kentucky. And as soon as I thought about it, I saw that this was the only choice. That was where I needed to go. Something had opened out, inside me, in the last months, something that required, demanded at least a week in that silence, in that austerity, praying together with the monks in their cold choir.

And my heart expanded with anticipation and happiness.

Meanwhile, suddenly, one day, towards the beginning of Lent, I began to write poems. I cannot assign any special cause for the ideas that began to crowd on me from every side. I had been reading the Spanish poet, Lorca, with whose poetic vein I felt in the greatest sympathy: but that was not enough, in itself, to account for all the things I now began to write. In the first weeks of Lent, the fasting I took on myself—which was not much, but at least it came up to the standard required by the Church for an ordinary Christian, and did not evade its obligations under some privilege to which I was not entitled—instead of cramping my mind, freed it, and seemed to let loose the string of my tongue.

Sometimes I would go several days at a time, writing a new poem every day. They were not all good, but some of them were better than I had written before. In the end, I did not altogether reject more than half a dozen of them. And, having sent many of the others to various magazines, I at last had the joy of seeing one or two of them accepted.

Towards the beginning of March, I wrote to the Trappists at Gethsemani asking if I could come down there for a retreat during Holy Week. I had barely received their reply, telling me they would be glad to have me there, when another letter came.

It was from the Draft Board, telling me that my number was up for the army.

I was surprised. I had forgotten about the draft, or rather I had made calculations that put all this off until at least after Easter. However, I had thought out my position with regard to the war, and knew what I had to do in conscience. I made out my answers to the questionnaires with peace in my heart, and not much anticipation that it would make any difference to my case.

It was about eight years since we had all stood under the banner in the gymnasium at Columbia, and the Reds had shouted and stamped on the platform, and we had all loudly taken a pledge that we weren't going to fight in any war whatever. Now America was moving into position to enter a war as the ally of countries that had been attacked by the Nazis: and the Nazis had, as their ally, Communist Russia.

Meanwhile in those eight years, I had developed a conscience. If I had objected to war before, it was more on the basis of emotion than anything else. And my unconditional objection had, therefore, been foolish in more ways than one. On the other hand, I was not making the mistake of switching from one emotional extreme to the other. This time, as far as I was able, I felt that I was called upon to make clear my own position as a moral duty.

To put it in terms less abstract and stuffy: God was asking me, by the light and grace that He had given me, to signify where I stood in relation to the actions of governments and armies and states in this world overcome with the throes of its own blind wickedness. He was not asking me to judge all the nations of the world, or to elucidate all the moral and political motives behind their actions. He was not demanding that I pass some critical decision defining the innocence and guilt of all those concerned in the war. He was asking me to make a choice that amounted to an act of love for His Truth, His goodness, His charity, His Gospel, as an individual, as a member of His Mystical Body. He was asking me to do, to the best of my knowledge, what I thought Christ would do.

For a war to be just, it must be a war of defence. A war of aggression is not just. If America entered the war now, would it be a war of aggression? I suppose if you wanted to get subtle about it, you could work out some kind of an argument to that effect. But I personally could not see that it would be anything else than legitimate self-defence. How legitimate? To answer that, I would have had to be a moral theologian and a diplomat and a historian and a politician and probably also a mind-reader. And still I would not have had more than a probable answer. Since there was such strong probable evidence that we were really defending ourselves, that settled the question as far as I was concerned.

I had more of a doubt on the question of whether it was really necessary or not. Did we really have to go to war? A lot of people were asking themselves that question, and argument about it was rather hot among some of the Friars at St. Bonaventure's. As far as I could see, it was a question that no private individual was capable of answering: and the situation was getting to be grave enough for it to be necessary to leave the government to make its own choice. The men in Washington presumably knew what was going on better than we did, and if, in a situation as obscure as this one was, and as perilous, they thought war was getting to be necessary—what could we do about it? If they called us to the army, I could not absolutely refuse to go.

The last and most crucial doubt about the war was the morality of the means used in the fight: the bombing of open cities, the wholesale slaughter of civilians. . . . To my mind, there was very little doubt about the immorality of the methods used in modern war. Self-defence is good, and a necessary war is licit: but methods that descend to wholesale barbarism and ruthless, indiscriminate slaughter of non-combatants practically without defence are hard to see as anything else but mortal sins. This was the hardest question of all to decide.

Fortunately the draft law was framed in such a way that I did not have to decide it. For there was a provision made for those who were willing to help the country without doing any killing. As I say, I couldn't tell just how much those provisions would mean in actual practice, but they looked nice on paper, and the least I could do was take advantage of them.

And therefore I made out my papers with an application to be considered as a non-combatant objector: that is, one who would willingly enter the army, and serve in the medical corps, or as a stretcher bearer, or a hospital orderly or any other thing like that, so long as I did not have to drop bombs on open cities, or shoot at other men.

After all, Christ did say: "Whatsoever you have done to the least of these my brethren, you did it to me." I know that it is not the mind of the Church that this be applied literally to war—or rather, that war is looked upon as a painful but necessary social surgical operation in which you kill your enemy not out of hatred but for the common good. That is all very fine in theory. But as far as I could see, since the government was apparently holding out an opportunity to those who wanted to serve in the army without killing other men, I could avoid the whole question and follow what seemed to me to be a much better course.

After all, I might be able to turn an evil situation into a source of much good. In the medical corps—if that was where they put me—I would not be spared any of the dangers that fell upon other men, and at the same time I would be able to help them, to perform works of mercy, and to overcome evil with good. I would be able to leaven the mass of human misery with the charity and mercy of Christ, and the bitter, ugly, filthy business of the war could be turned into the occasion for my own sanctification and for the good of other men.

If you set aside the practically insoluble question of cooperation that might be brought up, it seemed to me that this was what Christ Himself would have done, and what He wanted me to do.

I put down all my reasons, and quoted St. Thomas for the edification of the Draft Board and got the whole business notarized and sealed and put it in an envelope and dropped it in the wide-open mouth of the mailbox in the Olean post office.

And when it was done, I walked out into the snowy street, and an ineffable sense of peace settled in my heart.

It was a late, cold afternoon. The frozen piles of snow lay along the swept sidewalks, in the gutters, in front of the small, one-story buildings on State Street. Presently Bob O'Brien, the plumber at the Olean house, who lived in Alleghany, and who used to fix the pipes when they went wrong up at the cottage, came by in his car. He stopped to give me a ride.

He was a big, jovial, family man, with white hair and several sons who served as altar boys at St. Bonaventure's Church in Alleghany, and as we passed out of town on the wide road, he was talking about peaceful and ordinary things.

The country opened out before us. The setting sun shone as bright as blood, along the tops of the hills, but the snow in the valleys and hollows was blue and even purple with shadows. On the left of the road, the antennae of the radio station stood up into the clean sky, and far ahead of us lay the red-brick buildings of the College, grouped in an imitation Italy in the midst of the alluvial valley. Beyond that, on the side of the hill were the redder buildings of St. Elizabeth's convent, past the high bridge over the railroad tracks.

My eyes opened and took all this in. And for the first time in my life I realized that I no longer cared whether I preserved my place in all this or lost it: whether I stayed here or went to the army. All that no longer mattered. It was in the hands of One Who loved me far better than I could ever love myself: and my heart was filled with peace.

It was a peace that did not depend on houses, or jobs, or places, or times, or external conditions. It was a peace that time and material created situations could never give. It was peace that the world could not give.

The weeks went by, and I wrote some more poems, and continued to fast and keep my Lent. All I prayed was that God should let me know His will—and, if it pleased Him, there was only one other thing I asked for myself besides: if I had to go to the army, I begged Him at least to let me make a retreat with the Trappist monks before I went.

However, the next thing I got from the Draft Board was a notice to present myself for medical examination before the doctors in Olean.

I had not been expecting things to develop that way, and at first I interpreted this to mean that my request for consideration as a non-combatant had simply been ignored. There were three days before the examination, and so I got permission to go down to New York. I thought I might see the Draft Board and talk to them: but that was not possible. In any case, it was not necessary.

So the week-end turned out to be a sort of a festival with my friends. I saw Lax, who was now working for the *New Yorker,* and had a desk of his own in a corner of their offices where he wrote letters to pacify the people who complained about the humor, or the lack of it, in the pages of the magazine. Then we went out to Long Beach and saw Seymour. And then Seymour and I and Lax all together got in a car and went to Port Washington and saw Gibney.

The next day was St. Patrick's Day, and the massed bands of all the boys and girls in Brooklyn who had never had an ear for music were gathering under the windows of the *New Yorker* offices and outside the Gotham Book Mart. And I, an Englishman, wearing a shamrock which I had bought from a Jew, went walking around the city, weaving in and out of the crowds, and thinking up a poem called April, although it was March. It was a fancy poem about javelins and leopards and lights through trees like arrows and a line that said: "The little voices of the rivers change." I thought it up in and out of the light and the shade of the Forties, between Fifth and Sixth avenues, and typed it on Lax's typewriter in the *New*

Yorker office, and showed it to Mark Van Doren in a subway station.

And Mark said, of the shamrock I was wearing:

"That is the greenest shamrock I have ever seen."

It was a great St. Patrick's Day. That night I got on the Erie train, and since I was so soon, I thought, to go to the army, I paid money to sleep in the Pullman. Practically the only other Pullman passenger was a sedate Franciscan nun, who turned out to be going to St. Elizabeth's: and so we got off at Olean together and shared a taxi out to Alleghany.

On Monday I prepared to go and be examined for the army. I was the first one there. I climbed the ancient stairs to the top floor of the Olean City Hall. I tried the handle of the room marked for the medical board, and the door opened. I walked in and stood in the empty room. My heart was still full of the peace of Communion.

Presently the first of the doctors arrived.

"You got here early," he said, and began to take off his coat and hat.

"We might as well begin," he said, "the others will be along in a minute."

So I stripped, and he listened to my chest, and took some blood out of my arm and put it in a little bottle, in a water-heater, to keep it cosy and warm for the Wassermann test. And while this was going on, the others were coming in, two other doctors to do the examining, and lanky young farm boys to be examined.

"Now," said my doctor, "let's see your teeth."

I opened my mouth.

"Well," he said, "you've certainly had a lot of teeth out!"

And he began to count them.

The doctor who was running the Medical Board was just coming in. My man got up and went to talk to him. I heard him say:

"Shall we finish the whole examination? I don't see much point to it."

The head doctor came over and looked at my mouth.

"Oh, well," he said, "finish the examination anyway."

And he sat me down and personally took a crack at my reflexes and went through all the rest of it. When it was over, and I was ready to get back into my clothes, I asked:

"What about it, Doctor?"

"Oh, go home," he said, "you haven't got enough teeth."

Once again I walked out into the snowy street.

So they didn't want me in the army after all, even as a stretcher bearer! The street was full of quiet, full of peace.

And I remembered that it was the Feast of St. Joseph.

iii

There were still about three weeks left until Easter. Thinking more and more about the Trappist monastery where I was going to spend Holy Week, I went to the library one day and took down the *Catholic Encyclopaedia* to read about the Trappists. I found out that the Trappists were Cistercians, and then, in looking up Cistercians, I also came across the Carthusians, and a great big picture of the hermitages of the Camaldolese.

What I saw on those pages pierced me to the heart like a knife.

What wonderful happiness there was, then, in the world! There were still men on this miserable, noisy, cruel earth, who tasted the marvelous joy of silence and solitude, who dwelt in forgotten mountain cells, in secluded monasteries, where the news and desires and appetites and conflicts of the world no longer reached them.

They were free from the burden of the flesh's tyranny, and their clear vision, clean of the world's smoke and of its bitter sting, were raised to heaven and penetrated into the deeps of heaven's infinite and healing light.

They were poor, they had nothing, and therefore they were free and possessed everything, and everything they touched struck off something of the fire of divinity. And they worked with their hands, silently ploughing and harrowing the earth, and sowing seed in obscurity, and reaping their small harvests to feed themselves and the other poor. They built their own houses and made, with their own hands, their own furniture and their own coarse clothing, and everything around them was simple and primitive and poor, because they were the least and the last of men, they had made themselves outcasts, seeking, outside the walls of the world, Christ poor and rejected of men.

Above all, they had found Christ, and they knew the power and the sweetness and the depth and the infinity of His love, living and working in them. In Him, hidden in Him, they had become the "Poor Brothers of God." And for His love, they had thrown away everything, and concealed themselves in the Secret of His Face. Yet because they had nothing, they were the richest men in the world, possessing everything: because in proportion as grace emptied their hearts of created desire, the Spirit of God entered in and filled the place that had been made for God. And the Poor Brothers of God, in their cells, they tasted within them the secret glory, the hidden manna, the infinite nourishment and strength of the Presence of God. They tasted the sweet exultancy of the fear of God, which is the first intimate touch of the reality of God, known and experienced on earth, the beginning of heaven. The fear of the Lord is the beginning of heaven. And all day long, God spoke to them: the clean voice of God, in His tremendous peacefulness, spending truth within them as simply and directly as water wells up in a spring. And grace was in them, suddenly, always in more and more abundance, they knew not from where, and the coming of this grace to them occupied them altogether, and filled them with love, and with freedom.

And grace, overflowing in all their acts and movements, made everything they did an act of love, glorifying God not by drama, not by gesture, not by outward show, but by the very simplicity and economy of utter perfection, so utter that it escapes notice entirely.

Outside in the world were holy men who were holy in the sense that they went about with portraits of all the possible situations in which they could show their love of God displayed about them: and they were always conscious of all these possibilities. But these other hidden men had come so close to God in their hiddenness that they no longer saw anyone but Him. They themselves were lost in the picture: there was no comparison between them receiving and God giving, because the distance by which such comparison could be measured had dwindled to nothing. They were in Him. They had dwindled down to nothing and had been transformed into Him by the pure and absolute humility of their hearts.

And the love of Christ overflowing in those clean hearts made them children and made them eternal. Old men with limbs like the roots of trees had the eyes of children and lived, under their grey woolen cowls, eternal. And all of them, the young and the old, were ageless, the little brothers of God, the little children for whom was made the Kingdom of Heaven.

Day after day the round of the canonical hours brought them together and the love that was in them became songs as austere as granite and as sweet as wine. And they stood and they bowed in their long, solemn psalmody. Their prayer flexed its strong sinews and relaxed again into silence, and suddenly flared up again in a hymn, the color of flame, and died into silence: and you could barely hear the weak, ancient voice saying the final prayer. The whisper of the *amens* ran around the stones like sighs, and the monks broke up their ranks and half emptied the choir, some remaining to pray.

And in the night they also rose, and filled the darkness with the strong, patient anguish of their supplication to God: and the strength of their prayer (the Spirit of Christ concealing His strength in the words their voices uttered) amazingly held back the arm of God from striking and breaking at last the foul world full of greed and avarice and murder and lust and all sin.

The thought of those monasteries, those remote choirs, those cells, those hermitages, those cloisters, those men in their cowls, the poor monks, the men who had become nothing, shattered my heart.

In an instant the desire of those solitudes was wide open within me like a wound.

I had to slam the book shut on the picture of Camaldoli and the bearded hermits standing in the stone street of cells, and I went out of the library, trying to stamp out the embers that had broken into flame, there, for an instant, within me.

No, it was useless: I did not have a vocation, and I was not for the cloister, for the priesthood. Had I not been told that definitely enough? Did I have to have that beaten into my head all over again before I could believe it?

Yet I stood in the sun outside the dining hall, waiting for the noon Angelus, and one of the Friars was talking to me. I could not contain the one thing that filled my heart:

"I am going to a Trappist monastery to make a retreat for Holy Week," I said. The things that jumped in the Friar's eyes gave him the sort of expression you would expect if I had said: "I am going to go and buy a submarine and live on the bottom of the sea."

"Don't let them change you!" he said, with a sort of a lame smile. That meant "Don't go reminding the rest of us that all that penance might be right, by getting a vocation to the Trappists."

I said: "It would be a good thing if they did change me."

It was a safe, oblique way of admitting what was in my heart—the desire to go to that monastery and stay for good.

On the morning of the Saturday before Palm Sunday I got up before five, and heard part of a Mass in the dark chapel and then had to make a run for the train. The rain fell on the empty station straight and continuous as a tower.

All the way down the line, in the pale, growing day, the hills were black, and rain drenched the valley and flooded the sleeping valley towns. Somewhere past Jamestown I took out my Breviary and said the Little Hours, and when we got into Ohio the rain stopped.

We changed stations at Galion, and on the fast train down to

Columbus I got something to eat, and in southern Ohio the air was drier still, and almost clearing. Finally, in the evening, in the long rolling hills that led the way in to Cincinnati, you could see the clouds tearing open all along the western horizon to admit long streaks of sun.

It was an American landscape, big, vast, generous, fertile, and leading beyond itself into limitless expanses, open spaces, the whole West. My heart was full!

So when we entered Cincinnati, in the evening, with the lights coming on among all the houses and the electric signs shining on the hills, and the huge freight yards swinging open on either side of the track and the high buildings in the distance, I felt as if I owned the world. And yet that was not because of all these things, but because of Gethsemani, where I was going. It was the fact that I was passing through all this, and did not desire it, and wanted no part in it, and did not seek to grasp or hold any of it, that I could exult in it, and it all cried out to me: God! God!

I went to Mass and Communion the next morning in Cincinnati, and then took the train for Louisville, and waited in Louisville all the rest of the day because I did not have the sense to take a bus to one of the towns near Gethsemani and buy a ride from there to the monastery.

It was not until after night fell that there was a train out to Gethsemani, on the line to Atlanta.

It was a slow train. The coach was dimly lighted, and full of people whose accents I could hardly understand, and you knew you were in the South because all the Negroes were huddled in a separate car. The train got out of the city into country that was abysmally dark, even under the moon. You wondered if there were any houses out there. Pressing my face to the window, and shading it with my hands, I saw the outline of a bare, stony landscape with sparse trees. The little towns we came to looked poor and forlorn and somewhat fierce in the darkness.

And the train went its slow way through the spring night, branching off at Bardstown junction. And I knew my station was coming.

I stepped down out of the car into the empty night. The station was dark. There was a car standing there, but no man in sight. There was a road, and the shadow of a sort of a factory a little distance away, and a few houses under some trees. In one of them was a light. The train had hardly stopped to let me off, and immediately gathered its ponderous momentum once again and was gone around the bend with the flash of a red tail light, leaving me in the middle of the silence and solitude of the Kentucky hills.

I put my bag down in the gravel, wondering what to do next. Had they forgotten to make arrangements for me to get to the monastery? Presently the door of one of the houses opened, and a man came out, in no hurry.

We got in the car together, and started up the road, and in a minute we were in the midst of moonlit fields.

"Are the monks in bed?" I asked the driver. It was only a few minutes past eight.

"Oh, yes, they go to bed at seven o'clock."

"Is the monastery far?"

"Mile and a half."

I looked at the rolling country, and at the pale ribbon of road in front of us, stretching out as grey as lead in the light of the moon. Then suddenly I saw a steeple that shone like silver in the moonlight, growing into sight from behind a rounded knoll. The tires sang on the empty road, and, breathless, I looked at the monastery that was revealed before me as we came over the rise. At the end of an avenue of trees was a big rectangular block of buildings, all dark, with a church crowned by a tower and a steeple and a cross: and the steeple was as bright as platinum and the whole place was as quiet as midnight and lost in the all-absorbing silence and solitude of the fields. Behind the monastery was a dark curtain of woods, and over to the west was a wooded valley, and beyond that a rampart of wooded hills, a barrier and a defence against the world.

And over all the valley smiled the mild, gentle Easter moon, the full moon in her kindness, loving this silent place.

At the end of the avenue, in the shadows under the trees, I could make out the lowering arch of the gate, and the words: *"Pax Intrantibus."*

The driver of the car did not go to the bell rope by the heavy wooden door. Instead he went over and scratched on one of the windows and called, in a low voice:

"Brother! Brother!"

I could hear someone stirring inside.

Presently the key turned in the door. I passed inside. The door closed quietly behind me. I was out of the world.

The effect of that big, moonlit court, the heavy stone building with all those dark and silent windows, was overpowering. I could hardly answer the Brother's whispered questions.

I looked at his clear eyes, his greying, pointed beard.

When I told him I came from St. Bonaventure's, he said drily:

"I was a Franciscan once."

We crossed the court, climbed some steps, entered a high, dark hall. I hesitated on the brink of a polished, slippery floor, while the Brother groped for the light switch. Then, above another heavy door, I saw the words: "God alone."

"Have you come here to stay?" said the Brother.

The question terrified me. It sounded too much like the voice of my own conscience.

"Oh, no!" I said. "Oh, no!" And I heard my whisper echoing around the hall and vanishing up the indefinite, mysterious heights of a dark and empty stair-well above our heads. The place smelled frighteningly clean: old and clean, an ancient house, polished and swept and repainted and repainted over and over, year after year.

"What's the matter? Why can't you stay? Are you married or something?" said the Brother.

"No," I said lamely, "I have a job . . ."

We began to climb the wide stairs. Our steps echoed in the empty darkness. One flight and then another and a third and a fourth. There was an immense distance between floors; it was a building with great high ceilings. Finally we came to the top floor, and the Brother opened the door into a wide room, and put down my bag, and left me.

I heard his steps crossing the yard below, to the gate house.

And I felt the deep, deep silence of the night, and of peace, and of holiness enfold me like love, like safety.

The embrace of it, the silence! I had entered into a solitude that was an impregnable fortress. And the silence that enfolded me, spoke to me, and spoke louder and more eloquently than any voice, and in the middle of that quiet, clean-smelling room, with the moon pouring its peacefulness in through the open window, with the warm night air, I realized truly whose house that was, O glorious Mother of God!

How did I ever get back out of there, into the world, after tasting the sweetness and the kindness of the love with which you welcome those that come to stay in your house, even only for a few days, O Holy Queen of Heaven, and Mother of my Christ?

It is very true that the Cistercian Order is your special territory and that those monks in white cowls are your special servants, *servitores Sanctae Mariae*. Their houses are all yours—Notre Dame, Notre Dame, all around the world. Notre Dame de Gethsemani: there was still something of the bravery and simplicity and freshness of twelfth-century devotion, the vivid faith of St. Bernard of Clairvaux and Adam of Perseigne and Guerric of Igny and Ailred of Rievaulx and Robert of Molesme, here in the hills of Kentucky: and I think the century of Chartres was most of all your century, my Lady, because it spoke you clearest not only in word but in glass and stone, showing you for who you are, most powerful, most glorious, Mediatrix of All Grace, and the most High Queen of Heaven, high above all the angels, and throned in glory near the throne of your Divine Son.

And of all things, it is the Rules of the Religious Orders dedicated to you, that are loudest and truest in proclaiming your honor, showing forth your power and your greatness obliquely by the sacrifices that love of you drives men to make. So it is that the Usages of the Cistercians are a Canticle for your glory, Queen of Angels, and those who live those Usages proclaim your tremendous prerogatives louder than the most exalted sermons. The white cowl of the silent Cistercian has got the gift of tongues, and the flowing folds of that grey wool, full of benediction, are more fluent than the Latin of the great monastic Doctors.

How shall I explain or communicate to those who have not seen these holy houses, your consecrated churches and Cistercian cloisters, the might of the truths that overpowered me all the days of that week?

Yet no one will find it hard to conceive the impression made on a man thrown suddenly into a Trappist monastery at four o'clock in the morning, after the night office, as I was the following day.

Bells were flying out of the tower in the high, astounding darkness as I groped half blind with sleep for my clothing, and hastened into the hall and down the dark stairs. I did not know where to go, and there was no one to show me, but I saw two men in secular clothes, at the bottom of the stairs, going through a door. One of them was a priest with a great head of white hair, the other was a young man with black hair, in a pair of dungarees. I went after them, through the door. We were in a hallway, completely black, except I could see their shadows moving towards a big window at the end. They knew where they were going, and they had found a door which opened and let some light into the hall.

I came after them to the door. It led into the cloister. The cloister was cold, and dimly lit, and the smell of damp wool astounded me by its unearthliness. And I saw the monks. There was one, right there, by the door; he had knelt, or rather thrown himself down before a *pietà* in the cloister corner, and had buried his head in the huge sleeves of his cowl there at the feet of the dead Christ, the Christ Who lay in the arms of Mary, letting fall one arm and a pierced hand in the limpness of death. It was a picture so fierce that it scared me: the abjection, the dereliction of this seemingly shattered monk at the feet of the broken Christ. I stepped into the cloister as if into an abyss.

The silence with people moving in it was ten times more gripping than it had been in my own empty room.

And now I was in the church. The two other seculars were kneeling there beside an altar at which the candles were burning. A priest was already at the altar, spreading out the corporal and opening the book. I could not figure out why the secular priest with the great shock of white hair was kneeling down to serve Mass. Maybe he wasn't a priest after all. But I did not have time to speculate about that: my heart was too full of other things in that great dark church, where, in little chapels, all around the ambulatory behind the high altar, chapels that were caves of dim candlelight, Mass was simultaneously beginning at many altars.

How did I live through that next hour? It is a mystery to me. The silence, the solemnity, the dignity of these Masses and of the church, and the overpowering atmosphere of prayers so fervent that they were almost tangible choked me with love and reverence that robbed me of the power to breathe. I could only get the air in gasps.

O my God, with what might You sometimes choose to teach a man's soul Your immense lessons! Here, even through only ordinary channels, came to me graces that overwhelmed me like a tidal wave, truths that drowned me with the force of their impact: and all through the plain, normal means of the liturgy—but the liturgy used properly, and with reverence, by souls inured to sacrifice.

What a thing Mass becomes, in hands hardened by gruelling and sacrificial labor, in poverty and abjection and humiliation! "See, see," said those lights, those shadows in all the chapels. "See Who God is! Realize what this Mass is! See Christ here, on the Cross! See His wounds, see His torn hands, see how the King of Glory is crowned with thorns! Do you know what Love is? Here is Love, Here on this Cross, here is Love, suffering these nails, these thorns, that scourge loaded with lead, smashed to pieces, bleeding to death because of your sins and bleeding to death because of people that will never know Him, and never think of Him and will never remember His Sacrifice. Learn from Him how to love God and how to love men! Learn of this Cross, this Love, how to give your life away to Him."

Almost simultaneously all around the church, at all the various altars, the bells began to ring. These monks, they rang no bells at the *Sanctus* or the *Hanc igitur*, only at the Consecration: and now, suddenly, solemnly, all around the church, Christ was on the Cross, lifted up, drawing all things to Himself, that tremendous Sacrifice tearing hearts from bodies, and drawing them out to Him.

"See, see Who God is, see the glory of God, going up to Him out of this incomprehensible and infinite Sacrifice in which all history begins and ends, all individual lives begin and end, in which every story is told, and finished, and settled for joy or for sorrow: the one point of reference for all the truths that are outside of God, their center, their focus: Love."

Faint gold fire flashed from the shadowy flanks of the upraised chalice at our altar.

"Do you know what Love is? You have never known the meaning of Love, never, you who have always drawn all things to the center of your own nothingness. Here is Love in this chalice full of Blood, Sacrifice, mactation. Do you not know that to love means to be killed for glory of the Beloved? And where is your love? Where is now your Cross, if you say you want to follow Me, if you pretend you love Me?"

All around the church the bells rang as gentle and fresh as dew.

"But these men are dying for Me. These monks are killing themselves for Me: and for you, for the world, for the people who do not know Me, for the millions that will never know them on this earth . . ."

After Communion I thought my heart was going to explode.

When the church had practically emptied after the second round of Masses, I left and went to my room. When I next came back to Church it was to kneel in the high balcony in the far end of the nave, for Tierce and Sext and then None and the Conventual Mass.

And now the church was full of light, and the monks stood in their stalls and bowed like white seas at the ends of the psalms, those slow, rich, sombre and yet lucid tones of the psalms, praising God in His new morning, thanking Him for the world He had created and for the life He continued to give to it.

Those psalms, the singing of the monks, and especially the ferial tone for the Little Hours' Hymns: what springs of life and strength and grace were in their singing! The whole earth came to life and bounded with new fruitfulness and significance in the joy of their simple and beautiful chanting that gradually built up to the climax of the conventual Mass: splendid, I say, and yet this Cistercian liturgy in Lent was reduced to the ultimate in simplicity. Therefore it was all the more splendid, because the splendor was intellectual and affective, and not the mere flash and glitter of vestments and decorations.

Two candles were lit on the bare altar. A plain wooden crucifix stood above the Tabernacle. The sanctuary was closed off with a curtain. The white altar cloth fell, at both ends, almost to the floor. The priest ascended the altar steps in a chasuble, accompanied by a deacon in alb and stole. And that was all.

At intervals during the Mass, a monk in a cowl detached himself from the choir and went slowly and soberly to minister at the altar, with grave and solemn bows, walking with his long flowing sleeves dangling almost as low as his ankles . . .

The eloquence of this liturgy was even more tremendous: and what it said was one, simple, cogent, tremendous truth: this church, the court of the Queen of Heaven, is the real capital of the country in which we are living. This is the center of all the vitality that is in America. This is the cause and reason why the nation is holding together. These men, hidden in the anonymity of their choir and their white cowls, are doing for their land what no army, no congress, no president could ever do as such: they are winning for it the grace and the protection and the friendship of God.

iv

I discovered that the young man with black hair, in dungarees, was a postulant. He was entering the monastery that day. That evening, at Compline, we who were standing up in the tribune at the back of the church could see him down there, in the choir, in his dark secular clothes, which made him easy to pick out, in the shadows, among the uniform white of the novices and monks.

For a couple of days it was that way. Practically the first thing you noticed, when you looked at the choir, was this young man in secular clothes, among all the monks.

Then suddenly we saw him no more. He was in white. They had given him an oblate's habit, and you could not pick him out from the rest.

The waters had closed over his head, and he was submerged in the community. He was lost. The world would hear of him no more. He had drowned to our society and become a Cistercian.

Up in the guest house, somebody who happened to know who he was, told me a few facts about him, by way of a kind of obituary.

I don't know if I got them straight or not: but he was a convert. He came from a rather wealthy family in Pennsylvania, and had gone to one of the big Eastern universities, and had been on a vacation in the Bahama Islands when he had bumped into a priest who got to talking to him about the faith, and converted him. When he was baptised, his parents were so incensed that they cut him off, as the saying goes, without a penny. For a while he had worked as a pilot on one of the big air lines, flying planes to South America, but now that was all over. He was gone out of the world. *Requiescat in pace.*

The secular priest with the white hair was more of a mystery. He was a big, bluff fellow, with some kind of an accent which led me to place him as a Belgian. He was not entering the community, but it seemed he had been there in the guest house for some time. In the afternoons he put on a pair of overalls, and went about painting benches and other furniture, and he laughed and talked with the others.

As he talked, his talk seemed strange to me. In a place like this, you would expect someone to say something, at least indirectly, about religion. And yet that was a subject on which he seemed to be inarticulate. The only thing he seemed to know anything about was strength, strength and work. At the dinner table, he rolled up his sleeve and said:

"Huh! Look at dat mossel!"

And he flexed a huge biceps for the edification of the retreatants.

I found out afterwards that he was under ecclesiastical censure, and was in the monastery doing penance. The poor man, for some reason or another, had not lived as a good priest. In the end, his mistakes had caught up with him. He had come into contact with some schismatics, in a sect known as "the Old Catholics" and these people persuaded him to leave the Church and come over to them. And when he did so, they made him an archbishop.

I suppose he enjoyed the dignity and the novelty of it for a while: but the whole thing was obviously silly. So he gave it up and came back. And now here he was in the monastery, serving Mass every morning for a young Trappist priest who scarcely had the oils of his ordination dry on his hands.

As the week went on, the house began to fill, and the evening before Holy Thursday there must have been some twenty-five or thirty retreatants in the monastery, men young and old, from all quarters of the country. Half a dozen students had hitch-hiked down from Notre Dame, with glasses and earnest talk about the philosophy of St. Thomas Aquinas. There was a psychiatrist from Chicago who said he came down every Easter, and there were three or four pious men who turned out to be friends and benefactors of the monastery—quiet, rather solemn personages; they assumed a sort of command over the other guests. They had a right to. They practically lived here in this guest house. In fact, they had a kind of quasi-vocation all their own. They belonged to that special class of men raised up by God to support orphanages and convents and monasteries and build hospitals and feed the poor. On the whole it is a way to sanctity that is sometimes too much despised. It sometimes implies a more than ordinary humility in men who come to think that the monks and nuns they assist are creatures of another world. God will show us at the latter day that many of them were better men than the monks they supported!

But the man I most talked to was a Carmelite priest who had wandered about the face of the earth even more than I had. If I wanted to hear something about monasteries, he could tell me about hundreds of them that he had seen.

We walked in the guest house garden, in the sun, watching the bees fighting in the rich yellow tulips, and he told me about the Carthusians in England, at Parkminster.

There were no longer any pure hermits or anchorites in the world: but the Carthusians were the ones who had gone the farthest, climbed the highest on the mountain of isolation that lifted them above the world and concealed them in God.

We could see the Cistercians here going out to work in a long line with shovels tucked under their arms with a most quaint formality. But the Carthusian worked alone, in his cell, in his own garden or workshop, isolated. These monks slept in a common dormitory, the Carthusian slept in a hidden cell. These men ate together while someone read aloud to them in their refectory. The Carthusian ate alone, sitting in the window-alcove of his cell, with no one to speak to him but God. All day long and all night long the Cistercian was with his brothers. All day long and all night long, except for the offices in choir and other intervals, the Carthusian was with God alone. *O beata solitudo!* . . .

The words were written on the walls of this Trappist guest house, too. *O beata solitudo, o sola beatitudo!*

There was one thing the Cistercians had in their favor. The Carthusians had a kind of recreation in which they went out for walks together and conversed with one another, to prevent the possibilities of strain that might go with too uncompromising a solitude, too much of that *sola beatitudo*. Could there be too much of it, I wondered? But the Trappist with his unbroken silence—at least as far as conversations were concerned—had one advantage!

And yet what did it matter which one was the most perfect Order? Neither one of them was for me! Had I not been told definitely enough a year ago that I had no vocation to any religious Order? All these comparisons were nothing but fuel for the fire of that interior anguish, that hopeless desire for what I could not have, for what was out of reach.

The only question was not which Order attracted me more, but which one tortured me the more with a solitude and silence and contemplation that could never be mine.

Far from wondering whether I had a vocation to either one, or from instituting a comparison between them, I was not even allowed the luxury of speculation on such a subject. It was all out of the question.

However, since the Carthusians were, after all, far away, it was what I had before my eyes that tortured me the most. The Carthusians were more perfect, perhaps, and therefore more to be desired: but they were doubly out of reach because of the war and because of what I thought was my lack of a vocation.

If I had had any supernatural common sense I would have realized that a retreat like this would be the best time to take that problem by the horns and overcome it, not by my own efforts and meditations but by prayer and by the advice of an experienced priest. And where would I find anyone more experienced in such matters than in a monastery of contemplatives?

But what was the matter with me? I suppose I had taken such a beating from the misunderstandings and misapprehensions that had arisen in my mind by the time that Capuchin got through with me, in his confessional, the year before, that I literally feared to reopen the subject at all. There was something in my bones that told me that I ought to find out whether my intense desire to lead this kind of a life in some monastery were an illusion: but the old scars were not yet healed, and my whole being shrank from another scourging.

That was my Holy Week, that mute, hopeless, interior struggle. It was my share in the Passion of Christ which began, that year, in the middle of the night with the first strangled cry of the Vigils of Holy Thursday.

It was a tremendous thing to hear the terrible cries of Jeremias resounding along the walls of that dark church buried in the country. ". . . Attend and see if there be any sorrow like unto my sorrow . . . From above He hath sent fire into my bones, and hath chastised me: He hath spread a net for my feet, He hath turned me back, He hath made me desolate, wasted with sorrow all the day long."

It was not hard to realize Whose words these were, not difficult to detect the voice of Christ, in the liturgy of His Church, crying out in the sorrows of His Passion, which was now beginning to be relived, as it is relived each year, in the churches of Christendom.

At the end of the office, one of the monks came solemnly out and extinguished the sanctuary light, and the sudden impression froze all hearts with darkness and foreboding. The day went on solemnly, the Little Hours being chanted in a strange, mighty, and tremendously sorrowful tone, plain as its three monotonously recurring notes could possibly make it be, a lament that was as rough and clean as stone. After the *Gloria in Excelsis* of the conventual Mass, the organ was at last altogether silent: and the silence only served to bring out the simplicity and strength of the music chanted by the choir. After the general Communion, distributed to the long slow line of all the priests and monks and brothers and guests, and the procession of the Blessed Sacrament to the altar of repose—slow and sad, with lights and the *Pange Lingua*—came the Maundy, the *Mandatum,* when, in the cloister, the monks washed the feet of some seventy or eighty poor men, and kissed their feet, and pressed money into their hands.

And through all this, especially in the *Mandatum,* when I saw them at close range, I was amazed at the way these monks, who were evidently just plain young Americans from the factories and colleges and farms and high-schools of the various states, were nevertheless absorbed and transformed in the liturgy. The thing that was most impressive was their absolute simplicity. They were concerned with one thing only: doing the things they had to do, singing what they had to sing, bowing and kneeling and so on when it was prescribed, and doing it as well as they could, without fuss or flourish or display. It was all utterly simple and unvarnished and straightforward, and I don't think I had ever seen anything, anywhere, so unaffected, so un-self-conscious as these monks. There was not a shadow of anything that could be called parade or display. They did not seem to realize that they were being watched—and, as a matter of fact, I can say from experience that they did not know it at all. In choir, it is very rare that you even realize that there are any, or many, or few seculars in the house: and if you do realize it, it makes no difference. The presence of other people becomes something that has absolutely no significance to the monk when he is at prayer. It is something null, neutral, like the air, like the atmosphere, like the weather. All these external things recede into the distance. Remotely, you are aware of it all, but you do not advert to it, you are not conscious of it, any more than the eye registers, with awareness, the things on which it is not focussed, although they may be within its range of vision.

Certainly one thing the monk does not, or cannot, realize is the effect which these liturgical functions, performed by a group as such, have upon those who see them. The lessons, the truths, the incidents and values portrayed are simply overwhelming.

For this effect to be achieved, it is necessary that each monk as an individual performer be absolutely lost, ignored, overlooked.

And yet, what a strange admission! To say that men were admirable, worthy of honor, perfect, in proportion as they disappeared into a crowd and made themselves unnoticed, by even ceasing to be aware of their own existence and their own acts. Excellence, here, was in proportion to obscurity: the one who was best was the one who was least observed, least distinguished. Only faults and mistakes drew attention to the individual.

The logic of the Cistercian life was, then, the complete opposite to the logic of the world, in which men put themselves forward, so that the most excellent is the one who stands out, the one who is eminent above the rest, who attracts attention.

But what was the answer to this paradox? Simply that the monk in hiding himself from the world becomes not less himself, not less of a person, but more of a person, more truly and perfectly himself: for his personality and individuality are perfected in their true order, the spiritual, interior order, of union with God, the principle of all perfection. *Omnis gloria ejus filiae regis ab intus.*

The logic of worldly success rests on a fallacy: the strange error that our perfection depends on the thoughts and opinions and applause of other men! A weird life it is, indeed, to be living always in somebody else's imagination, as if that were the only place in which one could at last become real!

With all these things before me, day and night, for two days, I finally came to the afternoon of Good Friday.

After a tremendous morning of ten hours of practically uninterrupted chanting and psalmody, the monks, exhausted, had disappeared from the scene of their gutted church, with its stripped altars and its empty Tabernacle wide open to the four winds. The monastery was silent, inert. I could not pray, I could not read any more.

I got Brother Matthew to let me out the front gate on the pretext that I wanted to take a picture of the monastery, and then I went for a walk along the enclosure wall, down the road past the mill, and around the back of the buildings, across a creek and down a narrow valley, with a barn and some woods on one side, and the monastery on a bluff on the other.

The sun was warm, the air quiet. Somewhere a bird sang. In a sense, it was a relief to be out of the atmosphere of intense prayer that had pervaded those buildings for the last two days. The pressure was too heavy for me. My mind was too full.

Now my feet took me slowly along a rocky road, under the stunted cedar trees, with violets growing up everywhere between the cracks in the rock.

Out here I could think: and yet I could not get to any conclusions. But there was one thought running around and around in my mind: "To be a monk . . . to be a monk . . ."

I gazed at the brick building which I took to be the novitiate. It stood on top of a high rampart of a retaining wall that made it look like a prison or a citadel. I saw the enclosure wall, the locked gates. I thought of the hundreds of pounds of spiritual pressure compressed and concentrated within those buildings and weighing down on the heads of the monks, and I thought, "It would kill me."

I turned my eyes to the trees, to the woods. I looked up the valley, back in the direction from which I had come, at the high wooded hill that closed off the prospect. I thought: "I am a Franciscan. That is my kind of spirituality, to be out in the woods, under the trees . . ."

I walked back across the trestle over the sunny, narrow creek, embracing my fine new error. After all I had seen of the Franciscans, where did I get the idea that they spent their time under the trees? They often lived in schools in towns and in cities: and these monks, on the contrary, did go out every day and work in the very fields and woods that I was looking at.

Human nature has a way of making very specious arguments to suit its own cowardice and lack of generosity. And so now I was trying to persuade myself that the contemplative, cloistered life was not for me, because there was not enough fresh air. . . .

Nevertheless, back in the monastery I read St. Bernard's *De Diligendo Deo* and I read the life of a Trappist monk who had died in a monastery in France, ironically enough in my own part of France, near Toulouse: Father Joseph Cassant.

The Retreat Master, in one of his conferences, told us a long story of a man who had once come to Gethsemani, and who had not been able to make up his mind to become a monk, and had fought and prayed about it for days. Finally, went the story, he had made the Stations of the Cross, and at the final station had prayed fervently to be allowed the grace of dying in the Order.

"You know," said the Retreat Master, "they say that no petition you ask at the fourteenth station is ever refused."

In any case, this man finished his prayer, and went back to his room and in an hour or so he collapsed, and they just had time to receive his request for admission to the Order when he died.

He lies buried in the monks' cemetery, in the oblate's habit.

And so, about the last thing I did before leaving Gethsemani, was to do the Stations of the Cross, and to ask, with my heart in my throat, at the fourteenth station, for the grace of a vocation to the Trappists, if it were pleasing to God.

V

Back in the world, I felt like a man that had come down from the rare atmosphere of a very high mountain. When I got to Louisville, I had already been up for four hours or so, and my day was getting on towards its noon, so to speak, but I found that everybody else was just getting up and having breakfast and going to work. And how strange it was to see people walking around as if they had something important to do, running after busses, reading the newspapers, lighting cigarettes.

How futile all their haste and anxiety seemed.

My heart sank within me. I thought: "What am I getting into? Is this the sort of a thing I myself have been living in all these years?"

At a street corner, I happened to look up and caught sight of an electric sign, on top of a two-storey building. It read: "Clown Cigarettes."

I turned and fled from the alien and lunatic street, and found my way into the nearby cathedral, and knelt, and prayed, and did the Stations of the Cross.

Afraid of the spiritual pressure in that monastery? Was that what I had said the other day? How I longed to be back there now: everything here, in the world outside, was insipid and slightly insane.

There was only one place I knew of where there was any true order.

Yet, how could I go back? Did I not know that I really had no vocation? . . . It was the same old story again.

I got on the train for Cincinnati, and for New York.

Back at St. Bonaventure's, where the spring I had already met in Kentucky finally caught up with me again, several weeks later, I walked in the woods, in the sun, under the pale blossoms of the wild cherry trees.

The fight went on in my mind.

By now, the problem had resolved itself into one practical issue: why don't I consult somebody about the whole question? Why don't I write to the abbot of Gethsemani, and tell him all about my case, and ask him his opinion?

More practical still, here at St. Bonaventure's there was one priest whom I had come to know well during this last year, a wise and good philosopher, Father Philotheus. We had been going over some texts of St. Bonaventure and Duns Scotus together, and I knew I could trust him with the most involved spiritual problem. Why did I not ask him?

There was one absurd, crazy thing that held me up: it was a kind of a blind impulse, confused, obscure, irrational. I can hardly identify it as it actually was, because its true nature escaped me: it was so blind, so elemental. But it amounted to a vague subconscious fear that I would once and for all be told that I definitely had no vocation It was the fear of an ultimate refusal. Perhaps what I wanted was to maintain myself in an equivocal, indefinite position in which I would be free to dream about entering the monastery, without having the actual responsibility of doing so, and of embracing the real hardships of Cistercian life. If I asked advice, and was told I had no vocation, then the dream would be over: and if I was told I had a vocation, then I would have to walk right in to the reality.

And all this was complicated by that other dream: that of the Carthusians. If there had been a Carthusian monastery in America, things would have been much simpler. But there is still no such place in the whole hemisphere. And there was no chance of crossing the Atlantic. France was full of Germans and the Charterhouse in Sussex had been bombed flat to the ground. And so I walked under the trees, full of indecision, praying for light.

In the midst of this conflict, I suddenly got a notion which shows that I was not very far advanced in the spiritual life. I thought of praying God to let me know what I was going to do, or what I should do, or what the solution would be, by showing it to me in the Scriptures. It was the old business of opening the book and putting your finger down blindly on the page and taking the words thus designated as an answer to your question. Sometimes the saints have done this, and much more often a lot of superstitious old women have done it. I am not a saint, and I do not doubt that there may have been an element of superstition in my action. But anyway, I made my prayer, and opened the book, and put my finger down definitely on the page and said to myself: "Whatever it is, this is it."

I looked, and the answer practically floored me. The words were: "*Ecce eris tacens.*" "Behold, thou shalt be silent."

It was the twentieth verse of the first chapter of St. Luke where the angel was talking to John the Baptist's father, Zachary.

Tacens: there could not have been a closer word to "Trappist" in the whole Bible, as far as I was concerned, for to me, as well as to most other people, the word "Trappist" stood for "silence."

However, I immediately found myself in difficulties which show how silly it is to make an oracle out of books. As soon as I looked at the context, I observed that Zachary was being reproved for asking too many questions. Did the whole context apply to me, too, and was I also therefore reproved? And therefore was the news to be taken as ominous and bad? I thought about it a little, and soon found that I was getting completely mixed up. Besides, when I reflected, I realized that I had not put the question in any clear terms, so that, as a matter of fact, I had forgotten just what I had asked. I did not know whether I had asked God to tell me His will, or merely to announce to me what would happen in the future in point of fact. By the time I had got myself completely tied up in these perplexities, the information I had asked for was more of a nuisance, and a greater cause of uncertainty than my ignorance.

In fact, I was almost as ignorant as I was before, except for one thing.

Deep down, underneath all the perplexity, I had a kind of a conviction that this was a genuine answer, and that the problem was indeed some day going to end up that way: I was going to be a Trappist.

But as far as making any practical difference, there and then, it was no help at all.

I continued to walk in the woods, in the pastures, and in the old tank lots at the wood's edge, down towards the radio station. When I was out there alone, I would go about full of nostalgia for the Trappist monastery, singing over and over *Jam lucis orto sidere* on the ferial tone.

It was a matter of deep regret to me that I could not remember the wonderful *Salve Regina* with which the monks ended all their days, chanting in the darkness to the Mother of God that long antiphon, the most stately and most beautiful and most stirring thing that was ever written, that was ever sung. I walked along the roads, in Two Mile Valley, in Four Mile Valley, in the late afternoons, in the early evenings, in the dusk, and along the river where it was quiet, wishing I could sing the *Salve Regina*. And I could remember nothing but the first two or three neumes. After that, I had to invent, and my invention was not very good. It sounded awful. So did my voice. So I gave up trying to sing, humiliated and sorrowful, and complaining a little to the Mother of God.

The weeks went on, and the weather began to show signs of summer when John Paul suddenly arrived at St. Bonaventure's, on his way back from Mexico. The back seat of his Buick was full of Mexican records and pictures and strange objects and a revolver and big colored baskets, and he was looking relatively well and happy. We spent a couple of afternoons driving around through the hills, and talking, or just driving and not talking. He had been to Yucatan, as he had planned, and he had been to Puebla, and he had just missed being in an earthquake in Mexico City, and he had lent a lot of money to some gent who owned a ranch near St. Luis Potosi. On the same ranch he had shot, with his revolver, a poisonous snake some six feet long.

"Do you expect to get that money back?" I asked him.

"Oh, if he doesn't pay me, I'll have a share in his ranch," said John Paul without concern.

But at the moment he was heading back towards Ithaca. I could not be sure whether he was going to go to Cornell summer school, and finally get his degree, or whether he was going to take some more flying lessons, or what he was going to do.

I asked him if he had kept in touch with this priest he knew there.

"Oh, yes," he said, "sure."

I asked him what he thought about becoming a Catholic.

"You know," he said, "I've thought about that a little."

"Why don't you go to the priest and ask him to give you some instructions?"

"I think I will."

But I could tell from the tone of his voice that he was as indefinite as he was sincere. He meant well, but he would probably do nothing about it. I said I would give him a copy of the Catechism I had, but when I went to my room I couldn't find it.

And so John Paul, in the big shiny Buick built low on its chassis, drove off at a great speed, towards Ithaca, with his revolver and his Mexican baskets.

In the gay days of early June, in the time of examinations, I was beginning a new book. It was called *The Journal of My Escape from the Nazis* and it was the kind of book that I liked to write, full of double-talk and all kinds of fancy ideas that sounded like Franz Kafka. One reason why it was satisfying was that it fulfilled a kind of psychological necessity that had been pent up in me all through the last stages of the war because of my sense of identification, by guilt, with what was going on in England.

So I put myself there and, telescoping my own past with the air-raids that were actually taking place, as its result, I wrote this journal. And, as I say, it was something I needed to write, although I often went off at a tangent, and the thing got away up more than one blind alley.

And so, absorbed in this work, and in the final examinations, and in preparation for the coming summer school, I let the question of the Trappist vocation drop into the background, although I could not drop it altogether.

I said to myself: after summer school, I will go and make a retreat with the Trappists in Canada, at Our Lady of the Lake, outside Montreal.

3

The Sleeping Volcano

In the cool summer nights, when the road behind the powerhouse and the laundry and the garages was dark and empty, and you could barely see the hills, outlined in the dark against the stars, I used to walk out there, in the smell of the fields, towards the dark cow-barns. There was a grove along the west side of the football field, and in the grove were two shrines, one to the Little Flower and the other a grotto for Our Lady of Lourdes. But the grotto wasn't complicated enough to be really ugly, the way those artificial grottos usually are. It was nice to pray out there, in the dark, with the wind soughing in the high pine branches.

Sometimes you could hear one other sound: the laughter of all the nuns and clerics and Friars and the rest of the summer school students sitting in Alumni Hall, which was at the end of the grove, and enjoying the movies, which were shown every Thursday night.

On those nights, the whole campus was deserted and the Alumni Hall was crowded. I felt as if I were the only one in the place who did not go to the movies—except for the boy at the telephone switchboard in the Dormitory building. He had to stay there, he was being paid for that.

Even my friend Father Philotheus, who was editing fourteenth-century philosophical manuscripts, and who had taught me St. Bonaventure's way to God according to the *Itinerarium*, and with whom I had studied parts of Scotus' *De Primo Principio*, even he went to the movies in the hope that there would be a Mickey Mouse. But as soon as all the comedies were over, he left. He could not make anything much out of all those other dramas and adventures.

Oh, the gay laughter of the Sisters and the clerics in that old firetrap of a red-brick building! I suppose they deserved to have a little entertainment—at least the Sisters deserved it. I know that many of them got some severe headaches from the course I was giving in "Bibliography and Methods of Research." The traditional way of teaching methods of research was to throw out a lot of odd names and facts to the class, without any clue as to where they came from, and tell them all to come back the next day with a complete identification. So I asked them things like: "Who is Philip Sparrow?" "What Oxford College has on its coat of arms a Pelican vulning herself proper?" To find out these things—which I only gave them because I already knew them myself—they had to break their heads over all kinds of reference books, and thus they got practical training in methods of research. But the Sisters always came back with the right answer, although they sometimes had circles under their eyes. The clerics had the right answer but no circles, because they had got the answer from the Sisters. In the back of the room sat a priest who belonged to some teaching Order in Canada and who seldom got the answers at all, even from the Sisters. He just sat there and gave me black looks.

So, on the whole, it was good that they should relax and laugh, and sit in those rows of ancient and uncomfortable chairs indulging their innocent and unsophisticated taste for carefully selected movies.

I walked along the empty field, and thought of their life—sheltered and innocent and safe. A number of them were, in many ways, still children—especially the nuns. They looked out at you from under various kinds of caps and coifs and blinkers and what not they had on, with round, earnest eyes; the sober, clear eyes of little girls. Yet you knew they had responsibilities, and many of them had suffered a lot of things you could only half guess: but it was all absorbed in quiet simplicity and resignation. The most you could observe even in the most harassed of them was that they looked a little tired: perhaps some of the older ones, too, were a trifle too tight-lipped, a trifle too grim. But even then, some of the old ones still had that little girl simplicity in their look, not yet altogether extinct.

Their life was secure. It was walled in by ramparts of order and decorum and stability, in the social as much as in the religious sphere. But they nevertheless all had to work hard—much harder than most of their relatives outside in the world. Most of the Sisters had long hours in their schoolrooms and then other things to do besides that. I suppose they had their fair share of cooking, and washing clothes, and scrubbing floors when they were in their proper communities. Yet even then, was not the relative comfort of their life apt to make them impervious to certain levels of human experience and human misery?

I wondered if they were aware of all the degrees of suffering and degradation which, in the slums, in the war zones, in the moral jungles of our century, were crying out to the Church for help, and to Heaven for vengeance against injustice. The answer to that would probably be that some of them were, and some of them were not: but that they all sincerely wanted to be doing something about these things, if they could. But, it was true, they were sheltered, protected, separated, in large measure, from the frightful realities that had a claim upon their attention if they loved Christ.

But then, why should I separate myself from them? I was in the same condition. Perhaps I was slightly more conscious of it than some of them: but all of us were going to have an occasion to remember this paradox, this accusing paradox that those who are poor for the love of Christ are often only poor in a purely abstract sense, and that their poverty, which is designed among other things to throw them into the midst of the real poor, for the salvation of souls, only separates them from the poor in a safe and hermetically-sealed economic stability, full of comfort and complacency.

One night there came to those nuns and to those clerics and to St. Bonaventure in general and myself in particular, someone sent from God for the special purpose of waking us up, and turning our eyes in that direction which we all tended so easily to forget, in the safety and isolation of our country stronghold, lost in the upstate hills.

It was right, of course, that my interior life should have been concerned first of all with my own salvation: it must be that way. It is no profit for a man to gain the whole world, and suffer the loss of his own soul, and anyway, one who is losing his own soul is not going to be able to do much to save the souls of others, except in the case where he may be giving out Sacraments which work, as they say, *ex opere operato,* without any intrinsic dependence on the sanctity of the one dispensing them. But now it was necessary that I take more account of obligations to other men, born of the very fact that I was myself a man among men, and a sharer in their sins and in their punishments and in their miseries and in their hopes. No man goes to heaven all by himself, alone.

I was walking around the football field, as usual, in the dark. The Alumni Hall was full of lights. It was not the night for movies. There was some speaker there. I had not paid much attention to the list of speakers that had been invited to come and stand on that platform and tell the clerics and Sisters all about some important topic. I knew there would be one from *The Catholic Worker,* and that David Goldstein, who was a converted Jew and ran an organization for street-preaching by laymen, was invited to speak, and I knew Baroness de Hueck, who was working among the Negroes in Harlem, was also going to come.

As far as I knew, this night was the one listed for David Goldstein, and I hesitated for a moment wondering whether I wanted to go and hear him or not. At first, I thought: "No," and started off towards the grove. But then I thought: "I will at least take a look inside the door."

Going up the steps to the second floor of the Hall, where the theater was, I could hear someone speaking with great vehemence. However, it was not a man's voice.

When I stepped in to the room, there was a woman standing on the stage. Now a woman, standing all alone on a stage, in front of a big lighted hall, without any decorations or costume or special lighting effects, just in the glare of the hall-lights, is at a disadvantage. It is not very likely that she will make much of an impression. And this particular woman was dressed in clothes that were nondescript and plain, even poor. She had no artful way of walking around, either. She had no fancy tricks, nothing for the gallery. And yet as soon as I came in the door, the impression she was making on that room full of nuns and clerics and priests and various lay-people pervaded the place with such power that it nearly knocked me backwards down the stairs which I had just ascended.

She had a strong voice, and strong convictions, and strong things to say, and she was saying them in the simplest, most unvarnished, bluntest possible kind of talk, and with such uncompromising directness that it stunned. You could feel right away that most of her audience was hanging on her words, and that some of them were frightened, and that one or two were angry, but that everybody was intent on the things she had to say.

I realized it was the Baroness.

I had heard something about her, and her work in Harlem, because she was well known and admired in Corpus Christi parish, where I had been baptized. Father Ford was always sending her things they needed, down there on 135th Street and Lenox Avenue.

What she was saying boiled down to this:

Catholics are worried about Communism: and they have a right to be, because the Communist revolution aims, among other things, at wiping out the Church. But few Catholics stop to think that Communism would make very little progress in the world, or none at all, if Catholics really lived up to their obligations, and really did the things Christ came on earth to teach them to do: that is, if they really loved one another, and saw Christ in one another, and lived as saints, and did something to win justice for the poor.

For, she said, if Catholics were able to see Harlem, as they ought to see it, with the eyes of faith, they would not be able to stay away from such a place. Hundreds of priests and lay-people would give up everything to go there and try to do something to relieve the tremendous misery, the poverty, sickness, degradation and dereliction of a race that was being crushed and perverted, morally and physically, under the burden of a colossal economic injustice. Instead of seeing Christ suffering in His members, and instead of going to help Him, Who said: "Whatsoever you did to the least of these my brethren, you did it to Me," we preferred our own comfort: we averted our eyes from such a spectacle, because it made us feel uneasy: the thought of so much dirt nauseated us—and we never stopped to think that we, perhaps, might be partly responsible for it. And so people continued to die of starvation and disease in those evil tenements full of vice and cruelty, while those who did condescend to consider their problems, held banquets in the big hotels downtown to discuss the "Race situation" in a big rosy cloud of hot air.

If Catholics, she said, were able to see Harlem as they should see it, with the eyes of faith, as a challenge to their love of Christ, as a test of their Christianity, the Communists would be able to do nothing there.

But, on the contrary, in Harlem the Communists were strong. They were bound to be strong. They were doing some of the things, performing some of the works of mercy that Christians should be expected to do. If some Negro workers lose their jobs, and are in danger of starving, the Communists are there to divide their own food with them, and to take up the defence of their case.

If some Negro is dying, and is refused admission to a hospital, the Communists show up, and get someone to take care of him, and furthermore see to it that the injustice is publicized all over the city. If a Negro family is evicted, because they can't pay the rent, the Communists are there, and find shelter for them, even if they have to divide their own bedding with them. And every time they do these things, more and more people begin to say: "See, the Communists really love the poor! They are really trying to do something for us! What they say must be right: there is no one else who cares anything about our interests: there is nothing better for us to do than to get in with them, and work with them for this revolution they are talking about. . . ."

Do the Catholics e a labor policy? Have the Popes said anything about these problems in their Encyclicals? The Communists know more about those Encyclicals than the average Catholic. *Rerum Novarum* and *Quadrigesimo Anno* are discussed and analyzed in their public meetings, and the Reds end up by appealing to their audience:

"Now we ask you, do the Catholics practice these things? Have you ever seen any Catholics down here trying to do anything for you? When this firm and that firm locked out so many hundreds of Negro workers, whose side did the Catholic papers take? Don't you know that the Catholic Church is just a front for Capitalism, and that all their talk about the poor is hypocrisy? What do they care about the poor? What have they ever done to help you? Even their priests in Harlem go outside and hire white men when they want somebody to repaint their churches! Don't you know that the Catholics are laughing at you, behind the back of their hands, while they pocket the rent for the lousy tenements you have to live in? . . ."

The Baroness was born a Russian. She had been a young girl at the time of the October Revolution. She had seen half her family shot, she had seen priests fall under the bullets of the Reds, and she had had to escape from Russia the way it is done in the movies, but with all the misery and hardship which the movies do not show, and none of the glamour which is their specialty.

She had ended up in New York, without a cent, working in a laundry. She had been brought up a Roman Catholic, and the experiences she had gone through, instead of destroying her faith, intensified and deepened it until the Holy Ghost planted fortitude in the midst of her soul like an unshakeable rock. I never saw anyone so calm, so certain, so peaceful in her absolute confidence in God.

Catherine de Hueck is a person in every way big: and the bigness is not merely physical: it comes from the Holy Ghost dwelling constantly within her, and moving her in all that she does.

When she was working in that laundry, down somewhere near Fourteenth Street, and sitting on the kerbstone eating her lunch with the other girls who worked there, the sense of her own particular vocation dawned upon her. It was the call to an apostolate, not new, but so old that it is as traditional as that of the first Christians: an apostolate of a laywoman in the world, among workers, herself a worker, and poor: an apostolate of personal contacts, of word and above all of example. There was to be nothing special about it, nothing that savored of a religious Order, no special rule, no distinctive habit. She, and those who joined her, would simply be poor—there was no choice on that score, for they were that already—but they would embrace their poverty, and the life of the proletariat in all its misery and insecurity and dead, drab monotony. They would live and work in the slums, lose themselves, in the huge anonymous mass of the forgotten and the derelict, for the only purpose of living the complete, integral Christian life in that environment—loving those around them, sacrificing themselves for those around them, and spreading the Gospel and the truth of Christ most of all by being saints, by living in union with Him, by being full of His Holy Ghost, His charity.

As she spoke of these things, in that Hall, and to all these nuns and clerics, she could not help but move them all deeply, because what they were hearing—it was too patent to be missed—was nothing but the pure Franciscan ideal, the pure essence of the Franciscan apostolate of poverty, without the vows taken by the Friars Minor. And, for the honor of those who heard her, most of them had the sense and the courage to recognize this fact, and to see that she was, in a sense, a much better Franciscan than they were. She was, as a matter of fact, in the Third Order, and that made me feel quite proud of my own scapular, which was hiding under my shirt: it reminded me that the thing was not altogether without meaning or without possibilities!

So the Baroness had gone to Harlem. She stepped out of the subway with a typewriter and a few dollars and some clothes in a bag. When she went to one of the tenements, and asked to look at a room, the man said to her:

"Ma'am, you all don't want to live here!"

"Yes, I do," she said, and added, by way of explanation: "I'm Russian."

"Russian!" said the man. "That's different. Walk right in."

In other words, he thought she was a Communist. . . .

That was the way Friendship House had begun. Now they were occupying four or five stores on both sides of 135th Street, and maintained a library and recreation rooms and a clothing room. The Baroness had an apartment of her own, and those of her helpers who lived there all the time also had a place on 135th Street. There were more girls than men staying with her in Harlem.

When the meeting was over, and when the Baroness had answered all the usual objections like "What if some Negro wanted to marry your sister—or you, for that matter?" I went up and spoke to her, and the next day I ran into her on the path in front of the library, when I was going, with an arm full of books, to teach a class on Dante's *Divine Comedy*. These two times were the only chance I had to speak to her, but I said:

"Would it be all right if I came to Friendship House, and did a little work with you, there, after all this is over?"

"Sure," she said, "come on."

But seeing me with my arms full of all those books, maybe she didn't believe me.

ii

It was a hot day, a rainy day, in the middle of August when I came out of the subway into the heat of Harlem. There were not many people on the streets that afternoon. I walked along the street until I came to the middle of the block, and saw one or two stores marked "Friendship House" and "Bl. Martin de Porres Center" or some such title in big blue letters. There did not seem to be anyone around.

The biggest of the stores was the library, and there I found half a dozen young Negroes, boys and girls, high school students, sitting at a table. Some of them wore glasses, and it seemed they were having some kind of an organized intellectual discussion, because when I came in they got a little embarrassed about it. I asked them if the Baroness was there, and they said no, she had gone downtown because it was her birthday, and I asked who I should see, so they told me Mary Jerdo. She was around somewhere. If I waited she would probably show up in a few minutes.

So I stood there, and took down off the shelf Father Bruno's *Life of St. John of the Cross* and looked at the pictures.

The young Negroes tried to pick up their discussion where they had left off: but they did not succeed. The stranger made them nervous. One of the girls opened her mouth and pronounced three or four abstract words, and then broke off into a giggle. Then another one opened her mouth and said: "Yes, but don't you think . . . ?" And this solemn question also collapsed in embarrassed tittering. One of the young men got off a whole paragraph or so, full of big words, and everybody roared with laughter. So I turned around and started to laugh too, and immediately the whole thing became a game.

They began saying big words just because it was funny. They uttered the most profoundly dull and ponderous statements, and laughed at them, and at the fact that such strange things had come out of their mouths. But soon they calmed down, and then Mary Jerdo came along, and showed me the different departments of Friendship House, and explained what they were.

The embarrassment of those young Negroes was something that gave me a picture of Harlem: the details of the picture were to be filled in later, but the essentials were already there.

Here in this huge, dark, steaming slum, hundreds of thousands of Negroes are herded together like cattle, most of them with nothing to eat and nothing to do. All the senses and imagination and sensibilities and emotions and sorrows and desires and hopes and ideas of a race with vivid feelings and deep emotional reactions are forced in upon themselves, bound inward by an iron ring of frustration: the prejudice that hems them in with its four insurmountable walls. In this huge cauldron, inestimable natural gifts, wisdom, love, music, science, poetry are stamped down and left to boil with the dregs of an elementally corrupted nature, and thousands upon thousands of souls are destroyed by vice and misery and degradation, obliterated, wiped out, washed from the register of the living, dehumanized.

What has not been devoured, in your dark furnace, Harlem, by marihuana, by gin, by insanity, hysteria, syphilis?

Those who manage somehow to swim to the top of the seething cauldron, and remain on its surface, through some special spiritual quality or other, or because they have been able to get away from Harlem, and go to some college or school, these are not all at once annihilated: but they are left with the dubious privilege of living out the only thing Harlem possesses in the way of an ideal. They are left with the sorry task of contemplating and imitating what passes for culture in the world of the white people.

Now the terrifying paradox of the whole thing is this: Harlem itself, and every individual Negro in it, is a living condemnation of our so-called "culture." Harlem is there by way of a divine indictment against New York City and the people who live downtown and make their money downtown. The brothels of Harlem, and all its prostitution, and its dope-rings, and all the rest are the mirror of the polite divorces and the manifold cultured adulteries of Park Avenue: they are God's commentary on the whole of our society.

Harlem is, in a sense, what God thinks of Hollywood. And Hollywood is all Harlem has, in its despair, to grasp at, by way of a surrogate for heaven.

The most terrible thing about it all is that there is not a Negro in the whole place who does not realize, somewhere in the depths of his nature, that the culture of the white men is not worth the dirt in Harlem's gutters. They sense that the whole thing is rotten, that it is a fake, that it is spurious, empty, a shadow of nothingness. And yet they are condemned to reach out for it, and to seem to desire it, and to pretend they like it, as if the whole thing were some kind of bitter cosmic conspiracy: as if they were thus being forced to work out, in their own lives, a clear representation of the misery which has corrupted the ontological roots of the white man's own existence.

The little children of Harlem are growing up, crowded together like sardines in the rooms of tenements full of vice, where evil takes place hourly and inescapably before their eyes, so that there is not an excess of passion, not a perversion of natural appetite with which they are not familiar before the age of six or seven: and this by way of an accusation of the polite and expensive and furtive sensualities and lusts of the rich whose sins have bred this abominable slum. The effect resembles and even magnifies the cause, and Harlem is the portrait of those through whose fault such things come into existence. What was heard in secret in the bedrooms and apartments of the rich and of the cultured and the educated and the white is preached from the housetops of Harlem and there declared, for what it is, in all its horror, somewhat as it is seen in the eyes of God, naked and frightful.

No, there is not a Negro in the whole place who can fail to know, in the marrow of his own bones, that the white man's culture is not worth the jetsam in the Harlem River.

That night I came back to Harlem, since Mary Jerdo told me to, and had dinner with them all, and congratulated the Baroness on her birthday, and we saw a play that was put on by the little Negro children in the recreation room of the group called the "Cubs."

It was an experience that nearly tore me to pieces. All the parents of the children were there, sitting on benches, literally choked with emotion at the fact that their children should be acting in a play: but that was not the thing. For, as I say, they knew that the play was nothing, and that all the plays of the white people are more or less nothing. They were not taken in by that. Underneath it was something deep and wonderful and positive and true and overwhelming: their gratitude for even so small a sign of love as this, that someone should at least make some kind of a gesture that said: "This sort of thing cannot make anybody happy, but it is a way of saying: 'I wish you were happy.' "

Over against the profound and positive and elemental reality of this human love, not unmixed with Christ's charity and almost obtrusively holy, was the idiotic character of the play itself. Some one of those geniuses who write one-act plays for amateur theatricals had thought up the idea of having King Arthur and his Knights appear in modern dress, running around in a country club.

Let me tell you, this piece of wit became so devastating that it nearly gave me grey hairs, watching its presentation by little Negro children in the midst of that slum. The nameless author, speaking in the name of twentieth-century middle-class culture, said: "Here is something very jolly." God, replying through the mouths and eyes and actions of these little Negro children, and through their complete incomprehension of what the jokes and the scene and the situations could possibly be about, said: "This is what I think of your wit. It is an abomination in my sight. I do not know you, I do not know your society: you are as dead to me as hell itself. These little Negro children, I know and love: but you I know not. You are anathema."

Two or three nights later there was another play put on in the parish hall by an older group. It was the same kind of a play, all about rich people having a good time, presented by poor hapless Negro youths and girls who had no means of knowing anything about a good time that was so inane and idiotic—or so expensive. The very zest and gaiety and enthusiasm with which they tried to make something out of this miserable piece of trash only condemned its author and his inspiration all the more forcibly. And you were left with the sense that these Negroes, even in Harlem, would have been able to give all the rich men on Sutton Place lessons in how to be happy without half trying: and that was why their imitation of the ruling class was all the more damning an indictment.

If the Baroness had tried to face the tremendous paradox of Harlem with no other weapons than these, I think Friendship House would have closed down in three days. But the secret of her success and of her survival in the teeth of this gigantic problem was that she depended not on these frail human methods, not on theatricals, or meetings, or speeches, or conferences, but on God, Christ, the Holy Ghost.

According to the plan of her vocation, the Baroness herself had come to Harlem, and had started to live there for God, and God had brought her quickly into contact with the others who were serving in His secret police in this enemy city: the saints He had sent to sanctify and purify, not Harlem, but New York.

On Judgement Day the citizens of that fat metropolis with its mighty buildings and its veins bursting with dollars and its brains overreaching themselves with new optimistic philosophies of culture and progress, will be surprised, astounded when they find out who it was that was keeping the brimstone and thunderbolts of God's anger from wiping them long since from the face of the earth.

Living in the same building as most of the Friendship House workers was an ageing Negro woman, thin, quiet, worn out, dying of cancer. I only saw her once or twice, but I heard a lot about her; for everyone said that she had visions of Our Lady. About that I know nothing, except that if Our Lady were to act according to her usual custom, Harlem would be one of the first and only places I would expect her to appear—Harlem, or some share-cropper's cabin in Alabama, or some miner's shack in Pennsylvania.

The only time I spoke to her and got a good look at her, I realized one thing: she possessed the secret of Harlem, she knew the way out of the labyrinth. For her the paradox had ceased to exist, she was no longer in the cauldron, except by the pure accident of physical presence, which counts for nothing since the cauldron is almost entirely of the moral order. And when I saw her and spoke to her, I saw in this tired, screne, and holy face the patience and joy of the martyrs and the clear, unquenchable light of sanctity. She and some other Catholic women were sitting on chairs by the doorsteps of the building, in the relatively cool street, in the early evening: and the group they made, there, in the midst of the turmoil of the lost crowd, astounded the passer-by with the sense of peace, of conquest: that deep, deep, unfathomable, shining peace that is in the eyes of Negro women who are really full of belief!

Seeing the boys and girls in the library, I had got some insight into the problem of Harlem. Here, just across the street, I saw the solution, the only solution: faith, sanctity. It was not far to seek.

If the Baroness, biding her time, letting the children put on plays, giving them some place where they could at least be off the street and out of the way of the trucks, could gather around her souls like these holy women and could form, in her organization, others that were, in the same way, saints, whether white or colored, she would not only have won her way, but she might eventually, by the grace of God, transfigure the face of Harlem. She had before her many measures of meal, but there was at hand already more than a little leaven. We know the way Christ works. No matter how impossible the thing may look, from a human angle, we may wake up one morning and find that the whole is leavened. It may be done with saints!

For my own part, I knew that it was good for me to be there, and so for two or three weeks I came down every night and ate dinner with the little community of them, in the apartment, and recited Compline afterwards—in English—all together, lined up in the narrow room in two choirs. It was the only time they ever did anything that made them look like religious, and there was not much that was really formally choral about it. It was strictly a family affair.

After that, for two or three hours, I devoted myself to the task of what was euphemistically called "looking after the Cubs." I stayed in the store that was their play-room, and played the piano as much for my own amusement as for anything else, and tried, by some sort of moral influence, to preserve peace and prevent a really serious riot. If a true fight had ever started, I don't know what would have happened. But most of the time everything was peace. They played ping-pong and monopoly, and for one little kid I drew a picture of the Blessed Virgin.

"Who is that?" he said.

"It is Our Blessed Mother."

Immediately his expression changed, became clouded over with a wild and strong devotion that was so primitive that it astonished me. He began crooning over and over: "Blessed Mother . . . Blessed Mother," and seized the picture and ran out into the street.

When August ended, and Labor Day came, the Baroness had to leave and go to Canada and I left to make the second Trappist retreat, which I had been promising myself ever since I returned from Gethsemani in the spring. But I did not have the time or the money to go to Canada. Instead, I had written to the monastery of Our Lady of the Valley, outside Providence, Rhode Island, and had received an answer to come the day after Labor Day.

Driving through Harlem with Seymour, the Saturday before Labor Day, I felt for Friendship House a little of the nostalgia I had felt for Gethsemani. Here I was, once again thrown back into the world, alone in the turmoil and futility of it, and robbed of my close and immediate and visible association with any group of those who had banded themselves together to form a small, secret colony of the Kingdom of Heaven in this earth of exile.

No, it was all too evident: I needed this support, this nearness of those who really loved Christ so much that they seemed to see Him. I needed to be with people whose every action told me something of the country that was my home: just as expatriates in every alien land keep together, if only to remind themselves, by their very faces and clothes and gait and accents and expressions, of the land they come from.

I had planned to spend the week-end before going to the monastery in somewhat the same way that everybody else in the country spends Labor Day week-end: trying to get some rest and recreation, which is certainly a very legitimate thing for them to do, at least in itself. But God, in order to remind me of my exile, willed that this plan of mine, which was primarily ordered to please no one but myself, should not be completely successful.

I had gone about it the way I had done things in the old days: I had decided just where I wanted to go, and just what I wanted to do, for my own pleasure and recreation. I would go, I thought, to Greenport, at the end of Long Island. There I would find some quiet place, and spend the days reading and writing and praying and meditating and swimming. After that I would cross the Sound on the New London Ferry, and go from there to Providence and to Our Lady of the Valley. And Lax thought that if he could get away from the *New Yorker* office in time, that Saturday afternoon, he would go to Greenport too. But he did not seem very definite about it.

I called up Seymour. Seymour said: "I will drive you to Greenport."

Having exacted some assurance that he meant what he said, I went out to Long Beach.

Seymour was at the station, with a lot of his friends and associates, people in Long Beach with whom he had once started a kind of an enterprise for turning the whole town into a Greek City State—the Athens of Pericles. We all started out in the car.

Having gone three blocks, we stopped, and everybody got out. And he said: "We are going to have lunch in this restaurant."

We took a few spoonfuls of bad food. Then, back into the car.

As I expected, Seymour turned the car around and started off in the direction, not of Greenport, but of his own house.

"I forgot my camera," he explained. Seymour never had a camera.

So we spent the afternoon in Seymour's sailboat, in the bay, and we landed on a sand-bar, and Seymour taught me some tricks in ju-jitsu. He had been learning ju-jitsu in a gymnasium on Broadway, considering that he would be able to use it in the war, if he got drafted: a little something to surprise the Japanese.

The next day, we started out for Connecticut. That was when we passed through Harlem. Seymour was going to find his wife, in Greenwich Village, and drive her to New Haven, where she was in a play at a summer theater. He did not find his wife in Greenwich Village, but somewhere in the Seventies where it was decided, after a long, secret argument, that she was not going to Connecticut that afternoon. Meanwhile, I tried to sneak away and take a train from Grand Central to somewhere where I would find the equivalent of the nice quiet room in Greenport.

(At that precise moment, although I did not know anything about it, Lax, having gone to Greenport, was searching for me in all the hotels and boarding houses and in the Catholic church.)

Finally, very late, Seymour and I sat in a traffic-jam on the Boston Post Road, and argued about the war.

He drove me all the way out to Old Lyme, and it got darker and darker, and everything I saw made me miserable. I could nowhere identify anything to suit my Labor-Day-Week-End dream.

Just before midnight I threw down my suitcase in a dirty little hotel back in New Haven, and finished saying the Office of that day. Seymour had vanished, silent and nervous, into the darkness, with his car, alleging that Helen was even now arriving in New Haven on the train.

As far as I knew, the plan was she would go to the summer theater and pick up some sewing or knitting or something, and then they would both drive back, at once, to New York.

"You see—" said Divine Providence—"you see how things are in the world where you are living. You see how it is with the plans and projects of men."

On the bright Tuesday morning when I rang the bell at the monastery gate, at Our Lady of the Valley, the sky was full of blue, and walking into that deep silence was like walking into heaven.

Kneeling in the tribune, with the sun pouring through the windows on to a great, curiously bloodless Crucifix, and with the chanting of the monks taking my heart home to God and rocking it in the peace of those majestic thoughts and cadences, I worked my way, or was led, rather, into a retreat that was serious and practical and successful—more than I realized. There were none of the great, overwhelming consolations and lights that had practically swamped me at Gethsemani: and yet when I came out again at the end of the week I was conscious of having acquired nourishment and strength, of having developed secretly in firmness and certitude and depth.

For I had come out of Harlem with what might well have been the problem of another vocation. Was it that? In these eight days, ending with the Feast of the Nativity of Our Lady, the matter had made itself more or less clear. If I stayed in the world, I thought, my vocation would be first of all to write, second to teach. Work like that at Friendship House would only come after the other two. Until I got some more definite light, I should stay where I was, at St. Bonaventure's. Had I been afraid, or perhaps subconsciously hoping, that the question of becoming a Trappist would once again become a burning issue here? It did not. That whole business remained in its neutral, indefinite state: relegated to the area which my mind could not quite perceive, because it was in darkness, and clouded with almost infinite uncertainties. One thing I knew, here at the Valley I was filled with the same unutterable respect for the Cistercian life, but there was no special desire to enter that particular monastery.

And so, once again, I was back in the world. The New Haven train sped through all those industrial towns, with occasional flashes of blue water and pale sand and greyish grass all along the line at the left. I read a story in the *New Yorker* about a boy who, instead of becoming a priest, got married, or at least fell in love or something. And the emptiness and futility and nothingness of the world once more invaded me from every side. But now it could not disturb me or make me unhappy.

It was sufficient to know that even if I might be in it, that did not compel me to have any part of it, or to belong to it, or even to be seriously begrimed with its sorry, unavoidable contact.

iii

Back at St. Bonaventure's they gave me a room on the north side of the building, where you could see the sun shining on the green hillside which was a golf-course. And all day long you could hear the trains in the Olean freight-yards crying out and calling to one another and ringing their bells: the sound of journeys, sound of exile. I found that, almost without realizing it, I had little by little reorganized the pattern of my life on a stricter plan, getting up earlier in the morning, saying the Little Hours about dawn, or before it when the days got shorter, as a preparation for Mass and Communion. Now, too, I took three quarters of an hour in the morning for mental prayer. I was doing a lot of spiritual reading—Lives of Saints—Joan of Arc, St. John Bosco, St. Benedict. I was going through St. John of the Cross' *Ascent of Mount Carmel* and the first parts of the *Dark Night* for the second time in fact, but for the first time with understanding.

The big present that was given to me, that October, in the order of grace, was the discovery that the Little Flower really was a saint, and not just a mute pious little doll in the imaginations of a lot of sentimental old women. And not only was she a saint, but a great saint, one of the greatest: tremendous! I owe her all kinds of public apologies and reparation for having ignored her greatness for so long: but to do that would take a whole book, and here I have only a few lines to give away.

It is a wonderful experience to discover a new saint. For God is greatly magnified and marvelous in each one of His saints: differently in each individual one. There are no two saints alike: but all of them are like God, like Him in a different and special way. In fact, if Adam had never fallen, the whole human race would have been a series of magnificently different and splendid images of God, each one of all the millions of men showing forth His glories and perfections in an astonishing new way, and each one shining with his own particular sanctity, a sanctity destined for him from all eternity as the most complete and unimaginable supernatural perfection of his human personality.

If, since the fall, this plan will never be realized in millions of souls, and millions will frustrate that glorious destiny of theirs, and hide their personality in an eternal corruption of disfigurement, nevertheless, in re-forming His image in souls distorted and half destroyed by evil and disorder, God makes the works of His wisdom and love all the more strikingly beautiful by reason of the contrast with the surroundings in which He does not disdain to operate.

It was never, could never be, any surprise to me that saints should be found in the misery and sorrow and suffering of Harlem, in the leper-colonies like Father Damian's Molokai, in the slums of John Bosco's Turin, on the roads of Umbria in the time of St. Francis, or in the hidden Cistercian abbeys of the twelfth century, or in the Grande Chartreuse, or the Thebaid, Jerome's cave (with the lion keeping guard over his library) or Simon's pillar. All this was obvious. These things were strong and mighty reactions in ages and situations that called for spectacular heroism.

But what astonished me altogether was the appearance of a saint in the midst of all the stuffy, overplush, overdecorated, comfortable ugliness and mediocrity of the *bourgeoisie*. Thérèse of the Child Jesus was a Carmelite, that is true: but what she took into the convent with her was a nature that had been formed and adapted to the background and mentality of the French middle class of the late nineteenth century, than which nothing could be imagined more complacent and apparently immovable. The one thing that seemed to me more or less impossible was for grace to penetrate the thick, resilient hide of *bourgeois* smugness and really take hold of the immortal soul beneath that surface, in order to make something out of it. At best, I thought, such people might turn out to be harmless prigs: but great sanctity? Never!

As a matter of fact, such a thought was a sin both against God and my neighbor. It was a blasphemous underestimation of the power of grace, and it was an extremely uncharitable judgement of a whole class of people on sweeping, general and rather misty grounds: applying a big theoretical idea to every individual that happens to fall within a certain category!

I first got interested in St. Thérèse of Lisieux by reading Ghéon's sensible book about her—a fortunate beginning. If I had chanced on some of the other Little Flower literature that is floating around, the faint spark of potential devotion in my soul would have been quenched at once.

However, no sooner had I got a faint glimpse of the real character and the real spirituality of St. Thérèse, than I was immediately and strongly attracted to her—an attraction that was the work of grace, since, as I say, it took me, in one jump, clean through a thousand psychological obstacles and repugnances.

And here is what strikes me as the most phenomenal thing about her. She became a saint, not by running away from the middle class, not by abjuring and despising and cursing the middle class, or the environment in which she had grown up: on the contrary, she clung to it in so far as one could cling to such a thing and be a good Carmelite. She kept everything that was *bourgeois* about her and was still not incompatible with her vocation: her nostalgic affection for a funny villa called "Les Buissonnets," her taste for utterly oversweet art, and for little candy angels and pastel saints playing with lambs so soft and fuzzy that they literally give people like me the creeps. She wrote a lot of poems which, no matter how admirable their sentiments, were certainly based on the most mediocre of popular models.

To her, it would have been incomprehensible that anyone should think these things were ugly or strange, and it never even occurred to her that she might be expected to give them up, or hate them, or curse them, or bury them under a pile of anathemas. And she not only became a saint, but the greatest saint there has been in the Church for three hundred years—even greater, in some respects, than the two tremendous reformers of her Order, St. John of the Cross and St. Teresa of Avila.

The discovery of all this was certainly one of the biggest and most salutary humiliations I have ever had in my life. I do not say that it changed my opinion of the smugness of the nineteenth century *bourgeoisie:* God forbid! When something is revoltingly ugly, it is ugly, and that is that. I did not find myself calling the externals of that weird culture beautiful. But I did have to admit that as far as sanctity was concerned, all this external ugliness was, *per se,* completely indifferent. And, what is more, like all the other physical evil in the world, it could very well serve, *per accidens,* as an occasion or even as the secondary cause of great spiritual good.

The discovery of a new saint is a tremendous experience: and all the more so because it is completely unlike the film-fan's discovery of a new star. What can such a one do with his new idol? Stare at her picture until it makes him dizzy. That is all. But the saints are not mere inanimate objects of contemplation. They become our friends, and they share our friendship and reciprocate it and give us unmistakeable tokens of their love for us by the graces that we receive through them. And so, now that I had this great new friend in heaven, it was inevitable that the friendship should begin to have its influence on my life.

The first thing that Thérèse of Lisieux could do for me was to take charge of my brother, whom I put into her care all the more readily because now, with characteristic suddenness, he had crossed the border into Canada, and sent us word by mail that he was in the Royal Canadian Air Force.

Not that this was a very great surprise to anybody. As the time came closer for him to be drafted it began to be clear that he didn't care where he went so long as it was not into the infantry. Finally, just when he was about to be called, he had gone to Canada and volunteered as an airman. Since Canada was already long since actually at war, and since her fliers went relatively quickly into action, where they were badly needed, in England, it was at once evident that John Paul's chances of surviving a long war were very small. I suppose he was the only one who ignored this. As far as I could gather, he went into the air force as if flying a bomber were nothing more dangerous than driving a car.

So now he was in camp, somewhere near Toronto. He wrote to me of some vague hope that, since he was a photographer, they might send him out as an observer, to take pictures of bombed cities and to make maps and so on. But meanwhile he was doing sentry duty, on the ground, along the length of a great wire fence. And I set the Little Flower as a sentry to look out for him. She did the job well.

But the things that happened in my own life, before two more months had passed, also bore the mark of her interference.

In October I was writing long letters, full of questions, to the Baroness, who was still in Canada—and getting letters just as long in return, full of her own vivid and energetic wisdom. It was good for me to get those letters. They were full of strong and definite encouragement. "Go on. You are on the right path. Keep on writing. Love God, pray to Him more. . . . You have arisen and started on the journey that seeks Him. You have begun to travel that road that will lead you to sell all and buy the pearl of great price."

To sell all! The thing had not bothered me so much, in September, and I had left it aside, to wait and see what would develop. It was beginning to develop now.

For now, in these days, I was often alone in the chapel, under those plain beams, watching the quiet Tabernacle, and things began to speak inside me. This time, it was a much deeper impulsion, the expression of a much profounder need. It was not a movement of love stretching out to grasp some external, tangible good, and to possess it: not a movement of appetite—intellectual if you like, but still of appetite towards some good that could be seen and felt and enjoyed: a form of life, a religious existence, a habit, a Rule. It was not a desire to see myself vested in this or that kind of a robe or cloak or scapular, and praying this way or that way, or studying here, or preaching there, or living in this or that kind of a monastery. It was something quite different.

I no longer needed to get something, I needed to give something. But here I was, day after day, feeling more and more like the young man with great possessions, who came to Christ, asking for eternal life, saying he had kept the Commandments, asking, "What is yet wanting to me?" Had Christ said to me: "Go, sell what thou hast, and give to the poor, and come, follow me"?

As the days shortened and grew darker, and the clouds were getting iron grey with the threat of the first snows, it seemed to me that this was what He was asking of me.

Not that I was a man of great possessions. Everybody on the staff at St. Bonaventure's was called a professor. That was in order that the title might compensate us all, more or less, for what we did not get in pay. The salary I got was quite sufficient to enable me to practice evangelical poverty.

The thought that first came into my mind was this. I still had some money that my grandfather had left me in a bank in New York. Perhaps what should be done was to give that away, to the poor.

That was as far as I had advanced, when I decided to make a novena, asking for grace to know what to do next.

On the third day of the novena, Father Hubert, one of the Friars, said: "The Baroness is coming. We are going to drive up to Buffalo and meet her train from Canada, and bring her down here. Do you want to come along?" Early in the afternoon we got in the car, and started north, up one of those long parallel valleys that slant down towards the Alleghany.

When the Baroness got off the train, it was the first time I had seen her with a hat on. But the thing that most impressed me was the effect she had on these priests. We had been sitting around in the station, bored, complaining of this and that situation in the world. Now they were wide awake and cheerful and listening very attentively to everything she had to say. We were in a restaurant having something to eat, and the Baroness was talking about priests, and about the spiritual life and gratitude, and the ten lepers in the Gospel, of whom only one returned to give thanks to Christ for having cured them. She had made what seemed to me to be certainly a good point. But I suddenly noticed that it had struck the two Friars like a bombshell.

Then I realized what was going on. She was preaching to them. Her visit to St. Bonaventure's was to be, for them and the Seminarians and the rest who heard her, a kind of a mission, or a retreat. I had not grasped, before, how much this was part of her work: priests and religious had become, indirectly, almost as important a mission field for her as Harlem. It is a tremendous thing, the economy of the Holy Ghost! When the Spirit of God finds a soul in which He can work, He uses that soul for any number of purposes: opens out before its eyes a hundred new directions, multiplying its works and its opportunities for the apostolate almost beyond belief and certainly far beyond the ordinary strength of a human being.

Here was this woman who had started out to conduct a more or less obscure work helping the poor in Harlem, now placed in such a position that the work which had barely been begun was drawing to her souls from every part of the country, and giving her a sort of unofficial apostolate among the priesthood, the clergy and the religious Orders.

What was it that she had to offer them, that they did not already possess? One thing: she was full of the love of God; and prayer and sacrifice and total, uncompromising poverty had filled her soul with something which, it seemed, these two men had often looked for in vain in the dry and conventional and merely learned retreats that fell to their lot. And I could see that they were drawn to her by the tremendous spiritual vitality of the grace that was in her, a vitality which brought with it a genuine and lasting inspiration, because it put their souls in contact with God as a living reality. And that reality, that contact, is something which we all need: and one of the ways in which it has been decreed that we should arrive at it, is by hearing one another talk about God. *Fides ex auditu.* And it is no novelty for God to raise up saints who are not priests to preach to those who are priests—witness the Baroness's namesake, Catherine of Siena.

But she had something to say to me, too.

My turn came when we were in the car, driving south along the shining wet highway.

The Baroness was sitting in the front seat, talking to everybody. But presently she turned to me and said:

"Well, Tom, when are you coming to Harlem for good?"

The simplicity of the question surprised me. Nevertheless, sudden as it was, the idea struck me that this was my answer. This was probably what I had been praying to find out.

However, it was sudden enough to catch me off my guard, and I did not quite know what to say. I began to talk about writing. I said that my coming to Harlem depended on how much writing I would be able to do when I got there.

Both the priests immediately joined in and told me to stop making conditions and opening a lot of loopholes.

"You let her decide about all that," said Father Hubert.

So it began to look as if I were going to Harlem, at least for a while.

The Baroness said: "Tom, are you thinking of becoming a priest? People who ask all the questions you asked me in those letters usually want to become priests. . . ."

Her words turned the knife in that old wound. But I said: "Oh, no, I have no vocation to the priesthood."

When the conversation shifted to something else, I more or less dropped out of it to think over what had been said, and it soon became clear that it was the most plausible thing for me to do. I had no special sense that this was my vocation, but on the other hand I could no longer doubt that St. Bonaventure's had outlived its usefulness in my spiritual life. I did not belong there any more. It was too tame, too safe, too sheltered. It demanded nothing of me. It had no particular cross. It left me to myself, belonging to myself, in full possession of my own will, in full command of all that God had given me that I might give it back to Him. As long as I remained there, I still had given up nothing, or very little, no matter how poor I happened to be.

At least I could go to Harlem, and join these people in their tenement, and live on what God gave us to eat from day to day, and share my life with the sick and the starving and the dying and those who had never had anything and never would have anything, the outcasts of the earth, a race despised. If that was where I belonged, God would let me know soon enough and definitely enough.

When we got to St. Bonaventure's, I saw the head of the English Department standing in the dim light under the arched door to the monastery, and I said to the Baroness:

"There's my boss. I'll have to go and tell him to hire somebody else for next term if I'm leaving for Harlem."

And the next day we made it definite. In January, after the semester was finished, I would come down to live at Friendship House. The Baroness said I would have plenty of time to write in the mornings.

I went to Father Thomas, the President, in his room in the Library, and told him I was going to leave.

His face became a labyrinth of wrinkles.

"Harlem," he said slowly. "Harlem."

Father Thomas was a man of big silences. There was a long pause before he spoke again: "Perhaps you are being a bit of an enthusiast."

I told him that it seemed to be what I ought to do.

Another big silence. Then he said: "Haven't you ever thought about being a priest?"

Father Thomas was a very wise man, and since he was the head of a seminary and had taught theology to generations of priests, one of the things he might be presumed to know something about was who might or might not have a vocation to the priesthood.

But I thought: he doesn't know my case. And there was no desire in me to talk about it, to bring up a discussion and get all mixed up now that I had made up my mind to do something definite. So I said:

"Oh, yes, I have thought about it, Father. But I don't believe I have that vocation."

The words made me unhappy. But I forgot them immediately, when Father Thomas said, with a sigh:

"All right, then. Go to Harlem if you must."

iv

After that, things began to move fast.

On the day before Thanksgiving I abandoned my Freshman class in English Composition to their own devices and started to hitch-hike south to New York. At first I was in doubt whether to make for New York or Washington. My uncle and aunt were at the capital, since his company was putting up a hotel there, and they would be glad to see me; they were rather lonely and isolated there.

However, the first ride I got took me on the way to New York rather than Washington. It was a big Standard Oil truck, heading for Wellsville. We drove out into the wild, bright country, the late November country, full of the light of Indian summer. The red barns glared in the harvested fields, and the woods were bare, but all the world was full of color and the blue sky swam with fleets of white clouds. The truck devoured the road with high-singing tires, and I rode throned in the lofty, rocking cab, listening to the driver telling me stories about all the people who lived in places we passed, and what went on in the houses we saw.

It was material for two dozen of those novels I had once desired to write, but as far as I was now concerned it was all bad news.

While I was standing on the road at the edge of Wellsville, just beyond a corner where there was a gas station, near the Erie tracks, a big trailer full of steel rails went past me. It was a good thing it did not stop and pick me up. Five or six miles further on there was a long hill. It led down to a sharp turn, in the middle of a village called I forget what—Jasper, or Juniper, or something like that. By the time I got another ride, and we came down the hill, my driver pointed to the bottom and said:

"Man, look at that *wreck!*"

There was a whole crowd standing around. They were pulling the two men out of the cab of the truck. I never saw anything so flat as that cab. The whole thing, steel rails and all, had piled up in an empty yard between two small houses. The houses both had glass store windows. If the truck had gone into one of those stores the whole house would have come down on top of them.

And yet, the funny thing was, the two men were both alive. . . .

A mile further on the man who had given me a lift turned off the road, and I started once again to walk. It was a big, wide-open place, with a sweep of huge fields all down the valley, and quails flew up out of the brown grass, vanishing down the wind. I took the Breviary out of my pocket and said the *Te Deum* on account of those two men who were not killed.

Presently I got to another village. Maybe that one was called Jasper or Juniper too. The kids were just getting out of school, at lunch time. I sat on some concrete steps that led down to the road from one of those neat white houses and started to say Vespers while I had a chance. Presently a big old-fashioned car, old and worn-out but very much polished, came along and stopped, and picked me up. It was a polite old man and his wife. They had a son who was a freshman at Cornell and they were going to bring him home for Thanksgiving. Outside of Addison they slowed down to show me a beautiful old colonial house that they always admired when they passed that way. And it was indeed a beautiful old colonial house.

So they dropped me at Horseheads and I got something to eat, and I broke a tooth on some nickel candy, and went walking off down the road reciting in my head this rhyme:

So I broke my tooth
On a bar of Baby-Ruth.

It was not so much the tooth that I broke as something a dentist had put there. And then a business man in a shiny Oldsmobile gave me a ride as far as Owego.

At Owego I stood at the end of the long iron bridge and looked at the houses across the river, with all their shaky old balconies, and wondered what it was like to live in such a place. Presently a car with a geyser of steam spouting over the radiator pulled up and the door opened.

It was a man who said he had been working on an all night shift in some war industry in Dunkirk that was operating twenty-four hours a day. And he said: "This car is running on borrowed time."

However, he was going all the way down to Peekskill for Thanksgiving.

I think it was on the day after Thanksgiving, Friday, the Feast of the Presentation, that I saw Mark. I had lunch with him at the Columbia Faculty Club. The main reason why I wanted to talk to him was that he had just read the book I had written that summer, the *Journal of My Escape from the Nazis,* and he had an idea that somebody he knew might publish it. That was what I thought was important about that talk, that day.

But Providence had arranged it, I think, for another reason.

We were downstairs, standing among a lot of iron racks and shelves and things for keeping hats and brief-cases, putting on our coats, and we had been talking about the Trappists.

Mark asked me:

"What about your idea of being a priest? Did you ever take that up again?"

I answered with a sort of an indefinite shrug.

"You know," he said, "I talked about that to someone who knows what it is all about, and he said that the fact you had let it all drop, when you were told you had no vocation, might really be a sign that you had none."

This was the third time that shaft had been fired at me, unexpectedly, in these last days, and this time it really struck deep. For the reasoning that went with this statement forced my thoughts to take an entirely new line. If that were true, then it prescribed a new kind of an attitude to the whole question of my vocation.

I had been content to tell everybody that I had no such vocation: but all the while, of course, I had been making a whole series of adjustments and reservations with which to surround that statement in my own mind. Now somebody was suddenly telling me: "If you keep on making all those reservations, maybe you will lose this gift which you know you have. . . ."

Which I knew I had? How did I know such a thing?

The spontaneous rebellion against the mere thought that I might definitely *not* be called to the monastic life: that it might certainly be out of the question, once and for all—the rebellion against such an idea was so strong in me that it told me all I needed to know.

And what struck me most forcibly was that this challenge had come from Mark, who was not a Catholic, and who would not be expected to possess such inside information about vocations.

I said to him: "I think God's Providence arranged things so that you would tell me that today." Mark saw the point of that, too, and he was pleased by it.

As I was taking leave of him, on the corner of 116th Street, by the Law School, I said:

"If I ever entered any monastery, it would be to become a Trappist."

It did not seem to me that this should have any effect on my decision to go to Harlem. If it turned out that I did not belong there, then I would see about the monastery. Meanwhile, I had gone down to Friendship House, and discovered that on Sunday they were all going to make their monthly day of retreat in the Convent of the Holy Child, on Riverside Drive.

Bob Lax went up with me, that Sunday morning, and together we climbed the steps to the convent door, and a Sister let us in. We were about the first ones there, and had to wait some time before the others came, and Mass began, but I think Father Furfey, their spiritual director, who was teaching philosophy at the Catholic University and running something like Friendship House in the Negro quarter of Washington, spoke to us first at the beginning of Mass. Everything he said that day made a strong impression on both me and Lax.

However, when I came back from receiving Communion, I noticed that Lax had disappeared. Later, when we went to breakfast, I found him there.

After we had all gone to Communion, he said he began to get the feeling that the place was going to fall down on top of him, so he went out to get some air. A Sister who had noticed me passing the Missal back and forth to him and showing him the place, hurried out after him and found him sitting with his head between his knees—and offered him a cigarette.

That night when we left the convent, neither of us could talk. We just walked down Riverside Drive in the dusk, saying nothing. I got on the train in Jersey City and started back for Olean.

Three days went by without any kind of an event. It was the end of November. All the days were short and dark.

Finally, on the Thursday of that week, in the evening, I suddenly found myself filled with a vivid conviction:

"The time has come for me to go and be a Trappist."

Where had the thought come from? All I knew was that it was suddenly there. And it was something powerful, irresistible, clear.

I picked up a little book called *The Cistercian Life*, which I had bought at Gethsemani, and turned over the pages, as if they had something more to tell me. They seemed to me to be all written in words of flame and fire.

I went to supper, and came back and looked at the book again. My mind was literally full of this conviction. And yet, in the way, stood hesitation: that old business. But now there could be no delaying. I must finish with that, once and for all, and get an answer. I must talk to somebody who would settle it. It could be done in five minutes. And now was the time. Now.

Whom should I ask? Father Philotheus was probably in his room downstairs. I went downstairs, and out into the court. Yes, there was a light in Father Philotheus' room. All right. Go in and see what he has to say.

But instead of that, I bolted out into the darkness and made for the grove.

It was a Thursday night. The Alumni Hall was beginning to fill. They were going to have a movie. But I hardly noticed it: it did not occur to me that perhaps Father Philotheus might go to the movie with the rest. In the silence of the grove my feet were loud on the gravel. I walked and prayed. It was very, very dark by the shrine of the Little Flower. "For Heaven's sake, help me!" I said.

I started back towards the buildings. "All right. Now I am really going to go in there and ask him. Here's the situation, Father. What do you think? Should I go and be a Trappist?"

There was still a light in Father Philotheus' room. I walked bravely into the hall, but when I got within about six feet of his door it was almost as if someone had stopped me and held me where I was with physical hands. Something jammed in my will. I couldn't walk a step further, even though I wanted to. I made a kind of a push at the obstacle, which was perhaps a devil, and then turned around and ran out of the place once more.

And again I headed for the grove. The Alumni Hall was nearly full. My feet were loud on the gravel. I was in the silence of the grove, among wet trees.

I don't think there was ever a moment in my life when my soul felt so urgent and so special an anguish. I had been praying all the time, so I cannot say that I began to pray when I arrived there where the shrine was: but things became more definite.

"Please help me. What am I going to do? I can't go on like this. You can see that! Look at the state I am in. What ought I to do? Show me the way." As if I needed more information or some kind of a sign!

But I said this time to the Little Flower: "You show me what to do." And I added, "If I get into the monastery, I will be your monk. Now show me what to do."

It was getting to be precariously near the wrong way to pray—making indefinite promises that I did not quite understand and asking for some sort of a sign.

Suddenly, as soon as I had made that prayer, I became aware of the wood, the trees, the dark hills, the wet night wind, and then, clearer than any of these obvious realities, in my imagination, I started to hear the great bell of Gethsemani ringing in the night—the bell in the big grey tower, ringing and ringing, as if it were just behind the first hill. The impression made me breathless, and I had to think twice to realize that it was only in my imagination that I was hearing the bell of the Trappist Abbey ringing in the dark. Yet, as I afterwards calculated, it was just about that time that the bell is rung every night for the *Salve Regina*, towards the end of Compline.

The bell seemed to be telling me where I belonged—as if it were calling me home.

This fancy put such determination into me that I immediately started back for the monastery—going the long way 'round, past the shrine of Our Lady of Lourdes and the far end of the football field. And with every step I took my mind became more and more firmly made up that now I would have done with all these doubts and hesitations and questions and all the rest, and get this thing settled, and go to the Trappists where I belonged.

When I came into the courtyard, I saw that the light in Father Philotheus' room was out. In fact, practically all the lights were out. Everybody had gone to the movies. My heart sank.

Yet there was one hope. I went right on through the door and into the corridor, and turned to the Friars' common room. I had never even gone near that door before. I had never dared. But now I went up and knocked on the glass panel and opened the door and looked inside.

There was nobody there except one Friar alone, Father Philotheus.

I asked if I could speak with him and we went to his room.

That was the end of all my anxiety, all my hesitation.

As soon as I proposed all my hesitations and questions to him, Father Philotheus said that he could see no reason why I shouldn't want to enter a monastery and become a priest.

It may seem irrational, but at that moment, it was as if scales fell off my own eyes, and looking back on all my worries and questions, I could see clearly how empty and futile they had been. Yes, it was obvious that I was called to the monastic life: and all my doubts about it had been mostly shadows. Where had they gained such a deceptive appearance of substance and reality? Accident and circumstances had all contributed to exaggerate and distort things in my mind. But now everything was straight again. And already I was full of peace and assurance—the consciousness that everything was right, and that a straight road had opened out, clear and smooth, ahead of me.

Father Philotheus had only one question:

"Are you sure you want to be a *Trappist?*" he asked me.

"Father," I answered, "I want to give God everything."

I could see by the expression on his face that he was satisfied.

I went upstairs like somebody who had been called back from the dead. Never had I experienced the calm, untroubled peace and certainty that now filled my heart. There was only one more question: would the Trappists agree with Father Philotheus, and accept my application?

Without any delay, I wrote to the Abbot of Gethsemani, asking permission to come and make a retreat at Christmas time. I tried to frame my request in words that hinted I was coming as a postulant, without giving them an opportunity to refuse me before I had at least put one foot inside the door. I sealed the envelope and took it downstairs and dropped it in the mailbox, and walked outside, once more, into the darkness, towards the grove.

Things were moving fast, now. But soon they began to move still faster. I had barely got a reply from Gethsemani, telling me that I was welcome to come there at Christmas, when another letter came in the mail. The envelope was familiar and frightening. It bore the stamp of the Draft Board.

I ripped it open and stood face to face with a notice that I was to report at once for a fresh medical examination.

It was not hard to see what that would mean. They had tightened up their requirements, and I would probably no longer be exempt from military service. For a moment it seemed to me that Providence had become deliberately cruel. Was this going to be a repetition of the affair of the year before, when I had had my vocation snatched out of my hands when I was practically on the doorstep of the novitiate? Was that going to start all over again?

Kneeling in the chapel, with that crumpled paper in my pocket, it took a certain amount of choking before I could get out the words "Thy will be done." But I was determined that my vocation would not fall in ruins all around me, the moment after I had recovered it.

I wrote to the Draft Board at once, and told them that I was entering a monastery, and asked for time to find out when and under what conditions I would be admitted.

Then I sat down to wait. It was the first week of December, 1941.

Father Philotheus, hearing about the sudden call from the Army, smiled and said: "I think that is a very good sign—I mean, as far as your vocation is concerned."

The week ended, with no news from the Draft Board.

Sunday, December the seventh, was the second Sunday in Advent. During High Mass the Seminarians were singing the *Rorate Coeli*, and I came out into the unusually warm sun with the beautiful Gregorian plaint in my ears. I went over to the kitchen, and got one of the Sisters to make me some cheese sandwiches and put them in a shoe-box, and started out for Two Mile Valley.

I climbed up the hillside, on the eastern slope of the valley, and reached the rim of the thick woods, and sat down in a windless, sunny place where there were a lot of brown dried ferns. Down the hill by the road was a little country school house. Further out, at the mouth of the little valley, near the Alleghany, were a couple of small farms. The air was warm and quiet, you could hear nothing but the pounding and coughing of a distant oil-pump, back in the woods.

Who would think there was a war anywhere in the world? It was so peaceful here, and undisturbed. I watched some rabbits come out and begin to play among the ferns.

This was probably the last time I would see this place. Where would I be in a week from that day? It was in the hands of God. There was nothing I could do but leave myself to His mercy. But surely, by this time, I should have been able to realize that He is much more anxious to take care of us, and capable of doing so, than we could be ourselves. It is only when we refuse His help, resist His will, that we have conflict, trouble, disorder, unhappiness, ruin.

I started back in the afternoon towards the College. It was two or two and a half miles to the railway trestle over the river, then a half a mile home. I walked slowly along the tracks towards the red brick buildings of the College. The sky was getting cloudy, and it was not long before sunset. When I got to the campus, and was walking down the cement path towards the dormitory, I met two of the other lay-professors. They were talking animatedly about something or other, and as I approached they cried:

"Did you hear what happened? Did you hear the radio?"

America was in the war.

The next morning, the Feast of the Immaculate Conception, all the Sisters who worked in the kitchen and the laundry were at Mass in the College chapel. This was one of the rare occasions when they came out in public. It was their patronal feast. The front pews were full of blue and white habits, and after the Gospel, Father Conrad, a big burly Friar with a ruddy face, a professor of philosophy as stout as St. Thomas Aquinas, preached a sad little sermon, half hiding behind a corner of a buttress that held up the beam over the sanctuary. It was about Pearl Harbor.

When I left the chapel, and went to the Post Office, I found a letter from the Draft Board. They said the medical examination would be put off for one month.

I went to Father Thomas, and explained my situation, asked permission to leave at once, and asked, too, for a letter of recommendation. There was a meeting of the English Department, to share out my classes among my astonished confreres, for the remainder of the term.

I packed up most of my clothes, and put them in a big box for Friendship House and the Negroes of Harlem. I left most of my books on my shelf for Father Irenaeus and his library, and gave some to a friend in the Seminary, who had been reading Duns Scotus with me, under Father Philotheus. The rest I put in a box to take with me to Gethsemani. Apart from that, all my possessions fitted into one suitcase, and that was too much: except that the Trappists might not receive me in their monastery.

I took the manuscripts of three finished novels and one half-finished novel and ripped them up and threw them in the incinerator. I gave away some notes to people who might be able to use them, and I packed up all the poems I had written, and the carbon copy of the *Journal of My Escape from the Nazis*, and another *Journal* I had kept, and some material for an anthology of religious verse, and sent it all to Mark Van Doren. Everything else I had written I put in a binder and sent to Lax and Rice who were living on 114th Street, New York. I closed my checking account at the Olean bank, and collected a check, with a bonus, for my services in the English Department from the bursar who couldn't figure out why a man should want to collect his wages in the middle of the month. I wrote three letters—to Lax, the Baroness and my relatives—and some postcards, and by the afternoon of the following day, Tuesday, with an amazing and joyous sense of lightness, I was ready to go.

My train was in the evening. It was already dark when the taxi called for me at the College.

"Where you going, Prof?" said somebody, as I passed out of the building with my suitcase.

The cab door slammed on my big general good-bye, and we drove away. I did not turn to see the collection of heads that watched the parting cab from the shelter of the arched door.

When we got to town, there was still time for me to go to the church of Our Lady of the Angels, where I used to go to confession and where I often made the Stations of the Cross, when I was in Olean. The place was empty. There were one or two little candles burning out in front of the statue of St. Joseph, and the red sanctuary light flickered in the quiet shadows. I knelt there for ten or twelve minutes in the silence without even attempting to grasp or comprehend the immense, deep sense of peace and gratitude that filled my heart and went out from there to Christ in His Tabernacle.

Jim Hayes, who had taken over the main burden of my courses for me, was at the station, to present me with a note saying the English Department was having five Masses said for me. Then the Buffalo train came in through the freezing, sleety rain, and I got on, and my last tie with the world I had known snapped and broke.

It was nothing less than a civil, moral death.

This journey, this transition from the world to a new life, was like flying through some strange new element—as if I were in the stratosphere. And yet I was on the familiar earth, and the cold winter rain streaked the windows of the train as we travelled through the dark hills.

After Buffalo, we began to pass factory after factory, lit up with a blue glare in the rain, working all night on armaments: but it was like looking at something in an aquarium. The last city I remembered was Erie. After that I was asleep. We went through Cleveland and I knew nothing of it.

I had been getting up and saying the Rosary in the middle of the night, as a sort of a night office, for several months past. I asked God to wake me up at Galion, Ohio, so that I could do this, and so, in the middle of the night, I woke up, and we were just pulling out of Galion. I began to say the Rosary where our tracks crossed the Erie line, which was the way I had come there the first time, on my way to Gethsemani in the spring. Then I went back to sleep, rocked by the joyous music of the wheels.

At Cincinnati, where we arrived about dawn, I asked the Traveller's Aid girl the name of some Catholic churches, and got in a taxi to go to St. Francis Xavier's, where I arrived just as Mass was beginning at the high altar; so I heard Mass and received Communion and went back to the station and had breakfast and got on the train for Louisville.

And now the sun was up. It was shining on bare, rocky valleys, poor farm land, thin, spare fields, with brush and a few trees and willows growing along the creeks, and grey cabins, from time to time, along the line. Outside one of the cabins a man was splitting a log with an axe and I thought: that is what I will be doing, if God wills it, pretty soon.

It was a strange thing. Mile after mile my desire to be in the monastery increased beyond belief. I was altogether absorbed in that one idea. And yet, paradoxically, mile after mile my indifference increased, and my interior peace. What if they did not receive me? Then I would go to the army. But surely that would be a disaster? Not at all. If, after all this, I was rejected by the monastery and had to be drafted, it would be quite clear that it was God's will. I had done everything that was in my power; the rest was in His hands. And for all the tremendous and increasing intensity of my desire to be in the cloister, the thought that I might find myself, instead, in an army camp no longer troubled me in the least.

I was free. I had recovered my liberty. I belonged to God, not to myself: and to belong to Him is to be free, free of all the anxieties and worries and sorrows that belong to this earth, and the love of the things that are in it. What was the difference between one place and another, one habit and another, if your life belonged to God, and if you placed yourself completely in His hands? The only thing that mattered was the fact of the sacrifice, the essential dedication of one's self, one's will. The rest was only accidental.

That did not prevent me from praying harder and harder to Christ and to the Immaculate Virgin and to my whole private litany, St. Bernard, St. Gregory, St. Joseph, St. John of the Cross, St. Benedict, St. Francis of Assisi, the Little Flower and all the rest to get me by hook or by crook into that monastery.

And yet I knew that if God wanted me to go to the army, that would be the better and the happier thing. Because there is happiness only where there is coordination with the Truth, the Reality, the Act that underlies and directs all things to their essential and accidental perfections: and that is the will of God. There is only one happiness: to please Him. Only one sorrow, to be displeasing to Him, to refuse Him something, to turn away from Him, even in the slightest thing, even in thought, in a half-willed movement of appetite: in these things, and these alone, is sorrow, in so far as they imply separation, or the beginning, the possibility of separation from Him Who is our life and all our joy. And since God is a Spirit, and infinitely above all matter and all creation, the only complete union possible, between ourselves and Him, is in the order of intention: a union of wills and intellects, in love, charity.

I stepped on to the platform of Louisville station in the glory of that freedom, and walked out into the streets with a sense of triumph, remembering the time I had come that way before, the previous Easter. I was so happy and exultant that I didn't look where I was going and walked into the Jim Crow waiting room: whose shadows, full of Negroes, became somewhat tense with resentment. I hastened out again apologetically.

The Bardstown bus was half full, and I found a somewhat dilapidated seat, and we rode out into the wintry country, the last lap of my journey into the desert.

When I finally got off in Bardstown, I was standing across the road from a gas station. The street appeared to be empty, as if the town were asleep. But presently I saw a man in the gas station. I went over and asked where I could get someone to drive me to Gethsemani. So he put on his hat and started his car and we left town on a straight road through level country, full of empty fields. It was not the kind of landscape that belonged to Gethsemani, and I could not get my bearings until some low, jagged, wooded hills appeared ahead of us, to the left of the road, and we made a turn that took us into rolling, wooded land.

Then I saw that high familiar spire.

I rang the bell at the gate. It let fall a dull, unresonant note inside the empty court. My man got in his car and went away. Nobody came. I could hear somebody moving around inside the Gatehouse. I did not ring again. Presently, the window opened, and Brother Matthew looked out between the bars, with his clear eyes and greying beard.

"Hullo, Brother," I said.

He recognized me, glanced at the suitcase and said: "This time have you come to stay?"

"Yes, Brother, if you'll pray for me," I said.

Brother nodded, and raised his hand to close the window.

"That's what I've been doing," he said, "praying for you."

4

The Sweet Savor of Liberty

THE MONASTERY IS a school—a school in which we learn from God how to be happy. Our happiness consists in sharing the happiness of God, the perfection of His unlimited freedom, the perfection of His love.

What has to be healed in us is our true nature, made in the likeness of God. What we have to learn is love. The healing and the learning are the same thing, for at the very core of our essence we are constituted in God's likeness by our freedom, and the exercise of that freedom is nothing else but the exercise of disinterested love—the love of God for His own sake, because He is God.

The beginning of love is truth, and before He will give us His love, God must cleanse our souls of the lies that are in them. And the most effective way of detaching us from ourselves is to make us detest ourselves as we have made ourselves by sin, in order that we may love Him reflected in our souls as He has re-made them by His love.

That is the meaning of the contemplative life, and the sense of all the apparently meaningless little rules and observances and fasts and obediences and penances and humiliations and labors that go to make up the routine of existence in a contemplative monastery: they all serve to remind us of what we are and Who God is—that we may get sick of the sight of ourselves and turn to Him: and in the end, we will find Him in ourselves, in our own purified natures which have become the mirror of His tremendous Goodness and of His endless love. . . .

ii

So Brother Matthew locked the gate behind me and I was enclosed in the four walls of my new freedom.

And it was appropriate that the beginning of freedom should be as it was. For I entered a garden that was dead and stripped and bare. The flowers that had been there last April were all gone. The sun was hidden behind low clouds and an icy wind was blowing over the grey grass and the concrete walks.

In a sense my freedom had already begun, for I minded none of these things. I did not come to Gethsemani for the flowers, or for the climate—although I admit that the Kentucky winters were a disappointment. Still, I had not had time to plan on any kind of a climate. I had been too busy with the crucially important problem of finding out God's will. And that problem was still not entirely settled.

There still remained the final answer: would I be accepted into this monastery? Would they take me in to the novitiate, to become a Cistercian?

Father Joachim, the guest master, came out the door of the monastery and crossed the garden with his hands under his scapular and his eyes fixed on the cement walk. He only raised them when he was near me and then he grinned.

"Oh, it's you," he said. I suppose he had been doing some praying for me too.

I did not give him a chance to ask if I had come to stay. I said: "Yes, Father, this time I want to be a novice—if I can."

He just smiled. We went into the house. The place seemed very empty. I put the suitcase down in the room that had been assigned to me, and hastened to the church.

If I expected any grand welcome from Christ and His angels, I did not get it—not in the sensible order. The huge nave was like a tomb, and the building was as cold as ice. However, I did not mind. Nor was I upset by the fact that nothing special came into my head in the way of a prayer. I just knelt there more or less dumb, and listened to the saw down at the sawmill fill the air with long and strident complaints and the sound of labor.

That evening at supper I found that there was another postulant—an ancient, toothless, grey-haired man hunched up in a huge sweater. He was a farmer from the neighborhood who had lived in the shadow of the abbey for years and had finally made up his mind to enter it as a lay brother. However, he did not stay.

The next day I found out there was still a third postulant. He arrived that morning. He was a fat bewildered youth from Buffalo. Like myself, he was applying for the choir. Father Joachim put the two of us to work together washing dishes and waxing floors, in silence. We were both absorbed in our own many thoughts, and I dare say he was no more tempted to start a conversation than I was.

In fact every minute of the day I was secretly congratulating myself that conversations were over and done with—provided always I was accepted.

I could not be quite sure whether someone would call me and tell me to go down for an interview with the Father Abbot, or whether I was expected to go down to him on my own initiative, but that part of the problem was settled for me towards the end of the morning work.

I went back to my room and started puzzling my head over the copy of the *Spiritual Directory* that Father Joachim had brought me. Instead of settling down quietly and reading the chapter that directly concerned me, the one that said what postulants were supposed to do while they were waiting in the Guest House, I started leafing through the two thin volumes to see if I could not discover something absolutely clear and definite as to what the Cistercian vocation was all about.

It is easy enough to say, "Trappists are called to lead lives of prayer and penance," because after all there is a sense in which everybody is called to lead that kind of a life. It is also easy enough to say that Cistercians are called to devote themselves entirely to contemplation without any regard for the works of the active life: but that does not say anything precise about the object of our life and it certainly does not distinguish the Trappists from any of the other so-called "contemplative Orders." Then the question always arises: "What do you mean by contemplation, anyway?"

From the *Spiritual Directory* I learned that "the Holy Mass, the Divine Office, Prayer and pious reading which form the exercises of the contemplative life occupy the major part of our day."

It was a frigid and unsatisfying sentence. The phrase "pious reading" was a gloomy one, and somehow the thought that the contemplative life was something that was divided up into "exercises" was of a sort that would have ordinarily depressed me. But I think I had come to the monastery fully resigned to the prospect of meeting that kind of language for the rest of my life. In fact, it is a good thing that I was resigned to it, for it is one of the tiresome minor details of all religious life today, that one must receive a large proportion of spiritual nourishment dished up in the unseasoned jargon of transliterated French.

I had no way of saying what the contemplative life meant to me then. But it seemed to me that it should mean something more than spending so many hours a day in a church and so many more hours somewhere else, without having to go to the bother of preaching sermons or teaching school or writing books or visiting the sick.

A few lines further on in the *Directory* there were some cautious words about mystical contemplation which, I was told, was "not required" but which God sometimes "vouchsafed." That word "vouchsafe"! It almost sounded as if the grace came to you dressed up in a crinoline. In fact, to my way of interpreting it, when a spiritual book tells you that "infused contemplation is sometimes vouchsafed" the idea you are supposed to get is this: "infused contemplation is all right for the saints, but as for *you:* hands off!" The original French of the *Directory* is not so icy as the translation, and the book goes on to add that monks can ask God for these graces, if they do so with a right intention, and that the Cistercian life should normally be a perfect preparation for them. In fact, the French edition also adds that the Cistercian has the *duty* of leading the kind of life that would dispose him for mystical prayer.

And yet I was left with the impression that contemplation in a Trappist monastery was liable to be pretty much *secundum quid* and that if I had a secret desire for what the lingo of the pious manuals would call the "summits" I had better be cautious about the way I manifested it. Under other circumstances the situation might have disturbed me: but now it did not bother me at all. After all, it was largely a theoretical question anyway. All that I needed to worry about was to do God's will, to enter the monastery if I were allowed to do so, and take things as I found them, and if God wanted to do any of this "vouchsafing" He could go ahead and "vouchsafe." And all the other details would take care of themselves.

As I was laying aside the *Directory* to take up another small volume of pidgin English, someone knocked on the door.

It was a monk I had not seen before, a rather burly man with white hair and an extremely firm jaw, who introduced himself as the Master of Novices. I took another look at the determination in that jaw and said to myself: "I bet he doesn't take any nonsense from novices, either."

But as soon as he started to talk I found that Father Master was full of a most impressive simplicity and gentleness and kindness and we began to get along together very well from that hour. He was no man that stood on ceremony and he would have nothing to do with the notorious technique of elaborately staged humiliations which have given La Trappe a bad name in the past. By those standards he should have walked into the room and slammed the door with an insult and then asked me if I were entering the monastery in order to get away from the police.

But he just sat down and said: "Does the silence scare you?"

I almost fell over myself in my eagerness to assure him that the silence not only did not scare me but that I was entranced with it and already felt myself to be in heaven.

"Aren't you cold in here?" he asked. "Why don't you shut the window? Is that sweater warm enough?"

I assured him with consummate bravery that I was as warm as toast but he made me shut the window anyway.

Of course, what had happened was that Brother Fabian, who worked in the Guest House that year, had been feeding me with horror stories about how cold it was when you got up in the morning and went creeping down to choir with your knees knocking together and your teeth chattering so loud that you could hardly hear the prayers. So I was trying to get myself in trim for the ordeal by sitting with the windows open, without a coat on.

"Have you ever learned any Latin?" asked Father Master. I told him all about Plautus and Tacitus. He seemed satisfied.

After that we talked about many other things. Could I sing? Did I speak French? What made me want to become a Cistercian? Had I ever read anything about the Order? Had I ever read the *Life of St. Bernard* by Dom Ailbe Luddy?—and a lot of other things like that.

It was such a pleasant conversation that I was getting to be more and more unwilling to unload the big shadowy burden that still rested on my conscience, and tell this good Trappist all the things about my life before my conversion that had once made me think I could not possibly have a vocation to the priesthood. However, I finally did so in a few sentences.

"How long is it since you were baptized?" said Father Master.

"Three years, Father."

He did not seem to be disturbed. He just said that he liked the way I had told him all that there was to be told, and that he would consult Father Abbot about it. And that was all.

I was still half expecting to be called down for a cross-examination by the First Superior, but that never came. The Fat Boy from Buffalo and I waxed floors for the next couple of days, and went down to church and knelt at the benches in front of St. Joseph's altar while the monks chanted the Office, and then came back to the Guest House to eat our scrambled eggs and cheese and milk. At what Brother Fabian would have described as our "last meal," he slipped us each a bar of Nestle's chocolate, and afterwards whispered to me:

"Tom, I think you are going to be very disappointed with what you see on the table when you go into the refectory this evening . . ."

That evening? It was the Feast of St. Lucy and a Saturday. I went back to the room and nibbled on the chocolate and copied out a poem I had just written by way of a farewell to Bob Lax and Mark Van Doren. Father Joachim came in and hid his face behind his hands to laugh when I told him what I was doing.

"A *poem?*" he said, and hastened out of the room.

He had come to get me to wax the floors some more, so presently the Fat Boy from Buffalo and I were on our knees again in the hall, but not for very long. Father Master came up the stairs and told us to get our things together and follow him.

So we put on our coats and got our bags and started downstairs, leaving Father Joachim to finish waxing the floor by himself.

The noise of our footsteps resounded in the great stair well. Down at the bottom of the flight, by the door, under the sign that said "God Alone" there were half a dozen local farmers standing around with their hats in their hands. They were waiting to go to confession. It was a kind of an anonymous, abstract delegation bidding us farewell in the name of civil society. As I passed one of them, a solemn polite old man with a four days' growth of beard, I suddenly got a somewhat melodramatic impulse and leaned over towards him whispering:

"Pray for me."

He nodded gravely that he was willing to do that, and the door closed behind us leaving me with the sense that my last act as a layman in the world still smacked of the old Thomas Merton who had gone around showing off all over two different continents.

The next minute we were kneeling by the desk of the man who had absolute temporal and spiritual authority over the monastery and everybody in it. This priest, who had been a Trappist for nearly fifty years, looked much younger than he was because he was so full of life and nervous energy. They had been fifty years of hard work which, far from wearing him out, had only seemed to sharpen and intensify his vitality.

Dom Frederic was deep in a pile of letters which covered the desk before him, along with a mountain of other papers and documents. Yet you could see that this tremendous volume of work did not succeed in submerging him. He had it all under control. Since I have been in the monastery I have often had occasion to wonder by what miracle he manages to *keep* all that under control. But he does.

In any case, that day Father Abbot turned to us with just as much ease and facility as if he had nothing else whatever to do but to give the first words of advice to two postulants leaving the world to become Trappists.

"Each one of you," he said, "will make the community either better or worse. Everything you do will have an influence upon others. It can be a good influence or a bad one. It all depends on you. Our Lord will never refuse you grace . . ."

I forget whether he quoted Father Faber. Reverend Father likes to quote Father Faber, and after all it would be extraordinary if he failed to do so on that day. But I have forgotten.

We kissed his ring as he blessed us both, and went out again. His parting shaft had been that we should be joyful but not dissipated, and that the Names of Jesus and Mary should always be on our lips.

At the other end of the long dark hall we went into a room where three monks were sitting at typewriters, and we handed over our fountain pens and wristwatches and our loose cash to the Treasurer, and signed documents promising that if we left the monastery we would not sue the monks for back wages for our hours of manual labor.

And then we passed through the door into the cloister.

Now I began to see the part of the monastery I had never seen—the long wing beyond the cloister, in the back of the building, where the monks actually live, where they gather in the intervals.

It was a contrast to the wide-open, frigid formality of the cloister itself. To begin with, it was warmer. There were notice boards on the walls, and there was a warm smell of bread coming from the bakery which was somewhere in those parts. Monks moved about with their cowls over their arms, waiting to put them on when the bell rang for the end of work. We stopped in the tailor shop and were measured for our robes, and then passed through the door to the novitiate.

Father Master showed us where the novitiate chapel was, and we knelt a moment before the Blessed Sacrament in that plain, whitewashed room. I noticed a statue of my friend St. Joan of Arc on one side of the door, and on the other was, of course, the Little Flower.

Then we went down to the basement where all the novices were milling around in the clatter of washbasins, groping for towels with their eyes full of soap and water.

Father Master picked the one who seemed to be the most badly blinded by suds and I heard him tell him to take care of me when we got to church.

"That's your guardian angel," Father explained, and added: "He used to be a Marine."

iii

Liturgically speaking, you could hardly find a better time to become a monk than Advent. You begin a new life, you enter into a new world at the beginning of a new liturgical year. And everything that the Church gives you to sing, every prayer that you say in and with Christ in His Mystical Body is a cry of ardent desire for grace, for help, for the coming of the Messiah, the Redeemer.

The soul of the monk is a Bethlehem where Christ comes to be born—in the sense that Christ is born where His likeness is re-formed by grace, and where His Divinity lives, in a special manner, with His Father and His Holy Spirit, by charity, in this "new incarnation," this "other Christ."

The Advent Liturgy prepares that Bethlehem with songs and canticles of ardent desire.

It is a desire all the more powerful, in the spiritual order, because the world around you is dead. Life has ebbed to its dregs. The trees are stripped bare. The birds forget to sing. The grass is brown and grey. You go out to the fields with mattocks to dig up the briars. The sun gives its light, as it were, in faint intermittent explosions, "squibs," not rays, according to John Donne's conceit in his Nocturnal on St. Lucy's Day. . . .

But the cold stones of the Abbey church ring with a chant that glows with living flame, with clean, profound desire. It is an austere warmth, the warmth of Gregorian chant. It is deep beyond ordinary emotion, and that is one reason why you never get tired of it. It never wears you out by making a lot of cheap demands on your sensibilities. Instead of drawing you out into the open field of feelings where your enemies, the devil and your own imagination and the inherent vulgarity of your own corrupted nature can get at you with their blades and cut you to pieces, it draws you within, where you are lulled in peace and recollection and where you find God.

You rest in Him, and He heals you with His secret wisdom.

That first evening in choir I tried to sing my first few notes of Gregorian chant with the worst cold I had ever had in my life—the fruit of my experiment in preparing myself for the low temperature of the monastery before I was even inside the place.

It was the second vespers of St. Lucy and we chanted the psalms of the *Commune virginum*, but after that the *capitulum* was of the second Sunday of Advent, and presently the cantor intoned the lovely Advent hymn, *Conditor Alme Siderum.*

What measure and balance and strength there is in the simplicity of that hymn! Its structure is mighty with a perfection that despises the effects of the most grandiloquent secular music—and says more than Bach without even exhausting the whole range of one octave. That evening I saw how the measured tone took the old words of St. Ambrose and infused into them even more strength and suppleness and conviction and meaning than they already had and made them flower before God in beauty and in fire, flower along the stones and vanish in the darkness of the vaulted ceiling. And their echo died and left our souls full of peace and grace.

When we began to chant the *Magnificat* I almost wept, but that was because I was new in the monastery. And in fact it was precisely because of that that I had reason to weep with thanksgiving and happiness as I croaked the words in my dry, hoarse throat, in gratitude for my vocation, in gratitude that I was really there at last, really in the monastery, and chanting God's liturgy with His monks.

Every day, from now on, the office would ring with the deep impassioned cries of the old prophets calling out to God to send the Redeemer. *Veni, Domine, noli tardare: relaxa facinora plebis tuae.* And the monks took up the cry with the same strong voices, and armed with the confidence of grace and God's own presence within them, they argued with Him and chided Him as His old prophets had done before. What is the matter with You, *Domine?* Where is our Redeemer? Where is the Christ You have promised us? Are You sleeping? Have You forgotten us, that we should still be buried in our miseries and in the shadow of war and sorrow?

Yet if I had been stirred with a movement of feeling during that first evening in choir, I had little opportunity in those first days to enjoy what are commonly called "consolations." Consolations cannot get a good hold on you when you are half stupefied with the kind of cold I had. And then there was all the business of getting used to the thousand material details of monastic life.

Now I saw the monastery from within, from the church floor, so to speak, not from the visitor's gallery. I saw it from the novitiate wing, not from the shiny and well-heated Guest House. Now I was face to face with monks that belonged not to some dream, not to some medieval novel, but to cold and inescapable reality. The community which I had seen functioning as a unity, in all the power of that impressive and formal liturgical anonymity which clothes a body of men obscurely in the very personality of Christ Himself, now appeared to me broken up into its constituent parts, and all the details, good and bad, pleasant and unpleasant, were there for me to observe at close range.

By this time God had given me enough sense to realize at least obscurely that this is one of the most important aspects of any religious vocation: the first and most elementary test of one's call to the religious life—whether as a Jesuit, Franciscan, Cistercian, or Carthusian—is the willingness to accept life in a community in which everybody is more or less imperfect.

The imperfections are much smaller and more trivial than the defects and vices of people outside in the world: and yet somehow you tend to notice them more and feel them more, because they get to be so greatly magnified by the responsibilities and ideals of the religious state, through which you cannot help looking at them.

People even lose their vocations because they find out that a man can spend forty or fifty or sixty years in a monastery and still have a bad temper. Anyway, now that I was a part of Gethsemani I looked about me to see what it was really like.

I was in a building with huge thick walls, some painted green, some white and most of them with edifying signs and sentiments painted on them. "If any man think himself to be a religious, not bridling his tongue, that man's religion is vain." And so on. I never quite discovered the value of those signs, because for my own part as soon as I had read them once I never noticed them again. They are there before me all the time but they simply don't register on my mind. However, perhaps some people are still pondering on them after years in the house. In any case it is a Trappist custom. You find it practically everywhere in the Order.

What was important was not the thick, unheated walls, but the things that went on within them.

The house was full of people, men hidden in white cowls and brown capes, some with beards, the lay brothers, others with no beards but monastic crowns. There were young men and old men, and the old ones were in the minority. At a rough guess, with all the novices we have in the house now I think the average age of the community cannot be much over thirty.

There was, I could see, something of a difference between the community proper and the novices. The monks and the professed brothers were more deeply absorbed in things that the novices had not yet discovered. And yet looking around at the novices there was a greater outward appearance of piety in them—but you could sense that it was nearer the surface.

It can be said, as a general rule, that the greatest saints are seldom the ones whose piety is most evident in their expression when they are kneeling at prayer, and the holiest men in a monastery are almost never the ones who get that exalted look, on feast days, in the choir. The people who gaze up at Our Lady's statue with glistening eyes are very often the ones with the worst tempers.

With the novices, their sensible piety was innocent and spontaneous, and it was perfectly proper to their state. As a matter of fact I liked the novitiate at once. It was pervaded with enthusiasm and vitality and good humor.

I liked the way they kidded one another in sign language, and I liked the quiet storms of amusement that suddenly blew up from nowhere and rocked the whole "scriptorium" from time to time. Practically all the novices seemed to be very enlightened and sincere about their duties in the religious life; they had been quick in catching on to the rules and were keeping them with spontaneous ease rather than hair-splitting exactitude. And the ingenuous good humor that welled up from time to time in the middle of all this made their faces all shine like the faces of children—even though some of them were no longer young.

You felt that the best of them were the simplest, the most unassuming, the ones who fell in with the common norm without fuss and without any special display. They attracted no attention to themselves, they just did what they were told. But they were always the happiest ones, the most at peace.

They stood at the mean between two extremes. On one hand there were one or two who exaggerated everything they did and tried to carry out every rule with scrupulousness that was a travesty of the real thing. They were the ones who seemed to be trying to make themselves saints by sheer effort and concentration—as if all the work depended on them, and not even God could help them. But then there were also the ones who did little or nothing to sanctify themselves, as if none of the work depended on them—as if God would come along one day and put a halo on their heads and it would all be over. They followed the others and kept the Rule after a fashion, but as soon as they thought they were sick they started pleading for all the mitigations that they did not already have. And the rest of the time, they fluctuated between a gaiety that was noisy and disquieting, and a sullen exasperation that threw a wet blanket over the whole novitiate.

It was usually the ones that belonged to these two extremes that left and went back to the world. Those who stayed were generally the normal, good-humored, patient, obedient ones who did nothing exceptional and just followed the common rule.

On Monday morning I went to confession. It was Ember week, and the novices all went to their extraordinary confessor who was Father Odo that year. I knelt at the little open confessional and confessed with deep contrition that when Father Joachim had told me, one day in the Guest House, to go and tell the Fat Boy from Buffalo to go down to the church for the canonical office of None, I had failed to do so. Having unburdened my soul of this and other similar offences, I got so mixed up at the unfamiliar Cistercian ritual that I was all ready to leave the confessional and run away as soon as Father Odo had finished the first prayer and before he had given me any absolution.

In fact I was already on my feet and about to walk away when he started talking to me so I thought I had better stay.

I listened to the things he had to say. He spoke very kindly and simply. And the burden of it was this:

"Who knows how many souls are depending on your perseverance in this monastery? Perhaps God has ordained that there are many in the world who will only be saved through your fidelity to your vocation. You must remember them if you are ever tempted to leave. And you probably will be tempted to leave. Remember all those souls in the world. You know some of them. Others you may never know until you meet them in heaven. But in any case, you did not come here alone . . ."

All the time I was in the novitiate I had no temptations to leave the monastery. In fact, never since I have entered religion have I ever had the slightest desire to go back to the world. But when I was a novice I was not even bothered by the thought of leaving Gethsemani and going to any other Order. I say I was not *bothered* by the thought: I had it, but it never disturbed my peace because it was never anything but academic and speculative.

I remember once how Father Master questioned me on that subject.

So I admitted: "I have always liked the Carthusians. In fact if I had had a chance I would have entered the Charterhouse rather than coming here. But the war made that impossible. . . ."

"You wouldn't get the penance there that we have here," he said, and then we began to talk of something else.

That did not become a problem until after profession.

The next morning Father Master called me in at the end of work and gave me an armful of white woolen garments, telling me to put them on. Postulants used to receive the oblate's habit a few days after their admission—one of those anomalous customs that grow up in isolated houses. It survived at Gethsemani until one of the recent visitations. And so within three days of my admission to the novitiate I was out of my secular clothing and glad to get rid of it for ever.

It took me a few minutes to figure out the complications of the fifteenth-century underwear that Trappists wear under their robes, but soon I was out of the cell in a white robe and scapular, and a white cloth band tied around my waist, with the white, shapeless oblate's cloak around my shoulders. And I presented myself to Father Master to find out my name.

I had spent hours trying to choose a name for myself when I thought I was going to become a Franciscan—and now I simply took what I got. In fact, I had been too busy to bother with such trivial thoughts. And so it turned out that I was to be called Frater Louis. The Fat Boy from Buffalo was Frater Sylvester. I was glad to be Louis rather than Sylvester, although I would probably never have dreamed of choosing either name for myself.

Still, it would seem that the only reason why God wanted me to remember all my life that I had first sailed for France on the twenty-fifth of August was in order that I should realize at last that it was the Feast of my patron saint in religion. That sailing was a grace. Perhaps ultimately my vocation goes back to the days I spent in France, if it goes back to anything in the natural order. . . . Besides, I remembered that I used rather frequently to pray at the altar of St. Louis and St. Michael the Archangel in the apse of St. Patrick's cathedral in New York. I used to light candles to them when I got in trouble in those first days of my conversion.

I went immediately into the scriptorium and took a piece of paper and printed on it "FRATER MARIA LUDOVICUS" and stuck it on the front of the box that was to represent all the privacy I had left: one small box, in which I would keep a couple of notebooks full of poems and reflections, and a volume of St. John of the Cross and Gilson's *Mystical Theology of St. Bernard*, and the letters I would receive from John Paul at his R.A.F. camp in Ontario, and from Mark Van Doren and from Bob Lax.

I looked out the window at the narrow rocky valley beyond the novitiate parapet, and the cedar trees beyond and the bare woods on the line of jagged hills. *Haec requies mea in saeculum saeculi, hic habitabo quoniam elegi eam!*

iv

In January the novices were working in the woods near the lake which the monks made by throwing a dam across a gulley. The woods were quiet and the axes echoed around the sheet of blue-grey water sleek as metal among the trees.

You are not supposed to *pause* and pray when you are at work. American Trappist notions of contemplation do not extend to that: on the contrary you are expected to make some act of pure intention and fling yourself into the business and work up a sweat and get a great deal finished by the time it is all over. To turn it into contemplation you can occasionally mutter between your teeth: "All for Jesus! All for Jesus!" But the idea is to keep on working.

That January I was still so new that I had not flung myself into the complex and absurd system of meditation that I afterwards tried to follow out. And occasionally I looked up through the trees to where the spire of the abbey church rose up in the distance, behind a yellow hill skirted with cedars, and with a long blue ridge of hills for background. It was peaceful and satisfying, that scene, and I thought of a line from one of the gradual psalms: *Montes in circuitu ejus, et Dominus in circuitu populi sui.* Mountains are round about it, so the Lord is round about His people from henceforth, now and for ever.

It was true. I was hidden in the secrecy of His protection. He was surrounding me constantly with the work of His love, His wisdom and His mercy. And so it would be, day after day, year after year. Sometimes I would be preoccupied with problems that seemed to be difficult and seemed to be great, and yet when it was all over the answers that I worked out did not seem to matter much anyway, because all the while, beyond my range of vision and comprehension, God had silently and imperceptibly worked the whole thing out for me, and had presented me with the solution. To say it better, He had worked the solution into the very tissue of my own life and substance and existence by the wise incomprehensible weaving of His Providence.

I was now preparing for the reception of the habit of novice, which would make me canonically a member of the Order and start me out officially on my progress towards the vows. However, as my papers had not all come, no one knew exactly when I would be clothed in the white cloak. We were still waiting for a letter from the Bishop of Nottingham, whose diocese included Rutland and Oakham, my old school.

It turned out that I was to have a companion in the reception of the habit—and not the Fat Boy from Buffalo, either. He left the monastery at the beginning of Lent, after having slumbered peacefully through the choral offices for several weeks. He returned home to Buffalo and soon we heard that he was in the Army.

But no, my companion was to be, you might say, an old friend. One day when we had come back from the lake and had taken off our work shoes and washed up, I was hurrying up the stairs from the basement when I ran into Father Master and a postulant coming around the corner.

The fact that I was hurrying and ran into people only indicates that I was much less of a contemplative than I thought I was.

In any case, the postulant was a priest, in a Roman collar, and when I took a second look at his face I recognized those bony Irish features and the dark rimmed spectacles, the high cheek bones and the ruddy skin. It was the Carmelite with whom I had had all those conversations in the Guest House garden on my retreat, the Easter before, when we had discussed the relative merits of the Cistercians and the Carthusians.

We both looked at each other with looks that said: "You—here!" I did not actually say the words, but he did. And then he turned to Father Master and said:

"Father, here is a man who was converted to the faith by reading James Joyce." I don't think Father Master had heard of James Joyce. I had told the Carmelite that reading Joyce had contributed something to my conversion.

So we received the habit together on the first Sunday of Lent. He received the name of Frater Sacerdos. We stood together in our secular clothes in the middle of the Chapter Room. There was an eighteen-year-old novice with us making simple profession. Behind us was a table stacked with the books that were to be given out to the community as their formal "Lenten reading."

Father Abbot was ill. Everybody had become aware of that by the way he had struggled through the Gospel at the night office. He should have been in bed, because, as a matter of fact, he had a bad case of pneumonia.

However, he was not in bed. He was sitting on that rigid piece of woodwork euphemistically called a "throne," from which he presides in Chapter. Although he could hardly see us, he delivered an impassioned exhortation, telling us with deep conviction that we were making a big mistake if we came to Gethsemani expecting anything but the cross, sickness, contradictions, troubles, sorrows, humiliations, fasts, sufferings and, in general, everything that human nature hates.

Then we went up the steps to his throne one by one and he peeled off out coats (*Exuat te Dominus veterem hominem cum actibus suis* . . .) and helped by the cantor and Father Master, formally clothed us in the white robes we had been wearing as oblates, together with the scapulars and cloaks of full-fledged novices in the Order.

It cannot have been much more than two weeks after that that I was in the infirmary myself, not with pneumonia but with influenza. It was the Feast of St. Gregory the Great. I remember entering the cell assigned to me with a sense of secret joy and triumph, in spite of the fact that it had just been vacated two days before by Brother Hugh, whom we had carried out to the cemetery, lying in his open bier with that grim smile of satisfaction that Trappist corpses have.

My secret joy at entering the infirmary came from the thought: "Now at last I will have some solitude and I will have plenty of time to pray." I should have added: "And to do everything that I want to do, without having to run all over the place answering bells." I was fully convinced that I was going to indulge all the selfish appetites that I did not yet know how to recognize as selfish because they appeared so spiritual in their new disguise. All my bad habits, disinfected, it is true, of formal sin, had sneaked into the monastery with me and had received the religious vesture along with me: spiritual gluttony, spiritual sensuality, spiritual pride. . . .

I jumped into bed and opened the Bible at the Canticle of Canticles and devoured three chapters, closing my eyes from time to time and waiting, with raffish expectation, for lights, voices, harmonies, savors, unctions, and the music of angelic choirs.

I did not get much of what I was looking for, and was left with the vague disillusionment of the old days when I had paid down half a dollar for a bad movie. . . .

On the whole, the infirmary of a Trappist monastery is the worst place to go looking for pleasure. The nearest I came to luxury was in the purely material order, where I got plenty of milk and butter and one day—perhaps the Brother made some kind of a mistake—

I even got one sardine. If there had been two or three I would have known it was a mistake, but since there was precisely one, I am inclined to think it was intentional.

I got up every morning at four and served Mass and received Communion and then the rest of the day I sat up in bed reading and writing. I said the office and went to the Infirmary chapel to do the Stations of the Cross. And in the late afternoon Father Gerard, the infirmarian, made sure that I did not forget to meditate on the volume of Father Faber I had received as a Lenten book.

But as soon as I began to get better, Father Gerard made me get up and sweep the infirmary and do other odd jobs and when the Feast of St. Joseph came, I was glad to go down to church for the night office and sing a lesson in the Jube.

It must have been a surprise for all those who thought that I had left the monastery: and when we were back in the infirmary, Father Gerard said: "You sure can sing *loud!*"

Finally, on the Feast of St. Benedict, I picked up our blankets and went back to the novitiate, thoroughly satisfied to get off with no more than nine days of what Brother Hugh had called "not Calvary but Thabor."

That was the difference between me and Brother Hugh—between one who had just begun his religious life and one who had just finished his with signal success.

For, to judge by the way people keep mentioning him in sermons, Brother Hugh had been truly a success as a Cistercian. I had not known him, except by sight. And yet even that was enough to tell a great deal about him. I have never forgotten his smile—I don't mean the one he wore in the bier, but the one he had when he was alive, which was quite a different matter. He was an old Brother, but his smile was full of the ingenuousness of a child. And he had a great abundance of that one indefinite quality which everybody seems willing to agree in calling characteristically Cistercian: the grace of simplicity.

What that means is often hard to say: but in Brother Hugh and the others like him—and there are not a few—it meant the innocence and liberty of soul that come to those who have thrown away all preoccupation with themselves and their own ideas and judgements and opinions and desires, and are perfectly content to take things as they come to them from the hands of God and through the wishes and commands of their superiors. It meant the freedom of heart that one can only obtain by putting his whole life in the hands of another, with the blind faith that God wills to use our superiors, our directors, as instruments for our guidance and the formation of our souls.

From what I have heard, Brother Hugh had all that. And therefore he was also what they call a "man of prayer."

But this peculiar combination—a contemplative spirit and a complete submission to superiors who entrusted him with many distracting responsibilities around the monastery—sanctified Brother Hugh according to what is, as near as I can make out, the Cistercian formula.

For it seems to me that our monasteries produce very few pure contemplatives. The life is too active. There is too much movement, too much to do. That is especially true of Gethsemani. It is a powerhouse, and not merely a powerhouse of prayer. In fact, there is an almost exaggerated reverence for work in the souls of some who are here. Doing things, suffering things, thinking things, making tangible and concrete sacrifices for the love of God—that is what contemplation seems to mean here—and I suppose the same attitude is universal in our Order. It goes by the name of "active contemplation." The word active is well chosen. About the second half of the compound, I am not so sure. It is not without a touch of poetic license.

It is only in theory that our wills can be disinfected of all these poisons by the universal excuse of "obedience." Yet it has been the Cistercian formula ever since St. Bernard of Clairvaux and a score of Cistercian Bishops and Abbots in the Middle Ages. Which brings me back to my own life and to the one activity that was born in me and is in my blood: I mean writing.

I brought all the instincts of a writer with me into the monastery, and I knew that I was bringing them, too. It was not a case of smuggling them in. And Father Master not only approved but encouraged me when I wanted to write poems and reflections and other things that came into my head in the novitiate.

Already in the Christmas season I had half filled an old notebook that belonged to my Columbia days, with the ideas that came swimming into my head all through those wonderful feasts, when I was a postulant.

In fact, I had found that the interval after the night office, in the great silence, between four and five-thirty on the mornings of feast days, was a wonderful time to write verse. After two or three hours of prayer your mind is saturated in peace and the richness of the liturgy. The dawn is breaking outside the cold windows. If it is warm, the birds are already beginning to sing. Whole blocks of imagery seem to crystallize out as it were naturally in the silence and the peace, and the lines almost write themselves.

Or that was the way it went until Father Master told me I must not write poetry then. The Rule would keep that hour sacred for the study of Scripture and the Psalms. And as time went on, I found that this was even better than writing poems.

What a time that is for reading and meditation! Especially in the summer when you can take your book and go out under the trees. What shades of light and color fill the woods at May's end. Such greens and blues as you never saw! And in the east the dawn sky is a blaze of fire where you might almost expect to see the winged animals of Ezechiel, frowning and flashing and running to and fro.

For six years, at that time of the day, on feast days, I have been reading nothing but one or another of some three or four books. St. Augustine's Commentary on the Psalms, St. Gregory the Great's Moralia, St. Ambrose on some of the Psalms or William of St. Thierry on the *Song of Songs*. Sometimes I look at one or another of the Fathers, or else read Scripture *simpliciter*. As soon as I had entered into the world of these great saints, and begun to rest in the Eden of their writings, I lost all desire to prefer that time for any writing of my own.

Such books as these, and the succession of our offices, and all the feasts and seasons of the liturgical year, and the various times of sowing and planting and harvesting, and, in general, all the varied and closely integrated harmony of natural and supernatural cycles that go to make up the Cistercian year tend to fill a man's life to such overflowing satiety that there is usually no time, no desire for writing.

After the poems I wrote the first Christmas, and one or two in January, and one at the Purification, and one more in Lent, I was glad to be quiet. If there were no other reason for not writing, summer is too busy a season.

As soon as Paschal time was well begun, we were planting peas and beans, and when it ended we were picking them. Then in May they cut the first crop of alfalfa in St. Joseph's field, and from then on the novices were going out, morning and afternoon, in their long line, Indian file, straw hats on their heads, with pitchforks to hay fields in all quarters of the farm. From St. Joseph's we went to the upper bottom, in the extreme northeast corner of the property, in a hollow surrounded by woods, behind the knoll called Mount Olivet. After that we were down in the lower bottom, where I lifted up a shock of hay on the fork and a black snake tumbled out of it. When the big wagons were loaded, two or three of us would ride back and help unload them in the cow barn or the horse barn or the sheep barn. That is one of the hardest jobs we have around here. You get inside the huge, dark loft, and the dust begins to swirl and the ones on the wagon are pitching hay up at you as fast as they can, and you are trying to stow it back in the loft. In about two minutes the place begins to put on a very good imitation of purgatory, for the sun is beating down mercilessly on a tin roof over your head, and the loft is one big black stifling oven. I wish I had thought a little about that cow barn, back in the days when I was committing so many sins, in the world. It might have given me pause.

In June, when the Kentucky sun has worked up his full anger, and stands almost at the zenith, beating the clay furrows with his raging heat, it begins to be the season of the Cistercian's true penance. It is then that the little green flag begins to appear in the small cloister to announce that we no longer have to wear our cowls in the intervals and in the refectory. But even then, no matter how motionless you remain, out under the trees, everything you have on is soaked in sweat: and the woods begin to sizzle with a thousand crickets, and their din fills the cloister court and echoes around the brick walls and the tiled floors of the cloister and makes the monastery sound like a gigantic frying pan standing over a fire. This is the time when the choir begins to fill with flies, and you have to bite your lip to keep your resolution about never swatting them, as they crawl over your forehead and into your eyes while you are trying to sing. . . . And yet it is a wonderful season, fuller of consolations than it is of trials: the season of the great feasts: Pentecost, Corpus Christi—when we pave the cloister with whole mosaics of flowers—the Sacred Heart, St. John the Baptist, Sts. Peter and Paul.

This is when you really begin to feel the weight of our so-called active contemplation, with all the accidental additions that it acquires at Gethsemani. You begin to understand the truth of the fact that the old Trappists of the eighteenth and nineteenth centuries saw in the "exercises of contemplation"—the choral office and mental prayer and so on—principally a means of penance and self-punishment. And so it is the season when novices give up and go back to the world—they give up at other times too, but summer is their hardest test.

My friend Frater Sacerdos had already left in May. I remember, a few days before he vanished from our midst, the novices were dusting the church, and he was mooning around St. Patrick's altar with a woeful expression and great sighs and gestures. His former name, in religion, as a Carmelite, had been Patrick, and he was on the point of returning to the tutelage of the great apostle of Ireland.

But I had no desire to leave. I don't think I enjoyed the heat any more than anybody else, but with my active temperament I could satisfy myself that all my work and all my sweat really meant something, because they made me feel as if I were doing something for God.

The day Frater Sacerdos left we were working in a new field that had just been cleared over near the western limits of the farm, behind Aidan Nally's. And we came home in our long file over the hill past Nally's house, with the whole blue valley spread out before us, and the monastery and all the barns and gardens standing amid the trees below us under a big blue sweep of Kentucky sky, with those white, incomparable clouds. And I thought to myself: "Anybody who runs away from a place like this is crazy." But it was not as supernatural as I may have thought. It is not sufficient to love the place for its scenery, and because you feel satisfied that you are a spiritual athlete and a not inconsiderable servant of God.

Now, at the beginning of July, we were in the midst of the harvest, getting in the wheat. The big threshing machine was drawn up at the east end of the cow barn, and wagons loaded with sheaves were constantly coming in, from all directions, from the various fields. You could see the cellarer standing on top of the threshing machine, outlined against the sky, giving directions, and a group of lay brother novices were busily filling the sacks and tying them up and loading trucks as fast as the clean new grain poured out of the machine. Some of the choir novices were taking the grain down to the mill and unloading the sacks and spilling the wheat out on the granary floor: but most of us were out in the fields.

That year we had a phenomenal harvest: but it was always threatened with ruin by showers of rain. So practically every day the novices went out to the fields and dismantled the shocks and spread the damp sheaves around on the ground, in the sun, to dry before they began to get full of mildew: and then we would put them back together again and go home—and there would be another shower of rain. But in the end it was a good harvest, anyway.

How sweet it is, out in the fields, at the end of the long summer afternoons! The sun is no longer raging at you, and the woods are beginning to throw long blue shadows over the stubble fields where the golden shocks are standing. The sky is cool, and you can see the pale half-moon smiling over the monastery in the distance. Perhaps a clean smell of pine comes down to you, out of the woods, on the breeze, and mingles with the richness of the fields and of the harvest. And when the undermaster claps his hands for the end of work, and you drop your arms and take off your hat to wipe the sweat out of your eyes, in the stillness you realize how the whole valley is alive with the singing of crickets, a constant universal treble going up to God out of the fields, rising like the incense of an evening prayer to the pure sky: *laus perennis!*

And you take your rosary out of your pocket, and get in your place in the long file, and start swinging homeward along the road with your boots ringing on the asphalt and deep, deep peace in your heart! And on your lips, silently, over and over again, the name of the Queen of Heaven, the Queen also of this valley: "Hail Mary, full of grace, the Lord is with Thee. . . ." And the Name of her Son, for Whom all this was made in the first place, for Whom all this was planned and intended, for Whom the whole of creation was framed, to be His Kingdom. "Blessed is the fruit of Thy womb, Jesus!"

"Full of grace!" The very thought, over and over, fills our own hearts with more grace: and who knows what grace overflows into the world from that valley, from those rosaries, in the evenings when the monks are swinging home from work!

It was a few days after the Feast of the Visitation, which is, for me, the feast of the beginning of all true poetry, when the Mother of God sang her *Magnificat*, and announced the fulfilment of all prophecies, and proclaimed the Christ in her and became the Queen of Prophets and of poets—a few days after that feast, I got news from John Paul.

For the last few months he had been at a camp in the plains of the Canadian west, in Manitoba. Day after day he had been making long flights and doing bombing practice, and now he had his sergeant's stripes and was ready to be sent overseas.

He wrote that he was coming to Gethsemani before he sailed. But he did not say when.

V

The Feast of St. Stephen Harding, the founder of the Cistercian Order, went by, and every day I was waiting to be called to Reverend Father's room, and told that John Paul had come.

By now the corn was high, and every afternoon we went out with hoes, to make war against our enemies, the morning-glories, in the cornfields. And every afternoon, I would disappear into those rows of green banners, and lose sight of everybody else, wondering how anybody would be able to find me if he were sent out there to bring me in with the news that my brother had come. Often you did not even hear the signal for the end of work, and frequently one or two of the more recollected novices would get left in the cornfield, hoeing away diligently in some remote corner, after everybody else had gone home.

But I have discovered from experience that the rule, in these things, is that what you are expecting always comes when you are not actually expecting it. So it was one afternoon that we were working close to the monastery, within the enclosure, weeding a patch of turnips, that someone made me a sign to come in to the house. I had so far forgotten the object of my expectations that it took me a moment or two before I guessed what it was.

I changed out of work-clothes and went straight to Reverend Father's room and knocked on the door. He flashed the "Please wait" sign that is worked from a button at his desk, and so there was nothing for it but to sit down and wait, which I did, for the next half hour.

Finally Reverend Father discovered that I was there, and sent for my brother, who presently came along the hall with Brother Alexander. He was looking very well, and standing very straight, and his shoulders, which were always broad, were now completely square.

As soon as we were alone in his room, I began to ask him if he didn't want to get baptized.

"I sort of hoped I could be," he said.

"Tell me," I said, "how much instruction have you had, anyway?"

"Not much," he said.

After I had questioned him some more, it turned out that "not much" was a euphemism for "none at all."

"But you can't be baptized without knowing what it is all about," I said.

I went back to the novitiate before vespers feeling miserable.

"He hasn't had any instruction," I said gloomily to Father Master.

"But he wants to be baptized, doesn't he?"

"He says he does."

Then I said: "Don't you think I could give him enough instruction in the next few days to prepare him? And Father James could talk to him when he gets a chance. And of course he can go to all the conferences of the retreat."

One of the week-end retreats was just beginning.

"Take him some books," said Father Master, "and talk to him, and tell him everything you can. And I'll go and speak to Reverend Father."

So the next day I hurried up to John Paul's room with a whole armful of volumes purloined from the Novitiate Common Box—and soon he had a room full of all kinds of books that different people had selected for him to read. If he had wanted to read them all, he would have had to stay in the monastery for six months. There was an orange pamphlet with an American flag on the cover, called "The Truth About Catholics." There were, of course, *The Imitation of Christ* and a New Testament. Then my contribution was the Catechism of the Council of Trent, and Father Robert's suggestion was *The Faith of Millions* and Father James had come through with the *Story of a Soul*, the autobiography of the Little Flower. There were plenty of others besides, for Father Francis, who was guest-master that year, was also librarian. Perhaps he was the one who supplied the *Story of a Soul*, for he has great devotion to the Little Flower.

But in any case, John Paul looked them all over. He said: "Who is this Little Flower, anyway?" And he read the *Story of a Soul* all in one gulp.

Meanwhile, I spent practically the whole of the morning and afternoon work periods talking my head off about everything I could think of that had something to do with the faith. It was much harder work than my fellow novices were doing out there in the cornfield—and much more exhausting.

The existence of God and the creation of the world did not give him any difficulty, so we went over that in two sentences. He had heard something about the Holy Trinity at the Choir School of St. John the Divine. So I just said that the Father was the Father and the Son was the Father's idea of Himself and the Holy Ghost was the love of the Father for the Son, and that these Three were One nature, and that nevertheless they were Three Persons—and they dwelt within us by faith.

I think I talked more about faith and the life of grace than anything else, telling him all that I myself had found out by experience, and all that I sensed he wanted most to know.

He had not come here to find out a lot of abstract truths: that was clear enough. As soon as I had begun to talk to him, I had seen awaken in his eyes the thirst that was hiding within him, and that had brought him to Gethsemani—for he certainly had not come merely to see me.

How well I recognized it, that insatiable thirst for peace, for salvation, for true happiness.

There was no need of any fancy talk, or of elaborate argument: no need to try and be clever, or to hold his attention by tricks. He was my brother and I could talk to him straight, in the words we both knew, and the charity that was between us would do the rest.

You might have expected two brothers, at such a time as this, to be talking about the "old days." In a sense, we were. Our own lives, our memories, our family, the house that had served us as a home, the things we had done in order to have what we thought was a good time—all this was indeed the background of our conversation, and, in an indirect sort of a way, entered very definitely into the subject matter.

It was so clearly present that there was no necessity to allude to it, this sorry, complicated past, with all its confusions and misunderstandings and mistakes. It was as real and vivid and present as the memory of an automobile accident in the casualty ward where the victims are being brought back to life.

Was there any possibility of happiness without faith? Without some principle that transcended everything we had ever known? The house in Douglaston, which my grandparents had built, and which they maintained for twenty-five years with the ice-box constantly full and the carpets all clean and fifteen different magazines on the living-room table and a Buick in the garage and a parrot on the back porch screaming against the neighbor's radio, was the symbol of a life that had brought them nothing but confusions and anxieties and misunderstandings and fits of irritation. It was a house in which Bonnemaman had sat for hours every day in front of a mirror, rubbing cold-cream into her cheeks as if she were going to go to the opera—but she never went to the opera, except, perhaps, the ones she saw before her in her dreams as she sat there, in peaceless isolation, among the pots of ointment.

Against all this we had reacted with everything our own generation could give us, and we had ended up doing, in the movies, and in the cheap, amber-lit little bars of Long Island, or the noisier ones, fixed up with chromium, in the city, all that she had been doing at home. We never went to our own particular kind of operas either.

If a man tried to live without grace, not all his works were evil: that was true, certainly. He could do a lot of good things. He could drive a car. That is a good thing. He could read a book. He could swim. He could draw pictures. He could do all the things my brother had done at various times: collect stamps, post-cards, butterflies, study chemistry, take photographs, fly a plane, learn Russian. All these things were good in themselves and could be done without grace.

But there was absolutely no need to stop and ask him, now, whether, without the grace of God, any of those pursuits had come anywhere near making him happy.

I spoke about faith. By the gift of faith, you touch God, you enter into contact with His very substance and reality, in darkness: because nothing accessible, nothing comprehensible to our senses and reason can grasp His essence as it is in itself. But faith transcends all these limitations, and does so without labor: for it is God Who reveals Himself to us, and all that is required of us is the humility to accept His revelation, and accept it on the conditions under which it comes to us: from the lips of men.

When that contact is established, God gives us sanctifying grace: His own life, the power to love Him, the power to overcome all the weaknesses and limitations of our blind souls and to serve Him and control our crazy and rebellious flesh.

"Once you have grace," I said to him, "you are free. Without it, you cannot help doing the things you know you should not do, and that you know you don't really want to do. But once you have grace, you are free. When you are baptized, there is no power in existence that can force you to commit a sin—nothing that will be able to drive you to it against your own conscience. And if you merely will it, you will be free forever, because the strength will be given you, as much as you need, and as often as you ask, and as soon as you ask, and generally long before you ask for it, too."

From then on his impatience to get to the Sacrament was intense.

I went to Reverend Father's room.

"We can't baptize him here, of course," he said. "But it might be done at one of the parishes near here."

"Do you think there is a chance of it?"

"I will ask Father James to talk to him and tell me what he thinks."

By Saturday afternoon I had told John Paul everything I knew. I had got to the Sacramentals and Indulgences and then gone back and given him an explanation of that notion, so mysterious to some outside the Church: "The Sacred Heart." After that I stopped. I was exhausted. I had nothing left to give him.

And he sat calmly in his chair and said: "Go on, tell me some more."

The next day was Sunday, the Feast of St. Anne. After Chapter, in the long interval before High Mass, I asked Father Master if I could go over to the Guest House.

"Reverend Father told me your brother might be going over to New Haven to get baptized."

I went to the novitiate chapel and prayed.

But after dinner I found out that it was true. John Paul was sitting in his room, quiet and happy. It was years since I had seen him so completely serene.

Then I realized, obscurely, that in those last four days the work of eighteen or twenty years of my bad example had been washed away and made good by God's love. The evil that had been done by my boasting and showing off and exulting in my own stupidity had been atoned for in my own soul, at the same time as it had been washed out of his, and I was full of peace and gratitude.

I taught him how to use a Missal and how to receive Communion, for it had been arranged that his First Communion would be at Reverend Father's private Mass the following day.

The next morning, all through Chapter, the obscure worry that John Paul would get lost and not be able to find his way down to the chapel of Our Lady of Victories had been haunting me. As soon as Chapter was over I hurried to the church ahead of Reverend Father, and entered the big empty building, and knelt down.

John Paul was nowhere in sight.

I turned around. At the end of the long nave, with its empty choir stalls, high up in the empty Tribune, John Paul was kneeling all alone, in uniform. He seemed to be an immense distance away, and between the secular church where he was, and the choir where I was, was a locked door, and I couldn't call out to him to tell him how to come down the long way 'round through the Guest House. And he didn't understand my sign.

At that moment there flashed into my mind all the scores of times in our forgotten childhood when I had chased John Paul away with stones from the place where my friends and I were building a hut. And now, all of a sudden, here it was all over again: a situation that was externally of the same pattern: John Paul, standing confused and unhappy, at a distance which he was not able to bridge

Sometimes the same image haunts me now that he is dead, a though he were standing helpless in Purgatory, depending more o less on me to get him out of there, waiting for my prayers. But I hope he is out of it by now!

Father Master went off to get him and I started lighting the candles on the altar of Our Lady of Victories and by the time the Mass started I could see, out of the corner of my eye, that he was kneeling there at one of the benches. And so we received Communion together, and the work was done.

The next day, he was gone. I went to see him off at the Gate, after Chapter. A visitor gave him a ride to Bardstown. As the car was turning around to start down the avenue John Paul turned around and waved, and it was only then that his expression showed some possibility that he might be realizing, as I did, that we would never see each other on earth again.

The fall came, and the Great Tricenary in September when all the young monks have to recite ten psalters for the dead. It is a season of bright, dry days, with plenty of sun, and cool air, and high cirrus clouds, and the forest is turning rusty and blood color and bronze along the jagged hills. Then, morning and afternoon, we go out to cut corn. St. Joseph's field had long been finished—the green stalks had gone into the silo. Now we were working through the vast, stony fields in the middle and lower bottoms, hacking our way through the dry corn with each blow of the knife cracking like a rifle shot. It was as if those glades had turned into shooting galleries and we were all firing away with twenty-twos.

And behind us, in the wide avenues that opened in our wake, the giant shocks grew up, and the two novices that came last garrotted them with a big rope and tied them secure with twine.

Around November when the corn-husking was nearly finished, and when the fat turkeys were gobbling loudly in their pen, running from one wire fence to the other in dark herds, under the gloomy sky, I got news from John Paul in England. First he had been stationed at Bournemouth, from which he sent me a postcard that showed some boarding houses I recognized, along the West Cliff. It was only ten years since we had spent a summer there: but the memory of it was like something unbelievable, like another life—as if there were some such thing as the transmigration of souls!

After that he was sent somewhere in Oxfordshire. His letters arrived with little rectangles neatly cut out of them, here and there, but when he wrote: "I enjoy going into —— and seeing the —— and the bookstores," it was easy enough for me to insert "Oxford" in the first hole and "Colleges" in the other, since the postmark read "Banbury." Here he was still in training. I could not tell how soon he would get in to the actual fighting over Germany.

Meanwhile, he wrote that he had met a girl, whom he described, and it soon turned out that they were going to get married. I was glad on account of the marriage, but there was something altogether pathetic about the precariousness of it: what chance was there that they would ever be able to have a home and live in it, the way human beings were supposed to do?

Christmas came to the monastery bringing with it the same kind of graces and consolations as the year before, only more intense. On the Feast of St. Thomas the Apostle, Reverend Father had allowed me to make my vows privately to him, more than a year before public profession would be permissible. If I had been able to make ten different vows every day I would not have been able to express what I felt about the monastery and the Cistercian life.

And so 1943 began, and the weeks hastened on towards Lent.

Lent means, among other things, no more letters. The monks neither receive mail nor write it in Lent and Advent, and the last news I had, before Ash Wednesday, was that John Paul was planning to get married about the end of February. I would have to wait until Easter to find out whether or not he actually did.

I had fasted a little during my first Lent, the year before, but it had been broken up by nearly two weeks in the infirmary. This was my first chance to go through the whole fast without any mitigation. In those days, since I still had the world's ideas about food and nourishment and health, I thought the fast we have in Trappist monasteries in Lent was severe. We eat nothing until noon, when we get the regular two bowls, one of soup and the other of vegetables, and as much bread as we like, but then in the evening there is a light collation—a piece of bread and a dish of something like apple-sauce—two ounces of it.

However, if I had entered a Cistercian monastery in the twelfth century—or even some Trappist monasteries of the nineteenth, for that matter—I would have had to tighten my belt and go hungry until four o'clock in the afternoon: and there was nothing besides that one meal: no collation, no frustulum.

Humiliated by this discovery, I find that the Lenten fast we now have does not bother me. However, it is true that now in the morning work periods I have a class in theology, instead of going out to break rocks on the back road, or split logs in the woodshed as we did in the novitiate. I expect it makes a big difference, because swinging a sledge-hammer when you have an empty stomach is apt to make your knees a little shaky after a while. At least that was what it did to me.

Even in the Lent of 1943, however, I had some indoor work for part of the time, since Reverend Father had already put me to translating books and articles from French.

And so, after the conventual Mass, I would get out book and pencil and papers and go to work at one of the long tables in the novitiate scriptorium, filling the yellow sheets as fast as I could, while another novice took them and typed them as soon as they were finished. In those days I even had a secretary.

Finally the long liturgy of penance came to its climax in Holy Week, with the terrible cry of the Lamentations once more echoing in the dark choir of the Abbey Church, followed by the four hours' thunder of the Good Friday Psalter in the Chapter Room, and the hush of the monks going about the cloisters in bare feet, and the long sad chant that accompanies the adoration of the Cross!

What a relief it was to hear the bells once more on Holy Saturday, what relief to wake up from the sleep of death with a triple "alleluia." Easter, that year, was as late as it could possibly be —the twenty-fifth of April—and there were enough flowers to fill the church with the intoxicating smell of the Kentucky spring—a wild and rich and heady smell of flowers, sweet and full. We came from our light, five hours' sleep into a church that was full of warm night air and swimming in this rich luxury of odors, and soon began that Easter invitatory that is nothing short of gorgeous in its exultation.

How mighty they are, those hymns and those antiphons of the Easter office! Gregorian chant that should, by rights, be monotonous, because it has absolutely none of the tricks and resources of modern music, is full of a variety infinitely rich because it is subtle and spiritual and deep, and lies rooted far beyond the shallow level of virtuosity and "technique," even in the abysses of the spirit, and of the human soul. Those Easter "alleluias," without leaving the narrow range prescribed by the eight Gregorian modes, have discovered color and warmth and meaning and gladness that no other music possesses. Like everything else Cistercian—like the monks themselves, these antiphons, by submitting to the rigor of a Rule that would seem to destroy individuality, have actually acquired a character that is unique, unparalleled.

It was into the midst of all this that news from England came.

There had been a letter from John Paul among the two or three that I found under the napkin in the refectory at noon on Holy

Saturday. I read it on Easter Monday, and it said that he had been married more or less according to plan, and had gone with his wife to the English Lakes for a week or so, and that after that he had been stationed at a new base, which put him into the fighting.

He had been once or twice to bomb something somewhere: but he did not even give the censor a chance to cut anything out. You could see at once that there was a tremendous change in his attitude towards the war and his part in it. He did not want to talk about it. He had nothing to say. And from the way he said that he didn't want to talk about it, you could see that the experience was terrific.

John Paul had at last come face to face with the world that he and I had helped to make!

On Easter Monday afternoon I sat down to write him a letter and cheer him up a little, if I could.

The letter was finished, and it was Easter Tuesday, and we were in choir for the Conventual Mass, when Father Master came in and made me the sign for "Abbot."

I went out to Reverend Father's room. There was no difficulty in guessing what it was.

I passed the *pietà* at the corner of the cloister, and buried my will and my natural affections and all the rest in the wounded side of the dead Christ.

Reverend Father flashed the sign to come in, and I knelt by his desk and received his blessing and kissed his ring and he read me the telegram that Sergeant J. P. Merton, my brother, had been reported missing in action on April 17th.

I have never understood why it took them so long to get the telegram through. April 17th was already ten days ago—the end of Passion Week.

Some more days went by, letters of confirmation came, and finally, after a few weeks, I learned that John Paul was definitely dead.

The story was simply this. On the night of Friday the sixteenth, which had been the Feast of Our Lady of Sorrows, he and his crew had taken off in their bomber with Mannheim as their objective. I never discovered whether they crashed on the way out or the way home, but the plane came down in the North Sea. John Paul was severely injured in the crash, but he managed to keep himself afloat, and even tried to support the pilot, who was already dead. His companions had managed to float their rubber dinghy and pulled him in.

He was very badly hurt: maybe his neck was broken. He lay in the bottom of the dinghy in delirium.

He was terribly thirsty. He kept asking for water. But they didn't have any. The water tank had broken in the crash, and the water was all gone.

It did not last too long. He had three hours of it, and then he died. Something of the three hours of the thirst of Christ Who loved him, and died for him many centuries ago, and had been offered again that very day, too, on many altars.

His companions had more of it to suffer, but they were finally picked up and brought to safety. But that was some five days later.

On the fourth day they had buried John Paul in the sea.

Sweet brother, if I do not sleep
My eyes are flowers for your tomb;
And if I cannot eat my bread,
My fasts shall live like willows where you died.
If in the heat I find no water for my thirst,
My thirst shall turn to springs for you, poor traveller.

Where, in what desolate and smokey country,
Lies your poor body, lost and dead?
And in what landscape of disaster
Has your unhappy spirit lost its road?

Come, in my labor find a resting place
And in my sorrows lay your head,
Or rather take my life and blood
And buy yourself a better bed—
Or take my breath and take my death
And buy yourself a better rest.

When all the men of war are shot
And flags have fallen into dust,
Your cross and mine shall tell men still
Christ died on each, for both of us.

For in the wreckage of your April Christ lies slain,
And Christ weeps in the ruins of my spring:
The money of Whose tears shall fall
Into your weak and friendless hand,
And buy you back to your own land:
The silence of Whose tears shall fall
Like bells upon your alien tomb.
Hear them and come: they call you home.

Epilogue

Meditatio Pauperis in Solitudine

DAY UNTO DAY uttereth speech. The clouds change. The seasons pass over our woods and fields in their slow and regular procession, and time is gone before you are aware of it.

Christ pours down the Holy Ghost upon you from heaven in the fire of June, and then you look about you and realize that you are standing in the barnyard husking corn, and the cold wind of the last days of October is sweeping across the thin woods and biting you to the bone. And then, in a minute or so, it is Christmas, and Christ is born.

At the last of the three great Masses, celebrated as a Solemn Pontifical High Mass with Pontifical Tierce, I am one of the minor ministers. We have vested in the Sacristy, have waited in the sanctuary. In the thunder of the organ music, Reverend Father has come with the monks in procession through the cloister, and has knelt a moment before the Blessed Sacrament in the Chapel of Our Lady of Victories. Then Tierce begins. After that the solemn vesting and I present the crozier with the suitable bows, and they go to the foot of the altar and the tremendous introit begins, in the choir, summing up with the splendor of its meaning the whole of Christmas. The Child born on earth, in lowliness, in the crib, before the shepherds, is born this day in heaven in glory, in magnificence, in majesty: and the day in which He is born is eternity. He is born forever, All-Power, All-Wisdom, begotten before the daystar: He is the beginning and the end, everlastingly born of the Father, the Infinite God: and He Himself is the same God, God of God, Light of Light, True God of True God. God born of Himself, forever: Himself His own second Person: One, yet born of Himself forever.

He it is also that is born each instant in our hearts: for this unending birth, this everlasting beginning, without end, this everlasting, perfect newness of God begotten of Himself, issuing from Himself without leaving Himself or altering His one-ness, this is the life that is in us. But see: He is suddenly born again, also, on this altar, upon that cloth and corporal as white as snow beneath the burning lights, and raised up above us in the hush of the consecration! Christ, the Child of God, the Son, made Flesh, with His All-power. What will You say to me, this Christmas, O Jesus? What is it that You have prepared for me at Your Nativity?

At the *Agnus Dei* I put aside the crozier and we all go to the Epistle side, together, to receive the kiss of peace. We bow to one another. The salutation passes from one to the other. Heads bow. Hands are folded again. Now we all turn around together.

And suddenly I find myself looking straight into the face of Bob Lax. He is standing at the benches that are drawn up, there, for visitors. He is so close to the step of the sanctuary, that if he were any closer he would be in it.

And I say to myself: "Good, now he'll get baptized too."

After dinner I went to Reverend Father's room and told him who Lax was, and that he was an old friend of mine, and asked if I might speak to him. We are ordinarily only allowed to receive visits from our own families, but since I had practically nothing left of my family, Reverend Father agreed that I might speak to Lax for a little while. And I mentioned that I thought he might be ready to be baptized.

"Isn't he a Catholic?" said Reverend Father.

"No, Reverend Father, not yet."

"Well, in that case, why was he taking Communion last night at the midnight Mass? . . ."

Up in the Guest House, Lax told me how the Baptism had come about. He had been at the University of North Carolina teaching some earnest young men how to write radio plays. Towards the end of Advent he had got a letter from Rice which said, in so many words, "Come to New York and we will find a priest and ask him to baptize you."

All of a sudden, after all those years of debating back and forth, Lax just got on the train and went to New York. Nobody had ever put the matter up to him like that before.

They found a Jesuit in that big church up on Park Avenue and he baptized him, and that was that.

So then Lax had said: "Now I will go to the Trappists in Kentucky and visit Merton."

Bob Gibney told him: "You were a Jew and now you are a Catholic. Why don't you black your face? Then you will be all the three things the Southerners hate most."

The night had already fallen, Christmas Eve, when Lax got to Bardstown. He stood by the road to hitch a ride to the monastery. Some fellows picked him up, and while they were driving along, they began talking about the Jews the way some people talk about the Jews.

So Lax said that he was not only a Catholic but a converted Jew.

"Oh," said the fellows in the car, "of course, you understand we were talking about *orthodox* Jews."

From Lax I heard the first scraps of information about all the friends I had not forgotten: about Bob Gerdy who was in England in the Army, after having been baptized into the Church in September. Rice was working on one of those picture magazines. Gibney had got married, and soon he and Lax would also be working on another picture magazine—a new one that had started since I came to the monastery, called *Parade* or *Fanfare* or something like that. I don't know if Peggy Wells had already gone to Hollywood, but she went soon and is there still. Nancy Flagg was working either on *Vogue* or *Harper's Bazaar.* Somehow, too, I have the impression that all the people who had lived in the cottage at Olean the summer I did not enter the Franciscans, had at one point got themselves jobs on the magazine *House and Garden.* The whole thing is very obscure and mysterious. Perhaps it is something I dreamed. But for those three or four months, or however long it was, *House and Garden* must have been quite a magazine! Surely nothing like the old *House and Garden* I used to yawn over in the doctor's office.

And Seymour was in India. He was in the army. He had not yet, as far as I knew, found any practical application for his jujitsu. In India his chief task was to edit a paper for the boys in the army. So one day he walked in to the printing press, where all the typesetters working for him were Hindus, nice peaceful fellows. And Seymour, in the middle of the printing press and in full view of all his native staff, swatted a fly with a report that rang through the shop like a cannon. Instantly all the Hindus stopped work and filed out on strike. I suppose that was the time Seymour had leisure enough to travel to Calcutta and pay a visit to Bramachari.

When Lax went back to New York he took with him a manuscript of some poems. Half of them had been written since I entered the novitiate. The other half went back, mostly, to the days at St. Bonaventure. It was the first time I had looked at them since I had come to Gethsemani. Getting these poems together and making a selection was like editing the work of a stranger, a dead poet, someone who had been forgotten.

Lax took this collection to Mark Van Doren, and Mark sent it to James Laughlin at New Directions, and just before Lent I heard he was going to print it.

The exceedingly tidy little volume, *Thirty Poems*, reached me at the end of November, just before we began the annual retreat, in 1944.

I went out under the grey sky, under the cedars at the edge of the cemetery, and stood in the wind that threatened snow and held the printed poems in my hand.

ii

By this time I should have been delivered of any problems about my true identity. I had already made my simple profession. And my vows should have divested me of the last shreds of any special identity.

But then there was this shadow, this double, this writer who had followed me into the cloister.

He is still on my track. He rides my shoulders, sometimes, like the old man of the sea. I cannot lose him. He still wears the name of Thomas Merton. Is it the name of an enemy?

He is supposed to be dead.

But he stands and meets me in the doorway of all my prayers, and follows me into church. He kneels with me behind the pillar, the Judas, and talks to me all the time in my ear.

He is a business man. He is full of ideas. He breathes notions and new schemes. He generates books in the silence that ought to be sweet with the infinitely productive darkness of contemplation.

And the worst of it is, he has my superiors on his side. They won't kick him out. I can't get rid of him.

Maybe in the end he will kill me, he will drink my blood.

Nobody seems to understand that one of us has got to die.

Sometimes I am mortally afraid. There are the days when there seems to be nothing left of my vocation—my contemplative vocation—but a few ashes. And everybody calmly tells me: "Writing is your vocation."

And there he stands and bars my way to liberty. I am bound to the earth, in his Egyptian bondage of contracts, reviews, page proofs, and all the plans for books and articles that I am saddled with.

When I first began to get ideas about writing, I told them to Father Master and Father Abbot with what I thought was "simplicity." I thought I was just "being open with my superiors." In a way, I suppose I was.

But it was not long before they got the idea that I ought to be put to work translating things, writing things.

It is strange. The Trappists have sometimes been definite, even exaggerated, in their opposition to intellectual work in the past. That was one of the big battle cries of De Rancé. He had a kind of detestation for monkish dilettantes and he took up arms against the whole Benedictine Congregation of Saint Maur in a more or less quixotic battle that ended in a reconciliation scene between De Rancé and the great Dom Mabillon that reads like Oliver Goldsmith. In the eighteenth and nineteenth centuries, it was considered a kind of a monastic sin for a Trappist to read anything but Scripture and the lives of the saints: and I mean those lives that are a chain of fantastic miracles interspersed with pious platitudes. It was considered a matter worthy of suspicion if a monk developed too lively an interest in the Fathers of the Church.

But at Gethsemani I had walked into a far different kind of a situation.

In the first place, I entered a house that was seething with an energy and a growth that it had not known for ninety years. After nearly a century of struggle and obscurity, Gethsemani was suddenly turning into a very prominent and vital force in the Cistercian order and the Catholic Church in America. The house was crowded with postulants and novices. There was no longer any room to hold them all. In fact, on the Feast of St. Joseph, 1944, when I made my simple profession, Father Abbot read out the names of those who had been chosen for the first daughter house of Gethsemani. Two days later, on the Feast of St. Benedict, the colony left for Georgia and took up its abode in a barn thirty miles from Atlanta, chanting the psalms in a hayloft. By the time this is printed there will have been another Cistercian monastery in Utah and another in New Mexico, and still another planned for the deep South.

This material growth at Gethsemani is part of a vaster movement of spiritual vitality that is working throughout the whole Order, all over the world. And one of the things it has produced has been a certain amount of Cistercian literature.

That there should be six Cistercian monasteries in the United States and a convent of nuns soon to come: that there should also be new foundations in Ireland and Scotland, all this means a demand for books in English about the Cistercian life and the spirituality of the Order and its history.

But besides that, Gethsemani has grown into a sort of a furnace of apostolic fire. Every week-end, during the summer, the Guest House is crowded with retreatants who pray and fight the flies and wipe the sweat out of their eyes and listen to the monks chanting the office and hear sermons in the library and eat the cheese that Brother Kevin makes down in the moist shadows of the cellar that is propitious for that kind of thing. And along with this retreat movement, Gethsemani has been publishing a lot of pamphlets.

There is a whole rack of them in the lobby of the Guest House. Blue and yellow and pink and green and grey, with fancy printing on the covers or plain printing—some of them even with pictures—the pamphlets bear the legend: "A Trappist says . . ." "A Trappist declares . . ." "A Trappist implores . . ." "A Trappist asserts . . ." And what does a Trappist say, declare, implore, assert? He says things like this: It is time you changed your way of looking at things. Why don't you get busy and go to confession? After death: what? and things like that. These Trappists, they have something to tell laymen and laywomen, married men and single men, old men and young men, men in the army and men who have just come out of the army and men who are too crippled up to get into the army. They have a word of advice for nuns, and more than a word for priests. They have something to say about how to build a home, and about how to go through four years of college without getting too badly knocked about, spiritually, in the process.

And one of the pamphlets even has something to say about the Contemplative Life.

So it is not hard to see that this is a situation in which my double, my shadow, my enemy, Thomas Merton, the old man of the sea, has things in his favor. If he suggests books about the Order, his suggestions are heard. If he thinks up poems to be printed and published, his thoughts are listened to. There seems to be no reason why he should not write for magazines. . . .

At the beginning of 1944, when I was getting near the time for simple profession, I wrote a poem to Saint Agnes on her feast in January, and when I had finished it my feeling was that I did not care if I never wrote another poem as long as I lived.

At the end of the year, when *Thirty Poems* were printed, I still felt the same way, and more so.

So then Lax came down again for another Christmas, and told me I should be writing more poems. I did not argue about it. But in my own heart I did not think it was God's will. And Dom Vital, my confessor, did not think so either.

Then one day—the Feast of the Conversion of Saint Paul, 1945—I went to Father Abbot for direction, and without my even thinking of the subject, or mentioning it, he suddenly said to me:

"I want you to go on writing poems."

iii

It is very quiet.

The morning sun is shining on the gate-house which is bright with new paint this summer. From here it looks as though the wheat is already beginning to ripen on St. Joseph's knoll. The monks who are on retreat for their ordination to the diaconate are digging in the Guest House garden.

It is very quiet. I think about this monastery that I am in. I think about the monks, my brothers, my fathers.

There are the ones who have a thousand things to do. Some are busy with food, some with clothing, some with fixing the pipes, some with fixing the roof. Some paint the house, some sweep the rooms, some mop the floor of the refectory. One goes to the bees with a mask on and takes away their honey. Three or four others sit in a room with typewriters and all day long they answer the letters of the people who write here asking for prayers because they are unhappy. Still others are fixing tractors and trucks, others are driving them. The brothers are fighting with the mules to get them into harness. Or they go out in the pasture after the cows. Or they worry about the rabbits. One of them says he can fix watches. Another is making plans for the new monastery in Utah.

The ones who have no special responsibility for chickens or pigs or writing pamphlets or packing them up to send out by mail or keeping the complicated accounts in our Mass book—the ones who have nothing special to do can always go out and weed the potatoes and hoe the rows of corn.

When the bell rings in the steeple, I will stop typing and close the windows of this room where I work. Frater Sylvester will put away that mechanical monster of a lawn-mower and his helpers will go home with their hoes and shovels. And I will take a book and walk up and down a bit under the trees, if there is time, before the Conventual Mass. And most of the others will sit in the scriptorium and write their theological conferences or copy things out of books on to the backs of envelopes. And one or two will stand around in a doorway that leads from the Little Cloister to the monks' garden, and twine their rosaries around in their fingers and wait for something to happen.

After that we will all go to choir, and it will be hot, and the organ will be loud, and the organist, who is just learning, will make a lot of mistakes. But on the altar will be offered to God the eternal Sacrifice of the Christ to Whom we belong, and Who has brought us here together.

Congregavit nos in unum Christi amor.

America is discovering the contemplative life.

There are paradoxes in the history of Christian spirituality and not the least of them is the apparent contradiction in the way the Fathers and modern Popes have looked at the active and contemplative lives. Saint Augustine and Saint Gregory lamented the "sterility" of contemplation, which was in itself, as they admitted, superior to action. Yet Pope Pius XI came out in the constitution "Umbratilem" with the clear statement that the contemplative life was *much more* fruitful for the Church (*multo plus ad Ecclesiae incrementa et humani generis salutem conferre . . .*) than the activity of teaching and preaching. What is all the more surprising to a superficial observer is the fact that such a pronouncement should belong to our energetic times.

Practically anyone who realizes the existence of the debate can tell you that Saint Thomas taught that there were three vocations: that to the active life, that to the contemplative, and a third to the mixture of both, and that this last is superior to the other two. The mixed life is, of course, the vocation of Saint Thomas's own order, the Friars Preachers.

But Saint Thomas also comes out flatly with a pronouncement no less uncompromising than the one we read from "Umbratilem." *Vita contemplativa,* he remarks, *simpliciter est melior quam activa* (the contemplative life in itself, by its very nature, is superior to the active life). What is more, he proves it by natural reason in arguments from a pagan philosopher—Aristotle. That is how esoteric the question is! Later on he gives his strongest argument in distinctly Christian terms. The contemplative life directly and immediately occupies itself with the love of God, than which there is no act more perfect or more meritorious. Indeed that love is the root of all merit. When you consider the effect of individual merit upon the vitality of other members of the Mystical Body it is evident that there is nothing sterile about contemplation. On the contrary Saint Thomas's treatment of it in this question shows that the contemplative life establishes a man in the very heart of all spiritual fecundity.

When he admits that the active life *can* be more perfect under certain circumstances, accidentally, he hedges his statement in with half a dozen qualifications of a strictness that greatly enhances what he has already said about contemplation. First, activity will only be more perfect than the joy and rest of contemplation if it is undertaken as the result of an overflow of love for God (*propter abundantiam divini amoris*) in order to fulfill His will. It is not to be continuous, only the answer to a temporary emergency. It is purely for God's glory, and it does not dispense us from contemplation. It is an added obligation, and we must return as soon as we morally can to the powerful and fruitful silence of recollection that disposes our souls for divine union.

First comes the active life (practice of virtues, mortification, charity) which prepares us for contemplation. Contemplation means rest, suspension of activity, withdrawal into the mysterious interior solitude in which the soul is absorbed in the immense and fruitful silence of God and learns something of the secret of His perfections less by seeing than by fruitive love.

Yet to stop here would be to fall short of perfection. According to Saint Bernard of Clairvaux it is the comparatively weak soul that arrives at contemplation but does not overflow with a love that must communicate what it knows of God to other men. For all the great Christian mystics without exception, Saint Bernard, Saint Gregory, Saint Theresa, Saint John of the Cross, Blessed John Ruysbroeck, Saint Bonaventure, the peak of the mystical life is a marriage of the soul with God which gives the saints a miraculous power, a smooth and tireless energy in working for God and for souls, which bears fruits in the sanctity of thousands and changes the course of religious and even secular history.

With this in mind, Saint Thomas could not fail to give the highest place to a vocation which, in his eyes, seemed destined to lead men to such a height of contemplation that the soul must overflow and communicate its secrets to the world.

Unfortunately Saint Thomas's bare statement "the religious institutes which are ordered to the work of preaching and teaching hold the highest rank in religion" is, frankly, misleading. It conjures up nothing more than a mental image of some pious and industrious clerics bustling from the library to the classroom. If it meant no more than this the solution would be hardly comprehensible to a

Christian. Yet the tragedy is that many—including members of those "mixed" Orders—cannot find in it any deeper significance. If you can give a half-way intelligent lecture applying some thoughts from scholastic philosophy to the social situation, that alone places you very near the summit of perfection. . . .

No, we keep our eyes on those flaming words which lay down the conditions under which it is valid to leave contemplation for action. First of all *propter abundantiam divini amoris.* The "mixed life" is to be rated above that of the pure contemplatives only on the supposition that their love is *so much more vehement, so much more abundant* that it has to pour itself out in teaching and preaching.

In other words Saint Thomas is here teaching us that the so-called mixed vocation can only be superior to the contemplative vocation if it is itself *more contemplative.* This conclusion is inescapable. It imposes a tremendous obligation. Saint Thomas is really saying that the Dominican, the Franciscan, the Carmelite must be supercontemplatives. Either that or he is contradicting everything he said about the superiority of the contemplative.

Whether the "mixed" Orders today in America are actually as contemplative as this program would demand is a question I have no intention of answering. But at any rate it seems that most of them have reached, in practice, a sort of compromise to get out of the difficulty. They divide up their duties between their nuns and their priests. The nuns live in cloisters and do the contemplating and the priests live in colleges and cities and do the teaching and preaching. In the light of "*Umbratilem*" and the doctrine of the Mystical Body this solution is at least possible, if conditions leave them with no other way out. Saint Thomas, however, envisaged a program that was far more complete and satisfactory, for the individual and for the Church!

But what about the contemplative Orders? Their rules and usages at least grant them all they need to dispose themselves for contemplation and if their members do not reach it, it is not because of any difficulty inherent in their actual way of life. Granting that they are, or can be, as contemplative as they were meant to be by their founders: are they anything else?

The fact is, there does not exist any such thing as a purely contemplative Order of men—an Order which does not have, somewhere in its constitution, the note of *contemplata tradere.* The Carthusians, with all their elaborate efforts to preserve the silence and solitude of the hermit's life in their monasteries, definitely wrote into their original "Customs" the characteristic labor of copying manuscripts and writing books in order that they might preach to the world by their pen even though their tongues were silent.

The Cistercians had no such legislation, and they even enacted statutes to limit the production of books and to forbid poetry altogether. Nevertheless they produced a school of mystical theologians which, as Dom Berlière says, represents the finest flower of Benedictine spirituality. I just quoted what Saint Bernard, the head of that school, had to say on the subject, and in any case even if the Cistercians never wrote anything to pass on the fruit of their contemplation to the Church at large, *contemplata tradere* would always be an essential element in Cistercian life to the extent that the abbot and those charged with the direction of souls would always be obliged to feed the rest of the monks with the good bread of mystical theology as it comes out in smoking hot loaves from the oven of contemplation. This was what Saint Bernard told the learned cleric of York, Henry Murdach, to lure him from his books into the woods where the beeches and elms taught the monks wisdom.

And these "purely active" Orders, what about them? Do any such things exist? The Little Sisters of the Poor, the nursing sisterhoods cannot truly fulfil their vocations unless there is something of that *contemplata tradere,* the sharing of the fruits of contemplation. Even the active vocation is sterile without an interior life, and a deep interior life at that.

The truth is, in any kind of a religious Order there is not only the possibility but even in some sense the obligation of leading, at least to some extent, the highest of all lives—contemplation, and the sharing of its fruits with others. Saint Thomas's principle stands firm: the greatest perfection is *contemplata tradere*. But that does not oblige us to restrict this vocation, as he does, to the teaching Orders. They only happen to be the ones that seem to be best equipped to pass on the knowledge of God acquired by loving Him —if they have acquired that knowledge in contemplation. Yet others may perhaps be better placed for acquiring it.

In any case, there are many different ways of sharing the fruits of contemplation with others. You don't have to write books or make speeches. You don't have to have direct contact with souls in the confessional. Prayer can do the work wonderfully well, and indeed the fire of contemplation has a tendency to spread of itself throughout the Church and vivify all the members of Christ in secret without any conscious act on the part of the contemplative. But if you argue that Saint Thomas's context limits us at least to some sort of visible and natural communication with our fellow men (though it is hard to see why this should be so) nevertheless even in that event there exists a far more powerful means of sharing the mystical and experimental knowledge of God.

Look in Saint Bonaventure's *Itinerarium* and you will find one of the best descriptions ever written of this highest of all vocations. It is a description which the Seraphic Doctor himself learned on retreat and in solitude on Mount Alvernia. Praying in the same lonely spot where the great founder of his Order, Saint Francis of Assisi, had had the wounds of Christ burned into his hands and feet and side, Saint Bonaventure saw, by the light of a supernatural intuition, the full meaning of this tremendous event in the history of the Church. "There," he says, "Saint Francis 'passed over into God' (*in Deum transiit*) in the ecstasy (*excessus*) of contemplation and thus he was set up as an example of perfect contemplation just as he had previously been an example of perfection in the active life in order that God, through him, might draw all truly spiritual men to this kind of 'passing over' (*transitus*) and ecstasy, *less by word than by example*."

Here is the clear and true meaning of *contemplata tradere*, expressed without equivocation by one who had lived that life to the full. It is the vocation to transforming union, to the height of the mystical life and of mystical experience, to the very transformation into Christ that Christ living in us and directing all our actions might Himself draw men to desire and seek that same exalted union because of the joy and the sanctity and the supernatural vitality radiated by our example—or rather because of the secret influence of Christ living within us in complete possession of our souls.

And notice the tremendously significant fact that St. Bonaventure makes no divisions and distinctions: Christ imprinted His own image upon Saint Francis in order to draw not some men, not a few privileged monks, but *all* truly spiritual men to the perfection of contemplation which is nothing else but the perfection of love. Once they have reached these heights they will draw others to them in their turn. So any man may be called at least *de jure*, if not *de facto*, to become fused into one spirit with Christ in the furnace of contemplation and then go forth and cast upon the earth that same fire which Christ wills to see enkindled.

This means, in practice, that there is only one vocation. Whether you teach or live in the cloister or nurse the sick, whether you are in religion or out of it, married or single, no matter who you are or what you are, you are called to the summit of perfection: you are called to a deep interior life perhaps even to mystical prayer, and to pass the fruits of your contemplation on to others. And if you cannot do so by word, then by example.

Yet if this sublime fire of infused love burns in your soul, it will inevitably send forth throughout the Church and the world an influence more tremendous than could be estimated by the radius reached by words or by example. Saint John of the Cross writes: "A very little of this pure love is more precious in the sight of God and of greater profit to the Church, even though the soul appear to be doing nothing, than are all other works put together."

Before we were born, God knew us. He knew that some of us would rebel against His love and His mercy, and that others would love Him from the moment that they could love anything, and never change that love. He knew that there would be joy in heaven among the angels of His house for the conversion of some of us, and He knew that He would bring us all here to Gethsemani together, one day, for His own purpose, for the praise of His love.

The life of each one in this abbey is part of a mystery. We all add up to something far beyond ourselves. We cannot yet realize what it is. But we know, in the language of our theology, that we are all members of the Mystical Christ, and that we all grow together in Him for Whom all things were created.

In one sense we are always travelling, and travelling as if we did not know where we were going.

In another sense we have already arrived.

We cannot arrive at the perfect possession of God in this life, and that is why we are travelling and in darkness. But we already possess Him by grace, and therefore in that sense we have arrived and are dwelling in the light.

But oh! How far have I to go to find You in Whom I have already arrived!

For now, oh my God, it is to You alone that I can talk, because nobody else will understand. I cannot bring any other man on this earth into the cloud where I dwell in Your light, that is, Your darkness, where I am lost and abashed. I cannot explain to any other man the anguish which is Your joy nor the loss which is the

Possession of You, nor the distance from all things which is the arrival in You, nor the death which is the birth in You because I do not know anything about it myself and all I know is that I wish it were over—I wish it were begun.

You have contradicted everything. You have left me in no-man's land.

You have got me walking up and down all day under those trees, saying to me over and over again: "Solitude, solitude." And You have turned around and thrown the whole world in my lap. You have told me, "Leave all things and follow me," and then You have tied half of New York to my foot like a ball and chain. You have got me kneeling behind that pillar with my mind making a noise like a bank. Is that contemplation?

Before I went to make my solemn vows, last spring, on the Feast of St. Joseph, in the thirty-third year of my age, being a cleric in minor orders—before I went to make my solemn vows, this is what it looked like to me. It seemed to me that You were almost asking me to give up all my aspirations for solitude and for a contemplative life. You were asking me for obedience to superiors who will, I am morally certain, either make me write or teach philosophy or take charge of a dozen material responsibilities around the monastery, and I may even end up as a retreat master preaching four sermons a day to the seculars who come to the house. And even if I have no special job at all, I will always be on the run from two in the morning to seven at night.

Didn't I spend a year writing the life of Mother Berchmans who was sent to a new Trappistine foundation in Japan, and who wanted to be a contemplative? And what happened to her? She had to be gate-keeper and guest-mistress and sacristan and cellaress and mistress of the lay sisters all at the same time. And when they relieved her of one or two of those jobs it was only in order to give her heavier ones, like that of Mistress of Novices.

Martha, Martha, sollicita eris, et turbaberis erga plurima . . .

When I was beginning my retreat, before solemn profession, I tried to ask myself for a moment if those vows had any condition attached to them. If I was called to be a contemplative and they did not help me to be a contemplative, but hindered me, then what?

But before I could even begin to pray, I had to drop that kind of thinking.

By the time I made my vows, I decided that I was no longer sure what a contemplative was, or what the contemplative vocation was, or what my vocation was, and what our Cistercian vocation was. In fact I could not be sure I knew or understood much of anything except that I believed that You wanted me to take those particular vows in this particular house on that particular day for reasons best known to Yourself, and that what I was expected to do after that was follow along with the rest and do what I was told and things would begin to become clear.

That morning when I was lying on my face on the floor in the middle of the church, with Father Abbot praying over me, I began to laugh, with my mouth in the dust, because without knowing how or why, I had actually done the right thing, and even an astounding thing. But what was astounding was not my work, but the work You worked in me.

The months have gone by, and You have not lessened any of those desires, but You have given me peace, and I am beginning to see what it is all about. I am beginning to understand.

Because You have called me here not to wear a label by which I can recognize myself and place myself in some kind of a category. You do not want me to be thinking about what I am, but about what You are. Or rather, You do not even want me to be thinking about anything much: for You would raise me above the level of thought. And if I am always trying to figure out what I am and where I am and why I am, how will that work be done?

I do not make a big drama of this business. I do not say: "You have asked me for everything, and I have renounced all." Because I no longer desire to see anything that implies a distance between You and me: and if I stand back and consider myself and You as if something had passed between us, from me to You, I will inevitably see the gap between us and remember the distance between us.

My God, it is that gap and that distance which kill me.

That is the only reason why I desire solitude—to be lost to all created things, to die to them and to the knowledge of them, for they remind me of my distance from You. They tell me something about You: that You are far from them, even though You are in them. You have made them and Your presence sustains their being, and they hide You from me. And I would live alone, and out of them. O *beata solitudo!*

For I knew that it was only by leaving them that I could come to You: and that is why I have been so unhappy when You seemed to be condemning me to remain in them. Now my sorrow is over, and my joy is about to begin: the joy that rejoices in the deepest sorrows. For I am beginning to understand. You have taught me, and have consoled me, and I have begun again to hope and learn.

I hear You saying to me:

"I will give you what you desire. I will lead you into solitude. I will lead you by the way that you cannot possibly understand, because I want it to be the quickest way.

"Therefore all the things around you will be armed against you, to deny you, to hurt you, to give you pain, and therefore to reduce you to solitude.

"Because of their enmity, you will soon be left alone. They will cast you out and forsake you and reject you and you will be alone.

"Everything that touches you shall burn you, and you will draw your hand away in pain, until you have withdrawn yourself from all things. Then you will be all alone.

"Everything that can be desired will sear you, and brand you with a cautery, and you will fly from it in pain, to be alone. Every created joy will only come to you as pain, and you will die to all joy and be left alone. All the good things that other people love and desire and seek will come to you, but only as murderers to cut you off from the world and its occupations.

"You will be praised, and it will be like burning at the stake. You will be loved, and it will murder your heart and drive you into the desert.

"You will have gifts, and they will break you with their burden. You will have pleasures of prayer, and they will sicken you and you will fly from them.

"And when you have been praised a little and loved a little I will take away all your gifts and all your love and all your praise and you will be utterly forgotten and abandoned and you will be nothing, a dead thing, a rejection. And in that day you shall begin to possess the solitude you have so long desired. And your solitude will bear immense fruit in the souls of men you will never see on earth.

"Do not ask when it will be or where it will be or how it will be: On a mountain or in a prison, in a desert or in a concentration camp or in a hospital or at Gethsemani. It does not matter. So do not ask me, because I am not going to tell you. You will not know until you are in it.

"But you shall taste the true solitude of my anguish and my poverty and I shall lead you into the high places of my joy and you shall die in Me and find all things in My mercy which has created you for this end and brought you from Prades to Bermuda to St.

Antonin to Oakham to London to Cambridge to Rome to New York to Columbia to Corpus Christi to St. Bonaventure to the Cistercian Abbey of the poor men who labor in Gethsemani:

"That you may become the brother of God and learn to know the Christ of the burnt men."

SIT FINIS LIBRI, NON FINIS QUAERENDI

Index

OXFORD WORLD'S CLASSICS

A CHILD OF THE JAGO

ARTHUR MORRISON (1863–1945) was born in Poplar. His father, an engine-fitter in the docks, died when Arthur was a child. Morrison rapidly bettered himself, rising through the Architect's Department of the London School Board to a post at the People's Palace on the Mile End Road. This was an ambitious educational institution (a 'University for the People') offering facilities designed to enhance the social, intellectual, and cultural awareness of London's respectable working and lower middle class. Morrison organized events and sub-edited the institution's *Journal*. As a teenager he wrote light verse for cycling periodicals and in his early twenties had serious journalism accepted. In 1888 he published a series of sketches of London life in the *People* and in 1890 resigned from the People's Palace to become a full-time journalist and contributor to the proliferating magazines of the period. He married in 1892. *Tales of Mean Streets* (1894), short stories that had mostly appeared in W. E. Henley's *National Observer*, gained him instant notoriety. *A Child of the Jago* (1896) turned from the commonplace streets of the East End to its worst slums. Morrison conducted on-the-spot research under the tutelage of the Revd Arthur Osborne Jay, Vicar of Holy Trinity, Shoreditch. *To London Town* (1899) extended the concerns of *Mean Streets* and *A Child of the Jago*, while the much admired *The Hole in the Wall* (1902) put similar material to use in a thriller. *Cunning Murrell* (1903) was a Hardyesque tale of Essex rural life. Morrison also produced detective fiction. Eventually his scholarly and commercial interest in Japanese art took over. His influential *Painters of Japan* appeared in 1911, while his dealing appears to have provided him with the means to retire from his journalistic and literary career. Morrison died in 1945.

PETER MILES is an Emeritus Fellow of the English Association and a former Head of English at the University of Wales, Lampeter. He is co-author (with Malcolm Smith) of *Cinema, Literature and Society: Elite and Mass Culture in Britain between the Wars* (1987) and author of *The Critics Debate: 'Wuthering Heights'* (1990). With David Skilton he has co-edited Wilkie Collins's *The Woman in White* (1982) and Anthony Trollope's *Framley Parsonage* (1984). He has also edited Tobias Smollett's *The Expedition of Humphry Clinker* (1993) and, in the Oxford World's Classics series, Robert Tressell's *The Ragged Trousered Philanthropists* (2005).

OXFORD WORLD'S CLASSICS

For over 100 years Oxford World's Classics have brought readers closer to the world's great literature. Now with over 700 titles—from the 4,000-year-old myths of Mesopotamia to the twentieth century's greatest novels—the series makes available lesser-known as well as celebrated writing.

The pocket-sized hardbacks of the early years contained introductions by Virginia Woolf, T. S. Eliot, Graham Greene, and other literary figures which enriched the experience of reading. Today the series is recognized for its fine scholarship and reliability in texts that span world literature, drama and poetry, religion, philosophy, and politics. Each edition includes perceptive commentary and essential background information to meet the changing needs of readers.

OXFORD WORLD'S CLASSICS

ARTHUR MORRISON

A Child of the Jago

Edited with an Introduction and Notes by
PETER MILES

OXFORD
UNIVERSITY PRESS

OXFORD
UNIVERSITY PRESS

Great Clarendon Street, Oxford OX2 6DP

Oxford University Press is a department of the University of Oxford.
It furthers the University's objective of excellence in research, scholarship,
and education by publishing worldwide in

Oxford New York

Auckland Cape Town Dar es Salaam Hong Kong Karachi
Kuala Lumpur Madrid Melbourne Mexico City Nairobi
New Delhi Shanghai Taipei Toronto

With offices in

Argentina Austria Brazil Chile Czech Republic France Greece
Guatemala Hungary Italy Japan Poland Portugal Singapore
South Korea Switzerland Thailand Turkey Ukraine Vietnam

Published in the United States
by Oxford University Press Inc., New York

First published as a World's Classics paperback 2012

British Library Cataloguing in Publication Data
Data available

Library of Congress Cataloging in Publication Data
Library of Congress Control Number: 2011942630

Typeset by Cenveo, Bangalore, India
Printed in Great Britain
on acid-free paper by
Clays Ltd, St Ives plc

ISBN 978–0–19–960551–4

5

CONTENTS

INTRODUCTION

Readers who are unfamiliar with the plot of A Child of the Jago *may prefer to treat this Introduction as an Afterword.*

'THIS ALSO', pronounces Joseph Conrad's Marlow, musing on the Thames and 'the monstrous town' of London at the beginning of *Heart of Darkness*, 'has been one of the dark places of the earth.' Arthur Morrison's novel *A Child of the Jago*, first published in 1896, just three years before Conrad's novella, is a classic, sensational depiction of city life at its darkest and most dysfunctional: a disturbing vision of the cost of London as history's greatest experiment in urban living. *A Child of the Jago*, as well as being the best remembered of Morrison's writings, is the most celebrated example of British 'slum fiction' of the 1890s, an extraordinary construction of the sights, sounds, cultural traits, and life trajectories of the late Victorian underclass. The critic Jane Findlater recalled at the end of that decade that 'in the 1890s we all read the books of Arthur Morrison and shuddered over them' (Appendix, p. 184). In this particular book such shudders are triggered not just by the account of appalling social conditions, but also by the graphic presentation of crime and brutal violence. A woman walks down a road with a bloody hank of hair torn from an opponent in a tribal conflict; a man fired by revenge battles through a bare-knuckle fight before a howling crowd; a teenage boy is knifed to death in a running street battle: these scenes are just some of the stuff of Morrison's at times near-apocalyptic vision of the savagery at the heart of his city. In 1899 the critic Leslie Cope Cornford reflected that Morrison

> limns the hideous growth that ravens at our very doors—whether passively engendered by greed, or neglect, or modern civilisation, or modern Christianity, or modern heathendom—by any of these, or none, or what you will: and bids us to consider the picture. He has gone down into the lair of the dragon, the monstrous worm.[1]

It comes then as no surprise to find *A Child of the Jago* recently

[1] Leslie Cope Cornford, 'The Work of Mr Arthur Morrison', in H. Morrah (ed.), *The Literary Year-Book and Bookman's Directory 1900* (London, 1900), 83–5, at 84.

dubbed by Martin J. Wiener 'the most important literary work of the 1890s focusing on criminality'.[2] Beyond this, Morrison's novel is a challenging exploration of a debate whose key terms may change through the centuries but which in essence persists in all our attempts to understand ourselves, our lives, and our societies, and most evidently, as voices within the novel recognize, in our formulations of social policy and our responses to it. Whether with Shakespeare's Prospero we talk in terms of 'nature' and 'nurture', or with Charles Darwin's successors we set 'heredity' or 'genetic determinism' against 'environmental factors', this is a debate entered whenever we respond to issues of personal responsibility, social welfare, and political intervention. For the novel's first readers, such as H. G. Wells, its bearing on such debate was emphatic, pressing, and controversial.

The neighbourhood that Arthur Morrison chose as the basis for his pursuit of these concerns was, he confirmed in a letter to the Revd W. Priest in 1899, 'the worst I have ever known' (Appendix, p. 168). This was the Old Nichol slum in the East End of London, for the purposes of his novel renamed 'The Jago'. 'Jago', Morrison explained to the same correspondent, though not in a wholly illuminating manner, 'is a Cornish surname and is pronounced to rhyme with "sago", the "J" having the ordinary English sound' (Appendix, p. 168). (It seems at least possible that Priest was wondering whether 'Jago' had been intended as an allusion to Shakespeare's villain Iago.) Morrison's imaginative rendering of the Jago is a considerable part of the achievement of the book; any reader will find it hard not to carry away a powerful image of the world within a world that is the Jago: 'the dense gloom, the unspeakable squalor, the whole swarming welter of wickedness, misery, and oppression', as Cornford put it.[3] Significantly, the frontispiece to the novel was not a portrait of a character or a picture of some moment in the novel's drama, but a sketch-map of the entire Jago as place, its dark heart clearly indicated as Jago Court. The map is an abstracted aerial view, suggesting that in the tale that follows, it is the labyrinthine Jago itself that to a large extent should command the reader's attention. Morrison's sketch-map can be seen as offering a rather distant perspective on the Jago, a way of keeping aloof from it, analogous to the perspectives of the city planner or

[2] Martin J. Wiener, *Deconstructing the Criminal: Culture, Law and Policy in England, 1890–1913* (Cambridge, 1990), 242.

[3] Cornford, 'Work of Morrison', 83.

cartographer: it denotes and makes seem broadly comprehensible what at street level hardly lends itself to so confident an essay in intellectual possession. However, it is into the chaos of the view from the street that Morrison's text immediately plunges his readers, a view that even some of the inhabitants of that street have difficulty in distinguishing from a prospect of hell. Morrison's characters are to a considerable extent subservient and secondary to the Jago as place: what happens to them serves to reinforce his judgement of the nurture that the Jago provides those who in effect have been socialized into it and even into a perverse pride in bearing its imprint, characters who freely and fiercely term themselves—as Morrison grimly names them—'Jagos'.

The original Old Nichol was an area of some thirty streets located off Shoreditch High Street, a mixture of decayed late seventeenth- and eighteenth-century houses and a swarm of early nineteenth-century jerry-built infilling that crowded and jumbled smaller buildings cheek by jowl into what once had been largely town-house gardens. The consequence was a district of barely mapped alleyways, sunless cellars, tunnels and courts, cul-de-sacs, stables, barrows, and sheds. Arthur Harding, an inhabitant of the area in the 1880s, remarked that the landlords and the builders 'had to congest the buildings to a small dimension because they never had the space available'.[4] Here, in what was a whirlpool of poverty and exploitation, inadequate sanitation and decaying construction, lived some 6,000 people, many of them in families who could afford to rent no more than a single room in a rotting tenement or barrack-like building. The writer W. E. Henley was not making an aesthetic judgement on Morrison's novel when he called *A Child of the Jago* 'a dreadful book':[5] rather he was recognizing the sheer power of the book to display the dreadful. And that the Old Nichol was a very bad place to live is not in doubt: inside it the mortality rate was twice as high as in the surrounding area of Bethnal Green—four times higher than London in general. However, that the Old Nichol was literally quite the breeding place of crime and criminality, of mugging and murder that Morrison conveyed to his readers through the Jago was avidly discussed at the time of the book's

[4] Raphael Samuel (ed.), *East End Underworld: Chapters in the Life of Arthur Harding* (London, 1981), 3.

[5] W. E. Henley, 'Some Novels of 1899', *North American Review*, 170/519 (Feb. 1900), 253–62, at 258.

publication, a discussion that has been renewed in more recent times. In particular, in the 1980s, Raphael Samuel's retrieval of Arthur Harding's memories of his childhood in the Old Nichol initiated a revisionism among historians that has been notably furthered by Sarah Wise in her recent documentary study of the Old Nichol, *The Blackest Streets*. The growth of local history and family history—not to mention tendencies in the community solidarity of the East End—has retrospectively thrown a more humane and protective light over lives that in Morrison's day were arguably an easy prey to misrepresentation or, indeed, translation into the status of folk devils. Today one does not have to go far to find views of *A Child of the Jago* that characterize the book as a vilification of, or a libel on, the community it depicts. Sarah Wise emphasizes the degree of responsibility for the condition of the Old Nichol that lay at the doors of landlords and local and national government rather than the inhabitants themselves; she also emphasizes how many successful businesses freely operated in the area. Stan Newens, whose great-grandfather was a member of the Salvation Army living in the Old Nichol, notes that in the area there were 'many law-abiding, industrious residents who brought up their children on the basis of strict moral principles'.[6] However, that the Old Nichol was an extraordinary place, distinctive in character, tradition, and identity from surrounding areas of the East End and its respectable working class, is undeniable. Even Arthur Harding described it as 'something like a ghetto', 'a place on its own', and remarked that 'in the Nichol there seemed to be a wall enclosing you' and indeed that on account of its 'evil reputation' some 'would have liked to build a wall right round it'.[7] Morrison persisted in his conviction of the criminal influence of the Jago—even after the buildings had been demolished and the area redeveloped. In 1899 he remarked in his letter to Priest that 'many of the people still live near; last Monday evening, indeed, there was an affray in Church Street (which I have called Meakin Street) in which the woman figured whom I have called Norah Walsh, and in which I am told that one person was killed and two others injured' (Appendix, p. 168).

The drama that Morrison projected into this setting was an engaging and disturbing one of the fate of a young boy of the underclass

[6] Stan Newens, *Arthur Morrison: The Novelist of Realism in East London and Essex* (Loughton, 2008), 36.

[7] Samuel (ed.), *East End Underworld*, 1.

growing up not only in deprivation but also in a world marked strongly by criminality as a way of life, where the language of daily life and even the nicknames of those about him are permeated by thieves' slang. The result was a novel that lent itself to consumption by a range of readers that encompassed seekers of exotic sensation, or of realistic depiction of a terra incognita, or of grist to a liberal conscience—and also readers prone to the worst fears of the conservative-minded concerning the social threat represented by, as the American novelist Jack London was to call them, the people of the abyss. Indeed, Morrison drily reported to his American publisher that in Britain *A Child of the Jago* had 'vogue (though you mightn't expect it) chiefly in the West End, among the most exclusive swells, who have taken to asking me to dine, and causing a waste of invention in excuses' (Appendix, p. 167).

The Elusive Arthur Morrison

Arthur Morrison wrote no autobiography and there has yet to be published a full biography or even a collection of his widely dispersed correspondence. On his death, many of his papers were burnt. What is known about Morrison has emerged in fragments over the decades, in part for the good and fascinating reason that he himself concealed or actively misrepresented details of his background. Stan Newens has recently remarked that Morrison's 'early life was a closed book up to and after his death'.[8] One surviving letter that Newens reproduces throws a strong light on the reason. Written late in the year of publication of *A Child of the Jago*, the letter refers to a visit that Morrison's correspondent had made to the author's mother in search of details of Morrison's life, ostensibly to help a friend who was due to review his latest book—*A Child of the Jago* itself. Politely, but unmistakably firmly, Morrison made clear his aversion to the idea:

> As a matter of fact, I prefer my private concerns not to be written about. They are my own business, and a book is best reviewed just as this book has been already by many others, with the information the book itself affords, and no other.
>
> *Entre nous*, and not for your friend's information, a man has only to

[8] Newens, *Arthur Morrison*, 16.

make a very small success to make a great many enemies, and the less they know of him, the less harm they can do. I am sure you won't mind my telling you this and that you will see your friend understands, that kind as his interest in me is, he will please me best by dealing with the book alone, if he thinks it worth his while, since it is the book alone that is offered for criticism and comment.[9]

At times literary criticism has been happy to reach its conclusions within just such constraints, as in the era of twentieth-century formalist or 'practical' criticism. Moreover, Morrison himself seems to have genuinely foreshadowed such a critical direction, as in a paragraph on the subject of writing short stories that he contributed to the *Bookman* a few months later: there he remarked 'of things that may be cultivated, the command of form is the first; indeed, I think it is all'. As an exercise, he suggested that the budding writer take a story by Guy de Maupassant, extract the facts of the story, and then compare them with the words of the achieved story:

He will see where the unessential is rejected; he will observe how everything receives its just proportion in the design; he will perceive that every incident, every sentence, and every word, has its value, its meaning, and its part in the whole. He will see the machinery, and in time he may learn to apply it for himself. But only by experience, inspired by natural gift, will he learn this, and will thus achieve the instinctive eye for the essential, and that severe command of material that will admit nothing else. Then, it may be, his critics will complain of his 'sketchiness', and cry aloud for a 'finished picture', meaning the industrious transcript of the incapable. But he will know that he has done well, and he will judge them at their worth. [. . .] Every story has its length—to a word. It is the aim of the artist to determine that length, and the first lesson is to reject.[10]

This is a valuable and generally overlooked insight into Morrison's priorities as a writer, as relevant to *A Child of the Jago* as to his short stories; but at the very least it was also a happy coincidence that his valuation of form, economy, and aesthetic design before all else should so coincide with his desire to keep his personal hinterland out of the range of critics' curiosity—as when, again in 1897, he disingenuously informed *Who's Who* that he had been born in Kent and had attended private schools. (Morrison habitually and variously

[9] Newens, *Arthur Morrison*, 37.
[10] 'How to Write a Short Story: A Symposium', *Bookman*, 5/1 (Mar. 1897), 45–6.

misled census enumerators about his place of birth.) However, *A Child of the Jago* and his preceding collection of short stories, *Tales of Mean Streets* (1894), did immediately highlight the question for Morrison's contemporaries of just how this writer could—as he evidently did—know so much about the working class and the underclass. The default position of reviewers was to read him as a fellow middle-class onlooker: one reviewer even gently explained what often went wrong when a gentleman of culture and education (presumably like Morrison and himself) tried to make sense of the lower classes. The truth that Morrison wished to conceal was that his own roots were indeed working class, perhaps, as he indicated in the above letter, on account of fears concerning the use some specific 'enemies' might make of that truth, perhaps out of a fundamental insecurity, or perhaps, as an ambitious and upwardly mobile writer, he simply saw no need to give a hostage to fortune in the face of the class prejudice of his society, from wherever it might come.

It is now known that Morrison was born on 1 November 1863 in the East End district of Poplar, in the Isle of Dogs. His father, George Richard Morrison, was an engine-fitter in the docks who died young, aged 31, in 1871, probably from tuberculosis, leaving his widow Jane to bring up Arthur and his two siblings on her income from working in, and eventually running, a haberdashery shop. Morrison, however, seems never to have defended the accuracy of his version of the East End on the basis of his authority as an East Ender. Instead, he asserted that his first-hand knowledge of the area had come by other means. In the preface to *A Child of the Jago* he wrote tendentiously of having lived there 'for certain years' and of his intimacy with its people being based on 'familiar and equal' friendships. Poplar, of course, was not the Jago or even the Old Nichol, but it was still the East End, and Morrison's equivocations allowed the reader to be quite unaware of his having experienced his upbringing there.

Morrison's working life began as a clerk in the Architect's Department of the London School Board, an occupation he retrospectively categorized as 'civil servant'. Probably while he was there, aged 17 or 18, his first publications appeared in popular periodicals about cycling. Indeed, he recalled in one letter that the very first manuscript he submitted—a blackly comic piece of verse involving a bicycle and a presumed murder—had been accepted for publication. By the mid-1880s he had graduated from the cycling periodicals (he recalled half a dozen significant ones) to such organs of what he termed the 'regular press' as the *Globe*, one of the club-land evening newspapers of the day that, as a group, also included such influential titles as the *Pall Mall Gazette*, the *St James's Gazette*, and the *Westminster Gazette*. In the meantime he had moved on to the People's Palace in the Mile End Road, a body that doubtless contributed some elements to his creation of the 'Pansophical Institute' in *A Child of the Jago*. There he organized social, cultural, and educational events for its respectable working-class clientele and also subedited and contributed to the institution's publication, the *Palace Journal*. It seems to have been the practical experience of his work on the *Journal* that gave him the confidence in the later 1880s to move into full-time work in journalism. By the time he was 30 Morrison was married, a father, and had a house in Loughton in Essex. (His property adjoined that of the successful popular writer W. W. Jacobs who later inscribed one of his books 'to my old neighbour, Arthur Morrison'.) Morrison himself was finding success through his writing in newspapers, magazines, and then books, developing his various journalistic and literary skills, and making new contacts. In short, he was succeeding as an exceptionally hard-working denizen of what the novelist George Gissing termed 'New Grub Street': the burgeoning late nineteenth-century commercial world of magazines and newspapers. It is thus apparent that it was essentially out of the world of journalism that Morrison's art grew. *Tales of Mean Streets* and *A Child of the Jago* each first appeared partially or in serial form in such magazines as *Macmillan's*, the *National Observer*, and the *New Review*. In this modern Grub Street Morrison was very adaptable. He could write stories of the life of the working class and the underclass, but he could also put together a newspaper, knock out a 'pot-boiler' about the spirit world (a term he himself used to describe some of his work), and weave around such commitments the composition of a number of volumes of Martin Hewitt detective stories that rivalled the adventures of Sherlock Holmes in their popularity and which, like Arthur Conan Doyle's stories, first appeared in the *Strand* with illustrations by Sidney Paget. Indeed it is in his *Chronicles of Martin Hewitt* of 1895 that one arguably finds the most telling image of Morrison at this period mirrored in his own Dr Watson, a hard-working journalist by the name of Brett who makes copy out of Martin Hewitt's investigations. In 'The Ivy Cottage Mystery' Brett reports:

I had been working double tides for a month: at night on my morning paper as usual; and in the morning on an evening paper as *locum tenens* for another man who was taking a holiday. This was an exhausting plan of work, although it only actually involved some six hours' attendance a day, or less, at the two offices. I turned up at the headquarters of my own paper at ten in the evening, and by the time I had seen the editor, selected a subject, written my leader, corrected the slips, chatted, smoked, and so on, and cleared off, it was very usually one o'clock. This meant bed at two, or even three, after supper at the club.

This was all very well at ordinary periods, when any time in the morning would do for rising, but when I had to be up again soon after seven, and round at the evening paper office by eight, I naturally felt a little worn and disgusted with things by midday, after a sharp couple of hours' leaderette scribbling and paragraphing, with attendant sundries.

The edge of the mirror of art catches a reflection of the professional writer himself: the busy Arthur Morrison, on a working day.

And Morrison already had a further string to his bow at this period, one which became increasingly important and increasingly defining through the years. This was an interest in visual art and, as his preface to *A Child of the Jago* amply demonstrates, in Japanese painting and prints in particular. It was a taste that may have been influenced by his early editor at the *National Observer*, W. E. Henley, to whom Morrison had dedicated *Tales of Mean Streets* and with whom James MacArthur described Morrison as enjoying a 'good fellowship'. Henley's poem 'Ballade of a Toyokuni Colour Print' was published in 1888; in 1895 Morrison was himself weaving that subject into a ghostly short story, 'A Vision of Toyokuni', a story that doubtless depicts something of Morrison's own response to Japanese art in what is there described as the narrator's 'morbid excess of sensibility to colour'. However exactly it arose, Morrison's taste for oriental art became a lifelong enthusiasm and, just as clearly, a commercial opportunity. Turn-of-the-century gossip portrayed Morrison haunting the East End seeking oriental rarities in its junkshops as much as material for his next story or novel. At the time of the publication of *A Child of the Jago*, studies in the field of oriental art were already making reference to artworks in his collection while in the early years of the twentieth century Morrison is himself found contributing on the subject of Chinese and Japanese art to the *Monthly Review*, *Macmillan's*, and the prestigious *Burlington Magazine*. Through the

1890s Morrison had been busy cultivating friendships with Japanese scholars and artists in London and also with figures associated with the oriental collections at the British Museum. One consequence was that by 1907 the *Connoisseur* magazine could devote an article in several parts to Morrison's collection which it characterized as 'astonishing' for its extent, completeness, and rarities. In the first decade of the twentieth century Morrison sold works directly to the British Museum and eventually his collection to that point was significant enough to be sold and thereafter to be donated by the purchaser to the British Museum. Morrison had also by then published his well-respected two-volume study *The Painters of Japan* (1911) and been engaged in a number of exhibitions. The American novelist and socialist Jack London may have fumed about those who organized exhibitions of Japanese art for the people—and he may well have had Morrison in mind—but more recently critics have shown interest in the connections in mode and subject matter to be made between the literary art of *A Child of the Jago* and the kind of pictorial art that fascinated Morrison—linking the two rather than seeing them as discrete aspects of his sensibility. Jessica Maynard has suggested that both emerged from a desire to capture 'the floating world' of everyday life, 'from attempts to sketch urban life and to engage with a marginalized reality'[11]—be that a matter of Japanese pleasure-garden courtesans and their clients, or of East End prostitutes and the High Mob. Morrison's preface to *A Child of the Jago* certainly shows that he found it perfectly natural to discuss his own literary technique through the medium of Japanese aesthetics. Beyond this, Morrison's interest in the art of the East and the contacts he made through it were an enduring and substantive aspect of his life, for with the waning of his activity in the field of fiction there exists little evidence to counter an impression of him as a man who no longer felt quite the same need to write for a living when he could well afford not to do so—as someone who in his middle and later years was no longer a comparatively poor man and who had found his own comfortable way out of his East End inheritance. The relatively little that is known of him after the First World War thus suggests a modestly successful

[11] Jessica Maynard, 'Arthur Morrison, the Floating World and the Pictorial Method in *A Child of the Jago*: Painters of the East', *English Literature in Transition (1880–1920)*, 51/1 (2008), 44–56, at 54.

survivor from the world of the Edwardian men-of-letters turned knowledgeable collector and dealer in art.

Morrison lived until 1945, but the energy and achievement of his writing career belonged principally to the last decade of the nineteenth century and the first decade of the twentieth. Jocelyn Bell observed of Morrison that he was 'one of those contemporary bestsellers who could be found on every Edwardian bookshelf, but who vanished in the Great War and were unknown to the new and changed generation which followed'.[12] Between the world wars many of his books slipped out of print; scholarship took little heed of them. Besides, fiction by and about the lower classes tended to shift its focus from the East End of London to the distressed areas of the Depression. After the Russian Revolution, writing by and about the working class took new directions; such 1930s novelists as Lewis Grassic Gibbon in Scotland, Lewis Jones in Wales, and Walter Greenwood in Salford depicted the working class from viewpoints and on premises very different to Arthur Morrison's. *A Child of the Jago* had allegiances to the genre of documentary style 'descent into the abyss'—texts revealing to the middle-class reader the life of the lower classes through the eyes of an adventurer descending into the 'dragon's lair' and briefly participating in their lives, to the extent that that was ever really possible. This was the case not only on account of the nature of the first-hand research that Morrison conducted for the novel, but through the dramatic role of its fictional Father Sturt and the historical role of that character's model, Father Arthur Osborne Jay, the enterprising vicar of Holy Trinity, Shoreditch. The genre was often presented and consumed in a spirit similar to works offering explorations of unknown regions in Africa and the Far East—and it had continued to flourish: Jack London's *The People of the Abyss* (1903), Ada Chesterton's *In Darkest London* (1926), her egregiously titled *I Lived in a Slum* (1936), and George Orwell's *The Road to Wigan Pier* (1937) carried further the spirit of Jay's and Morrison's descents into the Shoreditch slums. As James MacArthur had written of *Tales of Mean Streets* on its publication in the USA, 'so far as our knowledge of the existing conditions of human life in that community are concerned, we remained, until as it were

[12] Jocelyn Bell, 'A Study of Arthur Morrison', *Essays and Studies*, 5 (1952), 77–89, at 77.

yesterday, almost as ignorant as of the undiscovered territories in Central Africa'.[13] Yet the second, discursively political part of *The Road to Wigan Pier* signals what had changed. *A Child of the Jago* and Frank Griffin's *October Day* are both East End novels, but by the time of Griffin's in 1939 the issue in the East End's streets had moved beyond the mobilization of liberal compassion towards slum-dwellers (or fears concerning them) to class politics and the outright confrontations of fascism and socialism. The politics of interwar representation of the working class hardly fostered rediscovery of a novelist Jane Findlater had assigned to a 'School of Pity'. If it was later than one thought, it was certainly too late for pity.

Children and Parents

When asked by the *Bookman* for his opinion of Dickens's works, Morrison remarked that he would consider it a matter of 'national decadence' if Dickens were no longer appreciated. *A Child of the Jago* is evidence of Dickens's influence on Morrison in terms of its eye for London locale and picturesque character, its ear for language, its interest in criminality, and, most particularly, in the figure and situation of Dicky Perrott as latter-day Oliver Twist. Dicky Perrott, the child of the Jago himself, is Morrison's control experiment: what happens to Dicky defines, as Morrison saw them, the tensions of nature and nurture in the working-out of destiny, the workings of heredity and environment, and the mechanics of will and circumstance.

Placing Dicky centre stage was also very much in tune with the pragmatic priorities and strategies of social commentators and reformers in relation to an urban growth that in the later nineteenth century was often seen as spiralling out of control. In 1878, referring to New York in *The Night Sides of City Life*, the Revd Charles de Witt Talmadge stressed, 'You see I speak more in regard to the youth and the children of the country, because old villains are seldom reformed, and therefore I talk more of the little ones'; Jacob Riis, in *How the Other Half Lives* (1890), observed 'Nothing is now better understood than that the rescue of the children is the key to the

[13] James MacArthur, 'Introduction to the American Edition', in Arthur Morrison, *Tales of Mean Streets* (Boston, 1895), 9–14, at 9–10.

problem of city poverty as presented for our solution today; that character may be formed where to reform it would be a hopeless task'. In *The Children of the Poor* (1892) Riis specifically commented that 'No investment gives a better return to-day than work among the children of the poor'. Walter Besant, author of *All Sorts and Conditions of Men* (1882) and founder of the People's Palace, reiterated that view in words and action, while in his sketch 'Whitechapel' Morrison himself remarked, 'Children must not be left in these unscoured corners. Their fathers and mothers are hopeless, and must not be allowed to rear a numerous and equally hopeless race.'[14] To the Revd W. Priest he specifically confirmed that the story of *A Child of the Jago* was 'designed by me to [. . .] show that children brought up in such surroundings had no chance of a decent life' (Appendix, p. 168). The idea of the 'child' appeared frequently in late nineteenth-century formulations of the social problems of the day: Morrison's 'child of the Jago' is one variant on a persistent motif in journalism and fiction where 'child' might be substituted by such terms as 'children', 'daughter', 'son', or 'girl', and 'the Jago' by 'gutter', 'ghetto', 'street', or some related term. Israel Zangwill's *Children of the Ghetto* appeared in 1892 while as late as 1914 the Irish navvy-poet Patrick MacGill published a novel entitled *Children of the Dead End*. Such formulations gained further rhetorical force through their barely concealed opposition to the idea of humankind as Child of God: in this implicit opposition there was thus placed at issue the definition of humankind as spiritual or—as the animal and body imagery of *A Child of the Jago* so much functions to suggest—as merely material being. In *Culture and Anarchy* Matthew Arnold had commented scathingly on the 'immense pretension' of society terming itself 'children of God': 'and the work which we collective children of God do, our grand centre of life, our *city* which we have builded for us to dwell in, is London!' Not the city of God, but a London of dark places: not children of God, but children—as it were—of the Jago. On first publication in England of Stephen Crane's *Maggie*, the novel's subtitle was altered from '*A Girl of the Streets*' to '*A Child of the Streets*'; it is a minor change to modern eyes, but to a late Victorian sensibility the first phrase risked indecency while the second obliquely appealed to a sense of the sacred. In consequence, *A Child of the Jago*

[14] Arthur Morrison, 'Whitechapel', *Palace Journal*, 24 Apr. 1899, 1022–3, at 1023.

is partly about spiritual and material parentage, about a battle between various parents for Dicky Perrott.

Dicky is the child of his petty-criminal father Josh and his debilitated mother Hannah, but also the child of the Jago and thus heir to what Morrison calls 'a black inheritance'. While he remains pathetically loyal to his biological parents, he is morally confused, neglected, and emotionally blocked by them at every turn: his tears and secrets are confided principally to a battered donkey; odd shillings in his hand raise the possibility (sadly disappointed) of 'buying sympathy of his father and mother' (p. 101). In this situation Dicky is fought over by surrogate fathers in the form of the fortuitously titled 'Father' Sturt and the fence Aaron Weech, as Oliver Twist had been fought over by Mr Brownlow and Fagin. Ironically, the only character firmly identified with the epithet 'mother' in a world where women tend to be either ineffective or feral is the publican and exploitative landlady 'Mother' Gapp. Sturt and Weech each possess, or pose as having, an authoritative 'omniscience' that commands Dicky's attention. Sturt attempts to salvage Josh as Dicky's true father by teasing him away from crime, encouraging him into church and towards honest work; at the same time Sturt draws out of Dicky the kind of love, respect, trust—and briefly the will and aspiration—that might normally be expected to stem from the relationship of parent and child. Meanwhile Weech, as the living instrument of the Jago, self-interestedly but by no means ineffectively parodies the moral guidance of a parent, keeping Dicky's rate of thieving up to scratch while maintaining that he gives Dicky 'good advice like a father'. More than this, Weech actively undermines his rivals for the parental role by engineering Dicky's dismissal from a steady job arranged for him by Father Sturt and by betraying Josh to the police, thus clearing the way for his own continued influence over the boy. Father Sturt's faith in the possibility of improving Dicky's situation is justified by the evidence of Dicky's love for his sister Looey, his bursts of generosity, his response to what music and art comes his way—if only in the form of a decorated musical box—his interest in reading, his intuition of, and desire for, a decent way of living beyond what the Jago offers. What in other circumstances might have existed between biological father and son is shadowed in Dicky's excitement at the fight with Billy Leary ('"Go it, father! Fa–ther! Fa–ther!" Dicky screamed from the window', p. 69) and even in Josh's motivations in his hatred of Weech ('My boy was goin' straight, an' earnin' wages; someone got 'im chucked', p. 150). Going into his last fight Dicky paradoxically yells 'Come on Father Sturt's boys' (p. 164); before he dies the slum's battle-cry 'Hold tight, Jago' (p. 164) rings out—the same cry from which his father gains strength as he goes to the gallows. In the drama of parentage and destiny, such ironies and pathos reinforce the tragic victory of the Jago and Weech, the fence finally revealed beneath Josh's bludgeoning as a mere 'bubbling Thing' (p. 150). That Hannah Perrott's last child is named 'Little Josh' constitutes a bitter confirmation of the cycle of parentage and inheritance. In the hideous extremes that the Jago presents, a child of God is lost as—in Yeats's words—another rough beast slouches towards Bethlehem to be born.

Negotiating the Real: The Accuracy of Fiction

In its day, *A Child of the Jago* was a synonym for realism, for the impartially photographic, or, as the French novelist Stendhal had expressed it, for a mirror walking down a road. The road in this case was the Old Nichol and the quality of the text's reflection, it was understood, could be tested by sampling the author's 'accuracy'. The text was assumed to offer a proxy seeing that would allow readers to respond to social problems that the novel did not so much represent as disclose: the journalist and critic H. D. Traill, for example, actually faulted the novel for *not* giving him the feeling that he had 'just paid a visit to the actual district under the protection of the police' (Appendix, p. 175). Although by no means accepting all Traill's assumptions about the mode of his writing, Morrison and his allies were quick to defend the accuracy of *A Child of the Jago*. Morrison was at heart a journalist and so the originals of Father Sturt, Dicky and Josh Perrott, Aaron Weech, and Sally Green were all triumphantly brought forward as irrefutable testimony to the novel's 'truth'. The literary press was sprinkled with witnesses to life and events in the Old Nichol who confirmed or threw doubt on Morrison's portrait of the area and its life. At the same time, the realism of *A Child of the Jago* attracted hostility for its assumed insistence on the aesthetic necessity of both the investigative observation that underlay its composition and the kind of setting and spectrum of human behaviour with which it dealt. As the camera was seen to threaten painting, so the extremes of literary realism were seen to threaten literary art. For these reasons Morrison's 'notebook' and his journalistic 'methods' became totems in debate while his violation of artistic 'reticence' in his descriptions of squalor and violence also figured large. For his part, while insisting that 'many of the more striking incidents are actual matters of fact', Morrison also assured his correspondent Priest that equally 'there are matters which I have considerably toned down'. More damagingly, others saw Morrison's achievement in the book as vitiated by echoes between his text and Father Arthur Osborne Jay's earlier writings about his Shoreditch parish (see Explanatory Notes). Here contributors to the argument about the 'truth' of Morrison's realism found a labyrinth of issues to discuss in which the same piece of evidence might from one perspective provide corroboration of the author's 'accuracy', yet from another demonstrate barefaced 'plagiarism' of Father Jay's writings. It was certainly ironic that the novelist George Gissing should have accused Jay of plagiarizing Gissing's novel *The Nether World*, that others should then have accused Morrison of plagiarizing Jay, and that Gissing should then have read *A Child of the Jago* and have judged it 'poor stuff'. (Sour grapes, perhaps: Jay only courted Morrison to write up the Old Nichol after wooing Gissing and possibly the *Daily Telegraph*'s socially concerned journalist James Greenwood with the same object in mind. Gissing, indeed, had been planning a 'big book' on the subject.)

Debates over 'realism' in the nineteenth century were highly significant for estimates of the seriousness of novels as literary art. From the very beginning of the novel as a form, realism had been recognized as its defining characteristic; through the eighteenth and nineteenth centuries the rise in influence and authority of natural philosophy and the social sciences effectively worked to confirm and amplify the claim of realism to be the inevitable mode of representation and analysis of a responsible literature. Indeed, on such bases could be founded the claim of the realistic novel to approach the condition of a new moral science, particularly where notation of the causes or conditions of events tended towards a deterministic view of human behaviour. In reviews, Morrison's name was often associated with those of Balzac and Zola. Balzac had set himself the task of assembling through his novels a zoology of mankind. Zola compared the construction of a novel to the setting up of a scientific experiment: if the mechanics were correctly operated, conditions understood, and observations correctly taken, then the result would be not so much an entertainment as scientific knowledge of the sector of human life selected for investigation.

Although Morrison vigorously defended the truth of *A Child of the Jago* in terms of its accuracy of place, event, and persons, he himself resisted the artistic label of 'realist' and in part, there is room to conclude, because he knew better than the labellers. The reflections on Japanese art that preface *A Child of the Jago* reveal him distrustful of any monolithic concept of realism, acutely aware of realisms and concerned to see them, in effect, as matters of cultural history, cultural politics, and cultural relativity. In short, Morrison knew that one man's realism, as an artistic mode, was another man's stylization—a truth inevitably distilled from the cross-cultural contexts into which his artistic interests led him. Over the years, his preface to *A Child of the Jago* (especially in its version as the essay 'What is a Realist?') has been criticized for failing to develop a strong, coherent theory of realism. Yet the terms of his resistance to providing one are interesting because they suggest just how far he was from being a naive realist and how uneasy he may have been about the danger of locking himself into a commitment to such a mode. In his essay 'Whitechapel' he referred affectionately to *A Journal of the Plague Year* and referred to its author as that 'realistic old deceiver De Foe'.

Undoubtedly he used the term 'deceiver' to highlight the element of hoax in Defoe's book (which represented itself as an eyewitness account of the Great Plague of 1665); yet to see Morrison playing with a concept of 'realistic deception' is to see him moving beyond a commitment to mere 'realism'. In this context it becomes less surprising that in 'Whitechapel' Morrison should also allude to Beaumont and Fletcher's self-conscious play *The Knight of the Burning Pestle*, and that at one point in his sketch 'Christmas Eve in the Streets' he declares 'We *will* have our Christmas Eve frosted; there shall be snow on the roofs, but a dry, swept, pavement; enough snows in the corners to make an occasional snowball of, but no more because more in London gets dirty and sludgy. Our Christmas Eve is an ideal one, and we will not have bad weather on Christmas Eve when we can get good.' The Jago was real enough for those who knew the Old Nichol to recognize it; but as the product of the pen of a realistic deceiver who could change the weather on Christmas Eve, the Jago was also decidedly of Morrison's own making.

Social Politics

A Child of the Jago was not written to draw attention to the Old Nichol slum as a specific social issue waiting to be dealt with; indeed, by the time the novel was published the Old Nichol had virtually disappeared, transformed into the Boundary Street Estate—just as, in Morrison's novel, the Jago is beginning to disappear in the same manner. Morrison was certainly interested in the general question of where responsibility lay for the generation of such slums and in his preface he presented his position clearly:

> If the community have left horrible places and horrible lives [. . .] then the fault is the community's [. . .] For the existence of this place, and for the evils it engendered, the community was, and is responsible; so that every member of the community was, and is, responsible to his degree. (p. 5)

In effect, the 'community', in the form of the London County Council, did indeed take responsibility. Morrison's sense of communal responsibility, however, did not lead him towards socialism: his satirical short story 'The Rodd Street Revolution' (in his 1909 collection *Green Ginger*) makes that entirely evident. And except where the incompletely formed child is concerned, Morrison did not view the underclass with the eyes of a victimologist. For his own part Morrison valued 'firmness' over what he called 'false sentiment' in dealing with members of the underclass. While capable of expressing regret for their lack of 'a decent chance in life', he believed that in the main they would continue to have none. The ironic tone in his representation of their lifestyle, values, intellectual limitations, and moral failings frequently reveals distaste and also a deep scepticism towards possibilities of their amendment, rehabilitation, or redemption. Environment and heredity had done their work and—at a fundamental level—those factors were not to be undone. Alan Sillitoe, author of *Saturday Night and Sunday Morning*, took this judgement to the extreme of declaring that Morrison 'wrote from too far above his characters: they lived in a zoo, and were to be regarded with fear, hostility, and derision'.[15] This may be too hard, but as the conversation between Father Sturt and the Surgeon in Chapter 28 indicates, Morrison's ideal of communal responsibility for the 'horrible lives' of the underclass extended

[15] Alan Sillitoe, 'Introduction', in Robert Tressell, *The Ragged Trousered Philanthropists* (London, 1965), 7–10, at 8.

beyond the role of such as Father Jay to proposals concerning emigration, penal settlements, eugenic apartheid, and other constraints on their reproduction: any lasting solution, he thought, giving the last word to heredity, needed to be not just social and environmental but eugenic. 'Let the weed', Morrison chillingly maintained, 'die out'; only then can we 'raise the raisable' (Appendix, p. 172). Later, he softened his terms, talking instead more like the Salvation Army's General Booth in his study *In Darkest England and the Way Out* (1890), of transportation to a colony where the inhabitants might have any luxuries they wished. However, there is no trace of his endorsement of the principle of segregation having altered, a principle whereby slum-dwellers would cease to be a danger to the community by propagating their kind. In the light of this alliance of fierce idealism with such expediency, the death of Dicky Perrott in Morrison's novel becomes double-edged, still moving to pity and underwriting liberal urges towards intervention, but in its disturbing status as dramatized euthanasia also raising ghosts for today's reader of more than one twentieth-century horror fuelled by misguided idealism. 'That is why I killed Dicky Perrott,' mused Morrison in December 1896, 'he could not escape from his environment, and had he lived, would have become perforce, as bad as his surroundings' (Appendix, p. 172).

For his part, of course, Morrison was on his way to escaping his environment. His own father had died when he was a boy and the situation of all his principal heroes—Dicky Perrott, Johnny May in *To London Town* (1899), and Stephen Kemp in *The Hole in the Wall* (1902)—echo that death and project the scale of the horror, isolation, and fear so induced in casting these boys' bereavements as occurring through the excesses of murder, or imprisonment and execution (what P. J. Keating called 'the wholesale slaughter of parents or parent figures'[16] in Morrison's fiction). The recurring patterns of these texts also project a composite mother figure, either absent or poorly equipped to deal with difficult times and the practical consequences of widowhood. And there is also a composite adolescent child unfairly suffering anxieties over money and over the survival of the family. The early and notorious short story 'Lizerunt' from *Tales of Mean*

[16] P. J. Keating, 'Biographical Study', in Arthur Morrison, *A Child of the Jago*, ed. Keating (Woodbridge, 1969), 11–36, at 16.

Streets and *A Child of the Jago* figured the bleakest versions of that anxiety—ejection onto the windy street and the desperate lives of the prostitute and the street arab and the consequence, unstated or stated, of death. In 1899, however, *To London Town*, while portraying the same deep anxiety, also shows it being steadily overcome by a Johnny May who commits himself to work and the dignity of its skills, who courageously takes charge of family affairs, and who ultimately returns to the site of his grandfather's murder to confront what he now regards as the mundane nature of the event. In *The Hole in the Wall* the typical situation and fears are as ingrained as ever and crucially shape the consciousness of Stephen Kemp, but they are here romantically displaced into an adventure story. Through these works, in short, there is a progressive accommodation and finally a romanticizing of deep childhood insecurity. This unifying thread offers a psychological perspective on Morrison's rather awkward retrospective trilogization of *Tales of Mean Streets*, *A Child of the Jago*, and *To London Town*. The graph of that accommodation of insecurity through those books runs in parallel to the literary success and the social rise of Arthur Morrison himself, leaving one, however, with the paradox that Morrison evidently felt that others could not do what he was himself doing. Poplar was not the Jago; the son of a skilled engine-fitter was not the same as the son of a petty thief and ne'er-do-well; the working class were not the underclass of the worst corners of the Old Nichol. Not everyone had Morrison's work ethic, energy, ambition, or talent. He was not 'hopeless'. These may have been some of the considerations that caused Morrison to draw such a sharp line between his own experience and trajectory in life and those of the inhabitants of the Old Nichol. They, perhaps, after his father's death, were what he had most feared becoming. If so, the Jago needs to be recognized as a domain of the imagination as much as a journalist's transcript of reality: the labyrinth, in part, of an anxious mind.

NOTE ON THE TEXT

THIS is a revised issue of an edition of *A Child of the Jago* previously published in 1996. The text follows the first book-form edition of the novel (London: Methuen, 1896). The text of Morrison's 'Preface' follows its first printing in the third edition (1897). Obvious mistakes have been corrected. Chapters have been so designated and their numbers modernized from Roman to Arabic. Some practices in punctuation (such as the use of a comma in association with a dash) have been modernized. Emendation has otherwise been light and principally directed towards maintaining the consistency of the first edition's compositorial and editorial practices. The original dedication and sketch-map have been retained.

SELECT BIBLIOGRAPHY

Biography

Keating, P. J., 'Biographical Study', in Arthur Morrison, *A Child of the Jago*, ed. Keating (Woodbridge, 1969).

Krzak, M., 'Preface', in Arthur Morrison, *Tales of Mean Streets*, ed. Krzak (Woodbridge, 1983).

Newens, S., *Arthur Morrison: The Novelist of Realism in East London and Essex* (Loughton, 2008).

Bibliography

Calder, R., 'Arthur Morrison: A Commentary with an Annotated Bibliography of Writings about Him', *English Literature in Transition (1880–1920)*, 28/3 (1985), 276–97.

Parrott, J., *Arthur Morrison (1863–1945): A Bibliography of First Editions* (Szeged, 2007).

Historical and Critical Works

Benvenuto, R., 'The Criminal and the Community: Defining Tragic Structure in *A Child of the Jago*', *English Literature in Transition (1880–1920)*, 31/2 (1988), 153–61.

Brome, V., *Four Realist Novelists* (London, 1965).

Colby, R. A., 'Oliver's Progeny—Some Unfortunate Foundlings', *Dickens Quarterly*, 4/2 (1987), 109–21.

Davies, G., 'Foreign Bodies: Images of the London Working Class at the End of the Nineteenth Century', *Literature and History*, 14/1 (Spring 1988), 64–77.

Fishman, W. J., *East End 1888: Life in a London Borough among the Labouring Poor* (London, 1988).

Fox, P., *Class Fictions: Shame and Resistance in the British Working-Class Novel, 1890–1940* (London, 1994).

Greenfield, J., 'Arthur Morrison's Sherlock Clone: Martin Hewitt, Victorian Values, and London Magazine Culture 1894–1903', *Victorian Periodicals Review*, 35 (2002), 18–36.

Hardy, A., 'Diagnosis, Death and Diet: The Case of London, 1750–1909', *Journal of Interdisciplinary History*, 18/3 (1988), 387–401.

Henkle, R., 'Morrison, Gissing and the Stark Reality', *Novel*, 25/3 (1992), 302–20.

Joyce, S., 'Castles in the Air: The People's Palace, Cultural Reformism, and the East End Working Class', *Victorian Studies*, 39/4 (1996), 513–38.

Keating, P. J., *The Working Classes in Victorian Fiction* (London, 1971).
——(ed.), *Into Unknown England 1866–1913* (London, 1976).
Kijinski, J. L., 'Ethnography in the East End: Native Customs and Colonial Solutions in *A Child of the Jago*', *English Literature in Transition (1880–1920)*, 37/4 (1994), 490–501.
Klaus, H. G. (ed.), *The Rise of Socialist Fiction 1880–1914* (London, 1987).
Krzak, M., 'Arthur Morrison's East End of London', in J.-P. Hulin and P. Coustillas (eds.), *Victorian Writers and the City* (Lille, 1979), 147–81.
Kumar, K., 'Versions of the Pastoral: Poverty and the Poor in English Fiction from the 1840s to the 1950s', *Journal of Historical Sociology*, 8/1 (1995), 1–37.
Ledger, S., 'In Darkest England: The Terror of Degeneration in *Fin de-Siècle* Britain', *Literature and History*, III, 4/2 (Autumn 1995), 71–86.
Le May, F., 'Memories of Bethnal Green', *East London Record*, 4 (1981), 30–5.
McCarthy, T. (ed.), *The Great Dock Strike 1889* (London, 1988).
Maynard, J., 'Arthur Morrison, the Floating World and the Pictorial Method in *A Child of the Jago*: Painters of the East', *English Literature in Transition (1880–1920)*, 51/1 (2008), 44–56.
Miles, P., 'Road Rage: Urban Trajectories and the Working Class', in E. Tabuteau and P. Laplace (eds.), *Cities on the Margin: On the Margin of Cities* (Paris, 2003), 43–62.
Pick, D., *Faces of Degeneration: A European Disorder* (Cambridge, 1986).
Pollock, G., '"With my own eyes": Fetishism, the Labouring Body and the Colour of its Sex', *Art History*, 17/3 (1994), 342–82.
Reed, J. S., 'Ritualism Rampant in East London—Anglo-Catholicism and the Urban Poor', *Victorian Studies*, 31/3 (1988), 375–403.
Ross, E., 'Not the Sort that Would Sit on the Doorstep—Respectability in Pre-World-War-I London Neighbourhoods', *International Labour and Working-Class History*, 27 (1985), 39–59.
Samuel, R. (ed.), *East End Underworld: Chapters in the Life of Arthur Harding* (London, 1981). Extracts from recordings of Arthur Harding's memories are available at the Bishopsgate Institute website: <http://www.bishopsgate.org.uk>.
Schwarzbach, F. S., 'Terra Incognita—An Image of the City in English Literature, 1820–1855', in P. Dodd (ed.), *The Art of Travel: Essays on Travel-Writing* (London, 1982), 61–84.
Smith, T. H., 'Re-Readings 2: The Jago', *East London Papers*, 2/1 (1959), 39–47.
Stoll, R. H., 'The Unthinkable Poor in Edwardian Writing', *Mosaic: A Journal for the Interdisciplinary Study of Literature*, 15/4 (1982), 23–45.

Swafford, K. R., 'Translating the Slums: The Coding of Criminality and the Grotesque in Arthur Morrison's *A Child of the Jago*', *Journal of the Midwest Modern Language Association*, 35 (2002), 50–64.

White, A., 'The City: the Sewer, the Gaze and the Contaminating Touch', in A. White and P. Stallybrass, *The Politics and Poetics of Transgression* (London, 1986), 125–48.

Wiener, M. J., *Reconstructing the Criminal: Culture, Law, and Policy in England, 1890–1913* (Cambridge, 1990).

Wise, S., *The Blackest Streets: The Life and Death of a Victorian Slum* (London, 2008).

Sources from the Period

Besant, W., *East London* (London, 1899).

——*As We Are and As We May Be* (London, 1903).

Booth, B. (ed.), *Essays and Sketches: The Salvation Army* (London, 1906).

Booth, W., *In Darkest England and the Way Out* (London, 1890).

Cornford, L. C., 'The Work of Mr Arthur Morrison', in H. Morrah (ed.), *The Literary Year-Book and Bookman's Directory 1900* (London, 1900), 84–5.

Findlater, J., 'The Slum Movement in Fiction', *National Review*, 35 (1900), 447–54.

Jay, A. O., *Life in Darkest London: With a Hint to General Booth* (London, 1891).

——*The Social Problem and Its Possible Solution* (London, 1893).

——*A Story of Shoreditch: A Sequel to Life in Darkest London* (London, 1896).

H. B. N., *Penal Servitude* (London, 1903).

Sturt, G., *A Small Boy in the Sixties* (1927; repr. 1982).

Further Reading in Oxford World's Classics

Arnold, Matthew, *Culture and Anarchy*, ed. Jane Garnett.

Dickens, Charles, *Oliver Twist*, ed. Kathleen Tillotson, introduction and notes by Stephen Gill.

Gissing, George, *The Nether World*, ed. Stephen Gill.

Mayhew, Henry, *London Labour and the London Poor*, ed. Robert Douglas-Fairhurst.

Tressell, Robert, *The Ragged Trousered Philanthropists*, ed. Peter Miles.

A CHRONOLOGY OF ARTHUR MORRISON

1863 Arthur Morrison born in Poplar, London (Nov.); his father George an engine-fitter in the docks.

1867 Second Reform Bill, enfranchising a million urban workers. Holy Trinity parish, Shoreditch, created.

1868 Disraeli becomes prime minister; succeeded by Gladstone.
Matthew Arnold, *Culture and Anarchy*

1870 Forster's Education Act; death of Dickens.

1871 George Morrison dies from tuberculosis, leaving his wife Jane with Arthur and two other children. Suppression of Paris Commune; trade unions legalized.
Charles Darwin, *The Descent of Man*
E. B. Tylor, *Primitive Culture*

1872 Charles Loring Brace, *The Dangerous Classes of New York*

1873 David Livingstone dies in Africa.
Zola, *The Belly of Paris*

1874 Disraeli's new ministry promotes slum clearance and public health; Factory Act establishes fifty-six-and-a-half-hour week; modern bicycle invented. Morrison's adolescence spent in the East End.

1875 Octavia Hill, *Homes of the London Poor*

1877 Outbreak of Russo-Turkish War.

1879 Morrison begins work as office boy in the Architect's Department of the London School Board at seven shillings a week. He later recalls, possibly at this period, frequenting second-hand bookshops in the Whitechapel Road.

1880 Morrison's mother takes over haberdasher's shop in Grundy Street; Morrison's first publication—humorous verse in the magazine *Cycling*. Subsequently contributes to various cycling journals; engages in boxing and cycling. Later recalls, possibly at this period, holidays in Essex in company with John Louis Wimbush.
George Gissing, *Workers in the Dawn*
Zola, *Nana*

1882 Society for Psychical Research founded.
Walter Besant, *All Sorts and Conditions of Men*
R. A. Woods, 'The University Settlement Idea', in *Philanthropy and Social Progress*

1883 Fabian Society founded.
Alfred Alsop, *Street Children Sought and Found, and Other Stories*
Andrew Mearns, *The Bitter Cry of Outcast London*
George Sims, *How the Poor Live*

1884 Third Reform Act extends vote to many rural workers; Socialist League founded; Royal Commission on Housing; Edwin Chadwick, pioneer of housing and sanitation reform, knighted.
Gissing, *The Unclassed*

1885 Morrison's first serious journalism, in the *Globe*. Death of General Gordon at Khartoum.
Alsop, *Below the Surface: or, Down in the Slums, by A. Delver*
Eleanor Grundy, *Life below the Surface; Being the True Incidents of Child Life in the Slums of Manchester*
Rider Haggard, *King Solomon's Mines*
Zola, *Germinal*

1886 Having risen to 'junior' and then 'third-class clerk', Morrison appointed secretary to the Beaumont Trustees, the body administering the People's Palace (Sept.); in charge of social and educational facilities. Pall Mall and Trafalgar Square riots; Colonial and Indian Exhibition.
Gissing, *Demos: A Story of English Socialism*
Thomas Hardy, *The Mayor of Casterbridge*

1887 Arthur Osborne Jay takes up parish duties in Shoreditch and the Old Nichol.
Queen Victoria opens the People's Palace. 'Bloody Sunday' rioting in Trafalgar Square broken up by the Lifeguards. Queen Victoria's Golden Jubilee.
Arthur Conan Doyle, *A Study in Scarlet*
Margaret Harkness, *A City Girl: A Realistic Story*

1888 Morrison obtains reader's ticket to British Museum. Contributes thirteen sketches entitled 'Cockney Corners' to the *People* on such districts as Poplar, Soho, Clerkenwell, Bow Street, Whitechapel, Jacob's Island, Greenwich Park, and Epping Forest: describes markets, trades, the condition of the unemployed and the ill. Jack the Ripper murders in Whitechapel continue into 1889. London Matchgirls' Strike.
Harkness, *Out of Work*

1889 Morrison becomes subeditor of *Palace Journal*; reprints such pieces as 'Whitechapel' (Apr.), 'On Blackwall Pier' (May), and 'Christmas Eve in the Streets' (Dec.); subeditorials commenting on books, pictures, critical taste, and urging membership of the Literary Society.

Writes of the suffering of the poor. Gas Workers' Strike wins eight-hour working day. Great Dock Strike, inspiring Morrison's story 'Without Visible Means'. Imprisonment of Vizetelly, Zola's English publisher.
Charles Booth, *East London*, 1-vol. version of *Life and Labour of the People in London*
Gissing, *The Nether World*
Harkness, *Captain Lobe*, reissued in 1891 as *In Darkest London*
George Sims, *Horrible London*

1890 Resigns (from 30 Sept.) from People's Palace. Joins editorial staff of the evening *Globe*; takes lodgings in the Strand. Subsequently free-lances, publishing another short story in the *People*. His friend Harold Parlett goes to the British Embassy in Japan and later helps Morrison acquire paintings. London's first underground railway line.
William Booth, *In Darkest England and the Way Out*
Rudyard Kipling, 'The Record of Badalia Herodsfoot' in *Harper's Weekly*
W. M. Stanley, *In Darkest Africa*
Jacob Riis, *How the Other Half Lives: Studies among the Tenements of New York*

1891 Morrison's first book, *The Shadows around Us*: narratives of the supernatural originally published in the *People*. Contributes 'A Street' to *Macmillan's* (Oct.).
Booth, *Life and Labour of the People in London* (2 vols.)
Gissing, *New Grub Street*
Hardy, *Tess of the d'Urbervilles*
Revd A. O. M. Jay, *Life in Darkest London: A Hint to General Booth*

1892 Collaborates with illustrator J. A. Shepherd on 'My Neighbours' Dogs' and other animal sketches for the *Strand*. Marries Elizabeth Thatcher at Forest Gate (Aug.). They live at Chingford and then Salcombe House, Loughton, Essex. Success of 'The Legend of Lapwater Hall' (ghost story) in *Macmillan's*. W. E. Henley, editor of the *National Observer* and continuing friend, provides an outlet for more stories of working-class life (to 1894); Morrison joins Kipling, Barrie, Hardy, Wells, and Yeats as one of Henley's 'Regatta' of writers.
Booth, *Life and Labour of the People in London* (9 vols., to 1897)
Doyle, The *Adventures of Sherlock Holmes*

1893 Guy Morrison born. Jay, *The Social Problem and Its Possible Solution*. Gissing accuses Jay of plagiarizing *The Nether World* in *The Social Problem*. Independent Labour Party formed.

Robert Blatchford, *Merrie England*
Stephen Crane, *Maggie: A Girl of the Streets*
Benjamin Orange Flower, *Civilization's Inferno: Studies in the Social Cellar*

1894 First Martin Hewitt detective story, 'The Lenten Croft Robberies', appears in the *Strand* (Mar.). Two working-class stories published in *Pall Mall Budget* (Aug.–Sept.). With some revision and addition of 'The Red Cow Group', *Tales of Mean Streets* collects these and most of the sketches from the *National Observer*; published 25 Nov. and dedicated to Henley. Removed from Clerkenwell Library by local authorities; W. H. Smith temporarily refuse to supply it to circulating libraries; Morrison later writes of it having been 'banned'. Also publishes *Martin Hewitt, Investigator* and *Zig-Zags at the Zoo*. Jay invites Gissing to visit him in Shoreditch. Anarchist attack at Greenwich.
George Moore, *Esther Waters*

1895 *Bookman* publishes interview (Jan.). Writes to *Spectator* (Mar.) about reviewers' over-reaction to 'Lizerunt'. Revd Jay writes letter of appreciation; invites Morrison to visit the Old Nichol. Morrison's interest in Japanese art grows. Publishes *Chronicles of Martin Hewitt*. Gissing visits Jay and sees 'his way to a big book'. LCC Boundary Street Scheme demolishing Old Nichol. Jay invites Gissing to opening of new church.
Crane, *The Red Badge of Courage*
Hardy, *Jude the Obscure*
H. W. Nevinson, *Neighbours of Ours: Slum Stories of London*

1896 Begins writing up *A Child of the Jago* (Apr.); published by Methuen (Nov.) after part-serialization (chs. 1–13) in Henley's *New Review*; published in USA. Also publishes *Adventures of Martin Hewitt*. Jacob Riis, great American social commentator, reviews *Tales of Mean Streets* in *Book Buyer*. 'How Realistic Fiction is Written' appears anonymously in *St James's Gazette* (Dec.), claiming plagiarism of Jay's *Life in Darkest London*; Jay defends Morrison in *Gazette*; 'C.R.' similarly defends Morrison in the *Academy*. *Daily News* publishes interview (Dec.). Jay interviewed for *London* under the headline 'To Check the Survival of the Fittest'. First English edn. (with bowdlerized title) of Crane's *Maggie: A Child of the Streets.*
Jay, *A Story of Shoreditch: Being a Sequel to 'Life in Darkest London'*
Wells, *The Island of Dr Moreau*

1897 Harold Boulton reviews *Jago* in *British Review* (Jan.). Second edition of *Jago*. H. D. Traill's 'The New Realism' (*Fortnightly Review*) attacks 'extraordinary unreality' of *Jago*. Jay responds in *Fortnightly* (Feb.) but Traill extends attack in *The New Fiction and Other Essays*.

Morrison completes 'What is a Realist?' for *New Review* (Feb.–Mar.), subsequently adapted as preface to third edition of *Jago*. Publishes *The Dorrington Deed-Box* (detective stories). Tauchnitz issues *Jago*.
Joseph Conrad, *The Nigger of the Narcissus*
Somerset Maugham, *Liza of Lambeth*
Bram Stoker, *Dracula*

1899 Publishes *To London Town* as completion of trilogy begun with *Mean Streets* and *Jago*. Anglo-Boer War begins.
W. Besant, *East London*
Blatchford, *Dismal England*
Clarence Rook, *The Hooligan Nights*
Conrad, *Heart of Darkness* (serial)

1900 Publishes *Cunning Murrell*.
Blatchford, 'On Realism', in his *My Favourite Books*

1901 'A Workman's Budget' (Apr.) in *Cornhill* and 'Hooliganism' in *Pall Mall*. Queen Victoria dies; accession of Edward VII.
S. Rowntree, *Poverty: A Study of Town Life*

1902 Publishes *The Hole in the Wall*; also series of articles on Japanese art in *Monthly Review*. Fourth edition of *Jago*. Anglo-Boer War ends; Jack London visits East End; death of Zola.
Booth, *Life and Labour of the People in London* (17 vols.)
C. F. G. Masterman, *From the Abyss*

1903 Publishes *The Red Triangle* (short stories).
Besant, *As We Are and As We May Be*
Jack London, *The People of the Abyss*
H.B.N., *Penal Servitude*
Pett Ridge, *Up Side Streets*

1904 Publishes *The Green Eye of Goona: Stories of a Case of Tokay* (as *The Green Diamond* in USA); also successful one-act play version of 'That Brute Simmons' from *Mean Streets*, in collaboration with Herbert C. Sargent. Russo-Japanese War begins.

1905 Publishes *Divers Vanities* (short stories). First Russian Revolution; Russia defeated by Japan.

1906 Sells collection of Japanese woodcuts to British Museum. Liberal election victory; Labour electoral successes.
Bramwell Booth (ed.), *Essays and Sketches: The Salvation Army*
Upton Sinclair, *The Jungle*

1907 Morrison's one-act play *A Stroke of Business* is well received. Another, *The Dumb-Cake*, published; an adaptation in collaboration with Richard Pryce from *Divers Vanities*.
Conrad, *The Secret Agent*

1909 Publishes *Green Ginger* (short stories). Old age pension introduced.
E. M. Forster, *Howards End*
Masterman, *The Condition of England*

1910 Parlett made Consul at Dairen. Death of Edward VII; accession of George V.
Wells, *The History of Mr Polly*

1911 Publishes the authoritative *Painters of Japan*, 2 vols., largely illustrated with paintings in his own collection. *Jago* reaches sixth edition. Liberal Government brings in national unemployment and medical insurance.
Sidney Webb, *The Prevention of Destitution*

1913 Retires from journalism; moves to 'Arabins' in High Beech, near Epping; continues interest in art collecting and dealing.
D. H. Lawrence, *Sons and Lovers*

1914 Outbreak of First World War: Guy Morrison serves in army. Morrison's collection of Japanese art bought by Sir Watkin Gwynne Evans (for £4,000) and presented to British Museum; publication of *Guide to an Exhibition of Japanese and Chinese Paintings Principally from the Arthur Morrison Collection* and *Exhibition of Japanese Screens Decorated by Old Masters, Held at the Galleries of the Royal Society of British Artists, January 26th to February 26th, 1914.*
Robert Tressell, *The Ragged Trousered Philanthropists*

1915 Morrison acting as special constable in Essex, credited with telephoning news of the first Zeppelin raid on London. Gallipoli.
Lawrence, *The Rainbow*

1916 Contributes commentary to propaganda edition of *Raemaekers's Cartoons*. Battles of Verdun and Somme.

1918 First World War ends in Armistice; women over 30 and men over 21 obtain the vote.

1921 Guy Morrison dies from malaria at his parents' home in Cavendish Square, London. Marie Stopes founds first birth-control clinic.

1922 Mussolini comes to power in Italy.
T. S. Eliot, *The Waste Land*
James Joyce, *Ulysses*

1924 Morrison elected member of Royal Society of Literature. Ramsay MacDonald becomes first Labour prime minister.

1925 Stanley Baldwin heads Conservative government.

1926 General Strike.
Mrs Cecil Chesterton, *In Darkest London*
Franz Kafka, *The Castle*

1928 Women aged 21 and over obtain the vote.

1929 Publication of retrospective volume by Morrison in *Short Stories of Today and Yesterday* series. Wall Street Crash.
Ernest Hemingway, *A Farewell to Arms*

1930 Moves to final home, 'High Barn', Chalfont St Peter, Buckinghamshire.

1933 Publishes *Fiddle O'Dreams and More* (short stories). Hitler becomes Chancellor of Germany; first concentration camps.
Walter Greenwood, *Love on the Dole*
George Orwell, *Down and Out in Paris and London*

1935 Morrison elected to Council of Royal Society of Literature.
Walter Brierley, *Means Test Man*
A. J. Cronin, *The Stars Look Down*

1936 Presents manuscript of *Jago* to Bethnal Green Library. Spanish Civil War begins. Battle of Cable Street in East End. George V dies; Edward VIII succeeds and abdicates; accession of George VI.

1937 Orwell, *The Road to Wigan Pier*
Wal Hannington, *The Problem of the Distressed Areas*

1939 Germany invades Poland; outbreak of Second World War.
John Steinbeck, *The Grapes of Wrath*

1940 Germany invades Denmark and Norway; Battle of Britain; Blitz begins, particularly affecting East End.

1942 Beveridge Report, laying foundations of Welfare State.
Evelyn Waugh, *Put Out More Flags*

1945 Second World War ends. Arthur Morrison dies (Dec.). His will bequeaths 140 Japanese paintings and woodcuts and collection of tea ceremony porcelain to British Museum. He directs his library to be sold and his notebooks and papers to be burned.

A CHILD OF THE JAGO

TO

ARTHUR OSBORNE JAY

VICAR OF HOLY TRINITY, SHOREDITCH

PREFACE TO THE THIRD EDITION*

I AM glad to take this, the first available opportunity, to acknowledge the kindness with which *A Child of the Jago* has been received: both by the reading public, from which I have received many gratifying assurances that what I have tried to say has not altogether failed of its effect: and by the reviewers, the most of whom have written in very indulgent terms.

I think indeed, that I am the more gratified by the fact that this reception has not been unanimous: because an outcry and an opposition, even from an unimportant minority, are proofs that I have succeeded in saying, however imperfectly, something that was worth being said. Under the conditions of life as we know it there is no truth worth telling that will not interfere with some hearer's comfort. Various objections have been made to *A Child of the Jago*, and many of them had already been made to *Tales of Mean Streets*. And it has been the way of the objectors as well as the way of many among the kindest of my critics, to call me a 'realist'. The word has been used sometimes, it would seem, in praise; sometimes in mere indifference as one uses a phrase of convenient description; sometimes by way of an irremediable reproach. It is natural, then, not merely that I should wish to examine certain among the objections made to my work, but that I should feel some interest in the definition and description of a realist. A matter never made clear to me.

Now it is a fact that I have never called myself a 'realist', and I have never put forth any work as 'realism'. I decline the labels of the schoolmen and the sophisters: being a simple writer of tales, who takes whatever means lie to his hand to present life as he sees it; who insists on no process; and who refuses to be bound by any formula or prescription prepared by the cataloguers and the pigeon-holers of literature.

So it happens that when those who use the word 'realist' use it with no unanimity of intent and with a loose, inapprehensive application, it is not easy for me, who repudiate it altogether, to make a guess at its meaning. Nevertheless, it seems to me that the man who is called a 'realist' is one who, seeing things with his own eyes, discards the conventions of the schools, and presents his matter in individual terms of art. For a while the schoolmen abuse him as a realist; and in twenty years' time, if his work have life in it, he becomes a classic. Constable* was called a realist; so was Corot.* Who calls these painters realists now? The history of Japanese art affords a continuous illustration. From the day when Iwasa Matahei* impudently arose and dared to take his subjects from the daily life of the people, to the day when Hiroshigé,* casting away the last rag of propriety, adventurously drew a cast shadow, in flat defiance of all the canons of Tosa and Kano*—in all this time, and through all the crowded history of the School of Ukioyé,* no artist bringing something of his own to his art but was damned for a realist. Even the classic Harunobu* did not escape. Look now at the work of these men, and the label seems grotesque enough. So it goes through the making of all art. A man with the courage of his own vision interprets what he sees in fresh terms, and gives to things a new reality and an immediate presence. The schoolmen peer with dulled eyes from amid the heap of precedents and prescriptions about them, and, distracted by seeing a thing sanctioned neither by precedent nor by prescription, dub the man realist, and rail against him for that his work fits none of their pigeon-holes. And from without the schools many cry out and complain: for truth is strong meat, and the weakling stomach turns against it, except in minim doses smothered in treacle. Thus we hear the feeble plea that the function of imagination is the distortion of fact: the piteous demand that the artist should be shut up in a flower-garden,* and forbidden to peep through the hedge into the world. And they who know nothing of beauty, who are innately incapable of comprehending it, mistake it for mere prettiness, and call aloud for comfits; and among them that cannot understand, such definitions of the aims of art are bandied, as mean, if they mean anything, that art finds its most perfect expression in pink lollipops and gilt boxes. But in the end the truth prevails, if it be well set forth; and the schoolmen, groaning in their infinite labour, wearily write another prescription, admit another precedent, and make another pigeon-hole.

I have been asked, in print,* if I think that there is no phase of life which the artist may not touch. Most certainly I think this. More, I know it. It is the artist's privilege to seek his material where he pleases, and it is no man's privilege to say him nay. If the community have left horrible places and horrible lives before his eyes, then the fault is the community's; and to picture these places and these lives becomes not merely his privilege, but his duty. It was my fate to encounter a place in Shoreditch, where children were born and reared in circumstances which gave them no reasonable chance of living decent lives: where they were born fore-damned to a criminal or semi-criminal career. It was my experience to learn the ways of this place, to know its inhabitants, to talk with them, eat, drink, and work with them. For the existence of this place, and for the evils it engendered, the community was, and is, responsible; so that every member of the community was, and is, responsible in his degree. If I had been a rich man I might have attempted to discharge my peculiar responsibility in one way; if I had been a statesman I might have tried another. Being neither of these things, but a mere writer of fiction, I sought to do my duty by writing a tale wherein I hoped to bring the conditions of this place within the apprehension of others. There are those who say that I should have turned away my eyes and passed by on the other side: on the very respectable precedent of the priest and the Levite* in the parable.

Now, when the tale was written and published it was found, as I have said, to cause some discomfort to some persons. It is needless to say more of the schoolmen. Needless, too, to say much of the merely genteel: who were shocked to read of low creatures, as Kiddo Cook and Pigeony Poll, and to find my pages nowhere illuminated by a marquis. Of such are they who delight to read of two men in velvet and feathers perforating each other's stomachs with swords; while Josh Perrott and Billy Leary, punching each other's heads, present a scene too sickening and brutal to consider without disgust. And it was in defiance of the maunderings of such as these that Charles Lamb wrote much of his essay *On the Genius and Character of Hogarth*.* But chiefly this book of mine disturbed those who had done nothing, and preferred to do nothing, by way of discharging their responsibility toward the Jago and the people in it. The consciousness of duty neglected is discomforting, and personal comfort is the god of their kind. They firmly believe it to be the sole function of art to minister to their personal comfort—as upholstery does. They find it comfortable to shirk consideration of the fate of the Jago children, to shut their eyes to it, to say that all is well and the whole world virtuous and happy. And this mental attitude they nickname optimism, and vaunt it—exult in it as a quality. So that they cry out at the suggestion that it is no more than a selfish vice; and finding truth where they had looked for the materials of another debauch of self-delusion, they moan aloud: they protest, and they demand as their sacred right that the bitter cup be taken from before them. They have moaned and protested at *A Child of the Jago*, and, craven and bewildered, any protest seemed good enough to them. And herein they have not wanted for allies among them that sit in committee-rooms, and tinker. For your professed philanthropist, following his own spirit,* and seeing nothing, honestly resents the demonstration that his tinkering profits little. There is a story current in the East End of London, of a distracted lady who, being assailed with a request for the loan of a saucepan, defended herself in these words:—'Tell yer mother I can't lend 'er the saucepan, consekince o' 'avin' lent it to Mrs Brown, besides which I'm a-usin' of it meself, an' moreover it's gone to be mended, an' what's more I ain't got one.' In a like spirit of lavish objection* it has been proclaimed in a breath that I transgress:—because (1) I should not have written of the Jago in all the nakedness of truth; (2) my description is not in the least like; (3) moreover, it is exaggerated; (4) though it may be true, it is quite unnecessary, because the Jago was already quite familiar, and everybody knew all about it; (5) the Jago houses have been pulled down; and (6) there never was any such place as the Jago at all.

To objections thus handsomely variegated it is not easy to reply with the tripping brevity wherewith they may be stated; and truly it is little reply that they call for, except, perhaps, in so far as they may be taken to impugn the sincerity of my work and the accuracy of my picture. A few of the objectors have caught up enough of their wits to strive after a war in my own country. They take hold of my technical method, and accuse me of lack of 'sympathy';* they claim that if I write of the Jago I should do so 'even weeping'. Now, my technical method is my own, and is deliberately designed to achieve a certain result, as is the method of every man—painter, poet, sculptor, or novelist—who is not the slave and the plaything of his material. My tale is the tale of my characters, and I have learned better than to thrust myself and my emotions between them and my reader. The cant of the charge stares all too plainly from the face of it. It is not that these good people wish me to write 'even weeping': for how do they know whether I weep or not? No: their wish is, not that I shall weep, but that I shall weep obscenely in the public gaze. In other words, that I shall do their weeping for them, as a sort of emotional bedesman: that I shall make public parade of sympathy in their behalf, so that they may keep their own sympathy for themselves, and win comfort from the belief that they are eased of their just responsibility by vicarious snivelling.

But the protest that my picture of the Jago is untrue, is another thing. For the most part it has found very vague expression, but there are instances of rash excursion into definiteness. Certain passages have been denoted as exaggerations—as impossibilities. Now, I must confess that, foreseeing such adventurous indiscretions, I had, for my own diversion, set *A Child of the Jago* with traps. For certain years I have lived in the East End of London, and have been, not an occasional visitor, but a familiar and equal friend in the house of the East-Ender in all his degrees; for, though the steps between be smaller, there are more social degrees in the East End than ever in the West. In this experience I have seen and I have heard things that persons sitting in committee-rooms would call diabolical fable; nevertheless, I have seen them, and heard them. But it was none of my design to write of extreme instances: typical facts were all I wanted; these, I knew, would be met—or shirked—with incredulity; so that, whenever I saw reason to anticipate a charge of exaggeration—as for instance, in the matter of faction fighting—I made my typical incident the cold transcript of a simple fact, an ordinary, easy-going fact, a fact notorious in the neighbourhood, and capable of any amount of reasonable proof. If I touched my fact at all, it was to subdue it; that and no more. The traps worked well. Not one definite charge of exaggeration has been flung but it has been aimed at one of the normal facts I had provided as a target: not one. Sometimes the effect has had a humour of its own; as when a critic in a literary journal, beginning by selecting two of my norms as instances of 'palpable exaggeration',* went on to assure me that there was no need to describe such life as the life in the Jago, because it was already perfectly familiar to everybody.

Luckily I need not vindicate my accuracy. That has been done for me publicly by independent and altogether indisputable authority. In particular, the devoted vicar of the parish, which I have called the Jago, has testified* quite unreservedly to the truth of my presentation. Others also, with special knowledge,* have done the same; and though I refer to them, and am grateful for their support, it is with no prejudice to the validity of my own authority. For not only have

I lived in the East End of London (which one may do, and yet never see it) but observation is my trade.

I have remarked in more than one place the expression of a foolish fancy that because the houses of the Old Jago have been pulled down, the Jago difficulty has been cleared out of the way. That is far from being the case. The Jago, as mere bricks and mortar, is gone.* But the Jago in flesh and blood still lives, and is crowding into neighbourhoods already densely over-populated.

In conclusion: the plan and the intention of my story made it requisite that, in telling it, I should largely adhere to fact; and I did so. If I write other tales different in scope and design, I shall adhere to fact or neglect it as may seem good to me: regardless of anybody's classification as a realist, or as anything else. For though I have made a suggestion, right or wrong, as to what a realist may be, whether I am one or not is no concern of mine; but the concern (if it be anybody's) of the tabulators and the watersifters.

A.M.

February 1897.

. . . Woe unto the foolish prophets, that follow their own spirit, and have seen nothing! . . .*

Because, even because they have seduced my people, saying, Peace; and there was no peace; and one built up a wall, and lo, others daubed it with untempered mortar:

Say unto them which daub it with untempered mortar, that it shall fall: there shall be an overflowing shower; and ye, O great hailstones, shall fall; and a stormy wind shall rend it.

Lo, when the wall is fallen, shall it not be said unto you, Where is the daubing wherewith ye have daubed it?

EZEKIEL xiii. 3 . . . 10–12.

The Old Jago

Sketch Plan.

CHAPTER 1

It was past the mid of a summer night in the Old Jago. The narrow street was all the blacker for the lurid sky; for there was a fire in a farther part of Shoreditch, and the welkin was an infernal coppery glare. Below, the hot, heavy air lay, a rank oppression, on the contorted forms of those who made for sleep on the pavement: and in it, and through it all, there rose from the foul earth and the grimed walls a close, mingled stink—the odour of the Jago.

From where, off Shoreditch High Street, a narrow passage, set across with posts,* gave menacing entrance on one end of Old Jago Street, to where the other end lost itself in the black beyond Jago Row; from where Jago Row began south at Meakin Street, to where it ended north at Honey Lane—there the Jago, for one hundred years the blackest pit in London,* lay and festered; and half way along Old Jago Street a narrow archway gave upon Jago Court, the blackest hole in all that pit.

A square of two hundred and fifty yards or less—that was all there was of the Jago. But in that square the human population swarmed in thousands. Old Jago Street, New Jago Street, Half Jago Street lay parallel, east and west: Jago Row at one end and Edge Lane at the other lay parallel also, stretching north and south: foul ways all. What was too vile for Kate Street, Seven Dials, and Ratcliff Highway in its worst day,* what was too useless, incapable and corrupt—all that teemed in the Old Jago.

Old Jago Street lay black and close under the quivering red sky; and slinking forms, as of great rats, followed one another quickly between the posts in the gut by the High Street, and scattered over the Jago. For the crowd about the fire was now small, the police was there in force, and every safe pocket had been tried. Soon the incursion ceased, and the sky, flickering and brightening no longer, settled to a sullen flush. On the pavement some writhed wearily, longing for sleep; others, despairing of it, sat and lolled, and a few talked. They were not there for lack of shelter, but because in this weather repose was less unlikely in the street than within doors: and the lodgings of the few who nevertheless abode at home were marked here and there by the lights visible from the windows. For in this place none ever slept without a light, because of three sorts of vermin that light in some sort keeps at bay: vermin which added to existence here a terror not to be guessed by the unafflicted: who object to being told of it. For on them that lay writhen and gasping on the pavement; on them that sat among them; on them that rolled and blasphemed in the lighted rooms; on every moving creature in this, the Old Jago, day and night, sleeping and walking,* the third plague of Egypt,* and more, lay unceasing.

The stifling air took a further oppression from the red sky. By the dark entrance to Jago Court a man rose, flinging out an oath, and sat with his head bowed in his hands.

'Ah—h—h—h,' he said. 'I wish I was dead: an' kep' a cawfy shop.'* He looked aside from his hands at his neighbours; but Kiddo Cook's* ideal of heaven was no new thing, and the sole answer was a snort from a dozing man a yard away.

Kiddo Cook felt in his pocket and produced a pipe and a screw of paper.* 'This is a bleed'n' unsocial sort o' evenin' party, this is,' he said. 'An' 'ere's the on'y real toff in the mob with 'ardly 'arf a pipeful left, an' no lights. D' y' 'ear, me lord'—leaning toward the dozing neighbour—'got a match?'

'Go t' 'ell!'

'O wot 'orrid langwidge! It's shocking, blimy.* Arter that y' ought to find me a match. Come on.'

'Go t' 'ell!'

A lank, elderly man, who sat with his back to the wall, pushed up a battered tall hat from his eyes, and, producing a box of matches, exclaimed 'Hell? And how far's that? You're in it!'* He flung abroad a bony hand, and glanced upward. Over his forehead a greasy black curl dangled and shook as he shuddered back against the wall. 'My God, there can be no hell after this!'

'Ah,' Kiddo Cook remarked, as he lit his pipe in the hollow of his hands, 'that's a comfort, Mr Beveridge, any'ow.' He returned the matches, and the old man, tilting his hat forward, was silent.

A woman, gripping a shawl about her shoulders, came furtively along from the posts, with a man walking in her tracks—a little unsteadily. He was not of the Jago, but a decent young workman, by his dress. The sight took Kiddo Cook's idle eye, and when the couple had passed, he said meditatively: 'There's Billy Leary in luck ag'in: 'is missis do pick 'em up, s'elp me. I'd carry the cosh meself if I'd got a woman like 'er.'

Cosh-carrying was near to being the major industry of the Jago. The cosh was a foot length of iron rod, with a knob at one end, and a hook (or a ring) at the other. The craftsman carrying it in his coat sleeve, waited about dark staircase corners till his wife (married or not)* brought in a well drunken stranger: when, with a sudden blow behind the head, the stranger was happily coshed, and whatever was found on him as he lay insensible was the profit on the transaction. In the hands of capable practitioners this industry yielded a comfortable subsistence for no great exertion. Most, of course, depended on the woman: whose duty it was to keep the other artist* going in subjects. There were legends of surprising ingatherings achieved by wives of especial diligence: one of a woman who had brought to the cosh some six-and-twenty on a night of public rejoicing. This was, however, a story years old, and may have been no more than an exemplary fiction designed, like a Sunday School book, to convey a counsel of perfection to the dutiful matrons* of the Old Jago.

The man and woman vanished in a doorway near the Jago Row end, where, for some reason, dossers were fewer than about the portal* of Jago Court. There conversation flagged, and a broken snore was heard. It was a quiet night, as quietness was counted in the Jago; for it was too hot for most to fight in that stifling air—too hot to do more than turn on the stones and swear. Still the last hoarse yelps of a combat of women came intermittently from Half Jago Street in the further confines.

In a little while something large and dark was pushed forth from the door-opening near Jago Row which Billy Leary's spouse had entered. The thing rolled over, and lay tumbled on the pavement, for a time unnoted. It might have been yet another would-be sleeper, but for its stillness. Just such a thing it seemed, belike, to two that lifted their heads and peered from a few yards off, till they rose on hands and knees and crept to where it lay: Jago rats both. A man it was; with a thick smear across his face, and about his head the source of the dark trickle that sought the gutter deviously over the broken flags. The drab stuff of his pockets peeped out here and there in a crumpled bunch, and his waistcoat gaped where the watch-guard had been. Clearly, here was an uncommonly remunerative cosh—a cosh so good that the boots had been neglected, and remained on the man's feet. These the kneeling two unlaced deftly, and, rising, prize in hand, vanished in the deeper shadow of Jago Row.

A small boy, whom they met full tilt at the corner, staggered out to the gutter and flung a veteran curse after them. He was a slight child, by whose size you might have judged his age at five. But his face was of serious and troubled age. One who knew the children of the Jago, and could tell, might have held him eight, or from that to nine.

He replaced his hands in his trousers pockets, and trudged up the street. As he brushed by the coshed man he glanced again toward Jago Row, and, jerking his thumb that way, 'Done 'im for 'is boots,' he piped. But nobody marked him till he reached Jago Court, when old Beveridge, pushing back his hat once more, called sweetly and silkily, 'Dicky Perrott!' and beckoned with his finger.

The boy approached, and as he did so the man's skeleton hand suddenly shot out and gripped him by the collar. 'It—never—does—to—see—too—much!' Beveridge said, in a series of shouts, close to the boy's ear. 'Now go home,' he added, in a more ordinary tone, with a push to make his meaning plain: and straightway relapsed against the wall.

The boy scowled and backed off the pavement. His ragged jacket was coarsely made from one much larger, and he hitched the collar over his shoulder as he shrank toward a doorway some few yards on. Front doors were used merely as firewood* in the Old Jago, and most had been burnt there many years ago. If perchance one could have been found still on its hinges, it stood ever open and probably would not shut. Thus at night the Jago doorways were a row of black holes, foul and forbidding.

Dicky Perrott entered his hole with caution, for anywhere, in the passage and on the stairs, somebody might be lying drunk, against whom it would be unsafe to stumble. He found nobody, however, and climbed and reckoned his way up the first stair-flight with the necessary regard for the treads that one might step through and the rails that had gone from the side. Then he pushed open the door of the first-floor back* and was at home.

A little heap of guttering grease, not long ago a candle end, stood and spread on the mantelpiece, and gave irregular light from its drooping wick. A thin-railed iron bedstead, bent and staggering, stood against a wall, and on its murky coverings a half-dressed woman sat and neglected a baby that lay by her, grieving and wheezing. The woman had a long dolorous face, empty of expression and weak of mouth.*

'Where 'a' you bin, Dicky?' she asked, rather complaining than asking. 'It's sich low hours for a boy.'

Dicky glanced about the room. 'Got anythink to eat?' he asked.

'I dunno,' she answered listlessly. 'P'raps there's a bit o' bread in the cupboard. I don't want nothin', it's so 'ot. An' father ain't bin 'ome since tea-time.'

The boy rummaged and found a crust. Gnawing at this, he crossed to where the baby lay. ''Ullo, Looey,' he said, bending and patting the muddy cheek. ''Ullo!'

The baby turned feebly on its back, and set up a thin wail. Its eyes were large and bright, its tiny face was piteously flea-bitten and strangely old. 'Wy, she's 'ungry, mother,' said Dicky Perrott, and took the little thing up.

He sat on a small box, and rocked the baby on his knees, feeding it with morsels of chewed bread. The mother, dolefully inert, looked on and said: 'She's that backward I'm quite wore out; more 'n ten months old, an' don't even crawl yut. It's a never-endin' trouble, is children.'

She sighed, and presently stretched herself on the bed. The boy rose, and carrying his little sister with care, for she was dozing, essayed to look through the grimy window. The dull flush still spread overhead, but Jago Court lay darkling below, with scarce a sign of the ruinous back yards that edged it on this and the opposite sides, and nothing but blackness between.

The boy returned to his box, and sat. Then he said: 'I don't s'pose father's 'avin' a sleep outside, eh?'

The woman sat up with some show of energy. 'Wot?' she said sharply. 'Sleep out in the street like them low Ranns an' Learys? I should 'ope not. It's bad enough livin' 'ere at all, an' me being used to different things once, an' all. You ain't seen 'im outside, 'ave ye?'

'No, I ain't seen 'im: I jist looked in the court.' Then, after a pause: 'I 'ope 'e's done a click,'* the boy said.

His mother winced. 'I dunno wot you mean, Dicky,' she said, but falteringly. 'You—you're gittin' that low an' an'—'

'Wy, copped somethink, o' course. Nicked somethink. You know.'

'If you say sich things as that I'll tell 'im wot you say, an' 'e'll pay you. We ain't that sort o' people, Dicky, you ought to know. I was alwis kep' respectable an' straight all my life, I'm sure, an'—'

'I know. You said so before, to father—I 'eard: w'en 'e brought 'ome that there yuller prop—the necktie pin. Wy, where did 'e git that? 'E ain't 'ad a job for munse and munse: where's the yannups come from wot's bin for to pay the rent, an' git the toke, an' milk for Looey? Think I dunno? I ain't a kid. I know.'

'Dicky, Dicky! you mustn't say sich things!' was all the mother could find to say, with tears in her slack eyes. 'It's wicked an'—an' low. An' you must alwis be respectable an' straight, Dicky, an' you'll—you'll git on then.'

'Straight people's fools, *I* reckon. Kiddo Cook says that, an' 'e's as wide as Broad Street. W'en I grow up I'm goin' to git toffs' clo'es an' be in the 'igh mob. They does big clicks.'

'They git put in a dark prison for years an' years, Dicky—an'—an' if you're sich a wicked low boy, father'll give you the strap—'ard,' the mother returned, with what earnestness she might. 'Gimme the baby, an' you go to bed, go on; 'fore father comes.'

Dicky handed over the baby, whose wizen face was now relaxed in sleep, and slowly disencumbered himself of the ungainly jacket, staring at the wall in a brown study. 'It's the mugs wot git took,' he said, absently. 'An' quoddin' ain't so bad.' Then, after a pause, he turned and added suddenly: 'S'pose father'll be smugged some day, eh, mother?'

His mother made no reply, but bent languidly over the baby, with an indefinite pretence of settling it in a place on the bed. Soon Dicky himself, in the short and ragged shirt he had worn under the jacket, burrowed head first among the dingy coverings at the foot, and protruding his head at the further side, took his accustomed place crosswise at the extreme end.

The filthy ceiling lit and darkened by fits as the candle-wick fell and guttered to its end. He heard his mother rise and find another fragment of candle to light by its expiring flame, but he lay still wakeful. After a time he asked: 'Mother, why don't you come to bed?'

'Waitin' for father. Go to sleep.'

He was silent for a little. But brain and eyes were wide awake, and soon he spoke again. 'Them noo 'uns in the front room,' he said. 'Ain't the man give 'is wife a 'idin' yut?'

'No.'

'Nor yut the boy—'umpty-backed 'un?'

'No.'

'Seems they're mighty pertickler. Fancy theirselves too good for their neighbours; I 'eard Pigeony Poll say that; on'y Poll said—'

'You mustn't never listen to Pigeony Poll, Dicky. Ain't you 'eard me say so? Go to sleep. 'Ere comes father.' There was, indeed, a step on the stairs, but it passed the landing, and went on to the top floor. Dicky lay awake, but silent, gazing upward and back through the dirty window just over his head. It was very hot, and he fidgeted uncomfortably, fearing to turn or toss lest the baby should wake and cry. There came a change in the hue of the sky, and he watched the patch within his view, until the red seemed to gather in spots, and fade a spot at a time. Then at last there was a tread on the stairs, that stayed at the door; and father had come home. Dicky lay still, and listened.

'Lor, Josh, where ye bin?' Dicky heard his mother say. 'I'm almost wore out a-waitin'.'

'Awright, awright'—this in a hoarse grunt, little above a whisper. 'Got any water up 'ere? Wash this 'ere stick.'

There was a pause, wherein Dicky knew his mother looked about her in vacant doubt as to whether or not water was in the room. Then a quick, undertoned scream, and the stick rattled heavily on the floor. 'It's sticky!' his mother said. 'O my Gawd, Josh, look at that—an' bits o' 'air, too!' The great shadow of an open hand shot up across the ceiling and fell again. 'O Josh! O my Gawd! You ain't, 'ave ye? Not—not—not that?'

'Not wot? Gawblimy, not what? Shutcher mouth. If a man fights, you're got to fight back, ain' cher? Any one 'ud think it was a murder, to look at ye. I ain't sich a damn fool as that. 'Ere—pull up that board.'

Dicky knew the loose floor-board that was lifted with a slight groaning jar. It was to the right of the hearth, and he had shammed sleep when it had been lifted once before. His mother whimpered and cried quietly. 'You'll git in trouble, Josh,' she said. 'I wish you'd git a reg'lar job, Josh, like what you used—I do—I do.'

The board was shut down again. Dicky Perrott through one opened eye saw the sky a pale grey above, and hoped the click had been a good one: hoped also that it might bring bullock's liver for dinner.

Out in the Jago the pale dawn brought a cooler air and the chance of sleep. From the paving of Old Jago Street sad grey faces, open-mouthed, looked upward as from the Valley of Dry Bones.* Down by Jago Row the coshed subject, with the blood dry on his face, felt the colder air, and moved a leg.

CHAPTER 2

THREE-QUARTERS of a mile east of the Jago's outermost limit was the East End Elevation Mission and Pansophical Institute:* such was the amazing success whereof, that a new wing had been built, and was now to be declared open by a Bishop of great eminence and industry.

The triumphs of the East End Elevation Mission and Pansophical Institute were known and appreciated far from East London, by people who knew less of that part than of Asia Minor.* Indeed, they were chiefly appreciated by these. There were kept, perpetually on tap for the aspiring East Ender, the Higher Life, the Greater Thought, and the Wider Humanity: with other radiant abstractions, mostly in the comparative degree,* specifics all for the manufacture of the Superior Person. There were many Lectures given on still more subjects. Pictures* were borrowed and shown, with revelations to the Uninformed of the morals ingeniously concealed by the painters. The Uninformed were also encouraged to debate and to produce papers on literary and political matters, while still unencumbered with the smallest knowledge thereof: for the Enlargement of the Understanding and the Embellishment of the Intellect. And there were classes, and clubs, and newspapers, and games of draughts, and musical evenings,* and a brass band, whereby the life of the Hopeless Poor might be coloured, and the Misery of the Submerged* alleviated. The wretches who crowded to these benefits were tradesmen's sons, small shopkeepers* and their families, and neat clerks, with here and there a smart young artisan of one of the especially respectable trades. They freely patronised the clubs, the musical evenings, the brass band, and the bagatelle board;* and those who took themselves seriously debated and Mutually-Improved* with pomp. Others, subject to savage fits of wanting-to-know, made short rushes at random evening classes, with intervals of disgusted apathy. Altogether, a number of decently-dressed and mannerly young men passed many evenings at the Pansophical Institute in harmless pleasures, and often with an agreeable illusion of intellectual advance.

Other young men, more fortunately circumstanced, with the educational varnish fresh and raw upon them, came from afar, equipped with a foreign mode of thought and a proper ignorance of the world and the proportions of things, as Missionaries.* Not without some anxiety to their parents, they plunged into the perilous deeps of the East End, to struggle—for a fortnight—with its suffering and its brutishness. So they went among the tradesmen's sons and the shopmen, who endured them as they endured the nominal subscription; and they came away with a certain relief, and with some misgiving as to what impression they had made, and what they had done to make it. But it was with knowledge and authority that they went back among those who had doubted their personal safety in the dark region.* The East End, they reported, was nothing like what it was said to be. You could see much worse places up West.* The people were quite a decent sort, in their way: shocking Bounders, of course; but quite clean and quiet, and very comfortably dressed, with ties and collars and watches.

But the Missionaries were few, and the subscribers to the Elevation Mission were many. Most had been convinced, by what they had been told, by what they had read in charity appeals, and perhaps by what they had seen in police-court and inquest reports,* that the whole East End was a wilderness of slums: slums packed with starving human organisms without minds and without morals, preying on each other alive. These subscribers visited the Institute by twos and threes, on occasions of particular festivity among the neat clerks, and were astonished at the wonderful effects of Pansophic Elevation on the degraded classes, their aspect and their habits. Perhaps it was a concert where nobody was drunk: perhaps a little dance where nobody howled a chorus, nor wore his hat, nor punched his partner in the eye. It was a great marvel, whereunto the observers testified: so that more subscriptions came, and the new wing was built.

The afternoon was bright, and all was promising. A small crowd of idlers hung about the main door of the Institute, and stared at a string of flags. Away to the left stood the new wing, a face of fair, clean brick; the ornamentation, of approved earnestness, in terra-cotta squares at regular intervals. Within sat many friends and relations of the shopmen and superior mechanics, and waited for the Bishop; the Eminences of the Elevation Mission sitting apart on the platform. Without, among the idlers, waited Dicky Perrott. His notions of what were going on were indistinct, but he had a belief, imbibed through rumour and tradition, that all celebrations at such large buildings were accompanied by the consumption, in the innermost recesses, of cake and tea. Even to be near cake was something. In Shoreditch High Street was a shop where cake stood in the window in great slabs, one slab over another, to an incalculable value. At this window—against it, as near as possible, his face flattened white—Dicky would stand till the shopkeeper drove him off: till he had but to shut his eyes to see once more, in the shifting black, the rich yellow sections with their myriad raisins. Once a careless errand-boy, who had bought a slice, took so clumsy a bite as he emerged that near a third of the whole piece broke and fell; and this Dicky had snatched from the paving and bolted with, ere the owner quite saw his loss. This was a superior sort of cake, at a penny. But once he had managed to buy himself a slice of an inferior sort for a halfpenny, in Meakin Street.

Dicky Perrott, these blessed memories in his brain, stood unobtrusively near the door, with the big jacket buttoned over as decently as might be, full of a desperate design: which was to get inside by whatsoever manner of trick or opportunity he might, and so, if it were humanly possible, to the cake.

The tickets were being taken at the door by an ardent young Elevator—one of the missionaries. Him, and all such washed and well-dressed people, Dicky had learnt to hold in serene contempt when the business in hand was dodging. There was no hurry: the Elevator might waste his vigilance on the ticket-holders for some time yet. And Dicky knew better than to betray the smallest sign of a desire for entrance while his enemy's attention was awake.

Carriages drew up, and yielded more Eminences: toward the end the Bishop himself, whom Dicky observed but as a pleasant-looking old gentleman in uncommon clothes; and on whom he bestowed no more thought than a passing wonder at what might be the accident to his hat which had necessitated its repair with string.*

But at the spikes of the Bishop's carriage* came another; and out of that there got three ladies, friends of the ticket-receiver, on whom they closed, greeting and shaking hands; and in a flash Dicky Perrott was beyond the lobby and moving obscurely along the walls of the inner hall, behind pillars and in shadow, seeking cake.

The Choral Society sang their lustiest, and there were speeches. Eminences expressed their surprise and delight at finding the people of the East End, gathered in the Institute building, so respectable and clean, thanks to persistent, indefatigable, unselfish Elevation.

The good Bishop, amid clapping of hands and fluttering of handkerchiefs, piped cherubically of everything. He rejoiced to see that day, whereon the helping hand of the West was so unmistakably made apparent in the East. He rejoiced also to find himself in the midst of so admirably typical an assemblage—so representative, if he might say so, of that great East End of London, thirsting and crying out for—for Elevation: for that—ah—Elevation which the more fortunately circumstanced denizens of—of other places, had so munificently—laid on. The people of the East End had been sadly misrepresented—in popular periodicals and in—in other ways.* The East End, he was convinced, was not so black as it was painted.* (Applause.) He had but to look about him. *Etcetera, etcetera.* He questioned whether so well-conducted, morally-given, and respectable a gathering could be brought together in any West End parish with which he was acquainted. It was his most pleasant duty on this occasion—and so on and so forth.

Dicky Perrott had found the cake. It was in a much smaller room at the back of the hall, wherein it was expected that the Bishop and certain Eminences of the platform would refresh themselves with tea after the ceremony. There were heavy, drooping curtains at the door of this room, and deep from the largest folds the ratling from the Jago watched. The table was guarded by a sour-faced man—just such a man as drove him from the window of the cake shop in Shoreditch High Street. Nobody else was there yet, and plainly the sour-faced man must be absent or busy ere the cake could be got at.

There was a burst of applause in the hall: the new wing had been declared open. Then there was more singing, and after that much shuffling and tramping, for everybody was free to survey the new rooms on the way out; and the Importances from the platform came to find the tea.

Filling the room and standing about in little groups; chatting, munching, and sipping, while the sour-faced man distractedly floundered amid crockery: not a soul of them all perceived an inconsiderable small boy, ducking and dodging vaguely among legs and round skirts, making, from time to time, a silent snatch at a plate on the table: and presently he vanished altogether. Then the amiable Bishop, beaming over the tea-cup six inches from his chin, at two courtiers of the clergy, bethought him of a dinner engagement, and passed his hand downward over the rotundity of his waistcoat.

'Dear, dear,' said the Bishop, glancing down suddenly, 'why—what's become of my watch?'*

There hung three inches of black ribbon, with a cut end. The Bishop looked blankly at the Elevators about him.

Three streets off, Dicky Perrott, with his shut fist deep in his breeches pocket, and a gold watch in the fist, ran full drive for the Old Jago.

CHAPTER 3

THERE was nobody in chase; but Dicky Perrott, excited by his novel exploit, ran hard: forgetting the lesson first learnt by every child of the Jago, to avoid, as far as may be, suspicious flight in open streets. He burst into the Old Jago from the Jago Row corner, by Meakin Street; and still he ran. A small boy a trifle bigger than himself made a sharp punch at him as he passed, but he took no heed. The hulking group at the corner of Old Jago Street, ever observant of weaklings with plunder, saw him, and one tried to catch his arm, but he had the wit to dodge. Past the Jago Court passage he scudded, in at the familiar doorway, and up the stairs. A pale hunchbacked child, clean and wistful, descended, and him Dicky flung aside and half downstairs with 'Git out, 'ump!'

Josh Perrott sat on the bed, eating fried fish from an oily paper; for it was tea-time. He was a man of thirty-two, of middle height and stoutly built, with a hard, leathery face as of one much older. The hair about his mouth seemed always three days old—never much less nor much more. He was a plasterer—had, at least, so described himself at police-courts. But it was long since he had plastered, though he still walked abroad splashed and speckled, as though from an eruption of inherent plaster. In moments of pride he declared himself the only member of his family who had ever learned a trade, and worked at it. It was a long relinquished habit, but while it lasted he had married a decent boiler-maker's daughter,* who had known nothing of the Jago till these latter days. One other boast Josh Perrott had: that nothing but shot or pointed steel could hurt him.* And this, too, was near being a true boast; as he had proved in more than one fight in the local arena—which was Jago Court. Now he sat peaceably on the edge of the bed, and plucked with his fingers at the oily fish, while his wife grubbed hopelessly about the cupboard shelves for the screw of paper which was the sugar-basin.

Dicky entered at a burst. 'Mother—father—look! I done a click! I got a clock—a red 'un!'

Josh Perrott stopped, jaw and hand, with a pinch of fish poised in air. The woman turned, and her chin fell. 'O, Dicky, Dicky,' she cried, in real distress, 'you're a awful low, wicked boy. My Gawd, Josh, 'e—'e'll grow up bad: I said so.'

Josh Perrott bolted the pinch of fish, and sucked his fingers as he sprang to the door. After a quick glance down the stairs he shut it, and turned to Dicky. 'Where d'je get that, ye young devel?' he asked, and snatched the watch.

'Claimed it auf a ol' bloke w'en 'e was drinkin' 'is tea,' Dicky replied, with sparkling eyes. 'Let's 'ave a look at it, father.'

'Did 'e run after ye?'

'No—didn't know nuffin' about it. I cut 'is bit o' ribbin with my knife.' Dicky held up a treasured relic of blade and handle, found in a gutter. 'Ain' cher goin' to let's 'ave a look at it?'

Josh Perrott looked doubtfully toward his wife: the children were chiefly her concern. Of her sentiments there could be no mistake. He slipped the watch into his own pocket, and caught Dicky by the collar.

'I'll give you somethink, you dam young thief,' he exclaimed, slipping off his belt. 'You'd like to have us all in stir for a year or two, I s'pose; goin' thievin' watches like a growed-up man.' And he plied the belt savagely, while Dicky, amazed, breathless and choking, spun about him with piteous squeals, and the baby woke and puled in feeble sympathy.

There was a rip, and the collar began to leave the old jacket. Feeling this, Josh Perrott released it, and with a quick drive of the fist in the neck sent Dicky staggering across the room. Dicky caught at the bed frame, and limped out to the landing, sobbing grievously in the bend of his sleeve.

It was more than his mother had intended, but she knew better than to attempt interference. Now that he was gone, she said, with some hesitation: ''Adn't you better take it out at once, Josh?'

'Yus, I'm goin',' Josh replied, turning the watch in his hand. 'It's a good 'un—a topper.'

'You—you won't let Weech 'ave it, will ye, Josh? 'E—'e never gives much.'

'No bloomin' fear. I'm goin' up 'Oxton with this 'ere.'

Dicky sobbed his way down the stairs and through the passage to the back. In the yard he looked for Tommy Rann, to sympathise. But Tommy was not, and Dicky paused in his grief to reflect that perhaps, indeed, in the light of calm reason, he would rather cast the story of the watch in a more heroic mould, for Tommy's benefit, than was compatible with tears and a belted back. So he turned and squeezed through a hole in the broken fence, sobbing again, in search of the friend that shared his inmost sorrows.

The belting was bad—very bad. There was broken skin on his shins where the strap had curled round, and there was a little sticky blood under the shirt half way up his back: to say nothing of bruises. But it was the hopeless injustice of things that shook him to the soul. Wholly unaided, he had done, with neatness and credit, a click that anybody in the Jago would have been proud of. Overjoyed, he had hastened to receive the commendations of his father and mother, and to place the prize in their hands, freely and generously, though perhaps with some hope of hot supper by way of celebration. And his reward was this. Why? He could understand nothing: could but feel the wrong that broke his heart. And so, sobbing, he crawled through two fences to weep on the shaggy neck of Jerry Gullen's canary.

Jerry Gullen's canary was no bird, but a donkey: employed by Jerry Gullen in his occasional intervals of sobriety to drag a cranky shallow, sometimes stored with glass bottles, rags, and hearthstone:* sometimes with firewood manufactured from a convenient hoarding, or from the joinery of an empty house: sometimes with empty sacks covering miscellaneous property suddenly acquired and not for general inspection. His vacations, many and long, Jerry Gullen's canary spent, forgotten and unfed, in Jerry Gullen's back yard: gnawing desperately at fences, and harrowing the neighbourhood with his bray. Thus the nickname, facetiously applied by Kiddo Cook in celebration of his piteous song, grew into use; and 'Canary' would call the creature's attention as readily as a mouthful of imprecations.

Jerry Gullen's canary was gnawing, gnawing, with a sound as of a crooked centre-bit.* Everywhere about the foul yard, ten or twelve feet square, wood was rounded and splintered and bitten white, and as the donkey turned his heavy head, a drip of blood from his gums made a disc on the stones. A twitch of the ears welcomed Dicky, grief-stricken as he was; for it was commonly thus that he bethought him of solace in Jerry Gullen's back yard. And so Dicky, his arms about the mangy neck, told the tale of his wrongs till consolation came in composition of the heroic narrative designed for Tommy Rann.

'O, Canary, it is a blasted shame!'

CHAPTER 4

When Dicky Perrott came running into Jago Row with the Bishop's watch in his pocket, another boy punched a fist at him, and at the time Dicky was at a loss to guess the cause—unless it were a simple caprice—but stayed neither to inquire nor to retaliate. The fact was that the Ranns and the Learys were coming out, fighting was in the air, and the small boy, meeting another a trifle smaller, punched on general principles. The Ranns and the Learys, ever at war or in guarded armistice, were the great rival families—the Montagues and the Capulets*—of the Old Jago. The Learys indeed, scarce pretended to rivalry—rather to factious opposition. For the Ranns gloried in the style and title of the 'Royal Family', and dominated the Jago; but there were mighty fighters, men and women, among the Learys, and when a combat arose it was a hard one and an animated. The two families ramified throughout the Jago; and under the Rann standard, whether by kin or by custom, were the Gullens, the Fishers, the Spicers, and the Walshes; while in the Leary train came Dawsons, Greens, and Harnwells. So that near all the Jago was wont to be on one side or the other, and any of the Jago which was not, was apt to be the worse for it; for the Ranns drubbed all them that were not of their faction in the most thorough and most workmanlike manner, and the Learys held by the same practice; so that neutrality meant double drubbing. But when the Ranns and Learys combined, and the Old Jago issued forth in its entire might against Dove Lane, then the battle was one to go miles to see.

This, however, was but a Rann and Leary fight; and it was but in its early stages when Dicky Perrott, emerging from Jerry Gullen's back yard, made for Shoreditch High Street by way of the 'Posties'—the passage with posts at the end of Old Jago Street. His purpose was to snatch a handful of hay from some passing waggon, or of mixed fodder from some unguarded nosebag, wherewith to reward the sympathy of Jerry Gullen's canary. But by the 'Posties', at the Edge Lane corner, Tommy Rann, capless, and with a purple bump on his forehead, came flying into his arms, breathless, exultant, a babbling braggart. He had fought Johnny Leary and Joe Dawson, he said, one after the other, and pretty nigh broke Johnny Leary's blasted neck; and Joe Dawson's big brother was after him now with a bleed'n' shovel. So the two children ran on together, and sought the seclusion of their own back yard; where the story of Johnny Rann's prowess, with scowls and the pounding of imaginary foes, and the story of the Bishop's watch, with suppressions and improvements, mingled and contended in the thickening dusk. And Jerry Gullen's canary went forgotten and unrequited.

That night fighting was sporadic and desultory in the Jago. Bob the Bender* was reported to have a smashed nose, and Sam Cash had his head bandaged at the hospital. At the Bag of Nails in Edge Lane, Snob Spicer* was knocked out of knowledge* with a quart pot,* and Cocko Harnwell's* missis had a piece bitten off of one ear. As the night wore on, taunts and defiances were bandied from window to door, and from door to window, between those who intended to begin fighting tomorrow; and shouts from divers corners gave notice of isolated scuffles. Once a succession of piercing screams seemed to betoken that Sally Green had begun. There was a note in the screams of Sally Green's opposites which the Jago had learned to recognise. Sally Green, though of the weaker faction, was the female champion of the Old Jago: an eminence won and kept by fighting tactics peculiar to herself. For it was her way, reserving teeth and nails, to wrestle closely with her antagonist, throw her by a dexterous twist on her face, and fall on her, instantly seizing the victim's nape in her teeth, gnawing and worrying. The sufferer's screams were audible afar, and beyond their invariable eccentricity of quality—a quality vaguely suggestive of dire surprise—they had mechanical persistence, a pump-like regularity that distinguished them, in the accustomed ear, from other screams.

Josh Perrott had not been home all the evening: probably the Bishop's watch was in course of transmutation into beer. Dicky, stiff and domestically inclined, nursed Looey and listened to the noises without till he fell asleep, in hopeful anticipation of the morrow. For Tommy Rann had promised him half of a broken iron railing wherewith to fight the Learys.

CHAPTER 5

SLEEP in the Jago was at best a thing of intermission, for reasons—reasons of multitude—already denoted; nevertheless Dicky slept well enough to be unconscious of his father's homecoming. In the morning, however, there lay Josh Perrott, snoring thunderously on the floor, piebald with road-dust. This was not a morning whereon father would want breakfast—that was plain: he would wake thirsty and savage. So Dicky made sure of a crust from the cupboard, and betook himself in search of Tommy Rann. As to washing, he was never especially fond of it, and in any case there were fifty excellent excuses for neglect. The only water was that from the little tap in the back yard. The little tap was usually out of order, or had been stolen bodily by a tenant; and if it were not, there was no basin there, nor any soap, nor towel; and anything savouring of moderate cleanliness was resented in the Jago* as an assumption of superiority.*

Fighting began early, fast and furious. The Ranns got together soon, and hunted the Learys up and down, and attacked them in their houses: the Learys' chances only coming when straggling Ranns were cut off from the main body. The weapons in use, as was customary, rose in effectiveness by a swiftly ascending scale. The Learys, assailed with sticks, replied with sticks torn from old packing-cases, with protruding nails. The two sides bethought them of coshes simultaneously, and such as had no coshes—very few—had pokers and iron railings. Ginger Stagg,* at bay in his passage, laid open Pud Palmer's* cheek with a chisel; and, knives thus happily legitimised with the least possible preliminary form, everybody was free to lay hold of whatever came handy.

In Old Jago Street, half way between Jago Court and Edge Lane, stood the Feathers, the grimiest and vilest of the four public-houses in the Jago. Into the Feathers some dozen Learys were driven, and for a while they held the inner bar and the tap-room against the Ranns, who swarmed after them, chairs, bottles, and pewter pots flying thick, while Mother Gapp, the landlady, hung hysterical on the beer-pulls in the bar, supplicating and blubbering aloud. Then a partition came down with a crash, bringing shelves and many glasses with it, and the Ranns rushed over the ruin, beating the Learys down, jumping on them, heaving them through the back windows. Having thus cleared the house of the intruding enemy, the Ranns demanded recompense of liquor, and took it, dragging handles off beer-engines, seizing bottles, breaking into the cellar, and driving in bungs.* Nobody better than Mother Gapp could quell an ordinary bar riot—even to knocking a man down with a pot; but she knew better than to attempt interference now. Nothing could have made her swoon, but she sat limp and helpless, weeping and blaspheming.

The Ranns cleared off, every man with a bottle or so, and scattered, and this for a while was their undoing. For the Learys rallied and hunted the Ranns in their turn: a crowd of eighty or a hundred sweeping the Jago from Honey Lane to Meakin Street. Then they swung back through Edge Lane to Old Jago Street, and made for Jerry Gullen's—a house full of Ranns. Jerry Gullen, Bill Rann, and the rest took refuge in the upper floors and barricaded the stairs. Below, the Learys broke windows and ravaged the rooms, smashing whatsoever of furniture was to be found. Above, Pip Walsh, who affected horticulture on his window-sill, hurled down flower-pots. On the stairs, Billy Leary, scaling the barricade, was flung from top to bottom, and had to be carried home. And then Pip Walsh's missis scattered the besiegers on the pavement below with a kettleful of boiling water.

There was a sudden sortie of Ranns from Jago Court, but it profited nothing; for the party was small, and, its advent being unexpected, there was a lack of prompt co-operation from the house. The Learys held the field.

Down the middle of Old Jago Street came Sally Green: red faced, stripped to the waist, dancing, hoarse and triumphant. Nail-scores wide as the finger striped her back, her face, and her throat, and she had a black eye; but in one great hand she dangled a long bunch of clotted hair,* as she whooped defiance to the Jago. It was a trophy newly rent from the scalp of Norah Walsh, champion of the Rann womankind, who had crawled away to hide her blighted head, and be restored with gin. None answered Sally's challenge, and, staying but to fling a brickbat at Pip Walsh's window, she carried her dance and her trophy into Edge Lane.

The scrimmage on Jerry Gullen's stairs was thundering anew, and parties of Learys were making for other houses in the street, when there came a volley of yells from Jago Row, heralding a scudding mob of Ranns. The defeated sortie-party from Jago Court, driven back, had gained New Jago Street by way of the house-passages behind the Court, and set to gathering the scattered faction. Now the Ranns came, drunk, semi-drunk, and otherwise, and the Learys, leaving Jerry Gullen's, rushed to meet them. There was a great shock, hats flew, sticks and heads made a wooden rattle, and instantly the two mobs were broken into an uproarious confusion of tangled groups, howling and grappling. Here a man crawled into a passage to nurse a broken head; there a knot gathered to kick a sprawling foe. So the fight thinned out and spread, resolving into many independent combats, with concerted rushes of less and less frequency, till once again all through the Jago each fought for his own hand. Kiddo Cook, always humorous, ran hilariously through the streets, brandishing a long roll of twisted paper, wherewith he smacked the heads of Learys all and sundry, who realised too late that the paper was twisted round a lodging-house poker.*

Now, of the few neutral Jagos: most lay low. Josh Perrott, however, hard as nails and respected for it, feared neither Rann nor Leary, and leaving a little money with his missis, carried his morning mouth in search of beer. Pigeony Poll,* harlot and outcast, despised for that she neither fought nor kept a cosh-carrier, like a respectable married woman, slunk and trembled in corners and yards, and wept at the sight of bleeding heads. As for old Beveridge, the affair so grossly excited him that he neglected business (he cadged and wrote begging screeves)* and stayed in the Jago, where he strode wildly about the streets, lank and rusty, stabbing the air with a carving knife, and incoherently defying 'all the lot' to come near him. Nobody did.

Dicky Perrott and Tommy Rann found a snug fastness in Jago Row. For there was a fence with a loose board, which, pushed aside, revealed a hole where through a very small boy might squeeze; and within were stored many barrows and shallows, mostly broken, and of these one, tilted forward and bottom up, made a hut or den, screened about with fence and barrows. Here they hid while the Learys swept the Jago, and hence they issued from time to time to pound such youngsters of the other side as might come in sight. The bits of iron railing made imposing weapons, but were a trifle too big and heavy for rapid use in their puny hands. Still, Dicky managed to double up little Billy Leary with a timely lunge in the stomach, and Tommy Rann made Bobby Harnwell's nose bleed very satisfactorily.

On the other hand, the bump on Tommy Rann's forehead was widened by the visitation of a stick, and Dicky Perrott sustained a very hopeful punch in the eye, which he cherished enthusiastically with a view to an honourable blackness. In the snuggery intervals they explained their prowess one to another, and Dicky alluded to his intention, when he was a man, to buy a very long sword wherewith to cut off the Learys' heads: Tommy Rann inclining, however, to a gun, with which one might also shoot birds.

The battle flagged a little toward midday, but waxed lively again as the afternoon began. It was then that Dicky Perrott, venturing some way from the retreat, found himself in a scrimmage, and a man snatched away his piece of iron and floored a Leary with it. Gratifying as was the distinction of aiding in the exploit, Dicky mourned the loss of the weapon almost unto tears, and Tommy Rann would not go turn-about with the other, but kept it wholly for himself; so Dicky was fain to hunt sorrowfully for a mere stick. Even a disengaged stick was not easy to find just then. So Dicky, emerging from the Jago, tried Meakin Street, where there were shops, but unsuccessfully, and so came round by Luck Row, a narrow way from Meakin Street by Walker's cook shop, up through the Jago.

Dicky's mother, left with the baby, fastened the door as well as she might, and trembled. Indeed she had reason. The time of Josh Perrott's return was a matter of doubt, but when he did come he would want something to eat; it was for that he had left the money. But Dicky was out, and there was nothing in the cupboard. From the window she saw divers fights in Jago Court; and a man lay for near two hours on the stones with a cut on his temple. As for herself, she was no favourite in the neighbourhood at any time. For one thing, her husband did not carry the cosh. Then she was an alien who had never entirely fallen into Jago ways; she had soon grown sluttish and dirty, but she was never drunk, she never quarrelled, she did not gossip freely. Also her husband beat her but rarely, and then not with a chair nor a poker. Justly irritated by such superiorities as these, the women of the Jago were ill-disposed to brook another: which was, that Hannah Perrott had been married in church. For these reasons she was timid at the most peaceful of times, but now, with Ranns and Learys on the war-path, and herself obnoxious to both, she trembled. She wished Dicky would come and do her errand. But there was no sign of him, and midday wore into afternoon. It was late for Josh as it was, and he would be sure to come home irritable: it was his way when a bad head from overnight struggled with morning beer. If he found nothing to eat there would be trouble.

At length she resolved to go herself. There was a lull in the outer din, and what there was seemed to come from the farther parts of Honey Lane and Jago Row. She would slip across by Luck Row to Meakin Street and be back in five minutes. She took up little Looey and went.

And as Dicky, stickless, turned into Luck Row, there arose a loud shriek and then another, and then in a changed voice a succession of long screams with a regular breath-pause. Sally Green again! He ran, turned into Old Jago Street, and saw.

Sprawled on her face in the foul road lay a writhing woman and screamed; while squeezed under her arm was a baby with mud in its eyes and a cut cheek, crying weakly; and spread over all, clutching her prey by hair and wrist, Sally Green hung on the nape like a terrier, jaws clenched, head shaking.

Thus Dicky saw it in a flash, and in an instant he had flung himself on Sally Green, kicking, striking, biting and crying, for he had seen his mother and Looey. The kicks wasted themselves among the woman's petticoats, and the blows were feeble; but the sharp teeth were meeting in the shoulder-flesh, when help came.

Norah Walsh, vanquished champion, now somewhat recovered, looked from a window, saw her enemy vulnerable, and ran out armed with a bottle. She stopped at the kerb to knock the bottom off the bottle, and then, with an exultant shout, seized Sally Green by the hair and stabbed her about the face with the jagged points. Blinded with blood, Sally released her hold on Mrs Perrott and rolled on her back, struggling fiercely; but to no end, for Norah Walsh, kneeling on her breast, stabbed and stabbed again, till pieces of the bottle broke away. Sally's yells and plunges ceased, and a man pulled Norah off. On him she turned, and he was fain to run, while certain Learys found a truck* which might carry Sally to the hospital.

Hannah Perrott was gone indoors, hysterical and helpless. She had scarce crossed the street on her errand when she had met Sally Green in quest of female Ranns. Mrs Perrott was not a Rann, but she was not a Leary, so it came to the same thing. Moreover, there was her general obnoxiousness. She had tried to run, but that was useless; and now, sobbing and bleeding, she was merely conscious of being gently led, almost carried, indoors and upstairs. She was laid back on the bed, and somebody loosened her hair and wiped her face and neck, giving her hoarse, comforting words. Then she saw the face—scared though coarse and pitted, and red about the eyes—that bent over her. It was Pigeony Poll's.

Dicky had followed her in, no longer the hero of the Jago Row retreat, but with his face tearful and distorted, carrying the baby in his arms, and wiping the mud from her eyes. Now he sat on the little box and continued his ministrations, with fear in his looks as he glanced at his mother on the bed.

Without, the fight rallied once more. The Learys ran to avenge Sally Green, and the Ranns met them with a will. Down by the Bag of Nails a party of Ranns was driven between the posts and through the gut into Shoreditch High Street, where a stand was made until Fag Dawson* dropped, with a shoemaker's knife sticking under his armpit. Then the Ranns left, with most of the Learys after them, and Fag Dawson was carried to a chemist's by the police, never to floor a Rann again. For he was chived in the left lung.

Thus the fight ended. For a faction fight in the Jago, with a few broken heads and ribs and an odd knife wound here and there—even with a death in the hospital from kicks or what not—was all very well; but when it came to homicide in the open High Street, the police drew the line, and entered the Jago in force. Ordinarily, a peep now and again from a couple of policemen between the 'Posties' was all the supervision the Jago had, although three policemen had been seen to walk the length of Old Jago Street together, and there were raids in force for special captures. There was a raid in force now, and the turmoil ceased. Nothing would have pleased both Ranns and Learys better than to knock over two or three policemen, for kicking-practice; but there were too many for the sport, and for hours they patrolled the Jago's closest passages. Of course nobody knew who chived Fag Dawson. No inquiring policeman ever found anybody in the Old Jago who knew anything, even to the harm of his bitterest foe. It was the sole commandment that ran there:—'Thou shalt not nark.'

That night it was known that there would be a fight between Josh Perrott and Billy Leary, once the latter grew well. For Josh Perrott came home, saw his wife, and turned Rann on the spot. But for the police in the Jago that night, there would have been many a sore head, if no worse, among the Learys, by visitation of Josh Perrott. Sally Green's husband had fled years ago, and Billy Leary, her brother, was the obvious mark for Josh's vengeance. He was near as eminent a fighter among the men as his sister among the women, and a charming scrap was anticipated. It would come off, of course, in Jago Court one Sunday morning, as all fights of distinction did; and perhaps somebody in the High Mob would put up stakes.

CHAPTER 6

IN the morning the police still held the Jago. Their presence embarrassed many, but none more than Dicky Perrott, who would always take a turning, or walk the other way, at sight of a policeman. Dicky got out of Old Jago Street early, and betook him to Meakin Street, where there were chandlers' shops with sugar in their windows, and cook-shops with pudding. He designed working through by these to Shoreditch High Street, there to crown his solace by contemplation of the cake-shop. But, as he neared Weech's coffee-shop, scarce half through Meakin Street, there stood Weech himself at the door, grinning and nodding affably, and beckoning him. He was a pleasant man, this Mr Aaron Weech,* who sang hymns aloud in the back parlour, and hummed the tunes in the shop: a prosperous, white-aproned, whiskered, half-bald, smirking tradesman, who bent and spoke amiably to boys, looking sharply in their eyes, but talked to a man mostly with his gaze on the man's waistcoat.

Indeed, there seemed to be something about Mr Aaron Weech especially attractive to youth. Nearly all his customers were boys and girls, though not boys and girls who looked likely to pay a great deal in the way of refreshment, much as they took. But he was ever indulgent, and at all times accessible to his young clients. Even on Sunday (though, of course, his shutters were kept rigidly up on the Day of Rest) a particular tap would bring him hot-foot to the door: not to sell coffee, for Mr Weech was no Sabbath-breaker.*

Now he stood at his door, and invited Dicky with nods and becks. Dicky, all wondering, and alert to dodge in case the thing were a mere device to bring him within striking distance, went.

'W'y Dicky Perrott,' quoth Mr Weech in a tone of genial surprise, 'I b'lieve you could drink a cup o' cawfy!'

Dicky, wondering how Mr Weech had learnt his name, believed he could.

'An' eat a slice o' cake too, I'll be bound,' Mr Weech added.

Dicky's glance leapt. Yes, he could eat a slice of cake too.

'Ah, I knew it,' said Mr Weech, triumphantly; 'I can always tell.' He rubbed Dicky's cap about his head, and drew him into the shop, at this hour bare of customers. At the innermost compartment they stopped, and Mr Weech, with a gentle pressure on the shoulders, seated Dicky at the table.

He brought the coffee, and not a single slice of cake, but two. True, it was not cake of Elevation Mission quality, nor was it so good as that shown at the shop in High Street: it was of a browner, dumpier, harder nature, and the currants were gritty and few. But cake it was, and to consider it critically were unworthy. Dicky bolted it with less comfort than he might, for Mr Weech watched him keenly across the table. And, indeed, from some queer cause, he felt an odd impulse to cry. It was the first time that he had ever been given anything, kindly and ungrudgingly.*

He swallowed the last crumb, washed it down with the dregs of his cup, and looked sheepishly across at Mr Weech.

'Goes down awright, don't it?' that benefactor remarked. 'Ah, I like to see you enjoyin' of yerself. I'm very fond o' you young 'uns: 'specially clever 'uns like you.'

Dicky had never been called clever before, so far as he could recollect, and he wondered at it now. Mr Weech, leaning back, contemplated him smilingly for some seconds, and then proceeded. 'Yus,' he said, 'you're the sort o' boy as can 'ave cawfy and cake w'enever you want it, you are.'

Dicky wondered more, and his face said as much. 'You know,' Mr Weech pursued, winking amain, grinning and nodding. 'That was a fine watch you found the other day. Y'ought to 'a' brought it to me.'

Dicky was alarmed. How did Mr Weech learn about the watch? Perhaps he was a friend of the funny old man who lost it. Dicky half rose, but his affable patron leaned across and pushed him back on the seat. 'You needn't be frightened,' he said. 'I ain't goin' to say nothink to nobody. But I know all about it, mind, an' I could if I liked. You found the watch, an' it was a red 'un, on a bit o' ribbin. Well, then you went and took it 'ome, like a little fool. Wot does yer father do? W'y 'e ups an' lathers you with 'is belt, an' 'e keeps the watch 'isself. That's all you git for yer pains. See—I know all about it.' And Mr Weech gazed on Dicky Perrott with a fixed grin.

'Oo toldjer?' Dicky managed to ask at last.

'Ah!'—this with a great emphasis and a tapping of the forefinger beside the nose*—'I don't want much tellin': it ain't much as goes on 'ereabout I don't know of. Never mind 'ow. P'raps I got a little bird as w'ispers—p'raps I do it some other way. Any'ow I know. It ain't no good any boy tryin' to do somethink unbeknownst to me, mindjer.'

Mr Weech's head lay aside, his grin widened, his glance was sidelong, his forefinger pointed from his temple over Dicky's head, and altogether he looked so very knowing that Dicky shuffled in his seat. By what mysterious means was this newfound friend so well informed? The doubt troubled him, for Dicky knew nothing of Mr Aaron Weech's conversation, an hour before, with Tommy Rann.

'But it's awright, bless yer,' Mr Weech went on presently. 'Nobody's none the wuss for me knowin' about 'em . . . Well, we was a-talkin' about the watch, wasn't we? All you got after sich a lot o' trouble was a woppin' with a belt. That was too bad.' Mr Weech's voice was piteous and sympathetic. 'After you a-findin' sich a nice watch—a red 'un an' all!—you gits nothink for yerself but a beltin'. Never mind, you'll do better next time—I'll take care o' that. I don't like to see a clever boy put upon. You go an' find another, or somethink else—anythink good—an' then you bring it 'ere.'

Mr Weech's friendly sympathy extinguished Dicky's doubt. 'I didn't find it,' he said, shy but proud. 'It was a click—I sneaked it.'

'Eh?' ejaculated Mr Weech, a sudden picture of blank incomprehension. 'Eh? What? Click? Wot's a click? Sneaked? Wot's that? I dunno nothink about no talk o' that sort, an' I don't want to. It's my belief it means somethink wrong—but I dunno, an' I don't want to. 'Ear that? Eh? Don't let me 'ave no more o' that, or you'd better not come near me agin. If you *find* somethink, awright: you come to me an' I'll give ye somethink for it, if it's any good. It ain't no business of anybody's *where* you find it, o' course, an' I don't want to know. But clicks and sneaks—them's Greek to me, an' I don't want to learn 'em. Unnerstand that? Nice talk to respectable people, with yer clicks an' sneaks!'

Dicky blushed a little, and felt very guilty without in the least understanding the offence. But Mr Weech's virtuous indignation subsided as quickly as it had arisen, and he went on as amiably as ever.

'When you *find* anythink,' he said, 'jist like you found that watch, don't tell nobody, an' don't let nobody see it. Bring it 'ere quiet, when there ain't any p'liceman in the street, an' come right through to the back o' the shop, an' say, "I come to clean the knives."* Unnerstand? "I come to clean the knives." There ain't no knives to clean—it's on'y a way o' tellin' me you got somethink without other people knowin'. An' then I'll give you somethink for it—money p'raps, or p'raps cake or wot not. Don't forgit. "I come to clean the knives." See?'

Yes, Dicky understood perfectly; and Dicky saw a new world of dazzling delights. Cake—limitless cake, coffee, and the like whenever he might feel moved thereunto; but more than all, money—actual money. Good broad pennies,* perhaps whole shillings—perhaps even more still: money to buy bullock's liver for dinner, or tripe, or what you fancied: saveloys, baked potatoes from the can on cold nights, a little cart to wheel Looey in, a boat from a toy-shop with sails!

'There's no end o' things to be found all over the place, an' a sharp boy like you can find 'em every day. If you don't find 'em, someone else will; there's plenty on 'em about on the lookout, an' you got jist as much right as them. On'y mind!'—Mr Weech was suddenly stern and serious, and his forefinger was raised impressively—'you know you can't do anythink without I know, an' if you say a word—if you say a word,' his fist came on the table with a bang, 'somethink'll happen to you. Somethink bad.'

Mr Weech rose, and was pleasant again, though business-like. 'Now, you just go an' find somethink,' he said. 'Look sharp about it, an' don't go an' git in trouble. The cawfy's a penny, an' the cake's a penny—ought prop'ly to be twopence, but say a penny this time. That's twopence you owe me, an' you better bring somethink an' pay it off quick. So go along.'

This was an unforeseen tag to the entertainment. For the first time in his life Dicky was in debt. It was a little disappointing to find the coffee and cake no gift after all: though, indeed, it now seemed foolish to have supposed they were; for in Dicky Perrott's world people did not give things away—that were the act of a fool. Thus Dicky, with his hands in his broken pockets, and thought in his small face, whereon still stood the muddy streaks of yesterday's tears, trudged out of Mr Aaron Weech's shop-door, and along Meakin Street.

Now he was beginning the world seriously, and must face the fact. Truly the world had been serious enough for him hitherto, but that he knew not. Now he was of an age when most boys were thieving for themselves, and he owed money like a man. True it was, as Mr Weech had said, that everybody—the whole Jago—was on the look-out for himself. Plainly he must take his share, lest it fall to others. As to the old gentleman's watch, he had but been beforehand. Through foolish ingenuousness he had lost it, and his father had got it, who could so much more easily steal one for himself; for he was a strong man, and had but to knock over another man at any night-time. Nobody should hear of future clicks but Mr Weech. Each for himself? Come, he must open his eyes.

CHAPTER 7

THERE was no chance all along Meakin Street. The chandlers and the keepers of cook-shops knew their neighbourhood too well to leave articles unguarded. Soon Dicky reached Shoreditch High Street. There things were a little more favourable. There were shops, as he well remembered, where goods were sometimes exhibited at the doors and outside the windows; but today there seemed to be no chance of the sort. As for the people, he was too short to try pockets, and indeed the High Street rarely gave passage to a more unpromising lot. Moreover, from robbery from the person he knew he must abstain, except for such uncommon opportunities as that of the Bishop's watch, for some years yet.

He hung about the doors and windows of shop after shop, hoping for a temporary absence of the shop-keeper, which might leave something snatchable. But he hoped in vain. From most shops he was driven away, for the Shoreditch trader is not slow to judge the purpose of a loitering boy. So he passed nearly two hours: when at last he saw his chance. It came in an advantageous part of High Street, not far from the 'Posties', though on the opposite side of the way. A nurse-girl had left a perambulator at a shop door, while she bought inside, and on the perambulator lay loose a little skin rug, from under which a little fat leg stuck and waved aloft. Dicky set his back to the shop, and sidled to within reach of the perambulator. But it chanced that at this moment the nurse-girl stepped to the door, and she made a snatch at his arm as he lifted the rug. This he dropped at once, and was swinging leisurely away (for he despised the chase of any nurse-girl) when a man took him suddenly by the shoulder. Quick as a weasel, Dicky ducked under the man's arm, pulled his shoulder clear, dropped forward and rested an instant on the tips of his fingers to avoid the catch of the other hand, and shot out into the road. The man tried to follow, but Dicky ran under the belly of a standing horse, under the head of another that trotted, across the fore-platform of a tramcar—behind the driver's back—and so over to the 'Posties'.

He slouched into the Jago, disappointed. As he crossed Edge Lane, he was surprised to perceive a stranger—a toff, indeed—who walked slowly along, looking up right and left at the grimy habitations about him. He wore a tall hat, and his clothes were black, and of a pattern that Dicky remembered to have seen at the Elevation Mission. They were, in fact, the clothes of a clergyman. For himself, he was tall and soundly built, with a certain square muscularity of face, and of age about thirty-five. He had ventured into the Jago because the police were in possession, Dicky thought; and wondered in what plight he would leave, had he come at another time. But losing view of the stranger, and making his way along Old Jago Street, Dicky perceived that indeed the police were gone, and that the Jago was free.

He climbed the broken stairs and pushed into the first-floor back, hopeful, though more doubtful, of dinner. There was none. His mother, tied about the neck with rags, lay across the bed nursing the damage of yesterday, and commiserating herself. A yard from her lay Looey, sick and ailing in a new way, but disregarded. Dicky moved to lift her, but at that she cried the more, and he was fain to let her lie. She rolled her head from side to side, and raised her thin little hand vaguely toward it, with feverishly working fingers. Dicky felt her head and she screamed again. There was a lump at the side, a hard, sharp lump; got from the stones of the roadway yesterday. And there was a curious quality, a rather fearful quality, in the little wails: uneasily suggestive of the screams of Sally Green's victims.

Father was out, prowling. There was nothing eatable in the cupboard, and there seemed nothing at home worth staying for. He took another look at Looey, but refrained from touching her, and went out.

The opposite door on the landing was wide open, and he could hear nobody in the room. He had never seen this door open before, and now he ventured on a peep: for the tenants of the front room were strangers, late arrivals, and interlopers. Their name was Roper. Roper was a pale cabinet-maker, fallen on evil times and out of work. He had a pale wife, disliked because of her neatly-kept clothes, her exceeding use of soap and water, her aloofness from gossip. She had a deadly pale baby; also there was a pale hunchbacked boy of near Dicky's age. Collectively the Ropers were disliked as strangers: because they furnished their own room, and in an obnoxiously complete style; because Roper did not drink, nor brawl, nor beat his wife, nor do anything all day but look for work; because all these things were a matter of scandalous arrogance, impudently subversive of Jago custom and precedent. Mrs Perrott was bad enough, but such people as these! . . .

Dicky had never before seen quite such a room as this. Everything was so clean: the floor, the windows, the bed-clothes. Also there was a strip of old carpet on the floor. There were two perfectly sound chairs; and two pink glass vases on the mantel-piece; and a clock. Nobody was in the room, and Dicky took a step farther. The clock attracted him again. It was a small, cheap, nickel-plated, cylindrical thing, of American make,* and it reminded him at once of the Bishop's watch. It was not gold, certainly, but it was a good deal bigger, and it could go—it was going. Dicky stepped back and glanced at the landing. Then he darted into the room, whipped the clock under the breast of the big jacket, and went for the stairs.

Half way down he met the pale hunchback ascending. Left at home alone, he had been standing in the front doorway. He saw Dicky's haste, saw also the suspicious bulge under his jacket, and straightway seized Dicky's arm. 'Where 'a' you bin?' he asked sharply. 'Bin in our room? What you got there?'

'Nothin' o' yours, 'ump. Git out o' that!' Dicky pushed him aside. 'If you don't le' go I'll corpse* ye!'

But one arm and hand was occupied with the bulge, and the other was for the moment unequal to the work of driving off the assailant. The two children wrangled and struggled downstairs, through the doorway and into the street: the hunchback weak, but infuriate, buffeting, biting and whimpering; Dicky infuriate too, but alert for a chance to break away and run. So they scrambled together across the street, Dicky dragging away from the house at every step; and just at the corner of Luck Row, getting his fore-arm across the other's face, he back-heeled him, and the little hunchback fell heavily, and lay breathless and sobbing, while Dicky scampered through Luck Row and round the corner into Meakin Street.

Mr Weech was busier now, for there were customers. But Dicky and his bulge he saw ere they were well over the threshold.

'Ah yus, Dicky,' he said, coming to meet him. 'I was expectin' you. Come in—

*In the swe-e-et by an' by,**
We shall meet on that beautiful shaw-er!

Come in 'ere.' And still humming his hymn, he led Dicky into the shop parlour.

Here Dicky produced the clock, which Mr Weech surveyed with no great approval. 'You'll 'ave to try an' do better than this, you know,' he said. 'But any'ow 'ere it is, sich as it is. It about clears auf wot you owe, I reckon. Want some dinner?'

This was a fact, and Dicky admitted it.

'Awright—

In the swe-e-e-t by an' by—

come out an' set down. I'll bring you somethink 'ot.'

This proved to be a very salt bloater, a cup of the usual muddy coffee, tasting of burnt toast, and a bit of bread: afterwards supplemented by a slice of cake. This to Dicky was a banquet. Moreover, there was the adult dignity of taking your dinner in a coffee-shop, which Dicky supported indomitably now that he began to feel at ease in Mr Weech's: leaning back in his seat, swinging his feet, and looking about at the walls with the grocers' almanacks* hanging thereto, and the Sunday School Anniversary bills* of past date, gathered from afar to signalise the elevated morals of the establishment.

'Done?' queried Mr Weech in his ear. 'Awright, don't 'ang about 'ere then. Bloater's a penny, bread a 'a'peny, cawfy a penny, cake a penny. You'll owe thrippence a'peny now.'

CHAPTER 8

When Dicky Perrott and the small hunchback were hauling and struggling across the street, Old Fisher came down from the top-floor back, wherein he dwelt with his son Bob, Bob's wife and two sisters, and five children: an apartment in no way so clean as the united efforts of ten people might be expected to have made it. Old Fisher, on whose grimy face the wrinkles were deposits of mud, stopped at the open door on the first floor, and, as Dicky had done, he took a peep. Perplexed at the monstrous absence of dirt, and encouraged by the stillness, Old Fisher also ventured within. Nobody was in charge, and Old Fisher, mentally pricing the pink glass vases at threepence, made for a small chest in the corner of the room, and lifted the lid. Within lay many of Roper's tools, from among which he had that morning taken such as he might want on an emergent call to work, to carry as he tramped Curtain Road. Clearly these were the most valuable things in the place;* and, slipping a few small articles into his pockets, Old Fisher took a good double handful of the larger, and tramped upstairs with them. Presently he returned with Bob's missis, and together they started with more. As they emerged, however, there on the landing stood the little hunchback, sobbing and smearing his face with his sleeve. At sight of this new pillage he burst into sharp wails, standing impotent on the landing, his streaming eyes following the man and woman ascending before him. Old Fisher, behind, stumped the stairs with a clumsy affectation of absent-mindedness; the woman, in front, looked down, merely indifferent. Scarce were they vanished above, however, when the little hunchback heard his father and mother on the lower stairs.

CHAPTER 9

DICKY came moodily back from his dinner at Mr Weech's, plunged in mystified computation: starting with a debt of twopence, he had paid Mr Weech an excellent clock—a luxurious article in Dicky's eyes—had eaten a bloater, and had emerged from the transaction owing threepence halfpenny. Of what such a clock cost he had no notion, though he felt it must be some inconceivable sum. As Mr Weech put it, the adjustment of accounts would seem to be quite correct; but the broad fact that all had ended in increasing his debt by three halfpence, remained and perplexed him. He remembered having seen such clocks in a shop in Norton Folgate. To ask the price, in person, were but to be chased out of the shop; but they were probably ticketed, and perhaps he might ask some bystander to read the ticket. This brought the reflection that, after all, reading was a useful accomplishment on occasion: though a matter of too much time and trouble to be worth while. Dicky had never been to school; for the Elementary Education Act ran in the Jago no more than any other Act of Parliament. There was a Board School,* truly, away out of the Jago bounds, by the corner of Honey Lane, where children might go free, and where some few Jago children did go now and again, when boots were to be given away, or when tickets were to be had,* for tea, or soup, or the like. But most parents were of Josh Perrott's opinion: that school-going was a practice best never begun; for then the child was never heard of, and there was no chance of inquiries or such trouble. Not that any such inquiries were common in the Jago, or led to anything.

Meantime Dicky, minded to know if his adventure had made any stir in the house, carried his way deviously toward home. Working through the parts beyond Jago Row, he fetched round into Honey Lane, so coming at New Jago Street from the farther side. Choosing one of the houses whose backs gave on Jago Court, he slipped through the passage, and so, by the back yard, crawled through the broken fence into the court. Left and right were the fronts of houses, four a side. Before him, to the right of the narrow archway leading to Old Jago Street, was the window of his own home. He gained the back yard quietly, and at the kitchen door met Tommy Rann.

'Come on,' called Tommy. ''Ere's a barney! They're a-pitchin' into them noo 'uns—Roperses. Roperses sez Fisherses is sneaked their things. They *are* a-gittin' of it!'

From the stairs, indeed, came shouts and curses, bumps and sobs and cries. The first landing and half the stairs were full of people, men and women, Ranns and Learys together. When Ranns joined Learys it was an ill time for them they marched against; and never were they so ready and so anxious to combine as after a fight between themselves, were but some common object of attack available. Here it was. Here were these pestilent outsiders, the Ropers, assailing the reputation of the neighbourhood by complaining of being robbed. As though their mere presence in the Jago, with their furniture and their superiority, were not obnoxious enough: they must turn about and call their neighbours thieves! They had been tolerated too long already. They should now be given something for themselves, and have some of their exasperating respectability knocked off; and if, in the confusion, their portable articles of furniture and bed-clothing found their way into more deserving hands—why, serve them right.

The requisite volleys of preliminary abuse having been discharged, more active operations began under cover of fresh volleys. Dicky, with Tommy Rann behind him, struggled up the stairs among legs and skirts, and saw that the Ropers, the man flushed, but the woman paler than ever, were striving to shut their door. Within, the hunchback and the baby cried, and without, those on the landing, skidding the door with their feet, pushed inward, and now began to strike and maul. Somebody seized the man's wrist, and Norah Walsh got the woman by the hair and dragged her head down. In a peep through the scuffle Dicky saw her face, ashen and sweat-beaded, in the jamb of the door, and saw Norah Walsh's red fist beat into it twice. Then somebody came striding up the stairs, and Dicky was pushed farther back. Over the shoulders of those about him, Dicky saw a tall hat, and then the head beneath it. It was the stranger he had seen in Edge Lane—the parson: active and resolute.* Norah Walsh he took by the shoulder, and flung back among the others, and as he turned on him, the man who held Roper's wrist released it and backed off.

'What is this?' demanded the new-comer, stern and hard of face. 'What is all this?' He bent his frown on one and another about him, and, as he did it, some shrank uneasily, and on the faces of others fell the blank lack of expression that was wont to meet police inquiries in the Jago. Dicky looked to see this man beaten down, kicked and stripped. But a well-dressed stranger was so new a thing in the Jago, this one had dropped among them so suddenly, and he had withal so bold a confidence, that the Jagos stood irresolute. A toff was not a person to be attacked without due consideration. After such a person there were apt to be inquiries, with money to back them, and vengeance sharp and certain: the thing, indeed, was commonly thought too risky. And this man, so unflinchingly confident, must needs have reason for it. He might have the police at instant call*—they might be back in the Jago at the moment. And he flung them back, commanded them, cowed them with his hard, intelligent eyes, like a tamer among beasts.

'Understand this, now,' he went on, with a sharp tap of his stick on the floor. 'This is a sort of thing I will *not* tolerate in my parish—in this parish: nor in any other place where I may meet it. Go away, and try to be ashamed of yourselves—go. Go, all of you, I say, to your own homes: I shall come there and talk to you again soon. Go along, Sam Cash—you've a broken head already, I see. Take it away: I shall come and see you too.'

Those on the stairs had melted away like punished schoolchildren. Most of the others, after a moment of averted face and muttered justification one to another, were dragging their feet, each with a hang-dog pretence of sauntering airily off from some sight no longer interesting. Sam Cash, who had already seen the stranger in the street, and was thus perhaps a trifle less startled than the others at his advent, stood, however, with some assumption of virtuous impudence, till amazed by sudden address in his own name:* whereat, clean discomfited, he ignominiously turned tail and sneaked downstairs in meaner case than the rest. How should this strange parson know him, and know his name? Plainly he must be connected with the police. He had brought out the name as pat as you please. So argued Sam Cash with his fellows in the outer street: never recalling that Jerry Gullen had called aloud to him by name, when first he observed the parson in the street; had called to him, indeed, to haste to the bashing of the Ropers; and thus had first given the stranger notice of the proceeding. But it was the way of the Jago that its mean cunning saw a mystery and a terror where simple intelligence saw there was none.

As the crowd began to break up, Dicky pushed his own door a little open behind him, and there stood on his own ground, as the others cleared off; and the hunchback ventured a peep from behind his swooning mother. 'There y'are, that's 'im!' he shouted, pointing at Dicky. ''E begun it! 'E took the clock!' Dicky instantly dropped behind his door, and shut it fast.

The invaders had all gone—the Fishers had made upstairs in the beginning—before the parson turned and entered the Ropers' room. In five minutes he emerged and strode upstairs: whence he returned, after a still shorter interval, herding before him Old Fisher and Bob Fisher's missis, sulky and reluctant, carrying tools.

And thus it was that the Reverend Henry Sturt first addressed his parishioners. The parish, besides the Jago, comprised Meakin Street and some small way beyond, and it was to this less savage district that his predecessor had confined his attention: preaching every Sunday in a stable, in an alley behind a disused shop, and distributing loaves and sixpences* to the old women who attended regularly on that account. For to go into the Jago were for him mere wasted effort. And so, indeed, the matter had been since the parish came into being.*

CHAPTER 10

WHEN Dicky retreated from the landing and shut the door behind him, he slipped the bolt, a strong one, put there by Josh Perrott himself, possibly as an accessory to escape by the window in some possible desperate pass. For a little he listened, but no sound hinted of attack from without, and he turned to his mother.

Josh Perrott had been out since early morning, and Dicky, too, had done no more than look in for a moment in search of dinner. Hannah Perrott, grown tired of self-commiseration, felt herself neglected and aggrieved—slighted in her state of invalid privilege. So she transferred some of her pity from her sore neck to her desolate condition as misprized wife and mother, and the better to feel it, proceeded to martyrise herself, with melancholy pleasure, by a nerveless show of 'setting to rights' in the room—a domestic novelty, perfunctory as it was. Looey, still restless and weeping, she left on the bed, for, being neglected herself, it was not her mood to tend the baby; she would aggravate the relish of her sorrows in her own way. Besides, Looey had been given something to eat a long time ago, and had not eaten it yet: with her there was nothing else to do. So that now, as she dragged a rag along the grease-strewn mantelpiece, Mrs Perrott greeted Dicky:—'There y'are, Dicky, comin' 'inderin' 'ere jest when I'm a-puttin' things to rights.' And she sighed with the weight of another grievance.

Looey lay on her back, faintly and vainly struggling to turn her fearful little face from the light. Clutched in her little fist was the unclean stump of bread she had held for hours. Dicky plucked a soft piece and essayed to feed her with it, but the dry little mouth rejected the morsel, and the head turned feverishly from side to side to the sound of that novel cry. She was hot wherever Dicky touched her, and presently he said:—'Mother, I b'lieve Looey's queer. I think she wants some med'cine.'

His mother shook her head peevishly. 'O, you an' Looey's a noosance,' she said. 'A lot you care about *me* bein' queer, you an' yer father too, leavin' me all alone like this, an' me feelin' ready to drop, an' got the room to do an' all. I wish you'd go away an' stop 'inderin' of me like this.'

Dicky took but another look at Looey, and then slouched out. The landing was clear, and the Ropers' door was shut. He wondered what had become of the stranger with the tall hat—whether he was in the Ropers' room or not. The thought hurried him, for he feared to have that stranger asking him questions about the clock. He got out into the street, thoughtful. He had some compunctions in the matter of that clock, now. Not that he could in any reasonable way blame himself. There the clock had stood at his mercy, and by all Jago custom and ethic it was his if only he could get clear away with it. This he had done, and he had no more concern in the business, strictly speaking. Nevertheless, since he had seen the woman's face in the jamb of the door, he felt a sort of pity for her—that she should have lost her clock. No doubt she had enjoyed its possession, as, indeed, he would have enjoyed it himself, had he not had to take it instantly to Mr Weech. And his fancy wandered off in meditation of what he would do with a clock of his own. To begin with, of course, he would open it, and discover the secret of its works and its ticking: perhaps thereby discovering how to make a clock himself. Also he would frequently wind it up, and he would show the inside to Looey, in confidence. It would stand on the mantelpiece, and raise the social position of the family. People would come respectfully to ask the time, and he would tell them, with an air. Yes, certainly a clock must stand eminent among the things he would buy, when he had plenty of money. He must look out for more clicks: the one way to riches.

As to the Ropers, again. Bad it must be, indeed, to be deprived suddenly of a clock, after long experience of the joys it brought; and Norah Walsh had punched the woman in the face, and clawed her hair, and the woman could not fight. Dicky was sorry for her, and straightway resolved to give her another clock, or, if not a clock, something that would please her as much. He had acquired a clock in the morning; why not another in the afternoon? Failing a clock, he would try for something else, and the Ropers should have it. The resolve gave Dicky a virtuous exaltation of spirit, the reward of the philanthropist.

Again he began the prowl after likely plunder that was to be his daily industry. Meakin Street he did not try. The chandlers' and the cook-shops held nothing that might be counted a consolatory equivalent for a clock. Through the 'Posties' he reached Shoreditch High Street at once, and started.

This time his movements aroused less suspicion. In the morning he had no particular prize in view, and loitered at every shop, waiting his chance at anything portable. Now, with a more definite object, he made his promenade easily, but without stopping or lounging by shop-fronts. The thing, whatsoever it might be, must be small, handsome, and of an interesting character—at least as interesting as the clock was. It must be small, not merely for facility of concealment and removal—though these were main considerations—but because stealthy presentation were then the easier. It would have pleased Dicky to hand over his gift openly, and to bask in the thanks and the consideration it would procure. But he had been accused of stealing the clock, and an open gift would savour of admission and peace-offering, whereas in that matter stark denial was his plain course.

A roll of print stuff would not do; apples would not do; and fish was wide of his purpose. Up one side and down the other side of High Street he walked, his eyes instant for suggestion and opportunity. But all in vain. Nobody exposed clocks out of doors, and of those within not one but an attempt on it were simple madness. And of the things less desperate of access nothing was proper to the occasion: all were too large, too cheap, or too uninteresting. Oddly, Dicky feared failure more than had he been hunting for himself.

He tried farther south, in Norton Folgate. There was a shop of cheap second-hand miscellanies: saddles, razors, straps,* dumb-bells, pistols, boxing gloves, trunks, bags, and billiard-balls. Many of the things hung about the door-posts in bunches, and within all was black, as in a cave. At one door-post was a pistol. Nothing could be more interesting than a pistol—indeed it was altogether a better possession than a clock; and it was a small, handy sort of thing. Probably the Ropers would be delighted with a pistol. He stood and regarded it with much interest. There were difficulties. In the first place it was beyond his reach; and in the second, it hung by the trigger-guard on a stout cord. Just then, glancing within the shop, he perceived a pair of fiery eyes regarding him, panther-like, from the inner gloom; and he hastily resumed his walk, as the Jew shopkeeper reached the door, and watched him safely away.

Now he came to Bishopsgate Street, and here at last he chose the gift. It was at a toy-shop: a fine, flaming toy-shop, with carts, dolls, and hoops dangling above, and wooden horses standing below, guarding two baskets by the door. One contained a mixed assortment of tops, whips, boats, and woolly dogs; the other was lavishly filled with shining, round metal boxes, nobly decorated with coloured pictures,* each box with a little cranked handle. As he looked, a tune, delightfully tinkled on some instrument, was heard from within the shop. Dicky peeped. There was a lady, with a little girl at her side who was looking eagerly at just such a shining, round box in the saleswoman's hands, and it was from that box, as the saleswoman turned the handle, that the tune came. Dicky was enchanted. This—this was the thing, beyond debate: a pretty little box that would play music whenever you turned a handle. This was a thing worth any fifty clocks. Indeed it was almost as good as a regular barrel-organ, the first thing he would buy if he were rich.

There was a shop-boy in charge of the goods outside the window, and his eyes were on Dicky. So Dicky whistled absently, and strolled carelessly along. He swung behind a large waggon, crossed the road, and sought a convenient doorstep; for his mind was made up, and his business was now to sit down before the toy-shop, and wait his opportunity.

A shop had been boarded up after a fire, and from its doorstep one could command a perfect view of the toy-shop across the broad thoroughfare with its crowded traffic—could sit, moreover, safe from interference. Here he took his seat, secure from the notice of the guardian shop-boy, whose attention was given to passengers on his own side. The little girl, gripping the new toy in her hand, came out at her mother's side and trotted off. For a moment Dicky reflected that the box could be easily snatched. But after all the little girl had but one: whereas the shopwoman had many, and at best could play on no more than one at a time.

He resumed his watch of the shop-boy, confident that sooner or later a chance would come. A woman stopped to ask the price of something, and Dicky had half crossed the road ere the boy had begun to answer. But the answer was short, and the boy's attention was released too soon.

At last the shopwoman called the boy within, and Dicky darted across—not directly, but so as to arrive invisibly at the side next the basket of music boxes. A quick glance behind him, a snatch at the box with the reddest picture, and a dash into the traffic did it.

The dash would not have been called for but for the sudden re-appearance of the shop-boy ere the box had vanished amid the intricacies of Dicky's jacket. Dicky was fast, but the boy was little slower, and was, moreover, bigger, and stronger on his legs; and Dicky reached the other pavement and turned the next corner into Widegate Street, the pursuer scarce ten yards behind.

It was now that he first experienced 'hot beef'—which is the Jago idiom denoting the plight of one harried by the cry 'Stop thief'. Down Widegate Street, across Sandys Row and into Raven Row he ran his best, clutching the hem of his jacket and the music box that lay within. Crossing Sandys Row a loafing lad shouldered against the shop-boy, and Dicky was grateful, for he made it a gain of several yards.

But others had joined in the hunt, and Dicky for the first time began to fear. This was a bad day—twice already he had been chased; and now—it was bad. He thought little more, for a stunning fear fell upon him: the fear of the hunted, that calculates nothing, and is measured by no apprehension of consequences. He remembered that he must avoid Spitalfields Market, full of men who would stop him; and he knew that in many places where a man would be befriended many would make a virtue of stopping a boy. To the right along Bell Lane he made an agonised burst of speed, and for a while he saw not nor remembered anything; heard no more than dreadful shouts drawing nearer his shoulders, felt only the fear. But he could not last. Quick enough when fresh, he was tiny and ill fed, and now he felt his legs trembling and his wind going. Something seemed to beat on the back of his head, till he wondered madly if it were the shop-boy with a stick. He turned corners, and chose his way by mere instinct, ashen-faced, staring, open-mouthed. How soon would he give in, and drop? A street more—half a street—ten yards? Rolling and tripping, he turned one last corner and almost fell against a vast, fat, unkempt woman whose clothes slid from her shoulders.

''Ere y' are, boy,' said the woman, and flung him by the shoulder through the doorway before which she stood.

He was saved at his extremity, for he could never have reached the street's end. The woman who had done it (probably she had boys of her own on the crook) filled the entrance with her frowsy bulk, and the chase straggled past. Dicky caught the stair-post for a moment's support, and then staggered out at the back of the house. He gasped, he panted, things danced blue before him, but still he clutched his jacket hem and the music box lying within. The back door gave on a cobble-paved court, with other doors, two coster's barrows, and a few dusty fowls. Dicky sat on a step where a door was shut, and rested his head against the frame.

The beating in his head grew slower and lighter, and presently he could breathe with no fear of choking. He rose and moved off, still panting, and feeble in the legs. The court ended in an arched passage, through which he gained the street beyond. Here he had but to turn to the left, and he was in Brick Lane, and thence all was clear to the Old Jago. Regaining his breath and his confidence as he went, he bethought him of the Jago Row retreat, where he might examine his prize at leisure, embowered amid trucks and barrows. Thither he pushed his way, and soon, in the shade of the upturned barrow, he brought out the music box. Bright and shiny, it had taken no damage in the flight, though on his hands he found scratches, and on his shins bruises, got he knew not how. On the top of the box was the picture of a rosy little boy in crimson presenting a scarlet nosegay to a rosy little girl in pink, while a red brick mansion filled the distance and solidified the composition. The brilliant hoop that made the sides (silver, Dicky was convinced) was stamped in patterns, and the little brass handle was an irresistible temptation. Dicky climbed a truck, and looked about him, peeping from beside the loose fence-plank. Then, seeing nobody very near, he muffled the box as well as he could in his jacket, and turned the handle.

This was indeed worth all the trouble. *Gently Does the Trick** was the tune, and Dicky, with his head aside and his ear on the bunch of jacket that covered the box, listened: his lips parted, his eyes seeking illimitable space. He played the tune through, and played it again, and then growing reckless, played it with the box unmuffled, till he was startled by a bang on the fence from without. It was but a passing boy with a stick, but Dicky was sufficiently disturbed to abandon his quarters and take his music elsewhere.

What he longed to do was to take it home and play it to Looey, but that was out of the question: he remembered the watch. But there was Jerry Gullen's canary, and him Dicky sought and found. Canary blinked solemnly when the resplendent box was flashed in his eyes, and set his ears back and forward as, muffled again in Dicky's jacket, it tinkled out its tune.

Tommy Rann should not see it, lest he prevail over its beneficent dedication to the Ropers. Truly, as it was, Dicky's resolution was hard to abide by. The thing acquired at such a cost of patience, address, hard flight, and deadly fear was surely his by right—as surely, quite, as the clock had been. And such a thing he might never touch again. But he put by the temptation manfully, and came out by Jerry Gullen's front door. He would look no more on the music box, beautiful as it was: he would convey it to the Ropers before temptation came again.

It was not easy to devise likely means. Their door was shut fast, of course. For a little while he favoured the plan of setting the box against the threshold, knocking, and running off. But an opportunity might arise of doing the thing in a way to give him some glimpse of the Ropers' delight, an indulgence he felt entitled to. So he waited a little, listened a little, and at last came out into the street, and loafed.

It was near six o'clock, and a smell of bloater hung about Jerry Gullen's door and window; under the raised sash Jerry Gullen, close-cropped and foxy of face, smoked his pipe, sprawled his elbows, and contemplated the world. Dicky, with the music-box stowed out of sight, looked as blank of design and as destitute of possession as he could manage; for there were loafers near Mother Gapp's, loafers at the Luck Row corner—at every corner—and loafers by the 'Posties', all laggard of limb and alert of eye. He had just seen a child, going with an empty beer can, thrown down, robbed of his coppers and a poor old top, and kicked away in helpless tears; and the incident was commonplace enough, or many would have lacked pocket-money. Whosoever was too young, too old, or too weak to fight for it must keep what he had well hidden, in the Jago.

Down the street came Billy Leary, big, flushed and limping, and hanging to a smaller man by a fistful of his coat on the shoulder. Dicky knew the small man for a good toy-getter—(which = watch stealer)—and judged he had had a good click, the proceeds whereof Billy Leary was battening upon in beer-shops. For Billy Leary rarely condescended to anything less honourable than bashing, and had not yet fallen so low as to go about stealing for himself. His missis brought many to the cosh, and his chief necessity—another drink—he merely demanded of the nearest person with the money to buy it, on pain of bashing. Or he walked into the nearest public-house, selected the fullest pot, and spat in it: a ceremony that deprived the purchaser of further interest in the beer, and left it at his own disposal. There were others, both Ranns and Learys, who pursued a similar way of life;

but Billy Leary was biggest among them—big men not being common in the Jago—and rarely came to a difficulty: as, however, he did once come, having invaded the pot of a stranger, who turned out to be a Mile End pugilist exploring Shoreditch. It was not well for any Jago who had made a click to have Billy Leary know of it; for then the clicker was apt to be sought out, clung to, and sucked dry; possibly bashed as well, when nothing more was left, if Billy Leary were still but sober enough for the work.

Dicky gazed after the man with interest. It was he whom his father was to fight in a week or so—perhaps in a few days: on the first Sunday, indeed, that Leary should be deemed fit enough. How much of the limp was due to yesterday's disaster and how much to today's beer, Dicky could not judge. But there seemed little reason to look for a long delay before the fight.

As Dicky turned away a man pushed a large truck round the corner from Edge Lane, and on the footpath beside it walked the parson, calm as ever, with black clothes and tall hat, whole and unsoiled. He had made himself known in the Jago in the course of that afternoon. He had traversed it from end to end, street by street and alley by alley. His self-possession, his readiness, his unbending firmness, abashed and perplexed the Jagos, and his appearance just as the police had left could but convince them that he must have some mysterious and potent connection with the force. He had attempted very little in the way of domiciliary visiting, being content for the time to see his parish, and speak here a word and there another with his parishioners. An encounter with Kiddo Cook did as much as anything toward securing him a proper deference. In his second walk through Old Jago Street, as he neared the Feathers, he was aware of a bunch of grinning faces pressed against the bar window, and as he came abreast, forth stepped Kiddo Cook from the door, impudently affable, smirking and ducking with mock obsequiousness, and offering a quart pot.*

'An' 'ow jer find jerself, sir?' he asked, with pantomime cordiality. 'Hof'ly shockin' these 'ere lower classes, ain't they? Er—yus; disgustin', weally. Er—might I—er—prepose—er—a little refreshment? Ellow me.'

The parson, grimly impassive, heard him through, took the pot, and instantly jerking it upward, shot the beer, a single splash, into Kiddo's face. 'There are things I must teach you, I see, my man,' he said, without moving a muscle, except to return the pot.

Kiddo Cook, coughing, drenched and confounded, took the pot instinctively and backed to Mother Gapp's door, while the bunch of faces at the bar window tossed and rolled in a joyous ecstasy: the ghost whereof presently struggled painfully among Kiddo's own dripping features, as he realised the completeness of his defeat, and the expedience of a patient grin. The parson went calmly on.

Before this, indeed when he left the Ropers' room, and just after Dicky had started out, he had looked in at the Perrotts' quarters to speak about the clock. But plainly no clock was there, and Mrs Perrott's flaccid indignation at the suggestion, and her unmistakable ignorance of the affair, decided him to carry the matter no further, at any rate for the present. Moreover, the little hunchback's tale was inconclusive. He had seen no clock in Dicky's possession—had but met him on the stairs with a bulging jacket. The thing might be suspicious, but the new parson knew better than to peril his influence by charging where he could not convict. So he duly commiserated Hannah Perrott's troubles, suggested that the baby seemed unwell and had better be taken to a doctor, and went his way about the Jago.

Now he stopped the truck by Dicky's front door and mounted to the Ropers' room. For he had seen that the Jago was no place for them now, and had himself found them a suitable room away by Dove Lane. And so, emboldened by his company, the Ropers came forth, and with the help of the man who had brought the truck, carried down the pieces of their bedstead, a bundle of bedding, the two chairs, the pink vases, and the strip of old carpet, and piled them on the truck with the few more things that were theirs.

Dicky, with his hand on the music box in the lining of his jacket, sauntered up by the tail of the truck, and, waiting his chance, plunged his gift under the bundle of bedding, and left it there. But the little hunchback's sharp eyes were jealously on him, and 'Look there!' he squealed, ''e put 'is 'and in the truck an' took somethink!'

'Ye lie!' answered Dicky, indignant and hurt, but cautiously backing off; 'I ain't got nothink.' He spread his hands and opened his jacket in proof. 'Think I got yer bloomin' bedstead?'

He had nothing, it was plain. In fact, at the tail of the truck there was nothing he could easily have moved at all, certainly nothing he could have concealed. So the rest of the little removal was hurried, for heads were now at windows, the loafers began to draw about the truck, and trouble might break out at any moment: indeed, the Ropers could never have ventured from their room but for the general uneasy awe of the parson. For nothing was so dangerous in the Jago as to impugn its honesty. To rob another was reasonable and legitimate, and to avoid being robbed, so far as might be, was natural and proper. But to accuse anybody of a theft was unsportsmanlike, a foul outrage, a shameful abuse, a thing unpardonable. You might rob a man, bash a man, even kill a man; but to 'take away his character'*—even when he had none—was to draw down the execrations of the whole Jago; while to assail the pure fame of the place—to 'give the street a bad name'—this was to bring the Jago howling and bashing about your ears.

The truck moved off at last, amid murmurings, mutterings, and grunts from the onlookers. The man of the truck pulled, Roper shoved behind, and his wife, with her threadbare decency and her meagre, bruised face, carried the baby, while the hunchbacked boy went by her side. All this under convoy of the Reverend Henry Sturt.

A little distance gave more confidence to a few, and, when the group had reached within a score of yards of Edge Lane, there came a hoot or two, a 'Yah!' and other less spellable sounds, expressive of contempt and defiance. Roper glanced back nervously, but the rest held on their way regardless. Then came a brickbat, which missed the woman by very little and struck the truck wheel. At this the parson stopped and turned on his heel, and Cocko Harnwell, the flinger, drove his hands into his breeches pockets and affected an interest in Mother Gapp's window; till, perceiving the parson's eyes directed sternly upon him, and the parson's stick rising to point at him, he ingloriously turned tail and scuttled into Jago Court.

And so the Ropers left the Jago. Dove Lane was but a stone's-throw ahead when some of the load shifted, and the truck was stopped to set the matter right. The chest was pushed back, and the bedding was lifted to put against it, and so the musical box came to light. Roper picked it up and held it before the vicar's eyes. 'Look at that, sir,' he said. 'You'll witness I know nothing of it, won't you? It ain't mine, an' I never saw it before. It's bin put in for spite to put a theft on us. When they come for it you'll bear me out, sir, won't you? That was the Perrott boy as was put up to do that, I'll be bound. When he was behind the truck.'

But nobody came for Dicky's gift, and in the Jago twilight Dicky vainly struggled to whistle the half-remembered tune, and to persuade himself that he was not sorry that the box was gone.

CHAPTER 11

JOSH PERROTT reached home late for tea but in good humour. He had spent most of the day at the Bag of Nails, dancing attendance on the High Mobsmen. Those of the High Mob* were the flourishing practitioners* in burglary, the mag,* the mace,* and the broads,* with an outer fringe of such dippers—such pickpockets—as could dress well, welshers,* and snidesmen.* These, the grandees of rascality, lived in places far from the Jago, and some drove in gigs and pony traps. But they found the Bag of Nails a convenient and secluded exchange and house of call,* and there they met, made appointments, designed villainies, and tossed for sovereigns: deeply reverenced by the admiring Jagos, among whom no ambition flourished but this—to become also of these resplendent ones. It was of these that old Beveridge had spoken one day to Dicky, in language the child but half understood. The old man sat on a kerb in view of the Bag of Nails, and smoked a blackened bit of clay pipe. He hauled Dicky to his side, and, pointing with his pipe, said:—'See that man with the furs?'

'What?' Dicky replied. 'Mean 'im in the ice-cream coat,* smokin' a cigar? Yus.'

'And the other with the brimmy* tall hat, and the red face, and the umbrella?'

'Yus.'

'What are they?'

''Igh mob. 'Ooks. Toffs.'

'Right. Now, Dicky Perrott, you Jago whelp, look at them—look hard. Some day, if you're clever—cleverer than anyone in the Jago now—if you're only scoundrel enough, and brazen enough, and lucky enough—one of a thousand—maybe you'll be like them: bursting with high living, drunk when you like, red and pimply. There it is—that's your aim in life—there's your pattern. Learn to read and write, learn all you can, learn cunning, spare nobody and stop at nothing, and perhaps—' he waved his hand toward the Bag of Nails. 'It's the best the world has for you, for the Jago's got you, and that's the only way out,* except gaol and the gallows. So do your devilmost, or God help you, Dicky Perrott—though he won't: for the Jago's got you!'

Old Beveridge had eccentric talk and manners, and the Jago regarded him as a trifle 'barmy', though anything but a fool. So that Dicky troubled little to sift the meaning of what he said.

Josh Perrott's mission among the High Mob had been to discover some Mobsman who might be disposed to back him in the fight with Billy Leary. For though a private feud was the first cause of the turn-up, still business must never be neglected, and a feud or anything else that could produce money must be made to produce it, and when a fight of exceptional merit is placed before spectators, it is but fair that they should pay for their diversion.

But few High Mobsmen were at the Bag of Nails that day. Sunday was the day of the chief gatherings of the High Mob: Sunday the market day, so to speak, of the Jago, when such rent as was due weekly was paid (most of the Jago rents were paid daily and nightly) and other accounts were settled or fought out. Moreover, the High Mob were perhaps a trifle shy of the Jago at the time of a faction fight; and one was but just over, and that cut short at a third of the usual span of days.* So that Josh waited long and touted vainly, till a patron arrived who knew him of old; who had employed him, indeed, as 'minder'—which means a protector or a bully, as you please to regard it—on a racecourse adventure involving bodily risk. On this occasion Josh had earned his wages with hard knocks given and taken, and his employer had conceived a high and thankful opinion of his capacity. Wherefore he listened now to the tale of the coming fight, and agreed to provide something in the way of stakes, and to put something on for Josh himself: looking for his own profit to the bets he might make at favourable odds with his friends. For Billy Leary was notorious as being near prime ruffian of the Jago, while Josh's reputation was neither so evil nor so wide. And so it was settled, and Josh came pleased to his tea; for assuredly Billy Leary would have no difficulty in finding another notable of the High Mob to cover the stakes.

Dicky was at home, sitting by Looey on the bed; and when he called his father it seemed pretty plain to Josh that the baby was out of sorts. 'She's rum about the eyes,' he said to his wife. 'Blimy if she don't look as though she was goin' to squint.'

Josh was never particularly solicitous as to the children, but he saw that they were fed and clothed—perhaps by mere force of the habit of his more reputable days of plastering. He had brought home tripe, rolled in paper, and stuffed into his coat pocket, to make a supper on the strength of the day's stroke of business. When this tripe was boiled, he and Dicky essayed to drive morsels into Looey's mouth, and to wash them down with beer; but to no end but choking rejection. Whereat Josh decided that she must go to the dispensary in the morning. And in the morning he took her, with Dicky at his heels; for not only did his wife still nurse her neck, but in truth she feared to venture abroad.

The dispensary was no charitable institution,* but a shop so labelled in Meakin Street, one of half a dozen such kept by a medical man who lived away from them, and bothered himself as little about them as was consistent with banking the takings and signing the death-certificates. A needy young student, whose sole qualification was cheapness, was set to do the business of each place, and the uniform price for advice and medicine was sixpence. But there was a deal of professional character in the blackened and gilt-lettered front windows, and the sixpences came by hundreds. For hospital letters* but rarely came Meakin Street way. Such as did were mostly in the hands of tradesmen, who subscribed* for the purpose of getting them, and gave them to their best customers, as was proper and business-like. And so the dispensary flourished, and the needy young student grew shifty and callous, and no doubt there were occasional faith-cures. Indeed, cures of simple science were not at all impossible. For there was always a good supply of two drugs in the place—Turkey rhubarb and sulphuric acid: both very useful, both very cheap, and both going very far in varied preparation, properly handled. An ounce or two of sulphuric acid, for instance, costing something fractional, dilutes with water into many gallons of physic. Excellent medicines they made too, and balanced each other very well by reason of their opposite effects.* But indeed they were not all, for sometimes there were two or three other drugs in hand,* interfering, perhaps troublesomely, with the simple division of therapeutics into the two provinces of rhubarb and sulphuric acid.

Business was brisk at the dispensary: several were waiting, and medicine and advice were going at the rate of two minutes for sixpence. Looey's case was not so clear as most of the others: she could not describe its symptoms succinctly, as 'a pain here', or 'a tight feeling there'. She did but lie heavily, staring blankly upward (she did not mind the light now), with the little cast in her eyes, and repeat her odd little wail; and Dicky and his father could tell very little.

The young student had a passing thought that he might have known a trifle more of the matter if he had had time to turn up Ross on nerve and brain troubles*—were such a proceeding consistent with the dignity of the dispensary; but straightway assigning the case to the rhubarb province, made up a powder, ordered Josh to keep the baby quiet, and pitched his sixpence among the others, well within the two minutes.

And faith in the dispensary was strengthened, for indeed Looey seemed a little better after the powder; and she was fed with spoonfuls of a fluid bought at a chandler's shop, and called milk.*

CHAPTER 12

'DICKY PERROTT, come 'ere,' said Mr Aaron Weech in a voice of sad rebuke, a few days later. 'Come 'ere, Dicky Perrott.'

He shook his head solemnly as he stooped. Dicky slouched up.

'What was that you found the other day an' didn't bring to me?'

'Nuffin'.' Dicky withdrew a step.

'It's no good you a-tellin' me that, Dicky Perrott, when I know better. You know very well you can't pervent me knowin'.' His little eyes searched Dicky's face, and Dicky sulkily shifted his own gaze. 'You're a wicked, ungrateful young 'ound, an' I've a good mind to tell a p'liceman to find out where you got that clock. Come 'ere now—don't you try runnin' away. Wot! after me a-takin' you in when you was 'ungry, an' givin' you cawfy an' cake, an' good advice like a father, an' a bloater an' all, an' you owin' me thrippence a'peny besides, then you goes an'—an' takes yer findin's somewhere else!'

'I never!' protested Dicky stoutly. But Mr Weech's cunning, equal to a shrewd guess that since his last visit Dicky had probably had another 'find', and quick to detect a lie, was slack to perceive a truth.

'Now don't you go an' add on a wicked lie to yer sinful ungratefulness, wotever you do,' he said, severely. 'That's wuss, an' I alwis know. Doncher know the little 'ymn?*—

> An' 'im as does one fault at fust
> An' lies to 'ide it, makes it two.

It's bad enough to be ungrateful to me as is bin so kind to you, an' it's wuss to break the fust commandment.* If the bloater don't inflooence you, the 'oly 'ymn ought. 'Ow would you like me to go an' ask yer father for that thrippence a'peny you owe me? That's wot I'll 'ave to do if you don't mind.'

Dicky would not have liked it at all, as his frightened face testified.

'Then find somethink an' pay it at once, an' then I won't. I won't be 'ard on you, if you'll be a good boy. But don't git playin' no more tricks—'cos I'll know all about 'em. Now go an' find somethink quick.' And Dicky went.

CHAPTER 13

TEN days after his first tour of the Old Jago, the Reverend Henry Sturt first preached in the parish church made of a stable, in an alley behind Meakin Street, but few yards away, though beyond sight and sound of the Jago. There, that Sunday morning was a morning of importance, a time of excitement, for the fight between Billy Leary and Josh Perrott was to come off in Jago Court. The assurance that there was money in the thing was a sovereign liniment for Billy Leary's bruises—for they were but bruises—and he hastened to come by that money, lest it melt by caprice of the backers, or the backers themselves fall at unlucky odds with the police. He made little of Josh Perrott, his hardness and known fighting power notwithstanding. For was there not full a stone and a half between their weights? And had Billy not four or five inches the better in height and a commensurate advantage in reach? And Billy Leary's own hardness and fighting power were well proved enough.

It was past eleven o'clock. The weekly rents—for the week forthcoming—had been extracted, or partly extracted, or scuffled over. Old Poll Rann, who had made money in sixty-five years of stall-farming* and iniquity, had made the rounds of the six houses she rented, to turn out the tenants of the night who were disposed to linger. Many had already stripped themselves to their rags at pitch-and-toss* in Jago Court; and the game still went busily on in the crowded area and in overflow groups in Old Jago Street; and men found themselves deprived, not merely of the money for that day's food and that night's lodging, but even of the last few pence set by to back a horse for Tuesday's race. A little-regarded fight or two went on here and there as usual, and on kerbs and doorsteps sat women, hideous at all ages, filling the air with the rhetoric of the Jago.

Presently down from Edge Lane and the 'Posties' came the High Mobsmen, swaggering in check suits and billycocks, gold chains and lumpy rings: stared at, envied, and here and there pointed out by name or exploit. 'Him as done the sparks in from Regent Street for nine centuries o' quids';* 'Him as done five stretch* for a snide bank bill an' they never found the oof'; 'Him as maced the bookies in

France an' shot the nark in the boat'; and so forth. And the High Mob being come, the fight was due.

Of course, a fight merely as a fight was no great matter of interest: the thing was too common. But there was money on this; and again, it was no common thing to find Billy Leary defied, still less to find him challenged. Moreover, the thing had a Rann and Leary complexion, and it arose out of the battle of less than a fortnight back. So that Josh Perrott did not lack for partisans, though not a Rann believed he could stand long before Billy Leary. Billy's cause, too, had lost some popularity because it had been reported that Sally Green, in hospital, had talked of 'summonsing' Norah Walsh in the matter of her mangled face: a scandalous device to overreach, a piece of foul practice repugnant to all proper feeling; more especially for such a distinguished Jago as Sally Green—so well able to take care of herself. But all this was nothing as affecting the odds. They ruled at three to one on Billy Leary, with few takers, and went to four to one before the fight began.

Josh Perrott had been strictly sober for a full week. And the family had lived better, for he had brought meat home each day. Now he sat indifferently at the window of his room, and looked out at the crowd in Jago Court till such time as he might be wanted. He had not been out of the room that morning: he was saving his energy for Billy Leary.

As for Dicky, he had scarce slept for excitement. For days he had enjoyed consideration among his fellows on account of this fight. Now he shook and quivered, and nothing relieved his agitation but violent exertion. So he rushed downstairs a hundred times to see if the High Mob were coming, and back to report that they were not. At last he saw their overbearing checks, and tore upstairs, face before knees, with ''Ere they are, father! 'Ere they are! They're comin' down the street, father!' and danced frenzied about the room and the landing.

Presently Jerry Gullen and Kiddo Cook came, as seconds, to take Josh out, and then Dicky quieted a little externally, though he was bursting at the chest and throat, and his chin jolted his teeth together uncontrollably. Josh dragged off his spotted coat and waistcoat and flung them on the bed, and then was helped out of his ill-mended blue shirt. He gave a hitch to his trousers-band, tightened his belt, and was ready.

'Ta-ta, ol' gal,' he said to his wife, with a grin; 'back agin soon.'

'With a bob or two for ye,' added Kiddo Cook, grinning likewise.

Hannah Perrott sat pale and wistful, with the baby on her knees. Through the morning she had sat so, wretched and helpless, sometimes putting her face in her hands, sometimes breaking out hopelessly:—'Don't, Josh, don't—good Gawd, Josh, I wish you wouldn't!' or 'Josh, Josh, I wish I was dead!' Josh had fought before, it was true, and more than once, but then she had learned of the matter afterward. This preparation and long waiting were another thing. Once she had even exclaimed that she would go with him—though she meant nothing.

Now, as Josh went out at the door, she bent over Looey and hid her face again. 'Good luck, father,' called Dicky, 'go it!' Though the words would hardly pass his throat, and he struggled to believe that he had no fear for his father.

No sooner was the door shut than he rushed to the window, though Josh could not appear in Jago Court for three or four minutes yet. The sash-line was broken, and the window had been propped open with a stick. In his excitement Dicky dislodged the stick, and the sash* came down on his head, but he scarce felt the blow, and readjusted the stick with trembling hands, regardless of the bruise rising under his hair.

'Aincher goin' to look, mother?' he asked. 'Wontcher 'old up Looey?'

But his mother would not look. As for Looey, she looked at nothing. She had been taken to the dispensary once again, and now lay drowsy and dull, with little more movement than a general shudder and a twitching of the face at long intervals. The little face itself was thinner and older than ever: horribly flea-bitten still, but bloodlessly pale. Mrs Perrott had begun to think Looey was ailing for something; thought it might be measles or whooping-cough* coming, and complained that children were a continual worry.

Dicky hung head and shoulders out of the window, clinging to the broken sill and scraping feverishly at the wall with his toes. Jago Court was fuller than ever. The tossing went on, though now with more haste, that most might be made of the remaining time. A scuffle still persisted in one corner. Some stood to gaze at the High Mob, who, to the number of eight or ten, stood in an exalted group over against the back fences of New Jago Street; but the thickest knot was about Cocko Harnwell's doorstep, whereon sat Billy Leary, his head just visible through the press about him, waiting to keep his appointment.

Then a close group appeared at the archway, and pushed into the crowd, which made way at its touch, the disturbed tossers pocketing their coppers, but the others busily persisting, with no more than a glance aside between the spins. Josh Perrott's cropped head and bare shoulders marked the centre of the group, and as it came, another group moved out from Cocko Harnwell's doorstep, with Billy Leary's tall bulk shining pink and hairy in its midst.

''E's in the court, mother,' called Dicky, scraping faster with his toes.

The High Mobsmen moved up toward the middle of the court, and some from the two groups spread and pushed back the crowd. Still half a dozen couples, remote by the walls, tossed and tossed faster than ever, moving this way and that as the crowd pressed.

Now there was an irregular space of bare cobble stones and house refuse, five or six yards across, in the middle of Jago Court, and all round it the shouting crowd was packed tight, those at the back standing on sills and hanging to fences. Every window was a clump of heads, and women yelled savagely or cheerily down and across. The two groups were merged in the press at each side of the space, Billy Leary and Josh Perrott in front of each, with his seconds.

'Naa then, any more 'fore they begin?' bawled a High Mobsman, turning about among his fellows. 'Three to one on the big 'un—three to one! 'Ere, I'll give fours—four to one on Leary! Fourer one! Fourer one!'

But they shook their heads; they would wait a little. Leary and Perrott stepped out. The last of the tossers stuffed away his coppers, and sought for a hold on the fence.

'They're a-sparrin', mother!' cried Dicky, pale and staring, elbows and legs a-work, till he was like to pitch out of window. From his mother there but jerked a whimpering sob, which he did not hear.

The sparring was not long. There was little of subtlety in the milling of the Jago: mostly no more than a rough application of the main hits and guards,* with much rushing and ruffianing. What there was of condition in the two men was Josh's: smaller and shorter, he had a certain hard brownness of hide that Leary, in his heavy opulence of flesh, lacked; and there was a horny quality in his face and hands that reminded the company of his boast of invulnerability to anything milder than steel. Also his breadth of chest was great. Nevertheless all odds seemed against him, by reason of Billy Leary's size, reach, and fighting record.

The men rushed together, and Josh was forced back by weight. Leary's great fists, left and right, shot into his face with smacking reports, but left no mark on the leathery skin, and Josh, fighting for the body, drove his knuckles into the other's ribs with a force that jerked a thick grunt from Billy's lips at each blow.

There was a roar of shouts. 'Go it, father! Fa—ther! Fa—ther!' Dicky screamed from the window, till his voice broke in his throat and he coughed himself livid. The men were at holds, and swaying this way and that over the uneven stones. Blood ran copiously from Billy Leary's nose over his mouth and chin, and, as they turned, Dicky saw his father spit away a tooth over Leary's shoulder. They clipped and hauled to and fro, each striving to break the other's foothold. Then Perrott stumbled at a hole, lost his feet, and went down, with Leary on top.

Cheers and yells rent the air, as each man was taken to his own side by his seconds. Dicky let go the sill and turned to his mother, wild of eye, breathless with broken chatter.

'Father 'it 'im on the nose, mother, like that—'is ribs is goin' black where father pasted 'em—'e was out o' breath fust—there's blood all over 'is face, mother—father would 'a' chucked 'im over if 'e 'adn't tumbled in a 'ole—father 'it 'im twice on the jore—'e—O!'

Dicky was back again on the sill, kicking and shouting, for time was called, and the two men rushed again into a tangled knot. But the close strife was short. Josh had but closed to spoil his man's wind, and, leaving his head to take care of itself, stayed till he had driven left and right on the mark, and then got back. Leary came after him, gasping and blowing already, and Josh feinted a lead and avoided, bringing Leary round on his heel and off again in chase. Once more Josh met him, drove at his ribs, and got away out of reach. Leary's wind was going fast, and his partisans howled savagely at Josh—perceiving his tactics—taunting him with running away, daring him to stand and fight. 'I'll take that four to one,' called a High Mobsman to him who had offered the odds in the beginning. 'I'll stand a quid on Perrott!'

'Not with me you won't,' the other answered. 'Evens, if you like.'

'Right. Done at evens, a quid.'

Perrott, stung at length by the shouts from Leary's corner, turned on Billy and met him at full dash. He was himself puffing by this time, though much less than his adversary, and, at the cost of a heavy blow (which he took on his forehead), he visited Billy's ribs once more.

Both men were grunting and gasping now, and the sound of blows was as of the confused beating of carpets. Dicky, who had been afflicted to heart-burst by his father's dodging and running, which he mistook for simple flight, now broke into excited speech once more:—

'Father's 'it 'im on the jore ag'in—'is eye's a-bungin' up—*Go it, father, bash 'i-i-i-m!* Father's landin' 'im—'e—'

Hannah Perrott crept to the window and looked. She saw the foul Jago mob, swaying and bellowing about the shifting edge of an open patch, in the midst whereof her husband and Billy Leary, bruised, bloody and gasping, fought and battered infuriately; and she crept back to the bed and bent her face on Looey's unclean little frock: till a fit of tense shuddering took the child, and the mother looked up again.

Without, the round ended. For a full minute the men took and gave knock for knock, and then Leary, wincing from another body-blow, swung his right desperately on Perrott's ear, and knocked him over.

Exulting shouts rose from the Leary faction, and the blow struck Dicky's heart still. But Josh was up almost before Kiddo Cook reached him, and Dicky saw a wide grin on his face as he came to his corner. The leathery toughness of the man, and the advantage it gave him, now grew apparent. He had endured to the full as much and as hard punching as had his foe—even more, and harder; once he had fallen on the broken cobble-stones with all Leary's weight on him; and once he had been knocked down on them. But, except for the sweat that ran over his face and down his back, and for a missing front tooth and the lip it had cut, he showed little sign of the struggle; while Leary's left eye was a mere slit in a black wen, his nose was a beaten mass, which had ensanguined him (and indeed Josh) from crown to waist, and his chest and flanks were a mottle of bruises.

'Father's awright, mother—I see 'im laughin'! And 'e's smashed Leary's nose all over 'is face!'

Up again they sprang for the next round, Perrott active and daring, Leary cautious and a trifle stiff. Josh rushed in and struck at the tender ribs once more, took two blows callously on his head, and sent his left at the nose, with a smack as of a flail on water. With that Leary rushed like a bull, and Josh was driven and battered back, for the moment without response. But he ducked, and slipped away, and came again, fresh and vicious. And now it was seen that Perrott's toughness of hand was lasting. Leary's knuckles were raw, cut, and flayed, and took little good by the shock when they met the other's stubborn muzzle; while Josh still flung in his corneous fists, hard and lasting as a bag of bullets.

But suddenly, stooping to reach the mark once more, Josh's foot turned on a projecting stone, and he floundered forward into Billy's arms. Like a flash his neck was clipped in the big man's left arm: Josh Perrott was in chancery. Quick and hard Leary pounded the imprisoned head, while Jerry Gullen and Kiddo Cook danced distracted and dismayed, and the crowd whooped and yelled.

Dicky hung delirious over the sill, and shrieked he knew not what. He saw his father fighting hard at the back and ribs with both hands, and Leary hammering his face in a way to make pulp of an ordinary mazzard. Then suddenly Josh Perrott's right hand shot up from behind, over Leary's shoulder, and gripped him at the chin. Slowly, with tightened muscles, he forced his man back over his bent knee, Leary clinging and swaying, but impotent to struggle. Then, with an extra wrench from Josh, up came Leary's feet from the ground, higher, higher, till suddenly Josh flung him heavily over, heels up, and dropped on him with all his weight.

The Ranns roared again. Josh was up in a moment, sitting on Kiddo Cook's knee, and taking a drink from a bottle. Billy Leary lay like a man fallen from a house-top. His seconds turned him on his back, and dragged him to his corner. There he lay limp and senseless, and there was a cut at the back of his head.

The High Mobsman who held the watch waited for half a minute and then called 'Time!' Josh Perrott stood up, but Billy Leary was knocked out of knowledge, and heard not. He was beaten.

Josh Perrott was involved in a howling, dancing crowd, and was pushed, grinning, this way and that, slapped on the back, and offered drinks. In the outskirts the tossers, inveterate, pulled out their pence and resumed their game.

Dicky spun about, laughing, flushed, and elated, and as soon as the door was distinct to his dazzled sight, he ran off downstairs.

His mother, relieved and even pleased, speculated as to what money the thing might bring. She put the baby on the bed, and looked from the window.

Josh, in the crowd, shouted and beckoned her, pointing and tapping his bare shoulder. He wanted his clothes. She gathered together the shirt, the coat, and the waistcoat, and hurried downstairs. Looey could come to no harm lying on the bed for a few minutes. And, indeed, Hannah Perrott felt that she would be a person of distinction in the crowd, and was not sorry to have an excuse for going out.

'Three cheers for the missis!' sang out Kiddo Cook as she came through the press. 'I said 'e'd 'ave a bob or two for you, didn't I?' Josh Perrott, indeed, was rich—a capitalist of five pounds. For a sovereign a side had been put up, and his backer had put on a sovereign for him at three to one. So that now it became him to stand beer to many sympathisers. Also, he felt that the missis should have some part in the celebration, for was it not her injury that he had avenged on Sally Green's brother? So Hannah Perrott, pleased though timorous, was hauled away with the rest to Mother Gapp's.

Here she sat by Josh's side for an hour. Once or twice she thought of Looey, but with native inertness she let the thought slip. Perhaps Dicky would be back, and at any rate it was hard if she must not take half an hour's relaxation once in a way. At last came Dicky, urgent perplexity in his face, looking in at the door. Josh, minded to be generous all round, felt for a penny.

'Mother,' said Dicky, plucking at her arm, 'Pigeony Poll's at 'ome, nussin' Looey; she told me to tell you to come at once.'

Pigeony Poll? What right had she in the room? The ghost of Hannah Perrott's respectability rose in resentment. She supposed she must go. She arose, mystified, and went, with Dicky at her skirts.

Pigeony Poll sat by the window with the baby in her arms, and pale misgiving in her dull face. 'I—I come in, Mrs Perrott, mum,' she said, with a hush in her thick voice, 'I come in 'cos I see you goin' out, an' I thought the baby'd be alone. She—she's 'ad a sort o' fit—all stiff an' blue in the face and grindin' 'er little mouth. She's left auf now—but I—I dunno what to make of 'er. She's so—so—'

Hannah Perrott stared blankly, and lifted the child, whose arm dropped and hung. The wizen age had gone from Looey's face, and the lids were down on the strained eyes; her pale lips lay eased of the old pinching—even parted in a smile. For she looked in the face of the Angel that plays with the dead children.

Hannah Perrott's chin fell. 'Lor',' she said bemusedly, and sat on the bed.

An odd croaking noise broke in jerks from Pigeony Poll as she crept from the room, with her face bowed in the bend of her arm, like a weeping schoolboy. Dicky stared, confounded. . . . Josh came and gazed stupidly, with his mouth open, walking tip-toe. But at a word from Kiddo Cook, who came in his tracks, he snatched the little body and clattered off to the dispensary, to knock up the young student.

The rumour went in the Jago that Josh Perrott was in double luck. For here was insurance money without a doubt. But in truth that was a thing the Perrotts had neglected.

Hannah Perrott felt a listless relief; Josh felt nothing in particular, except that there was no other thing to be done, and that Mother Gapp's would be a cheerful place to finish the day in, and keep up the missis's pecker.

So that eight o'clock that evening at Perrotts' witnessed a darkening room wherein an inconsiderable little corpse lay on a bed; while a small ragamuffin spread upon it with outstretched arms, exhausted with sobbing, a soak of muddy tears:—'O Looey, Looey! Can't you 'ear? Won't you never come to me no more?'

And the Reverend Henry Sturt, walking from church through Luck Row toward his lodgings in Kingsland Road, heard shouts and riot behind the grimy panes of Mother Gapp's, and in the midst the roar of many voices joined in the Jago chant:—

Six bloomin' long months in a prison,
Six more bloomin' months I must stay,
For meetin' a bloke in our alley
An' takin' 'is uxter away!

Toora-li—toora-li—looral,
Toora-li—toora-li—lay,
A-coshin' a bloke in our alley,
*An' takin' 'is uxter away!**

CHAPTER 14

On an autumn day four years after his first coming to the Jago, the Reverend Henry Sturt left a solicitor's office in Cheapside, and walked eastward, with something more of hope and triumph in him than he had felt since the Jago fell to his charge. For the ground was bought whereon should be built a church and buildings accessory, and he felt, not that he was like to see any great result from his struggle, but that perhaps he might pursue it better armed and with less of grim despair than had been his portion hitherto.

It had taken him four years to gather the money for the site, and some of it he was paying from his own pocket. He was unmarried, and had therefore no reason to save. Still, he must be careful, for the sake of the parish: the church must be built, and some of the money would probably be wanted for that. Moreover, there were other calls. The benefice brought a trifle less than £200 a year, and out of that, so far as it would go, he paid (with some small outside help) £130 for rent of the temporary church and the adjacent rooms; the organist's salary; the rates and the gas-bills; the cost of cleaning, care, and repair; the sums needed for such relief as was impossible to be withheld; and a thousand small things beside. While the Jagos speculated wildly among themselves as to the vast sums he must make by his job. For what toff would come and live in the Jago except for a consideration of solid gain? What other possible motive could there be, indeed?

Still, he had an influence among them such as they had never known before. For one thing, they feared in him what they took for a sort of supernatural insight. The mean cunning of the Jago, subtle as it was, and baffling to most strangers, foundered miserably before his relentless intelligence; and crafty rogues—'wide as Broad Street',* as their proverb went—at first sulked, faltered and prevaricated transparently, but soon gave up all hope or effort to deceive him. Thus he was respected. Once he had made it plain that he was no common milch-cow in the matter of gratuities: to be bamboozled for shillings, cajoled for coals, and bullied for blankets: then there became apparent in him qualities of charity and loving-kindness, well-judged and governed, that awoke in places a regard that was in a way akin to affection. And the familiar habit of the Jago slowly grew to call him Father Sturt.

Father Sturt was not to be overreached: that was the axiom gloomily accepted by all in the Jago who lived by what they accounted their wits. You could not juggle shillings and clothing (convertible into shillings) out of Father Sturt by the easy fee-faw-fum of repentance and salvation that served with so many. There were many of the Jagos (mightily despised by some of the sturdier ruffians) who sallied forth from time to time into neighbouring regions in pursuit of the profitable sentimentalist: discovering him—black-coated, earnest, green—sometimes a preacher, sometimes a layman, sometimes one having authority on the committee of a charitable institution; dabbling in the East End on his own account, or administering relief for a mission, or disbursing a Mansion House Fund.* He was of two chief kinds: the Merely-Soft*—the 'man of wool' as the Jago word went—for whom any tale was good enough, delivered with the proper wistful misery: and the Gullible-Cocksure, confident in a blind experience, who was quite as easy to tap, when approached with a becoming circumspection. A rough and ready method, which served well in most cases with both sorts, was a profession of sudden religious awakening. For this, one offered an aspect either of serene happiness or of maniacal exaltation, according to the customer's taste. A better way, but one demanding greater subtlety, was the assumption of the part of Earnest Inquirer, hesitating on the brink of Salvation. For the attitude was capable of indefinite prolongation, and was ever productive of the boots, the coats, and the half-crowns used to coax weak brethren into the fold. But with Father Sturt, such trouble was worse than useless; it was, indeed, but to invite a humiliating snub. Thus, when Fluffy Pike* first came to Father Sturt with the intelligence that he had at last found Grace, then Father Sturt asked if he had found it in a certain hamper—a hamper hooked that morning from a railway van—and if it were of a quality likely to inspire an act of restoration to the goods office. Nothing was to be done with a man of this disgustingly practical turn of mind, and the Jagos soon ceased from trying.

Father Sturt had made more of the stable than the make-shift church he had found. He had organised a club in a stable adjoining, and he lived in the rooms over the shut-up shop. In the club he gathered the men of the Jago indiscriminately, with the sole condition of good behaviour on the premises. And there they smoked, jumped, swung on horizontal bars, boxed,* played at cards and bagatelle, free from interference save when interference became necessary. For the women there were sewing-meetings and singing. And all governed with an invisible discipline, which, being brought to action, was found to be of iron.

Now there was ground on which might be built a worthier church; and Father Sturt had in mind a church which should have by its side a cleanly lodging-house, a night-shelter, a club, baths and washhouses. And at a stroke he would establish this habitation and wipe out the blackest spot in the Jago. For the new site comprised the whole of Jago Court and the houses that masked it in Old Jago Street.

This was a dream of the future—perhaps of the immediate future, if a certain new millionaire* could only be interested in the undertaking—but of the future certainly. The money for the site alone had been hard enough to gather. In the first place the East London Elevation Mission and Pansophical Institute was asking very diligently for funds—and was getting them. It was to that, indeed, that people turned by habit when minded to invest in the amelioration of the East End. Then about this time there had arisen a sudden quacksalver, a Panjandrum of philanthropy, a mummer of the market-place, who undertook, for a fixed sum, to abolish poverty and sin together;* and many, pleased with the new gaudery,* poured out before him the money that had gone to maintain hospitals and to feed proved charities. So that gifts were scarce and hard to come by—indeed, were apt to be thought unnecessary, for was not misery to be destroyed out of hand? Moreover, Father Sturt wanted not for enemies among the Sentimental-Cocksure. He was callous and cynical in face of the succulent penitence of Fluffy Pike and his kind. He preferred the frank rogue before the calculating snivelmonger. He had a club at which boxing was allowed, and dominoes—flat ungodliness.* He shook hands familiarly every day with the lowest characters: his tastes were vulgar and brutal. And the company at his club was really dreadful. These things the Cocksure said, with shaking of heads; and these they took care should be known among such as might give Father Sturt money. Father Sturt!—the name itself was sheer papistry.* And many comforted themselves by writing him anonymous letters, displaying hell before his eyes, and dealing him vivid damnation.

So Father Sturt tramped back to the Jago, and to the strain and struggle that ceased not for one moment of his life, though it left never a mark of success behind it. For the Jago was much as ever. Were the lump once leavened by the advent of any denizen a little less base than the rest, were a native once ridiculed and persuaded into a spell of work and clean living, then must Father Sturt hasten to drive him from the Jago ere its influence suck him under for ever; leaving for his own community none but the entirely vicious. And among these he spent his life: preaching little, in the common sense, for that were but idle vanity in this place; but working, alleviating, growing into the Jago life, flinging scorn and ridicule on evil things, grateful for tiny negative successes—for keeping a few from ill-behaviour but for an hour; conscious that wherever he was not, iniquity flourished unreproved; and oppressed by the remembrance that albeit the Jago death-rate ruled full four times that of all London* beyond, still the Jago rats bred and bred their kind unhindered, multiplying apace and infecting the world.

In Luck Row he came on Josh Perrott, making for home with something under the skirt of his coat.

'How d'ye do, Josh?' said Father Sturt, clapping a hand on Josh's shoulder, and offering it as Josh turned about.

Josh, with a shifting of the object under his coat, hastened to tap his cap-peak with his forefinger before shaking hands. He grinned broadly, and looked this way and that, with mingled gratification and embarrassment, as was the Jago way in such circumstances. Because one could never tell whether Father Sturt would exchange a mere friendly sentence or two, or, with concealed knowledge, put some disastrous question about a watch, or a purse, or a breastpin, or what not.

'Very well, thanks, Father,' answered Josh, and grinned amiably at the wall beyond the vicar's elbow.

'And what have you been doing just lately?'

'Oo—odd jobs, Father.' Always the same answer, all over the Jago.

'Not quite such odd jobs as usual, I hope, Josh, eh?' Father Sturt smiled, and twitched Josh playfully by the button-hole as one might treat a child. 'I once heard of a very odd job in the Kingsland Road that got a fine young man six months' holiday. Eh, Josh?'

Josh Perrott wriggled and grinned sheepishly; tried to frown, failed, and grinned again. He had only been out a few weeks from that six moon.* Presently he said:—'Awright, Father; you do rub it into a bloke, no mistake.'

The grin persisted as he looked first at the wall, then at the pavement, then down the street, but never in the parson's face.

'Ah, there's a deal of good in a blister* sometimes, isn't there, Josh? What's that I see—a clock? Not another odd job, eh?'

It was indeed a small nickel-plated American clock which Josh had under his coat, and which he now partly uncovered with positive protests. 'No, s'elp me, Father, it's all straight—all fair trade, Father—jist a swop for somethink else, on me solemn davy. That's wot it is, Father—straight.'

'Well, I'm glad you thought to get it, Josh,' Father Sturt pursued, still twitching the button-hole. 'You never have been a punctual church-goer, you know, Josh, and I'm glad you've made arrangements to improve. You'll have no excuse now, you know, and I shall expect you on Sunday morning—promptly. Don't forget: I shall be looking for you.' And Father Sturt shook hands again, and passed on, leaving Josh Perrott still grinning dubiously, and striving to assimilate the invitation to church.

The clock was indeed an exchange, though not altogether an innocent one: the facts being these. Early that morning Josh had found himself scrambling hastily along a turning out of Brick Lane, accompanied by a parcel of nine or ten pounds of tobacco, and extremely conscious of the hasty scrambling of several other people round the corner. Some of these people turned that corner before Josh reached the next, so that his course was observed, and it became politic to get rid of his parcel before a possible heading-off in Meakin Street. There was one place where this might be done, and that was at Weech's. A muddy yard, one of a tangle of such places behind Meakin Street, abutted on Weech's back fence; and it was no uncommon thing for a Jago on the crook, hard pressed, to pitch his plunder over the fence, double out into the crowd, and call on Mr Aaron Weech for the purchase-money as soon as opportunity served. The manœuvre was a simple one, facilitated by the plan of the courts; but it was only adopted in extreme cases, because Mr Aaron Weech was at best but a mean paymaster, and with so much of the upper hand in the bargain as these circumstances conferred, was apt to be meaner than ever. But this case seemed to call for the stratagem, and Josh made for the muddy yard, dropped the parcel over the fence, with a loud whistle, and backed off by the side passage in the regular way.

When he called on Mr Aaron Weech a few hours later, that talented tradesman, with liberal gestures, told out shillings singly in his hand, pausing after each as though that were the last. But Josh held his hand persistently open, till Mr Weech, having released the fifth shilling, stopped altogether, scandalised at such rapacity. But still Josh was not satisfied, and as he was not quite so easy a customer to manage as the boys who commonly fenced at the shop, Mr Weech compromised, in the end, by throwing in a cheap clock. It had been in hand for a long time; and Josh was fain to take it, since he could get no more. And thus it was that Dicky, coming in at about five o'clock, was astonished to see on the mantelpiece, amid the greasy ruins of many candle ends, the clock that had belonged to the Ropers four years before.

CHAPTER 15

As for Dicky, he went to school. That is to say, he turned up now and again, at irregular intervals, at the Board School just over the Jago border in Honey Lane. When anything was given away, he attended as a matter of course; but he went now and again without such inducement—perhaps because he fancied an afternoon's change, perhaps because the weather was cold and the school was warm. He was classed as a half-timer, an arrangement which variegated the register, but otherwise did not matter. Other boys, half-timers or not, attended as little as he. It was long since the managers had realised the futility of attempting compulsion in the Jago.*

Dicky was no fool, and he had picked up some sort of reading and writing as he went along. Moreover, he had grown an expert thief, and had taken six strokes of a birch-rod by order of a magistrate. As yet he rarely attempted a pocket, being, for most opportunities, too small; but he was comforted by the reflection that probably he would never get really tall, and thus grow out of pocket-picking when he was fully experienced, as was the fate of some. For no tall man can be a successful pickpocket, because he must bend to his work, and so advertise it to every beholder.

Meantime Dicky practised that petty larceny which is possible in every street in London; and at odd times he would play the scout among the practitioners of the 'fat's a-running'* industry. If one crossed Meakin Street by way of Luck Row and kept his way among the courts ahead, he presently reached the main Bethnal Green Road, at the end whereof stood the great goods depot of a railway company.* Here carts and vans went to and fro all day, laden with goods from the depot, and certain gangs among the Jagos preyed on these continually. A quick-witted scout stood on the look-out for such vehicles as went with unguarded tailboards. At the approach of one such he sent the shout '*Fat's a-runnin'!*' up Luck Row, and, quick at the signal, a gang scuttled down, by the court or passage which his waved hand might hint at, seized whatever could be snatched from the cart, and melted away into the courts, sometimes leaving a few hands behind to hinder and misdirect pursuit. Taking one capture with another, the thing paid very well; and besides, there were many vans laden with parcels of tobacco, not from the railway depot but from the tobacco factories hard by,* a click from which was apt to prove especially lucrative. Dicky was a notable success as scout. The department was a fairly safe one, but it was not always easy to extract from the gang the few coppers that were regarded as sufficient share for service done. Moreover, Mr Weech was not pleased; for by now Dicky was near to being his most remunerative client, and the cart robberies counted nothing, for the fat's a-running boys fenced their swag with a publican at Hoxton. And though Dicky had grown out of his childish belief that Mr Weech could hear a mile away and see through a wall, he had a cautious dread of the weapon he supposed to lie ever to his patron's hand—betrayal to the police. In other respects things were easier. His father took no heed of what he did, and even his mother had so far accepted destiny as to ask if he had a copper or two, when there was a scarcity. Indeed Hannah Perrott filled her place in the Jago better than of old. She would gossip, she drew no very rigid line as to her acquaintance, and Dicky had seen her drunk. Still, for Old Jago Street she was a quiet woman, and she never brawled nor fought. Of fighting, indeed, Josh could do enough for the whole family, once again four in number. For the place of Looey, forgotten, was supplied by Em, aged two.

When Dicky came home and recognised the clock on the mantelpiece, being the more certain because his mother told him it had come from Weech's, the thing irritated him strangely. Through all those four years since he had carried that clock to Mr Weech, he had never got rid of the wretched hunchback. He, too, went to the Board School in Honey Lane (it lay between Dove Lane and the Jago), but he went regularly, worked hard, and was a favourite with teachers. So far, Dicky was unconcerned. But scarce an ill chance came to him but, sooner or later, he found the hunchback at the back of it. If ever a teacher mysteriously found out that it was Dicky who had drawn his portrait, all nose and teeth, on the blackboard, the tale had come from Bobby Roper. Whenever Dicky, chancing upon school by ill luck on an afternoon when sums were to be done, essayed to copy answers from his neighbour's slate, up shot the hunchback's hand in an instant, the tale was told, and handers were Dicky's portion. Once, dinnerless and hungry, he had stolen a sandwich from a teacher's desk; and, though he had thought himself alone and unseen, the hunchback knew it, and pointed him out, white malice in his thin face and eager hate in his thrust finger. For a fortnight Dicky dared not pass a little fruit shop in Meakin Street, because of an attempt on an orange, betrayed by his misshapen schoolfellow, which brought him a hard chase from the fruiterer and a bad bruise on the spine from a board flung after him. The hunchback's whole energies—even his whole time—seemed to be devoted to watching him. Dicky, on his part, received no injuries meekly. In the beginning he had tried threats and public jeers at his enemy's infirmity. Then, on some especially exasperating occasion, he pounded Bobby Roper savagely about the head and capsized him into a mud-heap. But bodily reprisal, though he erected it into a practice, proved no deterrent. For the little hunchback, though he might cry at the pummelling, retorted with worse revenge of his own sort. And once or twice bystanders, seeing a deformed child thus treated, interfered with clouts on Dicky's ears. The victim, moreover, designed another retaliation. He would go to some bigger boy with a tale that Dicky had spoken vauntingly of fighting him and beating him hollow, with one hand. This brought the big boy after Dicky at once, with a hiding: except on some rare occasion when the hunchback rated his instrument of vengeance too high, and Dicky was able to beat him in truth. But this was a very uncommon mistake. And after this Dicky did not wait for specific provocation: he 'clumped' Bobby Roper, or rolled him in the gutter, as a matter of principle, whenever he could get hold of him.

That afternoon Dicky had suffered again. Two days earlier, tea and cake had been provided by a benevolent manager for all who attended the school. Consequently the attendance was excellent, and included Dicky. But his attempt to secrete a pocketful of cake, to carry home for Em, was reported by Bobby Roper; and Dicky was hauled forth, deprived of his plunder, and expelled in disgrace. He waited outside and paid off the score fiercely, by the help of a very long and pliant cabbage stalk. But this afternoon Bill Bates, a boy a head taller than himself and two years older, had fallen on him suddenly in Lincoln Street, and, though Dicky fought desperately and kicked with much effect, had dealt him a thrashing that left him bruised, bleeding, dusty, and crying with rage and pain. This was the hunchback's doing, without a doubt. Dicky limped home, but was something comforted by an accident in Shoreditch High Street, whereby a coster's barrow-load of cough-drops was knocked over by a covered van, and the cough-drops were scattered in the mud.

For while the carman* and the coster flew at each other's name and address, and defamed each other's eyes and mother,* Dicky gathered a handful of cough-drops, muddy, it is true, but easy to wipe. And so he made for home more cheerfully disposed: till the sight of the Ropers' old clock brought the hunchback to mind once more, and in bitter anger he resolved to search for him forthwith, and pass on the afternoon's hiding, with interest.

As he emerged into the street, a hand was reached to catch him, which he dodged by instinct. He rushed back upstairs, and emptied his pockets, stowing away in a safe corner the rest of the cough-drops, the broken ruin he called his knife, some buttons and pieces of string, a bit of chalk, three little pieces of slate pencil* and two marbles. Then he went down again into the street, confident in his destitution, and watched, forgetting the hunchback in the excitement of the spectacle.

The loafers from the corners had conceived a sudden notion of co-operation* and had joined forces to the array of twenty or thirty. Confident in their numbers, they swept the street, stopping every passenger—man, woman or child—and emptying all pockets. A straggler on the outskirts of the crowd, a hobbledehoy like most of the rest, had snatched at but had lost Dicky, and was now busy, with four or five others, rolling a woman, a struggling heap of old clothes and skinny limbs, in the road. It was Biddy Flynn, too old and worn for anything but honest work, who sold oranges and nuts from a basket, and who had been caught on her way out for her evening's trade in High Street. She was a fortunate capture, being a lone woman with all her possessions about her. Under her skirt, and tied round her waist with string, she kept her money-bag; and it was soon found and dragged away, yielding two and eightpence farthing and a lucky shoe-tip, worn round and bright. She had, moreover, an old brass brooch; but unfortunately her wedding ring, worn to pin-wire, could not be got past the knotted knuckle—though it would have been worth little in any case. So Biddy Flynn, exhausted with plunging and screaming, was left, and her empty basket was flung at her. She staggered away, wailing and rolling her head, with her hand to the wall; and the gang, sharing out, sucked oranges with relish, and turned to fresh exploits. Dicky watched from the Jago Court passage.

Business slackened for a little while, and the loafers were contemplating a raid in force on Mother Gapp's till, when a grown lad ran in pell-mell from Luck Row with a square parcel clipped under his arm—a parcel of aspect well known among the fat's a-running boys—a parcel that meant tobacco. He was collared at once.

'Stow it, Bill!' he cried breathlessly, recognising his captor. 'The bloke's a-comin'!'

But half-a-dozen hands were on his plunder, it was snatched away, and he was flung back on the flags. There was a clatter on the stones of Luck Row, and a light van came rattling into Old Jago Street, the horse galloping, the carman lashing and shouting:—'Stop 'im! Stop thief!'

The sight was so novel that for a moment the gang merely stared and grinned. This man must be a greenhorn—new to the neighbourhood—to venture a load of goods up Luck Row. And it was tobacco, too. He was pale and flustered, and he called wildly, as he looked this way and that:—'A man's stole somethin' auf my van. Where's 'e gawn?'

'No good, guv'nor,' cried one. 'The ball's stopped rollin'.* You're lawst 'im.'

'My Gawd!' said the man, in a sweat, 'I'm done. There's two quid's worth o' 'bacca—an' I on'y got the job o' Monday—bin out nine munse!'

'Was it a parcel like this 'ere?' asked another, chuckling, and lifting a second packet over the tailboard.

'Yus—put it down! Gawd—wotcher up to? 'Ere—'elp! 'elp!'

The gang were over the van, guffawing and flinging out the load. The carman yelled aloud, and fought desperately with his whip—Bill Hanks is near blind of an eye now from one cut; but he was the worse for it. For he was knocked off the van in a heap, and, as he lay, they cleared his pockets, and pulled off his boots; those that had caught the sting of the whip kicking him about the head till it but shifted in the slime at the stroke, an inanimate lump.

There was talk of how to deal with the horse and van. To try to sell them was too large a job, and too risky. So, as it was growing dusk, the senseless carman was put on the floor of the van, the tailboard was raised, and one of the gang led the horse away, to lose the whole thing in the busy streets.

Here was a big haul, and many of the crowd busied themselves in getting it out of sight, and scouting out among the fences to arrange sales. Those who remained grew less active, and hung at the corner of Luck Row, little more than an ordinary corner-group of loafers.

Then Dicky remembered the hunchback, and slouched off to Dove Lane. But he could see nothing of Bobby Roper. The Jago and Dove Lane were districts ever at feud, active or smouldering, save for brief intervals of ostentatious reconciliation, serving to render the next attack on Dove Lane the more savage—for invariably the Jagos were aggressors and victors. Dicky was careful in his lurkings, therefore: lest he should be recognised and set upon by more Dove Lane boys than would be convenient. He knew where the Ropers lived, and he went and hung about the door. Once he fancied he could hear a disjointed tinkle, as of a music-box grown infirm, but he was not sure of it. And in the end he contented himself, for the present, with flinging a stone through the Ropers' window, and taking to his heels.

The Jago was black with night, the rats came and went, and the cosh-carriers lurked on landings. On a step, Pigeony Poll, drunk because of a little gin and no food, sang hideously and wept. The loafers had dispersed to spend their afternoon's makings. The group which Dicky had left by Luck Row corner, indeed, had been discouraged early in the evening in consequence of an attempt at 'turning over' old Beveridge, as he unsuspectingly stalked among them, in from his city round. For the old man whipped out his case-knife and drove it into the flesh of Nobber Sugg's* arm, at the shoulder—stabbed, too, at another, and ripped his coat. So Nobber Sugg, with blood streaming through his sleeve, went off with two more to tie up the arm; and old Beveridge, grinning and mumbling fiercely, strode about the street, knife in hand, for ten minutes, ere he grew calm enough to go his way. This Tommy Rann told Dicky, sitting in the back yard and smoking a pipe; a pipe charged with tobacco pillaged from a tin-full which his father had bought, at about fourpence a pound, from a loafer. And both boys crawled indoors deadly sick.

CHAPTER 16

JOSH PERROTT was at church on Sunday morning, as Father Sturt had bid him. Not because of the bidding, but because the vicar overtook him and Kiddo Cook in Meakin Street, and hauled them in, professing to be much gratified at their punctuality, and charging them never to fall away from the habit. The two Jagos, with dubious grins, submitted as they must, and were in a little while surprised to find others arriving, friends and acquaintances never suspected of church-going. The fact was, that Father Sturt, by dint of long effort, had so often brought so many to his stable-church, as he had now brought Josh and Kiddo, that the terrors and embarrassments of the place had worn off, and many, finding nothing more attractive elsewhere, would make occasional attendances of their own motion. Wet Sundays, particularly, inclined them to church: where there might be a fire, where at least there was a clean room, with pictures on the wall, where there were often flowers,* where there was always music, and where Father Sturt made an address of a quarter of an hour, which nobody ever suspected of being a sermon; an address which one might doze over or listen to, as one might be disposed; but which most listened to, more or less, partly because of an uneasy feeling that Father Sturt would know if they did not, and partly because it was very easy to understand, was not oppressively minatory, was spoken with an intimate knowledge of themselves, and was, indeed, something of a refreshing novelty, being the simple talk of a gentleman.

Josh Perrott and Kiddo Cook were not altogether sorry they had come. It was a rest. Stable though it had been, they had never sat in so pleasant a room before. There was nothing to do, no constant watch to be kept, no police to avoid, and their wits had a holiday. They forgot things. Their courage never rose so high as to build the thought; but in truth pipes would have made them happy.

The address being done, Father Sturt announced the purchase of the site for the new church, and briefly described his scheme. He would give tenants good notice, he said, before the houses were destroyed. Meantime, they must pay rent; though most of the amounts would be reduced.*

And after the benediction, Father Sturt, from his window over the closed shop, saw Josh Perrott and Kiddo Cook guffawing and elbowing one another up Luck Row. Each was accusing the other of having tried to sing.

CHAPTER 17

THERE was much talk of Father Sturt's announcement. Many held it a shame that so much money, destined for the benefit of the Jago, should be spent in bricks and mortar, instead of being distributed among themselves. They fell to calculating the price of the land and houses, and to working it out laboriously in the denomination of pots and gallons. More: it was felt to be a grave social danger that Jago Court should be extinguished. What would become of the Jago without Jago Court? Where would Sunday morning be spent? Where would the fights come off, and where was so convenient a place for pitch and toss? But mainly they feared the police. Jago Court was an unfailing sanctuary, a city of refuge ever ready, ever secure. There were times when two or three of the police, hot in the chase, would burst into the Jago at the heels of a flying marauder. Then the runaway would make straight for the archway, and, once he was in Jago Court, danger was over. For he had only to run into one of the ever-open doors at right or left, and out into back yards and other houses; or, better, to scramble over the low fence opposite, through the back door before him, and so into New Jago Street. Beyond the archway the police could not venture, except in large companies. A young constable who tried it once, getting ahead of two companions in his ardour, was laid low as he emerged from the passage, by a fire-grate adroitly let drop* from an upper window.

The blotting out of such a godsend* of a place as this would be a calamity. The Jago would never be the same again. As it was, the Old Jago was a very convenient, comfortable sort of place, they argued. They could not imagine themselves living anywhere else. But assuredly it would be the Jago no longer without Jago Court. And this thing was to be done, too, with money got together for their benefit! The sole explanation the Jago could supply was the one that at last, with arithmetical variations, prevailed. The landlords were to be paid a sum (varying in Jago estimation from a hundred pounds to a hundred thousand) for the houses and the ground, and of this they were secretly to return to Father Sturt a certain share (generally agreed on as half), as his private fee for bringing about so desirable a transaction. Looked at from all points, this appeared to be the most plausible explanation: for no other could reasonably account for Father Sturt's activity. No wonder he could afford to reduce some of the rents! Was he not already receiving princely wages* (variously supposed to be something from ten pounds to thirty pounds a week) from the Government, for preaching every Sunday?

Still the rents were to be reduced: that was the immediate consideration, and nothing but an immediate consideration carried weight in the Jago,* where a shilling today was to be preferred to a constant income beginning in a month's time. The first effect of the announcement was a rush of applications for rooms in the doomed houses, each applicant demanding to be accommodated by the eviction of somebody already established, but now disinterestedly discovered to be a bad tenant. They were all disappointed, but the residents had better luck than they had hoped. For the unexpected happened, and the money for a part of the new buildings was suddenly guaranteed. Wherefore Father Sturt, knowing that many would be hard put to it to find shelter when the houses came down, and guessing that rents would rise with the demand, determined to ask none for the little while the tenements endured. Scarce had he made his decision known ere he regretted it, popular as it was. For he reflected that the money saved would merely melt, and that at the inevitable turning out, not a soul would be the better off for the relief, but, indeed, might find it harder than ever to pay rent after the temporary easement. It would have been better rigidly to exact the rent, and return it in lump to each tenant as he left. The sum would have been an inducement to leave peaceably—a matter in which trouble was to be expected. But then, what did any windfall of shillings bring in the Jago? What but a drunk? This was one of Father Sturt's thousand perplexities, and he could but hope that, perhaps, he had done right after all.

The old buildings were sold, as they stood, to the house-wreckers, and on the house-wreckers devolved the work of getting the lodgers out. For weeks the day was deferred, but it drew very near at last, and a tall hoarding was put up. Next morning it had vanished; but there was a loud crackling where the Jagos boiled their pots; Dicky Perrott and Tommy Rann had a bonfire in Edge Lane; and Jerry Gullen's canary sweated abroad before a heavy load of cheap firewood.

Then Josh Perrott and Billy Leary, his old enemy, were appointed joint guardians of the new hoarding, each to get half-a-crown on every morning when the fence was found intact. And in the end there came eviction day, and once more the police held the Jago in force, escorting gangs of men with tumbrils.*

As for the Perrotts, they could easily find another room, at the high rent always charged for the privilege of residence in the Jago. To have remained in one room four or five years, and to have paid rent with indifferent good regularity was a feat sufficiently rare to be notorious, and to cause way to be made for them wherever a room was falling vacant, or could be emptied. They went no farther than across the way, to a room wherein a widow had died over her sack-making two days before, and had sat on the floor with her head between her knees for hours, while her children, not understanding, cried that they were hungry. These children were now gone to the workhouse: more fortunate than the many they left behind. And the room was a very fair one, ten feet square or so.

The rest of the tenants thought not at all of new quarters, and did nothing to find them, till they found themselves and their belongings roofless in Old Jago Street. Then with one accord they demanded lodgings of the vicar. Most of them had never inhabited any rooms so long as they had these which they must now leave—having been ejected again and again because of unpaid rent. Nevertheless, they clamoured for redress as they might have clamoured had they never changed dwellings in their lives.

Nobody resisted the police; for there were too many of them. Moreover, Father Sturt was there, and few had hardihood for any but their best behaviour in his presence. Still, there were disputes among the Jagos themselves, that sometimes came very near to fights. Ginger Stagg's missis professed to recognise a long-lost property in a tin kettle brought into the outer air among the belongings of Mrs Walsh. The miscellaneous rags and sticks that were Cocko Harnwell's household goods got mingled in the roadway with those appertaining to the Fishers; and their assortment without a turn of family combat was a task which tried the vicar's influence to the utmost. Mrs Rafferty, too, was suspected of undue pride in a cranky deal washstand, and thereby of a disposition to sneer at the humbler turn-out of the Regans from the next floor: giving occasion for a shrill and animated row.

The weather was dry, fortunately, and the evicted squatted in the roadway, by their heaps, or on them, squabbling and lamenting. Ginger Stagg, having covered certain crockery with the old family mattress, forgetfully sat on it, and came upon Father Sturt with an indignant demand for compensation.

Father Sturt's efforts to stimulate a search for new lodgings met with small success at first. It was felt that, no doubt, there were lodgings to be had, but they would be open to the fatal objection of costing something; and the Jago temperament could neither endure nor understand payment for what had once been given for nothing. Father Sturt, the Jagos argued, had given them free quarters for so long. Then why should he stop now? If they cleared out in order to make room for his new church, in common fairness he should find them similar lodging on the same terms. So they sat and waited for him to do it.

At length the vicar set to work with them in good earnest, carried away with him a family or two at a time, and inducted them to rooms of his own finding. And hereat others, learning that in these cases rent in advance was exacted, bestirred themselves: reflecting that if rent must be paid they might as well choose their own rooms as take those that Father Sturt might find. Of course the thing was not done without payments from the vicar's pocket.* Some were wholly destitute; others could not muster enough to pay that advance of rent which alone could open a Jago tenancy. Distinguishing the genuine impecuniosity from the merely professed, with the insight that was now a sixth sense with him, Father Sturt helped sparingly and in secret; for a precedent of almsgiving was an evil thing in the Jago, confirming the shiftlessness which was already a piece of Jago nature, and setting up long affliction for the almsgiver. Enough of such precedents existed; and the inevitable additions thereto were a work of anxious responsibility and jealous care.

So the bivouac in Old Jago Street melted away. For one thing, there were those among the dispossessed who would not waste time in unproductive inactivity just then; for war had arisen with Dove Lane, and spoils were going. Dove Lane was no very reputable place, but it was not like the Jago. In the phrase of the district, the Dove Laners were pretty thick, but the Jagos were thick as glue. There were many market-porters among the Dove Laners, and at this, their prosperous season,* they and their friends resorted to a shop in Meakin Street, kept by an 'ikey' tailor, there to buy the original out-and-out downy benjamins,* or the celebrated bang-up kicksies, cut saucy, with artful buttons and a double fakement* down the sides.

And hereabout they were apt to be set upon by Jagos; overthrown by superior numbers; bashed; and cleaned out. Or, if the purchases had been made, they were flimped of their kicksies, benjies or daisies,* as the case might be. So that a fight with Dove Lane might be an affair of some occasional profit; and it became no loyal Jago to idle in the stronghold.

Father Sturt's task was nearly over, when, returning to Old Jago Street, he saw Dicky Perrott sitting by a still-remaining heap—a heap small and poor even among those others. The Perrotts had been decorously settled in their new home since early morning; but here was Dicky, guarding a heap with a baby on it, and absorbed in the weaving of rush bags.

'That's right, Dicky my boy,' said Father Sturt in the approving voice that a Jago would do almost anything—except turn honest—to hear. And Dicky, startled, looked up, flushed and happy, over his shoulder.

'Rush bags, eh?' the vicar went on, stooping and handing Dicky another rush from the heap. 'And whose are they?'

The bags, the rushes, the heap, and the baby belonged to Mrs Bates, the widow, who was now in search of a new room. Dicky had often watched the weaving of fishmongers' frails,* and, since it was work in which he had had no opportunity of indulging, it naturally struck him as a fascinating pastime. So that he was delighted by the chance which he had taken, and Mrs Bates, for her part, was not sorry to find somebody to mind her property. Moreover, by hard work and the skill begot of much practice, she was able to earn a sum of some three farthings an hour at the rush bags: a profit which her cupidity made her reluctant to lose, for even half an hour. And thus to have Dicky carry on the business*—and in his enthusiasm he did it very well—was a further consideration.

Father Sturt chatted with Dicky till the boy could scarce plait for very pride. Would not Dicky like to work regularly every day, asked Father Sturt, and earn wages? Dicky could see no graceful answer but the affirmative; and in sober earnest he thought he would. Father Sturt took hold of Dicky's vanity. Was he not capable of something better than other Jago boys? Why should he not earn regular wages, and live comfortably, well fed and clothed, with no fear of the police, and no shame for what he did? *He* might do it, when others could not. They were not clever enough. They called themselves 'clever' and 'wide'; 'but,' said Father Sturt, 'is there one of them that can deceive me?' And Dicky knew there was not one. Most did no work, the vicar's argument went on, because they had neither the pluck to try nor the intelligence to accomplish. Else why did they live the wretched Jago life instead of take the pleasanter time of the decent labourer?

Dicky, already zealous at work as exampled in rush bag-making, listened with wistful pride. Yes, if he could, he would work and take his place over the envious heads of his Jago friends. But how? Nobody would employ a boy living in the Jago. That was notorious. The address was a topsy-turvy testimonial for miles round.

All the same when Mrs Bates at last took away her belongings, Dicky ran off in delighted amaze to tell his mother and Em that he was going to tea at Father Sturt's rooms.

And the wreckers tore down the foul old houses, laying bare the secret dens of a century of infamy; lifting out the wide sashes of the old 'weavers' windows'*—the one good feature in the structures; letting light and air at last into the subterraneous basements where men and women had swarmed, and bred, and died, like wolves in their lairs; and emerging from clouds of choking dust, each man a colony of vermin. But there were rooms which the wreckers—no jack-a-dandies neither—flatly refused to enter;* and nothing would make them but much coaxing, the promise of extra pay, and the certainty of much immediate beer.

CHAPTER 18

Mr Grinder* kept a shop in the Bethnal Green Road. It was announced in brilliant lettering as an 'oil, colour and Italian warehouse', and there, in addition to the oil and the colour, and whatever of Italian there might have been, he sold pots, pans, kettles, brooms, shovels, mops, lamps, nails, and treacle. It was a shop ever too tight for its stock, which burst forth at every available opening, and heaped so high on the paving that the window was half buried in a bank of shining tin. Father Sturt was one of the best customers: the oil, candles and utensils needed for church and club all coming from Mr Grinder's. Mr Grinder was losing his shop-boy, who had found a better situation; and Father Sturt determined that, could but the oilman be persuaded, Dicky Perrott should be the new boy. Mr Grinder was persuaded. Chiefly perhaps, because the vicar undertook to make good the loss, should the experiment end in theft; partly because it was policy to oblige a good customer; and partly, indeed, because Mr Grinder was willing to give such a boy a chance in life, for he was no bad fellow, as oil-and-colourmen go, and had been an errand boy himself.

So that there came a Monday morning when Dicky, his clothes as well mended as might be (for Hannah Perrott, no more than another Jago, could disobey Father Sturt), and a cut-down apron of his mother's tied before him, stood by Mr Grinder's bank of pots and kettles, in an eager agony to sell something, and near blind with the pride of the thing. He had been waiting at the shop-door long ere Mr Grinder was out of bed; and now, set to guard the outside stock—a duty not to be neglected in that neighbourhood—he brushed a tin pot here and there with his sleeve, and longed for some Jago friend to pass and view him in his new greatness. The goods he watched over were an unfailing source of interest; and he learned by much repetition the prices of all the saucepans, painted in blue distemper on the tin, and ranging from eightpence-halfpenny, on the big pots in the bottom row, to three-halfpence on the very little ones at the top. And there were long ranks of little paraffin lamps at a penny—the sort that had set fire to a garret in Half Jago Street a month since, and burnt old Mother Leary to a greasy cinder. With a smaller array of a superior quality at fourpence-halfpenny—just like the one that had burst at Jerry Gullen's, and burnt the bed. While over his head swung doormats at one-and-eightpence, with penny mousetraps dangling from their corners.

When he grew more accustomed to his circumstances, he bethought him to collect a little dirt, and rub it down the front of his apron,* to give himself a well-worked and business-like appearance; and he greatly impeded women who looked at the saucepans and the mouse-traps, ere they entered the shop, by his anxiety to cut them off from Mr Grinder and serve them himself. He remembered the boy at the toy-shop in Bishopsgate Street, years ago, who had chased him through Spitalfields; and he wished that some lurching youngster would snatch a mousetrap, that he might make a chase himself.

At Mr Grinder's every call Dicky was prompt and willing; for every new duty was a fresh delight, and the whole day a prolonged game of real shopkeeping. And at his tea—he was to have tea each day in addition to three and sixpence every Saturday—he took scarce five minutes. There was a trolley—just such a thing as porters used at railway stations, but smaller—which was his own particular implement, his own to pack parcels on for delivery to such few customers as did not carry away their own purchases: and to acquire the dexterous management of this trolley was a pure joy. He bolted his tea to start the sooner on a trolley-journey to a public-house two hundred yards away.

His enthusiasm for work as an amusement cooled in a day or two, but all his pride in it remained. The fight with Dove Lane waxed amain, but Dicky would not be tempted into more than a distant interest in it. In his daydreams he saw himself a tradesman, with a shop of his own and the name 'R. Perrott', with a gold flourish, over the door. He would employ a boy himself then; and there would be a parlour, with stuff-bottomed chairs and a shade of flowers, and Em grown up and playing on the piano. Truly Father Sturt was right: the hooks were fools, and the straight game was the better.

Bobby Roper, the hunchback, went past the shop once, and saw him. Dicky, minding his new dignity, ignored his enemy, and for the first time for a year and more, allowed him to pass without either taunt or blow. The other, astonished at Dicky's new occupation, came back and back again, staring, from a safe distance, at Dicky and the shop. Dicky, on his part, took no more notice than to assume an ostentatious vigilance: so that the hunchback, baring his teeth in a snigger of malice, at last turned on his heel and rolled off.

Twice Kiddo Cook passed, but made no sign of recognition beyond a wink; and Dicky felt grateful for Kiddo's obvious fear of compromising him. Once old Beveridge came by, striding rapidly, his tatters flying, and the legend 'Hard Up' chalked on his hat, as was his manner in his town rambles. He stopped abruptly at sight of Dick, stooped, and said:—'Dicky Perrott? Hum—hum—hey?' Then he hurried on, doubtless conceiving just such a fear as Kiddo Cook's. As for Tommy Rann, his affections were alienated by Dicky's outset refusal to secrete treacle in a tin mug for a midnight carouse; and he did not show himself. So matters went for near a week.

But Mr Weech missed Dicky sadly. It was rare for a day to pass without a visit from Dicky, and Dicky had a way of bringing good things. Mr Weech would not have sold Dicky's custom for ten shillings a week. So that when Mr Weech inquired, and found that Dicky was at work in an oil-shop, he was naturally annoyed. Moreover, if Dicky Perrott got into *that* way of life, he would have no fear for himself, and might get talking inconveniently among his new friends about the business affairs of Mr Aaron Weech. And at this reflection that philanthropist grew thoughtful.

CHAPTER 19

DICKY had gone on an errand, and Mr Grinder was at the shop door, when there appeared before him a whiskered and smirking figure, with a quick glance each way along the street, and a long and smiling one at the oil-man's necktie.

'Good mornin', Mr Grinder, good mornin' sir.' Mr Weech stroked his left palm with his right fist and nodded pleasantly. 'I'm in business meself, over in Meakin Street—name of Weech: p'r'aps you know the shop? I—I just 'opped over to ask'—Grinder led the way into the shop—'to ask (so's to make things quite sure y'know, though no doubt it's all right) to ask if it's correct you're awfferin' brass roastin'-jacks at a shillin' each.'

'Brass roastin'-jacks at a shillin'?' exclaimed Grinder, shocked at the notion. 'Why, no!'

Mr Weech appeared mildly surprised. 'Nor yut seven-poun' jars o' jam an' pickles at sixpence?' he pursued, with his eye on those ranged behind the counter.

'No!'

'Nor doormats at fourpence?'

'Fourpence? Cert'nly not!'

Mr Weech's face fell into a blank perplexity. He pawed his ear with a doubtful air, murmuring absently:—'Well I'm sure 'e *said* fourpence: an' sixpence for pickles, an' bring 'em round after the shop was shut. But there,' he added, more briskly, 'there's no 'arm done, an' no doubt it's a mistake.' He turned as though to leave, but Grinder restrained him.

'But look 'ere,' he said, 'I want to know about this. Wotjer mean? '*Oo* was goin' to bring round pickles after the shop was shut? '*Oo* said fourpence for doormats?'

'Oh, I expect it's jest a little mistake, that's all,' answered Weech, making another motion toward the door; 'an' I don't want to git nobody into trouble.'

'Trouble? Nice trouble I'd be in if I sold brass smoke-jacks* for a bob! There's somethink 'ere as I ought to know about. Tell me about it straight.'

Weech looked thoughtfully at the oil-man's top waistcoat button for a few seconds, and then said:—'Yus, p'raps I better. I can feel for you, Mr Grinder, 'avin' a feelin' 'art, an' bein' in business meself. Where's your boy?'

'Gawn out.'

'Comin' back soon?'

'Not yut. Come in the back-parlour.'

There Mr Weech, with ingenuous reluctance, assured Mr Grinder that Dicky Perrott had importuned him to buy the goods in question at the prices he had mentioned, together with others—readily named now that the oil-man swallowed so freely—and that they were to be delivered and paid for at night when Dicky left work. But perhaps, Mr Weech concluded, parading an obstinate belief in human nature, perhaps the boy, being new to the business, had mistaken the prices, and was merely doing his best to push his master's trade.

'No fear o' that,' said Grinder, shaking his head gloomily. 'Not the least fear o' that. 'E knows the cheapest doormats I got's one an' six—I 'eard him tell customers so outside a dozen times; an' anyone can see the smoke-jacks is ticketed five an' nine'—as Mr Weech had seen, when he spoke of them. 'I thought that boy was too eager an' willin' to be quite genavin,' Dicky's master went on. ''E ain't 'ad me yut, that's one comfort: if anythin' 'ud bin gawn I'd 'a' missed it. But out 'e goes as soon as 'e comes back: you can take yer davy o' that!'

'Ah,' replied Mr Weech, 'it's fearful the wickedness there is about, ain't it? It's enough to break yer 'art. Sich a neighb'r'ood too! Wy, if it was known as I'd give you this 'ere little friendly information, bein' in business meself an' knowin' wot it is, my life wouldn't be safe a hower. It wouldn't, Mr Grinder.'

'Wouldn't it?' said Mr Grinder. 'You mean them in the Jago, I s'pose.'

'Yus. They're a awful lot, Mr Grinder—you've no idear. The father o' this 'ere boy as I've warned you aginst, 'e's in with a desprit gang, an' they'd murder me if they thought I'd come an' told you honest, w'en you might 'a' bin robbed, as is my nature to. They would indeed. So o' course you won't say wot I toldjer, nor 'oo give you this 'ere honourable friendly warnin'—not to nobody.'

'That's awright,' answered the simple Grinder, 'I won't let on. But out 'e goes, promp'. I'm obliged to ye, Mr Weech. Er—r wot'll ye take?'

Weech put away the suggestion with a virtuous palm:—'Nothink at all, Mr Grinder, thanks all the same. I never touch nothink; an' I'm glad to—to do any moral job, so to speak, as comes in my way. "Scatter seeds o' kindness" you know, as the—the Psalm says,* Mr Grinder. Your boy ain't back, is 'e?'

And after peering cautiously, Mr Weech went his way.

CHAPTER 20

DICKY completed his round, and pushed his unladen trolley Grinderward with a fuller sense of responsibility than ever. For he carried money. A publican had paid him four and threepence, and he had taken two and tenpence elsewhere. He had left his proud signature, pencilled large and black, on two receipts, and he stopped in a dozen doorways to count the money over again, and make sure that all was right. Between the halts he added four and three to two and ten mentally, and proved his sum correct by subtracting each in turn from seven and a penny. And at last he stood his trolley on end by the bank of saucepans, and entered the shop.

'Walker's is paid, an' Wilkins is paid,' said Dicky, putting down the money. 'Two an' ten an' four an' three's seven an' a penny.'

Mr Grinder looked steadily and sourly at Dicky, and counted. He pitched the odd penny into the till and shook the rest of the coins in his closed hand, still staring moodily in the boy's face. 'It's three an' six a week you come 'ere at,' he said.

'Yus sir,' Dicky replied, since Grinder seemed to expect an answer. The supreme moment when he should take his first wages had been the week's beacon to him, reddening and brightening as Saturday night grew nearer.

'Three an' six a week an' yer tea.'

Dicky wondered.

'So as if I found out anythink about—say Brass Roastin'-jacks for instance—I could give ye yer three an' six an' start y' auf, unless I did somethin' wuss.'

Dicky was all incomprehension; but something made him feel a little sick.

'But s'posin' I *didn't* find out anythink about—say Seven-pun' Jars o' Pickles—an' s'pose I wasn't disposed to suspect anythink in regard to—say Doormats; then I could either give ye a week's notice or pay y' a week's money an' clear y' out on the spot, without no more trouble.'

Mr Grinder paused, and still looked at Dicky with calm dislike. Then he added, as though in answer to himself, 'Yus.' . . .

He dropped the money slowly from his right hand to his left.

Dicky's mouth was dry, and the drawers and pickle-jars swam before him at each side of Grinder's head. What did it mean?

'Ere y' are,' cried Mr Grinder, with sudden energy, thrusting his hand across the counter. 'Two three-and-sixes is seven shillin's, an' you can git yer tea at 'ome with yer dirty little sister. Git out o' my shop!'

Dicky's hand closed mechanically on the money, and after a second's pause, he found broken speech. 'W—w—wot for, sir?' he asked, huskily. 'I ain't done nothink!'

'No, an' you sha'n't do nothink, that's more. Out ye go! If I see ye near the place agin I'll 'ave ye locked up!'

Dicky slunk to the door. He felt the sobs coming, but he turned at the threshold and said with tremulous lips:—'Woncher gimme a chance, sir? S'elp me, I done me best. I—'

Mr Grinder made a short rush from the back of the shop, and Dicky gave up and fled.

It was all over. There could never be a shop with 'R. Perrott' painted over it, now; there would be no parlour with stuff-bottomed chairs and a piano for Em to play. He was cut off from the trolley for ever. Dicky was thirteen, and at that age the children of the Jago were past childish tears; but tears he could not smother, even till he might find a hiding-place: they burst out shamefully in the open street.

He took dark turnings, and hid his head in doorways. It was very bitter. At last, when the sobs grew fewer, he remembered the money gripped in his wet fist. It was a consolation. Seven shillings was a vast sum in Dicky's eyes; until that day he had never handled so much in his life. It would have been handsome recompense, he thought, for any trouble in the world but this. He must take it home, of course; it might avail to buy sympathy of his father and mother. But then, to think he might have had as much every fortnight of his life, a good tea every day, and the proud responsibility, and the trolley! At this his lips came awry again, his eyes sought his sleeve, and he turned to another doorway.

His glance fell on the white apron, now smudged and greased in good earnest. It made him feel worse; so he untied it and stuffed it away under his jacket. He wondered vaguely what had occurred to irritate Mr Grinder, and why he talked of pickles and doormats; but the sorrow of it all afflicted him to the extinction of such minor speculation. And in this misery he dragged his reluctant feet toward the Old Jago.

CHAPTER 21

HE handed his father the seven shillings, and received a furious belting for losing his situation. He cried quietly, but it was not because of the strap. All he feared now was to meet Father Sturt. He had rather fifty beltings than Father Sturt's reproaches; and, having disgraced himself with Mr Grinder in some mysterious way which it was beyond his capacity to understand, what but reproaches could he expect from the vicar? The whole world was against him. As for himself, he was hopeless: plainly he must have some incomprehensible defect of nature, since he offended, do as he might, and could neither understand nor redeem his fault. He wondered if it had been so with little Neddy Wright, who had found the world too ruthless for him at ten; and had tied a brick to his neck, as he had seen done with needless dogs, and let himself timidly down into the canal at Haggerstone Bridge.

So he shuffled through Jago Row, when a hand came on his shoulder and a hoarse voice said:—'Wot's the matter, Dicky?'

He turned, and saw the mild, coarse face of Pigeony Poll, the jaw whereof was labouring on something tough and sticky. Poll pulled from her pocket a glutinous paper, clinging about a cohesive lump of broken toffee—the one luxury of her moneyed times. ''Ave a bit,' she said. 'Wot's the matter?'

But Dicky thrust the hand away and fled, for he feared another burst of tears. His eyes were bad enough as it was, and he longed to hide himself in some hole.

He turned into New Jago Street. Hither it was that Jerry Gullen had betaken himself with his family and the canary, after the great eviction. Dicky slackened his pace, loitered at Jerry's doorway, and presently found himself in the common passage. It was long since he had had a private interview with Jerry Gullen's canary: for, indeed, he was thirteen—he was no longer a child, in fact!—and it was not well that he should indulge in such foolish weakness. Nevertheless he went as far as the back door. There stood the old donkey, mangy and infirm as ever, but apparently no nearer the end. The wood of the fence was bitten in places, but it was not as yet gnawed to the general whiteness and roundness of that in Canary's old abode. Canary, indeed, was fortunate today, for at the sound of Dicky's step he lifted his nose from a small heap of straw, dust, and mouldy hay, swept into a corner. Dicky stepped into the yard, and put his hand on Canary's neck; presently he glanced guiltily at the windows above. Nobody was looking. And in five minutes Dicky, aged as he was, had told Canary his troubles, while new tears wetted the ragged crest* and dropped into the dusty straw.

Now his grief lost some of its edge. Ashamed as he was, he had a shapeless, unapprehended notion that Canary was the sole creature alive that could understand and feel with him. And Canary poked his nose under the old jacket and sniffed in sympathy, as the broken lining tickled him. Dicky's intellectuals began to arrange themselves. Plainly, Mr Weech's philosophy was right after all. He was of the Jago, and he must prey on the outer world, as all the Jago did; not stray foolishly off the regular track in chase of visions, and fall headlong. Father Sturt was a creature of another mould. Who was he, Dicky Perrott, that he should break away from the Jago habit, and strain after another nature? What could come of it but defeat and bitterness? As old Beveridge had said, the Jago had got him. Why should he fight against the inevitable, and bruise himself? The ways out of the Jago old Beveridge had told him, years ago. Gaol, the gallows and the High Mob. There was his chance, his aspiration, his goal: the High Mob. To dream of oil-shops or regular wages was foolishness. His bed was made in the Jago, and he must lie on it. His hope in life, if he might have a hope at all, was to be of the High Mob. Spare nobody, stop at nothing, do his devilmost: old Beveridge had said that years ago. The task was before him, and he must not balk at it. As for gaol and the gallows, well! There they were, and he could not help it; ill ways out of the Jago, both, but still—ways out.

He rubbed his face carefully with his sleeve, put away his foolish ambitions, and went forth with a brave heart: to accomplish his destiny for well or ill—a Jago rat. To do his devilmost. But to avoid Father Sturt.

Out he went into Shoreditch High Street, and there he prowled the evening away; there and in Norton Folgate. But he touched for* nothing—nothing at all. He feared lest his week's honesty had damaged his training. Even an apple on a stall he failed at, and had to run. And then he turned into Bethnal Green Road.

But here a thought checked him suddenly. What of Mr Grinder? He had threatened to have Dicky locked up if he came near the shop again. But a child of the Jago knew too much to be frightened by such a threat as that. He went on. He felt interested to see how his late employer was getting along without him, and who was minding the goods outside the shop. Probably there was nobody: and this gave Dicky an idea.

He had forgotten his smudgy apron, folded and tucked away in the lining of his jacket. Now he pulled it out, and fastened it before him once more. He knew Mr Grinder's habits in the shop, and if he could seize a fitting opportunity he might be able, attired in his apron, to pick up or reach down any article that struck his fancy, fearless of interference from passers-by; for he would seem to be still shop-boy.

With that he hastened, for it was near closing time at Grinder's. He took the opposite side of the road, the better to observe unseen in the darkness. But Mr Grinder had already begun to carry things in from the pavement. As Dicky looked he came out with a long pole wherewith he unhooked from above a clattering cluster of pails and watering-pots, and a bunch of doormats. The doormats he let fall on the flags, while he carried in the pots and pails. Dicky knew that these pots and pails were kept at night in a shed behind the house; so he scuttled across the road, opening the blade of his old knife as he ran. He cut the string that held the mats together, selected a thick one, rolled it under his arm, and edged off into the shadow. Then he ran quietly across to the nearest turning.

Presently Mr Grinder came out, hooked his finger in the string among the mats, and pulled up nothing. He stooped, and saw that the string was cut. He looked about him suspiciously, flung the mats over, and counted them. Then he stood erect; stared up the street, down the street, and across the road, with his mouth open; and made short rushes left and right into the gloom. Then he returned to the mats and scratched his head. Finally, he gave another glance about the street, picked up the mats in his arms and carried them in, counting them as he went. And, the mats bestowed, whenever he came forth for a fresh armful of saucepans, he stood and gazed doubtfully, now this way, now that, about the Bethnal Green Road.

Mr Aaron Weech was pushing his last shutter into its place when 'Clean the knives,' said Dicky Perrott, in perfunctory repetition of the old formula.

Mr Weech seemed taken aback. 'Wot, that?' he asked, doubtfully, pointing at the doormat. Then, after a sharp look about the almost deserted street, he ran to Jago Row corner, twenty yards away, and looked down there. Nobody was hiding, and he came back. He led the way into the shop, and closed the door. Then, looking keenly in Dicky's face, he suddenly asked—''Oo toldjer to bring that 'ere?'

'Told me?' Dicky answered sullenly. 'Nobody told me. Don'cher want it?'

'Ow much did 'e tell ye t' ask for it?'

'Tell me? 'Oo?'

'*You* know. 'Ow much didjer say 'e said?'

Dicky was mystified. 'Dunno wotcher mean,' he replied.

Mr Weech suddenly broke into a loud laugh, but kept his keen look on the boy's face nevertheless. 'Ah, it's a good joke, Dicky, ain't it?' he said, and laughed again. 'But you can't 'ave me, ye know! Mr Grinder's a old friend o' mine, an' I know 'is little larks. Wot did 'e tell ye to do if I wouldn't 'ave that doormat?'

'Tell me?' asked Dicky, plainly more mystified than ever. 'Wy 'e never told me nothink. 'E gimme the sack this afternoon, an' chucked me out.'

'Then wotcher got yer apron on now for?'

'Oh,' said Dicky, looking down at it, 'I jist put it on agin—o' purpose.' And he glanced at the mat.

Mr Weech understood, and grinned—a genuine grin this time. 'That's right Dicky,' he said, 'never let yer wits go a-ramblin'. A sharp boy like you's a lot too good for a shop-boy, slavin' away from mornin' till night, an' treated ungrateful. Wot did 'e sack ye for?'

'I dunno. Took a fit in 'is 'ead, I s'pose. Wotcher goin' to gimme for this mat? It's a two an' three mat.'

'Want somethink to eat, doncher?' suggested Mr Weech, glancing at a heap of stale cake.

'No I don't,' Dicky answered, with sulky resolution. 'I want money.'

'Awright,' said Mr Weech, resignedly. 'You ain't 'ad much to eat an' drink 'ere for a long time, though. But I'll do the 'an'some, seein' you're bin treated ungrateful by Grinder. 'Ere's twopence.'

But Dicky held to the mat. 'Twopence ain't enough,' he said. 'I want fourpence.' He meant to spare nobody—not even Mr Weech.

'Wot? Fourpence?' gasped Mr Weech indignantly. 'Wy, you're mad. Take it away.'

Dicky rolled the mat under his arm and turned to the door.

‘’Ere,’ said Mr Weech, seeing him going, ‘I’ll make it thrippence, seein’ you’re bin treated so bad. Thrippence—*and* a slice o’ cake,’ he added, perceiving that Dicky did not hesitate.

‘I don’t want no cake,’ Dicky answered doggedly. ‘I want fourpence, an’ I won’t take no less.’

The good Weech was unwilling that Dicky should find another market after all, so he submitted to the extortion. ‘Ah well,’ he said, with a sigh, pulling out the extra coppers, ‘jist for this once, then. You’ll ’ave to make it up next time. Mindjer, it’s on’y ’cos I’m sorry for ye bein’ treated ungrateful. Don’t *you* go an’ treat *me* ungrateful, now.’

Dicky pocketed his pence and made for home, while Mr Weech, chuckling gently at his morning prophecy of a doormat for fourpence, carried the plunder to the room reserved for new and unused stock; promising himself, however, a peep at Grinder’s shop in the morning, to make quite sure that Dicky had really left.

So ended Dicky’s dealings with the house of Grinder. When Father Sturt next saw the oil-man, and inquired of Dicky’s progress, he was met with solemn congratulations that no larcenies were to pay for. Mr Grinder’s sagacity, it seemed, had enabled him to detect and crush at the outset Dicky’s plans for selling stock wholesale on his own account. Out of consideration for the vicar’s recommendation he had refrained from handing the boy over to the police, but had paid him a week in advance and dismissed him. Father Sturt insisted on repaying the money, and went his way with a heavy heart. For if this were what came of the promising among his flock, what of the others? For some while he saw nothing of Dicky; and the incident fell back among a crowd of others in his remembrance: for Dicky was but one among thousands, and the disappointment was but one of many hundreds.

Lying awake that night, but with closed eyes, Dicky heard his mother, talking with his father, suggest that perhaps an enemy had earwigged Grinder, and told him a tale that had brought about Dicky’s dismissal: somebody, perhaps, who wanted the situation for somebody else. Josh Perrott did no more than grunt at the guess, but it gave a new light to Dicky. Clearly that would account for Grinder’s change. But who could the mischief-maker be?

The little clock on the mantelpiece ticked away busily in the silence, and Dicky instantly thought of the hunchback. He it must have been, without a doubt. Who else? Was he not hanging about the shop, staring and sneering, but a day or two back? And was it not he who had pursued him with malice on every occasion, in school and out? Had not Bobby Roper this very trick of lying tales? Where was the gratuitous injury in all these four years that had not been Bobby Roper's work? Dicky trembled with rage as he lay, and he resolved on condign revenge. The war with Dove Lane was over for the time being, but that made it easier for him to catch his enemy.

CHAPTER 22

THE feud between the Jago and Dove Lane was eternal, just as was that between the Ranns and the Learys; but, like the Rann and Leary feud, it had its paroxysms and its intervals. And, in both cases, the close of a paroxysm was signalised by a great show of amity between the factions. Bob Rann and Billy Leary would drink affably from the same pot, and Norah Walsh and Sally Green would call each other 'mum'; while Jagos and Dove-Laners would mingle in bars and lend pinches of tobacco, and call each other 'matey'. A paroxysm in the war had now passed, and reconciliation was due. The Dove-Laners had been heavily thrashed: their benjamins and kicksies had been impounded in Meakin Street, and they had ceased from buying. Dove Lane itself had been swept from end to end by the victorious Jago, and the populations of both were dotted thickly with bandaged heads. This satisfactory state of things achieved, there was little reason left for fighting. Moreover, if fighting persisted too long at a time, the police were apt to turn up in numbers, subjecting the neighbourhood to much inconvenient scrutiny, and very often coming across Jagos—or even Dove-Laners—'wanted' on old accounts. So peace was declared; and, as a visible sign thereof, it was determined that the Dove-Laners should visit the Jago in a body, there to join in a singsong at Mother Gapp's. Mother Gapp's was chosen, not only because it *was* Mother Gapp's—an important consideration—but also because of the large room behind the bar, called the 'club-room', which had long ago been made of two rooms and a big cupboard, by the cutting away of crazy partitions from the crazy walls.

Scarce was it dark when the Dove-Laners, in a succession of hilarious groups—but withal a trifle suspicious—began to push through Mother Gapp's doors. Their caps pulled down to their ears, their hands in their pockets, their shoulders humped, and their jackets buttoned tight, they lurched through the Jago, grinning with uneasy affability at the greetings that met them, being less practised than the Jagos in the assumption of elaborate cordiality.

In the club-room of the Feathers there were but three or four of the other party, though the bar was packed. The three or four, of whom Josh Perrott was one, were by way of a committee of stewards deputed to bid the Dove-Laners welcome, and to help them to seats. The Jagos were in some sort in the situation of hosts, and it had been decided after debate that it would ill become them to take their places till their guests were seated. The punctilio of the Jago on such occasions was a marvel ever.

So Josh Perrott stood at one side of the club-room door and Billy Leary at the other, shaking hands with all who entered, and strenuously maintaining cheerful grins. Now the Jago smile was a smile by itself, unlike the smiles in other places. It faded suddenly, and left the face—the Jago face—drawn and sad and startling by contrast, as of a man betrayed into mirth in the midst of great sorrow. So that a persistent grin was known for a work of conscious effort.

The Dove-Laners came in still larger numbers than had been expected, and before long it was perceived that there would be little space in the club-room, if any at all, for the Jagos. Already the visitors seemed to fill the place, but they still kept coming, and found places by squeezing. There was some doubt as to what had best be done. Meanwhile the sing-song began, for at least a score were anxious to 'oblige' at once, and every moment fresh volunteers arose. Many Dove-Laners stood up, and so made more room; but more came, and still more, till the club-room could hold not another, and the very walls were like to burst. Under the low ceiling hung a layer of smoke that obscured the face of the man standing on the table at the end to sing; and under the smoke was a close-packed array of heads, hats, and clay pipes, much diversified by white bandages and black eyes.

Such Dove-Laners as came in now were fain to find places in the bar, if they could; and a crowd of Jagos, men and women, hung about the doors of the Feathers. More fortunate than other boys, Dicky, who would go anywhere to hear what purported to be music, had succeeded in worming himself through the bar and almost to the door of the club-room; but he could get no farther, and now he stood compressed, bounded on the face by Cocko Harnwell's coat-tails, and on the back of the head by Fluffy Pike's moleskin waistcoat, with pearlies down the front and the artful dodge over the pockets.* Pud Palmer—one of the reception committee—was singing. He accompanied his chorus by a step dance, and all the company stamped in sympathy:—

'She's a fighter, she's a biter, she's a swearer, she's a tearer,
The gonophs down aar alley they calls 'er Rorty Sal;
But as I'm a pertikiler sort o' bloke. I calls 'er Rorty SAIRER,*
I'm goin'—'

Crack!—CRASH!

Dicky clung to Cocko Harnwell's coat-tails lest he were trampled to death; and for a while he was flung about, crushed and bruised, among rushing men, like a swimmer among breakers, while the air was rent with howls and the smash of glass. For the club-room floor had given way.

It had been built but slightly in the beginning, as floor for two small rooms and a cupboard, with little weight to carry. Old and rotten now, and put to the strain of a multitude, stamping in unison, it had failed utterly, and had let down a struggling mob of men five feet on the barrels in the cellar, panic-stricken and jumbled with tables, pots, wooden forms, lighted pipes and splintered joinery.

From the midst of the stramash a Dove-Laner bawled aloud that it was a trap,* and instantly Jagos and Dove-Laners were at each others' throats, and it was like to go hard with the few Jagos among the ruins. Billy Leary laid about him desperately with a ragged piece of flooring, while Josh Perrott and Pud Palmer battered Dove-Laners with quart pots. Then it was shouted without that the Dove-Laners were exterminating the Jagos within, and a torrent of Jagos burst through the doors, poured through the bar, and over the club-room threshold into the confusion below.

Dicky, bruised, frightened and flung like a rag this way and that, at last made shift to grasp a post, and climb up on the bar counter. Mother Gapp, a dishevelled maniac, was dancing amid pots and broken glass, black in the face, screaming inaudibly. Dicky stumbled along the counter, climbed over the broken end of a partition, and fell into the arms of Kiddo Cook, coming in with the rush. 'Put the boy out!' yelled Kiddo, turning and heaving him over the heads behind him. Somebody caught Dicky by a leg and an arm, his head hit the door post, the world turned a double-somersault about him, and he came down with a crash. He was on the flags of Old Jago Street, with all his breath driven out of him.

But he was quickly on his feet again. A crowd beat against the front of Mother Gapp's, and reinforcements came running from everywhere, with the familiar rallying-cry, 'Jago! Jago 'old tight!'

Dove Lane had abused the Jago hospitality; woe to the Dove-Laners!

There were scuffles here and there, where Dove-Laners, who had never reached the club-room, or who had been crowded out of it, made for escape. Dicky was shaken and sore, but he pulled himself together resolutely. He had seen a few Dove Lane boys about before he had got into the Feathers, and plainly it was his duty to find them and bash them. Moreover, he wondered what had become of his father. He hastened through the dark passage of the house next to Mother Gapp's, into the back yard, and through the broken fence. There was a door in the club-room wall, and through this he thought to see what was going forward.

The cellar—at any rate, at the farther end—was a pit of writhing forms, and the din rose loud as ever. A short figure stood black against the light, and held by the doorpost, looking down at the riot. Dicky knew it. He sprang at Bobby Roper, pulled him by the arm, and struck at him furiously. The hunchback, whimpering, did his best to retaliate and to get away; but Dicky, raging at the remembrance of his fancied injury, struck savagely, and struck again, till Bobby Roper tripped backward over the projecting end of a broken floor-board, and pitched headlong into the cellar. He struck a barrel and rolled over, falling into the space between that and two other barrels. Dicky looked, but the hunchback did not move. Then some of the Dove-Laners flung pots at the lamps hanging against the club-room walls. Soon they were smashed and fell, and there was a darkness; and under cover thereof the aliens essayed flight.

Dicky was a little frightened at what he had done, but he felt that with Bobby Roper anything was justifiable. Some Dove-Laners escaped by the back door—the cellar was low, and there was not five feet between the barrels and the broken joists—and these Dicky avoided by getting back through the fence. In the end, most of the enemy struggled away by one means or another, and when lights were brought at last the Jagos were found pummelling each other savagely in the gloom.

Father Sturt, apprised of something uncommon by the exodus of members from the club, finally locked the doors and came to investigate. He arrived as the Jagos were extricating themselves from the cellar, and it was he who lifted the little hunchback from among the barrels and carried him into the open air; he also who carried him home.

No bone was broken, and no joint was disturbed, but there was a serious shock, many contusions, and a cut on the scalp. So said the surgeon whom Father Sturt took with him to Dove Lane. And Bobby Roper lay a fortnight in bed.

More plaster than ever embellished the heads of Dove Lane and the Jago that night; but for the Jagos there was compensation. For down among the barrels lay many a packet of tobacco, many a pair of boots, and many a corner stuffed with mixed property of other sorts: which Mother Gapp had fenced for many a month back. So that it happened to more than one warrior to carry home again something with which he had run between the 'Posties' long before, and had sold to Mother Gapp for what she would give.

The ground floor of the Feathers stood a battered shell. The damage of four years ago was inconsiderable compared to this. With tears and blasphemy Mother Gapp invaded the hoard of her long iniquity to buy a new floor; but it was the larceny—the taking of the tobacco and the boots, and the many other things from among the barrels—that cut her to the soul. A crool—a crool thing was such robbery—sheer robbery, said Mother Gapp.

Josh Perrott got a bad sprain in the cellar and had to be helped home. More, he took with him not a single piece of plunder, such was his painful disablement.

CHAPTER 23

For more than a week Josh Perrott could not walk about. And it was a bad week. For some little while his luck had been but poor, and now he found himself laid up with a total reserve fund of fourteenpence. A coat was pawned with old Poll Rann (who kept a leaving shop* in a first floor back in Jago Row) for ninepence. Then Josh swore at Dicky for not being still at Grinder's, and told him to turn out and bring home some money. Dicky had risen almost too sore and stiff to stand, on the morning after the fight at the Feathers, and he was little better now. But he had to go, and he went, though he well knew that a click was out of the question, for his joints almost refused to bend. But he found that the fat's a-running boys were contemplating business, and he scouted for them with such success as to bring home sevenpence in the evening. Then Kiddo Cook, who had left Mother Gapp's with a double armful on the night of the sing-song, found himself rich enough, being a bachelor, to lend Josh eighteenpence. And a shawl of Hannah Perrott's was pawned. That, though, was redeemed the next day, together with the coat. For Dicky brought home a golden sovereign.

It had been an easy click—scarce a click at all, perhaps, strictly speaking. Dicky had tramped into the city, and had found a crowd outside St Paul's—a well-dressed crowd, not being moved on: for something was going forward in the cathedral. He recognised one of the High Mob, a pogue-hunter—that is a pickpocket who deals in purses. Dicky watched this man's movements, by way of education; for he was an eminent practitioner, and worked alone, with no assistant to cover him. Dicky saw him in the thick of the crowd, standing beside and behind one lady after another; but it was only when his elbow bent to slip something into his own pocket that Dicky knew he had 'touched'. Presently he moved to another part of the crowd, where mostly men were standing, and there he stealthily let drop a crumpled newspaper, and straightway left the crowd. He had 'worked' it as much as he judged safe. Dicky wriggled toward the crumpled paper, slipped it under his jacket, and cleared away also. He knew that there was something in the paper besides news: that, in fact, there were purses in it—purses emptied and shed as soon as might be, because nobody can swear to money, but strange purses lead to destruction. Dicky recked little of this danger, but made his best pace to a recess in a back street, there to examine his pogues; for though the uxter was gone from them, they might yet bring a few coppers from Mr Weech, if they were of good quality. They were a fairly sound lot. One had a large clasp that looked like silver, and another was quite new, and Dicky was observing with satisfaction the shop-shininess of the lining, when he perceived a cunning pocket at the back, lying flat against the main integument—and in it was a sovereign! He gulped at the sight. Clearly the pogue-hunter, emptying the pogues in his pocket by sense of touch, had missed the flat pocket. Dicky was not yet able to run with freedom, but he never ceased from trotting till he reached his own staircase in Old Jago Street. And so the eight or nine days passed, and Josh went out into the Jago with no more than a tenderness about his ankle.

Now, he much desired a good click; so he went across High Street Shoreditch, to Kingsland Railway Station and bought a ticket for Canonbury.

Luck was against him, it was plain. He tramped the northern suburbs from three o'clock till dark, but touched for nothing. He spent money, indeed, for he feared to overwork his ankle, and for that reason rested in divers public-houses. He peeped in at the gates of quiet gardens, in the hope of garden-hose left unwatched, or tennis-rackets lying in a handy summer-house. But he saw none. He pried about the doors of private stable-yards, in case of absent grooms and unprotected bunches of harness, but in vain. He inspected quiet areas and kitchen entrances in search of unguarded spoons—even descended into one area, where he had to make an awkward excuse about buying old bottles, in consequence of meeting the cook at the door. He tramped one quiet road after another on the look out for a dead 'un—a house furnished, but untenanted. But there was never a dead 'un, it seemed, in all the northern district. So he grew tired and short-tempered, and cursed himself for that he had not driven off with a baker's horse and cart that had tempted him early in the afternoon.

It grew twilight, and then dark. Josh sat in a public-house, and took a long rest and some bread and cheese. It would never do to go home without touching, and for some time he considered possibilities with regard to a handful of silver money, kept in a glass on a shelf behind the bar. But it was out of reach, and there were too many people in the place for any attempt by climbing on the counter. Josh grew savage and soured. Plastering itself was not such troublesome work; and at least the pay was certain. It was little short of ten o'clock when he left the public-house and turned back toward Canonbury. He would have *something* on the way, he resolved, and he would catch the first train home. He would have to knock somebody over in a dark street, that was all. It was nothing new, but he would rather have made his click another way this time, because his tender ankle might keep him slow, or even give way altogether; and to be caught in a robbery with violence might easily mean something more than mere imprisonment; it might mean a dose of the 'cat':* and the cat was a thing the thought or the mention whereof sent shudders through the Old Jago.

But no: nobody worth knocking down came his way. Truly luck was out tonight. There was a spot by the long garden wall of a corner house that would have suited admirably, and as Josh lingered there, and looked about him, his eye fell on a ladder, reared nearly upright against the back wall of that same corner house, and lashed at the roof. It passed by the side of the second floor window, whereof the top sash was a little open. That would do. It was not his usual line of work, but it looked very promising.

He stuck his stick under his waistcoat by way of the collar, and climbed the wall with gingerly care, giving his sound foot all the hard work. The ladder offered no difficulty, but the bottom sash of the window was stiff, and he cracked a pane of glass in pushing at the frame with his stick. The sash lifted, however, in the end, and he climbed into the dark room, being much impeded by the dressing-table. All was quiet in the house, and the ticking of a watch on the dressing-table was distinct in the ear. Josh felt for it and found it, with a chain hanging from the bow.*

The house was uncommonly quiet. Could it possibly be a dead 'un after all? Josh felt that he ought to have inspected the front windows before climbing the wall, but the excitement of the long-delayed chance had ruined his discretion. At any rate he would reconnoitre. The door was ajar and the landing was dark.

Down in the drawing-room a gross, pimply man, in shirtsleeves and socks, sat up on the sofa at the sound of an opened window higher in the house. He took a drink from the glass by his side, and listened. Then he rose and went softly upstairs.

Josh Perrott came out on the landing. It was a long landing, with a staircase at the end, illuminated from somewhere below: so that it was not a case of a dead 'un after all. He tiptoed along to take a look down the stairs, nevertheless. Then he was conscious of a loud breathing, as of an over-gorged cow, and up behind the stair-rails rose a fat head, followed by a fat trunk, between white shirt-sleeves.

Josh sank into the shadow. The man had no light, but discover him he must, sooner or later, for the landing was narrow. Better sooner, and suddenly. As the man's foot was on the topmost stair, Josh sprang at him with a straight left-hander that took him on the broad chin, and sent him downstairs in a heap, with a crash and a roar. Josh darted back to the room he had just left, scrambled through the window, and slid down the ladder, as he had slid down many another when he was a plasterer's boy. He checked himself short of the bottom, sprang at the wall-coping, flung himself over, and ran up the dark by-street, with the sound of muffled roars and screams faint in his ears.

He ran a street or two, taking every corner as he came to it, and then fell into a walk. In his flight he had not spared his ankle, and now it was painful. Moreover, he had left his stick behind him, in the bedroom. But he was in Highbury, and Canonbury Road Station was less than half a mile away. He grinned silently as he went, for there was something in the aspect of the overfed householder, and in the manner of his downfall, that gave the adventure a comic flavour. He took a peep at his spoil as he passed under a street lamp, for all watches and chains are the same in the dark, and the thing might be a mere Waterbury on a steel guard.* But no: both were gold, and heavy: a red clock and slang* if ever there was one. And so Josh Perrott hobbled and chuckled his way home.

CHAPTER 24

BUT indeed Josh Perrott's luck was worse than he thought. For the gross, pimply man was a High Mobsman—so very high a mobsman that it would have been slander and libel, and a very great expense, to write him down a mobsman at all. He paid a rent of a hundred and twenty pounds a year, and heavy rates, and put half-a-crown into the plate at a very respectable chapel every Sunday. He was, in fact, the King of High Mobsmen, spoken of among them as the Mogul.* He did no vulgar thievery: he never screwed a chat, nor claimed a peter,* nor worked the mace. He sat easily at home, and financed (sometimes planned) promising speculations: a large swindle requiring much ground-baiting and preliminary outlay; or a robbery of specie from a mail train: or a bank fraud needing organization and funds. When the results of such speculations consisted of money he took the lion's share. When they were expressed in terms of imprisonment they fell to active and intelligent subordinates. So that for years the Mogul had lived an affluent and a blameless life, far removed from the necessity of injudicious bodily exercise, and characterised by every indulgence consistent with a proper suburban respectability. He had patronised, snubbed, or encouraged High Mobsmen of more temerarious habit, had profited by their exploits, and had read of their convictions and sentences with placid interest in the morning papers. And after all this, to be robbed in his own house and knocked downstairs by a casual buster was an outrage that afflicted the Mogul with wrath infuriate. Because that was a sort of trouble that had never seemed a possibility, to a person of his eminence: and because the angriest victim of dishonesty is a thief.

However, the burglar had got clean away, that was plain; and he had taken the best watch and chain in the house, with the Mogul's initials on the back. So that respectable sufferer sent for the police, and gave his attention to the alleviation of bumps and the washing away of blood. In his bodily condition a light blow was enough to let a great deal of blood—no doubt with benefit;* and Josh Perrott's blows were not light in any case.

So it came to pass that not only were the police on the look-out for a man with a large gold watch with the Mogul's monogram on the back; but also the word was passed as by telegraph through underground channels, till every fence in London was warned that the watch was the Mogul's; and ere noon next day there was not one but would as lief have put a scorpion in his pocket as that same toy and tackle that Josh Perrott was gloating over in his back room in Old Jago Street.

As for Josh, his ankle was bad in the morning, and swelled. He dabbed at it perseveringly with wet rags, and rubbed it vigorously, so that by one o'clock he was able to lace up his boot and go out. He was anxious to fence his plunder without delay, and he made his way to Hoxton. The watch seemed to be something especially good, and he determined to stand out for a price well above the usual figure. For the swag of common thieves commanded no such prices as did that of the High Mob. All of it was bought and sold on the simple system first called into being seventy years back and more by the prince of fences, Ikey Solomons.* A breast-pin brought a fixed sum, good or bad, and a roll of cloth brought the fixed price of a roll of cloth, regardless of quality. Thus a silver watch fetched six shillings, never more and never less; a gold watch was worth twice as much; an uncommonly good one—a rich man's watch—would bring as much as eighteen shillings, if the thief were judge enough of its quality to venture the demand. And as it commonly took three men to secure a single watch in the open street—one to 'front',* one to snatch, and a third to take from the snatcher—the gains of the toy-getting trade were poor, except to the fence. This time Josh resolved to put pressure on the fence, and to do his best to get something as near a sovereign as might be. And as to the chain, so thick and heavy, he would fight his best for the privilege of sale by weight. Thus turning the thing in his mind, he entered the familiar doorway of the old clothes shop.

'Vot is id?' asked the fence, holding out his hand with the customary air of contempt for what was coming, by way of discounting it in advance. This particular fence, by-the-bye, never bought anything himself.* He inspected whatever was brought on behalf of an occult friend; and the transaction was completed by a shabby third party in an adjoining court. But he had an amazingly keen regard for his friend's interests.

Josh put the watch into the extended hand. The fence lifted it to his face, turned it over, and started. He looked hard at Josh, and then again at the watch, and handed it hastily back, holding it gingerly by the bow. 'Don' vant *dot*', he said; 'nod me—nod 'im, I mean. No, no.' He turned away, shaking his hand as though to throw off contamination. 'Take id avay.'

'Wot's the matter?' Josh demanded, astonished. 'Is it 'cos o' the letters on the back? You can easy send it to church, can't ye?'

A watch is 'sent to church' when it is put into another case. But the fence waved away the suggestion. 'Take id avay I tell you,' he said. 'I—'e von't 'ave nodden to do vid id.'

'Wot's the matter with the chain, then?' asked Josh. But the fence walked away to the back of the shop, wagging his hands desperately, like a wet man seeking a towel, and repeating only:—'Nodden to do vid id—take id avay—nodden to do vid id.'

Josh stuffed his prize back into his pocket, and regained the street. He was confounded. What was wrong with Cohen? Did he suspect a police trick to entrap him? Josh snorted with indignation at the thought. He was no nark! But perhaps the police were showing a pressing interest in Cohen's business concerns just now, and he had suspended fencing for a while. The guess was a lame one, but he could think of none better at the moment, as he pushed his way to the Jago. He would try Mother Gapp.

Mother Gapp would not even take the watch in her hands; her eyes were good enough at that distance. 'Lor', Josh Perrott,' she said, 'wot 'a' ye bin up to now? Want to git me lagged now, do ye? Ain't satisfied with breakin' up the 'ouse an' ruinin' a pore widder that way, ain't ye? You git out, go on. I 'ad 'nough o' you!'

It was very extraordinary. Was there a general reclamation of fences? But there were men at work at the Feathers, putting down boards and restoring partitions; and two of them had been 'gone over' ruinously on their way to work, and now they came and went with four policemen. Possibly Mother Gapp feared the observation of carpenters. Be it as it might, there was nothing for it now but Weech's.

Mr Weech was charmed. 'Dear me, it's a wonderful fine watch, Mr Perrott—a wonderful fine watch. An' a beautiful chain.' But he was looking narrowly at the big monogram as he said it. 'It's reely a wonderful article. 'Ow they do git 'em up, to be sure! Cost a lot o' money too, I'll be bound. Might you be thinkin' o' sellin' it?'

'Yus o' course,' replied Josh. 'That's wot I brought it for.'

'Ah, it's a lovely watch, Mr Perrott—a lov-erly watch; an' the chain matches it. But you mustn't be too 'ard on me. Shall we say four pound for the little lot?'

It was more than double Josh's wildest hopes, but he wanted all he could get. 'Five,' he said doggedly.

Weech gazed at him with tender rebuke. 'Five pound's a awful lot o' money, Mr Perrott,' he said. 'You're too 'ard on me, reely. I 'ardly know 'ow I can scrape it up. But it's a beautiful little lot, an' I won't 'aggle. But I ain't got all that money in the 'ouse now. I never keep so much money in the 'ouse—sich a neighb'r'ood, Mr Perrott! Bring it round tomorrer mornin' at eleven.'

'Awright, I'll come. Five quid, mind.'

'Ah yus,' answered Mr Weech, with a reproving smile. 'It's reely more than I ought!'

Josh was jubilant, and forgot his sore ankle. He had never handled such a sum as five pounds since his fight with Billy Leary, years ago; when, indeed, he had stooped to folly in the shape of lavish treating, and so had not enjoyed the handling of the full amount.

Mr Weech, also, was pleased. For it was a great stroke of business to oblige so distinguished a person as the Mogul. There was no telling what advantages it might not lead to in the way of trade.

That night the Perrotts had a hot supper, brought from Walker's cookshop in paper. And at eleven the next morning Josh, twenty yards from Mr Weech's door, with the watch and chain in his pocket, was tapped on the arm by a constable in plain clothes, while another came up on the other side. 'Mornin', Perrott,' said the first constable, cheerily. 'We've got a little business with you at the station.'

'Me? Wot for?'

'Oh well, come along; p'raps it ain't anything—unless there's a gold watch an' chain on you, from Highbury. It's just a turnin' over.'

'Awright,' replied Josh, resignedly. 'It's a fair cop. I'll go quiet.'

'That's right, Perrott; it ain't no good playin' the fool, you know.' They were moving along; and as they came by Weech's shop, a whiskered face, with a patch of shining scalp over it, peeped from behind a curtain that hung at the rear of the bloaters and plumcake in the window. As he saw it, Josh ducked suddenly, wrenching his arm free, and dashed over the threshold. Mr Weech, whiskers and apron flying, galloped through the door at the back, and the constables sprang upon Josh instantly and dragged him into the street. 'Wotcher mean?' cried the one who knew him, indignantly, and with a significant glance at the other. 'Call that goin' quiet?'

Josh's face was white and staring with rage. 'Awright,' he grunted through his shut teeth, after a pause. 'I'll go quiet now. I ain't got nothin' agin *you*.'

CHAPTER 25

DICKY'S morning theft that day had been but a small one—he had run off with a new two-foot rule that a cabinet-maker had carelessly left on an unfinished office table at his shop door in Curtain Road. It was not much, but it might fetch some sort of a dinner at Weech's, which would be better than going home, and, perhaps, finding nothing. So about noon, all ignorant of his father's misfortune, he came by way of Holywell Lane and Bethnal Green Road to Meakin Street.

Mr Weech looked at him rather oddly, Dicky fancied, when he came in, but he took the two-foot rule with alacrity, and brought Dicky a rasher of bacon, and a slice of cake afterward. This seemed very generous. More: Mr Weech's manner was uncommonly amiable, and when the meal was over, of his own motion, he handed over a supplementary penny. Dicky was surprised; but he had no objection, and he thought little more about it.

As soon as he appeared in Luck Row he was told that his father had been 'smugged'. Indeed the tidings had filled the Jago within ten minutes. Josh Perrott was walking quietly along Meakin Street—so went the news—when up comes Snuffy* and another split, and smugs him. Josh had a go for Weech's door, to cut his lucky out at the back, but was caught. That was a smart notion of Josh's, the Jago opinion ran, to get through Weech's and out into the courts behind. But it was no go.

Hannah Perrott sat in her room, inert and lamenting. Dicky could not rouse her, and at last he went off by himself to reconnoitre about Commercial Street Police Station, and pick up what information he might; while a gossip or two came and took Mrs Perrott for consolation to Mother Gapp's. Little Em, unwashed, tangled and weeping, could well take care of herself and the room, being more than two years old.

Josh Perrott would be brought up tomorrow, Dicky ascertained, at the North London Police Court. So the next morning found Dicky trudging moodily along the two miles of flags to Stoke Newington Road; while his mother and three sympathising friends, who foresaw an opportunity for numerous tiny drops with interesting circumstances to flavour them, took a penny cast* on the way in a tramcar.

Dicky, with some doubt as to the disposition of the door-keeping policeman toward ragged boys, waited for the four women, and contrived to pass in unobserved among them. Several Jagos were in the court, interested not only in Josh's adventure, but in one of Cocko Harnwell's, who had indulged, the night before, in an animated little scramble with three policemen in Dalston; and they waited with sympathetic interest while the luck was settled of a long string of drunk-and-disorderlies.

At last Josh was brought in, and lurched composedly into the dock, in the manner of one who knew the routine. The police gave evidence of arrest, in consequence of information received, and of finding the watch and chain in Josh's trousers pocket. The prosecutor,* with his head conspicuously bedight with sticking-plaster, puffed and grunted up into the witness-box, kissed the book, and was a 'retired commission agent'.* He positively identified the watch and chain, and he not less positively identified Josh Perrott, whom he had picked out from a score of men in the police-yard. This would have been a feat indeed for a man who had never seen Josh, and had only once encountered his fist in the dark, had it not been for the dutiful though private aid of Mr Weech: who, in giving his information had described Josh and his one suit of clothes with great fidelity, especially indicating a scar on the right cheek-bone which would mark him among a thousand. The retired commission agent was quite sure of the prisoner. He had met him on the stairs, where there was plenty of light from a lamp, and the prisoner had attacked him savagely, beating him about the head and flinging him downstairs. The policeman called by the prosecutor's servant deposed to finding the prosecutor bruised and bleeding. There was a ladder against the back of the house; a bedroom window had been opened; there were muddy marks on the sill; and he had found the stick—produced—lying in the bedroom.

Josh leaned easily on the rail before him while evidence was being given, and said 'No, yer worship', whenever he was asked if he desired to question a witness. He knew better than to run the risk of incriminating himself by challenging the prosecutor's well-coloured evidence; and, as it was a certain case of committal for trial, it would have been useless in any event. He made the same reply when he was asked if he had anything to say before being committed: and straightway was 'fullied'. He lurched serenely out of the dock, waving his cap at his friends in the court, and that was all. The Jagos waited till Cocko

Harnwell got his three months and then retired to neighbouring public-houses; but Dicky remembered his little sister, and hurried home.

The month's session at the Old Bailey had just begun, so that Josh had no long stay at Holloway.* Among the Jagos it was held to be a most creditable circumstance that Josh was to take his trial with full honours at the Old Bailey, and not at mere County Sessions at Clerkenwell, like a simple lob-crawler* or peter-claimer. For Josh's was a case of burglary with serious violence, such as was fitting for the Old Bailey, and not even a High Mobsman could come to trial with greater glory. 'As like as not it's laggin' dues,* after 'is other convictions,' said Bill Rann. And Jerry Gullen thought so too.

Dicky went, with his mother and Em, to see Josh at Newgate. They stood with other visitors, very noisy, before a double iron railing* covered with wire-netting, at the farther side whereof stood Josh and other prisoners, while a screaming hubbub of question and answer filled the air. Josh had little to say. He lounged against the farther railing with his hands in his pockets, asked what Cocko Harnwell had got, and sent a message to Bill Rann. While his wife did little more than look dolefully through the wires, and pipe:—'Oh, Josh, wotever shall I do?' at intervals, with no particular emotion; while Em pressed her smudgy little face against the wires, and stared mightily; and while Dicky felt that if he had been younger he would have cried. When time was up, Josh waved his hand and slouched off, and his family turned out with the rest: little Em carrying into later years a memory of father as a man who lived in a cage.

In such a case as this, the Jago would have been for ever disgraced if Josh Perrott's pals had neglected to get up a 'break' or subscription to pay for his defence. Things were never very flourishing in the Jago. But this was the sort of break a Jago could not shirk, lest it were remembered against him when his own turn came. So enough was collected to brief an exceedingly junior counsel, who did his useless best. But the facts were too strong even for the most experienced advocate; the evidence of the prosecutor was nowhere to be shaken, and the jury found a verdict of guilty without leaving the box—indeed, with scarce the formality of collecting their heads together over the rails. Then Josh's past was most unpleasantly raked up before him. He had been convicted of larceny, of assaulting the police, and of robbery with violence. There were two sentences of six months' imprisonment recorded against him, one of three months, and two of a month. Besides fines. The Recorder* considered it a very serious offence. Not deterred by the punishments he had already received the prisoner had proceeded to a worse crime—burglary; and with violence. It was plain that lenience was wasted in such a case, and simple imprisonment was not enough. There must be an exemplary sentence. The prisoner must be kept in penal servitude for five years.

Lagging dues it was, as Bill Rann had anticipated. That Josh Perrott agreed with him was suggested by the fact that from the very beginning he described himself as a painter; because a painter in prison is apt to be employed at times in painting—a lighter and a more desirable task than falls to the lot of his fellows in other trades.

In a room by the court Josh saw his wife, Dicky, and Bill Rann (Josh's brother-in-law for the occasion) before his ride to Holloway, his one stopping place on the way to Chelmsford Gaol. Little Em had been left sprawling in the Jago gutters. This time Hannah Perrott wept in good earnest, and Dicky, notwithstanding his thirteen years, blinked very hard at the wall before him. The arrangement of Josh's affairs was neither a long nor a difficult labour. 'S'pose you'll 'ave to do wot you can with rush bags, an' sacks, and match-boxes, an' wot not,' he said to his wife, and she assented. Josh nodded:—'An' if you 'ave to go in the 'ouse'—he meant the workhouse—'well, it can't be 'elped. You won't be no wuss auf 'n me.'

'Oh, *she'll* be awright,' said Bill Rann, jerking his thumb cheerfully toward the missis. 'Wot about you? Think they'll make it Parkhurst?'

Josh shook his head moodily. Parkhurst being the prison reserved for convicts of less robust habit, he had little hope of enjoying its easier conditions.* Presently he said:—'I bin put away this time—fair put away.'

'Wot?' answered Bill, 'narkin' dues is it?'

Josh nodded.

''Oo done it then? 'Oo narked?'

Josh shook his head. 'Never mind,' he said, 'I don't want 'im druv out o' the Jago 'fore I come out. I'd be sorry to miss 'im. *I* know 'im—that's enough.'

And then time was up. Josh suffered the missis to kiss him, and shook hands with Bill Rann. 'Good luck to all you Jagos,' he said. Dicky shook hands too, and said 'Goodbye, father!' in a voice of such laboured cheerfulness that a grin burst for a moment amid Josh's moody features as he was marched away, and so departed for the place—in Jago idiom—where the dogs don't bite.

CHAPTER 26

It was Father Sturt's practice to visit every family in his parish in regular order. But small as the parish was—insignificant, indeed, in mere area—its population exceeded eight thousand: so that the round was one of many months, for visiting was but one among innumerable duties. But Josh Perrott's lagging secured his family a special call. Not that the circumstances were in any way novel or at all uncommon; nor even that the vicar had any hope of being able to help. He was but the one man who could swim in a howling sea of human wreckage.* In the Jago, wives like Hannah Perrott, temporarily widowed by the absence of husbands 'in the country',* were to be counted in scores, and most were in worse case than she, in the matter of dependent children. Father Sturt's house-list revealed the fact that in Old Jago Street alone, near seventy of the males were at that moment on ticket-of-leave.*

In the Perrott case, indeed, the sufferers were fortunate, as things went. Mrs Perrott had but herself and the child of two to keep, for Dicky could do something, whether good or bad, for himself. The vicar might try to get regular work for Dicky, but it would be a vain toil, for he must tell an employer what he knew of Dicky's past and of that other situation. He could but give the woman the best counsel at his command, and do what he might to quicken any latent spark of energy. So he did his best, and that was all. The struggle lay with Hannah Perrott.

She had been left before, and more than once; but then the periods had been shorter, and, as a matter of fact, things had fallen out so well that scarce more than a meal here and there had had to be missed, though, when they came, the meals were apt to be but of crusts. And now there was more trouble ahead; for though she began her lonely time with but one small child on hand, she knew that ere long there would be two.

Of course, she had worked before; not only when Josh had been 'in' but at other times, to add to the family resources. She was a clumsy needle woman: else she might hope to earn some ninepence or a shilling a day at making shirts,* by keeping well to the needle for sixteen hours out of the twenty-four; and from the whole sum there would be no deductions, except for needles and cotton, and what the frugal employer might choose to subtract for work to which he could devise an objection. But, as it was, she must do her best to get some sack-making. They paid one-and-sevenpence a hundred for sacks, and, with speed and long hours, she could make a hundred in four days. Rush bag-making would bring even more, which would be desirable, considering the three-and-sixpence a week for rent: which, with the payments for other rooms, made the rent of the crazy den in Old Jago Street about equal, space for space, to that of a house in Onslow Square. Then there was a more lucrative employment still, but one to be looked for at intervals only: one not to be counted on at all, in fact, for it was a prize, and many sought after it. This was the making of matchboxes. For making one hundred and forty-four outside cases with paper label and sandpaper, and the same number of trays to slide into them—a gross of complete boxes, or two hundred and eighty-eight pieces in all—one got twopence farthing; indeed, for a special size one even got a farthing a gross more; and all the wood and the labels and the sandpaper were provided free: so that the fortunate operative lost nothing out of the twopence farthing but the cost of the paste, and the string for tying up the boxes into regularly numbered batches, and the time employed in fetching the work and taking it back again. And if seven gross were to be got, and could be done in a day—and it was really not very difficult for the skilful hand who kept at work long enough—the day's income was one-and-threepence three-farthings, less expenses: still better, that, than the shirts. But the work was hard to get. As the public-spirited manufacturers complained: people would buy Swedish matches, whereas if people would Support Home Industries* and buy no matches but theirs, they would be able to order many a twopence-farthingsworth of boxes more.

There might be collateral sources of income, but these were doubtful and irregular. Probably Dicky would bring in a few coppers now and again. Then judicious attendance at churches, chapels and prayer-meetings beyond the Jago borders was rewarded by coal-tickets, boots, and the like. It was necessary to know just where and when to go and what to say, else the sole result might be loss of time. There was a church in Bethnal Green, for instance, which it would be foolish to enter before the end of the Litany, for then you were in good time to get your half-quarter hundredweight of coals;* but at other places they might object to so late an appearance. Above all, one must know the ropes. There were several women in the Jago who made almost a living in this way alone. They were experts; they knew every fund, every meeting-house, all the comings and goings of the gullible; insomuch that they would take black umbrage at any unexpected difficulty in getting what they demanded. 'Wy,' one would say, 'I 'ad to pitch sich a bleed'n' 'oly tale I earned it twice over.' But these were the proficient, and proficiency in the trade was an outcome of long experience working on a foundation of natural gifts; and Hannah Perrott could never hope to be among them.

Turning these things in her mind, she addressed herself to her struggle. She managed to get some sacks, but for a week or two she could make nothing like twenty-five a day, though Dicky helped. Her fingers got raw; but she managed to complete a hundred within the first week. They might have been better done, as the employer said when he saw them. But she got her full one-and-sevenpence. She pawned her boots for fourpence, and wore two old odd ones of Josh's; and she got twopence on a petticoat. Dicky also helped a little; and at the end of a fortnight there came a godsend in the shape of material for matchboxes. Mrs Perrott was slow with them at first; but Dicky was quick, and even little Em began to learn to spread paste.

CHAPTER 27

DICKY grew slighter and lanker, dark about the eyes, and weaker. He was growing longitudinally, and that made his lateral wasting the quicker and the more apparent. A furtive, frighted look hung ever in his face, a fugitive air about his whole person. His mother's long face was longer than ever, and blacker under the eyes than Dicky's own, and her weak open mouth hung at the corners as that of a woman faint with weeping. Little Em's knees and elbows were knobs in the midst of limbs of unnatural length. Rarely could a meal be seen ahead; and when it came, it made Dicky doubtful whether or not hunger were really caused by eating. But his chief distress was to see that little Em cried not like a child, but silently, as she strove to thread needles or to smear matchbox labels. And when good fortune brought matchboxes, there was an undue loss on the twopence farthing in the matter of paste. The stuff was a foul mess, sour and faint, and it was kept in a broken tea-cup, near which Dicky had detected his sister sucking her fingers; for in truth little Em stole the paste.

On and off, by one way and another, Mrs Perrott made enough to keep the rent paid with indifferent regularity, and sometimes there was a copper or so left over. She did fairly well, too, at the churches and prayer-meetings; people saw her condition, and now and again would give her something beyond the common dole; so that she learned the trick of looking more miserable than usual at such places.

The roof provided, Dicky felt that his was the task to find food. Alone, he might have rubbed along clear of starvation, but there were his mother and his sister. Lack of victuals shook his nerve and made him timid. Moreover, his terror grew greater than ever at the prospect of being caught in a theft. He lay awake at night and sweated to think of it. Who would bring in things from the outer world for mother and Em then? And the danger was worse than ever. He had felt the police-court birch,* and it was bad, very bad. But he would take it every day and take it almost without a tear, rather than the chance of a reformatory. Magistrates were unwilling to send boys to reformatories while both father and mother were at hand to control them, for that were relieving the parents of their natural responsibility;

but in a case like Dicky's, a 'schooling'* was a very likely thing. So that Dicky, as he prowled, was torn between implacable need and the fear of being cut off from all chance of supplying it.

It was his rule never to come home without bringing something, were it no more than a mildewed crust. It was a resolve impossible to keep at times, but at those times it was two in the morning ere he would drag himself, pallid and faint, into the dark room where the others might be—probably were—lying awake and unfed. Rather than face such a home-coming he had sometimes ventured on a more difficult feat than stealing in the outer world: he had stolen in the Jago. Sam Cash, for instance, had lost a bloater.

Dicky never ate at Weech's now. Rarely, indeed, would he take payment in kind, unless it were for something of smaller value than the average of his poor pilferings; and then he carried the food home. But cheaper things could be bought elsewhere, so that more usually he insisted on money payments: to the grief of Mr Weech, who set forth the odiousness of ingratitude at length; though his homilies had no sort of effect on Dicky's morals.

Father Sturt saw that Hannah Perrott gained no ground in her struggle, and urged her to apply for outdoor parish relief, promising to second her request with the guardians.* But with an odd throw-back to the respectability of her boiler-making ancestry, she disliked the notion of help from the parish, and preferred to remain as she was; for there at least her ingrained inertness seemed to side with some phantom of self-respect. To her present position she had subsided by almost imperceptible degrees, and she was scarce conscious of a change. But to parish relief there was a distinct and palpable step: a step that, on the whole, it seemed easier not to take. But it was with eagerness that she took a Maternity Society's letter, wherewith the vicar had provided himself on her behalf. For her time was drawing near.

CHAPTER 28

JOSH PERROTT well understood the advantage of good prison-behaviour, and after six months in his Chelmsford cell he had earned the right to a visit from friends. But none came. He had scarcely expected that anybody would, and asked for the order merely on the general principle that a man should take all he can get, useful or not. For there would have been a five-shilling fare to pay for each visitor from London, and Hannah Perrott could as easily have paid five pounds. And indeed she had other things to think of.

Kiddo Cook had been less observed of late in the Jago. In simple fact he was at work. He found that a steady week of porterage at Spitalfields Market would bring him sixteen shillings and perhaps a little more: and he had taken Father Sturt's encouragement to try another week, and a week after that. Father Sturt too, had cunningly stimulated Kiddo's ambitions: till he cherished aspirations to a fruit and vegetable stall, with a proper tarpaulin cover for bad weather; though he cherished them in secret, confident that they were of his own independent conception. Perhaps the Perrotts saw as much of Kiddo as did anybody at this time. For Kiddo, seeing how it went with them (though indeed it went as badly with others too) built up laboriously a solemn and most circumstantial Lie.* There was a friend of his, a perfect gentleman, who used a beer-shop by Spitalfields Market, and who had just started an extensive and complicated business in the general provision line. He sold all sorts of fruit and vegetables fresh, and all sorts of meat, carrots, cabbages, saveloys, fried fish and pease-pudding cooked. His motto was:—'Everything *of* the best.' But he had the misfortune to be quite unable himself to judge whether his goods were really of the best or not, in consequence of an injury to his palate, arising from a blow on the mouth with a quart pot, inflicted in the heat of discussion by a wealthy acquaintance. So that he, being a perfect gentleman, had requested Kiddo Cook, out of the friendship he bore him, to drop in occasionally and test his samples. 'Take a good big whack, you know,' said he, 'and get the advice of a friend or two, if *you* ain't sure.' So Kiddo would take frequent and handsome whacks accordingly, to the perfect gentleman's delight; and, not quite knowing what to do with all the whacks, or being desirous of an independent opinion on them (there was some confusion between these two motives) he would bring Mrs Perrott samples, from time to time, and hope it wouldn't inconvenience her. It never did.

It was late in the dusk of a rainy day that Kiddo Cook stumped into Old Jago Street with an apple in his pocket for Em. It was not much, but money was a little short, and at any rate the child would be pleased. As he climbed the stairs he grew conscious of sounds of anguish, muffled by the Perrotts' door. There might have been sobs, and there seemed to be groans; certainly little Em was crying, though but faintly, and something—perhaps boot-heels—scraped on the boards. Kiddo hesitated a little, and then knocked softly. The knock was unnoticed, so in the end he pushed the door open.

The day had been a bad one with the Perrotts. Dicky had gone out early, and had not returned. His mother had tramped unfed to the sackmakers, but there was no work to be got. She tried the rush bag people, with a like result. Nor was any matchbox material being given out. An unregarded turnip* had rolled from a shop into the gutter, and she had seized it stealthily. It was not in nature to take it home whole, and once a corner was cleared, she dragged herself Jago-ward, gnawing the root furtively as she went. And so she joined Em at home late in the afternoon.

Kiddo pushed the door open and went in. At his second step he stood staring, and his chin dropped. 'Good Gawd!' said Kiddo Cook.

He cleared the stairs in three jumps. He stood but an instant on the flags before the house, with a quick glance each way, and then dashed off through the mud.

Pigeony Poll was erratic in residence, but just now she had a room by the roof of a house in Jago Row, and up the stairs of this house Kiddo ran, calling her by name.

'Go over to Perrotts', quick!' he shouted from the landing below as Poll appeared at her door. 'Run, for Gawd's sake, or the woman'll croak! I'm auf to Father's.' And he rushed away to the vicar's lodgings.

Father Sturt emerged at a run, and made for a surgeon's in Shoreditch High Street. And when the surgeon reached Hannah Perrott he found her stretched on her ragged bed, tended, with anxious clumsiness, by Pigeony Poll; while little Em, tearful and abashed, sat in a corner and nibbled a bit of turnip.

Hannah Perrott had anticipated the operation of the Maternity Society letter, and another child of the Jago had come unconsenting into its black inheritance.

Father Sturt met the surgeon as he came away in the later evening, and asked if all were well. The surgeon shrugged his shoulders. 'People would call it so,' he said. 'The boy's alive, and so is the mother. But you and I may say the truth. You know the Jago far better than I. Is there a child in all this place that wouldn't be better dead—still better unborn? But does a day pass without bringing you just such a parishioner? Here lies the Jago, a nest of rats, breeding, breeding, as only rats can; and we say it is well. On high moral grounds we uphold the right of rats to multiply their thousands.* Sometimes we catch a rat. And we keep it a little while, nourish it carefully, and put it back into the nest to propagate its kind.'

Father Sturt walked a little way in silence. Then he said:—'You are right, of course. But who'll listen, if you shout it from the housetops? I might try to proclaim it myself, if I had time and energy to waste. But I have none—I must work, and so must you. The burden grows day by day, as you say. The thing's hopeless, perhaps, but that is not for me to discuss. I have my duty.'

The surgeon was a young man, but Shoreditch had helped him over most of his enthusiasms. 'That's right,' he said, 'quite right. People are so very genteel, aren't they?' He laughed, as at a droll remembrance. 'But, hang it all, men like ourselves needn't talk as though the world was built of hardbake. It's a mighty relief to speak truth with a man who knows—a man not rotted through with sentiment. Think how few men we trust with the power to give a fellow creature a year in gaol, and how carefully we pick them! Even damnation is out of fashion, I believe, among theologians. But any noxious wretch may damn human souls to the Jago, one after another, year in year out, and we respect his right: his sacred right.'

At the 'Posties' the two men separated. The rain, which had abated for a space, came up on a driving wind, and whipped Dicky Perrott home to meet his new brother.

CHAPTER 29

THINGS grew a little easier with the Perrotts. Father Sturt saw that there was food while the mother was renewing her strength, and he had a bag of linen sent. More, he carried his point as to parish relief by main force. It was two shillings and three quartern loaves a week. Unfortunately the loaves were imprinted with the parish mark, or they might have been sold at the chandler's, in order that the whole measure of relief might be passed on to the landlord (a very respectable man, with a chandler's shop of his own) for rent. As it was, the bread perforce was eaten, and the landlord had the two shillings, as well as eighteenpence which had to be got in some other way. Of course, Hannah Perrott might have 'taken in lodgers' in the room, as others did, but she doubted her ability to bully the rent out of them, or to turn them out if they did not pay. Whatever was pawnable had gone already, of course, except the little nickel-plated clock. That might have produced as much as sixpence, but she had a whim to keep it. She regarded it as a memorial of Josh, for it was his sole contribution to the family appointments.

Dicky, with a cast-off jacket from the vicar's store, took to hanging about Liverpool Street Station in quest of bags to carry. Sometimes he got bags, and coppers for carrying them: sometimes he got kicks from porters. An hour or two of disappointment in this pursuit would send him off on the prowl to 'find' new stock for Mr Weech. He went farther afield now: to the market-places in Mile End and Stepney, and to the riverside, where there were many chances—guarded jealously, however, by the pirate boys of the neighbourhood, who would tolerate no interlopers at the wharves. In the very early morning, too, he practised the sand-bag fake, in the Jago. For there were those among the Jagos who kept (two even bred) linnets and such birds, and prepared them for julking, or singing matches at the Bag of Nails. It was the habit of the bird-fanciers to hang their little wooden cages on nails out of windows, and there they hung through the night: for it had been noted, as a surprising peculiarity in linnets, that a bird would droop and go off song after a dozen or so of nights in a Jago room, in company with eight, ten or a dozen human sleepers, notwithstanding the thoughtful shutting of windows. So that any early riser provided with a little bag packed with a handful or so of sand, could become an opulent bird-owner in half-an-hour. Let but the sandbag be pitched with proper skill at the bottom of a cage, and that cage would leave the nail, and come tumbling and fluttering down into the ready hands of the early riser. The sand-bag brought down the cage and fell quietly on the flags, which was why it was preferred before a stone. The sand-bag faker was moved by no particular love of linnets. His spoil was got rid of as soon as the bird-shops opened in Club Row. And his craft was one of danger.

Thus the months went with Dicky, and the years. There were changes in the Jago. The baby was but three months old when Father Sturt's new church was opened, and the club set going in new buildings; and it was at that time that Josh Perrott was removed to Portland. Even the gradual removal of the Old Jago itself was begun. For the County Council* bought a row of houses at the end of Jago Row, by Honey Lane, with a design to build big barrack dwellings on the site. The scenes of the Jago Court eviction were repeated, with less governed antics. For the County Council knew not Jago ways; and when deputations came forth weeping, protesting the impossibility of finding new lodgings, and beseeching a respite, they were given six weeks more, and went back delighted into free quarters. At the end of the six weeks a larger deputation protested a little louder, wept a great deal more, and poached another month; for it would seem an unpopular thing to turn the people into the street. Thus in the end, when the unpopular thing had to be done, it was with sevenfold trouble, loud cursing of the County Council in the public street, and many fights. But this one spot of the Jago cleared, the County Council began to creep along Jago Row and into Half Jago Street; and after long delay the crude yellow brick of the barrack dwellings* rose above the oft-stolen hoardings, and grew, storey by storey. Dicky was fourteen, fifteen, sixteen. If Josh Perrott had only earned his marks,* he would soon be out now.

CHAPTER 30

JOSH PERROTT earned his marks, and in less than four years from his conviction he came away from Portland. It was a mere matter of hours ere his arrival in London, when Dicky, hands in pockets, strolled along Old Jago Street, and by the 'Posties' to High Street.

Dicky was almost at his seventeenth birthday. He had grown his utmost, and stood five feet two. He wore a cap with a cloth peak and ear-laps tied at the top with strings, slap-up kicksies, cut saucy, and a bob-tail coat of the out-and-out description: though all these glories were torn and shabby, and had been bought second-hand. He was safe from any risk of the reformatory now, being well over the age;* and he had had the luck never to have been taken by the police since his father's lagging—though there were escapes too narrow to be thought about with comfort. It was a matter for wonderment, and he spoke of it with pride. Here he was, a man of long experience, and near seventeen years old, yet he had never been in prison. Few, very few of such an age could say that.

Sometimes he saw his old enemy, the hunchback, who worked at a shoemaker's, but he saw him with unconcern. He cared nothing for tale-bearing now. The memory of old injuries had dulled, and, after all, this was a merely inconsiderable hunchback, whom it were beneath his dignity to regard with anything but tolerant indifference. Bob Roper steered clear at such encounters, and showed his teeth like a cat, and looked back malevolently. It didn't matter.

Dicky was not married, either in the simple Jago fashion or in church. There was little difference, as a matter of fact, so far as facility went. There was a church in Bethnal Green where you might be married for sevenpence if you were fourteen years old, and no questions asked—or at any rate they were questions answers whereunto were easy to invent. You just came in, drunk if possible, with a batch of some scores, and rowdied about the church with your hat on, and the curate worked off the crowd at one go, calling the names one after another. You sang, or you shouted, or you drank out of a bottle, or you flung a prayer-book at a friend, as the fancy took you; and the whole thing was not a bad joke for the money, though after all sevenpence is half-a-gallon,* and not to be wasted. But Dicky had had enough to do to look after his mother and Em and little Josh—as Hannah Perrott had called the baby. Dicky, indeed, had a family already. More: the Jago girls affected him with an odd feeling of repulsion. Not of themselves, perhaps, though they were squalid drabs long ere they were ripe for the sevenpenny church: but by comparison with the clean, remote shop-girls who were visible through the broad windows in the outer streets.

Dicky intended the day to be a holiday. He was not going 'out', as the word went, for ill-luck had a way of coming on notable days like this, and he might easily chance to 'fall'* before his father got home. He was almost too big now for carrying bags at Liverpool Street, because small boys looked cheaper than large ones—not that there was anything especially large about Dicky, beyond his height of five feet two; and at the moment he could think of nothing else that might turn a copper. He stood irresolute on the High Street footway, and as he stood, Kiddo Cook hove in sight, dragging a barrow-load of carrots and cabbages. Kiddo had not yet compassed the stall with the rain-proof awning. But it was almost in sight, for the barrow could scarce hold all that he could sell; and there was a joke abroad that he was to be married in Father Sturt's church: some facetiously suggesting that Mother Gapp would prove a good investment commercially, while others maintained the greater eligibility of old Poll Rann.

''Tcheer, Dicky!' said Kiddo, pulling up and wiping his cap-lining with a red cotton handkerchief. 'Ol' man out today, ain't 'e?'

'Yus,' Dicky answered. ''Spect 'im up tonight.'*

Kiddo nodded, and wiped his face. ''Spose the mob'll git up a break for 'im,' he said; 'but 'e'll 'ave a bit o' gilt from stir as well, won't 'e? So 'e'll be awright.' And Kiddo stuffed his handkerchief into his trousers pocket, pulled his cap tight, and bent to his barrow-handles.

Dicky turned idly to the left, and slouched to the corner of Meakin Street. There he loafed for a little while, and then went as aimlessly up the turning. Meakin Street was much as ever. There were still the chandlers' shops, where tea and sugar were sold by the farthingsworth, and the barber's where hair was fashionably cut for three halfpence: though Jago hair was commonly cut in another place* and received little more attention. There was still Walker's cook-shop, foggy with steam, its windows all a-trickle, and there was the Original Slap-up Tog Emporium, with its kicksies and its benjamins cut saucy as ever, and its double fakements still artful. At the 'dispensary' there was another young student, but his advice and medicine were sixpence, just as his remote predecessor's had been for little Looey, long forgotten. And farther down on the opposite side, Mr Aaron Weech's coffee-shop, with its Sunday-school festival bills, maintained its general Band-of-Hope* air, and displayed its shrivelled bloaters, its doubtful cake, and its pallid scones in an odour of respectability and stale pickles. Dicky glanced in as he came by the door, and met the anxious eye of Mr Weech, whom he had not seen for a fortnight. For Dicky was no boy now, but knew enough to sell at Cohen's or elsewhere whenever possible, and to care not a rap for Mr Weech.

As that tradesman saw Dicky, he burst into an eager smile, and came forward. 'Good mornin'—er—' with a quick glance—'Mr Perrott! Good mornin'! You're quite a stranger, reely!'

Mister Perrott! Mr Weech was very polite. Dicky stopped, and grunted a cautious salutation.

'Do come in, Mr Perrott. Wy, is the good noos right wot I 'ear, about yer father a-comin' 'ome from—from the country?'

Dicky confirmed the news.

'Well I *am* glad t' 'ear that now.' Mr Weech grinned exceedingly, though there was something lacking in his delight. 'But there, wot'll you 'ave, Mr Perrott? Say anythink in the 'ole shop and welcome! It's sich an 'appy occasion, Mr Perrott, I couldn't think o' chargin' you a 'a'peny. 'Ave a rasher, now, do. There's one on at this very moment. Sairer! ain't that rasher done yut?'

Dicky did not understand this liberality, but he had long since adopted the policy of taking all he could get. So he sat at a table, and Mr Weech sat opposite.

'Jist like ole times, ain't it?' said Mr Weech. 'An' that reminds me I owe you a shillin'. It's that pair o' noo boots you chucked over the back fence a fortnight ago. W'en I come to look et 'em, they was better'n wot I thought, an' so I says to meself, "This won't do," says I. "On'y ninepence for a pair o' boots like them ain't fair," I says, "an' I'd rayther be at a lawss on 'em than not be fair. Fair's fair, as the apostle David says in the Proverbs,* an' them boots is worth very near *one*-an'-nine. So I'll give Mr Perrott another shillin'," I says, "the very next time I see 'im." An' there it is.'

He put the shilling on the table, and Dicky pocketed it, nothing loth. The thing might be hard to understand, but that concerned him not. There was the shilling. Likewise, there was the bacon, and the coffee that went with it, and Dicky went at them with a will, recking nothing of why they were there, and nothing of any matter which might make the giver anxious in the prospect of an early meeting with Josh.

'Ah,' Mr Weech went on, 'it'll be quite a pleasure to see yer father agin, that it will. Wot a blessed release!* "Free from the lor O 'appy condition," as the 'ymn says. I 'ope 'e'll be well an' 'arty. An' if—*if* there should be anythink in the way of a friendly lead* or a subscription or wot not, I 'ope—remember this, Mr Perrott, won'tcher?—I 'ope you'll let me 'ave a chance to put down somethink good. Not as I can reely afford it, ye know, Mr Perrott—trade's very pore, an' it's sich a neighb'r'ood!—but I'll do it for yer father—yus, if it's me last copper. Ye won't forgit that, will ye? An' if 'e'd like any little relish* w'en 'e comes 'ome—sich as a 'addick or a bit o' 'am—wy, I'll wrop it up an' send it.'

This was all very handsome, and Dicky wished some notion of the sort had occurred to Mr Weech on a few of the dinnerless days of the past four years. But he went away wondering if it might not be well to regard Mr Weech with caution for a while. For there must be a reason for all this generosity.

CHAPTER 31

It was in Mother Gapp's that Josh Perrott and his family met. Hannah had started out with an idea of meeting him at Waterloo Station; but, finding herself an object of distinction and congratulation among the women she met, she had lingered by the way, accepting many little drops, to prove herself not unduly proud, and so had failed of her intent. Josh, on his part, had not been abstinent. He had successfully run the gauntlet of Prisoners' Aid Societies* and the like, professing to have 'a job waiting for him' in Shoreditch, and his way across London had been freely punctuated at public-houses; for his prison gratuity* was a very pleasant and useful little sum. And now, when at last they met, he was not especially gracious. He wanted to know, not only why he had found nobody at home, but also why Hannah had never been to see him at Portland. As to the second question, the obvious and sufficient answer was that the return fare to Portland would have been some twenty-five shillings: a sum that Hannah had never seen together since Josh left her. As to the first, she protested, with muddled vehemence, that she had gone to meet him, and had missed him by some mistake as to arrival platforms. So that at length, urged thereto by the rest of the hour's customers at the Feathers, Josh kissed her sulkily and ordered her a drink. Em was distrustful at first, but drank her allowance of gin* with much relish, tipping the glass again and again to catch the last drop; and little Josh, now for the first time introduced to Josh the elder, took a dislike to his father's not particularly sober glare and grin, and roared aloud upon his knee, assailing him, between the roars, with every curse familiar in the Jago, amid the genial merriment of the company. Dicky came in quietly, and stood at his father's elbow with the pride natural to a dutiful son on such an occasion. And at closing-time they all helped each other home.

In the morning Josh rose late. He looked all the better for his lagging, browner than ever in the face, smarter and stouter. In a corner he perceived a little heap of made match-boxes, and, hard by, the material for more. It was Em's work of yesterday morning. 'Support 'ome ind*us*teries,' said Josh, musingly. 'Yus. Twopence-farden a gross.' And he kicked the heap to splinters.

He strolled out into the street, to survey the Jago. In the bulk it was little changed, though the County Council had made a difference in the north-east corner, and was creeping farther and farther still. The dispossessed Jagos had gone to infect the neighbourhoods across the border, and to crowd the people a little closer. They did not return to live in the new barrack-buildings; which was a strange thing, for the County Council was charging very little more than double the rents which the landlords of the Old Jago had charged. And so another Jago, teeming and villainous as the one displaced, was slowly growing, in the form of a ring, round about the great yellow houses. But the new church and its attendant buildings most took Josh's notice. They were little more than begun when last he walked Old Jago Street in daylight, and now they stood, large and healthy amid the dens about them, a wonder and a pride. As he looked, Jerry Gullen and Bill Rann passed.

'Wayo, brother-in-law!' sang out Bill Rann, who remembered the Old Bailey fiction of four years back, and thought it a capital joke.

'Nice sort o' thing, ain't it?' said Jerry Gullen with indignant sarcasm, jerking his thumb toward the new church. 'The street's clean ruined. Wot's the good o' livin' 'ere now? Wy, a man mustn't even do a click, blimy!'

'An' doncher?' asked Josh with a grin. Hereat another grin broke wide on Jerry Gullen's face, and he went his way with a wink and a whistle.

'And so you're back again, Josh Perrott!' said old Beveridge, seedier than ever, with the 'Hard Up' fresh chalked on the changeless hat. 'Back again! Pity you couldn't stay there, isn't it? Pity we can't all stay there.'

Josh looked after the gaunt old figure with much doubt and a vague indignation: for such a view was foreign to his understanding. And as he looked Father Sturt came out of the church, and laid his hand on Josh's shoulder.

'What!' exclaimed the vicar, 'home again without coming to see me! But there, you must have been coming. I hope you haven't been knocking long? Come in now, at any rate. You're looking wonderfully well. What a capital thing a holiday is, isn't it—a good long one?' Taking Josh by the arm he hauled him, grinning, sheepish and almost blushing, toward the club door. And at that moment Sam Cash came hurrying round Luck Row corner, with his finger through a string, and on that string a bunch of grouse.

'Dear me,' said Father Sturt, turning back, but without releasing Josh's arm. 'Here's our dear friend, Sam Cash, taking home something for his lunch. Come, Sam, with such a fine lot of birds as that, I'm sure you'll be proud to tell us where they came from. Eh?'

For a moment Sam Cash was a trifle puzzled, even offended. Then there fell over his face the mask of utter inexpression which the vicar had learned to know. Said Sam Cash, stolidly: 'I bin 'avin' a little shootin' with a friend.'

'Dear, dear, what a charming friend! And where are his moors? Nowhere about the Bethnal Green Road, I suppose, by the goods depot? Come now, I'm sure Josh Perrott would like to know. You didn't get any shooting in your little holiday, did you, Josh?' Josh grinned, delighted, but Sam shuffled uneasily, with a hopeless sidelong glance as in search of a hole wherein to hide. 'Ah, you see,' Father Sturt said, 'he doesn't want his friend's hospitality to be abused. Let me see—two, four, six—why there must be nine or ten brace, and all at one shot, too! Sam always makes his bag at one shot, you know, Josh, whatever the game is. Yes, wonderful shooting. And did you shoot the label at the same time, Sam? Come, I *should* like to look at that label!'

But the wretched Sam was off at a bolt, faster than a police pursuit would have sent him, while Josh guffawed joyously. To be 'rotted' by Father Sturt was the true Jago terror, but to the Jagos looking on it was pure delight. Theft was a piece of the Jago nature; but at least Father Sturt could wither the pride of it by such ridicule as the Jago could understand.

'There—he's very bashful for a sportsman, isn't he, Josh?' the vicar proceeded. 'But you must come and see the club at once. You shall be a member.'

Josh spent near an hour in the new buildings. Father Sturt showed him the club, the night shelter, the church, and his own little rooms. He asked, too, much about Josh's intentions for the future. Of course, Josh was 'going to look for a job'. Father Sturt knew he would say that. Every Jago had been going to look for a job ever since the vicar first came to the place. But he professed to take Josh's word seriously, and offered to try to get him taken on as a plasterer at some of the new County Council buildings. He flattered Josh by reminding him of his command of a regular trade. Josh was a man with opportunities, and he should be above the pitiable expedients of the poor untradesmanlike about him. Indeed, he should leave the Jago altogether, with his family, and start afresh in a new place, a reputable mechanic.

To these things Josh Perrott listened with fidgety deference, answering only 'Yus, Father', when it seemed to be necessary. In the end he promised to 'think it over', which meant nothing, as the parson well knew. And in the mood in which Josh came away he would gladly have risked another lagging to serve Father Sturt's convenience; but he would rather have suffered one than take Father Sturt's advice.

He made the day a holiday. He had been told that he was in for a little excitement, for it was held that fitting time had arrived for another scrap with Dove Lane; but the affair was not yet moving. Snob Spicer had broken a window with a Dove-Laner's head, it was true, but nothing had come of it, and etiquette demanded that the next card should be played by Dove Lane. For the present, the Jago was content to take thought for Josh's 'friendly lead'. Such a thing was everybody's right on return from a lagging, and this one was fixed for a night next week.

All that day Mr Weech looked out anxiously, but Josh Perrott never passed his way.

CHAPTER 32

BILL RANN called for Josh early the next morning, and they strolled down Old Jago Street in close communion.

'Are you on for a job?' asked Bill. ''Cos I got one cut an' dried—a topper, an' safe as 'ouses.'

'Wot sort o' job's this?'

'Wy a bust—unless we can screw it.'

This meant a breaking-in, with a possibility of a quieter entrance by means of keys. It was unpleasantly suggestive of Josh's last exploit, but he answered: 'Awright. Depends, o' course.'

'O, it's a good un.' Bill Rann grinned for no obvious reason, and slapped his leg to express rapturous amusement. 'It's a good un—you can take yer davy o' that. I bin a thinkin' about it for a fortnight, but it wants two. Damme, it's nobby!' And Bill Rann grinned again, and made two taps of a step-dance.* 'Wotjer think,' he pursued, suddenly serious, 'wotjer think o' screwin' a fence?'

It was a novel notion, but in Josh's mind, at first flush, it seemed unsportsmanlike. 'Wot fence?' asked Josh.

Bill Rann's grin burst wide again. He bent low, with outstretched chin, and stuck his elbows out as he answered: 'Wy, ole Weech!'

Josh bared his teeth—but with no smile—looking sharply in the other's upturned face. Bill Rann, bent nearly double, and with hands in pockets, flapped his arms in the manner of wings, chuckled aloud, and, jerking his feet back and forth, went elaborately through the first movement of the gallows-flap.* 'Eh? eh?' said he. ''Ow's that strike ye, ole cock?'

Josh answered not, but his parted lips stretched wide, and his tongue-tip passed quickly over them while he thought.

'It'll be a fair cop for 'im,' Bill pursued, eagerly. ''E's treated us all pretty mean, one time or other. Wy, I bet 'e *owes* us fifty quid atween us, wot with all the times 'e's squeeged us for a bit. It'll on'y be goin' to bring away our own stuff!'

'G-r-r-r!' Josh growled, glaring fiercely; 'it was 'im as put me away for my laggin'! Bleed'n' swine!'

Bill Rann stopped, surprised. 'Wot—'im?' he exclaimed. 'Ole Weech narked ye? 'Owjer know that?'

Josh told the tale of his negotiations in the matter of the Mogul's watch, and described Weech's terror at sight of his dash at the shop-door. 'I'm on,' said Josh in conclusion. 'It's one way o' payin' 'im, an' it'll bring a bit in. On'y '*e* better not show 'isself w'ile I'm abaat! '*E* wouldn't git auf with a punch on the chin, like the bloke at 'Ighbury!' Josh Perrott ended with a tigerish snarl and a white spot at the curl of each of his nostrils.

'Blimy!' said Bill Rann; 'an' so it was 'im, was it? I often wondered 'oo you meant. Well, flimpin' 'im's the best way. Won't 'e sing a bleed'n' 'ymn w'en 'e finds 'is stuff weeded!' Bill flung back his head, and laughed again. 'But there—let's lay it out.' And the two men fell to the discussion of methods.

Weech's back fence was to be his undoing. It was the obvious plan. The front shutters were impracticable in such a place as Meakin Street; but the alleys in the rear were a perfect approach. Bill Rann had surveyed the spot attentively, and, after expert consideration, he had selected the wash-house window as the point of entrance. Old boxes and packing-wood littered the yard, and it would be easy to mount a selected box, shift the catch of the little window, and wriggle in, feet first, without noise. True, the door between the wash-house and the other rooms might be fastened, but it could be worked at under cover; and Bill Rann had a belief that there must be a good deal of 'stuff' in the wash-house itself. There would be nobody in the house but Weech, because the wretched old woman, who swept the floors and cooked bloaters, was sent away at night; so that every room must be unoccupied but one.

As for tools, Josh had none, but Bill Rann undertook to provide them; and in the matter of time it was considered that that same night would be as good as any. It would be better than most, in fact, for it was Wednesday, and Bill Rann had observed that Mr Weech went to the bank in High Street, Shoreditch, pretty regularly on Thursday mornings.

This day also Mr Weech kept a careful watch for Josh Perrott, but saw him not.

CHAPTER 33

HANNAH PERROTT did her best to keep Josh from going out that night. She did not explain her objections, because she did not know precisely what they were, though they were in some sort prompted by his manner; and it was solely because of her constitutional inability to urge them with any persistence that she escaped forcible retort. For Josh was in a savage and self-centred mood.

'Wy, wot's up?' asked Bill Rann, when they met, looking doubtfully in his pal's face. 'You ain't bin boozin', 'ave ye?'

Josh repelled the question with a snarl. 'No I ain't,' he said. 'Got the tools?' There was a thickness in his voice, with a wildness in his eye, that might well explain his partner's doubt.

'Yus. Come under the light. I couldn't git no twirls, an' we sha'n't want 'em. 'Ere's a screwdriver, an' two gimlets, an' a knife for the winderketch, an' a little james, an' a neddy—'

'A neddy!' Josh cut in, scornfully pointing his thumb at the instrument, which some call life-preserver. 'A neddy for Weech! G-r-r-r! I might take a neddy to a *man*!'

'That's awright,' Bill replied. 'But it 'ud frighten 'im pretty well, wouldn't it? Look 'ere. S'pose we can't find the oof. W'y shouldn't we wake up Mr Weech very quiet an' respeckful, an' ask 'im t' 'elp us? 'E's all alone, an' I'm sure 'e'll be glad to 'blige, w'en 'e sees this 'ere neddy, without waitin' for a tap. W'y, blimy, I b'lieve 'e'd be afraid to sing out any'ow, for fear o' bringin' in the coppers to find all the stuff 'e's bought on the crook! It's all done, once we're inside!'

It was near midnight, and Bill Rann had observed Weech putting up his shutters at eleven. So the two Jagos walked slowly along Meakin Street, on the side opposite Weech's, with sharp eyes for the windows.

All was quiet; there was no visible light—none from the skylight over the shop door, none from the window above, none from the garret window above that. They passed on, crossed the road, strolled back, and listened at the door; there was no sound from within. The clock in a distant steeple struck twelve, and was joined at the fourth stroke by the loud bell of St Leonard's, hard by;* and ere the last mild note had sounded from the farthest clock in the awakened chorus, Josh Perrott and Bill Rann had taken the next turning, and were pushing their way to the alleys behind Weech's.

Foul rat-runs these alleys, not to be traversed by a stranger. Josh and Bill plunged into one narrow archway after another, each of which might have been the private passage of a house, and came at last, stealthy and unseen, into the muddy yard.

Weech's back fence was before them, and black house-backs crowded them round. There were but one or two lights in the windows, and those windows were shut and curtained. The rear of Weech's house was black and silent as the front. They peered over the fence. The yard was pitch-dark, but faint angular tokens here and there told of heaped boxes and lumber. 'We won't tip 'im the whistle this time,' whispered Bill Rann, with a smothered chuckle. 'Over!'

He bent his knee, and Josh straddled from it over the rickety fence with quiet care, and lowered himself gingerly on the other side. 'Clear 'ere,' he whispered. 'Come on.' Since Bill's display of the tools Josh had scarce spoken a word. Bill wondered at his taciturnity, but respected it as a business-like quality in the circumstances.

It was but a matter of four or five yards to the wash-house window, but they bent and felt their way. Josh took up an old lemonade-case as he went, and planted it on the ground below the window, stretching his hand for the knife as he did so. And now he took command and foremost place.

It was an old shoemaker's knife, with too long a handle; for there was a skew-joint in the sash, and the knife would not bend. Presently Bill Rann, below, could see that Josh was cutting away the putty from the pane, and in five minutes the pane itself was put into his hand. He stooped, and laid it noiselessly on the soft ground.

Josh turned the catch and lifted the sash. There was some noise, but not much, as he pushed the frame up evenly, with a thumb at each side. They waited; but it was quite still, and Josh, sitting on the sill, manœuvred his legs, one at a time, through the narrow opening. Then, turning over, he let himself down, and beckoned Bill Rann to follow.

Bill Rann had a small tin box, with an inch of candle on the inside of one end, so that when the wick was lit the contrivance made a simple but an effective lantern, the light whereof shone in front alone, and could be extinguished at a puff. Now a match was struck, and a quick view taken of the wash-house.

There was not much about; only cracked and greasy plates, jars, tins, pots and pans, and in a corner a miscellaneous heap, plainly cheap pilferings, covered with a bit of old carpet. The air was offensive with the characteristic smell of Weech's—the smell of stale pickles.

'There ain't nothin' to waste time over 'ere,' said Josh, aloud. 'Come on!'

'Shut up, you damn fool!' exclaimed Bill Rann, in a whisper. 'D'jer want to wake 'im?'

'Umph! Why not?' was the reply, still aloud. Bill began to feel that his pal was really drunk. But, silent once more, Josh applied himself to the door of the inner room. It was crank and old, worn and battered at the edges. Josh forced the wedge end of the jemmy through the jamb, splintering the perished wood of the frame, and, with a push, forced the striking-box* of the lock off its screws. There was still a bolt at the top; that at the bottom had lost its catch—but this gave as little trouble as the lock. Bill Rann strained the door open from below, the jemmy entered readily, and in a few seconds the top bolt was in like case with the bottom.

They entered the room behind the shop, and it was innocent and disappointing. A loo table,* four horse-hair covered chairs, a mirror, three coloured wall-texts,* two china figures and a cheap walnut sideboard—that was all. The slow step of a policeman without stopped, with a push at the shop-door, to test its fastenings, and then went on; and stronger than ever was the smell of stale pickles.

To try the shop would be mere waste of time. Weech's pocket was the till, and there could be no other prize. A door at the side of the room, latched simply, gave on the stairs. 'Take auf yer boots,' Bill whispered, unlacing his own, and slinging them across his shoulder by the tied laces.

But Josh would not, and he said so, with an oath. Bill could not understand him. *Could* it be drink? Bill wished him a mile away. 'Awright,' he whispered, 'you set down 'ere w'ile I slip upstairs an' take a peep. I bet the stuff's in the garret. Best on'y one goes, quiet.'

Josh sat, and Bill, taking his lantern, crept up the stairs noiselessly, save for one creak. He gained the stair-head, listened a moment, tiptoed along the small landing, and was halfway up the steep and narrow garret-stairs, when he heard a sound, and stopped. Somebody was on the lower flight.

There was a heavy tread, with the kick of a boot against stair or skirting-board; and then came noisy steps along the landing. Josh was coming up in his boots! Bill Rann was at his wits' end. He backed down the garret-stairs, and met Josh at the foot. 'Are ye barmy?' he hissed fiercely, catching Josh by the collar and pulling him into the turn of the stairs. 'D'ye want another five stretch?'

A loud creak and a soft thump sounded from behind the door at the other end of the landing; and then a match was struck. 'Keep back on the stairs,' Bill whispered. ''E's 'eard you.' Josh sat on a stair, perfectly still, with his legs drawn up out of sight from the door. Bill blew out his light. He would not venture open intimidation of Weech now, with Josh half muzzy, lest some burst of lunacy brought in the police.

A soft treading of bare feet, the squeak of a door-handle, a light on the landing, and Aaron Weech stood at his open door in his shirt, candle in hand, his hair rumpled, his head aside, his mouth a little open, his unconscious gaze upward; listening intently. He took a slight step forward. And then Bill Rann's heart turned over and over.

For Josh Perrott sprang from the stair, and, his shoulders humped and his face thrust out, walked deliberately across the landing. Weech turned his head quickly; his chin fell on his chest as by jaw-break; there were but dots amid the white of his eyes; his head lay slowly back, as the candle tilted and shot its grease on the floor. The door swung wider as his shoulder struck it, and he screamed, like a rabbit that sees a stoat. Then, with a wrench, he turned, letting drop the candle, and ran shrieking to the window, flung it open, and yelled into the black street. ''Elp! 'Elp! P'lice! *Murder! Murder! Murder! Murder!*'

'Run, Josh—run, ye blasted fool!' roared Bill Rann, bounding across the landing, and snatching at his arm.

'Go on—go on! I'm comin'!' Josh answered without turning his head. And Bill took the bottom flight at a jump. The candle flared as it lay on the floor, and spread a greasy pool about it.

'*Murder! Murder! Mu-r-r—*'

Josh had the man by the shoulder, swung him back from the window, gripped his throat, and dragged him across the carpet as he might drag a cat, while Weech's arms waved uselessly, and his feet feebly sought a hold on the floor.

'Now!' cried Josh Perrott, glaring on the writhen face below his own, and raising his case-knife in the manner of a cleaver, 'sing a hymn! Sing the hymn as'll do ye most good! You'll cheat me when ye can, an' when ye can't you'll put me five year in stir, eh? Sing a hymn, ye snivellin' nark!'

From the street there came the noise of many hurrying feet and of a scattered shouting. Josh Perrott made an offer at slashing the slaty face, checked his arm, and went on.

'You'll put down somethin' 'an'some at my break, will ye? An' you'll starve my wife an' kids all to bones an' teeth four year! Sing a hymn, ye cur!'

He made another feint at slashing. Men were beating thunderously at the shop door, and there were shrill whistles.

'Won't sing yer hymn? There ain't much time! My boy was goin' straight, an' earnin' wages: someone got 'im chucked. A man 'as time to think things out, in stir! Sing, ye son of a cow! Sing! Sing!'

Twice the knife hacked the livid face. But the third hack was below the chin; and the face fell back.

The bubbling Thing dropped in a heap, and put out the flaring candle. Without, the shouts gathered to a roar, and the door shook under heavy blows. 'Open—open the door!' cried a deep voice.

He looked from the open window. There was a scrambling crowd, and more people were running in. Windows gaped, and thrust out noisy heads. The flash of a bull's-eye* dazzled him, and he staggered back. 'Perrott! Perrott!' came a shout. He had but glanced out, but he was recognised.

He threw down his knife, and made for the landing, slipping on the wet floor and stumbling against the Heap. There were shouts from behind the house now; they were few, but they were close. He dashed up the narrow stairs, floundered through the back garret, over bags and boxes and heaps of mingled commodities, and threw up the sash. Men were stumbling invisibly in the dark yard below. He got upon the sill, swung round by the dormer-frame, and went, hands and knees, along the roof. Yells and loud whistles rose clamant in the air, and his own name was shouted to and fro. Then the blows on the shop-door ceased with a splintering crash, and there was a trampling of feet on floor-boards.

The roofs were irregular in shape and height, and his progress was slow. He aimed at reaching the roof of Father Sturt's old club building, still empty. He had had this in mind from the moment he climbed from the garret-window; for in the work of setting the drains in order an iron ventilating pipe had been carried up from the stable-yard to well above the roof. It was a stout pipe, close by the wall, to which it was clamped with iron attachments. Four years had passed since he had seen it, and he trusted to luck to find it still standing, for it seemed his only chance. Down below people scampered and shouted. Crowds had sprung out of the dark night as by magic; and the police—they must have been lying in wait in scores. It seemed a mere matter of seconds since he had scaled the back fence; and now people were tearing about the house behind him, and shouting out of windows to those below. He hoped that the iron pipe might not be gone.

Good—it was there. He peered from the parapet down into the stable-yard, and the place seemed empty. He gripped the pipe with hands and knees, and descended.

The alley had no back way: he must take his chance in Meakin Street. He peeped. At the street end there was a dark obstruction, set with spots of light: a row of police. That way was shut; he must try the Jago—Luck Row was almost opposite, and no Jago would betray him. The hunters were already on the roofs. Men shouted up to them from the street, and kept pace with them, coming nearer. He took a breath and dashed across, knocking a man over at the corner.

Up Luck Row, into Old Jago Street he ran, past his own home, and across to a black doorway, just as Father Sturt, roused by the persistent din, opened his window. The passage was empty, and for an instant he paused, breathless. But there were howls without, and the pelting of many feet. The man knocked over at the corner had given the alarm, and the hunt was up.

Into the back yard and over the fence; through another passage into New Jago Street; with a notion to gain the courts by Honey Lane and so away. But he was thinking of the Jago as it had been—he had forgotten the demolishment. As he neared Jago Row the place of it lay suddenly before him—an open waste of eighty yards square, skirted by the straight streets and the yellow barracks, with the Board School standing dark among them. And along the straight streets more men were rushing, and more police. They were newcomers: why not venture over? He rubbed his cheek, for something like a film of gum clung to it. Then he remembered, and peered closely at his hands. Blood, sticking and drying and peeling; blood on hands and face, blood on clothes, without a doubt. To go abroad thus were to court arrest, were he known or not. It must be got off; but how?

To go home was to give himself up. The police were there long since—they swarmed the Jago through. Some half-dismantled houses stood at hand, and he made for the nearest.

There were cellars under these houses, reached from the back yards. Many a Jago had been born, had lived, and had died in such a place. A cellar would hide him for an hour, while he groped himself clean as he might. Broken brickwork littered the space that had been the back yard. Feeling in the dark for the steps, which stood in a little pit, his foot turned on a stone, and he pitched headlong.

The cellar itself was littered with rubbish, and he lay among it a little while, breathless and bruised. When he tried to rise, he found his ankle useless. It was the old sprain, got at Mother Gapp's before his lagging, and ever ready to assert itself. He sat among the brickbats to pull off the boot—that was foul and sticky too—and he rubbed the ankle. He had been a fool to think of the cellar: why not any corner among the walls above? He had given way to the mere panic instinct to burrow, to hide himself in a hole, and he had chosen one wherefrom there was no second way of escape—none at all but by the steps he had fallen in at. Far better to have struck out boldly across the streets by Columbia Market to the canal: who could have seen the smears in the darkness? And in the canal he might have washed the lot away, secure from observation, under a bridge. The thing might be possible, even now, if he could stand the pain. But no, the foot was useless when he tried it. He was trapped like a rat. He rubbed and kneaded the ankle diligently, and managed to draw the boot on. But stand on both legs he could not. He might have crawled up the steps on hands and knees, but what was the use of that? So he sat, and waited.

Knots of men went hurrying by, and he caught snatches of their talk. There had been a murder—a man was murdered in his bed—it was a woman—a man had murdered his wife—there were two murders—three—the tale went every way, but it was always Murder, Murder, Murder. Everybody was saying Murder: till in the passing footsteps, in the vague shouts in the distance, and presently in the mere black about him he heard the word still—Murder, Murder, Murder. He fell to contrasting the whispered fancy with the real screams in that bedroom. He wondered what Bill Rann thought of it all, and what had become of the james and the gimlets. He pictured the crowd in Old Jago Street, pushing into his room, talking about him, telling the news. He wondered if Hannah had been asleep when they came, and what she said when they told her. And more people hurried past the ruined house, all talking Murder, Murder, still Murder.

The foot was horribly painful. Was it swelling? Yes, he thought it was; he rubbed it again. What would Dicky do? If only Dicky knew where he was! That might help. There was a new burst of shouts in the distance. What was that? Perhaps they had caught Bill Rann; but that was unlikely. They knew nothing of Bill—they had seen but one man. Perhaps they were carrying away the Heap on a shutter:* that would be no nice job, especially down the steep stairs. There had been very little in the wash-house, and nothing in the next room; the garrets were pretty full of odd things, but no doubt the money was in the bedroom. The smell of stale pickles was very strong.

So his thoughts chased one another—eager, trivial, crowded—till his head ached with their splitting haste. To take heed for the future, to plan escape, to design expedients—these were merely impossible, sitting there inactive in the dark. He thought of the pipe he had slid down, what it cost, why they put it there, who the man was that he ran against at Luck Row, whether or not he hurt him, what the police would do with the bloaters and cake and bacon at the shop, and—again—of the smell of stale pickles.

Father Sturt was up and dressed, standing guard on the landing outside the Perrotts' door. The stairs were full of Jagos—mostly women—constantly joined by new-comers, all anxious to batter the door and belabour the hidden family with noisy sympathy and sedulous inquiries: all, that is, except the oldest Mrs Walsh in the Jago, who, possessed by an unshakable conviction that Josh's wife must have 'druv 'im to it', had come in a shawl and a petticoat to give Hannah a piece of her mind. But all were driven back and sent grumbling away, by Father Sturt.

Every passage from the Jago was held by the police, and a search from house to house was begun. With clear consciences the Jagos all could deny any knowledge of Josh Perrott's whereabouts; but a clear conscience was little valued in those parts, and one after another affirmed point blank that the man seen at the window was not Perrott at all, but a stranger who lived a long way off. This, of course, less by way of favouring the fugitive than of baffling the police: the Jago's first duty. But the police knew the worth of such talk, and the search went on.

Thus it came to pass that in the grey of the morning a party in New Jago Street, after telling each other that the ruins must be carefully examined, climbed among the rubbish, and were startled by a voice from underground.

'Awright,' cried Josh Perrott in the cellar. 'I'm done; it's a cop. Come an' 'elp me out o' this 'ole.'

CHAPTER 34

THE Lion and Unicorn* had been fresh gilt since he was there before, but the white-headed old gaoler in the dock was much the same. And the big sword—what did they have a big sword for, stuck up there, over the red cushions, and what was the use of a sword six foot long? But perhaps it wasn't six foot after all—it looked longer than it was; and no doubt it was only for show, and probably a dummy with no blade. There was a well-dressed black man sitting down below among the lawyers. What did he want? Why did they let him in? A nice thing—to be made a show of, for niggers! And Josh Perrott loosened his neckcloth with an indignant tug of the forefinger, and went off into another train of thought. He had a throbbing, wavering headache, the outcome of thinking so hard about so many things. They were small things, and had nothing to do with his own business; but there were so many of them, and they all had to be got through at such a pace, and one thing led to another.

Ever since they had taken him he had been oppressed by this plague of galloping thought, with few intervals of rest, when he could consider immediate concerns. But of these he made little trouble. The thing was done. Very well then, he would take his gruel* like a man. He had done many a worse thing, he said, that had been thought less of.

The evidence was a nuisance. What was the good of it all? Over and over and over again. At the inquest, at the police-court, and now here. Repeated, laboriously taken down, and repeated again. And now it was worse than ever, for the judge insisted on making a note of everything, and wrote it down slowly, a word at a time. The witnesses were like barrel-organs, producing the same old tune mechanically, without changing a note. There was the policeman who was in Meakin Street at twelve-thirty on the morning of the fourth of the month, when he heard cries of Murder, and proceeded to the coffee-shop. There was the other policeman who also 'proceeded' there, and recognised the prisoner, whom he knew, at the first-floor window. And there was the sergeant who had found him in the cellar, and the doctor who had made an examination, and the knife, and the boots, and all of it. It was Murder, Murder, Murder still. Why? Wasn't it plain enough? He felt some interest in what was coming—in the sentence, and the black cap, and so on—never having seen a murder trial before. But all this repetition oppressed him vaguely amid the innumerable things he had to think of, one thing leading to another.

Hannah and Dicky were there, sitting together behind the glass partition that rose at the side of the dock. Hannah's face was down in her hands, and Dicky's face was thin and white, and he sat with his neck stretched, his lips apart, his head aside to catch the smallest word. His eyes, too, were red with strained, unwinking attention. Josh felt vaguely that they might keep a bolder face, as he did himself. His sprained foot was still far from well, but he stood up, putting his weight on the other. He might have been allowed to sit if he had asked, but that would look like weakness.

There was another judge this time, an older one, with spectacles. He had come solemnly in, after lunch, with a bunch of flowers* in his hand, and Josh thought he made an odd figure in his long red gown. Why did he sit at the end of the bench, instead of in the middle, under the long sword? Perhaps the old gentleman, who sat there for a little while and then went away, was the Lord Mayor. That would account for it. There was another room behind the bedroom at Weech's, which he had never thought about. Perhaps the money was there, after all. Could they have missed any hiding-place in the shop parlour? No: there was the round table, with the four chairs about it, and the little sideboard; besides the texts on the wall, and two china figures on the mantelpiece—that was all. There was a copper in the wash-house, but there was nothing in it. The garret was a very good place to keep things in; but there was a strong smell of stale pickles. He could smell it now—he had smelt it ever since.

The judge stopped a witness to speak of a draught from a window. Josh Perrott watched the shutting of the window—they did it with a cord. He had not noticed a draught himself. But pigeons were flying outside the panes and resting on the chimney-stacks. Pud Palmer tried to keep pigeons in Jago Row, but one morning the trap* was found empty. A poulterer gave fourpence each for them. They were ticketed at eighteenpence a pair in the shop, and that was fivepence profit apiece for the poulterer. Tenpence a pair profit on eleven pairs was nearly ten shillings—ten shillings all but tenpence. They wouldn't have given any more in Club Row.* A man had a four-legged linnet in Club Row, but there was a show in Bethnal Green

Road with a two-headed sheep.* It was outside there that Ginger Stagg was pinched for lob-crawling. And so on, and so on, till his head buzzed again.

His counsel was saying something. How long had he been talking? What was the good of it? He had told him that he had no defence. The lawyer was enlarging on the dead man's iniquities, talking of provocation, and the heat of passion, and the like. He was aiming desperately at a recommendation to mercy. That was mere foolery.

But presently the judge began to sum up. They were coming to something at last. But it was merely the thrice-told evidence once more. The judge blinked at his notes, and went at it again; the policeman with his whistle, and the other with his lantern, and the doctor, and the sergeant, and the rest. It was shorter this time, though. Josh Perrott turned and looked at the clock behind him, with the faces over it, peering from the gallery. But when he turned to face the judge again he had forgotten the time, and crowded trivialities were racing through the narrow gates of his brain once more.

There was a cry for silence, and then a fresh voice spoke. 'Gentlemen of the jury, have you agreed upon your verdict?'

'We have.' The foreman was an agitated, colourless man, and he spoke in a low tone.

'Do you find the prisoner at the bar guilty, or not guilty?'

'Guilty.'

Yes, that was right; this was the real business. His head was clear and ready now.

'And is that the verdict of you all?'

'Yes.'

Was that Hannah sobbing?

A pale parson in his black gown came walking along by the bench, and stood like a tall ghost at the judge's side, his eyes raised and his hands clasped. The judge took a black thing from the seat beside him, and arranged it on his head. It was a sort of soft mortarboard* Josh noted curiously, with a large silk tassel hanging over one side, giving the judge, with his wig and his spectacles and his red gown, a horribly jaunty look. No brain could be clearer than Josh Perrott's now.

'Prisoner at the bar, have you anything to say why sentence of death should not be passed on you according to law?'

'No sir—I done it. On'y 'e was a worse man than me!'

The Clerk of Arraigns* sank into his place, and the judge spoke.

'Joshua Perrott, you have been convicted, on evidence that can leave no doubt whatever of your guilt in the mind of any rational person, of the horrible crime of wilful murder. The circumstances of your awful offence there is no need to recapitulate, but they were of the most brutal and shocking character. You deliberately, and with preparation, broke into the house of the man whose death you have shortly to answer for in a higher court than this: whether you broke in with a design of robbery as well as of revenge by murder I know not, nor is it my duty to consider: but you there, with every circumstance of callous ferocity, sent the wretched man to that last account which you must shortly render for yourself. Of the ill-spent life of that miserable man, your victim, it is not for me to speak, nor for you to think. And I do most earnestly beseech you to use the short time yet remaining to you on this earth in true repentance, and in making your peace with Almighty God. It is my duty to pronounce sentence of that punishment which not I, but the law of this country, imposes for the crime which you have committed. The sentence of the Court is: that you be taken to the place whence you came, and thence to a place of execution: and that you be there Hanged by the Neck till you be Dead: and may the Lord have Mercy on your Soul!'

'Amen!' It was from the tall black figure.

Well, well, that was over. The gaoler touched his arm. Right. But first he took a quick glance through the glass partition. Hannah was falling over, or something—a mere rusty swaying bundle—and Dicky was holding her up with both arms. Dicky's face was damp and grey, and twitching lines were in his cheeks. Josh took a step toward the partition, but they hurried him away.

CHAPTER 35

ALL this hard thinking would be over in half an hour or so. What was to come now didn't matter; no more than a mere punch in the eye. The worst was over on Saturday, and he had got through that all right. Hannah was very bad, and so was Dicky. Em cried in a bewildered sort of way, because the others did. Little Josh, conceiving that his father was somehow causing all the tears, kicked and swore at him. He tried to get Hannah to smile at this, but it was no go; and they had to carry her out at last. Dicky was well-plucked though, bad as he was. He felt him shake and choke when he kissed him, but he walked out straight and steady, with the two children. Well, it was over . . .

He hoped they would get up a break in the Jago for Hannah and the youngsters. His own break had never come off—they owed him one. The last break he was at was at Mother Gapp's, before the Dove-Laners fell through the floor. It must have cost Mother Gapp a deal of money to put in the new floor; but then she must have made a lot in her time, what with one thing and another. There was the fencing, and the houses she had bought in Honey Lane, and the two fourpenny doss-houses* in Hoxton that they said were hers, and—well, nobody could say what else. Some said she came of the gipsies that used to live at the Mount years ago.* The Mount was a pretty thick place now, but not so thick as the Jago: the Jagos were thick as glue and wide as Broad Street. Bob the Bender fell in Broad Street, toy-getting, and got a stretch and a half . . .

Yes, yes, of course, they always tolled a bell. But it was rather confusing, with things to think about.

Ah, they had come at last. Come, there was nothing more to think about now; nothing but to take it game. Hold tight—Jago hold tight . . . 'No thank you, sir—nothing to say, special. On'y much obliged to ye, thank ye kindly, for the grub an'—an' bein' kind an' wot not. Thanks all of ye, come to that. Specially you, sir.' It was the tall black figure again . . .

What, this was the chap, was it? Seedy-looking. Sort of undertaker's man to look at. All right—straps. Not cords to tie, then. Waist; wrists; elbows; more straps dangling below—do them presently. This was how they did it, then . . . This way?

'I am the resurrection and the life, saith the Lord: he that believeth in Me, though he were dead, yet shall he live: and whosoever liveth and believeth in Me shall never die.'

A very big gate, this, all iron, painted white. Round to the right. Not very far, they told him. It was dark in the passage, but the door led into the yard, where it was light and open, and sparrows were twittering. Another door: in a shed.

This was the place. All white, everywhere—frame too; not black after all. Up the steps . . . Hold tight: not much longer. Stand there? Very well.

'Man that is born of woman hath but a short time to live, and is full of misery. He cometh up, and is cut down, like a flower: he fleeth as it were a shadow, and never continueth in one stay.

'In the midst of life . . .'*

CHAPTER 36

It was but a little crowd that stood at the Old Bailey corner while the bell tolled, to watch for the black flag. This was not a popular murder. Josh Perrott was not a man who had been bred to better things; he did not snivel and rant in the dock; and he had not butchered his wife nor his child, nor anybody with a claim on his gratitude or affection; so that nobody sympathised with him, nor got up a petition for pardon, nor wrote tearful letters to the newspapers. And the crowd that watched for the black flag was a small one, and half of it came from the Jago.

While it was watching, and while the bell was tolling, a knot of people stood at the Perrotts' front-doorway, in Old Jago Street. Father Sturt went across as soon as the sleepers of the night had been seen away from the shelter, and spoke to Kiddo Cook, who stood at the stair-foot to drive off intruders.

'They say she's been settin' up all night, Father,' Kiddo reported, in a hushed voice. 'An' Poll's jest looked in at the winder from Walsh's, and says she can see 'em all kneelin' round a chair with that little clock o' theirs on it. It's—it's more'n 'alf an hour yut.'

'I shall come here myself presently, and relieve you. Can you wait? You mustn't neglect trade, you know.'

'I'll wait all day, Father, if ye like. Nobody sha'n't disturb 'em.'

When Father Sturt returned from his errand, 'Have you heard anything?' he asked.

'No, Father,' answered Kiddo Cook. 'They ain't moved.'

There were two faint notes from a distant steeple, and then the bell of St Leonard's beat out the inexorable hour.

CHAPTER 37

KIDDO COOK prospered. The stall was a present fact, and the awning was not far off; indeed, he was vigilantly in search of a second-hand one, not too much worn. But with all his affluence he was not often drunk. Nothing could be better than his pitch—right out in the High Street, in the busiest part, and hard by the London and County branch bank. They called it Kiddo's Bank in the Jago, and made jokes about alleged deposits of his. If you bought a penn'orth of greens from Kiddo, said facetious Jagos, he didn't condescend to take the money himself; he gave you a slip of paper, and you paid at the bank. And Kiddo had indulged in a stroke of magnificence that no other Jago would have thought of. He had taken *two* rooms, in the new County Council dwellings. The secret was that Father Sturt had agreed to marry Kiddo Cook and Pigeony Poll. There would be plenty for both to do, what with the stall and the regular round with the barrow.

The wedding-day came when Hannah Perrott had been one week a widow. For a few days Father Sturt had left her alone, and had guarded her privacy. Then, seeing that she gave no sign, he went with what quiet comfort he might, and bespoke her attention to her concerns. He invented some charing work in his rooms for her. She did it very badly, and if he left her long alone, she would be found on the floor, with her face in a chair-seat, crying weakly. But the work was something for her to do and to think about, and by dint of bustling it and magnifying its importance, Father Sturt brought her to some degree of mindfulness and calm.

Dicky walked that morning in a sort of numb, embittered fury. What should he do now? His devilmost. Spare nobody and stop at nothing. Old Beveridge was right that morning years ago. The Jago had got him, and it held him fast. Now he went doubly sealed of the outcasts:* a Jago with a hanged father. Father Sturt talked of work, but who would give *him* work? And why do it, in any case? What came of it before? No, he was a Jago and the world's enemy; Father Sturt was the only good man in it; as for the rest, he would spoil them when he could. There was something for tomorrow night, if only he could get calmed down enough by then. A builder's yard in Kingsland with an office in a loft, and money in a common desk. Tommy Rann had found it, and they must do it together; if only he could get this odd numbness off him, and have his head clear. So much crying, perhaps, and so much trying not to, till his head was like to burst. Deep-eyed and pale, he dragged round into Edge Lane, and so into New Jago Street.

Jerry Gullen's canary was harnessed to the barrow, and Jerry himself was piling the barrow with rags and bottles. Dicky stood and looked; he thought he would rub Canary's head, but then he changed his mind, and did not move. Jerry Gullen glanced at him furtively once or twice, and then said: 'Good ole moke for wear, ain't 'e?'

'Yus,' Dicky answered moodily, his talk half random. ''E'll peg out soon now.'

''Im? Not 'im. Wy, I bet 'e'll live longer'n you will. '*E* ain't goin' to die.'

'I think 'e'd like to,' said Dicky, and slouched on.

Yes, Canary would be better off, dead. So would others. It would be a comfortable thing for himself if he could die quietly then and there. But it would never do for mother and the children to be left helpless. How good for them all to go off easily together,* and wake in some pleasant place, say a place like Father Sturt's sitting-room, and perhaps find—but there, what foolishness!

What was this unendurable stupor that clung about him like a net? He knew everything clearly enough, but it was all in an atmosphere of dull heedlessness. There would be some relief in doing something violent—in smashing something to little pieces with a hammer.

He came to the ruined houses. There was a tumult of yells, and a crowd of thirty or forty lads went streaming across the open waste, waving sticks.

'Come on! Come on, Jago! 'Ere they are!'

A fight! Ah, what more welcome! And Dove Lane, too—Dove Lane, that had taken to bawling the taunt, 'Jago cut-throats', since . . .

He was in the thick of the raid. 'Come on, Jago! Jago! 'Ere they are!' Past the Board School and through Honey Lane they went, and into Dove Lane territory. A small crowd of Dove-Laners broke and fled. Straight ahead the Jagos went, till they were suddenly taken in flank at a turning by a full Dove Lane mob. The Jagos were broken by the rush, but they fought stoutly, and the street was filled with a surge of combat.

'Jago! Jago hold tight!'

Thin, wasted and shaken, Dicky fought like a tiger. He had no stick till he floored a Dove-Laner and took his from him, but then he bludgeoned apace, callous to every blow, till he fought through the thick, and burst out at the edge of the fray. He pulled his cap tight, and swung back, almost knocking over, but disregarding, a leather-aproned,* furtive hunchback, who turned and came at his heels.

'Jago! Jago hold tight!' yelled Dicky Perrott. 'Come on, Father Sturt's boys!'

He was down. Just a punch under the arm from behind. As he rolled, face under, he caught a single glimpse of the hunchback, running. But what was this—all this?

A shout went up. 'Stabbed! Chived! They chived Dicky Perrott!'

The fight melted. Somebody turned Dicky on his back, and he moaned, and lay gasping. He lifted his dabbled hands, and looked at them, wondering. They tried to lift him, but the blood poured so fast that they put him down. Somebody had gone for a surgeon.

'Take me 'ome,' said Dicky, faintly, with an odd gurgle in his voice. 'Not 'awspital.'

The surgeon came running, with policemen at his heels. He ripped away the clothes from about the wound, and shook his head. It was the lung. Water was brought, and cloths, and an old door. They put Dicky on the door, and carried him toward the surgery; and two lads who stayed by him were sent to bring his friends.

The bride and bridegroom, meeting the news on the way home, set off at a run, and Father Sturt followed.

'Good Gawd, Dicky,' cried Poll, tearing her way to the shutter as it stopped at the surgery door, 'wot's this?'

Dicky's eye fell on the flowered bonnet that graced the wedding, and his lip lifted with the shade of a smile. 'Luck, Pidge!'

He was laid out in the surgery. A crowd stood about the door, while Father Sturt went in. The vicar lifted his eyebrows questioningly, and the surgeon shook his head. It was a matter of minutes.

Father Sturt bent over and took Dicky's hand. 'My poor Dicky,' he said, 'who did this?'

'Dunno, Fa'er.'

The lie—the staunch Jago lie. Thou shalt not nark.

'Fetch mother an' the kids. Fa'er!'

'Yes, my boy?'

'Tell Mist' Beveridge there's 'nother way out—better.'

THE END

APPENDIX

MORRISON AND HIS CRITICS

Arthur Morrison reflects on his earliest ventures in writing:

Salcombe House
Loughton
Essex

August 19th 1907

Dear Sir,

My first published manuscript was the first manuscript I wrote for publication—in other words my first effort was accepted. It was nothing very ambitious, though I was very young at the time, for it was twenty-six or perhaps twenty-seven years ago. The thing was verse—people used to begin with verse in those days—and I earnestly intended it to be comic. It appeared in a cycling magazine well known at the time, called, I think, *Cycling*. It was in the time of the tall bicycle and some genius had invented a machine of that sort which would double up and go into a carpet bag. My verse described certain tragic misunderstandings on the part of somebody who ~~heard~~ overheard a conversation about a carpet bag wherein were stowed a 'head', a 'neck', a 'backbone', different ~~parts~~ pieces of a 'felloe' and similar parts of a bicycle. I had no idea of taking to literature as a vocation at that time, ~~but I~~—I was a boy—but afterwards contributed very extensively to the cycling press of the eighties; which consisted, as a fact, of some half a dozen flourishing periodicals. My first attempt on the more regular press was a sketch printed in the Globe. I forget its subject and its date, except that it must have been about 1885. ~~or 1886~~

Yours faithfully,
Arthur Morrison

Walter J. Roberts Esq.

(Reproduced courtesy of the Bancroft Library, University of California, Berkeley, and the Regents of the University of California)

In this previously unpublished letter Morrison writes light-heartedly to Herbert S. Stone, his American publisher, about the news he has received of the prospects for A Child of the Jago *in the USA—but also with amazement at how some of the first American reviews had distorted the plot of the novel.*

Salcombe House
Loughton
Essex
England

December 9th 1896

Dear Stone,

Just a line to congratulate and thank you. You have put 'A Child of the Jago' into stunning clobber (as they would say in the Jago) and the book is altogether so handsome that I don't care how soon you send me a few copies. It beats the English edition. If only you had stretched the 397 pages into 400 I should have been a foot higher and got my hat broken. One would feel voluminous with a book of 400 pages. Here it makes but 345. Someday I must do you a worse done book so that you may sell more.

As it is, however, I trust you are well going with the second million. Here it has vogue (though you mightn't expect it) chiefly in the West End, among the most exclusive swells, who have taken to asking me to dine, and causing a waste of invention in excuses. But it is selling, too.

Your American reviews are amazing. Start a paper, will you, and get books read as well as reviewed? A new thing like that might 'catch on'. The reviews are full of a desire to be kind, but disregard of the formality of reading has caused improvements in my story that come upon me like a punch in the stomach. One paper assures me that Dicky's father was in a machine shop, that the cosh-carriers invariably killed their victims, which he only did once. The wretchedness of everything has infected the Pansophic Institute, which becomes a 'wretched little mission room'. Dicky joins the pawnbroking interest, and Weech, having [*deletion*] suddenly transformed himself into the pawnbroker (like a pig in a nightmare) gives him the sack—and then there is a complaint that I don't sufficiently explain this part of the tangle. I'd like someone else to try first; and it all tops up with praise of the dedication (which is to the original of Sturt) as a 'grim bit of satire'?!!

Hope you're well. I <u>know</u> the business is good from what I hear. Go ahead. But especially take care to get through that second million of the Jago and start on the third.

Yours very truly,
Arthur Morrison.

(Reproduced courtesy of the Donald C. Davidson Library, University of California, Santa Barbara, and the University of California Regents)

In this previously unpublished letter, Morrison explains the nature and purposes of A Child of the Jago *to the Revd W. Priest:*

Salcombe House,
Loughton

September 30th 1899

Dear Sir,

'A Child of the Jago' is my picture of life in a neighbourhood a plan of which is printed in the book. Almost the whole of the place is now demolished, though many of the people still live near; ~~and~~ last Monday evening, indeed, there was an affray in Church Street (which I have called Meakin Street) in which the woman figured whom I have called Norah Walsh, and in which I am told that one person was killed and two others injured. If you substitute the word 'Nichol' for 'Jago' wherever you see it in the plan, you will have the true names of the streets, except in the case of Jago Court, which was Orange Court, Luck Row is Chance Street, and Edge Lane is Boundary Lane. The neighbourhood ~~is the~~ was the worst I have ever known.

The story, of course, was original and designed by me to picture the life and to show that children brought up in such surroundings had no chance of a decent life. Many of the chief characters are actual persons under new names and many of the more striking incidents are actual matters of fact, though there are matters which I have considerably toned down. The word 'Jago' is a Cornish surname, and is pronounced to rhyme with 'sago', the 'J' having the ordinary English sound.

I am, dear Sir
Yours faithfully
Arthur Morrison

The Revd W. Priest

H. G. Wells identifies conflicts in Morrison's presentation of nature and nurture:

The son of the alcoholic proletarian, the apparently exhausted topic of Dr Barnardo, has suddenly replaced the woman with the past in the current novel . . . Next year the artful publisher will be asking his young authors for books about poor boys born in sin and vermin and displaying with infinite pathos the stunted rudiments of a soul . . . It is indisputable that the rediscovery of Oliver Twist is upon us . . .

'A Child of the Jago' is indeed indisputably one of the most interesting novels this year has produced. We have admired Mr Morrison already for his 'Lizerunt'; we have disliked him for his despicable detective stories; and we will frankly confess we did not think Mr Morrison capable of anything nearly so good as this admirably conceived and excellently written story . . . It is beyond doubt that Mr Morrison must be full of East End material, and never once through this book does he drop into the pitfall of reporting. 'A Child of the Jago' is one of those rare and satisfactory novels in which almost every sentence has its share in the entire design.

The design, it must be confessed, is a little narrow. It is as if Mr Morrison had determined to write of the Jago and nothing but the Jago. It is the Jago without relativity. The reader will remember the spacious effect at the end of Mr Conrad's 'Outcast of the Islands' when Almayer shook his fist at the night and silence outside his sorrows. Mr Morrison never gets that spacious effect, although he carries his readers through scenes that would light into grandeur at a glance, at the mere turn of a phrase. The trial scene of Josh Perrott for the murder of Weech, and the execution scene that follows, show this peculiar want of breadth in its most typical manner . . . The execution is got off in three pages with a flavour of having been written in a hurry, is, indeed a mere sketch of one of the characters for the fuller picture there should have been. It seems all the slighter, because it comes immediately after an elaborately written murder, action as finely executed as one could well imagine, and just before the equally stirring concluding chapter, the killing of Dick Perrott in a street faction fight. Moreover, by this brevity the latter chapter is brought too close to the murder chapter. Instead of crest and trough, a rise and cadence of emotion, we end in a confusion, like water breaking on a rocky beach. Had the father and son been presented in antagonism with some clearly indicated creative and destroying force, with Destiny, with Society or with human Stupidity, the book might have concluded with that perfect unity of effect it needs and does not possess . . .

The origin of the Jago, the place of the Jago in the general scheme of things, the trend of change in it, its probable destiny—such matters are not in his mind. [*Quotes the discussion between Father Sturt and the surgeon.*] Thus speaks Mr Morrison. It is practical on the face of it, and quite what would occur to a man looking so nearly at Whitechapel that the wider world where the races fight together was hidden. But the fact is that neither ignorance, wrong moral suggestions, nor parasites are inherited; the baby that survives in the Jago must needs have a good physique, the Jago people are racially indistinguishable from the people who send their children to Oxford, and the rate of increase of the Jago population is entirely irrelevant to the problem. The Jago is not a 'black inheritance', it is a black contagion—which alters the whole problem. And Mr Morrison knocks his surgeon's case entirely to pieces by his own story; for he shows, firstly, in Mrs Perrott that to come into the Jago is to assimilate oneself to the Jago; and, secondly, in Kiddo Cook, that a vigorous, useful citizen may come out of it.

('A Slum Novel', *Saturday Review*, 82 (28 Nov. 1896), 573)

The Athenaeum *is glad to find no 'immorality' in* A Child of the Jago—*but finds too many fights, exaggeration, and uncertain purpose:*

Realism is so often an excuse for immorality in what is called art, that one can gladly praise Mr Arthur Morrison for a realism which deals frankly with dirt, brutality, and crime . . . [*Quotes the fight between Norah Walsh and Sally Green to show the 'zest of the narrator'*.] The human frame can bear a great deal; but if this description is taken literally it is pretty clear that Sally must have been killed on the spot. At another place it is said that a constable was laid low by a fire-grate adroitly let drop from an upper window. 'Laid low' may, of course, mean killed, but if so, the author for once fails to choose the plainest word; if it does not, the exaggeration is palpable. Many pages are devoted to elaborate accounts of free fights, and one chapter describing a single combat furnishes the most disgusting passages in all the book. What is the object of it all? Those who have to pass their time in police courts or in the Central Criminal Court know very well that villainy such as Mr Morrison depicts, and worse, exists in London . . . Mr Morrison has nothing new to tell. He is sarcastic about the philanthropists, who surely do not deserve his sarcasm. If his aim is to beguile novel-readers into taking an interest in the slums, it is not to be commended . . . Better directed efforts are not wanting and those who are in earnest must deplore the methods of the novelist who dwells upon revolting details of blood and blows.

('A Child of the Jago', *Athenaeum*, 3607 (12 Dec. 1896), 832–3)

With an opportunity to weigh Morrison against Stephen Crane, Wells's verdict goes to Morrison the 'heavyweight':

The literature of the slum multiplies apace, and just as the mud of the Port of London has proved amenable to Mr Whistler, so the mud of the New York estuary has furnished material for artistic treatment to Mr Crane. Mr Crane, in 'Maggie', shows himself the New York equivalent of Mr Morrison, with perhaps a finer sense of form and beauty and a slenderer physique. He is the light weight of the two. He is far more alert for what the industrious playwright calls the effective 'line', and every chapter cocks its tail with a point to it. He sketches, for instance, the career of Maggie's brother James, and tells of his lusts and brutality. 'Nevertheless,' ends the chapter, he had on a certain starlit evening said wonderingly and quite reverently, 'Dah moon looks like h—l, don't it?' And with that the chapter, rather self-consciously, pauses for your admiration. Of Mr Morrison's 'Dick Perrott' it is not recorded that he ever saw the beauty of moonlight or the stars. But one may doubt, even after the chromatic tumult of 'The Red Badge of Courage', whether Mr Crane is anywhere equal to Mr Morrison's fight between Perrott and Leary. To read that and to turn to Mr Crane's fight between Maggie's brother and her seducer is to turn from power to hysterics. The former is too strong and quiet to quote—it must be read: but of the latter: 'The arms of the combatants whirled in the air like flails. The faces of the men, at first flushed to flame-coloured anger, now began to fade to the pallor of warriors in the blood and heat of a battle . . . The quiet stranger had sprawled very pyrotechnically out on the sidewalk.'

Which is very fine, no doubt, but much more suggestive of a palette dipped in vodki than of two men fighting. Yet, on the other hand, the emotional power of that concluding chapter of 'Maggie' seems a little out of Mr Morrison's reach—the old woman, drink sodden and obese, stricken with the news of her daughter's death and recalling her one vivid moment of maternal pride.

'Jimmy, boy, go get yer sister! Go get yer sister an' we'll put dah boots on her feet!'

('Another View of "Maggie" ', *Saturday Review*, 82 (19 Dec. 1896), 655)

Morrison entertains Josh Perrott at Loughton, disputes with H. G. Wells on eugenic theory, and explains why he 'killed Dicky Perrott':

'Sometimes I had the people themselves down here to my house in Loughton. One of my chief characters, a fellow as hard as nails, who could stand a punch in the face without flinching, and whom it was said only steel or lead could affect, came several times, and told me gruesome stories and how the thieves made a sanctuary of Orange-court; the inner hell of this awful place . . .'

'Yes, you are right,' went on my host, 'heredity and environment are their greatest enemies. One of the critics in his notice of my book said that "neither ignorance, wrong moral suggestion, or parasites were hereditary", but he is wrong. Just look at this book of Charles Booth's, "Pictures of Pauperism", and see the influence of heredity. Look at these long lists of families going back to the third and fourth generation, and all criminals or lunatics. Now and again turns up a respectable artisan, but he is a freak, a "sport", to use the biological term, and he is so rare and startling an exception that he only goes to prove the point . . .'

'How can a half-starved girl of sixteen bear healthy children?' exclaimed Mr Morrison. 'One of the critics says that my Jago people are racially indistinguishable from the people who send their children to Oxford, but you never see a tall man amongst them, all the criminal classes are stunted. They have a certain strength, they can fight for a short time, but they have no staying-power. Take them a five-mile walk and you'll soon find that out. Therefore they have no quality that goes to make a good workman. It is monstrous that the weak should be destroyed by the strong, but still more so that the strong should be destroyed by the weak . . . For my own part, I believe, as Father Jay does, in penal settlements; it would be far cheaper than our present prison system. Why not confine them as lunatics are confined? Let the weed die out, and then proceed to raise the raisable. That is why I killed Dicky Perrott. He could not escape from his environment, and had he lived, would have become perforce, as bad as his surroundings.'

('The Children of the Jago: Slum-Life at Close Quarters: A Talk with Mr Arthur Morrison', *Daily News* (12 Dec. 1896), 6)

'C.R.', repudiating a charge of plagiarism, adduces information about the novel's sources and composition:

A writer in the *St. James's Gazette* claims to have discovered the secret of Mr Arthur Morrison's realism . . . 'In a sense,' says the reviewer, 'the book has been written before' . . . Now five years ago the Rev. Osborne Jay published a little book . . . dealing with the same district . . . For example, Mr Jay states in a passage of about thirty lines that faction fights are common in Old Nichol. Mr Morrison gives two chapters of vivid description of a definite faction fight. Mr Jay makes the plain statement that 'women even take part, biting at each other's faces and tearing out each other's hair', while Mr Morrison 'expands' this piece of information into the character of Sally Green, 'the female champion of the old Jago'. Such parallels as these, the writer urges, 'suffice to show how realistic fiction may be written'. Now it will occur to the least reflecting that Mr Morrison must be a much cleverer man than he is, to evolve a realistic story, full of the minutest details of slum-life, from the few bald facts that the *St. James's* reviewer discovers to be common to *Life in Darkest London* and *A Child of the Jago*. Moreover, my own knowledge of Mr Morrison convinced me that this was not the method on which he worked. And in answer to my request he was good enough to relate to me the genesis of his book, and to explain the origin of those points of resemblance which certainly exist between his work and that of Mr Jay.

It was shortly after the publication of *Tales of Mean Streets* that Mr Morrison made the acquaintance of Mr Jay and his parish. Mr Jay, struck by the grim truth of Mr Morrison's work, wrote him a letter of appreciation, which brought the author on a visit of inspection to Old Nichol. Already Mr Morrison had the idea of Dicky Perrott in his mind [I have seen it, among scores of other jotted notions, in one of his old note-books] and was hesitating whether to place him in Poplar, in Bethnal Green, or elsewhere . . . Hither, then, Mr Morrison came day after day for more than eighteen months, learning every inch of the half-dozen streets—now improved off the face of the earth—which makes up the Jago, haunting the public-houses, sitting with the people in their homes, and even trying in his own person what it feels like to earn a living by making match-boxes . . .

Now, given two men who spend eighteen months or so studying the lives of its inhabitants, and comparing notes of their discoveries and impressions, is it unlikely that when the one sets down the facts and the other weaves the facts into fiction a similarity should here and there appear?

('The Methods of Mr Morrison', *Academy*, 1284 (12 Dec. 1896), 531)

The Bookman *protests against 'orgies of physical violence':*

This new book of his has pages which it is almost impossible to read. We do not combat his general attitude at all . . . We do not accuse him of exaggeration, and as for his excesses of realism we can at least understand the temptation. But to understand does not take away the right of protest; and we do protest against the useless riot of brutality, the orgies of physical violence which we are made witnesses of if we read the book through. Zola has never outdone some of the pages here in their horrible defiance of any sensitive feelings we may have. But we declare our right to have these feelings respected, if not pampered, and our opinion that an unblinking perusal of these tales of brutal fights would show much more morbid effeminacy than any shrinking from them would do. They are no necessary part of Mr Morrison's strenuous and courageous purpose.

('A Child of the Jago', *Bookman* (London), 11 (Dec. 1896), 90–1)

Blackwood's *reviewer muses on the uses of fiction: recreation or missionary's medium?*

When [fiction] is not absorbed in the odious question of sex, it is so overstrained in the pursuit of the unusual, so determined at any hazard to humanity and with every possible breach of its prevailing laws to get something new . . . that its inventions are sometimes monstrous, and its call upon our attention rather an offence to us than an advantage . . .

There is nothing attractive at all in the world which he opens to our gaze. It is a world without hope or desire or any fair or pleasant thing, knowing nothing but the foullest sediment of existence, unable to conceive of anything better—brutal, filthy, miserable, yet in a measure content . . . It is strange to think upon what rule it is that pictures like these please the imagination, and are received by so many in the character of an entertainment, a portion of the relaxation of life. It may well be that we should see how another part of the world lives . . . But . . . what are they for? To make us all a kind of missionaries, impelled by disgust and horror, if by no better motive? . . . Are we then to take these doubtful tales for amusement? France has accepted a similar kind of amusement from M. Zola; but only when highly spiced with vice and the peculiar kind of garbage upon which the French novel-reader has chosen to feed. Seldom, however, does the historian of the Jago bring in this element to make his horrors palatable. He shows us all the uncleanness of the streets excepting that. So far as we can recollect, the appalling sketch called 'Lizerunt in the Mean Streets', in which the brutality becomes tragic and so justifies itself, is the only one in which the great pollution of all is so much as referred to . . .

Fiction is scarcely the medium for a lesson taught in such miserable detail, and in colours so dark and terrible . . . Perhaps he thinks it is the best way to seize the attention of the frivolous public; but we think he is mistaken . . . On the contrary, the gentlest of readers prefers to be seen with Nordau, or Kidd, or Pearson, quite superior kinds of literature, upon her table.

(Mrs Oliphant, 'A Raid Among Books', *Blackwood's Magazine*, 160 (Dec. 1896), 838–44)

George Gissing is annoyed—and then courted—by Father Jay; he records in his diary spending Christmas Day reading A Child of the Jago*:*

[8 Sept. 1893:] Reading *The Times* at news-room, yesterday, came across a review of a book called 'The Social Problem', by one Revd Osborne Jay, of Shoreditch. In a passage quoted from him I recognized whole sentences taken bodily from 'The Nether World'. Wrote letter to *The Times*.
[9 Sept.:] . . . My letter in *The Times*, headed, unfortunately, 'Borrowed Feathers' . . .
[11 Sept.:] . . . To-day the Revd O. J. writes in *The Times* that I am hard upon him, that he of course meant to quote me, that by some mistake he did not see the proofs of his book, etc. The lamest excuse . . .

[13 Sept.:] . . . One W. C. Hunt writes to *The Times* to say that the Revd O. Jay entrusted to him the correction of his proofs and *he* is responsible for the omission of inverted commas and of 'some names'. Referring to this the *Westminster Gazette* heads its para[graph] 'A Printer's Marvellous Confession'. Indeed, it is remarkable enough . . .
[21 Dec. 1894:] . . . Astonished by letter from Revd Osborne Jay, of Holy Trinity, Shoreditch (the man whose plagiarism I had to write to *The Times* about, last year) inviting me to visit him. Replied genially, of course, and promised to go some day.
[31 Mar. 1895] . . . Afternoon to Shoreditch, where I stayed till 6 o'clock with Father Jay, as he is called. Think I see my way to a big book.
[5 July:] . . . Invitation from Osborne Jay to the laying of the foundation stone of his new church; can't go . . .
[25 Dec. 1896:] Read A *Child of the Jago*. Poor stuff.

(Pierre Coustillas (ed.), *London and the Life of Literature in Late Victorian England: The Diary of George Gissing* (Hassocks, 1978), 314–430)

H. D. Traill launches his influential attack on A Child of the Jago, *detecting not the 'mud pies' of realism, but 'a fairyland of horror', another 'Voyage to the Houyhnhnms':*

It need not surprise us to find our attention solicited by a New Realism, of which the two most obvious things to be said are that it is unreal with the falsity of the half truth, and as old as the habit of exaggeration . . .

Mr Arthur Morrison, author of *Tales of Mean Streets* and *A Child of the Jago*, undoubtedly carries heavier guns than Mr Crane. To begin with, he can tell a story . . . Many of his characters are vividly and vigorously drawn . . . Mr Morrison . . . perceives . . . that the life of the criminal in his constant struggle with the law, and in perpetual danger from its officers, possesses at least the element of 'sport', and presents features of variety and interest which that of the mere sot and tavern-brawler [in Crane's *Maggie*] cannot possibly offer . . . In a word, the English writer differs from the American by all the difference which divides the trained craftsman from the crude amateur, and he deserves to that extent more serious and detailed criticism.

What, however, has most astonished one of Mr Morrison's critics fresh from a perusal of *A Child of the Jago,* is the impression of extraordinary unreality which, taken as a whole, it leaves behind it. . . . He comes out from the Jago with the feelings, not as he had expected, of a man who has just paid a visit to the actual district under the protection of the police, but of one who has just awakened from the dream of a prolonged sojourn in some fairyland of horror . . .

No wonder that those who know the East End of London have protested against this picture. The houses in that area of 'two hundred and fifty yards square' have been cleared of its former occupants and their dens, and the original of the Jago has, it is admitted, ceased to exist. But I will make bold to say that as described by Mr Morrison it never did exist. Mr Morrison has simply taken all the types of London misery, foulness and rascality, and 'dumped them down' on the area aforesaid . . . It is certainly not realism. It is the idealising method, and its result is as essentially ideal as the Venus of Milo. That it is the idealisation of ugliness, instead of beauty, is a mere detail . . . Unless words are to part with all their distinctions of meaning, it can no more be a realistic history of any community of human beings that ever existed on the earth, than is the *Voyage to the Houyhnhnms* . . . The total effect of the story is unreal and phantasmagoric . . .

('The New Realism', *Fortnightly Review*, 67, NS 61 (1897), 63–73)

Dicky Perrott lives; Harold Boulton asserts the accuracy of A Child of the Jago*:*

Incredible as it may appear, the Alsatia known in these pages as the Jago did exist up to three or four years ago, with all its reeking filth and horror, its absolute lawlessness, its frequent murders, its untainted heathendom, and its death-rate four times that of the rest of London. Perrott, the fighting man, the burglar, the murderer, was but one of many such, and the statement that eighty per cent of the male population in one street were ticket-of-leave men only leads to the conclusion that the remaining twenty per cent had served their time or not yet been caught. The blood-feuds and faction fights between the Ranns and the Learys, well as they are depicted, as matter of fact fall somewhat short of the hideous reality. In the great historic final fight, renewed at certain hours every day and lasting the best part of a week, one of the most striking incidents has escaped Mr Morrison's researches.

There had been for some days a *crescendo* of weapons as well as a *crescendo* of fury: fists had been discarded for sticks with nails in them, these for pieces of iron, and the climax was evidently at hand when one evening the Dove-Laners, as the author calls them, appeared before a certain house in the hostile quarter and, executing a savage war-dance, proceeded to sharpen knives upon the pavement in front of their foes, as an earnest of what might be expected on the morrow. It so happened that a youth, very much like the Dicky Perrott of the tale, who had at last succeeded in obtaining an honest situation, much to the derision of his friends, was a witness of this war-dance. The old Jago blood within him was too much for this recruit to the ranks of respectability; next day he sallied forth to battle in the ranks of the Jagos, only to fall horribly wounded by a butcher's cleaver, and to be borne off to hospital, where his depositions were taken. Contrary to expectation, after several months he recovered; but of course his situation is gone for ever, and he is to be seen to-day meditating among the ruins of the Jago and waiting for a job to turn up. Whether it is likely to be an honest one after such a failure, who can say?

Here, until quite lately, existed a state of things that no novelist could exaggerate, no reporter over-paint . . .

Mr Morrison's book has appeared just as the old order of things has vanished, and it is therefore timely. It should remain a *locus classicus* for a certain type of nineteenth century barbarism flourishing undisturbed for a while in the midst of our over-civilisation.

('A Novel of the Lowest Life', *British Review* (9 Jan. 1897), 349)

The Nation *measures the affective force of* A Child of the Jago *against Dickens:*

The story of the Jago is a terrible one, very modern in the manner of its telling, but dating back to Charles Dickens in matter, incident, and character. We seem to be reading about the 'Artful Dodger' and 'Poor Jo', 'Tom All-Alones', 'Bill Sykes', 'Nancy' and 'Pecksniff' converted into a fence slightly more degraded, but no more hypocritical and hateful. They are all done in a new way—a harder, more physical, brutal way. We have a stronger realization of their pitiable plight, but are more reconciled to it—it is so hopeless, so inevitable. Our horror is more vivid, our compassion feebler. Undoubtedly a great impetus to philanthropy was given by Dickens's slum stories. He controlled tears and laughter; he made emotional people feel that something must be done, and he forced sentimental people to go and do something at once. It is hardly probable that any burst of sympathetic activity can follow the reading of tales written by the more actual moderns. Literary worth does not spur the general reader to action, and perhaps, with such tales as the 'Child of the Jago', it is the force of the literary presentation which convinces those who can appreciate it of an impotence in action—a conviction to which that sort is ever predisposed.

('*Sir George Tressady* and Other Fiction', *Nation* (New York), 64/1648 (28 Jan. 1897), 70–1)

Mr Woodland Erlebach, a former manager of the Nichol Street Board School, writes to lend support to Traill's objections:

From a thirty years' acquaintance with the district [Mr Morrison's Jago] I boldly say that the district, though bad enough, was not even thirty years ago so hopelessly bad and vile as this book paints it.

(Letter presented by Traill, along with the names of other 'experts' demanded by Morrison, in publishing his revised critique in book form: *The New Fiction and Other Essays on Literary Subjects* (London, 1897), 25–6)

Aaron Weech lives; Jay describes and defends Morrison's methods:

SIR,—I have for ten years been an inhabitant [and indeed Vicar] of the district the existence of which Mr H. D. Traill appears to doubt—the district described by Mr Arthur Morrison in his novel *A Child of the Jago*. I have much respect for Mr Traill's abilities as a literary critic, and in that respect would not venture to question his opinions; but as regards simple facts I think I may with honesty claim to be an 'expert' in the matter of the life which Mr Morrison has described. I have one thing to say—a thing I have said publicly before—and that is that Mr Morrison's book exhibits with perfect truth the life of my parish as I have known it day by day for ten years.

Who the 'experts' may be who condemn the book I am at a loss to conceive, and Mr Traill does not mention their names. I can think of nobody more entitled to be styled an 'expert' in this matter than Mr Morrison himself, who, after many years of residence and personal study in other parts of the East-End, spent eighteen months in minute personal investigation of my parish—the 'Jago'—before beginning his book; and apart from myself, I have met nobody well-acquainted with the neighbourhood—and I think I know all such people—who does not agree with me that the book presents the place and the people with a sincerity and truth that is wonderful. So far from Mr Morrison's characters being selected from different districts, I know all the originals among my parishioners, and could point them out. As to Aaron Weech [his name is not Queech, nor is he a Jew as Mr Traill supposes], he is alive now, and carrying on in his shop. Mr Traill is surprised that readers are 'invited to believe' that cosh-carrying, as described by Mr Morrison, was a general feature in this unhappy parish. I also most earnestly invite Mr Traill to believe it, sad as the fact is. The Bishop of Stepney's organ, *The East London Church Chronicle*, supports Mr Morrison's facts unreservedly, though I trust my own testimony is sufficient. The professional philanthropists who live in the West and talk of the East may disagree with those on the spot who know, but I am sure Mr Traill will weigh their opinions in a just balance. The place is cleared away certainly—or nearly so. But the people still exist, and, it was the people who made the place bad, not the place that degraded the people. The problem still exists.

I am Sir, your obedient servant.
A. OSBORNE JAY

Holy Trinity Vicarage,
Shoreditch, E.

('The New Realism: To the Editor of the Fortnightly Review', *Fortnightly Review*, 67, NS 61 (Feb. 1897), 314)

Sally Green lives; Morrison contests Traill's label of 'realist' and assumptions about 'process':

To begin with, then, I have never called myself a 'realist', and I have never put forth any of my work as 'realism'. I decline the labels of the schoolmen and the sophisters: being a simple writer of tales, who takes whatever means lie to his hand to present life as he sees it; who 'insists' on no 'process'; and who refuses to be bound by any formula or prescription prepared by the cataloguers and pigeon-holers of literature. This, I am aware, may be an announcement of limited interest: but I think I am justified in making it by reason of the perplexing movements of Mr H. D. Traill in the course of an article on what he calls 'The New Realism' . . . The procedure, briefly, is this. The critic begins by calling me, quite gratuitously and of his own motion, a 'realist'; he announces, again quite gratuitously, that realists [and I presumably among them] 'insist' on a certain 'process' in the production of fiction; he proceeds himself to 'insist' on a particular 'process', which he presents ready mixed and of his own discovery; then he produces from his imagination, inspired by the completest ignorance of the life of which I have written, a theory that I have not worked by his process. He compares this theory with his label *Realist*, and decides that there is a disagreement somewhere. And in this way, amiably trotting after his own tail, he arrives at the conclusion that I am a very insincere sort of person, writing the thing which is not in base competition with other realists . . .

Mr H. D. Traill, however, has adventured farther than any other critic in this direction. The Jago, as I have described it, he 'makes bold to say' never existed. Truly, he makes very bold: even so did Dickens's 'amazing alderman' make bold to say that Jacob's Island never existed. In a like degree would he make bold were he to deny the existence of Franz Josef Land. For the only perceptible warrant for his denial is that he has never seen the Jago . . . He cites my description of the 'cosh' and its use—to stun or disable a drunken man decoyed into the Jago for purposes of robbery. He complains that he is invited to believe that 'coshing' was a regular industry of the Jago, practised throughout the whole district, at all times, and by every one who had the means of practising it with success. My actual words were that 'cosh-carrying was near to being the major industry of the Jago', and certainly he is invited to believe this. I know it, Mr Jay knows it, his lay-helper, his curate and his mission-woman know it. Mr Harold Boulton knows it. Mr Traill knows nothing of the Jago at all: therefore he refuses to believe it. That is all . . .

He will not believe in Sally Green, her trick of gnawing the nape, and the incident of the broken bottle assault . . . Sally Green is alive at this moment, and, as I write, it is scarce twenty-four hours since I had sight of a cheek, eye, and temple swollen to the size of a turnip by the application of her boot. Her actual name is not Sally Green—as matter of fact, she chances to bear the surname of one of the most inoffensive literary men alive; but her manner of fighting was such as I have described. She is growing older now, and is losing some of her quickness; consequently she fights rather less, and rarely attempts the difficult tactic that won her supremacy in earlier years. But her temper has not improved, and she is surprisingly ready with a heavy boot. If Mr Traill is willing to risk the boot, it will give me much pleasure to present him to Sally Green in person . . .

A definite accusation is that I have taken bad types from divers districts, and concentrated them in my picture of the Jago. But again Mr Traill mistakes. The original of my Jago was a place to which those types gravitated as by natural law from other parts . . . Not I, but their own propensity, brought these people together.

Mr Traill has discovered that in Josh Perrott's fight with Billy Leary 'every punch, with its effect on the punched part, is faithfully delineated in black and blue, picked out with crimson'. Surprised to learn this, I turned to the book, and succeeded in counting the mere mention [no more] of as many as a dozen blows. Has Mr Traill any conception of how many blows are delivered in, say, a quarter of an hour of a well-stricken fight? Has he ever seen such a fight? . . .

Why does he call my Weech a 'revival' of Fagin? True, he styles him 'Queech', and a Jew—which he isn't; but even that brings him little nearer. Aaron Weech is alive now, and in his shop [though it is not a coffee-shop], and there are hundreds of other men of his class. His likeness to Fagin is as the likeness of Cacus to Jack Sheppard: his trade is the same, and that is all . . .

One thing I regret, and that is that when Mr Traill speaks of Dicky Perrott's story being buried in a mass of squalid irrelevancies, he does not point to some, at least, of the irrelevancies to which he refers; because the information might have been of use to me. There is nothing I am more anxious to exclude from work of mine than irrelevancy.

But when I am attempting to depict the squalid surroundings of a boy in a thieves' neighbourhood, and their effect on his character, I am disposed to consider these surroundings no irrelevancies at all, but strict essentials of the picture . . .

('What is a Realist?', *New Review*, 16/94 (Mar. 1897), 326–36; see Explanatory Notes, note to p. 3)

The Critic *sounds the aesthetic note of the 1890s, finding Baudelaire without the beauty and Dickens without the poetry: a novel that leaves 'only a shudder behind':*

Many years ago, a French poet distinguished himself by a volume in which the worship of evil, the adoration of ugliness, was the dominant chord . . . In Baudelaire—in the 'Fleurs du Mal'—it allied itself with beautiful form, and had so far a reason for its existence; an exquisite vase held the fetid unguent, a rare and lovely rhythm threw a panoply of grace over the monstrous limbs . . .

But what can one say of ugliness unredeemed by beauty of form or grace of utterance—ugliness of toads and adders and creeping things, that freezes and thrills like the Medusa of Leonardo and leaves only a shudder behind? We have tried in vain to read Mr Morrison's book; we must frankly avow ourselves defeated. As a 'tract for the times', supplementing the revelations of Mr Jacob Riis and the philanthropic economists who are investigating East New York and East London, the book is undoubtedly powerful and may serve a good purpose; the very disgust with which we lay it down shows its power . . . The same talent, remarkable enough, which he displays in painting these brutal Salvador Rosa landscapes, might, if softened a little, have served his purpose infinitely better, and created or evoked the sympathy which he longs for the reader to feel. No one can read nearly 400 pages of unrelieved wretchedness, pessimism and ugliness without an effort too heroic to be expected in these days. The wonderful genius of Victor Hugo triumphed over us in 'Les Miserables'; but Victor Hugos are scarce. The 'children of the Jago' (the Five Points of London) are miserable enough in their gaunt poverty, but to make them interesting, a certain transfiguring touch must poetize their habitations, their lives and loves, as Dickens has made them beautiful in little Nell and other immortal figures. If we can neither smile nor weep, we are apt to fall into the rigidity of indifference.

('A Child of the Jago', *Critic* (New York), 30, NS 17 (24 Apr. 1897), 287–8)

The Academy *weighs up Morrison's career, suggesting that he should restore the priority of 'human nature' over 'environment':*

Mr Morrison appears to have arrived at a very interesting and critical stage of his career, for no one can say whether promise is going to ripen into performance or not. He is of the French school; Daudet might have taught him his method, and Zola selected his subjects. In his *Jago* he trusted little or nothing to imagination, but a great deal to his notebook . . . [But] human nature does not alter so much with conditions as he seems to think . . . Mr Albert Chevalier made his early success by recognising this fact; the coster of his songs is recognisably alive and human. The coster of Mr Morrison does not seem to be a man, but only a stuffed figure carrying a blotch of horrible characteristics . . . Moreover, his success has been achieved in pictures of the brutal. There are times when he seems to reflect that, after all, passion and hatred and love and tears and sorrow and forgiveness, if he could but see them, play the same part in the slum that they do in Piccadilly; but so far this discernment has resulted in no more than the reproduction of some of the worst faults of Charles Dickens, catch-penny pathos, and weak sentimentality where he intended real feeling. Mr Morrison never will do first-rate work till he shuts up his Dickens, a writer who had no command of the harsh, bitter cynicism in which Mr Morrison excels, and whose sunny love of what was bright and cheerful is inimitable.

To pronounce any final judgment upon Mr Morrison's writing would be absurd. The truth is, he has not yet found himself; he has not searched his mind so thoroughly as to be able to say how much of it is second-hand Kipling, second-hand Daudet, Dickens and Zola, and what remnant is pure Morrison . . . The imitation that is freely pardoned at the beginning of a career is not to be so easily forgiven in more ambitious tasks. So, also, the lack of sympathy—we do not mean pity or compassion so much as the power to enter into and share another's views and thoughts and passions—may be passed by once, but without it there can be no really great imaginative writing.

('Mr Arthur Morrison', *Academy* (4 Dec. 1897), 493)

With the evidence of To London Town, *the* Bookman *calls a halt to reproaches against Morrison:*

The reproaches sometimes cast at Mr Morrison that his 'Tales of Mean Streets' and his 'Child of the Jago' gave a one-sided and a very miserable account of East London life, must now cease. It was not a wanton delight in gloom that made him write so harshly of existence in the wildernesses of brick and mortar. He writes his report of life in chapters, and not in one alone can he tell the ultimate truth. But here he comes nearer to doing so. There is something idyllic in the story [of *To London Town*], much that is gentle. But it is no symptom of Mr Morrison's having begun to quail before the spectacle of poverty and sin and suffering. Beauty and goodness are seen in their common struggle against sordid ugliness, but beauty and goodness are uppermost.

('In London Town', *Bookman* (Nov. 1899), 58–9)

Looking back on his trilogy, Morrison focuses on the short-termism and reversal of moral code of the Jagos:

'I believe that if you could erect a machine at a cost of £500 which would supply them with food and clothes and all the necessities of life for ever, and if you went down to them with the £500 and said, "Here I have £500 to spend on you. Shall I build a machine, which I can do in a month, to keep you in food and clothes for ever after the month is over, or shall I divide the money among you and give you eighteenpence each on the spot"—I believe if you did that a great shout would go up, "Give us our eighteenpence". They are utterly unable to see beyond the present; the idea that at the end of the month the machine would supply them with all they wanted would be quite incomprehensible to them . . .

'The moral order of things was reversed in the Jago; this boy was brought up to stealing, and stealing became a moral habit to him. He had never known it was wrong, and could not understand being punished for it. He had no chance. So criminals are made and paupers are brought into the world.'

('New Light on London's Poverty: A Chat with Mr Arthur Morrison',
Cassell's Saturday Journal (19 Sept. 1900), 24)

Jane Findlater sketches the evolution of slum fiction, according Morrison a high place—though not the last word:

Many authors, many modes of presentation; but, in spite of this, it is easy to arrange our authors into distinct 'schools', each writing from their own standpoint. The slum and the slum-dweller, then, may be, and have been, treated in (at least) five different ways:

1. As a moral lesson.
2. As a social problem.

3. As an object of pity and terror.
4. As a gladiatorial show.
5. As an amusing study.

The first of these divisions belongs now, to a bygone age; the second and third merge into each other; the fourth has not very many exponents; the fifth is the latest evolution of the whole movement . . . Dickens from the outset is moralizing; and that is what no modern author would dare to do for a moment—because no one would read his books if he did. The awful retribution of sin, the hard way of the transgressor, is not what we wish to hear about in 1900, whatever the public of earlier days liked. It is much more to our taste to read of the triumph of the transgressor and the total defeat of innocency by inexorable fate . . .

The whole school of social reformers sprang into being with *Alton Locke*. . . . Surely every unwholesome trade has had its novel; every grievance of the toilers its special pleader in fiction. All honour to the reformers, and long may they blossom and bear fruit. What Kingsley began Besant went on into, and a host of smaller writers, well-intentioned but nameless, followed hard upon their masters . . . This interest in social reform books is certainly more healthy than the rush which was made for the two other classes of slum literature which I have mentioned—i.e. (1) the school of pity and terror, and (2) the school of brutality.

The demand for the first of these is, I hope, explained by the fact that the writers of this school have written so admirably.

It was in 1890 that Gissing brought out that extraordinary book *The Nether World* . . . Gissing writes the tragedy of Want. It is not written with brutality, and that is why it is so terrible and undeniable . . . As we read we know that every word is true—this is hunger, and heaven help the hungry;—this despair indeed—not the glib despair which the novelists deal in by the page, but that mortal disease of the mind which is past all cure. Gissing has no gospel of hope to offer his readers . . . The lower orders are, to his seeing, one huge tragedy . . . Arthur Morrison became the most prominent exponent of the School of Pity. His *Child of the Jago* continued the tradition at its best, and exhibited the 'relentless' modern method very plainly. For here is the story of a boy of originally good, tender instincts, who, like Oliver Twist, is in training for a thief. Does innocence triumph here? Is there a measure of hope and comfort at the close? Impossible. Dicky Perrott—the 'Oliver' of our day—has never a chance from the cradle to the grave . . . We all read the books of Arthur Morrison and shuddered over them; some people were apparently reading them without the shudder, for in 1897 appeared yet another recruit to the ranks of slum literature, who, in slang phrase, seemed to be determined to 'go one better' than his predecessors. The brutal school had appeared . . .

[Somerset Maugham's] *Liza of Lambeth* appeared in 1897. It is a story of brutal frankness and sickening import . . . We are spared nothing: the reek of the streets; the effluvia of unwashed humanity: but worse than all these outside things is the hopeless moral atmosphere in which the characters move . . . Nor does the author seem to write in any spirit of pity, or with any love for the creatures he has made. With a stolid indifference he chronicles their hopeless sufferings; without apparent disgust he details the loathsome vices which degrade them; the whole thing is so gratuitous. Why all these horrors? Why all this filth? . . . But this is just where these books fail. Life in the slums has its joys quite as surely if not as evidently, as a life in palaces, and it is ridiculous to suppose that it has not.

This was a fact which was working obscurely in the writings of Arthur Morrison. *The Child of the Jago* scarcely admits the joys of slum-life, but it gives a fair idea of its pleasurable, if savage, excitements—the ecstasy of Dicky Perrott's absorption in the prize fight, the lust of battle, the gratulation of successful thieving— all these dubious joys are freely admitted.

But it remained for yet newer recruits to the slum-writers to discover what I venture to say is more nearly the ultimate truth about slum-dwellers, and to describe this. [William Pett Ridge's] *'Mord Emly* and [Clarence Rook's] *The Hooligan Nights* both give voice to this new discovery, and with admirable art, that is quite without exaggeration, show the wild joys and excitements of slum-life . . . There comes the truth; every slum-dweller is not entirely depraved, or desperately miserable.

('The Slum Movement in Fiction', *National Review*, 35 (1900), 447–54)

Robert Blatchford, editor of the socialist Clarion, *focuses on Morrison's omissions and ultimate literary limitations:*

An infinite deal of nothing has been written about *A Child of the Jago*. The book has been foolishly praised, and as foolishly condemned, and both praise and condemnation have been a source of amusement and surprise to the few who possess real knowledge of both literature and the slums. For it is a fact within the memories of a legion of readers that nearly every feature of the 'Jago' life has been painted in literature before; and it is a fact within the knowledge of innumerable citizens of London, Glasgow, Dublin, Liverpool and Manchester, that the life of the 'Jago', and of all other slums of which the 'Jago' is a type, is more horrible, more miserable, more shameful, and more unspeakable than Mr Morrison has painted it. Mr Morrison . . . has *not* presented the 'Jago' in all the colours of its wretchedness and shame. On the contrary, he has exercised a stern artistic reticence.

Let anyone who knows the slums consider how the truth is toned down or evaded in *A Child of the Jago*. What are the two commonest adjectives of the low-life Cockney? No publisher dare print them: yet in 'Jago' conversation hardly a sentence is spoken without their use . . . Then nothing is said in Mr Morrison's book as to the sanitary arrangements of the 'Jago', nor is there any indication of the great prevalence of sicknesses, which . . . flourish in the slums as fungi flourish upon rotten trees . . . In the 'Jago' children are prostitutes before they reach their teens; and it is true that bad as are the morals of the East, they are exceeded by the vileness of the West of London.

There is not a newspaper nor a novelist in these islands who dare tell the whole truth and the real truth about Whitechapel, the Strand, and Piccadilly.

('On Realism', in *My Favourite Books* (London, 1900), 222–53)

Jack London visits the setting of A Child of the Jago *and reflects on the 'mean streets' of the East End:*

We next visited the municipal dwellings erected by the London County Council on the site of the slums where lived Arthur Morrison's 'Child of the Jago'. While the buildings housed more people than before, it was much healthier. But the dwellings were inhabited by the better-class workmen and artisans. The slum people had simply drifted on to crowd other slums or to form new slums . . .

The City of Dreadful Monotony, the East End is often called, especially by well-fed, optimistic sight-seers, who look over the surface of things and are merely shocked by the intolerable sameness and meanness of it all . . . But [it merits] a worse title. It should be called the City of Degradation.

While it is not a city of slums, as some people imagine, it may well be said to be one gigantic slum. From the standpoint of simple decency and clean manhood and womanhood, any mean street, of all its mean streets, is a slum . . . The mean streets merely look mean from the outside, but inside the walls are to be found squalor, misery, and tragedy.

(*The People of the Abyss* (1903; repr. London, 1977), 88–9)

A defender of William Booth turns on such clergy as Jay:

How has [General Booth] been received? And what has he done?

He has been received with an almost unbroken chorus of insult and abuse. Clergymen who have never been heard of outside their own little parishes—who have never shown themselves worthy to tie his shoe, and of whom any thousand put together cannot show as the fruit of their labours one tithe of the souls whom he has rescued from darkness to light and from the power of Satan unto God—have written about him in terms of positive fury. To me there is something absolutely shocking in this fact . . . Here is a man who to all his *religious work*—of which the results are incontestible, however much its methods may be disliked—has added a *social work* ample and fruitful enough to furnish out the glory of fifty ordinary reformers, and yet every fussy nobody, every commonplace and routine clergyman, thinks himself justified in speaking of him with scornful disapprobation, and looking down upon him from the whole height of his inferiority.

(The Ven. Archdeacon Farrar, 'The "Darkest England" Social Scheme', repr. from *The Review of the Churches*, in Bramwell Booth (ed.), *The Salvation Army: Essays and Sketches* (London, 1906), 206–34)

EXPLANATORY NOTES

ABBREVIATIONS

Jay	A. O. Jay, *Life in Darkest London*
Le May	F. Le May, 'Memories of Bethnal Green'
H.B.N.	H.B.N., *Penal Servitude*
McCarthy	T. McCarthy (ed.), *The Great Dock Strike 1889*
Smith	T. H. Smith, 'Re-Readings 2: The Jago'
Sturt	G. Sturt, *A Small Boy in the Sixties*

See the Select Bibliography for full details of the works cited in these notes.

3 *PREFACE TO THE THIRD EDITION*: variant, shorter version of Morrison's essay 'What is a Realist?'. The latter was an essay engaging in greater detail with H. D. Traill's objections to *A Child of the Jago* made in the *Fortnightly Review* (see Appendix, p. 175).

4 *Constable*: John Constable (1776–1837), English landscape painter, particularly known for his natural lighting effects, water reflections, and cloud studies.

Corot: Jean Baptiste Camille Corot (1796–1875), French figure and landscape painter who worked in Romantic and realist styles.

Iwasa Matahei: (or Matabei) (1578–1650); first Japanese artist publicly to identify himself with genre compositions depicting the lives of ordinary people. Previously such figures played mainly subsidiary roles in paintings of noble or saintly characters. See note below on Ukioyé; also Morrison's *The Painters of Japan* (1911).

Hiroshigé: (1797–1858) with Hokusai, master of colour-printed woodcuts of contemporary life and scenery of Japan. Exclusion of the natural cast shadow had been regarded as one of the defining characteristics of Japanese art; Hiroshigé's work was consequently better received in the West than in Japan.

Tosa and Kano: opposing traditions in Japanese art, each, from the earliest times, enjoying periods of dominance. Tosa, Buddhist in inspiration and typified by the art of Takayoshi, produced a native art of ceremony, grace, and formal convention. Kano, which supplanted Tosa in the fifteenth century, was Zen in inspiration, Chinese-influenced, and prioritized the subjective response of artist and viewer.

Ukioyé: (or, variously, Ukiyo-ye, Ukiyo-e); see notes above: Iwasa Matahei and Hiroshigé. Japanese school of genre painting and printmaking developed in the seventeenth and eighteenth centuries by such artists as Moronobu, Haronobu, Okumura Masanobu, Kiyonaga, and Utamora.

4 *Harunobu*: Suzuki Haronobu (1718–70); Japanese artist who advanced woodblock printing from the conventional two-colour technique to polychrome; he specialized in idyllic images of youth.

the artist should be shut up in a flower-garden: Morrison alludes, as in the reflection that follows concerning those who regard art as 'upholstery', to the *Bookman*'s review of *Jago*, which prioritized literature as 'a portion of the relaxation of life'. The *Critic*'s review, taking a similar stance even more emphatically, did not appear until April 1897 (see Appendix, p. 181).

I have been asked, in print: chiming of the word 'phase' indicates that Morrison is alluding to the *Blackwood's* review: 'Mr Morrison will say that he does not wish to please, but only to exhibit another phase of life' (see Appendix, p. 174).

5 *the priest and the Levite*: parable of the Good Samaritan, answering the question 'And who is my neighbour?': Luke 10: 29–37.

Hogarth: Charles Lamb (1775–1834), 'On the Genius and Character of Hogarth, with Some Remarks on a Passage in the Writings of the Late Mr Barry', an essay first published in Leigh Hunt's *Reflector* (1811). The essay praised the engraver, satirist, and comic history painter William Hogarth (1697–1764), particularly for the quality of 'the real' in his depiction of the principal character in *The Rake's Progress*. Lamb defended Hogarth against the strictures of Sir Joshua Reynolds and those who deprecated 'the low' in Hogarth's compositions. Lamb observed: 'Those persons seem to me to confound the painting of subjects in common or vulgar life with the being a vulgar artist. The quantity of thought which Hogarth crowds into every picture, would alone *unvulgarize* every subject which he might choose.' This reference to Lamb's essay only appears in the preface and not in 'What is a Realist?'.

6 *following his own spirit*: see note to p. 9.

a like spirit of lavish objection: the objections listed relate specifically to Traill's attack.

lack of 'sympathy': the *Bookman* found in *Jago* 'a horrible defiance of any sensitive feelings we may have'; Traill wrote of realists who 'sternly shut their eyes to the real pathos of the scenes and lives which they describe'. The *Critic* was shortly to suggest that some 'softening' might have 'created or evoked the sympathy which he [Morrison] longs for the reader to feel'; in December the *Academy* charged him with 'lack of sympathy', without which 'there can be no really great imaginative writing'. Morrison had already bridled at this charge in his *Daily News* interview (see Appendix, p. 171).

7 *'palpable exaggeration'*: review of *Jago* in the *Athenaeum*, 3607 (12 Dec. 1896) (see Appendix, p. 170).

the devoted vicar . . . has testified: Revd Arthur Osborne Jay, Vicar of Holy Trinity, Shoreditch, the novel's dedicatee and model for Father Sturt. 'What is a Realist?' mentions Jay corroborating Morrison's account 'four or five times at least in public print'. Jay wrote letters to the *St James's Gazette* and the *Fortnightly Review* and gave an interview to *London*; Morrison may also have had in mind one or more of Jay's books (see Select Bibliography).

Others . . . with special knowledge: these included Harold Boulton, 'C.R.', and the *East London Church Chronicle* (effectively, the Bishop of Stepney) (see Appendix, pp. 172, 176).

8 *The Jago . . . is gone*: see note to p. 135: County Council.

9 [*epigraph*] *Woe unto the foolish prophets*: attack on false prophets prophesying 'concerning Jerusalem, and which see visions of peace for her, and there is no peace' (Ezekiel 13: 16). The idea of the destruction of Jerusalem had been applied to London since the Renaissance. In his preface Morrison identified such prophets with 'your professed philanthropist, following his own spirit and seeing nothing'.

10 *The Old Jago: Sketch Plan*: excluding the historical (Shoreditch) High Street and Bethnal Green Road, Smith (pp. 42–3) translates this sketch-plan into the historical street system:

Old Jago Street:	Old Nichol Street
New Jago Street:	New Nichol Street
Half Jago Street:	Half Nichol Street
Jago Row:	Nichol Row
Edge Lane:	Boundary Street
Honey Lane:	Mead Street
Meakin Street:	Church Street

In his 1899 letter to W. Priest Morrison identified Luck Row as Chance Street. He also identified Jago Court as 'Orange Court' in his *Daily News* interview (see Appendix, p. 171, and Jay, 61). One reviewer suggested that 'Jago' was a play on the name 'Jay' (i.e. 'Jay-go' as opposed to a 'No-go' area): *Athenaeum*, 3607 (12 Dec. 1896), 832–3. Smith notes that Charles Booth's *Life and Labour of the People in London* contains 'a description of part of the Jago, really the "Nichol", house by house, under the name of Summer Gardens' (p. 40).

11 *set across with posts*: designed to exclude horses and carts from subsequently narrowing passageways.

for one hundred years the blackest pit in London: the enormous growth of the East End occurred during the nineteenth century: 'The whole of that great city of a million souls, now called East London, consisted, until the end of the last century, of Whitechapel and Bethnal Green, still preserving something of the old rusticity; of Mile End, Stepney and Bow, and West Ham, hamlets set among fields, and market-gardens, and of that long fringe of riverside-streets and houses': Walter Besant, 'A Riverside Parish' (1892); repr. in *As We Are and As We May Be*, 108. In the wake of development, the 'Old' Jago, first occupied by Huguenot silk-weavers or their successors, was left to decay through what Morrison termed 'a century of infamy'.

11 *What was too vile for Kate Street, Seven Dials, and Ratcliff Highway in its worst day*: 'the Kate Street mob dropped on him in Brick Lane and bashed him full sore': Morrison, 'A Conversion', in *Tales of Mean Streets* (1894), 260.

Dickens wrote of the 'Dials' with its 'seven dark passages' in *Sketches by Boz* (ch. 5): 'Where is there such another maze of streets, courts, lanes and alleys? Where such a pure mixture of Englishmen and Irishmen, as in this complicated part of London? [. . .] The unexperienced wayfarer [. . .] traverses streets of dirty straggling houses, with now and then an unexpected court composed of buildings as ill-proportioned and deformed as the half-naked children that wallow in the kennels.'

The folk song 'As I was a-walking along Ratcliff Highway' captures this principal dockland road's associations with sailors, prostitutes, and the press gang. Dickens called it 'that reservoir of dirt, drunkenness and drabs'. Besant characterized its history as 'street fighting and brawling all day long; the perpetual adoration of rum; quarrels over stolen goods; quarrels over drunken drabs [. . .] a never-ending, still-beginning debauch' ('A Riverside Parish', 117). Morrison set *The Hole in the Wall* (1902) here (vividly describing the Blue Gate slum): 'I think there could never have been another street in this country at once so foul and so picturesque as Ratcliff Highway at the time I speak of' (p. 83).

12 *sleeping and walking*: in his edition Keating prints the more idiomatic 'sleeping and waking'; the first edition reading, however, has the merit of extending the theme of motion through 'writhen', 'rolled', and 'moving'.

three sorts of vermin . . . third plague of Egypt: fleas, flies, and lice. Looey is 'horribly flea-bitten'; in Egypt, flies and lice followed the plague of frogs (Exodus 9); Jay observed that 'only those who reside [here] can know the abject terror of the awful curse "lice in all their quarters", or the extreme reasonableness of the ordinary summer ejaculation, "They do bite this weather!"' (p. 69).

'*I wish I was dead: an' kep' a cawfy shop*': Jay: '"I wish I were dead," is a common aspiration, "and kept a coffee-house"—a vision surely of peace which should touch the hearts of all the well-fed, who can get all they want as soon as they ask for it' (p. 118). In 1951 Francis Le May, an inhabitant of Huguenot descent, recalled Bethnal Green in the 1880s and 1890s and explained the role of coffee shops and cook shops (such as Weech's) in the community: 'Gas cookers were unknown, so most of the food was bought already cooked. Every eating house supplied hot meals, vegetables, puddings etc. [. . .] There were Cook Shops, Pie Shops and Coffee Shops everywhere, and people you passed carrying basins with a saucer for cover, or a beer can with soup, or a covered plate could be counted by the score' (pp. 31–2).

Kiddo Cook: Jago nicknames connote wiliness, bravado, or expertise. 'Kid' was a slang term of admiration for an expert young thief or pugilist. 'Kiddy' meant to fool ('kid'); as a noun it was what Morrison called 'a friendly synonym' for a professional thief assuming a 'flashness' of dress and manner (*OED*). 'Kiddy', meaning a 'bloke', survives in London and the south-east, as also does 'kiddo' as a term of address importing 'friend'.

screw of paper: nineteenth-century equivalent of a paper bag. George Sturt teased his readers 'Do you know how to twist up paper into a small bag?' (p. 135). At the Perrotts' a 'screw of paper' substitutes for a 'sugar basin'; Kiddo's keeping tobacco in this way (as Butson does in *To London Town*), indicates that he cannot afford a tobacco-pouch.

O wot 'orrid langwidge! It's shocking, blimy: Besant, in 'From Thirteen to Seventeen' (1886; repr. in *As We Are and As We May Be*), declared that he had never heard 'language more vile and depraved' than from 15-year-old working girls at Hampstead Heath fair; 'at mere profanity, of course, these girls would be easily defeated by men, but not in absolute vileness' (p. 34). Kiddo theatrically mimics the offended sensibility of superior classes or of the posturing working class whose dropped 'aitches' and unconscious profanity ('[Cor] blimey' = God blind me') inadvertently announce the affectation.

'Hell? And how far's that? You're in it!': infernal imagery pervades constructions of the East End, constituting a whole discourse as much as a discrete chain of literary transmission. Mephistophilis' 'Why, this is Hell, nor am I out of it' (Christopher Marlowe, *Dr Faustus*, iii. 78) offers a precedent, but so does Jay: '"There can be no hell hereafter," is a common expression of the people, "we live in it already"' (p. 108); this phrasing is echoed in Morrison's *Daily News* interview. However, the sentiment equally chimes with Gissing's *The Nether World* (which Gissing had accused Jay of plagiarizing) where Mad Jack reports his dream of the underclass living in 'a state of punishment' inflicted for their misusing wealth in a former life: 'This life you are now leading is that of the damned; this place to which you are confined is Hell! [. . .] This is Hell—Hell—Hell!' (ch. 37).

13 *wife (married or not)*: middle-class horror of the underclass partly focused on perceived sexual immorality. Domestic Christian Missions encouraged marriage of those joined, as Morrison put it, 'in the simple Jago fashion'—or as Jay phrased it, 'only married, not churched' (p. 110). Hence the later references to a Bethnal Green church 'where you might be married for sevenpence if you were fourteen years old and no questions asked'. Morrison's *Daily News* interviewer was himself a former East End curate and interpolated: 'my mind went back to a Christmas morning in an East End church, where I, as curate, stood marrying blaspheming youths and girls to one another [. . .] ghastly mockery'. Harold Boulton commented that 'the institution of the family as sanctioned by the narrow formulae of Church and State had been stamped out' in the Old Nichol. Besant saw

early marriage as a symptom of cultural poverty, indeed 'the greatest curse of East London' ('A Riverside Parish', 129). Kijinski ('Ethnography in the East End') notes that in evaluating cultures Victorian ethnographic methodology gave special weight to the status of marriage.

13 *industry . . . craftsman . . . profit . . . transaction . . . capable practitioners . . . duty . . . artist*: long-lived extended metaphor presenting the criminal urban poor in relation to work and business, notably enshrined in Hogarth's 'Industry and Idleness' (where the industrious apprentice becomes Lord Mayor and the idle apprentice, turning to crime, is hanged); also in Dickens's *Oliver Twist* where Fagin refers to his boys' activities as examples of industry and craftsmanship. Terms such as 'trade', 'tradesman', and 'training' are used ironically throughout *Jago*, while an ironic version of the idle and industrious apprentices ghosts through the presentation of Dicky Perrott and Bobby Roper at the Board School.

exemplary fiction . . . Sunday School book . . . dutiful matrons: Joseph Alleine and John Wesley ran Sunday schools earlier, but these institutions are particularly associated with Robert Raikes's organizing activity in the 1780s. They were subsequently promoted by Sunday school unions and participated in the project of educating the poor working class into 'respectability'. St Mary's Whitechapel, for example, was running a Sunday school in 1890 under its rector Arthur J. Robinson. Prize-books 'of the goody kind' for good attendance or scripture reading were produced for distribution by such specialist publishers as SPCK and Partridge (Besant, *East London* (London: Chatto, 1899; new edn., 1902), 13). Their idealized stories inculcated such virtues as temperance, chastity, stoicism, and filial duty.

portal: elaborate, quasi-medieval gateway; Orange Court was noted for its narrow, tunnel-like entrance.

14 *Front doors were used merely as firewood*: Jago houses are in multiple occupation (Smith mentions that 53 Old Nichol Street 'with ten rooms had ninety persons'); the dismantling of front doors destroys their function as symbols of artisan respectability or of middle-class domesticity and privacy. In 'That Brute Simmons', in *Mean Streets*, the punctilious Mrs Simmons regards even an open front door as 'low'. See E. Ross, 'Not the Sort that Would Sit on the Doorstep'.

first-floor back: 'back' rooms, having less light and looking out on walls, waste areas, or middens, commanded lower rents. (The Ropers, who with their 'threadbare decency' are seen as 'pertickler' and 'too good for their neighbours', occupy a 'front room'.) Visitors used coded knocks at the front door (when present) for particular tenants (see 'That Brute Simmons').

weak of mouth: physiognomy as a key to character flourished through the nineteenth century both in popular culture and in the novel. As a pseudo-science it cooperated in defining and locating 'degeneration'; while Hannah is 'weak of mouth', Father Sturt is 'tall and soundly built, with a certain square muscularity of face'. See Daniel Pick, *Faces of Degeneration*.

15 *done a click*: committed a theft; Jay draws attention to the expression (p. 98).

18 *Valley of Dry Bones*: the dead awaiting resurrection as a metaphor for the underclass awaiting 'a better way' (with an ironic quibble on the coshed man regaining consciousness). Ezekiel 37: 1–2.

19 *East End Elevation Mission and Pansophical Institute*: the location of the Institute suggests the satire is directed at Toynbee Hall, associated with St Jude's church, Whitechapel, rather than Morrison's former place of employment, the People's Palace, located in Stepney, further east along the Mile End Road. However, Morrison satirizes the premises and principles of philanthropic activity rather than any particular institution.

The ostentatious title combines the spirit of Victorian civic and educational development ('Institute') with democratic humanist ('Pansophical') and evangelical religious impulses ('Mission'). In Matthew Arnold's terms, the Institute offers 'sweetness and light', cultural development and moral improvement. 'Elevation' was part of philanthropic and eugenic discourses; it carried a residual religious meaning ('the lifting up of the soul [in adoration]; a devout exaltation of feeling' (*OED*)) but also denoted a 'raising' of the lower classes physically, socially, morally, and culturally. Besant saw the People's Palace as working for the 'purification and elevation of life'. Morrison saw such elevation as principally self-aggrandizement by the philanthropist: in *To London Town* 'superior visitors' to a Working Man's Institute come away 'oozing with inexpensive patronage' (p. 222) and other visitors 'went home virtuously conscious of having done their duty towards the Submerged' (p. 238). The term 'elevator' (as in 'ardent young Elevator') may be mildly ironic in that it principally meant a Salvation Army factory—such as Hanbury Street Elevator—resocializing the underclass into responsible work: see Besant, 'The Farm and the City', in Bramwell Booth (ed.), *Essays and Sketches: The Salvation Army* (London: Salvation Army, 1906), 60.

Besant defined the interests of the People's Palace as 'knowledge in all its branches'; 'its educational capacities are almost boundless [. . .] there will be founded here a University for the People of a kind hitherto unknown and undreamed of' ('The People's Palace' (1887), reprinted in *As We Are and As We May Be*, 50–1). The *OED* notes two principal meanings of 'Pansophy': 'universal encyclopaedic knowledge; a scheme or encyclopaedic work embracing the whole body of human knowledge' and 'the claim or pretension' to such.

people who knew less of that part than of Asia Minor: widespread ignorance concerning conditions in the East End is a common theme in writing about it. 'Asia Minor' here implies the Ottoman Empire and the Balkan politics which so exercised Gladstone and affected debate about the aims of British Liberalism. As a result of the Russo-Turkish War (1877–8),

Eastern Rumelia was placed under Ottoman control, but in 1885 a revolution led to the province joining Bulgaria. This in turn led to war between Serbia and Bulgaria and complex repercussions involving the Ottoman Empire, Russia, Austria, Greece, and Romania. The connotations of 'West' and 'East' thus oscillate between denoting parts of London and a larger ideological geography opposing the West, as Christendom, to a threatening 'other' along Europe's Eastern and Southern borders characterized as Muslim, Serb, or Semitic, often as pederastic, homosexual, or otherwise deviant or degenerative: see Edward Said, *Orientalism* (1978). The Transylvania of Bram Stoker's *Dracula* (1897) is patent evidence of such anxiety but the East End with its 'street arabs' and ethnic diversity also provided a domestic model of the opposition.

19 *Higher Life . . . comparative degree*: satire on the discourse of idealists and transcendentalists. 'Higher Life', denoting a state of personal spiritual sanctification, was a term common in evangelical and educational debate, as also in nonconformist theological stances. The theosophy movement (founded in 1875 by Madame Blavatsky), influenced by Indian thought, used the term to signify higher mystical planes of existence.

Lectures . . . Pictures: Besant judged Toynbee Hall's lecturers 'the most distinguished men in their own lines to be found; there is no talking "down" to the Whitechapel audience'. Easter art exhibitions were organized by the Revd Samuel Barnett, Vicar of St Jude. Besant elaborated: 'In the evening ladies go round with small parties and give little talks upon the pictures, explaining what the artist meant and how his design has been carried out' (*East London*, 311, 296).

papers on literary and political matters . . . musical evenings: Morrison may have in mind the People's Palace and his own former role in organizing such activities: see Michael Krzak's preface to *Mean Streets*. Besant recorded: 'What Barnett and Toynbee Hall have done for the intellectual side, the People's Palace has done for the musical side. Its cheap concerts have led the people, naturally inclined to music, insensibly into ways of good taste [. . .] They now have their own orchestra, vocal and instrumental [. . .] Here is the finest gymnasium in London, and here are many clubs—for foot-ball, cricket, and games of all kinds' (*East London*, 312–13). Besant's greatest disappointment was that a literary prize he instituted produced responses of very low quality.

Uninformed . . . Hopeless Poor . . . Misery of the Submerged: social problem discourse generated such terms as the Submerged, the Subterranean (prefiguring H. G. Wells's 'Morlocks'), the Unemployed, the Dispossessed, the Nether Worlders, the Great Unwashed, the Degraded Classes, and the Vicious Classes. Besant characterized the Submerged as those who had fallen to the gutter from any height, whether starting as professional man, tradesman or workman (*East London*, 229). Also see R. H. Stoll, 'The Unthinkable Poor in Edwardian Writing'. 'The Uninformed' may be Morrison's invention or satire on conflation of the condition of the outcast poor with the very different issue of educational provision for the artisan and lower middle class. In *To London Town* Morrison wrote mockingly of those who spoke of 'the Degraded Classes, who were to be Raised from the Depths' by cultural education (p. 222) or even of 'the Upraising of the Hopeless Residuum' (p. 235).

tradesmen's sons, small shopkeepers: Besant was clear about the constituency served by the People's Palace. In 'The Amusements of the People' (1884), reprinted in *As We Are and As We May Be*, he commented: 'It can do nothing, absolutely nothing, to relieve the great starvation and misery which lies all about London, but more especially at the East-end [. . .] We are concerned only with the well fed, those who are in steady work, the respectable artisans and *petits commis*, the artists in the hundred little industries which are carried on in the East-end; those, in fact, who have already acquired some power of enjoyment because they are separated by a sensible distance from their hand-to-mouth brothers and sisters' (pp. 288–9).

bagatelle board: popular from the Regency onwards, this forerunner of pinball machines was often found in pubs; it is also played in Father Sturt's club (as it was in Jay's, though not for money). It did not figure as one of the rational recreations demanding 'skill, patience, discipline, drill, and obedience to law' that Besant encouraged ('The People's Palace', 57); Morrison may be implying philanthropists' failure to inculcate desired recreational values.

Mutually-Improved: debating societies were sometimes termed 'Mutual Improvement Societies'; Morrison had already mocked them in *Mean Streets* (see 'A Street').

20 *Other young men . . . Missionaries*: the Society for the Propagation of the Gospel in Foreign Parts was established in 1701. Theological debate further enhancing the duty of mission, the missionary became an icon of Victorian culture. The domestic dimension of mission grew in parallel; the need was demonstrated in an 1886 census in the East End which found that some 92 per cent of the population attended no religious service. University Settlements enabled those in training for the Church to gain experience of mission in deprived areas.

perilous deeps . . . dark region: in social problem discourse deprived areas are typically constructed as deep (descent; the pit; the abyss; drowning at sea) and dark (night; the nether world; the African interior).

much worse places up West: Besant emphasized that the East End was not a city of slums, and singled out Devil's Acre (close to Westminster Abbey), as far worse than any in the East End (*East London*, 38). George Sturt wrote of the annual arrival in Farnham of hoppers 'from the slums of Reading or of West London' (p. 76).

police-court and inquest reports: 'police intelligence' was published in the daily newspapers; Besant suggested that publications like the *Police News Budget* represented the typical reading of the East Ender.

21 *accident to his hat . . . string*: a bishop's hat resembled a low top hat with strings running from its sides to the brim.

21 *spikes of the Bishop's carriage*: designed to prevent people jumping on the back. George Sturt recalled a bishop 'who could not drive to church without two flunkeys clinging to the back of his carriage' (p. 168).

22 *popular periodicals and in—in other ways*: the Bishop's hesitation suggests Morrison may be mischievously alluding to his own *Mean Streets*.

not so black as it was painted: the *Spectator*'s reviewer toyed with such a charge against *Mean Streets*: 'as if he were deluding consciously the public into taking too black a view of the East-End'. Charles Booth's Poverty Survey Maps of London used a seven-shade colour-coding system running between black ('lowest class') and yellow ('wealthy'). For Booth's map covering the Old Nichol see McCarthy, pp. 96–7.

23 *what's become of my watch?*: elaboration of Jay's account of his new church's foundation ceremony: 'Outside for many hundred yards a dense crowd gathered; and within a Bishop, a Bishop-elect, and an Archdeacon graced the proceedings with their presence. Some of these eminent persons were on their way to attend a garden party at Lambeth, and I personally conducted them afterwards through the crowd, feeling sure that otherwise they would attend that gathering minus their watches' (p. 65).

24 *decent boiler-maker's daughter*: boilermakers counted themselves among the aristocracy of skilled labour, far higher socially than a plasterer (such as Josh claims to be). Morrison, as in the preface and his sketch 'On Blackwall Pier', was acutely aware of lower-class social distinctions: 'Here, perhaps, would muse the democratic observer, are no social distinctions—here all men are equal. Arcadian republic of Blackwall! Happy province of peaceful anarchy! But the democratic observer would be making a mistake' (*Palace Journal* (8 May 1889), 1046). Boilermaking relates to Morrison's father's occupation as engine-fitter and to Tommy May's apprenticeship in engineering in *To London Town*.

nothing but shot or pointed steel could hurt him: attribute claimed by the original of Josh Perrott as reported by Morrison in his *Daily News* interview (see Appendix, p. 171).

26 *hearthstone*: soft stone or composition of pipe clay and pulverized stone used for scouring and whitening hearths or doorsteps; typically supplied by rag-and-bone men in exchange for metal, glass, bones (for glue), and rags (for shoddy or paper). Jerry may thus be an occasional rag-and-bone man. In *Sketches by Boz* (ch. 5) Dickens described the 'firewood and hearthstone line' as one requiring 'a floating capital of eighteenpence or thereabouts'.

centre-bit: carpenter's tool, favoured by burglars, used for making cylindrical holes: in *Oliver Twist* Bill Sykes requires only 'a centre-bit and a boy' to perform a burglary (ch. 19); Tennyson referred to 'the villainous centre-bits' that 'Grind on the wakeful ear in the hush of the moonless nights' (*Maud*, I. xi).

27 *Montagues and the Capulets*: feuding families in Shakespeare's *Romeo and Juliet*.

28 *Bob the Bender*: 'bender' was slang for a hard drinker. 'Jack the Bender' was a nickname in use in Jay's parish (p. 37).

Snob Spicer: 'snob' was slang for a shoemaker. Spicer is of the Rann persuasion; Fag Dawson (one of the Leary tribe) falls 'with a shoe-maker's knife sticking under his arm-pit'. Some element of the principal modern meaning of 'snob' may be involved, given a positive turn to imply flamboyance.

knocked out of knowledge: battered unconscious.

quart pot: i.e. a 2-pint pewter mug. Morrison observed: 'At a beer-house in such a locality (such a house as Mother Gapp's in my book) beer is only served in pewter pots [. . .] A customer specifically demanding beer in a glass is met with flat denial, though beer can be sold more profitably by the glass than by measure; and the reason is that brawlers, women especially, are apt to break a glass at the rim, and, taking the bottom in the palm of the hand, stab at faces with the jagged points' ('What is a Realist?', 333–4).

Cocko Harnwell: contraction of 'cock o'the walk' (crack man on the street) or an allusion to cock-fighting, meaning a spirited fighter. In noting 'cock' as 'a familiar term of appreciation among the vulgar', *OED* highlights the nuance 'swaggering'.

29 *cleanliness was resented in the Jago*: middle-class perception of the urban poor was structured by awareness of the need for improved sanitation in those slum areas that fuelled the cross-class threat from cholera and typhoid. Cleanliness being 'next to godliness' (Father Sturt appears 'whole and unsoiled'), a discourse of class difference structured the poor as by nature ungodly and dirty the 'Great Unwashed' versus 'washed and well-dressed people' (ch. 2). In *The Road to Wigan Pier* George Orwell recorded having to overcome precisely this inculcated sense of class difference.

assumption of superiority: like 'narking', a grievous fault in the culture of the urban poor and working class.

Ginger Stagg: by occupation Ginger Stagg is a lob-crawler (see note to p. 124), but 'Stag'—in addition to generating the pun 'at bay'—has some provenance in slang as meaning a person who provides false alibis for payment.

Pud Palmer: 'palmer' carries the meaning of a petty criminal adept at sleight of hand (palming coins, cards, or dice).

30 *driving in bungs*: breaking into unopened casks of beer or spirits by staving in the wood or cork used to stopper the 'bung-hole'.

Sally Green . . . dangled a long bunch of clotted hair: 'in this street are two great rival families, two different schools of philosophy, two claimants to the homage and honour of the rest [. . .] Women even take part, biting at each other's faces, and tearing at each other's hair' (Jay, 106).

31 *lodging-house poker*: with the implication of its being larger and heavier than the domestic version; iron rather than brass may be implied.

31 *Pigeony Poll*: *OED*, while not recording 'pigeony', notes use of 'pigeon' into the seventeenth century to mean 'a young woman, a girl; a sweetheart'. More common meanings of 'pigeon', still widely current in the nineteenth century, and not without some relevance to the presentation of Poll, were 'coward; simpleton, dupe'.

cadged and wrote begging screeves: to cadge is to beg (more literally than in the familiar modern use of the word). Systematic ('professional') writing of begging letters addressed to people known to have come into wealth was an attested occupation of the semi-criminal. See Mayhew, *London Labour*, i. 313: '"He writes a good hand," exclaimed one as the screever wrote the petition.'

33 *truck*: the wheelwright George Sturt described a 'truck': 'A little light hand-cart it was—a panelled box (made for strength) with T handle [. . .] Its main use was for the morning papers. Two boys took it to the station, threw into it the parcel of newspapers, then brought it at a run to the shop [. . .] You could hear divers trucks rattling about the ancient street' (p. 97).

34 *Fag Dawson*: 'fag' was thieves' slang for pickpocket.

36 *Aaron Weech*: despite the name 'Aaron', Morrison and Jay insisted that Weech was not Jewish (or, rather, that his original was not). The textual Weech has, however, been widely read as an anti-Semitic portrait in the same vein as Dickens's Fagin. If Weech is not Jewish, Morrison's fences usually were. Cohen plainly is, and Morrison's portrait of Issy Marks ('Snorkey Timms, His Marks', in *Green Ginger*) is hardly ambiguous. Weech's first name seems a pointed allusion to the first Jewish priest, the brother of Moses, significantly associated with making the golden calf while Moses was receiving the Ten Commandments.

no Sabbath-breaker: the Act of Uniformity (1551) first placed Sunday observance on the statute book and was followed through the centuries by a number of Sunday Observance, or Lord's Day Acts. An Act of 1871 had in fact considerably reduced the restrictions of the Lord's Day Acts on Sunday trading. Sabbatarianism, however, as it derived from the Ten Commandments, remained a strong tendency among the respectable.

37 *given anything, kindly and ungrudgingly*: an episode strongly echoing Oliver Twist's introduction to his 'benefactor' and 'patron' Fagin. See R. A. Colby, 'Oliver's Progeny'.

tapping of the forefinger beside the nose: gestural code for knowingness, but in particular a characteristic of Fagin: see Cruikshank's illustration to *Oliver Twist*, 'The Jew and Morris both begin to understand Each Other'.

39 *clean the knives*: to avoid corrosion, steel knives of the period required vigorous scouring; this was often done by a 'knife-boy', either manually on a 'knife-board' or using a 'knife-machine'.

broad pennies: possibly a reference to eighteenth-century 'cartwheel' pennies which remained in circulation into Victoria's reign.

43 *American make*: automated mass production and design innovations that reduced the number of working parts made mid-nineteenth-century United States the world's leading clock-making nation. The 'American clock' was consequently a byword for extreme cheapness.

corpse: *Notes and Queries* (1884) reported that 'to corpse' was 'one of many customary and coarse ways of menacing the infliction of death. It is horribly familiar in London' (*OED*).

In the swe-e-et by an' by: popular hymn by Sanford Fillmore Bennett (1836–98), included in Moody and Sankey's hymn-book and frequently printed separately for display purposes.

44 *grocers' almanacks*: pictorial calendars distributed as advertising; here serving as cheap substitutes for pictures.

Sunday School Anniversary bills: later termed 'Sunday-school festival bills'.

45 *Roper's tools . . . were the most valuable things in the place*: with Bethnal Green, Shoreditch was a woodworking and furniture-making area. As a cabinetmaker (and thus highly skilled) Roper would be responsible for supplying his own tools; in stealing them, Old Fisher steals Roper's means of living. In *To London Town* Butson's tools are in pawn 'and a man felt discouraged from looking for a job when his tools were "put away", and he had no money to redeem them' (p. 173).

46 *Elementary Education Act . . . Board School*: the 1870 Education Act established board schools: there was one in Nichol Street, and Morrison places one in Honey Lane (Mead Street). Elected school boards had powers to build and maintain schools out of the rates. Support by parliamentary grant was also available to board schools and existing schools in particularly poor areas.

tickets were to be had: philanthropists have often distributed dedicated vouchers rather than coin to ensure that welfare is applied to ends defined by the giver rather than the recipient. However, once vouchers were exchanged for goods, the underworld offered a 'regular tariff in gin for charity-given shirts and boots and groceries' (Morrison, 'A Blot on St Basil', in *Divers Vanities* (1905), 196). Jay opposed the manipulative use of tickets: 'I was not a ticket-machine' (p. 28).

47 *parson: active and resolute*: as the *Blackwood's* reviewer noted (see Appendix, p. 173), a description which suggests F. D. Maurice's 'Muscular Christianity' movement.

48 *have the police at instant call*: 'there was, for some time, a rooted suspicion that I might be in some way connected with the police' (Jay, 35).

amazed by sudden address in his own name: 'I soon learned [their right names], somewhat to their surprise' (Jay, 37).

49 *loaves and sixpences*: quibble on the 'loaves and fishes' of the feeding of the five thousand (Matthew 14: 17), widely used as a metaphor for the 'perks' of religious observance.

49 *since the parish came into being*: in 1867.

52 *straps*: i.e. leather strops for sharpening razors.

53 *shining, round metal boxes, notably decorated with coloured pictures*: presumably examples of popular German export tin-plate and clockwork manufacture of the period.

55 *Gently Does the Trick*: music-hall song by Punch and Browne associated with Arthur Corney, 'eccentric vocalist' of the 1890s. It includes the lines 'For sneaking ladies' lockets | Or for clearing out back pockets | Oh, 'tis gently does the trick'.

57 *offering a quart pot*: 'one of my new Club members rushed half-tipsy out of a public-house, and, to the evident enjoyment of his companions at the bar window, insulted me by offering me a pot of beer. I took the proffered pewter-pot, and, flinging the contents in his face, told him to recollect whom he was addressing; a rebuke, I am bound to say, he took in good part, and one apparently much appreciated by his friends': Jay, 35–6.

59 *'take away his character'*: a key point of tension when Jay accuses Tommy Irishman of stealing the Club's bagatelle balls: '"Do you," he cried, "take away my character?" "I do not," I calmly retorted, "You possess no character to take away"': Jay, 41.

60 *High Mob*: with deficiencies in policing and social administration, the East End has a long history of criminal gangs or mobs, including the Kray brothers in the post-war period, in which the gang (paradoxically, from a middle-class perspective) is a partly benign presence, 'deeply reverenced' by the community, 'stared at', and 'envied'.

flourishing practitioners: professional thieves were considered as belonging to the branch of thieving in which they excelled the most, and were named after it.

the mag: halfpenny, in the context of 'mag flying' or illegal pitch-and-toss rackets (see note to p. 65).

the mace: swindling, robbery by fraud. Snorkey Timms, one of Morrison's dramatized guides to the London underworld, renders 'macing the digs' as 'takin' lodgin's on the strength of 'is luggage an' slidin' off with anything 'e might find. So that a bag stuffed with bricks was just what 'e'd ave, natural enough' ('His Tale of Bricks', in *Divers Vanities*, 188).

the broads: playing cards, for such scams as 'Find the Lady' and 'Crown and Anchor'.

welshers: swindlers who act as bookmakers but abscond with the money laid as bets.

snidesmen: counterfeiters or passers of counterfeit coin ('snide-pitchers').

exchange and house of call: dealing room or 'stock exchange'; 'house where journeymen of a particular trade assemble, where carriers call for commissions, or where various persons in request may be heard of' (*OED*). The terms are used in part ironically, but in noting the 'vast systematic organized depredation' of shipping and the docks, Besant observed: 'To make robbery successful, there must be accomplices, receiving-houses, fences, a way to dispose of the goods [. . .] All the public-houses were secret markets attended by grocers and other tradesmen where the booty was sold by auction, and, to escape detection, fictitious bills and accounts were given and received' ('A Riverside Parish', 115).

ice-cream coat: fur coat. '"Half your luck!" called out a talkative youngster to a horrified lady-visitor from the West End in a new fur coat. "After you with the ice-cream coat! I suppose you did a click yesterday." It was in no sense meant as impertinence, but only as a cheerful and hearty greeting' (Jay, 119).

brimmy: presumably a contraction of 'brimmingly', with a figurative sense of 'complete' or 'excellent'.

the only way out: weighted phrase both in colloquial expression and in social problem discourse (repeated on the novel's last page). Jacob Riis wrote of the Bowery in *How the Other Half Lives* (1890): 'The one way out [that the sanitarian of the last generation] saw—rapid transit to the suburbs—has brought no relief. We know now that there is no way out.' William Booth gave the phrase a more optimistic (though to such as Jay and Morrison, foolishly blithe) colouring in the title of his *In Darkest England and the Way Out* (1890). That there are only two 'ways out' of the East End—boxing or crime—remains a common sentiment in the area.

61 *and that cut short at a third of the usual span of days*: i.e. the faction fight has only lasted a third of the normal period, and so the High Mobsmen are not yet back in circulation.

62 *The dispensary was no charitable institution*: charity-supported dispensaries did exist, supplying medicine and advice free of charge.

hospital letters: documents enabling the bearer to seek treatment in a charitable hospital. Cf. 'Maternity Society letter' (ch. 27) entitling prospective mother to assistance in childbirth.

who subscribed: i.e. contributed to the charity that ran the hospital concerned.

Turkey rhubarb and sulphuric acid . . . their opposite effects: Turkey (alternatively 'Russian') rhubarb was a medicinal rootstock originally imported from China and Tibet through Turkey or Russia; its effects were initially purgative but subsequently astringent. Sulphur and its compounds were used as laxatives.

two or three other drugs in hand: cf. George Sturt: 'You took risks, for it cost too much to go to a doctor. You took powders too! [. . .] There were convenient doses to be got at a grocer's—senna, rhubarb, camomile, Stedman's powders, and a loathsome brown powder we called 'Grandmother's powder' which we hated—fortunately, for it contained some form of mercury' (p. 134).

63 *Ross on nerve and brain troubles*: James Ross (1837–92), physician working in Newchurch, Rossendale, and subsequently at Manchester Infirmary;

appointed professor of medicine at Owens College, Manchester, in 1887; author of *Treatise on Diseases of the Nervous System* (1881).

63 *fluid bought at a chandler's shop, and called milk*: chandlers (sellers of hardware and domestic goods) often also sold food; adulteration of milk in London was an issue from the eighteenth century through to the twentieth. See A. Hardy, 'Diagnosis, Death and Diet'.

64 *little 'ymn*: Weech's smattering of religious knowledge derives from some contact with Sunday school. His 'little 'ymn' alludes to one of the innumerable collections of hymns for 'little children | folk | ones', of which Isaac Watts's (1674–1748), Ann Taylor's (1782–1866), and Mrs Cecil Alexander's (1818–95) were some of the best known. The phrase 'Little Hymn-Book' frequently occurs in the titles of such collections.

wuss . . . commandment: the first commandment is in fact 'Thou shalt have no other gods before me'; beyond the obvious irony, Weech presumably means the ninth: 'Thou shalt not bear false witness against thy neighbour': Exodus 20: 3, 16.

65 *stall-farming*: subletting subdivided properties (akin to stalls in a stable) on a nightly basis.

pitch-and-toss: gambling game endemic in the slums of Europe and the USA, hard to police because requiring no special equipment. Three coins are tossed in the air from the finger-ends; bets are made on the balance of heads and tails resulting. *OED* cites the *Standard* (1892): 'There were usually three or four in a gang, one acting as the "magflyer", the "mag" being the coin, another as the caller of the odds or amounts, a third as treasurer'. 'Tossing rings' attracted hundreds of gamblers, dealt in large sums of money and into the twentieth century their control was violently disputed. Besant notes Sunday as the great gambling day in the East End; Jay specifically records that in Orange Court [Jago Court] 'every Sunday crowds of men and boys assembled to play pitch-and-toss' (*Darkest London*, 61).

'Him as done the sparks in from Regent Street for nine centuries o' quids': the one who fenced the diamonds from the Regent Street robbery for £900. Regent Street was famous for both jewellery shops and its 'smash-and-grab' robberies.

five stretch: five-year term of imprisonment.

67 *sash-line . . . sash*: cord that controls the movement of a vertically sliding wooden window.

measles or whooping-cough: common and potentially fatal childhood diseases. Measles could cause brain damage, while complications of whooping cough included damage to the nervous system, haemorrhage, and pneumonia.

68 *rough application of the main hits and guards*: Morrison is reported to have boxed and his status as an afficionado of the ring and its technicalities is apparent in this description, as also in his short story 'Three Rounds' in

Mean Streets and the prizefight in *Cunning Murrell*. In his *Daily News* interview Morrison spoke of conversations with inhabitants of the Old Nichol: 'we used to talk of all kinds of things, especially boxing. The Nichol has sent out some of our best boxers.' However, with its 'holds' (including 'chancery', a wrestling head-hold) this is no purist's boxing match.

73 *Six bloomin' long months in a prison . . . away!*: song of the prostitute and her male accomplice, possibly from the music hall; more probably a street-song actually collected in the Old Nichol: cf. Jay, 116: 'the very sin which is most common in the streets of London is practised here more for the pure sake of robbery and theft than for anything else, and even children see no harm in the universal practice of the wretched street-walker who with her confederate persuades "A man to come down our alley | And then take his money away."'

74 *'wide as Broad Street'*: extremely knowing and crafty: Jay drew attention to the expression (p. 37).

75 *Mansion House Fund*: charitable fund initiated by the Lord Mayor of London (officially residing at the Mansion House), normally in response to a hard winter, an epidemic, or adverse trade. In context Morrison is almost certainly alluding to a fund for the unemployed opened in the 1880s—and with the same jaundiced view of it as Besant: a 'mighty migration' of 'hungry applicants arrived by every train'; 'they gave up work in order to be eligible'; 'when the day of distribution arrived they fought for admission, they threatened to brain the distributors, they took tickets which entitled them to food and sold them at the public house; in the end that act of charity developed and strengthened the pauper spirit in hundreds of thousands' (*East London*, 343).

Merely-Soft: utterly silly and sentimental. In his *Daily News* interview Morrison declared 'the false sentiment of the day is the curse of the country'.

Fluffy Pike: 'fluffy' was slang for drunk. *OED* quotes a report of a man being charged with being 'fluffy and disorderly'.

76 *jumped, swung on horizontal bars, boxed*: the Muscular Christianity movement and public school ethos of *mens sana in corpore sano* (a healthy mind in a healthy body) validated sport, including boxing, in the East End. The aim was to channel savage street violence into 'duello'. '[They] get rid of the devil in the gymnasium with the boxing-gloves and with single stick; they contract habits of order and discipline; they become infected with some of the upper-class ideals, especially as regards honour and honesty, purity and temperance' (Besant, *East London*, 172).

certain new millionaire: Jay reports courting 'a wealthy City magnate'; a donation of £1,000 through the trustees of a philanthropist Jay referred to as 'Betty Dash' largely enabled his church-building project (pp. 47, 56).

quacksalver, a Panjandrum of philanthropy, a mummer of the market-place, who undertook, for a fixed sum, to abolish poverty and sin together: Morrison endorses Jay's fears that William Booth's Salvation Army would monopolize charitable donation and damage parish-based social work. Booth complained of a 'whole vocabulary of vituperation' used against him. 'Sudden quacksalver' implies an upstart salesman of patent medicines. 'Panjandrum' was a mock-title invented by Samuel Foote (1720–77) in a passage of nonsense designed to test the memory of the actor Charles Macklin (*c.*1699–1797); Morrison might well have encountered its use in Henry Kingsley's novel *Ravenshoe* (1862). The 'Grand Panjandrum' of G. E. Farrow, whose children's books included *The Wallypug of Why* (1895), *The Little Panjandrum's Dodo* (1898), and *The New Panjandrum* (1902), is normally addressed as 'Your Supreme Importance'. Jay's parish was near Salvation Army headquarters at 188 Whitechapel Road: a contemporary print shows the name of the 'Rev. W. Booth' strikingly prominent on boards and placards (see McCarthy, 88). 'Mummer of the marketplace' refers to Booth's appearances at public meetings and use of modern advertising methods. The 'fixed sum' that Booth initially sought for his work was £100,000.

76 *new gaudery*: the Salvation Army's military-style ranks, its uniforms, standards, bands, and processions.

club at which boxing was allowed, and dominoes—flat ungodliness: Jay reports a Baptist preacher's objections to boxing and the circulation of fears among his parishioners that boxing resulted in damnation: 'so disturbed were the minds of some of my people, that I announced a sermon on the subject, "May a Christian box?"' (p. 88). Others were wary of dominoes: 'I recollect being surprised at the horror with which a few regarded dominoes—"devil's dice", as they called them—whilst all united in looking on cards as innocuous—a fact, no doubt, owing to the amount of gambling with dominoes in most public-houses' (p. 34).

Father Sturt!—the name itself was sheer papistry: the Oxford Movement had resulted in a largely accepted High Church presence in the Anglican Church, though middle-class suspicion of both Catholicism and Anglo-Catholicism was common enough. In the East End, St George's-in-the-East had been an influential centre of ritualism: see J. S. Reed, 'Ritualism Rampant in East London'. Besant noted some features of Jay's services that could have fuelled charges of 'papistry', including incense and processions involving 'banners and crosses'. Morrison, however, makes clear that Sturt's title of 'Father' principally stems from the Jagos themselves, a stock strongly indicated as Irish by such names as Leary, Flynn, Rafferty, and Regan. Jay indicated that an 'Irish element' was 'not wanting' in his parish and specifically mentioned parishioners nicknamed 'Tommy Irishman' and 'Wild Irishman' (pp. 37, 105). 'Father' also functions as a kind of practitioner-nickname in the world of aliases into which Henry Sturt enters.

77 *Jago death-rate . . . London*: Boulton confirmed this figure in writing about the novel for the *British Review*; Smith notes: 'In 1889 the death rate was 40 per 1000, nearly double that of Bethnal Green as a whole, and four times that of the rest of London' (p. 41).

78 *six moon*: i.e. period of six months' imprisonment.

blister: medical treatment for serious inflammation; figuratively, an unpleasant but salutary experience—such as Josh's prison sentence.

80 *futility of attempting compulsion in the Jago*: school boards had powers, at first discretionary, subsequently mandatory, to enforce school attendance. Jay wrote that in Shoreditch 'compulsion is a dead letter' (p. 133). It was one of the new school board attendance officers, John Reeves, working the area between 1872 and 1907, who left an account of the Old Nichol in *Recollections of a School Attendance Officer* (1913).

'fat's a-running': metaphor for theft on the move, presumably deriving from roasting meat over a fire. As the meat draws near to being cooked, the fat runs and there is the chance of catching some of the drips.

great goods depot of a railway company: the Great Eastern Goods Station was situated to the south of the junction of Bethnal Green Road and Shoreditch High Street and its goods depot a little way along the line.

81 *tobacco factories hard by*: Jay refers to theft of tobacco from carts in Shoreditch (p. 100). Arthur Harding recalled: 'There was a passage called Boundary Passage—it is still there—which used to be the getaway when they snatched the parcels from Hill's the tobacco people. It's on some of the maps. It is just a narrow place and Hill's used to be on the corner of New Inn Yard. The lads used to wait up there and when a fellow came out with a big parcel of tobacco, they used to snatch the parcel and run through the passage' (R. Samuel (ed.), *East End Underworld*, 9).

83 *carman*: van driver. Vans often carried a boy to load and unload goods and to ride at the back to protect the load from pilfering.

defamed each other's eyes and mother: euphemism for 'Damn your eyes, you bastard'.

slate pencil: schoolchildren wrote on wood-framed slates which could be wiped clean for reuse; the 'pencil' was a short rod of slate, sometimes in a paper wrapper, capable of being ground to a point. It produced a grey line on the writing slate. See Sturt, 94–5.

co-operation: significant political concept of the day. However, Morrison gave anarchism short shrift, was sceptical towards socialism, and deploys the term 'co-operation' in the ironic context of a criminal activity (one which survived into 1980s London as 'steaming').

84 *ball's stopped rollin'*: presumably an expression from bagatelle, meaning that the opportunity to achieve a large score has now passed.

85 *Nobber Sugg*: 'nobber' was slang for someone who collected money, though the implication here is probably of a fighter with a predilection for 'nobbing', or beating about the head.

86 *a clean room, with pictures on the wall, where there were often flowers*: Father Sturt's stable-church embodies Jay's priorities: 'The church I had in my mind's eye [. . .] was to be a home as well as a temple [. . .] warm, attractive, hung with pictures and decorated with colours' (p. 24).

86 *good notice . . . though most of the amounts would be reduced*: Morrison's account differs from Jay's, who emphasized that the site only came into his possession once the tenants had been evicted (pp. 60–1).

88 *fire-grate adroitly let drop*: 'two policemen tried one Sunday to go down the narrow entrance to the court, the first, on emerging, at the inner end, was levelled to the ground, though not seriously hurt, by a grate thrown by some one on him out of one of the empty rooms above' (Jay, 62). In his *Daily News* interview Morrison said that the original of Josh Perrott told him this story and 'C.R.' insisted that Morrison had himself told the story to Jay. However, Jay's book was completed by the end of 1890, so not dependent on Morrison. Perhaps Josh's original told the same story, independently, to both Jay and Morrison.

unfailing sanctuary . . . godsend: 'these facilities for escape were doubtless the reason why thieves so often chose this place as a temporary receptacle for what they had taken' (Jay, 62). The ironic liturgical discourse has a general rather than particular reference.

89 *princely wages*: Jay comments on the calls on his income and the difficulties of fund-raising throughout *Life in Darkest London*.

nothing but an immediate consideration carried weight in the Jago: 'when I first mentioned building a church, the people suggested instead that any money collected might be far better employed in providing them with food and clothes. I agreed, of course, partly with what they said, but deplored the trait of character which all, like so many wild beasts, exhibited, of clutching at any present advantage, utterly regardless of others, or of the future' (Jay, 46).

90 *tumbrils*: two-wheeled covered cart for carrying tools.

91 *not done without payments from the vicar's pocket*: 'one man demanded compensation on the ground that, in a moment of abstraction, he had placed an old mattress on the top of a cage containing a canary, and sitting down had crushed it flat. Another was so persistent in protesting his inability to provide a home for his family, that I felt almost forced to hire a room elsewhere for him, paying, however, only one week's rental' (Jay, 62).

their prosperous season: much casual work was seasonal; girls who made matches in winter might work in jam factories in the summer and autumn. Market-porters would be busiest in late summer or autumn. Winter generally produced less work and more social distress.

benjamins: a benjamin was 'a smart overcoat; so called from a tailor of the name, and rendered popular by its association with Joseph and his coat of many colours' (*Brewer's*).

bang-up kicksies, cut saucy, with artful buttons and a double fakement: splendid trousers (cf. 'kecks'), stylishly tailored with decoratively placed buttons and double trimming.

92 *daisies*: boots (Cockney rhyming slang, via 'daisy-roots'—from the idea of their being 'hard to pull up').

frails: woven rush-baskets.

weaving of rush bags . . . profit . . . the business: despite irony about the return on Mrs Bates's 'business', the idea of 'profit' is relevant since in many of the home-working trades (including garment-making), the worker had to take into account the cost of the materials that they themselves had to buy and supply.

93 *wide sashes of the old 'weavers' windows'*: 'there are silk-weavers in Spitalfields and Bethnal Green. An attempt has been made to revive the trade; meantime, many of the old houses remain with their wide windows on the first floor' (Besant, *East London*, 202–3).

rooms which the wreckers—no jack-a-dandies neither—flatly refused to enter: 'jack-a-dandies' implies weak, flashily dressed effeminate men. 'The workmen absolutely refused to enter this room at first, because it was so indescribably filthy. [. . .] The workmen at last only consented to enter it on the promise of a liberal allowance of beer to each' (Jay, 115).

94 *Mr Grinder*: a quibble on 'organ-grinder' (in the context of his 'Italian warehouse') may be involved, but principally an allusion to the trade of oil-and-colourman. Pigment, or 'colour', had to be 'ground' and mixed with oil to make paint. Robert Tressell was to use the name 'Grinder' for an exploiting employer (kin to 'Sweater'), but Morrison's character is an erstwhile errand boy and 'no bad fellow'.

95 *collect a little dirt, and rub it down the front of his apron*: the new apprentice dirtying himself to create the appearance of an old hand is part of the mythology of work. In *To London Town* Johnny May, as new engineering apprentice, wants to get his gleaming coffee can smoky. In Walter Greenwood's *Love on the Dole* the new apprentice dirties his face, is sent for the 'long stand' (the 'round square' in Johnny's case), and, like Johnny, encounters sordid and humiliating initiation rites.

97 *Brass roastin'-jacks . . . smoke-jacks*: appliances that kept meat in motion while roasting; machines for turning roasting-spits by making use of the current of hot air in the chimney.

99 *"Scatter seeds o' kindness" you know, as the—the Psalm says*: typical misattribution on Weech's part.

103 *crest*: tuft on a donkey's head.

touched for: stole successfully, in the context of picking pockets or petty theft.

109 *moleskin waistcoat, with pearlies down the front and the artful dodge over the pockets*: waistcoat of cotton fustian (a material shaved before dyeing); traditional cockney's mother-of-pearl buttons. The 'artful dodge' suggests a button-down flap to deflect pickpockets.

110 *She's a fighter . . . Rorty SAIRER*: 'rorty' is slang for fine, splendid, jolly. The internal rhymes suggest a music-hall song that encouraged audience participation.

trap: possibly echoing the planned entrapment of the Turks (and, in the event, Barabas himself) in Marlowe's *The Jew of Malta*; both episodes are legible as modelling the damned entering hell's mouth. Mother Gapp's cellar into which 'the aliens' fall is a 'pit of writhing forms', while the name 'Gapp' itself suggests a gaping mouth or chasm. (Morrison makes some allusion to Renaissance drama in his journalism.)

113 *leaving shop*: unlicensed pawnbroker's.

115 *dose of the 'cat'*: cat-o'-nine-tails: abolished in the services in 1881, but still part of the system of judicial corporal punishment. 'The cat [. . .], which is strictly reserved for the very worst cases of all—and then only for men of the strongest physique—is a punishment which leaves its marks in some cases both on body and on mind. It is the one thing the callous, depraved, dehumanized convict stands in fear of' (H.B.N., 136).

bow: ring on a pocket watchcase to which the chain or ribbon is attached.

116 *mere Waterbury on a steel guard*: cheap stem-wound American watch with a base metal chain. Waterbury watches used a stamped-out mechanism without jewels and were very cheap to buy.

red clock and slang: gold watch and chain.

117 *Mogul*: Emperor of Delhi; figuratively, a tycoon—usually in 'legitimate' business.

screwed a chat, nor claimed a peter: to screw a chat was to make a quiet entry into a house; peter-claiming was 'laying hands nonchalantly on unconsidered parcels and bags at railway stations', sometimes involving a swap ('A Conversion', 258). See 'His Tale of Bricks' for a disquisition on the technicalities of the crime (p. 180) and the confusions of three peter-claimers accidentally stealing each other's identical brick-filled bags.

let a great deal of blood—no doubt with benefit: ironic reference to cupping and bloodletting as a medical procedure.

118 *prince of fences, Ikey Solomons*: historical model for Dickens's Fagin in *Oliver Twist*.

'front': one who distracts a victim's attention, allowing an accomplice to pick the victim's pocket more easily (cf. 'front man').

never bought anything himself: see the activities of Captain Kemp in Morrison's *The Hole in the Wall* for a detailed elaboration of this method of the professional fence.

122 *Snuffy*: nickname for someone who takes snuff; also slang for drunken or tipsy.

penny cast: by analogy with a thrown object, the distance of journey by tram allowable for a penny.

123 *prosecutor*: in the sense of one agreeing to press charges.

commission agent: someone with authority to act in business for another party (though here used as a loosely defined occupation to conceal the Mobsman's true activities).

124 *Old Bailey . . . Holloway*: the Old Bailey, or Central Criminal Court, adjoined Newgate prison where prisoners due to make a court appearance

would be brought from such holding prisons as Holloway. A 'respectable' prisoner recorded being held in Holloway in 1898: 'I [. . .] was put into what is called a furnished cell—that is to say, a cell containing a table and some chairs, with a drugget on the floor, so that it looks something like a private room. [. . .] as long as I was in Holloway I was not altogether a close prisoner. I wore my own clothes, and I had my meals brought in from a restaurant. I also had newspapers and books to read, and I was allowed to write letters and receive visits' (H.B.N., 14).

lob-crawler: a robber of 'the till: not narrowly [. . .] the individual till, but broad-mindedly [. . .] the till as a general institution, to be approached in unattended shops by stealthy grovelling on the belly' ('A Conversion', 257).

laggin' dues: penal servitude; confinement and specified hard labour.

Newgate . . . before a double iron railing: this scene bears close comparison with Frank Holl's painting *Newgate—Committed for Trial* (1878)—so much so that the painting comes close to constituting a found illustration to the novel. Along with Luke Fildes and Hubert von Herkomer, Holl was a notable social realist painter whose work appeared in the *Graphic* during the 1870s. While not depicting a 'screaming hubbub' (though a baby may be crying), Holl does show a woman with two bewildered children looking at her husband through the wire-netted 'double iron railing'. The husband lounges against the bars on his side. Holl's prisoner is a young clerk rather than a Josh Perrott, but his manner suggests that he too has 'little to say'. As in Morrison's scene, the prisoner is among other prisoners while his wife must communicate with him in the presence of other visitors (and a prison officer). While the scene has a generic status, Morrison might well have seen Holl's painting or a reproduction of it.

125 *Recorder*: city or borough magistrate with criminal and civil jurisdiction.

Parkhurst . . . easier conditions: 'first offenders condemned to penal servitude, after a short time in a local gaol, are, as a rule, sent to Lewes prison to serve their separate confinement, and are afterwards removed either to Portland or to Parkhurst, the only two convict prisons where first offenders are sent' (H.B.N., 26–7). Josh serves what would normally have been nine months of separate (or effectively solitary) confinement (twenty-three hours a day alone in a cell, of which eight were spent in work) at Chelmsford Prison, and is then transferred to Portland. H.B.N. was in poor health and was duly sent to Parkhurst, 'a special place of confinement for invalid or weak-minded prisoners who are brought there from all the other convict prisons as soon as their condition is considered serious' (p. 148).

126 *howling sea of human wreckage*: significant metaphor in social problem discourse: see folding frontispiece to William Booth's *In Darkest England and the Way Out* and its image of drowning people pulled to safety by Salvation Army officers out of a sea labelled 'Starvation', 'Unemployed', 'Drunkenness', etc. (also reproduced in McCarthy, 96–7).

126 *'in the country'*: euphemism for imprisonment, playing on the upper-class idea of possessing town and country houses.

ticket-of-leave: colloquial name for an 'order of licence' giving a convict liberty before expiry of sentence, the remission involved being dependent on good conduct. The ticket could be remitted on petition to the Home Secretary.

making shirts: Mayhew isolated shirt-finishing as one of the most exploitative kinds of home-working. See also Morrison's 'Whitechapel'.

127 *twopence farthing . . . Support Home Industries*: Jay mentions a rate of tuppence farthing a gross, judging the task two hours' work (p. 22), seven gross representing a fourteen-hour day (not allowing for time for collection and delivery). Conditions at Bryant and May's factory had included harsh fines and poor ventilation (understood to foster phosphorus-induced skin and bone cancers); these considerations prompted Annie Besant's article 'White Slavery in London' and the Match-girls' strike of 1888. The ironic force of 'public-spirited' evokes the contrast between such matters and the public image of 'England's Glory' matchboxes decorated jingoistically with Union Jacks, an imperial dreadnought in full steam and the motto 'Support Home Industries'. 'C.R.' reported that Morrison tried 'in his own person what it feels like to earn a living by making match-boxes'. Sweden was the principal overseas competition in the manufacture of matches.

half-quarter hundredweight of coals: i.e. 1 stone or 14 pounds (slightly more than 6 kilograms).

129 *police-court birch*: corporal punishment; flogging with a birch rod. Magistrates could order up to twenty-five strokes for those less than 16 years of age; not more than twelve strokes for those less than 14.

130 *reformatories . . . 'schooling'*: young offenders were often sent to standard prisons; in 1903, H.B.N. commented, 'only ten years ago over two hundred children under twelve years of age, and over three thousand aged between twelve and sixteen, were annually committed to prison' (p. 251). Alternatively, for committing crimes otherwise punishable by penal servitude, detention in a reformatory school could be ordered for not less than two years and not more than five. The Prisons Committee of 1894 recommended great extension of provision for young offenders and the establishment of borstal followed.

outdoor parish relief . . . guardians: provision for the sick and destitute through the parish, or a union of parishes, took the form either of the workhouse or 'outdoor relief' given in the homes of the able-bodied. Boards of Guardians, administering such provision, were introduced by the Poor Law Amendment Act of 1834.

131 *solemn and most circumstantial Lie*: *As You Like It*, v. iv. 66–100. In Touchstone's seven-point scale of quarrelling, the charge of 'Lie Circumstantial' is the most extreme short of the 'Lie Direct': 'I durst go no further than the Lie Circumstantial, nor he durst not give me the Lie Direct. And so we measured swords and parted' (ll. 82–5).

132 *unregarded turnip*: episode echoing Jay, 113.

133 *right of rats to multiply their thousands*: as spoken by a surgeon, these words may be designed to refute the liberal East End doctor in Margaret Harkness's novel *Captain Lobe*: Ledger ('In Darkest England', 80) notes that Harkness's surgeon criticizes 'eugenic theorists who explain degeneration through theories of heredity'; 'They talk such rubbish. They cannot, or will not, see that while the environment of these people remains what it is, they will indulge in the only two enjoyments they can command.'

135 *County Council*: in 1889 London County Council took over responsibility for this area from the Metropolitan Board of Works; the 'Boundary Street Scheme' had the distinction of being the first major project in slum-clearance undertaken by the Council.

crude yellow brick of the barrack dwellings: in *East London*, Besant criticized the barrack-like nature of the new buildings and the tenants' lack of control over their new homes. Charles Booth observed that the rents were too high and the conditions of occupancy restrictive: 'the result is that the new buildings are occupied by a different class, largely Jews' (Smith, 44); in his *Daily News* interview Morrison observed of the Old Nichol that 'no jew would be tolerated there for a moment'. Also see Sarah Wise's discussion of the matter in *The Blackest Streets*.

earned his marks: good conduct system. 'Having earned the maximum number of marks for good conduct without forfeiting any, I was discharged' (H.B.N., 48). Josh earns enough to serve only four years.

136 *safe from . . . the reformatory now, being well over the age*: i.e. more than 16.

sevenpence is half-a-gallon: i.e. the price of 4 pints of beer.

137 *'out' . . . 'fall'*: go out thieving; get caught or arrested. Cf. 'Bob the Bender fell in Broad Street'.

''Spect 'im up tonight': i.e. Josh will arrive from Portland on the 'up' train.

Jago hair was commonly cut in another place: i.e. prison: 'Before, however, being taken to my cell in the hospital [at Wormwood Scrubs], I was measured and weighed, and had all my hair clipped off' (H.B.N., 25).

138 *Band-of-Hope*: influential total-abstinence association. 'The drunkenness was appalling. [. . .] Reeling men and women singing one minute, fighting and cursing the next were everywhere. [. . .] The Blue Ribbon Army and the Salvation Army together with the Bands of Hope, and Adult Temperance Societies, did a grand work in their campaign against intemperance in and around Bethnal Green, but the improved social conditions including education, better facilities for recreation and enjoyment have played a large part' (Le May, 33).

Fair's fair, as the apostle David says in the Proverbs: Weech's most egregious and complex biblical confusion: the saying is not biblical; the Book of Proverbs is associated with Solomon, David's son; David was not an apostle.

139 *Wot a blessed release!*: in his anxiety Weech misapplies a cliché, used of death as a release from illness; with inadvertent humour he pursues the idea of release into a misquotation that confuses the 'happy condition' of freedom in the Lord with freedom from the 'lor' (law, police).

friendly lead: 'among the poorer classes in London, an entertainment given by friends, for the benefit of a person in distress, etc.' (*OED*).

relish: savoury variation on a staple diet. Besant wrote of a factory girl: 'She made her breakfast on tea, bread and margarine, and a "relish". The relish included many possibilities. It depended mainly on the day of the week. It is obvious that what one can afford on a Monday is unattainable on a Friday. On Monday it might be a herring or a haddock, an egg or a rasher of bacon. On Friday and Saturday it would be a sprig of water-cress or a pickle' (*East London*, 137).

140 *run the gauntlet of Prisoners' Aid Societies*: part of the running joke about Josh's aversion to work; such societies met men leaving prison and aimed to guide them into work. Alfred Alsop's *Down in the Slums* suggests that they were easily evaded.

prison gratuity: in the case of a man serving three years, 'a few shillings' (H.B.N., 263).

Em . . . drank her allowance of gin: the early introduction of children to spirits was a strong theme in fictional and documentary accounts of the slums, accentuated by the participation of the Temperance Movement in social work. In Phil May's *In an East End Gin Shop* a mother stands calmly holding a tankard while her ragged little girl drinks from it (see Besant, *East London*, 125).

144 *step-dance*: 'dance intended for the display of special steps by an individual performer' (*OED*).

gallows-flap: possibly a specific dance, or a black-humoured pantomime of the movements of a man being hanged: cf. Cruikshank's illustration 'Master Bates Explains a Professional Technicality' in *Oliver Twist*.

146 *St Leonard's, hard by*: St Leonard, Shoreditch, was the parish adjoining Holy Trinity to its north and west, its church standing beyond Shoreditch High Street, on the eastern side of Kingsland Road, at the junction with Hackney Road. Keating, in his edition of the novel, prints 'close by' rather than the first edition's 'hard by'; the latter term may risk suggesting the church was rather nearer to Weech's establishment in Meakin Street than would have been the case.

148 *striking-box*: 'the metal box on a door-jamb which receives the end of the bolt of the lock when the door is locked' (*OED*).

loo table: Keating prints the simpler 'low table', but the first edition reading is quite coherent: 'loo table' was a general trade term for a kind of round table (originally associated with the popular card game 'loo'). Josh later recalls it specifically as a 'round table'.

coloured wall-texts: popular Victorian decoration: sentimental or biblical quotation, printed or embroidered and usually framed. Implied as the source of some of Weech's fractured pious sentiments.

150 *bull's-eye*: police-issue lantern with hemispherical lens giving a powerful beam.

153 *Heap on a shutter*: 'if you dropped dead "in a fit" you would be "brought home on a shutter", as there was no ambulance, but every shop had shutters' (Sturt, 133).

155 *Lion and Unicorn*: royal coat of arms.

take his gruel: gruel was standard prison fare; synecdoche for judicial punishment.

156 *bunch of flowers*: originally carried to ward off typhus (prison fever).

trap: cage with a contrivance for releasing the birds quickly.

They wouldn't have given any more in Club Row: if the pigeons had been sold live in the fancy bird market in Club Row, they would have fetched no more money than they did dead at the poulterer's.

157 *four-legged linnet . . . two-headed sheep*: freak shows, animal and human, authentic and fake, were common features of Victorian fairgrounds. On Fair Day at Farnham 'there was a rich selection of fat ladies, bearded ladies, abortions of all sorts' (Sturt, 108).

soft mortarboard: black cap, traditionally donned by judges in pronouncing the death sentence.

158 *Clerk of Arraigns*: court officer recording judicial decisions.

159 *fourpenny doss-houses*: some dosshouses, or common lodging houses, charged less than fourpence a night, though tuppence or less might only bring the chance of sleeping across a rope slung across the room. For a print, see McCarthy, 33.

the gipsies that used to live at the Mount years ago: Morrison reported that well into the eighteenth century a fort called 'The Mount' stood in the area of the Whitechapel Road ('down near the London Hospital, and opposite the Pavilion Theatre'). The site had subsequently been built over with a terrace of shops that maintained the name. See his article 'Whitechapel'. Local historians debate the matter.

160 *I am the resurrection and the life . . . In the midst of life . . .*: Book of Common Prayer. Morrison's ellipsis functions to highlight the words that follow in the Order for the Burial of the Dead: 'We are in death'.

162 *doubly sealed of the outcasts*: 'outcast' was a key word in social problem discourse, notably deployed in Andrew Mearns's *Bitter Cry of Outcast London* (1883).

163 *How good for them all to go off easily together*: suicide (e.g. Neddy Wright) and domicide were themes of turn-of-the-century depictions of poverty: cf. Thomas Hardy, *Jude the Obscure*; London, *The People of the Abyss*; and Tressell, *The Ragged Trousered Philanthropists*.

164 *leather-aproned*: emblem of the shoemaker (here, Bobby Roper).

GLOSSARY

Below are listed some less familiar words and meanings not treated in the Explanatory Notes.

amain with full force, violently
area yard, open place, basement stairwell
assortment unsorting

barney argument, fight, commotion
bedesman proxy paid or endowed to pray for others
beer-engines pumps drawing beer from cask to bar
billycock round, low-crowned felt hat
bob one shilling (twelve pence)
break collection, whip-round
brickbat broken brick (used as missile)
bust; buster burglary, burglar

case-knife sheath-knife
chive stab
claim steal, lift
clicker thief
compassed brought about
cop steal
copper laundry boiler made of iron or copper
corneous horny
crank (of machinery) weak, shaky
cranky shaky, crazy
croak die
crook, on the dishonestly, criminally
cut his lucky escaped, went when the going was good

davy affidavit, legal deposition
dipper pickpocket

faint (of glue) feeble, lacking in strength
farthing quarter of an old penny
fastness secure place, place of safety
fee-faw-fum nonsense fit only to terrify a child
fence receiver of stolen goods
flaming gaudy, 'loud'
flimped robbed, usually by a team of thieves
fullied committed for trial at a higher court

gilt money
gonoph petty thief
gossip old woman

half-a-crown two shillings and sixpence
handers caning on the hands
hardbake slab (almond) toffee
hook thief, steal (cf. 'Hookey Street')

ikey Jewish

james jemmy, burglar's crowbar

lag; lagging imprison, sentence to penal servitude; period of penal servitude
lathers beats, thrashes

mazzard head
mechanic workman, skilled labourer
milch-cow source of profit, person from whom money is easily taken

milling boxing
minim sixtieth part of a fluid drachm

neddy life-preserver, stick or bludgeon loaded with lead

oof money ('ooftish')
'ooks *see* **hook**
opposites opponents

pogue-hunter pickpocket dealing in purses
prop piece of jewellery with pin

quartern loaves four-pound loaves
quoddin' serving a prison sentence

red gold
rotted chaffed, bantered, teased
rum odd, queer
rusty (of clothes) showing age or use, shabby, worn, faded

shallow costermonger's cart
smug arrest
snuggery snug place or room; otherwise, small bar in a pub
sovereign gold coin worth one pound (twenty shillings)
specie coin, as opposed to (traceable) paper money
specifics medicines or remedies
split detective, informer
squeeged squeezed, compressed
stir prison
thick united, solid ('thick as thieves', 'thick as glue')
toff gentleman
tog(s) clothing, clothes
toke bread
toy and tackle watch and chain
turnin' over search on suspicion, fleece, rob
turn-up fight, commotion
twirls skeleton keys

uxter money

watch-guard chain, cord, or ribbon securing a watch to clothing
well-plucked full of pluck
wide knowing, streetwise, able to fence with the law
worked off disposed of and got done with
writhen subjected to writhing, contorted

yannups money
yuller 'yellow metal', gold

ACKNOWLEDGEMENTS

I AM grateful to the University of California Regents for permission to make use of Arthur Morrison's letters to Herbert S. Stone and Walter J. Roberts, and also to Ed Fields at the Donald C. Davidson Library, Santa Barbara, for his patient assistance. Staff in the Special Collections Department at the University of British Columbia were extremely helpful in making available Morrison's letter to the Revd W. Priest. I am also grateful to the Lilly Library, Bloomington, Indiana, for making available copies of letters to Morrison from Laurence Binyon and Cicely Powell; also to Jane Baxter, Local Studies Librarian at Richmond upon Thames, for making available copies of letters by Morrison to Douglas Sladen.

My thanks remain as ever to Barbara Dennis, Andrew Hassam, Michael Kakooza, William Price, Allen Samuels, Malcolm Smith, and Martin Wright, who all illuminated corners of Victorian culture which were dark to me. Sophie Gilmartin, John Scattergood, and George Walter gave generous long-distance assistance with bibliographical puzzles; Jim Walker, while treading a very different path, eased my introduction to Japanese art. For technical facilities I am grateful to the Media Centre, Library and Academic Computing Services at the former University of Wales, Lampeter.

This edition remains dedicated to John, Viv, Nicholas, and Jonathan.